Program Evaluation

Alternative Approaches and Practical Guidelines

Second Edition

Blaine R. Worthen
Utah State University

James R. Sanders
Western Michigan University

Jody L. Fitzpatrick
*University of Colorado
at Colorado Springs*

An imprint of Addison Wesley Longman, Inc.

New York • Reading, Massachusetts • Menlo Park, California • Harlow, England
Don Mills, Ontario • Sydney • Mexico City • Madrid • Amsterdam

Program Evaluation: Alternative Approaches and Practical Guidelines, Second Edition

The previous edition of *Program Evaluation* was published under the title *Educational Evaluation* (Longman, 1987).

Longman, 10 Bank Street, White Plains, N.Y. 10606

Acquisitions editor: Virginia L. Blanford
Associate editor: Arianne J. Weber
Editorial assistant: Mike Lee
Production editor: Ann P. Kearns
Production supervisor: Edith Pullman
Cover design: Betty Sokol
Text art: Hoyt Hemphill
Compositor: ExecuStaff Composition Services

Library of Congress Cataloging-in-Publication Data

Worthen, Blaine R.
     Program evaluation : alternative approaches and practical
guidelines / Blaine R. Worthen, James R. Sanders, Jody L.
Fitzpatrick.—2nd ed.
          p.   cm.
     Rev. ed. of: Educational evaluation. c1987.
     Includes bibliographical references and index.
     ISBN 0-8013-0774-0
     1. Educational evaluation—United States.   2. Evaluation research
(Social action programs)—United States.   3. Evaluation—Study and
teaching—United States.   I. Sanders, James R.   II. Fitzpatrick,
Jody L.   III. Worthen, Blaine R.   Educational evaluation.
IV. Title.
LB2822.75.W67   1997
379.1'54—dc20   96-28952
                                                                        CIP

          8 9 10-MA-00

Contents

CHAPTER 19 **REPORTING AND USING EVALUATION INFORMATION   407**

CHAPTER 20 **EVALUATING EVALUATIONS   439**

PART FIVE   EMERGING AND FUTURE SETTINGS FOR PROGRAM EVALUATION   459

CHAPTER 21 **CONDUCTING MULTIPLE-SITE EVALUATION STUDIES   461**

Preface

Those who are familiar with the 1987 Worthen and Sanders evaluation textbook will likely wonder why we have not retained that title for this book. Perhaps the simplest explanation is that while this volume is in part a revision of the earlier text, many of the changes are so substantial that this is a very different book, much broader than our 1987 text. The addition of a new author and the expanded focus of this book are the outgrowth of the following factors:

- Valued evaluation colleagues working in several different disciplines have encouraged us to broaden the focus of our earlier book to make it more relevant to them and their students.

- As the field of evaluation has continued to mature, it is apparent that some of the new and potentially most important developments transcend any one field or discipline within which evaluation might be conducted; restricting their discussion to education seems unwarranted.

- Although continuing to evaluate educational programs, the senior authors have had considerable experience during the past decade evaluating programs outside of education (e.g., health services, family planning, humane treatment of animals, corporate training, youth corrections, community development, United Way, and mental health services), thus broadening their perspectives and making it possible to expand the focus of the book without losing its relevance for educational evaluators.

- Evaluation of our earlier text by 55 members of the American Evaluation Association (AEA) Topical Interest Group on Teaching of Evaluation has emphasized the importance of producing a text that would continue to serve educational evaluators well while extending that same service to evaluation professors and practitioners in other disciplines and fields.

- Of the thousands of graduate students who have used the book in masters or doctoral evaluation courses, formal written (anonymous) feedback from 387 have identified important omissions or "parochialism" in the 1987 text that required attention; students majoring in psychology, public administration, social work, business, and health have pointed out how existing material could be made more relevant to their areas, without losing its relevance to education.

These are the forces that have prompted us to broaden the title—and the focus of the book—from *Educational Evaluation* to *Program Evaluation.*

BUT IS THIS BOOK STILL USEFUL FOR EDUCATIONAL EVALUATION?

Of the 55 AEA evaluation professors who completed and returned our evaluative questionnaire pertaining to the 1987 textbook, 37 teach a class on educational evaluation. Most of these requested—some quite fervently—that no revisions be made that would lessen the book's usefulness in training students to evaluate educational programs. We have been faithful, we believe, to that request. Every effort has been made to retain the portions of the earlier text that our education colleagues have found most helpful in the past. Although we have reduced somewhat the number of education examples and references to make room for those from other fields, we continue to draw more examples from education than from any other area.

We have asked a few colleagues who teach educational evaluation courses to review this manuscript. Based on their opinions, this book will serve to train educational evaluators every bit as well as did the earlier text. Indeed, as some have pointed out, there is merit in educational evaluators' being exposed to evaluation in other fields and vice versa. In a world where evaluators frequently are prompted by invitations or personal interest to stray beyond the discipline boundaries of their training, it may be advantageous for evaluators in every area to examine applications of their craft in other areas. Perhaps school-based evaluators may never evaluate programs aimed at reducing drunk driving, enhancing corporate training, or providing treatment for juvenile sex offenders, yet professionals increasingly find themselves drawn into the role of world citizens who are required to relate their own areas of expertise to that of others as societal needs and problems cut across disciplinary boundaries. Will an educator who is the only trained evaluator in Smalltown, U.S.A., refuse to design an evaluation of a community program aimed at reducing illicit use of drugs on the grounds that drug evaluations were not in her[1] curriculum? Similarly, we

---

[1] Until there is a singular pronoun in the English language that is both masculine and feminine, we will alternate between using feminine pronouns in one chapter and masculine pronouns in the next.

believe some exposure to evaluations in other fields is beneficial regardless of the disciplinary home base of the evaluator-in-training.

CAN THIS TEXT REALLY BE USED IN OTHER, NONEDUCATIONAL FIELDS?

Yes, for two reasons. First, as a new author for this book, Jody Fitzpatrick adds not only additional insight and expertise in evaluation methodology but also considerable experience in evaluating programs in health, social services, the environment, and training. Second, we have drawn not only examples but also concepts, principles, and procedural guidelines from a wide spectrum of fields of study as well as from diverse agency and institutional settings. Several colleagues who told us they were unable to use the prior text because of its exclusive focus on education have, upon reviewing this manuscript, declared their intention of using it. We hope that number expands and that feedback from new users will help us make this text useful across a wide variety of fields.

CONTINUITY AND CHANGES FROM THE 1987 TEXT

We have drawn into this volume those portions and features of the former text that our evaluation colleagues and students have suggested to us are most useful and that we judge still to be current. Although much of our content is new, we judge the best of the 1987 Worthen and Sanders text to be included here.

This book possesses the following features:

1. It is an **integrated textbook,** not an edited book of readings (though we have liberally quoted and excerpted what we consider the real nuggets from the evaluation literature and incorporated that content with our own).
2. Our **coverage of evaluation approaches and models is not only more current but also broader**, ranging across the entire spectrum of evaluation approaches that have been shown to be useful in evaluation. Empowerment evaluation, cluster evaluation, and **numerous other evaluation approaches** that were nonexistent or too underdeveloped for inclusion in the earlier text are treated at some length here.
3. We have **added** the following:
   - A chapter on **evaluation approaches used in business and industrial settings**, focusing on evaluation of corporate training and organizational improvement programs. Total Quality Management, front-end analysis, quality analysis, and customer satisfaction studies are only a few of the approaches we examine.

- A new chapter describing **how to conduct multisite evaluation studies** so as to minimize their risks and maximize their benefits.
- More emphasis on how to collect, analyze, and use **qualitative data.** A new section deals with the use of **focus groups** as an evaluation tool. **Performance assessment** and other alternative assessment techniques useful in evaluation are reviewed.
- The **newest standards for evaluation**, along with AEA guiding principles for evaluator behavior, in a revised chapter on meta-analysis.
- A chapter on **recent development in evaluation**, which examines new trends that have appeared in evaluation in the past several years.

4. More than half of this volume is still devoted to **practical guidelines** for planning, conducting, and using evaluations; **checklists and step-by-step procedural guides** are proposed to guide the inexperienced evaluator in conducting many essential evaluation activities.

5. We have kept **graphics and other visuals** that users have found helpful, attempting to accommodate diverse learning styles and preferences.

6. We have applied the content of each of the chapters in Parts Three and Four, "Practical Guidelines," to **a case study of a fictional evaluation** of a school curriculum to show how our suggestions might be carried out in "real life."

7. We have referenced and cited most of the **best contributions to the expanding literature in evaluation** and allied areas, so that this book will serve as both a useful reference source for the professor of evaluation and a text for the student of evaluation.

8. We have collaborated with a colleague to produce the following supplemental instructional aids to accompany this textbook:
   - A **Student Guide** to help the student master the contents of the book by using **synopses of each chapter's major points, guided study prompts,** and **application exercises**
   - An **Instructor's Manual**, constructed to provide (1) more **detailed discussions of several topics treated more briefly in the text**, for instructors who may wish to take students to a greater depth in those topics, (2) **suggestions for how the book may best be used** with courses of various lengths, and (3) a **TEST QUESTION BANK** containing test items for each chapter, in alternative item formats, from which the instructor can choose **items for midterm or final examinations**

9. We have added a **Glossary** at the end of the book and defined in it each term we anticipate will be unfamiliar to many readers. Each word that appears in the glossary is printed in boldface the first time it appears in the book in a way that may be unfamiliar to many readers; it may also be bolded the first time it is formally defined.

USES AND GOALS

This book can be used in a variety of ways, but its two major uses are described below.

Basic Evaluation Textbook

This book is designed primarily as an introductory text for graduate courses in program evaluation or related areas (e.g., quality improvement, enhancing organizational performance, improving school curricula, methods of social change, management training). It would be pertinent wherever courses are aimed at teaching practitioners how to assess the effectiveness of their endeavors. More ideally suited to a semester-length course or a two-quarter sequence, it can be readily adapted to a one-quarter course by judiciously selecting content to be covered. Selective picking and choosing of content will also allow portions of this book to be used in in-service seminars and workshops on program evaluation. The *Instructor's Manual* contains our suggestions for (1) sections, chapters, and pages to be used in one-quarter courses (with three alternatives that differ, depending on the instructor's purposes); (2) semester courses or two-quarter sequences; and (3) several topical in-service workshops or seminars.

Reference Resource

This book should also serve well as a reference for practicing evaluators, professors, graduate and advanced undergraduate students, and others who desire a comprehensive overview of program evaluation and references to additional sources of information.

In general, this book is intended (1) to familiarize readers with the variety of alternative approaches proposed for planning and conducting program evaluation and (2) to provide practical guidelines helpful with almost any general evaluation approach.

Within this general framework, the more specific goals of this book are these:

1. To help users develop an awareness of and sensitivity to critical concepts and issues in program evaluation
2. To help users develop a clear perspective about the role of evaluation in education, the social sciences, business, the health professions, the nonprofit sector, and government programs and services of all varieties and at various levels
3. To help readers become enlightened users of evaluation in their respective occupations and endeavors
4. To prepare evaluators to conduct useful, feasible, proper, and technically sound evaluation studies. (Of course, although this book will contribute substantially to the training of professional evaluators, additional education and experience will be necessary to develop

further the competencies they must possess to conduct high-quality evaluation studies.)

It may be helpful to say a word about **areas this book is *not* intended to cover.**

1. First, although tests, questionnaires, and interviews are used frequently to collect evaluation data, this book cannot devote space for detailed coverage of these or other data-collection or -analysis tools used in program evaluation.

2. Second, although many of the evaluation concepts and guidelines discussed here for evaluating programs (or their associated products, processes, or practices) also apply to evaluation of personnel, this text is not intended as a full treatment of personnel evaluation. We do discuss the topic very briefly in Chapter 22, in discussing evaluation in the corporate world, but meaningful treatment of teacher evaluation, university faculty evaluation, or general personnel evaluation is incidental and limited, for such topics deserve books of their own.

3. Third, although the authors have conducted a number of evaluations in other countries, the majority of our experience is with evaluations of programs in the United States, and we draw naturally for many of our examples from that which we know best. At the same time, the general concepts, principles, and guidelines offered in this text will generalize across most geographic boundaries and settings and transcend most differences in social and disciplinary context. In short, this book should prove as useful in evaluating a Barclays Bank managers' training program in Kent County, England, or a mental health clinic in Ottawa as it is in evaluating a vocational education curriculum in the San Francisco public schools.

TEACHING AND LEARNING AIDS

To assist instructors and readers in using this book, we include several teaching and learning aids. Each chapter contains the following:

- **Orienting questions** at the beginning of the chapter that readers should be able to answer at its conclusion
- **Application exercises** for students to test their understanding
- A list of **additional suggested readings**
- For each chapter including practical guidelines for planning, conducting, reporting, and using evaluation studies (Chapters 12–20), a listing of **evaluation standards** that pertain to that chapter

In addition, each chapter that provides practical guidelines for planning, conducting, reporting, or using an evaluation study contains an application of the chapter's content to a running **case study**, unfolded chapter by chapter to illustrate how the newly introduced concepts would be applied in a real-life evaluation situation.

SUGGESTIONS FOR IMPROVEMENT

We hope that this text will meet your needs, whether you are the instructor, student, or a practicing evaluator for whom this book might serve as a reference or handbook. Whatever your role, we have a request to make. We want very much to receive your comments or suggestions on how to improve future editions to make this work as helpful as possible to those who use it; your help will be gratefully received. Please send any suggestions to Blaine R. Worthen, Department of Psychology, Utah State University, Logan, UT 84322-2810, or e-mail to BLAINE@FS1.ED.USU.EDU, or fax to (801) 797-1448.

ACKNOWLEDGMENTS

We express our appreciation to the following:

- Our many colleagues and students whose urging and helpful suggestions have influenced us in the revision and redirection of the earlier textbook this volume will replace. We especially appreciate the candid feedback of the members of AEA's Topical Interest Group on Teaching of Evaluation who responded to our prerevision survey;
- Those colleagues our publishers selected as reviewers of the present manuscript. Their critiques—both compliments and criticisms—were very helpful in our final revisions:

  James W. Altschuld, Ohio State University

  Sarah M. Dinham, University of Arizona

  R. Tony Eichelberger, University of Pittsburgh

  Gonzalo Garcia Jr., Texas A&M University

  Mary E. Huba, Iowa State University

  Noreen Michael, Illinois State University

  Dianna L. Newman, University at Albany

  David A. Payne, University of Georgia

  Leslie J. C. Riggin, Florida State University

  William H. Scarbrough, Central Michigan University

  Wayne Welch, University of Minnesota

  David D. Williams, Brigham Young University

- Dune Ives for her very helpful and insightful work preparing many of the instructional aids published as supplements to this book;

- Joyce Brinck for her outstanding and tireless production of this manuscript (and the earlier textbook it replaced) and her dedication to the completion of myriad tasks associated with it; and to Ginafer Low and Karen Ranson, who frequently stepped into the breach to help with these tasks at critical points, and did so at the same high level of quality;

- Renee Snyder for her competent, complete, and cheerful search of electronic databases to ensure that nothing important was overlooked; and to Eric Gee, Michael Chen, and Audrey Matsumoto for their uncomplaining and useful technical assistance with obtaining necessary references and completing other tasks associated with the manuscript; and

- Our spouses, Barbara, Susan, and Jeff, and our families, without whose support and sacrifice this book could not have been written.

BLAINE R. WORTHEN
JAMES R. SANDERS
JODY L. FITZPATRICK

part ONE

Introduction
to Evaluation

This initial section of our text provides the background necessary for the beginning student to understand the chapters that follow. In it, we attempt to accomplish three things.

First, we discuss in Chapter 1 the basic purpose of evaluation, varying roles evaluation studies can play, current societal expectations of evaluation, and factors that influence how well evaluation can fulfill such expectations. We define evaluation more specifically. Finally, we introduce the reader to two basic distinctions important to evaluation.

Second, we discuss in Chapter 2 the origins of today's evaluation tenets and practices and the historical evolution of evaluation as a growing force in improving our societies' education, and other public, nonprofit, and private-sector programs.

Third, in Chapter 3, we summarize recent developments and trends in evaluation that have marked the past decade. These movements were either not apparent or still too embryonic to deserve attention when our 1987 text was written. Today, no discussion of evaluation should overlook the expanding uses of qualitative methods and "authentic assessment" techniques, the potential of theory-based evaluation, the impact of new technology on evaluation practice, the institutionalization of evaluation in several sectors of our society, and the emergence of evaluation as a viable profession with its own standards, literature, and professional organizations.

Our intent in Part One is to provide the reader with information essential to understanding not only the content of the sections that follow but also the broad wealth of material that exists in the literature on program evaluation. Although the content in the remainder of this book is intended to apply to evaluation of educational, social, or corporate *programs,* most of it applies as well to *projects, products,* and *processes* used in those areas—indeed, to *any* object of an evaluation. That breadth is especially true of these first three chapters. By the time we reach Part Two of this text, our discussion will focus somewhat more explicitly on *program evaluation,* and we will pause there to define precisely what a program is. Despite the fact that the content of most chapters is as pertinent to evaluation of projects, products, processes, or policies as to evaluation of programs, we avoid tedious redundancy and maintain our emphasis by using only the term *program* in each example or concept presented hereafter. The other possible objects of evaluation (e.g., products or projects) can often be assumed to be included by implication, as should be clear from the context.

chapter 1

Evaluation's Basic Purpose, Uses, and Conceptual Distinctions

ORIENTING QUESTIONS

1. How does evaluation serve society? Why is it important?

2. How many different ways can you list that evaluation has been defined? Which definition do you prefer, and why?

3. What is the difference between formal and informal evaluation?

4. What is the basic purpose of evaluation? What uses can evaluation play? Give some examples.

5. What is an evaluation object? What are some examples of important evaluation objects in education? In business and industry? In the health professions? In the criminal justice system?

6. What are some noninformational uses for evaluation? Which do you see as legitimate uses? As illegitimate?

7. What are the major differences between formative and summative evaluations?

8. What limitations of evaluation should its users keep in mind?

The challenges confronting our society in the twenty-first century will be enormous. Few of them are really new. Most were very apparent in the 1980s and especially in the 1990s, when many of society's current problems have become increasingly more evident. In the United States and many other countries, the public and nonprofit sectors are all grappling with complex issues such as educating children for the next century, reducing functional illiteracy, strengthening families, training versatile employees, and reducing crime, drug abuse, child and spouse abuse, and teenage pregnancy. Each new decade seems to add to the list of challenges as society and the problems it confronts become increasingly complex.

As society's concern over these pervasive and perplexing problems has intensified, so have its efforts to resolve them. Collectively, local, regional, and national agencies have launched a veritable flotilla of programs aimed at identifying and eliminating the underlying causes of these problems. Specific programs judged to have been ineffective have been "mothballed" or sunk outright, usually to be replaced by a new program designed to attack the problem in a different— and hopefully more effective—manner.

In more recent years, scarce resources and budget deficits have posed still more challenges as public and nonprofit agency officials have had to struggle to keep their most promising programs afloat. Increasingly, policy makers and program managers have been faced with tough choices, being forced to cancel some programs or program components to provide sufficient funds to launch or continue others.

To make such choices intelligently, policy makers need good information about the relative effectiveness of each program. Which programs are working well? Which poorly? What are the programs' relative costs and benefits? Similarly, each program manager needs to know how well each part of her program is working. Are some parts contributing more than others? What can be done to improve those parts of the program that are not contributing what they should? Have all aspects of the program planning proven effective, or is more planning needed? What adaptations would make the program more effective?

Answering such questions is the major task of program **evaluation**. And the major task of this book is to introduce you to evaluation and the vital role it plays in virtually every sector of modern society. However, before we can hope to convince you that good evaluation is an essential part of good programs, we must help you understand at least the basic concepts in each of the following areas:

- How we—and others—define evaluation
- How formal and informal evaluation differ
- The basic purpose—and various uses—of formal evaluation
- The distinction between formative and summative evaluation
- The distinction between internal and external evaluation
- Evaluation's importance and its limitations

Covering all of those areas thoroughly could fill a whole book, not just one chapter of an introductory text. Thus, in this chapter, we provide only brief coverage of each of these topics to orient you to concepts and distinctions necessary to understand the content of later chapters.

A BRIEF DEFINITION OF EVALUATION

In the previous section, the perceptive reader will have noticed that the term **evaluation** has been used rather broadly without definition except what was implicit in context. But the rest of this chapter could be rather confusing if we did not stop briefly to define the term more precisely.

Intuitively, it may not seem difficult to define evaluation. For example, one typical dictionary definition of evaluation is "to determine or fix the value of: to examine and judge." Seems quite straightforward, doesn't it? Yet among professional evaluators, there is no uniformly agreed-upon definition of precisely what the term *evaluation* means. It has been used by various evaluation theorists to refer to a great many disparate phenomena.

Of the various definitions proffered for evaluation, we most prefer that proposed by Scriven (1967), who defined evaluation as judging the worth or merit of something. Unfortunately, the evaluation literature has been clouded with other definitions we see as less useful. For example, some writers equate evaluation with research or measurement. Others define it as the assessment of the extent to which specific **objectives** have been attained. For some, evaluation is synonymous with and encompasses nothing more than professional judgment. Others equate evaluation with auditing or several of the variants of quality control. There are those who define evaluation as the act of collecting and providing information to enable decision makers to function more intelligently. And so on.

In later chapters, we will discuss alternative views of evaluation and how these differing conceptions lead to widely varied types of evaluation studies. Our purpose here is only to define evaluation briefly to help readers understand what we mean when we refer to "evaluation" in the remainder of this book.

A Simple Verbal Definition

Put most simply, we believe that evaluation is determining the worth or merit of an evaluation object (whatever is evaluated). Said more expansively, evaluation is the identification, clarification, and application of defensible criteria to determine an evaluation object's value (worth or merit), quality, utility, effectiveness, or significance in relation to those criteria.

Evaluation uses inquiry and judgment methods, including (1) determining **standards** for judging quality and deciding whether those standards should be relative or absolute, (2) collecting relevant information, and (3) applying the standards to determine value, quality, utility, effectiveness, or significance. It leads to recommendations intended to optimize the evaluation object in relation to its intended purpose(s).

In defining evaluation, we should also distinguish it from "**evaluation research**," a term popularized in the late 1960s and early 1970s, beginning with Suchman's 1967 book *Evaluative Research*. Since then, many social scientists have adopted this usage to differentiate between *evaluation research,* which they see as any evaluation that employs rigorous social science research methodology, and *evaluation,* which they use to describe evaluations conducted with other methods (e.g., Rossi, 1982). Throughout this text, we will use the more common and simpler term, *evaluation,* to refer to all evaluations, regardless of their methodology.

We will discuss shortly the matter of how one's definition of evaluation is the product of what one believes the purpose of evaluation to be. But first, we need to distinguish between systematic, formal evaluation studies—the focus of this book—and the much more informal, even casual evaluation that is a part of our everyday life.

INFORMAL VERSUS FORMAL EVALUATION

Evaluation is not a new concept. If one focuses on the aspect of "examining and judging, to determine value," then the practice of evaluation doubtlessly long preceded its definition, tracing its roots back to the beginning of human history. Neanderthals practiced it when determining which types of saplings made the best spears, as did Persian patriarchs in selecting the most suitable suitors for their daughters, or English yeomen who abandoned their own crossbows in favor of the Welsh longbow. They had observed that the longbow could send an arrow through the stoutest armor and was capable of launching three arrows while the crossbow sent only one. Although no formal evaluation reports on "bow comparisons" have been unearthed in English archives, it is clear that the English evaluated the longbow's value for their purposes, deciding that its use would strengthen them in their struggles with the French. So they relinquished their crossbows, perfected and improved upon the Welsh longbow, and the English armies proved invincible during most of the Hundred Years' War.

By contrast, French archers experimented briefly with the longbow, then went back to the crossbow—and continued to lose battles. Such are the perils of poor evaluation! Unfortunately, the faulty judgment that led the French to persist in using an inferior weapon represents an informal evaluation pattern that has been repeated too often throughout history.

Consider the state textbook committee chair that recommends use of a factually inaccurate and culturally insensitive book because it has "lovely illustrations." Or, consider the social worker who judges it best to leave a child at risk of abuse in her home, rather than seek foster home placement. The social worker has likely based her decision on a highly informal appraisal of the relative risks and benefits of these two alternatives. The police officer who decides to make an arrest for loitering has done an on-the-spot evaluation, although most informally. So has the corporate executive who reacts to a subordinate's insubordination with a termination notice. Everyone is, in his or her own way, an evaluator engaged in evaluation of a sort.

Groups also engage in informal evaluation. A city planning and zoning board may vote to down-zone a particular neighborhood without surveying the affected homeowners, examining economic or social impact, or considering possible alternative courses of action—all because of the impressive and polished manner in which the rezoning proposal was presented. Or a city council may impose a curfew for juveniles, even though they have no firm evidence that such a policy actually reduces or prevents juvenile crime. A corporate board may adopt "performance pay" as a way to improve employee productivity, without realizing that the plan could backfire because cooperation and collaboration among employees is an essential in their business. A state board of regents may base its mandate to move all state universities to a common calendar on conversations with a few university presidents or provosts, without examining the impact of such a decision on faculty, students, employers, and others affected by the decision.

These examples remind us that carelessly conducted evaluations often result in faulty judgments. But informal evaluation can also result in correct, even wise decisions. Though it lacks systematic procedures and formally collected evidence, informal evaluation does not occur in a vacuum. Experience, instinct, generalization, and reasoning can all influence the outcome of informal evaluations, and any or all of these may be the basis for sound judgments. When formal evaluation studies are not possible, informal evaluation carried out by knowledgeable, experienced, and fair people can be very useful indeed. It would be unrealistic to think any individual, group, or organization could evaluate formally everything it does. Often informality is the only practical approach. (In choosing an entree from a dinner menu, only the most compulsive individual would conduct exit interviews with restaurant patrons to gather data to guide that choice.)

Evaluation, then, is a basic form of human behavior. Sometimes it is thorough, structured, and formal. More often it is impressionistic and private. Informal evaluation occurs whenever one chooses from among available alternatives without having somehow collected formal evidence about the relative merit of those alternatives. This informal type of evaluation—choices based on highly subjective *perceptions* of which alternative is best—is not of concern in this book. Our focus is on more formal, structured, and public evaluation, where choices are based on *systematic* efforts to define *explicit* criteria and obtain *accurate* information about alternatives (thus enabling the real value of the alternatives to be determined).

DISTINGUISHING BETWEEN EVALUATION'S PURPOSE, USES, AND ESSENTIAL ACTIVITIES

We mentioned earlier that how one defines evaluation stems from what one perceives evaluation's basic purpose to be. We treat that topic somewhat more in depth in this section as we attempt to separate the basic *purpose* of evaluation from (1) the *uses* to which it may be put and (2) the *activities* that are necessary to conduct an evaluation.

Purposes of Evaluation

Just as evaluators are not all agreed on one final, authoritative definition of evaluation, they are by no means unanimous in what they believe evaluation's purpose to be. Consistent with our earlier definition of evaluation, we believe that the basic purpose of evaluation is to render judgments about the value of whatever is being evaluated. Many different *uses* may be made of those value judgments, as we shall discuss shortly, but in every instance the central *purpose* of the evaluative act is the same: to determine the merit or worth of some thing (in program evaluation, of the program or some part of it). This view parallels that of Scriven (1967), who was one of the earliest to outline the purpose of formal evaluation. In his seminal paper "The Methodology of Evaluation," he noted that evaluation plays many roles but argued that it has a single **goal**: to determine the worth or merit of whatever is evaluated. He made the distinction that the *goal* of evaluation is to provide answers to significant evaluative questions that are posed, whereas evaluation *roles* refer to the ways in which those answers are used. (His goal and roles of evaluation are roughly equivalent to what we have preferred to call evaluation's purpose and uses.) According to Scriven (1967), evaluation's goal usually relates to value questions, requires judgments of worth or merit, and is conceptually distinct from its roles. Scriven made the distinction this way:

> In terms of goals, we may say that evaluation attempts to answer certain *types of question* about certain *entities.* The entities are the various . . . instruments (processes, personnel, procedures, programs, etc.). The types of question include questions of the form: *How well* does this instrument perform (with respect to such-and-such criteria)? Does it perform *better* than this other instrument? *What* merits, or drawbacks does this instrument have . . . ? Is the use of this instrument *worth* what it's costing?
>
> . . . But the *roles* which evaluation has in a particular . . . context may be enormously various; it may form part of a . . . training activity, of the process of curriculum development, of a field experiment . . . of . . . an executive training program, a prison, or a classroom. (pp. 40–41)

In the decades since this original distinction between evaluation's basic purpose (goal) and its diverse uses (roles), Scriven (1980, 1991a, 1991b) has greatly elaborated his view without abandoning it. While he has more recently added that "evaluation is concerned with significance, not just merit and worth" (1994, p. 380), he continues to present powerful philosophical arguments that evaluation of any object (e.g., a marketing plan, a school curriculum, or a residential treatment facility for drug abusers) is undertaken to identify and apply defensible criteria to determine its worth, merit, or quality.

This view of evaluation's basic purpose has been most widely adopted by prominent evaluators working in the field of education, ultimately being incorporated into the Program Evaluation Standards developed by the Joint Committee on Standards for Educational Evaluation (1994). Yet while this view is broadly held, other articulate colleagues have argued that evaluation has several purposes. For example, Talmage (1982) notes that "three purposes appear most frequently in definitions of evaluation: (1) to render judgments on the worth of a program; (2) to assist decision makers responsible for deciding policy; and (3) to serve a political function" (p. 594). Talmage also notes that, while these purposes are not mutually exclusive, they are clearly different.

In general, we have no quarrel with Talmage's analysis, but we would note one point of departure. For us, the first purpose she lists for evaluation—to render judgments of the value of a program—*is* evaluation's purpose. Conversely, the other purposes do not describe what evaluation is but rather two of its most common *uses.* Holding that view does not require us to question or diminish the important uses evaluation plays in decision making and political activities. We agree with those who note that the important issues in most programs usually focus on decisions to be made, not judging value for the sake of judging value. But while this ties the purpose of evaluation closely to the decision-making context in which evaluation is typically used, it does not narrow the purpose of evaluation to serve only decision making.

Talmage's discussion of political "purposes" of evaluation ("uses," we would say) draws attention to another intriguing question evaluators have pondered. Is evaluation a scientific activity or a political activity? The answer is "Both." It draws on the methods of the sciences (although not only on those methods), while at the same time being used to serve a variety of political functions. (We discuss this topic further in Chapter 16.)

Before leaving this section, we should note that some highly regarded evaluators (e.g., Shadish, 1994; Fetterman, 1994) construe both the definition and purpose of evaluation to be broader than that which we have proposed here. Because those differences have somewhat more to do with what evaluators do— that is, the activities that are essential in being an evaluator—we will address their views briefly in the next two sections.

Essential Activities of Professional Evaluators

Shadish (1994) has argued that the definition of evaluation should encompass more than "scientific valuing," extending also to include other key activities and practices of the evaluator, such as seeing that the evaluation is used and providing recommendations aimed at program improvement. We applaud the high priority that he accords these critical activities, even as we eschew calling them evaluation. We note that much of what surgeons do (studying research reports on new surgical techniques, presenting papers at professional conferences, or selecting new surgical equipment, for example) is not surgery per se, although that does not make such activities unimportant. Similarly, professional evaluators can appropriately market their services, negotiate evaluation contracts, and help to collate and bind evaluation reports printed at the eleventh hour without calling such activities evaluation. Indeed, much of what evaluators do is *not* evaluation but yet is crucial in their professional practice.

Uses and Objects of Evaluation

Fetterman (1994) has also proposed broadening evaluation's definition and purpose to include using evaluation concepts and techniques to empower (or emancipate, liberate, or illuminate) those whose programs are evaluated. To us, these are wise suggestions of worthy *uses* to which evaluation might be put rather than examples that define evaluation or its central purpose. As important as these pivotal *uses of evaluation* are, they are made no more important, we suggest, by calling them evaluation.

Perhaps this point will be clarified by examining a few of the many uses to which formal evaluation has been put. An exhaustive list would be prohibitive, filling the rest of this book and more. Here we provide only a few representative examples of uses made of evaluation in selected sectors of society.

Examples of Evaluation Use in Education
1. To empower teachers to have more say about how school budgets are allocated
2. To judge the quality of school curricula in specific content areas
3. To accredit schools that meet minimum accreditation standards
4. To determine the value of a middle school's antiviolence program
5. To satisfy an external funding agency's demands for reports on effectiveness of school programs it supports

Examples of Evaluation Use in Other Public Sectors
1. To decide whether to implement an urban development program
2. To establish the value of a job training program
3. To decide whether to modify a low-cost housing project's rental policies
4. To improve a community training program for health care volunteers
5. To determine the impact of a prison's early release program on recidivism

Examples of Evaluation Use in Business and Industry
1. To improve a commercial product
2. To judge the effectiveness of a corporate training program
3. To evaluate new management initiatives (e.g., teamwork, employee participation in decision making, on-site day care, flextime, marketing, affirmative action efforts)

4. To identify the contribution of specific programs to corporate profits
5. To determine the public's perception of a corporation's environmental responsibility

One additional comment about the use of evaluation in business and industry may be warranted. Evaluators unfamiliar with the private sector are sometimes unaware that personnel evaluation is not the only use made of evaluation in business and industrial settings. Perhaps that is because the term "evaluation" has been absent from the descriptors for many corporate activities and programs that, when examined, are decidedly evaluative. Activities labeled as quality assurance, quality control, Total Quality Management (TQM), or Continuous Quality Improvement (CQI) turn out, on closer inspection, to possess many characteristics of program evaluation. In Chapter 22 we treat this topic more fully. Suffice it to say here that many uses are made of evaluation concepts in business and industry.

Uses of Evaluation Are Generally Applicable.   As should be obvious by now, uses of evaluation are clearly portable, if one wishes to use evaluation in the same way in another arena. The use of evaluation may remain constant, but the entity it is applied to—that is, the object of the evaluation—may vary widely. Thus, evaluation may be used *to improve* a commercial product, a community training program, or a school district's student assessment system. It could be used *to build organizational capacity* in the Xerox Corporation, the E. F. Lilly Foundation, the Minnesota Department of Education, or the Utah Division of Family Services. Evaluation can be used *to empower* parents in the San Juan County Migrant Education Program, workers in the U.S. Postal Service, employees of Barclays Bank of England, or residents in downtown Los Angeles. Evaluation can be used *to provide information for decisions about programs* in vocational education centers, community mental health clinics, university medical schools, or county cooperative extension offices. Such examples could be multiplied *ad infinitum,* but these should suffice to make our point.

A Word about the Objects of Formal Evaluation Studies.   As is evident from the previous discussion, formal evaluation studies have been conducted to answer questions about a wide variety of entities, which we have referred to as *evaluation objects.* The evaluation object is whatever is being evaluated. Like many disciplines, evaluation has developed its own technical terminology. For example, "evaluand" is often used to refer to the evaluation object, unless it is a person, who is then an "evaluee" (Scriven, 1991a).

While we do not mind precise language, we see no need to use new terminology when familiar terms will do. Thus, except as they may appear in quoted material, we will not use "evaluand" or "evaluee" further, preferring to refer to both as "objects" of the evaluation.

In some instances, so many evaluations are conducted of the same type of evaluation object that it prompts suggestions for evaluation techniques found to be particularly helpful in evaluating something of that particular type. An example would be Kirkpatrick's (1983) proposal for evaluating training efforts. In several areas, concern about how to evaluate broad categories of objects effectively has led to the development of various subareas within the field of evaluation, such as product evaluation, personnel evaluation, program evaluation, policy analysis, and performance evaluation.

Before we leave this discussion of evaluation uses and objects, we should also note that evaluation's uses are not always limited to providing information. In Chapter 12, we discuss noninformational uses of evaluation, such as the salutary effect that often results from the mere fact that people know their activities may be evaluated (analogous to the behavior of freeway drivers when following a state trooper). However, using evaluation for noninformational—but legitimate—uses is a far cry from *misusing* evaluations by providing erroneous information.

Mischief Caused by Misuse of Evaluation

Now and then a poorly conceived or executed "evaluation" yields information that is at best misleading and at worst absolutely false. While such occurrences are rare, they can cause serious problems. Because they typically carry an air of respectability, such pseudoevaluations are often not challenged, with the result that important decisions about essential programs and services are unwittingly based on fallacious information. Sometimes the damage may be slight, but at others it may be catastrophic. An example should serve to show what mischief can be caused when this form of evaluation misuse occurs.

In the United States, the National Commission on Excellence in Education was created in the early 1980s to investigate the widespread public perception that something was seriously wrong with the U.S. educational system. The essential message in the commission's public report, titled *A Nation at Risk: The Imperative for Educational Reform* (1983), was a scathing attack on the schools, concluding that they were failing so badly in educating the citizenry that America's very future as a nation and a people was threatened.

This report sparked a U.S. national pastime of school bashing that continues in today's media, although perhaps the tone is recently becoming more muted. Yet Americans have been bombarded for better than a decade with news stories about the deplorable state of education in the United States, while glowing news reports about the superiority of Japan's (and many other countries') schools have penetrated America's homes and minds. The impact of this one supposed "evaluation" study has been enormous. Its conclusions have sent many panicked educators scurrying about in search of a solution to the horrendous problems the report cited in America's schools. Countless changes in curricula in countless schools were efforts to correct problems cited in the *Nation at Risk* report. This report's conclusions have been trumpeted so loudly and so often that they have become embedded in the belief structure of the great majority of the American public, including school practitioners.

Fortunately, not everyone believed the pessimistic prophecies of the National Commission. Gerald Bracey (1995) has issued a series of five annual reports on "the condition of public education," in which he attacks the "myth" that America's schools and students are inferior. He specifically attacks the *Nation at Risk* report's claim that performance of American students is low in comparison to their Asian and European counterparts. He raised doubts about the validity of the National Commission's work.

Yet the magnitude of the mischief caused by the National Commission's conclusions was not fully evident until the recent publication of Berliner and Biddle's (1995) *The Manufactured Crisis,* in which the authors examine the "report's evidence" concerning the "sorry state" of American schools. They conclude that the report "made many claims about the 'failures' of American education, how those 'failures' were confirmed by 'evidence,' and how this would inevitably damage the nation. (Unfortunately, none of the supposedly supportive 'evidence' actually appeared in *A Nation at Risk,* nor did this work provide citations to tell Americans where that 'evidence' might be found)"(p. 3). They point out that the claims of this often quoted report were a combination of unsupported assertions, myths, and half-truths. Thankfully, that fact now appears to be leaking out to even the media, and there appears to be a possible "sea change" in the tide of public opinion that has been until now surging strongly against schools in the United States (Gough, 1996).

Space does not permit us to trace the inestimable damage done by the largely specious *Nation at Risk* report. Such pseudoevaluations can corrode the confidence policy makers and program managers hold in the usefulness of evaluation. Such flagrant and swashbuckling misuse of so-called evaluation evidence can do much to erode the promise that genuine evaluation holds for the improvement of educational—and other—programs and practices. To be helpful, evaluation must be used correctly and sensibly. Not a profound thought, we concede, but one that sometimes seems to escape even seasoned and distinguished panels of experts. Sometimes such problems arise from the failure to make the two simple but important distinctions in evaluation that we discuss in the next section.

TWO BASIC DISTINCTIONS IN EVALUATION

Prominent evaluation theorists differ widely in their views of what evaluation is and how it should be carried out. We will discuss these differences in some detail in Part Two. Despite these varying perspectives, however, some common concepts and distinctions exist about which there seems to be relatively little debate (not that everyone agrees as to their importance or utility but rather as to what they are and how they can be differentiated). These notions, though elemental, have proven powerful in shaping people's thinking about evaluation. In this section, we will discuss two basic distinctions in evaluation and how they apply to evaluation studies.

Formative and Summative Evaluation

Scriven (1967) first distinguished between the *formative* and *summative* roles of evaluation. Since then, the terms have become almost universally accepted in the field. Although in practice distinctions between these two types of evaluation may blur somewhat, it seems useful to summarize the major differences noted by Scriven, even at the risk of some oversimplification.

Formative evaluation is conducted to provide program staff evaluative information useful in improving the program. Three examples follow.

1. During the development of an innovative, elementary-school reading curriculum, formative evaluation would involve content inspection by reading experts, pilot tests with small numbers of children, field tests with larger numbers of children and teachers in several schools, and so forth. Each step would result in immediate feedback to those developing the curriculum, who would then use the information to make necessary revisions.

2. During implementation of a Total Quality Management (TQM) program in an organization, a formative evaluation might begin with an assessment of the organizational climate and culture to determine which aspects of the climate would facilitate the implementation of TQM and which might present barriers to its successful implementation. As the program unfolds, a formative evaluation could examine the interactions of TQM groups, the issues they choose to address, the methods they use, and acceptance of their recommendations. Such information could be used to improve the TQM training of employees, the structuring of groups, and issues to address.

3. A formative evaluation of a long-standing outreach program intended to improve the immunization of infants and preschoolers might begin with (1) determining which program goals are not being achieved to their desired level and (2) determining how attainment of those goals can be improved. For example, evaluators might examine the characteristics of children least likely to be immunized and identify reasons for the lack of immunization (perceived cost, location of facility, fear or ignorance regarding immunizations, etc.). Armed with that feedback, program personnel could then modify the existing program based on their improved understanding of the target group and their needs.

Summative evaluation is conducted and made public to provide program decision makers and potential consumers with judgments about that program's worth or merit in relation to important criteria, as can be seen by extending the three previous examples.

1. After the reading curriculum package is completely developed, a summative evaluation might be conducted to determine, with a

national sample of typical elementary schools, teachers, and students, how effective the package is in improving students' reading ability, attitude toward reading, and the like. The findings of the summative evaluation would then guide decisions about continuation of the program in the school(s) where it was developed, as well as being made available to other schools potentially interested in the new curriculum.

2. To determine whether the TQM program should continue, the director of the organization might ask the evaluator to determine the degree to which TQM has improved the productivity of the organization and the morale of employees.

3. A needs assessment could be carried out to determine whether a new outreach immunization program was needed in a community not previously served by such a program. Data could be collected to answer the following questions: (1) Are there enough children without immunization to warrant establishing the program; and (2) Would such a program, in fact, attract the desired target audience (children unlikely to be immunized without the program)? If answers to either of these questions were negative, the health administrators who requested the study might rightly conclude that the needs are not sufficient to warrant it, thus making a summative decision to terminate the entire outreach immunization planning effort.

Note that the **audiences** and uses for formative and summative evaluation are very different. In formative evaluation, the audience is program personnel— in our examples, those responsible for developing the reading curriculum, implementing the TQM program, or designing and running the outreach immunization program. Summative evaluation audiences include potential consumers (students, teachers, employees, managers, or health officials in agencies that could adopt the program), funding sources (taxpayers or funding agency), and supervisors and other officials, as well as program personnel. Formative evaluation leads to (or should lead to) decisions about program development (including modification, revision, and the like). Summative evaluation leads to decisions concerning program continuation, termination, expansion, adoption, and so on.

It should be apparent that both formative and summative evaluations are essential because decisions are needed during the developmental stages of a program to improve and strengthen it, and again, when it has stabilized, to judge its final worth or determine its future. Unfortunately, far too many agencies conduct only summative evaluation of their programs. This is unfortunate because the development process, without formative evaluation, is incomplete and inefficient. Consider the foolishness of developing a new aircraft design and submitting it to a "summative" test flight without first testing it in the "formative" wind tunnel. Program "test flights" can be expensive, too, especially when we haven't a clue about the probability of success.

Failure to use formative evaluation is myopic, for formative data collected early can help rechannel time, money, and all types of human and material resources into more productive directions. Evaluation conducted only when a project nears completion may simply come too late to be of much help. Apparently, many instructional designers and trainers understand this point. Zemke (1985) surveyed readers of *Training* magazine and found that over 60 percent reported that they used formative evaluation in their training activities. In a later survey of corporate training officials, Tessmer and Wedman (1992) found that nearly half of their respondents reported that they use formative evaluation.

Although formative evaluations more often occur in early stages of a program's development and summative evaluations more often occur in their later stages, as these two terms imply, it would be an error to think they are limited to those time frames. However, the relative emphasis on formative and summative evaluation changes throughout the life of a program, as suggested in Figure 1.1, although this generalized concept obviously may not precisely fit the evolution of any particular program.

Two important factors that influence the usefulness of formative evaluation are control and timing. If suggestions for improvement are to be implemented, then it is important that the formative study collect data on variables over which program administrators have some control. Also, information that reaches those administrators too late for use in improving the program is patently useless.

An effort to distinguish between formative and summative evaluation on several dimensions appears in Figure 1.2. As with most conceptual distinctions, formative and summative evaluation are often not as easy to distinguish in practice as they seem in these pages. Scriven (1991a) has acknowledged that the two are often profoundly intertwined in practice. For example, if a program continues beyond a summative evaluation study, the results of that study may be used for both summative and, later, formative evaluation purposes. In practice,

FIGURE 1.1 Relationship between formative and summative evaluation across life of a program

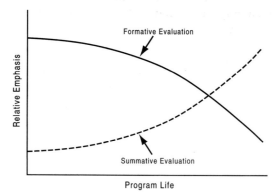

	Formative Evaluation	Summative Evaluation
Purpose	To determine value or quality	To determine value or quality
Use	To improve the program	To make decisions about the program's future or adoption
Audience	Program administrators and staff	Program administrators and/or potential consumer or funding agency
By Whom	Primarily internal evaluators, supported by external evaluators	External evaluators, supported by internal evaluators in unique cases
Major Characteristics	Provides feedback so program personnel can improve it	Provides information to enable program personnel to decide whether to continue it, or consumers to adopt it
Design Constraints	What information is needed? When?	What evidence is needed for major decisions?
Purpose of Data Collection	Diagnostic	Judgmental
Measures	Sometimes informal	Valid and reliable
Frequency of Data Collection	Frequent	Infrequent
Sample Size	Often small	Usually large
Questions Asked	What is working? What needs to be improved? How can it be improved?	What results occur? With whom? Under what conditions? With what training? At what cost?

FIGURE 1.2 Differences between formative and summative evaluation

the line between formative and summative is often rather fuzzy. Scriven (1986) himself suggested one reason why they sometimes blur, noting that when programs have many components, summative evaluations that result in replacing weak components have played a formative role in improving the program in its entirety.

Are All Evaluations Either Formative or Summative? Several other evaluators have suggested that Scriven's (1967) dichotomy is not sufficiently broad to encompass all forms of evaluation. For example, Misanchuk (1978) was quick to suggest that Scriven's summative evaluation needed to be followed by a delayed **confirmative evaluation**, conducted after the program had been implemented and in operation for a significant period to see how well it retains its effectiveness across time. Chen (1996) has recently proposed that Scriven's formative-summative dichotomy does not capture adequately all of the basic types of evaluation. He offers a typology that includes evaluation functions and program stages that he contends are overlooked by Scriven. Scriven (1996) has argued that Chen's typology is unnecessary and that the formative-summative dichotomy adequately accommodates all functions and program stages Chen proposes, but delving deeper into this issue would be beyond the scope of this introductory text. Those interested in more detail should peruse Chen's fuller description of Scriven and their differences. Suffice it to say here that the formative and summative distinction has not only served the field well in providing a usable language to describe important uses of evaluation but has also been a rich conceptual seedbed for the sprouting of many proposed refinements and extensions that may yet prove fruitful to the field.

The distinction between formative and summative evaluation is relevant to another important distinction, that of internal and external evaluation.

Internal and External Evaluation

The adjectives *internal* and *external* distinguish between evaluations conducted by program employees and those conducted by outsiders. An experimental year-round education program in the San Francisco public schools might be evaluated by a member of the school district staff (internal) or by a site-visit team appointed by the California State Board of Education (external). A large health maintenance organization (HMO) with facilities in six cities may have a member of each facility's staff evaluate the utility of their training of local residents to serve in paraprofessional roles (internal). Or the state may send a team out to look at that paraprofessional training program (external).

Seems pretty simple, right? And often it is. But assume that the HMO sends a team out from *their* headquarters to evaluate the program in *their* six separate facilities. Is that an **internal evaluation** or **external evaluation**? Write your answer here: _____ Actually, the correct answer is "Both," for such an evaluation is clearly external from the perspective of those in the individual facility, yet it clearly is an internal evaluation from the perspective of the headquarters administrators who assigned their staff to evaluate those parts of the parent HMO operation.

There are obvious advantages and disadvantages connected with both internal and external evaluation roles. The internal evaluator is almost certain to know more about the program than any outsider, but she may also be so close to the program that she is unable to be completely objective. Seldom is there as much reason to question the objectivity of the external evaluator (unless she is found to have a particular ax to grind), and this dispassionate perspective is perhaps her greatest asset. Conversely, it is difficult for an external evaluator to ever learn as much about the program as the insider knows. Note that when we say "as much," we refer only to quantity, not quality. One often finds an internal evaluator who is full of unimportant details about the program but overlooks several critical variables. If these bits of key information are picked up by the external evaluator, as is sometimes the case, she may end up knowing much less *overall* about the project but knowing much more of importance. On the other hand, the internal evaluator is much more likely to be familiar with important contextual information (for example, the serious illness of the director's husband, which is adversely affecting the director's work) that would temper evaluation recommendations.

Knowing who funds an evaluation and to whom the evaluator reports largely determines the evaluator's financial and administrative dependence. Most evaluation writers assume that the external evaluator's financial and administrative independence from the program generally enhances the credibility of the study, a point with which we agree.

Also, the belief has been present for decades that external evaluators who are selected for their expertise enhance the evaluation's credibility. We concur (hastening to add that when external evaluators are selected for other reasons—friendliness, old fraternity ties, "she owes me one" favors, and so on—all bets about heightened credibility are off).

Of course, under some circumstances, the objectivity and credibility of external evaluators may be little better than that of their internal counterparts. Even Scriven (1993), long the champion of external evaluation as the only sensible way to control bias, acknowledges this. While reiterating that internal evaluators are irrevocably biased toward favorable findings, he notes that can also be true of the external evaluator who is selected by the program manager for "friendliness" or who becomes caught up in social interactions with staff. But the greater problem for the external evaluator, he contends, is that "No one ever got rich from one evaluation contract. . . . we have to have satisfied clients if we want additional business from them. . . . And what pleases clients more, good news about their baby or bad news? Right. . . . even external evaluators [can have] direct conflicts of interest" (p. 84).

This only touches on some of the most obvious of internal and external evaluation's advantages and disadvantages.

Possible Role Combinations

The dimensions of formative and summative evaluation can be combined with the dimensions of internal and external evaluation to form the two-by-two matrix shown in Figure 1.3. The most common roles in evaluation might be indicated by cells 1 and 4 in the matrix. Formative evaluation is most often conducted by an internal evaluator, and there are clear merits in such an approach. Her knowledge of the program is of great value here, and possible lack of objectivity is not nearly the problem it would be in a summative evaluation. Summative evaluations are probably most often (and probably best) conducted by external evaluators. It is difficult, for example, to know how much credibility to accord a Ford Motor Company evaluation that concludes that a particular Ford automobile is far better than its competitors in the same price range. The credibility accorded to an internal summative program evaluation (cell 3) may be no better. In most organizations, summative evaluation is generally best conducted by an external evaluator or agency. But there are two circumstances in which we would alter that statement quite dramatically. First, in some instances, there

	INTERNAL	EXTERNAL
FORMATIVE	**1** Internal Formative	**2** External Formative
SUMMATIVE	**3** Internal Summative	**4** External Summative

FIGURE 1.3 Combination of evaluation roles

is simply no possibility of the program's obtaining such external help because of financial constraints or absence of competent personnel willing to do the job. In these cases, the summative evaluation is weakened by the lack of outside perspective, but it might be possible to retain a semblance of objectivity and credibility by choosing the internal summative evaluator from among those who are some distance removed from the actual development of the program or product being evaluated.

For example, assume that an elementary school in a large (in geography, not budget) rural district in Saskatchewan needs to have a summative evaluation of an innovative French language and culture program they have been running. No funds are available to bring an evaluator in from outside the district, and because much of the program is oral, it would be hard to bundle it up and send it off for review. Everyone in the school is either a zealous enthusiast or a bitter opponent of the program, so there is no way to get an unbiased internal evaluation. In this context, we see it far better to obtain a "quasi-external" summative evaluation than do none at all. By "quasi-external" we mean that one should conduct the evaluation so as to maximize its "externality." Why not ask the principal of another school in the district to evaluate the program in return for helping with a later task in that school? While still internal to the district, this principal would be external to the school, hence quasi-external. If the evaluation were commissioned with a strong request for the quasi-outsider to "tell-it-like-it-is," with no punches pulled and no weaknesses overlooked, there is good reason to suspect many of the advantages of a true external summative evaluation would occur. If one still worried that being in the same district tainted the outcomes, perhaps a principal from an adjacent district, or a school not too far beyond the province's boundary, would make it a true external evaluation. Whatever definitional cutoffs one chooses to use, it is important to remember that there is a continuum from external to internal; it is a matter of degree, not black or white.

The second circumstance where we might soften our cautions about the biases that abound in internal evaluations is where organizations have structured their internal evaluation unit (and its evaluators) to enhance their ability to be forthright about their findings. Such structuring can take many forms, but the key is that the internal evaluators are insulated and shielded from the consequences of displeasure of those whose program is evaluated. Otherwise, the buffeting sometimes experienced by evaluators who do not gild the sometimes unsightly truth about the agencies' programs can be painful. Over time, even the stouthearted may begin hiding any criticisms behind carefully worded doublespeak (e.g., using double-message statements such as "You will be very fortunate if you can get this department to work for you" or "I can recommend this department with no qualifications whatsoever").

Fortunately, a number of large agencies have structured their internal evaluation function to give it maximum independence (and avoid evaluators being placed in the untenable posture of evaluating programs developed by the boss or close associates). The larger the organization, the more insulated its evaluation staff can be and the fewer problems or pressures one might expect to be caused by hierarchial or close social relationships. Indeed, the unit (and its function) may even lose much of its internal flavor and appear more like a built-in external evaluation unit (if that non sequitur is permitted), free to pursue evaluations throughout the organization as need demands.

At the U.S. federal level, the Offices of the Inspectors General, though certainly not apolitical, perhaps comes closest to this description. In the private sector, Xerox Corporation's "Document University" is a good example, with numerous training programs being run and the internal evaluation unit they have supported providing targeted (and sometimes very pointed) criticisms of those training courses, but with little fear of repercussions typical of in-house evaluators obligated to evaluate in-house programs.

To return to Figure 1.3, a very important role—that of the external formative evaluator (cell 2)—is almost completely neglected in most program evaluations. As implied earlier, the internal evaluator may share many of the perspectives and blind spots of other program staff and, consequently, neglect even to entertain negative questions about the program. The external evaluator, who does not have lengthy familiarity with the program or its context, is much less likely to be influenced by a priori perceptions of its basic worth. This is not synonymous with saying that she is predisposed toward judging the program as ineffective. Her orientation should be neither positive nor negative. It should be neutral, uninfluenced by close associations with either the program or its competitors. In essence, the external formative evaluator introduces a cold, hard look of reality into the evaluation relatively early—in a sense, a preview of what a summative evaluator might say. This fresh outside perspective is important and can preclude the disaster that frequently occurs when program staff self-consciously select criteria and variables they believe will prove their program successful, only to have an outside agency (a governing board or site-visit team) later recommend terminating the program because their summative evaluation—which focused on other variables or criteria—suggested the program was ineffective. This fresh point of view allows the external formative evaluator to see issues overlooked by the insiders. Moreover, the external evaluator can prove helpful to the internal evaluator by suggesting additional methods for data collection that may be more feasible or cost-effective for the insider to use. Wisdom would urge the use of an outside evaluator as part of every formative evaluation. Scriven (1972), although accepting the utility of internal formative evaluation, also argued for this view, saying that "it now seems to me that a producer or staff evaluator who wants good *formative* evaluation has got to use some external evaluators to get it" (p. 2).

EVALUATION'S IMPORTANCE—AND ITS LIMITATIONS

Given its many formative and summative uses, it may seem almost axiomatic to assert that evaluation is not only valuable but essential in any effective system or society. Scriven (1991b) has said it well:

> The process of disciplined evaluation permeates all areas of thought and practice. . . . It is found in scholarly book reviews, in engineering's quality control procedures, in the Socratic dialogues, in serious social and moral criticism, in mathematics, and in the opinions handed down by appellate courts. . . . It is the process whose duty is the systematic and objective determination of merit, worth, or value. Without such a process, there is no way to distinguish the worthwhile from the worthless. (p. 4)

Scriven also argues the importance of evaluation in *pragmatic* terms ("bad products and services cost lives and health, destroy the quality of life, and waste the resources of those who cannot afford waste"), *ethical* terms ("evaluation is a key tool in the service of justice"), *social* and *business* terms ("evaluation directs effort where it is most needed, and endorses the 'new and better way' when it is better than the traditional way—and the traditional way where it's better than the new high-tech way"), *intellectual* terms ("it refines the tools of thought"), and *personal* terms ("it provides the only basis for justifiable self-esteem") (p. 43). Perhaps for these reasons, evaluation has increasingly been used as an instrument to pursue goals of business and governmental agencies at local, regional, national, and international levels.

Potential Limitations of Evaluation

The usefulness of evaluation has led some persons to look to it as a panacea for all the ills of society. But evaluation alone cannot solve all the problems of society. One of the biggest mistakes of evaluators is to promise results that cannot possibly be attained. Even ardent supporters of evaluation are forced to admit that many evaluation studies fail to lead to significant improvements in the programs they evaluate. Why? Partly it's a question of grave inadequacies in the conceptualization and conduct of many evaluations. It's also a question of understanding too little about other factors that affect the use of evaluation information, even from studies that are well conceptualized and well conducted. In addition, both evaluators and their clients may have been limited by an unfortunate tendency to view evaluation as a series of discrete studies rather than a continuing system of self-renewal.

A few poorly planned, badly executed, or inappropriately ignored evaluations should not surprise us; such failings occur in every field of human endeavor. The real problem is one of frequency and significance. So many key evaluations have been disappointing or have made such little impact that even some evaluation advocates have expressed reservations about evaluation's living up to its high potential. Indeed, unless evaluation practices improve significantly in the years ahead, its potential may never be realized. That need not happen. This book is intended to help evaluators, and those who use their results, to improve the practice and utility of evaluation.

A parallel problem exists when those served by evaluation naively assume that its magic wand need only be waved over an enterprise to correct all its malfunctions and inadequacies. Though evaluation can be enormously useful, it is generally counterproductive for evaluators or those who depend on their work to propose evaluation as the ultimate solution to every problem or, indeed, as any sort of solution, because evaluation in and of itself won't effect a solution—though it might suggest one. Evaluation serves to identify strengths and weaknesses, highlight the good, and expose the faulty, but it cannot singlehandedly correct problems, for that is the role of management and other **stakeholders**, using evaluation findings as one tool that will help them in that process.

Evaluation has a role to play in enlightening its consumers, and it may be used for many other roles. But it is only one of many influences on improving the policies, practices, and decisions in the institutions that are important to us.

APPLICATION EXERCISES

1. List the types of evaluation studies that have been conducted in an institution or agency of your acquaintance, noting in each instance whether the evaluator was internal or external to that institution. Determine whether each study was formative or summative and whether the study would have been strengthened by having someone with the *opposite* (internal/external) relationship to the institution conduct the study.

2. Think back to any formal evaluation study you have seen conducted (or if you have never seen one conducted, find a written evaluation report of one). Identify three things that make it different from informal evaluations. Then list 10 informal evaluations you have performed so far today. (Oh, yes you have!)

3. Discuss the potential and limitations of program evaluation. Identify some things evaluation can and cannot do for programs in your field.

4. Within your own institution (if you are a university student, you might choose your university), identify several evaluation objects that you believe would be appropriate

for study. For each, identify (a) the *use* the evaluation study would serve and (b) the basic *purpose* of the evaluation.

SUGGESTED READINGS

We suggest that you read the entire contents of *Evaluation Practice*, 15(3), a special issue devoted to "Evaluation: Review of the Past, Preview of the Future," including articles by several leading evaluation theorists and practitioners. If you must choose among the 17 papers, do not skip the Introduction by Smith; the articles by House, Reichardt, Lincoln, Patton, Stufflebeam, and Shadish; or the ones by Scriven, Bickman, . . .

Scriven, M. (1991). Beyond formative and summative evaluation. In M. W. McLaughlin & D. C. Phillips (Eds.) *Evaluation and education: At quarter century* (pp. 19–64). Ninetieth Yearbook of the National Society for the Study of Education. Chicago: National Society for the Study of Education.

Shadish, W. R. (1994). Need-based evaluation: What do you need to know to do good evaluation? *Evaluation Practice, 15*(3), 347-358.

chapter 2

Origins of Modern Program Evaluation

ORIENTING QUESTIONS

1. Cite two uses of formal evaluation prior to 1800.
2. How extensively was program evaluation used between 1800 and 1940?
3. What major political events occurred in the late 1950s and early 1960s that greatly accelerated the growth of evaluation thought?
4. What are the most significant events beginning in 1965 that precipitated the emergence of modern program evaluation? In what way did it contribute to the development of new evaluation approaches and methods?

Formal evaluation of educational, and other public, nonprofit and private-sector programs is still maturing as a field, with its most rapid development occurring during the past four decades. Nearly 15 years ago, some analysts already credited it with substantial growth:

> Evaluation, as an established field, is now in its late adolescent years. The bubbling, exciting, fast-developing childhood years of the late 1960s and early 1970s gave way in the mid to late 1970s to the less self-assured, serious, introspective early adolescent years. Now, in the early 1980s, evaluation is making the transition from late adolescence to adulthood. (Conner, Altman, & Jackson, 1984, p. 13)

Is the label of adulthood deserved for program evaluation? Perhaps if *young* adulthood is included. But it is a long way from the threshold of adulthood to full maturity achieved as a field reaches its prime, and that is a distance program evaluation must still travel. Yet, we should not overlook the fact that evaluation has progressed to the point where we are comfortable viewing it as a rapidly maturing profession and nearly agreeing with those who refer to it as an emerging discipline or **transdiscipline** (e.g., Scriven, 1991b, 1993).

In our next chapter we discuss the developments and trends that mark evaluation's progress toward becoming both a full-fledged profession and a discipline or transdiscipline. But first we invite you to probe briefly with us into the social, political, and methodological soils in which evaluation first took root and from which its more recent trends and developments have sprung. This chapter contains a brief history of formal evaluation up to 1965, a watershed year with key events many view as the beginning of modern program evaluation.

THE HISTORY AND INFLUENCE OF EVALUATION IN SOCIETY: STONE AGE TO 1965

It is instructive to examine, even though briefly, the early antecedents of evaluation that grew and intertwined into program evaluation as we know it today. In this chapter we trace briefly the early, general history of program evaluation. Readers interested in more complete coverage are referred to excellent summaries by Madaus, Scriven, and Stufflebeam (1983) and Baker and Niemi (in press), as well as to our earlier, detailed history of evaluation in education (Worthen & Sanders, 1987, chap. 2).

In this chapter we make no attempt to cover the history of research or other activities dependent on data collection (e.g., census taking), preferring to confine ourselves to the history of evaluation, except as we are sometimes forced to mention developments in measurement or other inquiry areas because of their particular pertinence to how program evaluation has evolved.

Our focus here is solely on *formal* evaluation, ignoring informal evaluation, which has been the ever present companion of humankind since the dawn of time. Yet even formal evaluation—the systematic use of accurate information and **criteria** to assign values and justify value judgments—has a much longer and more distinguished history than is generally recognized.

Early Forms of Formal Evaluation

Some evaluator-humorists have mused that formal evaluation was probably at work in determining which evasion skills taught in Sabertooth Avoidance 101 had the greatest survival value. Scriven (1991b) apparently was not tongue-in-cheek in suggesting that formal evaluation of crafts may reach back to evaluation of early stone-chippers' products, and he was obviously serious in asserting that it can be traced back to samurai sword evaluation.

In the public sector, formal evaluation was evident as early as 2000 B.C., when Chinese officials conducted civil service examinations to measure proficiency of public officials. And in education, Socrates used verbally mediated evaluations as part of the learning process. But centuries passed before formal evaluations began to compete with religious and political beliefs as the driving force behind social and educational decisions.

Some commentators (e.g., Cronbach et al., 1980) see the ascendancy of natural science in the seventeenth century as a necessary precursor to the premium that later came to be placed on direct observation. Occasional tabulations of mortality, health, and populations grew into a fledgling tradition of empirical social research that expanded to where "In 1797, *Encyclopaedia Britannica* could speak of statistics—'state-istics,' as it were—as a 'word lately introduced to express a view or survey of any kingdom, county, or parish'" (p. 24).

But quantitative surveys were not the only precursor of modern social research in the 1700s. Rossi and Freeman (1985) give an example of an early British sea captain who halved his crew into a "treatment group" forced to consume limes, while their control counterparts consumed the sailors' normal diet. Not only did the experiment show that "consuming limes could avert scurvy," but "British seamen eventually were forced to consume citrus fruits— this is the derivation of the label 'limeys,' which is still sometimes applied to the English" (pp. 20–21).

Program Evaluation: 1800–1940

During the 1800s, dissatisfaction with educational and social programs in Great Britain generated reform movements in which government-appointed royal commissions heard testimony and used other less formal methods to "evaluate" the respective institutions. This led to still-existing systems of external inspectorates for schools in England and Ireland.

In the United States, educational evaluation took a slightly different bent, being influenced by Horace Mann's comprehensive annual, empirical reports on Massachusetts's education in the 1840s and the Boston School Committee's 1845 and 1846 use of printed tests in several subjects (the first instance of wide-scale assessment of student achievement serving as the basis for school comparisons). These two developments in Massachusetts were the first attempts at objectively measuring student achievement to assess the quality of a large school system.

Later, during the late 1800s, liberal reformer Joseph Rice organized a similar assessment program in several large school systems throughout the United States to "document" his claims that schooltime was inefficiently used. On spelling tests, for example, he found negligible differences in students' spelling performance between schools, where one had students spend as much as 100 minutes a week on spelling instruction while another had students spend as little as 10 minutes per week. He used these data to flog educators into seeing the need to scrutinize their practices empirically.

The late 1800s also saw the beginning of efforts to accredit U.S. universities and secondary schools, although that movement did not really become a potent force for evaluating educational institutions until several strong regional accrediting associations were established in the 1930s. (The evaluation of that form of program evaluation will be traced further in Chapter 8). The early 1900s saw another example of **accreditation** (broadly defined) in Flexner's (1910) evaluation (backed by the American Medical Association and the Carnegie Foundation) of the 155 medical schools then operating in the United States and Canada. Although based only on one-day site visits to each school by himself and one colleague, Flexner argued that inferior training was immediately obvious: "A stroll through the laboratories disclosed the presence or absence of apparatus, museum specimens, library and students; and a whiff told the inside story regarding the manner in which anatomy was cultivated" (Flexner, 1960, p. 79). Flexner was not deterred by lawsuits or death threats from what the medical schools viewed as his "pitiless exposure" of their medical training practices. He delivered his evaluation findings in scathing terms (labeling, for example, Chicago's 15 medical schools as "the plague spot of the country in respect to medical education" [p. 84]), and soon "Schools collapsed to the right and left, usually without a murmur" (p. 87). No one was ever left to wonder whether Flexner's reports were evaluative.

Other areas of public interest were also subjected to evaluative surveys in the early 1900s; Cronbach and his colleagues (1980) cite surveys of slum conditions, management and efficiency studies in the schools, and investigations of local government corruption as examples.

Also in the early 1900s, the educational testing movement began to gain momentum as measurement technology made rapid advances under E. L. Thorndike and his students, and by 1918 objective testing was flourishing, pervading the military and private industry as well as all levels of education. The 1920s saw the rapid emergence of norm-referenced tests developed for use in measuring individual performance levels. By the mid-1930s, more than half of the United States had some form of statewide testing, and standardized, norm-referenced testing, including achievement tests and personality and interest profiles, became a huge commercial enterprise.

During this period, educators regarded measurement and evaluation as nearly synonymous, with the latter usually thought of as summarizing student test performance and assigning grades. Although the broader concept of evaluation, as we know it today, was still embryonic, useful measurement tools for the evaluator were proliferating rapidly, even though very few meaningful, formally published evaluations of school programs or curricula would appear for another 20 years. One notable exception was the ambitious landmark Eight Year Study (Smith & Tyler, 1942) that set a new standard for educational evaluation with its sophisticated methodology and its linkage of outcome measures to desired learning outcomes. Tyler's work, in this and subsequent studies (e.g., Tyler, 1950), also planted the seeds of **criterion-referenced testing**, a viable alternative to **norm-referenced testing**. (We will return in Chapter 5 to the profound impact that Tyler and those who followed in his tradition have had on program evaluation, especially in education.)

Meanwhile, foundations for evaluation were being laid in public administration and the private sector as well. The emergence of "efficiency experts" in industry soon permeated the business community and, as Cronbach et al. (1980) noted, "business executives sitting on the governing boards of social services pressed for greater efficiency in those services" (p. 27). Some cities and social agencies began to develop internal research units, and social scientists began to trickle into government service, where they began to conduct applied social research in specific areas of public health, housing needs, and work productivity. However, these ancestral, social-research "precursors to evaluation" were small, isolated activities that exerted little overall impact on the daily lives of the citizenry or the decisions of the government agencies that served them.

But then came the Great Depression and the sudden proliferation of government services and agencies as President Roosevelt's New Deal programs were implemented to salvage the U.S. economy. Federal agencies were established to oversee new national programs in welfare, public works, labor management, urban development, health, education, and numerous other human service areas, and increasing numbers of social scientists went to work in these agencies. Applied social research opportunities abounded, and soon social science academics began to join with their agency-based colleagues to study a wide variety of variables relating to these programs. While some scientists called for explicit evaluation of these new social programs (e.g., Stephan, 1935), most pursued applied research at the intersection of their agency's needs and their personal interests.

Program Evaluation: 1940–1965

Applied social research expanded during World War II as researchers investigated government programs intended to help military personnel in areas such as reducing their vulnerability to propaganda, increasing morale, and improving the training and job placement of soldiers. In the following decade, studies were directed at new programs in job training, housing, family planning, and community development. Such studies were often focused on particular facets of the program in which the researchers happened to be most interested. As these programs increased in scope and scale, however, social scientists began to focus their studies more directly on the entire programs rather than on the parts of them they found personally intriguing. With this broader focus came more frequent references to their work as "evaluation research" (social research methods applied to improve a particular program). If we are liberal in stretching the definition of evaluation to cover most types of data collection in health and human service programs, we can safely say evaluation flourished in those areas in the 1950s and early 1960s. Rossi and Freeman (1985) state that it was commonplace in that period to see social scientists "engaged in evaluations of delinquency-prevention programs, felon-rehabilitation projects, psychotherapeutic and psychopharmacological treatments, public housing programs, and community organization activities . . . [as well as] family planning, . . . nutrition and health care . . . and agricultural and community development" (p. 25). Most such studies drew on existing social research methods and did not extend the conceptual or methodological boundaries of evaluation beyond those already established for behavioral and social research. Such efforts would come later.

Developments in educational program evaluation between 1940 and 1965 were unfolding in a somewhat different pattern. The 1940s generally saw a period of consolidation of earlier evaluation developments. School personnel devoted their energies to improving standardized testing, teacher-made classroom tests, accreditation, and school surveys. The 1950s and early 1960s also saw considerable efforts to enhance the Tylerian approach by teaching educators how to state objectives in explicit, measurable terms and providing taxonomies of possible educational objectives in the cognitive domain (Bloom, Engelhart, Furst, Hill, & Krathwohl, 1956) and the affective domain (Krathwohl, Bloom, & Masia, 1964).

In 1957, the Soviets' successful launch of *Sputnik I* sent tremors through the U.S. establishment that were quickly amplified into calls for more effective teaching of math and science to American students. The reaction was immediate. Passage of the National Defense Education Act of 1958 poured millions of dollars into massive, new curriculum development projects, especially in mathematics and science. Only a few projects were funded, but their size and perceived importance led policy makers to fund evaluations of most of them.

The resulting studies revealed the conceptual and methodological impoverishment of evaluation in that era. Inadequate designs and irrelevant reports were only some of the problems. Most of the studies depended on imported behavioral and social science research concepts and techniques that were fine for such research but not very suitable for evaluation of school programs.

Theoretical work related directly to evaluation (as opposed to research) did not exist, and it quickly became apparent that the best theoretical and methodological thinking from social and behavioral research failed to provide guidance on how to carry out many aspects of evaluation. Thus, educational scientists and practitioners were left to glean what they could from applied social, behavioral, and educational research. Their gleanings were so meager that Cronbach (1963) penned a seminal article criticizing past evaluations and calling for new directions. Although his recommendations had little immediate impact, they did catch the attention of other educational scholars, helping to spark a greatly expanded conception of evaluation that would emerge in the next decade.

The Emergence of Modern Program Evaluation

Although the developments discussed so far were not sufficient in themselves to create a strong and enduring evaluation movement, each helped create a context that would give birth to such a movement. Conditions were right for accelerated conceptual and methodological development in evaluation, and the catalyst was found in the War on Poverty and the Great Society, the legislative centerpieces of the administrations of U.S. Presidents John Kennedy and Lyndon

Johnson. The underlying social agenda of these administrations was an effort to equalize and enhance opportunities for all citizens in virtually every sector of society. Billions of dollars were poured into programs in education, health, housing, criminal justice, unemployment, urban deterioration, and many other areas aimed at assuring equal opportunities for all citizens.

Unlike the private sector, where the well-established auditing profession and procedures provided constant feedback on corporate programs' productivity and profitability, these huge, new social investments had no similar mechanism in place to chart their success. There were government employees with some relevant competence—social scientists and technical specialists in the various federal departments, particularly in the General Accounting Office (GAO)—but they were too few and not well enough organized to deal even marginally with determining the effectiveness of these vast government innovations. (A decade would pass before program evaluation became a formal charge in many of the agencies.) To complicate matters, many inquiry methodologies and management techniques that worked on smaller programs proved inadequate or unwieldy with programs of the size and scope of these sweeping social reforms. For a time it appeared that another concept developed and practiced successfully in business and industry might be successfully adapted for evaluating these federal programs. This was an application of the systems approach used in the Ford Motor Company, the Planning, Programming, and Budgeting System (PPBS), brought to the U.S. Department of Defense (DOD) by Robert McNamara when he became Kennedy's secretary of defense. The PPBS was a variant of the systems approaches that were being used by many large aerospace, communications, and automotive industries. Aimed at improving system efficiency, effectiveness, and budget allocation decisions by defining organizational objectives and linking them to system outputs and budgets, the PPBS apparently would also be ideally suited for the federal agencies charged with administering the War on Poverty programs.

Perhaps it was, but few of the bureaucrats heading those agencies were eager to embrace the PPBS, and it was largely confined to the DOD during the Kennedy administration. Lyndon Johnson believed firmly in the efficacy of the PPBS, however, and decreed that all federal agencies implement it. They did—at least on paper. But many federal officials simply hunkered down and waited for this particular political wind to pass. For a time the pressure persisted, and not only did PPBS spread through federal agencies but its logical appeal carried it into many state governments, universities, and school systems as well. Gradually it mutated into various forms patterned loosely after PPBS, such as the "management by objectives" approach. But it never really developed into an effective program evaluation system and gradually waned in popularity. Within a few years it could only be found in use in isolated agencies. Perhaps its most lasting contribution was to increase program managers' receptivity to the objectives-oriented and management-oriented evaluation approaches we discuss at length in Chapters 5 and 6.

Meanwhile, the federal agencies charged with implementing the congressionally decreed War on Poverty and Great Society programs had little time to
worry about assessing these programs' impact. But gradually concerns over
whether the cost-benefit ratios of these enormous programs were acceptable
began to be voiced. A few U.S. senators and congressmen began to fret over
how Congress could discharge its oversight function adequately without better
direct evidence about program effectiveness. Concerns grew over how to hold
state and local recipients of the program grants accountable for expending the
funds as prescribed. And the inevitable cynicism of the media about government
waste, abuse, and mismanagement added to the growing unease about whether
these programs were a boon or boondoggle to the taxpaying public. The stage
for serious evaluation was set.

The first efforts to add an evaluative element to any of these programs were
small, consisting of congressionally mandated evaluations of a federal juvenile
delinquency program in 1962 (Weiss, 1987) and a federal manpower development and training program enacted that same year (Wholey, 1986). It matters
little which was first, however, since neither had any lasting impact on the
development of evaluation. Three more years would pass before Robert F.
Kennedy would trigger the event that would send a shock wave through the
U.S. education system, awakening both policy makers and practitioners to the
importance of systematic evaluation.

Evaluation Requirements in the 1965 Education Law

The one event that is most responsible for the emergence of contemporary
program evaluation is the passage of the Elementary and Secondary Education
Act (ESEA) of 1965. This bill proposed to provide a huge increase in federal
funding for education, with tens of thousands of federal grants to local schools,
state and regional agencies, and universities. The largest single component of
the bill was Title I (later Chapter 1), destined to be the most costly federal
education program in American history.

When Congress began its deliberations on the proposed ESEA, concerns
began to be expressed, especially on the Senate floor, that no convincing
evidence existed that any federal funding for education had ever resulted in
any real educational improvements. Indeed, there were some in Congress who
believed federal funds allocated to education prior to ESEA had sunk like stones
into the morass of educational programs with scarcely an observable ripple to
mark their passage.

Robert F. Kennedy was the most persuasive voice insisting that the ESEA
require each grant recipient to file an evaluation report showing what had
resulted from the expenditure of the federal funds. This congressional evaluation
mandate was ultimately approved for Title I (compensatory education) and Title III
(innovative educational projects).

Suddenly, thousands of educators were for the first time *required* to
evaluate their own efforts. The field of educational program evaluation had

been born overnight (although it would be a frail and ungainly child for yet some years).

Although the passage of the 1965 ESEA deserves its historical designation as the birth of contemporary program evaluation, it was a beginning marked by great travail. Overnight, thousands of educators were required to evaluate their own efforts. Few were up to the task. Teachers, administrators, and school psychologists were among those pressed into service as Title I or III evaluators. Their tasks included empirical data collection and analysis activities for which their training was ill-suited. The results were abysmal. Surprisingly, when well-trained educational, psychological, or sociological researchers were called to help, the results were little better. Despite their technical prowess, it quickly became apparent that their experimental research designs, standardized tests, and quantitative surveys were not suited to the rapidly shifting field conditions of the local Titles I and III projects.

From the perspective of the panicked project directors, however, these colleagues from more empirically oriented fields certainly seemed more qualified than shanghaied classroom teachers. And some help seemed better than none, so these technical experts were widely employed. Using the resources known to them, they borrowed heavily from the behavioral and social sciences to evaluate the local school projects.

In retrospect, it seems inevitable that the resulting "evaluations" would be inadequate. These researchers were unprepared for the complex tasks of ferreting out the influences attributable to each of several components in a school's Title I or III project, or even of separating out the effects of the project from other ongoing activities in the school. They were no better prepared to design and conduct studies that would simultaneously assess the accomplishment of specific local objectives and provide Congress with a complete portrait of how well Titles I and III were meeting their overall national objectives. Viewed collectively, these evaluations were of little use either to educators or to the Congress.

Clearly, new evaluation approaches, methods, and strategies were needed, and also, perhaps, professionals with a somewhat different training and orientation to apply them. In Chapter 3, we describe key developments in evaluation that have occurred since this rocky beginning for program evaluation in the 1960s, including development of new evaluation approaches and initiation of training programs designed expressly to prepare professional evaluators.

APPLICATION EXERCISES

1. Make a timeline of what you perceive as key events in the history of formal program evaluation prior to 1965.

2. Identify parallels as well as contrasts between the growth of evaluation thought in education and in the behavioral and social sciences. Use both to write a brief essay on similarities and differences in evaluation in those two areas.

3. What do you perceive as the major attributes of the ESEA of 1965 that served to provide such a springboard to the development of modern program evaluation?

SUGGESTED READINGS

Baker, E. L., & Niemi, D. (in press). School and program evaluation. In D. C. Berliner & R. C. Calfee (Eds.), *Handbook of education psychology.* New York: Macmillan.

Madaus, G., Stufflebeam, D., & Scriven, M. (1983). Program evaluation: A historical overview. In G. Madaus, M. Scriven, & D. L. Stufflebeam (Eds.), *Evaluation models: Viewpoints on educational and human services evaluation* (pp. 3–22). Boston: Kluwer-Nijhoff.

chapter 3

Recent Developments and Trends in Evaluation

ORIENTING QUESTIONS

1. How would you characterize the growth of program evaluation from 1965 to the present?
2. List 10 significant developments in program evaluation that have occurred since 1965, helping evaluation to mature as a profession.
3. Of those 10 developments, choose the 3 you believe have been most influential in helping evaluation mature as a profession. Why were they so significant?
4. What factors have contributed to the institutionalization of evaluation?
5. Do you think that evaluators should be certified or licensed? Why or why not?
6. Do you believe evaluation is a profession? A discipline? Explain your answer.
7. List all the emerging trends you can identify that appear likely to influence evaluation's future. Which three do you think will be most influential? Why?

In Chapter 2 we described how formal program evaluation had been used in earlier periods of history, briefly tracing its evolution from ancient times up to the mid-1960s. The purpose of this chapter is to examine evaluation's growth and maturation across the ensuing three decades, paying particular attention to trends and developments that have implications for practicing evaluators. This chapter includes two sections. The first section examines important activities and trends since 1965 that mark evaluation's coming of age as a profession. The second section outlines still other recent developments that may impact on the direction evaluation takes in the future. While most of the contents of these sections is well referenced, some content depends partially (or largely) on our personal observations and interpretations of the influence of these recent developments and trends on the field of program evaluation.

PROGRAM EVALUATION: TRENDS ACROSS THREE DECADES OF A MATURING PROFESSION

Much has transpired during the past three decades to help program evaluation through its growing pains to the point where it appears to have shed most of its adolescent awkwardness, taking on characteristics more typical of a maturing profession. In this section we try to impose order on the welter of interrelated activities and developments that have shaped evaluation during this era. At the same time, we attempt to determine how far evaluation has progressed toward becoming a full-fledged profession or, possibly, a discipline in its own right. To accomplish both of these purposes, we examine 10 separate criteria that we believe are useful in determining whether or not evaluation has attained the status of a true profession. These criteria are

- A need for specialists trained in evaluation
- Development of unique evaluation content
- Development of formal programs for preparing evaluators
- Stable career opportunities of evaluators
- Institutionalization of the function of evaluation
- Procedures for certification of evaluators
- Development of professional associations for evaluators
- Criteria for membership in those evaluation associations
- Influence of the evaluation association(s) on evaluator preparation programs
- Development of standards for evaluation practice

We do not suggest that every criterion must be met for evaluation to deserve being considered a profession, for even some venerable professions have not yet met all 10. But we do suggest that at least a majority of these criteria must be met before program evaluation could appropriately be accorded the designation of profession.

We will use these 10 criteria to examine how far program evaluation has come since its unprepossessing appearance on center stage in 1965. Evaluation's progress has not been fully successful, in our opinion, in all of these 10 areas. In some areas it may be more appropriate to refer to evaluation's struggles, rather than evaluation trends, but for simplicity we will not make that differentiation. As we discuss evaluation's progress on each of these 10 criteria, tracing it across the intervening years, we will be able to complete our history of modern-day program evaluation, interweaving in the tale some of the most intriguing social, political, economic, and intellectual forces that have nurtured or challenged evaluation during its formative years. We trust that the reader will note that we cover developments from 1965 to the present *within* each of these 10 areas, thus retracing that 30-year history several times, but each on a slightly different path. Then, at the end of this section, we reflect on evaluation's growth and share our opinion of whether it yet warrants being considered a profession and/ or a discipline.

1. Need for Evaluation Specialists

Let us return to 1965 and our summary in Chapter 2 of the general failure of the thousands of mandated Titles I and III project evaluations to produce information useful either to Congress or to local school officials. This failure made two things apparent. First, there was a need for evaluation specialists better prepared to respond to the needs imposed by the ESEA evaluation mandate. Second, the need would not be met easily: It would require large numbers of trained specialists. In short, there was a new and urgent demand for persons who could serve in the new role of "educational evaluator," and no supply was in sight. The need for trained evaluation specialists was sudden and acute.

And that was only in the education portion of the Great Society legislation. Meanwhile, other, noneducation areas were also experiencing burgeoning demands for evaluation (although it was often called applied social science or other names). By the late 1960s, Congress had authorized money for evaluation of social programs in areas as diverse as the Job Corps, vocational rehabilitation, child health, treatment of alcoholism, crime control, and community action.

As for the magnitude of this demand, Wholey, Scanlon, Duffy, Fukumoto, and Vogt (1970) studied evaluation in federal agencies and concluded that not much evaluation of social programs was occurring, but only two years later Buchanan and Wholey's follow-up survey (1972) revealed that evaluation funds had mushroomed, numerous evaluations had been completed, and large-scale evaluations of social programs were increasing. Whether the growth spurt had been that sudden or whether the 1970 report was an underestimate is less important than the fact that evaluation requirements had spread well beyond education, with the demand once again far outstripping the supply. Shadish, Cook, and Leviton (1991) reported that (1) the U.S. General Accounting Office compiled an index of 5,610 federal evaluations completed between 1973 and 1979 and (2) a UCLA data bank of program evaluations listed 3,027 local mental health center evaluations.

Managers of these and other specific projects and programs funded under this new wave of social legislation searched to find those best equipped to fill newly created evaluation roles. Faced with an absence of persons directly trained in evaluation, they frequently employed those trained for roles that contained some evaluative functions—professional accountants and auditors, management consultants, planning and systems analysts, and product development and test marketing specialists from the private sector—as well as economists and social and behavioral science researchers and academicians in areas relevant to collection and analysis of evaluative information. According to Shadish and his colleagues (1991),

> By the late 1960s, demand for feedback about social programs exceeded the supply of personnel with appropriate skills. That demand swept into evaluation many graduates of professional schools and social science departments. (p. 24)

Unfortunately, impressing such persons into evaluation often yielded evaluations that were little better than those that had resulted from pressing classroom teachers and educational psychologists into service as evaluators on federally funded education projects. While most of those drafted or recruited into health and human service evaluation roles were very skillful in *some* tasks required of evaluators, few were even aware of the broad range of tasks that were essential in any complete and adequate evaluation. Fewer yet possessed the skills necessary to complete those tasks. The need for persons with a new constellation of specialized skills beyond those typically possessed by even the best-trained social and behavioral scientists was becoming apparent.

Today the need for evaluation specialists is generally accepted, even though many policy makers and program managers (themselves naive about knowledge and skills evaluators should possess) credulously attribute evaluation expertise to self-appointed or self-anointed "evaluators" who lack most essential evaluation skills and knowledge. Despite these frequent lapses in discernment when *selecting* evaluators, the *need* for evaluation specialists now seems well established.

2. Development of Unique Evaluation Content

When demands for evaluation increased dramatically in the 1960s, the resulting evaluation studies revealed the conceptual and methodological impoverishment of evaluation in that era. Theoretical and methodological work related directly to evaluation did not exist, and evaluators were left to draw what they could from theories in cognate disciplines and to glean what they could from better developed methodologies, such as experimental design, psychometrics, survey research, and ethnography. The results were disappointing, underscoring the need for development of new conceptualizations and methods tailored to fit more precisely the needs of evaluators.

Scholars responded to this need, and by 1970 important seminal writings had provided conceptual foundations and scaffolding for the young field of evaluation (e.g., Cronbach, 1963; Scriven, 1967; Stake, 1967; Stufflebeam, 1968). Books of readings on evaluation were published (e.g., Worthen & Sanders, 1973). Articles about evaluation began to appear with increasing frequency in professional journals. Together, these publications resulted in a number of new evaluation "models" touted by the authors as responsive to the needs of specific types of evaluations (e.g., ESEA Title III evaluations, or evaluations of mental health programs). New evaluation approaches were proposed by evaluation theorist-practitioners in the United States, England, Australia, Israel, Sweden, and other countries.

Collectively these new conceptualizations of evaluation provided new ways of thinking about evaluation that greatly broadened earlier views. They made it clear that good program evaluation encompasses much more than simple application of the skills of the empirical scientists.

As these new frameworks for planning evaluation studies were refined, evaluators began increasingly to rely on them for guidance. Although these so-called models couldn't begin to solve all the evaluation problems of local evaluators, they did help them circumvent several of the more treacherous pitfalls common to earlier evaluation studies. Problems caused by mindless application of objectives-based (Tylerian) evaluation methods to every evaluation were revealed. The need to evaluate unintended outcomes of a curriculum, a drug treatment center, or a corporate training program was recognized. Values and standards were emphasized, and the importance of making judgments about merit and worth was made clear. These new and controversial ideas spawned dialogue and debate that fed a developing evaluation vocabulary and literature. The result has been an exponential growth in the evaluation literature during the past three decades. Contained in the numerous manuals, anthologies, articles, and textbooks were dozens of formalized or semi-formalized evaluation "models" proposed for use by program evaluators. (Fortunately, these specific models can be sorted and subsumed into only a few more general evaluation approaches, as shown later in Part Two.)

This burgeoning body of evaluation literature revealed sharp differences in the authors' philosophical and methodological preferences, but it also underscored a fact about which there was much agreement: Evaluation is a multidimensional technical and political enterprise that requires both new conceptualizations and new insights into when and how existing methodologies from other fields might be used appropriately. Shadish and his colleagues (1991) said it well when, in recognizing the need for unique theories for evaluation, they noted that "as evaluation matured, its theory took on its own special character that resulted from the interplay among problems uncovered by practitioners, the solutions they tried, and traditions of the academic discipline of each evaluator, winnowed by 20 years of experience" (p. 31).

Publications focused exclusively on evaluation appeared in the 1970s and 1980s, including journals and series such as *Evaluation and Program Planning, Evaluation Practice, Evaluation Review, Evaluation Quarterly, Educational Evaluation and Policy Analysis, Studies in Educational Evaluation, Canadian Journal of Program Evaluation, New Directions for Program Evaluation, Evaluation and the Health Professions, ITEA Journal of Test and Evaluation, Performance Improvement Quarterly,* and the *Evaluation Studies Review*

Annual. Others that omit evaluation from the title but highlight it in their contents include *Performance Improvement Quarterly, Policy Studies Review,* and *Journal of Policy Analysis and Management.* In the latter half of the 1970s and throughout the 1980s, the publication of evaluation books expanded markedly, including textbooks, reference books, and even compendia and encyclopedias of evaluation.

Conceptual and empirical efforts continue today to expand evaluation's knowledge base. A good example is Mertens's (1994) very useful analysis of unique skills and knowledge needed by evaluators. Clearly, the necessary conceptual underpinnings of a profession are accumulating in a body of evaluation literature that is largely unique.

Thus, on this criterion evaluation seems to qualify as a profession. A body of knowledge exists that outlines the content of the field—its unique (or adapted) theories, strategies, and methods.

3. Development of Formal Programs for Training Evaluators

When the U.S. Congress funded the ESEA in 1965, they recognized that several of its stipulations would create a need for well-trained researchers and evaluators in the schools. Foreseeing that education had few persons trained in these areas, the Congress also provided funds for universities to launch new graduate training programs in educational research and evaluation, including fellowship stipends for graduate study in those specializations. Several universities began ambitious, federally funded graduate programs aimed at training educational or social science evaluators. When federal funds disappeared in less than three years, so did most of the graduate programs they had supported (before they had time to graduate a single student). In 1971, graduate programs for training evaluators existed in more than 100 American universities (Worthen & Byers, 1971). Only 15 years later, such programs existed in only 44 U.S. universities (May, Fleischer, Scheirer, & Cox, 1986), and by 1993, the number had declined to 38 (Altschuld, Engle, Cullen, Kim, & Macce, 1994).

The U.S. evaluation training programs that did survive, however, were joined by 11 programs in Canada and Australia (Altschuld et al., 1994). Collectively, these 49 appeared to be maturing into programs offering unique training opportunities—training tailored to fit the reconceptualized views of evaluation that were emerging. Notions of how evaluators should be trained gradually expanded beyond traditional training. No longer were courses in research design, statistics, and measurement the only core training, and no longer was psychology the major discipline from which technical skills were drawn. Instead, evaluation began to draw on philosophy, sociology, anthropology, political science, economics, and other discipline bases. Venerable statistics and design courses began to be supplemented by a wide variety of courses in applied methods and techniques in areas such as naturalistic observation, interviewing techniques, content analysis, performance assessment, communication and writing skills, and unique evaluation techniques. Evaluation internships, assistantships, and practice became more central in preparation programs as evaluation mentors realized that in evaluation, as elsewhere, the best training is often apprenticeship training.

Bickman (1994) predicts that future training programs for evaluators will focus more on master's level training, feeling that most evaluation tasks do not require doctoral training. Sechrest (1994) seems to agree, in a rather critical analysis in which he concludes that few evaluation training programs exist, and those that do are usually ad hoc or second-priority operations, operated by staff for whom program evaluation is not their first calling. Our experience does not lend itself to such a cheerless view, and the evaluator training programs we know best do not fit that description. Indeed, we have seen excellent training programs at both master's and doctoral levels. Thus, we are comforted that Sechrest added this observation: "A few outstanding evaluation research training programs remain, and the students in those programs are exposed to concepts and methods of nearly astonishing sophistication" (p. 361). We favor doctoral students' reaching such levels of knowledge and skill, for some evaluation tasks require unusual proficiency. Yet we endorse heartily the notion of master's level training, for there obviously are many evaluation activities that can be carried out by professionals who are well-trained at the master's level in basic evaluation skills.

Whatever the degree level of training, it is also becoming increasingly clear that it may be folly to pattern evaluator training programs after traditional programs aimed at preparing social scientists. Fitzpatrick (1994) provides an analysis of alternative models for structuring professional preparation programs for evaluators, patterned loosely after the model of other professions' preparation programs. While beyond the scope of this section, we recommend that analysis to those interested in establishing university-based training programs for evaluators.

In recent years, training of evaluators has expanded in nonacademic settings. Mandates for program improvement and accountability are directed not only to governing boards but also to practitioners, who are often expected to perform in evaluation roles without the benefit of evaluation training. Many schools, state agencies, and businesses and several national professional associations have sponsored in-service evaluation training for practitioners to allow them to get evaluation training in their home settings. On occasion large corporations have established corporate training centers (such as Xerox Document University) that resemble mini-universities, providing training in evaluation (along with other techniques). In some, certificates are provided attesting that the recipient is qualified in the particular specialization in which they were trained. Some federal agencies have set up formal, in-service training programs in evaluation for their employees, with formal credits, certificates of completion, and the like. By far the largest of these is the ambitious program in the U.S. General Accounting Office.

In summary, evaluation training programs can be found in universities, government agencies, corporations, and other settings. Whether these existing programs can supply the flow of trained personnel needed for evaluation to thrive as a profession is unclear. When one sees persons with no evaluation training pressed into playing evaluation roles, however, there certainly appears to be room for additional programs for training evaluators. Perhaps this is what prompted the American Educational Research Association to announce in 1996 their intent to fund four doctoral-level Evaluation Training Programs at $325,000 each to increase the nation's capability to evaluate its mathematics and science education programs competently.

4. Emergence of Stable Career Opportunities in Evaluation, and
5. Institutionalization of the Function of Evaluation

Although we see these two trends as distinct, and each important in its own right, they are so closely interrelated that we prefer to discuss them together here.

One sign of a profession is that there is an enduring need for the services of personnel trained in that particular specialty. No field that is only a fad, flourishing only briefly before fading, would qualify as a profession. In judging evaluation on this dimension, therefore, it is important to consider whether evaluation's endurance in the face of uncertain social and economic trends provides the type of stable employment opportunities typical of mature professions.

Tracking the demand for evaluation personnel across the last 30 years is no small undertaking, and it is not possible to do justice to the topic in a short section here. Similarly, it would be different to describe adequately here the extent to which the institutionalization of evaluation in various types of agencies has affected the stability of career opportunities for evaluators. Both topics have been discussed in greater detail elsewhere (Worthen, 1994, 1995). Here we only cover a few of the high points very briefly to enable the reader to understand why we have drawn our conclusions about evaluation's degree of maturation as a profession in these two areas.

The Stability of Career Opportunities in Evaluation.   During the 1970s, evaluators were vigorously sought after by a variety of U.S. federal agencies, including the National Institute of Education; the U.S. Office of Planning, Budgeting, and Evaluation; the Congressional Research Service; the Office of Technology Assessment; and the General Accounting Office. The need for evaluators was not limited to these federal agencies, however, for many of the social and educational programs that provided large sums of money to state and local agencies were accompanied by evaluation mandates. Consequently, many evaluators were employed on local or state projects supported by federal funds. Thus, federal funding of evaluation, coupled with evaluation requirements, had created a three-tiered employment (or consulting) base for evaluators working on local, state, or national projects in a wide variety of programmatic areas. Evaluation was a booming business that appeared likely to provide career stability for those choosing to pursue it, prompting some commentators to opine that "professional evaluation became a viable career alternative to academic employment" (Shadish et al., 1991, p. 25).

The late 1970s saw a dip in the level of federal funding for evaluation, however, and it appeared likely that the U.S. job market for evaluators would decline proportionately. By the early 1980s, that possibility became a near certainty, as Ronald Reagan's shadow fell over the evaluation scene. Much of the categorical funding to states and local institutions that had carried evaluation mandates was replaced by block grants that had no evaluation requirements at all. Many evaluators and political commentators predicted that evaluation—which had only been conducted because of federal insistence—would dwindle, if not die outright, as soon as the federal evaluation requirements were abolished. Those who calculated the impact during the 1980s reported evaluation staff and budget cuts at around 50 percent (Levitan, 1992) and a 90 percent reduction in the number of evaluation studies conducted by some federal agencies (Cordray & Lipsey, 1987). Evaluators who had depended on federal funding (and the accompanying evaluation mandates) began to see their livelihood slipping away. To many it appeared that evaluators were a vanishing breed.

Institutionalization of the Evaluation Function.   Before long, however, it became apparent that many evaluators and evaluation agencies were not greatly affected by the decline in federally mandated and supported evaluations. Indeed, their evaluation business continued to expand. Some even wondered what their colleagues were concerned about. Gradually, the situation clarified. Despite the fact that most state and local agencies first became involved with evaluation when it was thrust upon them by federal mandates, many of these agencies apparently had come to value evaluation in its own right. Indeed, there were numerous instances of such agencies, along with foundations, corporations, and even churches, that were routinely building evaluation into their programs—even programs that had never had a dollar of federal support and were under absolutely no obligation to evaluate their efforts. So, while many state and local agencies did abandon evaluation when federal mandates were eliminated, many did not. Indeed, the function of evaluation appears to have been institutionalized in enough agencies that the career opportunities for evaluators once again looked promising.

Returning to our two criteria for determining whether evaluation can be considered a profession, it appears that the stability of evaluation careers and the institutionalization of evaluation in a sizable slice of society's institutions both signal that evaluation has matured enough to legitimize referring to it as a profession.

6. Procedures for Certification or Licensure of Evaluators

A central question for any emerging professional specialty is whether or not its practitioners should be certified or licensed. We believe the answer, for evaluators, *should, ideally,* be yes. But that prompts the simple question of whether there are existing (or near-future) mechanisms for certifying or licensing evaluators similar to those that mark physicians, teachers, psychologists, and certified public accountants as professionals. And the simple answer, of course, is no.

No professional association or governmental agency has yet assumed or accepted broad responsibility for licensing or certifying the competence of evaluation practitioners. Without some type of credentialing process, it is difficult for those who need evaluation services to determine in advance the competency of those they select. "Let the buyer beware" is still the watchword in retaining the services of evaluation specialists. In the absence of certification or licensure, uninformed amateurs and unprincipled hucksters can do much mischief and greatly tarnish the image of program evaluation in the process. Of course, licensing cannot guarantee ethical conduct, as we see readily when we find the occasional licensed lawyer or stockholder whose unscrupulous conduct is not prevented by their licensure.

Most evaluators and those who use evaluation seem to agree that it would be desirable if there were some straightforward way to certify that an individual evaluator is qualified for the evaluation tasks she proposes to conduct. That would require that the means and methods be established whereby certification and/or licensure of professional evaluators becomes a reality. Desirable? Indeed. Feasible? Not likely, at least not soon.

7. Development of Professional Associations for Evaluators

Several professional associations have emerged to provide homes for evaluators. One of the first was not a full-blown association, as such, but rather the American Educational Research Association's Division H, dedicated to providing a home for school evaluators. In 1976, however, two professional associations for practicing evaluators were founded in the United States. The Evaluation Network (EN), consisting largely of educational evaluators, and the Evaluation Research Society (ERS), devoted largely to serving social scientists and evaluators in government and allied professional fields, provided additional professional identification for evaluators.

In 1985, EN and ERS merged to form the American Evaluation Association (AEA), which, with more than 2,000 members, became the largest professional association that exists solely to serve the needs of practicing evaluators. The Canadian Evaluation Society (CES) was also launched to serve similar needs for Canadian evaluation practitioners filling evaluation roles in varied settings, ranging from provincial ministries to private consulting groups. The European Evaluation Society (EES) was founded in 1994, the Australasian Evaluation Society (AES) has developed into a strong organization for evaluators in the Pacific region, and a Latin American Evaluation Society is just emerging.

With professional associations beginning to span the globe, and the most venerable of them reaching out to include evaluators from other countries, it is clear that viable professional organizations exist for evaluators everywhere. On this criterion, evaluation fares as well as any profession.

Associations	Journals	Conferences
American Evaluation Association (AEA)	*Evaluation Practice* and *New Directions for Program Evaluation* (a quarterly sourcebook)	Annual AEA meeting (October–November)
American Educational Research Association (AERA)	*Educational Evaluation and Policy Analysis*	Annual AERA meeting (April)
Australasian Evaluation Society (AES)	*Evaluation Journal of Australasia* and *Evaluation News and Comment*	Annual AES conference (September)
Canadian Evaluation Society (CES)	*Canadian Journal of Program Evaluation*	Annual CES conference (October–November)
European Evaluation Society (EES)	*Evaluation*	Founding conference (December 1994)

FIGURE 3.1   Evaluation's major professional associations, journals, and conferences

The evaluation journals and other periodicals produced by major professional associations for evaluators are shown in Figure 3.1, along with a listing of annual conferences sponsored by these groups.

8. Criteria for Determining Membership in Evaluation Associations

In most professions, there are established criteria for denying membership in professional associations to those who are patently unqualified in whatever is the business of that profession. Not so with evaluation. The membership criteria for all of the professional evaluation associations mentioned previously are rather lenient, and none would effectively exclude from membership individuals who are unqualified as evaluators. On this criterion, it appears that evaluation has not yet reached full maturity as a profession, for reasons similar to those already mentioned when discussing certification (criterion 6), which is closely related.

9. Influence of Evaluation Associations on Preparation Programs for Evaluators

In many professions, the major professional association(s) plays a powerful role in shaping university preparation programs through accreditation or other similar mechanisms. No such influence exists in evaluation. None of the professional associations for evaluators listed previously exercises any direct control or influence over any preservice program that purports to train evaluators. In short, the evaluation associations do not accredit preservice training programs or control any decisions concerning curriculum content, essential internship experiences, or faculty qualifications. Here again, evaluation does not fully meet the criterion of a fully developed profession. The Canadian Evaluation Society has done some preliminary groundwork that could be used as a basis for a bona fide accreditation program for evaluator training programs (Love, 1994), but it is currently uncertain whether such a program will actually be established.

10. Development of Standards for Evaluation Practice

Most professions contain technical and/or ethical standards intended to ensure that professional practice is of high quality. Evaluation was without such standards during its early years. Then in 1981, a giant step was made toward qualifying evaluation as a profession. Several years of work by the Joint Committee on Standards for Eduational Evaluation, a coalition of professional associations concerned with evaluation in education and psychology, resulted in the publication of *Standards for Evaluations of Educational Programs, Projects, and Materials* (Joint Committee, 1981). These comprehensive standards were intended to guide both those who conduct evaluations and those who use evaluation reports.

In 1982, efforts of the Evaluation Research Society resulted in another set of standards for evaluation practice (Evaluation Research Society Standards Committee, 1982). In 1988, the Joint Committee published the *Personnel Evaluation Standards.* Then, in 1989, a set of standards intended to guide evaluation of federal programs was published in Canada (Office of the Comptroller General, 1989). In 1995 the American Evaluation Association published its "Guiding Principles" as a statement of professional responsibility of evaluators. Arguably the most widely recognized evaluation standards, however, are the Joint Committee's (1994) updated and significantly revised second edition of their 1981 standards, simply termed *The Program Evaluation Standards.* The states of Florida, Hawaii, and Louisiana have formally adopted these standards as their guide for evaluations of education and public sector programs.

We will forgo any further discussion of any of these sets of standards and how they may be used since that is a central topic in Chapter 20. We wish to note, however, that if a set of standards to guide professional practice is a hallmark of a profession, then evaluation certainly qualifies, for its standards are much better developed than those used to guide practice in several more venerable professions.

Program Evaluation: Profession or Discipline?

The past two decades in program evaluation may be called decades of "professionalization," as the shared knowledge and experience of a great many evaluators in education and the social sciences has grown and matured. But is it yet a profession? A discipline? We will attempt here to answer the first question, then turn our attention to the second.

To this point, 10 touchstones that seem useful in ascertaining when a field of endeavor has attained the status of a distinct profession have been proposed and briefly discussed. Considered together, what do they tell us about the progress of evaluation toward becoming a profession? Is evaluation yet separate and distinct from other professions and disciplines with which it has been intertwined for decades? In short, is evaluation a viable profession or not?

The answer depends on the rigor demanded in applying the 10 criteria outlined above. If all 10 must be met before an area of specialization can be thought of as a profession, then evaluation falls short. Figure 3.2, which summarizes the earlier discussion of how well evaluation meets each criterion, shows that evaluation lacks three characteristics possessed by most fully developed professions. For evaluation to be considered a fully mature profession, we believe these three areas would need to be dealt with. Yet some conditions will be difficult to change; for example, the challenge of certifying evaluators may never be met. Does this mean that evaluation will never qualify as a profession? Or can evaluation be considered a profession if it meets *most* of the criteria?

We believe that evaluation can appropriately be considered and treated as a profession, even if it does not yet have all the trappings of older professions, such as medicine or law. Others who have commented on evaluation's status as a profession are not of one voice. In the 1980s, most writers seemed to agree that evaluation had not yet attained the status of a distinct profession. For example, Rossi and Freeman (1985) concluded that

> evaluation is not a "profession," at least in terms of the formal criteria that sociologists generally use to characterize such groups. Rather, it can best be described as a "near-group," a large aggregate of persons who are not formally organized, whose membership changes rapidly, and who have little in common in terms of the range of tasks undertaken, competencies, work-sites, and shared outlooks. (p. 362)

FIGURE 3.2 Criteria for judging evaluation's progress toward becoming a profession

Does evaluation meet the criterion of

	Yes	No
1. A need for evaluation specialists?	✓	
2. Content (knowledge and skills) unique to evaluation?	✓	
3. Formal preparation programs for evaluators?	✓	
4. Stable career opportunities in evaluation?	✓	
5. Institutionalization of the function of evaluation?	✓	
6. Certification or licensure of evaluators?		✓
7. Appropriate professional associations for evaluators?	✓	
8. Exclusion of unqualified persons from membership in evaluation associations?		✓
9. Influence of evaluators' associations on preservice preparation programs for evaluators?		✓
10. Standards for the practice of evaluation?	✓	

More recently, several evaluation authors have been somewhat more liberal in their conclusions. For example, Patton (1990a) states unequivocally that evaluation has become a profession, and a demanding and challenging one at that. Shadish and his colleagues (1991) are slightly more cautious; in their opinion, "evaluation is a profession in the sense that it shares certain attributes with other professions and differs from purely academic specialties such as psychology or sociology. . . . Program evaluation is not fully professionalized, like medicine or the law; it has no licensure laws, for example. But it tends toward professionalization more than most disciplines" (p. 25). Love (1994) points out some areas of professionalism yet lacking in evaluation but speaks of "regulating the profession" of evaluation (p. 38). Chelimsky (1992) speaks of a "renascent evaluation profession" (p. 339) and House (1994a) flatly states that evaluation has become a "specialized profession" (p. 239).

In summary, evaluation seems to be increasingly viewed as a profession because it possesses most of the touchstones that collectively define a profession. While some may continue to see it as a "near-group" that "tends toward professionalization," because it lacks licensure laws and some other characteristics of professions such as law and medicine, we would step aside from such exacting distinctions. Whatever it is called, evaluation is a vital social force, an area of professional practice and specialization that has its own literature, preparation programs, standards of practice, and professional associations. If it is not a profession in all particulars, we are comfortable considering it such, even as we strive to make it more so.

Can Evaluation Be Considered a Discipline?

Again, evaluators are not univocal, but differences in their views on this question are much smaller. In our 1987 text, we asserted that "evaluation is not a discipline but merely a social process or activity aimed at determining the value of certain materials, programs, or efforts. As such, it necessarily cuts across disciplines" (Worthen & Sanders, 1987, p. 53). Sechrest (1994) says that "program evaluation is not a discipline or field and that is, probably in large part, because we who are involved in it have never worked hard enough at making it into a discipline/field" (p. 360).

Other prominent evaluators are slightly more optimistic. In an insightful and thought-provoking analysis of evaluation's progress toward beginning a discipline, Scriven (1991b) lists criteria for a new discipline and shows that evaluation—as presently conceived—meets them only partially. He argues that, because of its versatility in providing services to all disciplines, evaluation is emerging as one of the most powerful of the "'transdisciplines'—tool disciplines such as logic, design, and statistics—that apply across broad ranges of the human investigative and creative effort while maintaining the autonomy of a discipline in their own right" (p. 1). He has embellished but not materially altered his view in more recent discussion (Scriven, 1994). Morell (1990) views evaluation as less a discipline than a loosely knit coalition of professionals whose common interests, journals, associations, markets, and parent disciplines bind together into a distinct field of activity. House (1994a) describes evaluation as an "*emerging* discipline" (p. 240, italics added).

In the traditional sense, evaluation may not qualify as a discipline, even though it seems to be progressing in a direction where one day it may. Since most professions are not disciplines per se but rather areas of applied practice that draw from one or several disciplines, it may well be that evaluation cannot and should not aspire to be both a profession and a discipline, in the full sense, but rather continue its growth as a profession and its simultaneous contribution as a transdiscipline.

RECENT TRENDS INFLUENCING PROGRAM EVALUATION

There are many emerging trends that we believe are—or soon will be—influencing the practice of program evaluation. Rather than discuss them all in this section, we have preferred to treat most of these trends in whichever chapter we see as being most relevant. Those we discuss elsewhere are only listed in this section to serve as "advance organizers" for the student. We have added at the end of the list three emerging trends not discussed elsewhere in this volume; these three trends are discussed very briefly in this final section of Chapter 3.

Please note that no effort has been made to list here every new thing being proposed or used in evaluation. Some are still too new for us to judge their contribution. Others seem merely "trendy"—ideas or practices we do not expect will be in vogue for long.

Twelve emerging trends or issues we believe likely to influence the future of program evaluation significantly are

1. Increasing priority and legitimacy of internal evaluation (discussed in Chapter 1 and again at greater length in Chapter 12)
2. Expanded use of qualitative methods (discussed in Chapters 4 and 18)
3. A strong shift toward combining quantitative and qualitative methods in each program evaluation rather than depending exclusively on either method (discussed in Chapters 4, 17, and 18)
4. Increasing acceptance of and preference for multiple-method evaluations (discussed in Chapter 11)
5. Introduction and development of theory-based (or theory-driven) evaluation (discussed in Chapter 13)
6. Increasing concern over ethical issues in conducting program evaluations (discussed in Chapter 16)
7. Increased use of program evaluation within business and industry generally (discussed in Chapter 22) and foundations and other agencies in the private and nonprofit sectors (discussed in Chapters 21 and 22)

8. Increased use of evaluation to empower a program's stakeholders
9. Increasing opinions that program evaluators should assume the role of advocates for the programs they evaluate (discussed in Chapter 16)
10. Advances in technology available to evaluators, and communication and ethical issues such advances will raise
11. Educators' increased use of alternative assessment methods (as opposed to traditional testing) to assess students' performance, and increased pressure on educational evaluators to use such methods in evaluating school programs
12. Modifications in evaluation strategies to accommodate increasing trends of government decentralization and delegation of responsibilities to states/provinces and localities.

For those trends listed but not referenced to discussions in other chapters, a brief description is provided in the following sections.

Evaluators' Use of Technological Advances and Resulting Communication and Ethical Issues

The impact of electronic and other technological advances on the lives of today's citizens, in almost every country and society, has been enormous, perhaps incalculable. Its impact on evaluators will be no less. The power and efficiency of today's personal computers, statistical and text/theme processing software, optical scanners, and computerized laser visuals will likely be eclipsed by newer, faster, and more flexible technology even before the printer's ink on these pages is dry. Space does not permit much speculation about such future developments here, but they seem sure to alter the practice of evaluation if not our basic conception of its nature. Imagine pocket-size instruments that can scan a classroom or a city council chamber, record individual and group attitudes, and monitor each student's or citizen's level of intellectual readiness or grasp of specific content. Perhaps that day may never come, but it does seem certain that technological advances will permit data collection to be much more rapid, reliable, and valid than is now the case. Arguments about multiple realities may be moot as attention shifts from concern over how to collect better data to whether the capability of collecting unflawed data should be allowed to intrude upon individual privacy. In the meantime, and until such moral and ethical dilemmas occur, evaluators should take full advantage of technological advances to make their work more effective and efficient.

Technology will not impact only the way in which data are collected. Evaluation's users—policy makers, managers, and consumers—are becoming increasingly sophisticated in their use of technology, allowing evaluators to use new means of conveying evaluation results or including stakeholders in the evaluation (e.g., on an e-mail list server, or a home page on the Internet). Such media are also directly useful to evaluators. For example, the Internet is already familiar to many, perhaps most, evaluators, as indicated by the burgeoning enrollment of evaluators on the American Evaluation Association's list servers, EvalTalk and EvalInfo. The former provides an exchange of ideas and requests for help among evaluators, while the latter makes much important evaluation information, such as the Joint Committee's *Standards,* readily available to any evaluators who have an Internet connection for their personal computers.

Increased Use and Pressures for Evaluators to Use Alternative Assessment

As pressures for educational reform have mounted during recent years, educators have been cudgeled into more and more "high-stakes" standardized tests, where low scores could have dire consequences not only for students but also for teachers and school administrators. Not surprisingly, known limitations of traditional multiple-choice tests became magnified by their misuse. Soon those critical of standardized tests called for their replacement by alternative assessment devices—using nontraditional measures that depended on direct assessment of student performance, where actual performances allow students' behavior and capacities to be observed directly, rather than tests whose items are proxies for such performances. Soon long-familiar assessment alternatives such as oral debates, typing tests, and writing samples were joined by less familiar alternatives, such as student diaries, self-assessment checklists, writing portfolios, and "think aloud" observation sessions. No recent measurement trend has swept across the field of education as quickly and aroused such sudden interest as the movement toward alternative assessment.

Educational evaluators could hardly avoid the rising tide; soon they were being urged by practitioners and policy makers alike to scrap traditional tests and attitude scales and to base their evaluations on performance assessments rather than on paper-and-pencil measures. The most direct impact of this movement comes when educational policy makers mandate the use of alternative assessment in a particular program evaluation. There is nothing wrong with that, unless such measures won't answer the evaluation questions posed or are too costly for the budget allowed for the evaluation. As preferable as direct assessment of performance is to a test's indirect measurement, some circumstances do not permit the former. For example, one U.S. state department of education recently invited interested parties to bid on a mandated statewide assessment of all students. The request for proposals (RFP) specified that the successful bidder would be required to develop, administer, score, and report results from performance assessments of grade 3–12 students in math, reading, writing, and citizenship—for a total of $10,000! Another RFP, this time from a major corporation, specified that direct assessment instruments were to be developed and administered as the means for determining student achievement in a nationwide evaluation of their grade 1–6 math and reading programs. That would have been fine, but then they announced only a six-month time frame and a $25,000 budget for the evaluation!

Only enormous naïveté about the cost of developing and administering such a series of alternative assessment exercises can account for such mandates. Unfortunately, infeasible mandates are familiar to most evaluators, but they still spoil the digestion of those who prefer to fit the data-collection tool to the task and the time permitted for its completion.

We expect that program evaluators will increasingly be pressured to use direct performance assessment by educators and educational policy makers who know enough about such assessment to understand its desirability but not enough to be aware of constraints that may limit its feasibility. Such a tendency will not be limited to education or to only this one means of collecting data.

The Impact of Government Decentralization on Evaluation Strategies

In the last few years there has been an increasing trend for the U.S. federal government to shift issues, problems, and resources to states and localities. Large national programs are dwindling, and more and more major innovations in government are taking place at state and local levels, where small experiments permit more extensive formative evaluation. With decentralization comes opportunity for variation in program innovations, but such opportunities increase the obligation to use formative evaluation to make the best possible programs, and then summative evaluation to determine the ultimate effectiveness of those programs.

A closely related U.S. trend is that of **privatization** of services, an innovation being implemented to varying degrees by local governments. In some cases, services are delivered by private organizations, while in others, services are delivered by the rapidly growing **nonprofit sector**. Charter schools are an example. The U.S. secretary of labor has also proposed privatizing employment services for the unemployed. (We discuss privatization more in Chapter 22, for those interested in more detail about this movement). We believe the locus and focus of program evaluation is likely to shift increasingly to local and state levels as evaluation's role in improving programs becomes increasingly institutionalized at those levels.

APPLICATION EXERCISES

1. Select three other professions and compare them to evaluation on the characteristics of a profession discussed in this chapter. Tell what that suggests to you about evaluation's current and future status as a profession.

2. Identify the characteristics of a full-fledged profession on which evaluation does not yet qualify. Discuss whether or not you think evaluation will qualify on any of those characteristics anytime soon, and explain why or why not.

3. Examine the 10 characteristics of a profession listed in this chapter. On which 3 of the 10 do you feel evaluation has been *most* successful?

SUGGESTED READINGS

House, E. R. (1994). The future perfect of evaluation. *Evaluation Practice 15*, 239–247.

Levitan, S. A. (1992). *Evaluation of federal social programs: An uncertain impact.* Washington, DC: George Washington University Center for Social Policy Studies.

Love, A. J. (1994). Should evaluators be certified? In J. W. Altschuld & M. Engle (Eds.), *The preparation of professional evaluators: Issues, perspectives, and programs.* New Directions for Program Evaluation, No. 62, 29–40. San Francisco: Jossey-Bass.

part **TWO**

Alternative Approaches
to Program Evaluation

In Part One we referred to varying uses of evaluation in education, government, business, nonprofit agencies, and many related areas. Readers were introduced to some distinctions related to the concept of evaluation. We hinted at differences that exist among some major schools of evaluation thought. But we have not yet exposed the reader to the range and variety of alternative, often conflicting, conceptions of what evaluation is and how it should be carried out. Doing so is the purpose of the next eight chapters.

In Part Two we introduce the reader to the wealth of thought and writing that has taken place in evaluation in recent decades. In Chapter 4 we address the diversity of evaluation approaches proposed and examine the factors that have contributed to such differing views. Prior efforts to classify the many evaluation approaches into fewer categories are also discussed, along with presentation of the categories that we use throughout the remainder of this book.

In Chapters 5 through 10 we summarize six general approaches to evaluation, one per chapter. These general approaches include those we see as most prevalent in the literature and most popular in use. Within each chapter, we briefly summarize previous thinking and writing pertaining to that approach, discuss how that approach has been used, and examine its strengths and weaknesses. Space does not permit exhaustive coverage of any particular evaluation model or conception; the chapters are necessarily too brief to provide the detail about any particular author's view of evaluation that would have been possible had we been willing to limit coverage to the thoughts of only a few evaluation theorists. We have preferred to cover a broader array of evaluation approaches at less depth, providing in each chapter references to which interested individuals may turn for a more in-depth discussion of any particular evaluation model.

We have attempted to include the best of both the "old" and "new" approaches proposed for use in conducting program evaluation studies. Some readers will not find their preferred approach featured in our treatment of alternatives, and others may be distressed that we have included approaches they think we should have omitted. We may be viewed as "traditionalists" because we have not included several recently proposed types of evaluation (e.g., advocacy evaluation, empowerment evaluation, or developmental evaluation) that we view as important uses of evaluation but not as types of evaluation per se. Also, in deciding what approaches to include, our intent has been to avoid bandwagon enthusiasm and introduce approaches that have proven demonstrably useful in at least several actual evaluation studies, not those that have been merely written about, however provocatively.

In Chapter 11 the characteristics and contributions of the six general alternative approaches we have described are compared, along with cautions concerning discipleship to any one approach and a plea for thoughtful, eclectic use of alternatives, especially where such an approach would strengthen evaluations more than would adherence to a single view.

Before examining the various alternative approaches to program evaluation, we need to define two terms. We have so far referred to "program" and "stakeholders" in contexts that we trust have given readers a general sense of what they mean. These terms are so pivotal to the remaining content in this book, however, that we need to define and comment on each here.

Stakeholders are various individuals and groups who have a direct interest in and may be affected by the program being evaluated or the evaluation's results. They hold a stake in the future direction of that program and deserve to play a role in determining that direction by (1) identifying concerns and issues to be addressed in evaluating the program and (2) selecting the criteria and variables that will be used in judging its value. As Reineke (1991) has wisely reminded us, evaluators need to identify stakeholders for an evaluation and involve them early, actively, and continuously.

Program is a term that can be defined in many ways. In its simplest sense, a program is a "standing arrangement that provides for a . . . service" (Cronbach et al., 1980, p. 14). The Joint Committee on Standards for Educational Evaluation (1994) has defined program simply as "activities that are provided on a continuing basis" (p. 3). More expansively, it is a complex of people, organization, management, and resources that collectively make up a continuing endeavor to reach some particular educational, social, or commercial goal. Alternately, it might be defined as an ongoing, planned intervention that seeks to achieve some particular outcome(s), in response to some perceived educational, social, or commercial problem.

In their discussion of social programming theory, Shadish, Cook, and Leviton (1991) identify three components: (1) internal program structure, (2) external forces that shape programs, and (3) understanding of how programs change to enhance societal goals. They see the internal structure of a program as the pattern in which "staff, clients, resources, outcomes, administration, internal budget allocations, social norms, facilities, and internal organization" are combined so as to relate "inputs to activities to outputs" (pp. 37–38). External forces could be local economic capacity, external funding agencies, prevailing political sentiments, pressures from powerful stakeholder groups, social mores, logistic or geographical constraints, and the like. Evaluators must understand how programs change—with or without evaluation—and how evaluation information can make those changes more functional and effective. "Programs can change by introducing incremental improvements in small practices, by adopting or adapting demonstration projects that are more effective than existing ones, and by radical shifts in values and priorities" (pp. 38–39).

Examples of educational programs would include Junior Achievement, Inc.'s new elementary school economics program, a state's adult education program, a school district's year-round education program, or an elementary school's staggered reading schedule program.

Examples of programs in other sectors might include the U.S. Federal Aviation Association's program for certifying air traffic controllers, a state program for licensing and training local day-care centers, a community program aimed at reducing vandalism, or a county health center program to increase immunization of children against communicable diseases.

Examples of programs in business and industry would include Price-Waterhouse's national orientation and training program for first-year auditors; Texaco's Environmental Protection Program, aimed at preventing oil spills; Utah Power and Light Company's energy conservation program; or Jostens Learning Corporation's Vanguard program (an integrated, computer-based learning program for elementary schools). Any business or industry might run smaller, nontitled programs such as an employee orientation program, a training program for supervisors on performance appraisal, a new purchasing strategy, an in-house child care center, flextime, or job sharing.

In the nonprofit sector, examples of programs would include the W. K. Kellogg Foundation's national initiative to support land-grant universities in reconceptualizing the training of food systems professionals, the Knight Foundation's Fellowships and Training for Future Journalists of the Pacific Islands, or the Warren Buffett Foundation's program to prevent nuclear proliferation. Other foundations may have an interest in operating a program for preventing alcohol and drug abuse, or a program for increasing employee use of alternative means of transportation.

These previous examples of programs are relatively easy to define and describe, for they are relatively self-contained and have identifiable boundaries, administrators and staff, and budgets. But programs are not always quite that simple. Some are complex, interrelated, and multilevel, and it is decidedly more difficult to evaluate those not-so-simple programs. For example, an evaluation of a specific program often must probe beyond the boundaries of that program to examine the broader context of neighboring programs or antecedent and concurrent conditions that may affect it. Consider the evaluation of the University of California at Los Angeles (UCLA) Psychology Department's program for recruiting and retaining minority students. That program may have multiple components within it (e.g., separate procedures and recruitment pools for undergraduate and graduate students, separate managers and budgets for direct mailings to qualified minority students in their senior year, recruitment visits to schools with large populations of minority students, and fellowships for qualified minority candidates). If so, the evaluator already may be evaluating more than one "miniprogram" as he pulls the evaluation findings for these components together into one integrated evaluation report. But the evaluation of the entire effort of the Psychology Department to recruit minority students is nested within the broader context of dozens of other, separate minority student recruitment and retention efforts in other UCLA departments, as well as an interdepartmental program directed by an Office of Minority Affairs. And all of these programs, including Psychology's, likely have a predecessor, a program used previously for the same purposes, that will have influenced the current programs in either conspicuous or subtle ways.

Before continuing, we should pause to ask why we need to bother ourselves about any of these other programs, either past or present. If we define the boundaries of the Psychology Department's program carefully, why should we care about other similar programs conducted in other parts of UCLA? Are we not complicating matters more by widening the focus of our evaluation beyond psychology? Not really. The complications already exist; we are merely acknowledging them. Some minority students may have participated in more than one UCLA program; others may have enrolled without ever hearing of any of the programs. All students bring with them antecedent variables that interact with program variables. The centrally run, interdepartmental program likely impacts so directly on Psychology's efforts that it would be naïve to overlook the broader program's influence. The evaluator must be aware of such factors to avoid drawing incorrect inferences about the specific program he is evaluating.

To expand our example, assume now that an evaluation of UCLA's entire, institutionwide effort to recruit and retain minorities is requested. Here the evaluation would be very comprehensive, subsuming what could be dozens of individual program evaluations. Frequently one is confronted with situations where a comprehensive evaluation of a large, agencywide program finds many more specific program evaluations nested within it. In such cases, an individual program may be evaluated in relation to how well it succeeds in accomplishing its own objectives, while simultaneously providing data that will be used in causal modeling or longitudinal analyses that are part of a comprehensive evaluation for the entire institutionwide program. There could also be several parallel evaluation efforts currently under way, or recently completed, in other UCLA departments. Each may be designed to serve that specific program's political, decision making, and revision needs, yet each could also be part of the larger whole.

Any large organization, such as a prison system, a school district, or an international corporation, is nearly certain to be faced with this evaluation-nested-within-a-larger-evaluation issue. An evaluator conducting an evaluation of any specific program in such a context should identify and strive to understand the other parts of the bigger picture that could confound the evaluation if not handled carefully.

Another way to illustrate that programs are not always tidy, neatly wrapped packages handed to the evaluator is to examine program budgets. Often the evaluator finds that the program to be evaluated has several budgets, one for each of several program components. Alternately, the program may draw on only part of a large budget that supports multiple programs. Or the program may be funded from a variety of budgets. This makes it risky for the evaluator to assume that the boundaries of the program to be evaluated are congruent with the boundaries of the budget that supports it. Our Australian colleague Jerome Winston (1995) noted that managers often think of program evaluation narrowly, assuming it refers only to the evaluation of programs defined in their program budget. He lamented that

> This narrow view . . . of program evaluation often discourages managers from recommending, supporting or even seeing the need for evaluations that cut across program boundaries as set out in "program budgets." These managers are often pleased to discover that the term "program evaluation" exists independently of "program budgeting" and can refer to the evaluation of any planned intervention that seeks to achieve outcome(s)—even when aspects of the "program" to be evaluated are (1) but a small portion of a funded "program," or (2) funded through different "programs" in the budget.

An interesting problem occurs when governments opt for the terminology of program budgeting. Because the word "program" then refers to an element in a budget, governments may not have a well-understood word to use when referring to a government policy or intervention (i.e., program) that applies across the boundaries of programs that are defined in program budgets. (p. 1)*

While we will typically use simple programs in most of the evaluation examples provided in this text (after all, this *is* an *introductory* text on evaluation), we will use a few more complicated examples like those we have just described so that we do not oversimplify the world in which the evaluator must work.

---

* Jerome Winston, "Defining program," e-mail message, American Evaluation Association Discussion List EVALTALK, 1995.

chapter 4

Alternative Views of Evaluation

ORIENTING QUESTIONS

1. Why are there so many different approaches to evaluation?
2. How would objectivists and subjectivists differ in their approach to evaluation?
3. Why is evaluation theory, as reflected in different approaches to evaluation, important to learn?
4. Do you believe it is useful to champion quantitative evaluation methods over qualitative evaluation methods or vice versa? Why or why not?
5. What practical issues contribute to the diversity of evaluation approaches?

Like many other young, emerging fields and disciplines, evaluation is troubled by definitional and ideological disputes. Those who write about evaluation differ widely in their views of what evaluation is. And those who conduct evaluation studies bring to the task diverse conceptions of how one should go about doing it. During the past three decades, nearly 60 different proposals for how evaluations should be conducted have been developed and circulated. These various prescriptions—today's so-called evaluation models—are implemented with varying degrees of fidelity. To complicate the picture further, some evaluations are designed without conscious reference to any existing conceptual framework, thereby resulting, if successful, in yet another evaluation approach.

This proliferation of evaluation models has posed a perplexing dilemma for the practitioner who is puzzled about which is best for his purposes. Each proposed approach comes with its built-in assumptions about evaluation—what it is and how it should be done. Each emphasizes different aspects of evaluation, depending on the priorities and preferences of its author(s). Few come with careful step-by-step instructions practitioners can follow, and even fewer are useful in settings and circumstances beyond those in which they were created. In short, few of evaluation's proposed prescriptions are easy for the practitioner to follow.

The various approaches proposed by evaluators are the content of the field of evaluation. But no clear and singular image of evaluation can be drawn from that content. Trying to understand program evaluation by reading the various commentaries and prescriptions of evaluation's theoreticians is rather like trying to learn what an elephant is like by piecing together reports of several blind people, each of whom happens to grasp a different portion of the elephant's anatomy. The evaluation literature is rather fragmented and is often aimed more at fellow evaluation theorists than at practitioners. Busy practitioners can hardly be faulted for not expending the time necessary to interpret and consolidate these disparate bits of knowledge.

We shall not solve the problem totally in this book. But this chapter and those that follow (Chapters 5 through 11) should clarify the varied alternatives useful in conducting evaluation. Perhaps by the end we will know enough about the elephant to recognize it when we see it.

DIVERSE CONCEPTIONS OF PROGRAM EVALUATION

The many evaluation "models"[1] that have emerged since 1965 range from comprehensive prescriptions to checklists of suggestions. These models have greatly influenced present practices. Some authors opt for a systems approach, viewing evaluation as a process of identifying and collecting information to assist decision makers. Others view evaluation as synonymous with professional judgment, where judgments about a program's quality are based on opinions of experts (whether or not the data and criteria used in reaching those judgments are clear). In another school of thought, evaluation is viewed as the process of comparing performance data with clearly specified objectives, while in another, evaluation is seen as synonymous with carefully controlled experimental research on significant educational or social programs. Others focus on the importance of naturalistic inquiry or urge that value pluralism be recognized, accommodated, and preserved and that those individuals involved with the entity being evaluated play the prime role in determining what direction the evaluation study takes. Some writers propose that evaluations be structured in keeping with legal or forensic **paradigms** so that planned opposition—both pro and con—is built in. And this barely dents the list of current alternatives.

---

[1] The fact that these prescriptions may not really qualify for the designation of "models," in any of the customary uses of that term, has been discussed elsewhere (Worthen, 1977); in this text any use we make of the word *models* is reflective of common usage in the field of evaluation. We believe the more permissive word *approaches* better describes the diverse proposals for how evaluations should be conducted. Hereafter, we will forgo referring to the approaches as "so-called models," assuming we have by now made our point adequately.

The various models are built on differing—often conflicting—conceptions and definitions of evaluation, with the result that practitioners are led in very different directions, depending upon which model they follow. Let us consider an example from education.

- If one viewed evaluation as essentially synonymous with professional judgment, the worth of a curriculum would be assessed by experts (as judged by the evaluation client) who observed the curriculum in action, examined the curriculum materials, or in some other way gleaned sufficient information to record their considered judgments.

- If evaluation is viewed as a comparison between student performance indicators and objectives, behaviorally stated objectives would be established for the curriculum and relevant student behaviors would be measured against this yardstick, using either standardized or evaluator-constructed instruments. (Note that in this conception there is no built-in assessment of the worth of the objectives themselves.)

- Using a decision-oriented approach, the evaluator, working closely with the decision maker, would collect sufficient information about the relative advantages and disadvantages of each decision alternative to judge which was best. However, although the decision maker would judge the worth of each alternative, evaluation per se would be a shared role.

- If one accepted our earlier definition of evaluation (see Chapter 1), the curriculum evaluator would first identify the curriculum goals and then, using input from appropriate reference groups, determine whether the goals were good for the students, parents, and community served. He would then collect evaluative information relevant to those goals as well as to identifiable side effects resulting from the curriculum. When the data were analyzed and interpreted, the evaluator would judge the worth of the curriculum and (usually) make a recommendation to the individual or group responsible for final decisions.

Obviously, the way in which one views evaluation has direct impact on the type of evaluation activities conducted, whether the evaluation is of a curriculum, a corporate training program, or a state program for aiding displaced homemakers.

ORIGINS OF ALTERNATIVE VIEWS OF EVALUATION

The diversity of evaluation approaches described in this section has arisen from the varied backgrounds and worldviews of their authors, which have resulted in diverse philosophical orientations, methodological predilections, and practical preferences. These different predispositions have led the authors of the various evaluation approaches—and their adherents—to propose widely different designs, data-collection and analysis methods, and interpretive techniques. Thus, the differences in evaluation approaches can be traced directly to their proponents' rather different views of the nature of evaluation.

Baker and Niemi (in press) propose that there are four disparate sources from which much of the thinking about evaluation has been drawn: (1) experimentation, (2) measurement, (3) systems analysis, and (4) interpretative approaches. These authors see experimentation as the use in evaluation of the social science experimental research tradition, complete with randomization, careful attention to units of analysis, and statistical tests. Measurement is described as the style of evaluation that presumes that use of a behavioral measurement device will yield numerical scores that provide evidence of a program's effectiveness. Systems analysis is proposed as examination of the interrelationships between broad sets of variables in complex processes or organizations, conducted to help managers make more defensible decisions. Interpretative approaches are uses of hermeneutic philosophy and interpretive theories of knowledge in generating holistic descriptive interpretations and judgments of complex programs.

While we concur that each of these four sources has influenced the evaluation literature, they obviously are not all on the same dimension. Experimentation and "interpretative approaches" are really alternate methodologies for collecting and interpreting empirical data. Measurement is simply one process of recording observations of some entity and translating them into simple descriptions of that entity. Systems analysis is an organizational strategy for collecting and using empirical information to improve decision making in the organization. We believe that a more fruitful way to understand the origins of alternative conceptualizations of evaluation is to examine differences in their authors' (and adherents') philosophical and ideological beliefs, methodological preferences, and practical choices stemming from prior experience. Collectively, these three dimensions encompass most of what we see as the important factors that have contributed to the different schools of evaluation thought.

PHILOSOPHICAL AND IDEOLOGICAL DIFFERENCES

There is no univocal philosophy of evaluation, any more than there is a single, universally accepted philosophy of science. And perhaps that lack has not hurt us too much; after all, evaluation seems to be doing reasonably well without one. The lack of a guiding philosophy has not prevented extensive discourse and debate concerning philosophical assumptions about epistemology and value. Indeed, different approaches to establishing worth or merit are largely responsible for the diversity of views about program evaluation.

Objectivist and Subjectivist Epistemology

House (1980, 1983a, 1983b) has written thoughtfully about different philosophies of knowing or establishing truth (**epistemology**) and how they affect one's choosing an approach to evaluation. He has grouped evaluation approaches into two categories: *objectivism* and *subjectivism.*

Objectivism requires that evaluation information be "scientifically objective," that is, that it use data-collection and analysis techniques that yield results reproducible and verifiable by other reasonable and competent persons using the same techniques. In this sense, the evaluation procedures are "externalized," existing outside of the evaluator in clearly explicated form that is replicable by others and that will produce similar results from one evaluation to the next. Objectivism is derived largely from the social science tradition of empiricism.

Subjectivism bases its validity claims on "an appeal to experience rather than to scientific method. Knowledge is conceived as being largely tacit rather than explicit" (House, 1980, p. 252). The validity of a subjectivist evaluation depends on the relevance of the evaluator's background and qualifications and the keenness of his perceptions. In this sense, the evaluation procedures are "internalized," existing largely within the evaluator in ways that are not explicitly understood or reproducible by others.

Objectivism held sway in the social sciences and in educational inquiry for decades, at least until the 1980s. There have been, however, many more recent criticisms of objectivist epistemology, as well as the dominance of **logical positivism** in social and educational science. Campbell (1984) states that "twenty years ago logical positivism dominated the philosophy of science. . . . Today the tide has completely turned among the theorists of science in philosophy, sociology, and elsewhere. Logical positivism is almost universally rejected" (p. 27). Scriven (1984) argues that any lingering positivist bias in evaluation should be eliminated. Bailey (1992) argues that traditional positivist methods should not be the preferred approach to studying public-sector programs. And Guba and Lincoln (1981) challenge the "infallibility" of the hypothetico-deductive inquiry paradigm because of its limitations in dealing with complex, interactive phenomena in dynamic, septic, real-world settings. Although less sweeping and conclusive in his critique, House (1980) portrays objectivism as inattentive to its own credibility, presuming validity because of its methodology, and therefore credible only to those who value such a methodology. He also notes that objectivism conceals hidden values and biases of which its adherents are unaware, because even the choice of data-collection techniques and instruments is not value-neutral, an assumption seemingly taken for granted by objectivist evaluators.

To counter the objectivist hold upon the methodologies of evaluation, criticisms of objectivism have been extreme. Yet subjectivism has been no less soundly criticized, especially by those who see its procedures as "unscientific" and therefore of dubious worth. Critics (e.g., Boruch & Cordray, 1980) point out that subjectivist evaluation often leads to varying, sometimes contradictory, conclusions that defy reconciliation because that which led to the conclusions is largely obscured within the nonreplicable procedures of the evaluator. Similarly, as House (1980) puts it,

> Critics of the phenomenologist epistemology note that there is often confusion over whose common sense perceptions are to be taken as the

[handwritten margin note: Biased/free observations of the natural world.]

basis for understanding. Furthermore, if one takes everyday understanding as the foundation of inquiry, does one not merely reconstruct whatever ideologies, biases, and false beliefs already exist? How can one distinguish causal determinants and regularities, the strength of the positivist epistemology, from perceived beliefs? How can one evaluate conflicting interpretations? Phenomenology provides no way of doing so. (p. 254)

And so the dialogue continues. The objectivists depend upon replicable facts as their touchstone of truth, whereas subjectivists depend upon accumulated experience as their way to understanding. Although both epistemologies carry within them "tests" that must be met if their application is to be viewed as trustworthy, they lead to very different evaluation designs and methods, giving rise to much of today's diversity in evaluation approaches.

Utilitarian versus Intuitionist-Pluralist Evaluation

House (1976, 1983a) has also made a distinction closely related to that of objectivism and subjectivism, namely, **utilitarian** versus **intuitionist-pluralist evaluation**. Although this is a distinction concerning principles for assigning values, not epistemology, utilitarian and intuitionist-pluralist evaluation approaches parallel the objectivist and subjectivist epistemologies outlined above.

Utilitarian Evaluation. Utilitarian approaches determine value by assessing the *overall* impact of a program on those affected. These approaches have tended to follow objectivist epistemology. In his classic treatise on "justice in evaluation," House (1976) suggests that utilitarian evaluation accepts the value premise that the greatest good is that which will benefit the greatest number of individuals. Thus, "properly speaking, utilitarianism refers to the idea of maximizing happiness in society" (House, 1983a, p. 49). A single, explicitly defined ethical principle is operative. As a result, the evaluator will focus on total group gains by using average outcome scores (e.g., test scores, number of days absent from work) or some other common index of "good" to identify the "greatest good for the greatest number." The best programs are those that produce the greatest gains on the criterion or criteria selected to determine worth. Statewide assessment programs and large-scale comparative evaluations of welfare systems are utilitarian in nature. Most utilitarian evaluation approaches lend themselves to use by governments or others who mandate and/or sponsor evaluation studies for which managers and public program administrators are the major audiences.

Intuitionist-Pluralist Evaluation. At the opposite end of the continuum are intuitionist-pluralist approaches to evaluation, which are based on the idea that value depends upon the impact of the program on *each* individual. These approaches have tended to follow subjectivist epistemology. Here the value position is that the greatest good requires the attention to each individual's benefit. Thus,

> The ethical principles are [neither] single in number nor explicitly defined as in utilitarian ethics. There are several principles derived from intuition and experience, but no set rules for weighting them. This captures another meaning of ethical subjectivism—that the ultimate criterion of what is good and right are individual feelings or apprehensions. (House, 1983a, p. 50)

This approach leads to a focus on the distribution of gains by individuals and subgroups (e.g., ethnic groupings). There can be no common index of "good" but rather a plurality of criteria and judges, and the evaluator is no longer an impartial "averager" but a portrayer of different values and needs. Data may be test scores, hours of training received, changes in income, or recidivism levels, but intuitionist-pluralist evaluators often prefer data from personal interviews and testimonials of program participants. Weighing and balancing the many judgments and criteria inherent in this approach is largely intuitive, and there are no algorithms to help reduce complex evaluative information to any unequivocal recommendation. The perceived merit or worth of the program depends largely on the values and perspectives of whoever is judging, and each individual or constituent group is a legitimate judge. "Likewise, the subjective utility of something is based on personal judgment and personal desires. Each person is the best judge of events for himself" (House, 1983a, p. 56). Within limits of feasibility, most intuitionist-pluralist evaluations try to involve as "judges" all individuals and groups who are affected by the program being evaluated rather than leave decisions and judgments to governmental sponsors and high-level administrators—as is typically the case with utilitarian evaluation.

The Impact of Philosophical Differences

Historically, evaluators tended to line up along the several continua described above or, worse, become polarized in "either-or" dichotomies. This debate over epistemology was, in prior decades, a major cause of rifts that permeated the field of evaluation. What one considered acceptable program evaluation often depended on the position one took along one of these philosophical dimensions. Yet, although differences in philosophy have led to alternative views of evaluation, the philosophical differences are not incompatible; for thoughtful contemporary evaluators, polarization has given way to integration of perspectives. Multiple approaches to describing objects of study, drawn from both objectivist and subjectivist traditions, have been used in the same evaluations to achieve important goals (e.g., Chelimsky, 1994).

We recognize the right, if not the wisdom, of any evaluator to subscribe totally to the assumptions and premises of one particular ideology. Yet few evaluators who succeed in a wide range of evaluation settings can afford to consider philosophical ideologies as "either-or" decisions. The purist view that looks noble in print yields to practical pressures demanding that the evaluator use appropriate methods based on an epistemology that is right *for that evaluation,* or even multiple methods based on alternative epistemologies within the same evaluation.[2] There are precious few philosophical purists among today's evaluation practitioners. It is important to know, however, the assumptions and limitations of methods that are drawn from different worldviews about evaluation.

METHODOLOGICAL BACKGROUNDS AND PREFERENCES

Different philosophical assumptions about knowledge and value give rise naturally to different evaluation methods. Indeed, evaluation philosophy and methodology are so closely intertwined that we might well have discussed both together in the previous section. But we believe it useful to examine separately two methodological issues that have influenced greatly the conduct of evaluation studies: (1) the relevance and utility of **quantitative** and **qualitative inquiry** and (2) the difficulty encountered by evaluators in working across disciplinary and methodological boundaries.

Quantitative and Qualitative Evaluation

Much has been said in recent years about quantitative and qualitative evaluation, as evaluators have struggled to sort out the relative utility of these two distinct approaches. Before we can address this issue adequately, we must delineate (as clearly as we can in a short space) the differences between qualitative and quantitative data-collection methods. Several authors have provided useful distinctions between the two (e.g., Hedrick, 1994; House, 1994b), but we still find descriptions by Schofield and Anderson (1984) most useful for this purpose.[3] In their view, *qualitative* inquiry generally

    (a) is conducted in natural settings, such as schools or neighborhoods;
    (b) utilizes the researcher as the chief "instrument" in both data-gathering

---

[2] More will be said about such multiple methods in later chapters of this book.
[3] We are indebted to Schofield and Anderson for their contribution to our thinking and for permission to quote liberally from their work in this section.

and analysis, . . . (c) emphasizes "thick description," that is, obtaining "real," "rich," "deep," data which illuminate everyday patterns of action and meaning from the perspective of those being studied . . . , (d) tends to focus on social processes rather than primarily or exclusively on outcomes, (e) employs multiple data-gathering methods, especially participant-observation and interviews, and (f) uses an inductive approach to data analysis, extracting its concepts from the mass of particular detail which constitutes the data base.

By contrast, these authors state that *quantitative* inquiry generally

focuses on the testing of specific hypotheses that are smaller parts of some larger theoretical perspective. This approach follows the traditional natural science model more closely than qualitative research, emphasizing experimental design and statistical methods of analysis. Quantitative research emphasizes standardization, precision, objectivity, and reliability of measurement as well as replicability and generalizability of findings. Thus, quantitative research is characterized not only by a focus on producing numbers but on generating numbers which are suitable for statistical tests. (pp. 8–9)

Time Out for Definitions

As a backdrop for further discussion of the quantitative-qualitative distinction, we must pause to introduce several terms used in philosophy of science for readers unfamiliar with that language and literature.

A **paradigm** is, most simply, a pattern or example. Most loosely, it is a philosophy or school of thought. Philosophers of science give the term special meaning, however, using it to describe integrated worldviews held by individuals or groups that determine how those individuals or groups perceive and attempt to comprehend truth. The resulting worldview (paradigm) includes an epistemological belief and an ontological belief that together govern perceptions and choices made in the pursuit of scientific truth. There are paradigms in many areas (e.g., political paradigms), but here we are concerned with *inquiry* paradigms that determine how we conduct inquiry activities.

Epistemology is the theory of knowledge or the study of the nature of knowledge, especially with reference to its limits and validity. Many philosophers of science do not distinguish between epistemology, methodology, and philosophy of science (Kaplan, 1964). In practice, one's epistemological belief determines how one thinks knowledge or truth can be comprehended, what problems and inaccuracies are associated with various ways of pursuing and presenting knowledge, and how the inquirer views his relationship with the object of his inquiry.

Ontology is the theory of reality or existence. In practice, one's ontological belief determines how one thinks about reality and about what exists in fact and what exists only in thought.

Positivism is a paradigm that holds that knowledge is based on natural phenomena and their properties and relations as verified by the empirical sciences. Put simply, positivism also holds that reality exists independent of those who perceive it. Earlier forms of positivism that were marked by dogmatic certainty and unthinking determination and reductionism have been referred to as **logical positivism**, a paradigm that is widely discredited and generally abandoned. Conversely, **post-positivism** is a paradigm labeled because it succeeded positivism, not because it was based on the same epistemological or ontological assumptions. Rather, post-positivists see empirical facts as value-laden, knowledge as fallible, and any set of data (facts) as explainable by many different theories. These views are virtually opposite to the views held by logical positivists. *Multiple realities caused by different individuals*

Constructivism is a paradigm that holds that knowledge is constructed by people and that realities do not exist objectively, for no reality exists except that created by people. In short, the constructivist holds that reality is socially constructed through individual or collective definition of the perceived situation. This paradigm is also often referred to as **interpretivist**. Although not completely congruent, many scholars lump **phenomenology** here also, since it holds that all knowledge is of phenomena and all existence is phenomenal (drawing more on the senses than on thought).

Now, armed with this clarified terminology, let us return to our discussion of differences in quantitative and qualitative inquiry.

Understanding Differences between Paradigms and Quantitative and Qualitative Methods

Frequently those who discuss differences in qualitative and quantitative methods extend the terminology to discussions of paradigms, thus speaking of differences between the qualitative and quantitative paradigms (e.g., Datta, 1994). Others (e.g., Hedrick, 1994) speak of the paradigms from which qualitative and quantitative methods *are drawn* but choose to label the paradigms in more formal philosophical terms (e.g., positivist vs. constructivist) even though, in their view, each paradigm leads to the use of only one family of methods. For example, Hedrick (1994) nests the term "quantitative" within the positivist paradigm, associates it with experimental, quasi-experimental, and representative sample designs (methodologies), and specific methods such as structured interviews, questionnaires, and review of administrative records. Conversely, Hedrick nests "qualitative" within the constructivist paradigm and associates it with hermeneutic (interpretive) dialectic and pattern-matching designs, and specific methods such as unstructured interviews, focus groups, and thick description (p. 47). While we concur that data-collection methods are closely *associated with* particular paradigms, in our view they are not necessarily *limited by* those paradigms.

Qualitative data can be as useful to the positivists as to the phenomenologist, and both may make good use of quantitative data. The fact that those who favor a particular paradigm may be more at home with methods frequently used within that paradigm does not make those tools their peculiar province. (See, e.g., Dennis, Fetterman, and Sechrest's 1994 example of the use of qualitative methods in quasi-experimental evaluation designs.) We reject references to qualitative or quantitative *paradigms,* reserving those adjectives to differentiate between two types of data (and the methods used to collect them).

But back to the two paradigms. Various other terms have been used to refer to them, although subtle differences exist. Guba and Lincoln (1981) contrast the *naturalistic* and *scientific* paradigms. Fetterman (1992) contrasts the *phenomenological* and *positivist* paradigms. House (1994b) labels them as *positivist* and *interpretivist.* Middleton (1995) has used the dichotomy of *subjective* versus *objective* to describe those worldviews. We should note that all of the dichotomies are largely artificial and should more accurately be thought of as different ends of a continuum, although we will continue to use them dichotomously for simplicity, at least for now.

An Unfortunate Qualitative-Quantitative Debate

We cannot leave this discussion of qualitative and quantitative methods without considering briefly the unfortunate and unnecessary disagreements that have arisen between evaluators who favor quantitative methods and those who prefer to collect qualitative data. These disagreements are in part a result of how both methodologies have developed during the past half century.

Because so many (of the relatively few) people serving in evaluation roles during the late 1950s and 1960s were trained as researchers, it is not surprising that the experimental tradition quickly became the most generally accepted evaluation approach. The work of Campbell and Stanley (1966) gave enormous impetus to the predominance of experimental or quasi-experimental approaches. Although some evaluators cautioned that correct use of the experimental model in largely uncontrollable program settings might not be feasible, the elegance and precision of the experimental method led most program evaluators to view it as the ideal. Whatever coherence existed in the still toddling practice of program evaluators in the 1960s was centered around most practicing evaluators' endorsement of the "scientific method" (knowledge accumulated through successive research studies, objective ways of knowing, utilitarian values, and quantitative methods of collecting and interpreting evaluation data).

Not all program evaluators were enamored with the use of traditional quantitative methods for program evaluations, however, and their dissatisfaction led to a search for alternatives. Qualitative and naturalistic methods, largely shunned by most program evaluators during the 1960s as unacceptably "soft," gained wider acceptance in the 1970s and thereafter as proposals for their application to program evaluations were made by Stake (1978), Eisner (1979b), Guba and Lincoln (1981, 1989), Lincoln (1991), Peshkin (1993), and others.

Increasingly, evaluators embraced subjective ways of knowing, pluralistic values, and qualitative methods previously considered "nonscientific" by many.

The rise in popularity of qualitative inquiry methods has been noted by social, behavioral, and educational scientists (e.g., Chen, 1993; Shadish, Cook, & Leviton, 1991). The past two decades have seen a spectacular increase in acceptability of qualitative techniques in program evaluation. The rapidity with which qualitative techniques have gained favor is apparent in the fact that by 1992 the American Evaluation Association's topical interest group on qualitative methods had burgeoned to about 550 members, while its quantitative topical interest group remained at about 150 members (Sechrest, 1992). Where the evaluator's preferred tools were once quasi-experimental designs, operational definitions of key variables, objective measurement techniques, and statistical analyses, most contemporary evaluators would feel poorly armed if their tool-boxes lacked the means for them to provide careful, thorough, narrative description, portray process, glean people's perceptions through interviews, and construct meaning from those individual or collective perceptions.

Although some who favor qualitative methods are concerned that the sudden popularity and apparent simplicity of this approach have attracted innocents who employ qualitative inquiry without understanding its complexity or the competence it demands of its user (Schofield & Anderson, 1984), most advocates are delighted by its increasing acceptance. Indeed, most thoughtful evaluators have come to understand that qualitative and naturalistic approaches have methodological standards and rigor that are *different* but not *lacking*. Most evaluators have come to accept the reality of multiple realities, or at least of multiple perceptions of reality. With this awareness and increased legitimacy, qualitative evaluation has emerged as a serious alternative—or complement—to the traditional quantitative approach.

Those who favor exclusive or primary use of quantitative methods are, for the most part, distressed by the shift toward qualitative inquiry (notwithstanding the fact that quantitative work still clings to its position as the dominant approach to evaluation and research, if readings of the most influential journals in education, public administration, and human resource management are any indication). These critics of qualitative evaluation often complain about the subjectivity of many qualitative methods and techniques, expressing concern that evaluation has abandoned objectivity in favor of inexpertly managed subjectivity.

In summary, sharp disagreements developed during the 1960s between proponents of the newer qualitative approaches and adherents to the more broadly accepted quantitative methods. The 1970s and 1980s were marked by debates as the two schools of thought struggled for ascendancy. In short, the last three decades have been marked by acrimony between these seemingly irreconcilable methodological persuasions.

Beginning in 1979, however, the dialogue began to move beyond this debate, with analysts increasingly discussing the benefits of integrating both methods within an evaluation study (e.g., Howe, 1988; Kidder & Fine, 1987; Smith, 1986; Cook & Reichardt, 1979; Madey, 1982). Stone's (1984) comment about educational research seems to extend to program evaluation as well:

Today in educational research, . . . the trend is methodological pluralism and eclecticism. Many formerly devout quantitative researchers are now trying their hands at qualitative inquiry. The vigorous quantitative/qualitative debate, if not dead, is somehow buried. (p. 1)

Smith and Heshusius (1986) optimistically titled their treatise "Closing Down the Conversation: The End of the Quantitative-Qualitative Debate among Educational Inquirers." For a time it appeared they spoke too soon. The late 1980s and early 1990s saw salvos of broadsides fired back and forth between leading proponents of constructivist philosophy and qualitative methods (Lincoln, 1991; Lincoln & Guba, 1992; Lincoln & Guba, 1994) and positivist or post-positivist philosophy and quantitative methods (Sechrest, 1992; Sechrest, Babcock, & Smith, 1993). The rather acrimonious nature of the debate caused several other prominent evaluators to lament such schisms or to argue that they are pointless and unproductive (e.g., Datta, 1994; House, 1994b; Scriven, 1994; Reichardt & Rallis, 1994).

In any event, despite this flare-up early in this decade, it appears that interest in the quantitative-qualitative debate has generally waned. Worthen (in press) has reported results of a survey that found many evaluation practitioners to be weary of the debate and the wrangling about which is preferable, qualitative or quantitative methods. To most evaluators today, the obvious answer is "both." Insightful integration of both qualitative and quantitative methods within a single evaluation design is now so widely accepted that there seems little point to the debate. Most evaluation scholars share the opinion that qualitative and quantitative methods are compatible and that using both in an evaluation strengthens it (e.g., Reichardt & Cook 1979; Schofield & Anderson, 1984; Mark & Shotland, 1987; Chelimsky, 1995b).

Some evaluators have gone beyond merely advocating use of both qualitative and quantitative methods to illustrate how both can be integrated within the same evaluation design. The most insightful and useful work in this area is that of Greene, Caracelli, and Graham (1989), who have provided a conceptual framework for such mixed-method evaluation designs. From this framework they have developed five types of mixed-method designs, each to serve a different evaluation purpose but all five using some mixture of qualitative and quantitative methods. Greene and her colleagues have artfully drawn on the practice of evaluators (examining 57 actual mixed-method studies) in a way that has at once legitimized and categorized the various ways that thoughtful evaluators have been combining methods for decades, while also helping more one-dimensional colleagues to see the fruitfulness of combining qualitative and quantitative methods. Such work has provided evaluators with a framework to help them craft each evaluation to take advantage of the complementary strengths of these two data-collection methods without getting sidetracked in academic and sometimes arcane arguments about which method is best.

In short, the majority of contemporary evaluators clearly view quantitative and qualitative methods as compatible, complementary approaches in evaluation of educational, social, or corporate programs. Few paradigm purists are left to carry on a debate that has largely lost its audience.

Disciplinary Boundaries and Evaluation Methodology

It is ironic that in a field with such a rich array of alternative evaluation approaches, there still exists a tendency to fall prey to the "law of the instrument" fallacy[4] rather than adapt or invent evaluation methods to meet our needs. Our grasp of evaluation still seems partial and parochial, as may be expected in a young field. But it is unfortunate that we seem to carry with us into a new field the methodological allegiances we developed through earlier studies. Too often we fail to encourage methodological flexibility, unthinkingly adopting a single-minded perspective that can answer only questions stemming from that perspective. Today's typical evaluation studies depend largely on methodology adapted from agronomy and anthropology, some facets of psychology, sociology, philosophy, and mathematics, and, to a limited extent, economics and history. Those who interpret this statement as critical of these fields have missed the point, for these are esteemed disciplines with methodologies well suited to the pursuit of research questions within their respective spheres of inquiry. Rather, the point is that evaluation is not a traditional discipline but a transdiscipline that necessarily cuts across disciplines (Scriven, 1991b), and evaluators are thus denied the luxury of remaining within any single-inquiry paradigm.

Evaluation, unlike research, cannot fix the boundaries of its own inquiry; rather, evaluation questions are set by clients' needs and might be framed so as to require the tools of several disciplines to answer them. Evaluators need to have the flexibility to use econometrics to collect one type of data, psychometrics for another, sociometrics for a third, and so forth. Yet evaluators often go about the business of evaluation using their preferred methods and drawing little if at all on the alternative paradigms that may be more relevant to the evaluation problems at hand.

Some promising starts have been made at broadening our methodological base in evaluation. Colleagues have adapted aspects of the judicial model, aesthetic criticism, investigative journalism, and the like into evaluative terms, as noted in Chapters 7 through 10 of this text. But for the most part, the methods and techniques from one discipline remain relatively unknown terrain to evaluators in another. It is not an easy thing to shuck off the conceptual shackles forged by experience. It is harder yet to expect that busy evaluators will interrupt an evaluation study to set off on an intellectual expedition into the terra incognita of another discipline to discover new methods perhaps more relevant to the problem at hand. And advising evaluators to be methodologically interdisciplinary sounds somewhat hollow in the absence of graduate programs designed specifically to assist evaluators-to-be in learning how they might do so.

Evaluators' predispositions and preferences on both philosophical and methodological dimensions lead to differing designs, data-collection and analysis

---

[4] Kaplan (1964) described this fallacy by noting that if you give a small boy a hammer, suddenly everything he encounters needs hammering. The same tendency is true, he asserts, for scientists who gain familiarity and comfort in using a particular method or technique; suddenly all problems will be wrested into a form where they may be addressed in that fashion, whether or not that is appropriate.

methods, and interpretive techniques. Thus, the increasing variety of methodological perspectives gaining legitimacy in program evaluation is not only increasing the variety of ways evaluations are designed and conducted but also adding richness of perspective to a field still too young to opt for any single, ideal evaluation paradigm.

DIFFERENT METAPHORS OF EVALUATION

The importance of metaphors in evaluation has become increasingly clear during the past two decades.[5] Worthen (1978) described an early federally supported research effort to identify metaphors from various disciplines that might be adapted into useful new evaluation methodologies:

> If I may use a metaphor, we have proposed a planned expedition into other fields to find and capture those methods and techniques that might have relevance for evaluation and domesticate them so they will become tractable for our use. Again, limited resources will allow us to explore only so far, so we need to identify early those areas which appear most likely to contain good methodological candidates for domestication. (p. 3)

Continued under the direction of Smith (1981), this research effort examined the possibility of using a variety of metaphors, such as investigative journalism, photography, storytelling, philosophical analysis, and literary criticism, to mention only a few. Although several of these metaphors have proven of limited use for evaluation, others have yielded many useful new methods and techniques for program evaluators.

One need not consciously seek metaphors; they already underlie and influence much of our thinking. Indeed, one reason for differing evaluation approaches is the different evaluation metaphors held by writers and practitioners. House (1983b) has demonstrated that much of our everyday thinking is metaphorical in nature and extends that point to argue that evaluation thought is also largely metaphorical. Further, he suggests that conflicts between existing evaluation schemes stem from differences in the underlying metaphors held by proponents of those schemes. For example, metaphoric conceptions of many social programs equate those programs with industrial production (leading to metaphors based on machines, assembly lines, or pipelines) or with sports contests or games (leading to metaphors of targets and goals).

---

[5] A metaphor is a figure of speech in which the meaning of a term or phrase is transferred from the object it ordinarily designates to another object so as to provide new insight or perspective on the latter. For example, a researcher interested in how rumors spread might use epidemiology, the theory of how diseases spread, as a metaphor. This theory would suggest that the researcher look for carriers of rumor, that rumors spread from epicenters in regional clusters, and so on.

The influence of such metaphors on evaluation is obvious. For example, one who perceives evaluation as retrospective backtracking of a program to discover the causes of its outcomes is likely to use an approach that resembles forensic pathology, whereas one who holds a connoisseurial metaphor of evaluation will use an approach more akin to literary criticism. Those who see evaluation's role as helping public agencies respond to the constantly changing needs of its constituents and the broader citizenry will likely invoke metaphors of the opinion pollster in their approach. Those who see evaluation as the instrument for bureaucratic program monitoring likely depend primarily on auditing as their operative metaphor. Yes, different metaphors account for much of the variation in evaluation approaches.

RESPONDING TO DIFFERENT NEEDS

In proposing new evaluation approaches, evaluation theorists have not only been influenced by their different methodological and metaphorical preferences or their different ways of looking at knowledge and how it is achieved. They have also been responding to different needs that they perceived—needs such as corporate executives' wanting better information for decision making in a profit-making environment, educators' wanting a systematic way to determine which charter schools to establish, United Way personnel's struggling for a better way to identify the top priority health and human service needs in their county, federal and state legislators' monitoring resource allocations, and local stakeholders' hoping to identify ways to make their towns and cities more livable. Each of these audiences works in a different environmental context, struggling with different types of economic and budgetary concerns, client needs, stakeholder interests, employee and management expectations, and so on. The evaluator must learn about each context and adapt the evaluation to it to be successful in meeting the needs of each audience.

Various evaluation approaches were developed to address different needs. In the aggregate, these different approaches help us comprehend the wide range of needs for program evaluation. We must learn to identify what is useful in each approach when faced with a specific evaluation need, to use it wisely, and not to be distracted by irrelevant evaluation approaches constructed to deal with a different need.

PRACTICAL CONSIDERATIONS

We have traced how epistemological issues, methodological preferences, metaphoric views of evaluation, and different needs all contribute to the diversity of alternative evaluation approaches. Several practical issues also contribute to this diversity.

First, evaluators disagree about whether the intent of evaluation is to render a value judgment. Some are concerned only with the usefulness of the evaluation to the decision maker and believe that he, not the evaluator, should render the value judgment. Others believe the evaluator's report to the decision maker is complete only if it contains a value judgment. Such differences in views have obvious practical implications.

Second, evaluators differ in their general view of the political roles of evaluation. We discuss political aspects of evaluation in greater detail in Chapter 16. Suffice it here to say that the evaluator's political orientation affects greatly the style of evaluation conducted.

Third, evaluators are influenced by their prior experience. Each evaluator draws from certain strengths, from experience with certain types of problems and processes, and from a way of looking at things that grew out of his professional education and career. Each view is limited in perspective by the evaluator's prior experience.

Fourth, evaluators differ in their views about who should conduct the evaluation and the nature of the expertise that the evaluator must possess. Although this topic is too complex to be treated adequately in this chapter, an illustration might help. Considering one dimension of expertise—substantive knowledge about the content of that which is evaluated (e.g., knowledge of mathematics in evaluating a mathematics education program)—some evaluators (e.g., Eisner, 1975) see such expertise as the sine qua non of evaluation. Indeed, without such expertise, their evaluation approach would be futile. Other evaluators (e.g., Worthen & Sanders, 1984) not only question the need for the evaluator to possess such expertise but also suggest that there may sometimes be advantages in selecting evaluators who are not specialists in the content of that which they evaluate. Such differences in perspective lead to different approaches to both the program and the evaluation.

Finally, evaluators differ even in their perception of whether it is desirable to have a wide variety of approaches to evaluation. Earlier, Gephart (1978) lamented the proliferation of evaluation models and urged that an effort be made to synthesize existing models. Conversely, Raizen and Rossi (1981) argued that the goal of attaining uniformity in evaluation methods and measures cannot be attained without prematurely inhibiting needed development in the field of evaluation. We agree with this latter view, believing that efforts to synthesize existing evaluation models would be dysfunctional (an argument that will be expanded later in Chapter 11). Regardless of which view you subscribe to, it is clear that either the inability to generate an idealistic evaluation model (after all, none has been forthcoming since the call for synthesis two decades ago) or resistance to trading the diversity of models for a unified view accounts, at least in part, for the continued variety of approaches that confronts the evaluation practitioner.

THEMES AMONG THE VARIATIONS

Despite the diversity in evaluation approaches, commonalities do exist. Many individuals have attempted to bring order out of the chaos reflected in evaluation literature by developing classification schemes, or taxonomies. Each such effort selected one or more dimensions deemed useful in classifying evaluation approaches. But because evaluation is multifaceted and because it can be conducted at different phases of a program's development, the same evaluation model can be classified in diverse ways, depending on emphasis.

Those who have published classification schemata are too numerous to list here, but examples include Guba and Lincoln (1981); House (1983a); Madaus, Scriven, and Stufflebeam (1983); Popham (1975); Scriven (1993); Shadish et al. (1991); Stake (1975b); and Worthen and Sanders (1973, 1987). All have influenced our thinking about the categorization of evaluation approaches, but we have drawn especially on our own work and that of House in developing the schema proposed below.

A CLASSIFICATION SCHEMA FOR EVALUATION APPROACHES

We have chosen to classify many different approaches to evaluation into the six categories described below.

1. *Objectives-oriented approaches,* where the focus is on specifying goals and objectives and determining the extent to which they have been attained
2. *Management-oriented approaches,* where the central concern is on identifying and meeting the informational needs of managerial decision makers
3. *Consumer-oriented approaches,* where the central issue is developing evaluative information on "products," broadly defined, for use by consumers in choosing among competing products, services, and the like
4. *Expertise-oriented approaches,* which depend primarily on the direct application of professional expertise to judge the quality of whatever endeavor is evaluated
5. *Adversary-oriented approaches,* where planned opposition in points of view of different evaluators (pro and con) is the central focus of the evaluation
6. *Participant-oriented approaches,* where involvement of participants (stakeholders in that which is evaluated) are central in determining the values, criteria, needs, and data for the evaluation

These six categories seem to us to distribute (though not equally) along House's (1983a) dimension of utilitarian to intuitionist-pluralist evaluation, as shown in Figure 4.1.

Placement of individual evaluation approaches within these six categories is to some degree arbitrary. Several approaches are multifaceted and include characteristics that would allow them to be placed in more than one category; for convenience we have decided to place such approaches in one category and

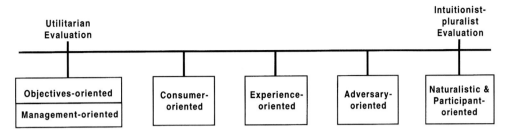

FIGURE 4.1   Distribution of six evaluation approaches on the dimension of utilitarian to intuitionist-pluralist evaluation

only reference in other chapters, where appropriate, their other features. Our classification is based on what we see as the driving force behind doing the evaluation: the major questions to be addressed and/or the major organizer(s) that underlie each approach (e.g., objectives or management decisions). Within each category, the approaches vary by level of formality and structure, some being relatively well developed philosophically and procedurally, others less developed. It should be noted that these frameworks deal with conceptual approaches to evaluation, not techniques; discussion of the many techniques that might be used in program evaluations is reserved for Parts Three and Four of this book. Also, we have not attempted to include, in any chapter, all of the proposed evaluation models that could fit there, for doing so would balloon this book by hundreds of more pages. Rather, we have selected for each chapter only an example or two of what we see as the most typical or influential example of that evaluation approach.

APPLICATION EXERCISES

1. Think about how you would approach evaluation. Describe the steps you think you would follow. Then, analyze your approach according to your philosophical and methodological preferences. Explain how your background and what you would be evaluating could have affected your approach. Describe other things that might have affected your approach to evaluation.
2. Identify a program in your area that you would like to see evaluated. List some qualitative evaluation methods that could be used. Now list some quantitative methods that you see as appropriate. Discuss whether it would be appropriate to combine both methods within the same study, including reasons for your conclusion.

SUGGESTED READINGS

House, E. R. (1983). Assumptions underlying evaluation models. In G. F. Madaus, M. Scriven, & D. L. Stufflebeam (Eds.), *Evaluation models: Viewpoints on educational and human services evaluation.* Boston: Kluwer-Nijhoff.

Lincoln, Y. S. (1994). Tracks toward a postmodern politics of evaluation. *Evaluation Practice, 15*(3), 299-309.

Mark, M. M., & Shotland, R. L. (1987). *Multiple methods in program evaluation.* New Directions for Program Evaluation, No. 35. San Francisco: Jossey-Bass.

Reichardt, C. S., & Rallis, S. F. (Eds.). (1994). *The qualitative-quantitative debate: New perspectives.* New Directions for Program Evaluation, No. 61. San Francisco: Jossey-Bass.

Sechrest, L., & Figueredo, A. J. (1993). Program evaluation. *Annual Review of Psychology, 44,* 645-674.

chapter 5

Objectives-Oriented Evaluation Approaches

ORIENTING QUESTIONS

1. What aspects of Tyler's approach to evaluation have permeated all later objectives-oriented evaluation approaches?
2. In what forms has the objectives-oriented evaluation approach been used in education? In health and human services? In business settings?
3. What are some major strengths and limitations of objectives-oriented evaluation approaches?
4. What is "goal-free evaluation"? Does it have a useful role to play in program evaluation?

The distinguishing feature of an **objectives**-oriented evaluation approach is that the purposes of some activity are specified, and then evaluation focuses on the extent to which those purposes are achieved. In education the activity can be as short as a one-day classroom lesson or as complex as a state's entire educational enterprise. In health and human services it is often a service or intervention. In business it may be as simple as a one-day meeting or as complex as a corporation's five-year strategic plan. The information gained from an objectives-oriented evaluation can be used to reformulate the purposes of the activity, the activity itself, or the assessment procedures and devices used to determine the achievement of purposes.

DEVELOPERS OF THE OBJECTIVES-ORIENTED EVALUATION APPROACH AND THEIR CONTRIBUTIONS

Many people have contributed to the evolution and refinement of the objectives-oriented approach to evaluation since its inception in the 1930s, but the individual credited with conceptualizing and popularizing it in education is Ralph W. Tyler (1942, 1950), for whom this approach has been named.

✳The Tylerian Evaluation Approach

Tyler's approach to evaluation was developed and used during the Eight Year Study of the late 1930s (Smith & Tyler, 1942). Travers (1983) did note, however, that an earlier work, Waples and Tyler's *Research Methods and Teacher Problems* (1930), set the stage for Tyler's later achievements in evaluation.

 (Behavioral)

Tyler conceived of evaluation as the process of determining the extent to which the objectives of a program are actually attained. His approach to evaluation followed these steps:

1. Establish broad **goals** or objectives.
2. Classify the goals or objectives.
3. Define objectives in behavioral terms.
4. Find situations in which achievement of objectives can be shown.
5. Develop or select measurement techniques.
6. Collect performance data.
7. Compare performance data with behaviorally stated objectives.

Discrepancies between **performance** and objectives lead to modifications intended to correct the deficiency, and the evaluation cycle is repeated.

Tyler's rationale was logical, scientifically acceptable, readily adoptable by evaluators (most of whose methodological upbringing was very compatible with the pretest-posttest measurement of behaviors stressed by Tyler), and had great influence on subsequent evaluation theorists.

Goodlad (1979) pointed out that Tyler advocated the use of general goals to establish purposes rather than premature preoccupation with formulating behavioral objectives. Of course, the broad goals for any activity eventually require operational definitions so that appropriate measurement devices and settings can be selected. Tyler's belief was that service providers primarily needed to discuss the importance and meaning of general goals of their service. Otherwise, in Goodlad's words, the premature specification of behavioral objectives results in objectives that "could only be arbitrary, restrictive, and ultimately dysfunctional" (p. 43). The service Tyler was interested in improving was education, but his thinking applies to services in other sectors as well.

Tyler described six categories of purpose for American schools (Goodlad, 1979). They were (1) acquisition of information; (2) development of work habits and study skills; (3) development of effective ways of thinking; (4) internalization of social attitudes, interests, appreciations, and sensitivities; (5) maintenance of physical health; and (6) development of a philosophy of life.

Over the years, educators have refined and reformulated the purposes of schooling into various forms. One publication that reflects the thinking of the past 60 years on purposes of education is *A Handbook of Educational Variables* (Nowakowski, Bunda, Working, Bernacki, & Harrington, 1985). The handbook divided elementary and secondary student development into these seven categories:

1. Intellectual
2. Emotional
3. Physical and recreational
4. Aesthetic and cultural
5. Moral
6. Vocational
7. Social

Each of these categories was analyzed in detail too extensive to reproduce here. Such a resource exemplifies the extent to which Tyler's approach to evaluation has been refined.

Goodlad (1979) stressed that evaluation and improvement of American schools cannot make much headway until their purposes have been discussed, accepted, operationally defined, and monitored. It should be clear that a single standardized test of achievement of basic skills provides insufficient data to evaluate our schools. Yet the use of standardized test results is still the most common form of school evaluation discussed in the popular media today. This oversimplification is one real danger of using only the objectives-oriented approach to evaluate programs.

Tyler stressed the importance of screening broad goals before accepting them as the basis for evaluating an activity. In education, the screen through which potential goals should be filtered includes value questions derived from three sources: philosophical (the nature of knowledge), social (the nature of society), and pedagogical (the nature of the learner and the learning process). Scriven (1967) reiterated the need to evaluate the purposes of any activity as a part of evaluating the activity and its consequences.

The question of how specifically to evaluate goals and objectives was addressed by Sanders and Cunningham (1973, 1974). Their approach was to consider both logical and empirical methods for evaluating goals. *Logical* methods include these:

1. Examining the cogency of the argument or rationale behind each objective. If there are no justifiable reasons for a goal or objective, it cannot have much value. The *need* for accomplishing the goal or objective is a critical consideration.
2. Examining the consequences of accomplishing the goal or objective. By projecting logically the consequences of achieving a goal, both

strengths and weaknesses in competing goals may be revealed. Criteria such as utility and feasibility (cost, acceptability, political palatability, training, or other requirements) of the goal or objective could be used here. A search of literature may reveal the results of past attempts to achieve certain goals or objectives.

3. Considering higher-order values, such as laws, policies, fit with existing practices, moral principles, or the ideals of a free society, to see whether a goal or purpose is required or whether it will conflict with such values.

Empirical methods for evaluating goals or objectives include these:

1. Collecting group data to describe judgments about the value of a goal or objective. Surveys are the most common form of gathering information about a group's value position.

2. Arranging for experts, hearings, or panels to review and evaluate potential goals or objectives. Specialists can draw from knowledge or experience that may not otherwise be available. Their informed judgment may be very different from the group value data that surveys produce.

3. Conducting content studies of archival records, such as speeches, minutes, editorials, or newsletters. Such content analyses may reveal value positions that conflict with, or are in support of, a particular goal or objective.

4. Conducting a pilot study to see whether the goal is attainable and in what form it may be attained. If no prior experience is available when evaluating a purpose or goal, it may be advisable to suspend judgment until some experience has been gained. Once a broad goal has been made operational or activities directed toward attaining the goal have been tried, it may take on a different meaning from that which it had in earlier discussions. This is one place where demonstration projects serve an important function in program evaluation.

Several evaluation approaches have used goals or objectives as a central focus in the evaluation procedure. These approaches may be seen, therefore, as further refinements of Tyler's approach. Noteworthy objectives-referenced evaluation approaches were those developed by Metfessel and Michael (1967) and Provus (1971). They are noteworthy because they add new insights into how programs may be studied within the Tylerian tradition.

Metfessel and Michael's Evaluation Paradigm

An early approach to evaluation suggested by Metfessel and Michael (1967) was heavily influenced by the Tylerian tradition. Eight steps in the evaluation process were proposed as follows:

1. Involve stakeholders as facilitators of program evaluation.
2. Formulate a cohesive model of goals and specific objectives.
3. Translate specific objectives into a communicable form.
4. Select or construct instruments to furnish measures allowing inferences about program effectiveness.
5. Carry out periodic observations using content-valid tests, scales, and other behavioral measures.
6. Analyze data using appropriate methods.
7. Interpret the data using standards of desired levels of performance over all measures.
8. Develop recommendations for the further implementation, modification, and revision of broad goals and specific objectives.

One of the primary contributions of Metfessel and Michael was in expanding the educational evaluator's vision of alternative instruments that might be used to collect evaluation data. Interested readers will find their lists of alternative instruments for data collection (Metfessel & Michael, 1967; Worthen & Sanders, 1973, pp. 276-279) to be a valuable guide.

Provus's Discrepancy Evaluation Model

Another approach to evaluation in the Tylerian tradition was developed by Malcolm Provus, who based his approach on his evaluation assignments in the Pittsburgh (Pennsylvania) public schools. Provus viewed evaluation as a continuous information-management process designed to serve as "the watchdog of program management" and the "handmaiden of administration in the management of program development through sound decision making" (Provus, 1973, p. 186). Although his was in some ways a management-oriented evaluation approach, the key characteristic of Provus's proposals stemmed from the Tylerian tradition. Provus viewed evaluation as a process of (1) agreeing upon standards (another term used in place of "objectives"[1]), (2) determining whether a discrepancy exists between the performance of some aspect of a program and the standards set for performance, and (3) using information about discrepancies to decide whether to improve, maintain, or terminate the program or some aspect of it. Provus called his approach, not surprisingly, the Discrepancy Evaluation Model.

Provus conceived that as a program is being developed, it goes through four developmental stages, to which he added a fifth optional stage.

---

[1] Although "standards" and "objectives" are not synonymous, they were used by Provus interchangeably. Stake (1970) also stated that "standards are another form of objective: those seen by outside authority-figures who know little or nothing about the specific program being evaluated but whose advice is relevant to programs in many places" (p. 185). Provus's use of the term is generally consistent with such accepted usage.

1. Definition
2. Installation
3. Process (interim products)
4. Product
5. Cost-benefit analysis (optional)

During the *definition,* or design, stage, the focus of work is on defining goals, processes, or activities, and delineating necessary resources and participants to carry out the activities and accomplish the goals. Provus considered programs to be dynamic systems involving inputs (antecedents), processes, and outputs (outcomes). Standards or expectations were established for each. These standards were the objectives on which all further evaluation work depends. The evaluator's job at the design stage is to see that a complete set of specifications is produced and that they meet certain criteria: theoretical and structural soundness.

At the *installation* stage, the program design or definition is used as the standard against which to judge program operation. The evaluator performs a series of congruency tests to identify any discrepancies between expected and actual implementation of the program or activity. The intent is to make certain that the program has been installed as it had been designed. This is important because studies have found that staff vary as much in implementing a single program as they do in implementing several different ones. The degree to which program specifications are followed is best determined through firsthand observation. If discrepancies are found at this stage, Provus proposed either changing the program definition, making adjustments in the installation (such as preparing a special in-service workshop), or terminating the activity if it appears that further development would be futile.

During the *process* stage, evaluation focuses on gathering data on the progress of participants to determine whether their behaviors changed as expected. Provus used the term *enabling objective* to refer to those gains that participants should be making if program goals are to be reached. If certain enabling objectives are not achieved, the activities leading to those objectives are revised or redefined. The validity of the evaluation data is also questioned. If the evaluator finds that enabling objectives are not being achieved, another option is to terminate the program if it appears that the discrepancy cannot be eliminated.

At the *product* stage, evaluation is to determine whether the *terminal objectives* for the program have been achieved. Provus distinguished between immediate outcomes, or *terminal objectives,* and long-term outcomes, or *ultimate objectives.* He encouraged the evaluator to go beyond the traditional emphasis on end-of-program performance and make follow-up studies a part of evaluation.

Provus also suggested an optional fifth stage that called for **cost-benefit analysis** and comparison of results with similar cost analyses of comparable programs. In recent times, with the funds for human services becoming scarcer, cost-benefit analyses have become an essential part of almost all program evaluations.

The Discrepancy Evaluation Model was designed to facilitate development of programs in a large public school system, and later it was applied to statewide evaluations by a federal bureau. A complex approach that works best in larger systems with adequate staff resources, the model's central focus is on use of discrepancies to help managers determine the extent to which program development is proceeding toward attainment of stated objectives. It attempts to ensure effective program development by preventing the activity from proceeding to the next stage until all identified discrepancies have been removed. Whenever a discrepancy is found, Provus suggested a cooperative problem-solving process for program staff and evaluators. The process involves asking, (1) Why is there a discrepancy? (2) What corrective actions are possible? and (3) Which corrective action is best? This process usually requires that additional information be gathered and criteria developed to allow rational, justifiable decisions about corrective actions (or terminations). This particular problem-solving activity was a new addition to the traditional objectives-oriented evaluation approach.

The evaluation approaches outlined here have been referred to not only as objectives-oriented evaluation approaches, the term we prefer, but also as "objectives-referenced" evaluations, "objectives-performance congruence" approaches, "performance congruence" models, and other similar terms. In each, assessment of the extent to which objectives have been attained is the central feature.

A Schema for Generating and Analyzing Objectives: The Evaluation Cube

Hammond (1973) developed a cube as a model for expanding thinking about the range of objectives that could be considered for educational programs. It was useful for evaluators to use in thinking about all the possibilities of objectives for programs. Building on the concept developed by Hammond, the Evaluation Center at Western Michigan University developed a three-dimensional framework for analyzing the objectives of community-based youth programs (see Figure 5.1). This is an example of how the idea of the cube can be adapted for use in analyzing any program. The approach can be easily modified to incorporate relevant dimensions for any objectives-oriented program.

The three dimensions of the cube are:

1. *Needs of youth* (the client). Categories developed by Stufflebeam (1977) and expanded by Nowakowski et al. (1985) are
   - Intellectual
   - Physical recreation
   - Vocational
   - Social
   - Moral
   - Aesthetic/cultural
   - Emotional

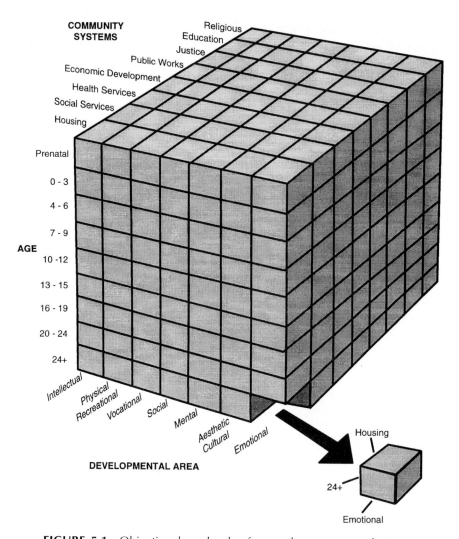

FIGURE 5.1   Objectives-based cube for youth program analysis

source: From "Interim summative evaluation: Assessing the value of a long term or ongoing program, during its operation" (p. 58) by S. C. Dodson, 1994. Unpublished doctoral dissertation, Western Michigan University, Kalamazoo. Reproduced by permission.

2. *Age of youth* (any relevant characteristic of the client), prenatal through young adult
3. *Source of service to youth* (the principle actors), such as
   - Housing
   - Social services
   - Health services

- Economic development
- Public works
- Justice
- Education
- Religious

In any category along any of the three dimensions, those planning a community-based youth program may choose to establish relevant objectives. Few if any stakeholders in community-based programs will be interested in every cell of the cube, but the categories contained in each of the three dimensions will provide a good checklist for making certain that important areas or categories of objectives are not overlooked. Obviously, use of the cube is not limited to community-based programs but could extend to other types of programs as well.

HOW THE OBJECTIVES-ORIENTED ⅄ EVALUATION APPROACH HAS BEEN USED

The objectives-oriented approach has dominated the thinking and development of evaluation since the 1930s, both in the United States and elsewhere (Madaus & Stufflebeam, 1989). Its straightforward procedure of letting achievement of objectives determine success or failure and justify improvements, maintenance, or termination of program activities has proved an attractive prototype.

The technology of objectives-oriented evaluation was refined by Mager (1962), who went beyond simple insistence that objectives be prespecified in behavioral terms to insist that objectives must also contain the desired attainment levels and the criteria for judging such attainment. Insistence on the use of behavioral objectives as defined by Mager sparked a widespread debate that began in the 1960s and still continues.

Whether or not one believes behavioral objectives are useful, one cannot help being distressed by the mindlessness that sometimes happens when program staff are encouraged to state every intent—however trivial—in behavioral terms. In some programs, the staffs spend so much time and energy stating everything they want to accomplish in behavioral terms that they hardly have time to deliver services or develop products. Training every staff member to use a recipe for translating every aspiration into a behavioral objective wastes time and resources and distorts the program's intent. This is especially true when staff members are used to writing objectives intended more for evaluation than for program implementation. It is, after all, the evaluator who is supposedly skilled in the language of operationalization. We think the evaluator should take the following stance in working with program personnel: "Give me an objective in any form, just so I understand what your intent is. As an evaluator, I will translate your objective into behavioral terms and have you review my statement to make certain I have not distorted your intent." That approach makes more sense than trying to train all program staff to be evaluators.

The pendulum obviously needed to move from the irresponsible position that program staff do not need objectives because, after all, they "know in their hearts they are right." But some moved too far to the opposite extreme when they spawned the religion of behaviorism and its disciples who applied it unintelligently. One can hardly oppose using objectives and assessing their attainment, but the use of dozens or even hundreds of objectives for each area of endeavor, not uncommon a few years ago, amounted to a monopolization of staff time and skills for a relatively small payoff. Although vestiges of this philosophy are still evident in some organizations, the press for behavioral reductionism seems to have diminished. Had the push for behavioral objectives not been contained, disenchanted program staff may well have refused to have anything to do with objectives—or evaluation—an outcome that would have had serious negative consequences for their programs. Though the debate has shifted from a focus on proper statement of objectives to that of how the objectives are to be measured, it still divides the field of evaluation.

Bloom and Krathwohl were influential in refining the objectives-oriented approach to evaluation with their work on the previously discussed taxonomies of educational objectives in both the cognitive domain (Bloom, Engelhart, Furst, Hill, & Krathwohl, 1956) and the affective domains (Krathwohl, Bloom, & Masia, 1964). With the development of these taxonomies of objectives, educators had powerful tools to aid them in using Tyler's approach. Bloom, Hastings, and Madaus (1971) also prepared a handbook for educators to use not only in identifying appropriate objectives for the subject matter taught in school but also in developing and using measurement instruments to determine students' levels of performance in each subject. Cronbach (1963), who also worked with Tyler on the Eight Year Study, developed an approach to using objectives and associated measurement techniques for purposes of course and curriculum improvement.

But the blockbuster in education, in terms of expenditure, has been the objectives-referenced or criterion-referenced testing movement originated in the 1960s and 1970s by federal and state governments. The National Assessment of Educational Progress (NAEP) was established in the mid-1960s under the leadership of Tyler. This federal program was designed to collect performance data periodically on samples of students and young adults in the essential subjects of American education. Great care was taken to select objectives generally accepted in this country as desirable achievements at the different stages of development measured (ages 9, 13, 17, and adult). Public reports have, since the mid-1960s, described the ability of Americans in these age groups to answer questions in subjects considered important.

Like those of the Eight Year Study, the specific instruments and objectives of NAEP have been made available to educators, but they have received limited use. Virtually every state has developed its own form of annual statewide testing, however, and many have generally followed the NAEP approach.

Derivative "objectives-oriented" movements appeared in the late 1960s in the form of school accountability (Lessinger & Tyler, 1971), competency or minimum competency testing (Berk, 1986; Jaeger, 1989; Madaus, 1983), objectives- and criterion-referenced test collections and exchanges, and federal project monitoring (Tallmadge & Wood, 1976); several of these movements continue to be influential. A useful objectives-oriented guide to outcomes measurement in drug and alcohol prevention programs has been developed and is available from the U.S. Department of Health and Human Services, Office for Substance Abuse Prevention (1991). Management techniques that were not evaluative but were still based on the objectives-oriented tradition included goal attainment scaling (Kiresuk, Smith, & Cardillo, 1994), Management by Objectives (MBO), Planning, Programming, and Budgeting System (PPBS), and outcome monitoring (Affholter, 1994). The tradition begun by Tyler over 60 years ago has had remarkable staying power.

Tyler's (1991) own statement on program evaluation has remained consistent for more than a half century.

> To summarize, a comprehensive evaluation of the outcomes of an educational program requires clear definitions of the desired patterns of behavior and of other possible outcomes both positive and negative. It then requires the selection or development of test situations that evoke such behavior from the students, and it necessitates the use of relevant and important criteria for appraising the students' reactions in these test situations. Finally, the reporting of these appraisals should be done in terms that can be understood by those who can use the results constructively.
>
> For social programs other than those in education, the rationale is similar. For example, for a program seeking to reduce the number of persons without jobs, there needs to be a definition of "having a job." Does one have a job if he or she is employed temporarily and is soon back on the street? Is it a job to have dead-end work with no opportunity for advancement or a "career"? Many job training programs place participants in jobs that are temporary or dead-end. The participants fail to attain employment in work that permits continued learning and achievement. Developing test situations in job training and placement are experiments with samples of trainees, and the results should be appraised in terms of the definition of desirable jobs. (p 14).

STRENGTHS AND LIMITATIONS OF THE OBJECTIVES-ORIENTED EVALUATION APPROACH

Probably the greatest strength and appeal of the objectives-oriented approach to evaluation lies in its simplicity. It is easily understood, easy to follow and implement, and produces information that program directors generally agree is relevant to their mission. This approach has stimulated so much technological development over the years that the processes of specifying objectives and developing or finding appropriate measurement procedures and instruments have been finely honed. The literature on objectives-oriented evaluation is extensive, filled with creative ideas for applying the approach (e.g., Cronbach, 1963; Popham, Eisner, Sullivan, & Tyler, 1969; Metfessel & Michael, 1967; Bloom et al., 1971; Morris & Fitz-Gibbon, 1978).

The objectives-oriented evaluation approach has caused program directors to reflect about their intentions and to clarify formerly ambiguous generalities about intended outcomes (Mager, 1962). Discussions of appropriate objectives with the community being served have given objectives-oriented evaluation the appeal of face validity—the program is, after all, merely being held accountable for what its designers said it was going to accomplish, and that is obviously legitimate. The objectives-oriented evaluation approach is one that directly addresses Standard U4, Values Identification, in *The Program Evaluation Standards* (Joint Committee, 1994). Its emphasis on clearly defining outcomes as the basis for judging the program helps evaluators and others to see the value basis for judging the program.

As a result of the attention placed on this approach, technically sound measurement practices have broadened to include unobtrusive measures (Webb, Campbell, Schwartz, & Sechrest, 1966) and non–paper-and-pencil evidence (Sanders & Sachse, 1977; Herman, Aschbacher, & Winters, 1992). These and other advances in the measurement of *outcomes* may be tied to the outcome orientation of Tyler. These advances, added to the many instruments, objectives pools, and step-by-step guides that have been placed in the hands of practitioners by various projects, have greatly expanded the available resources for evaluation during the twentieth century.

Useful as this approach to evaluation seems to its many adherents, critics have asserted that it (1) lacks a real evaluative component (facilitating measurement and assessment of objectives rather than result in explicit judgments of merit or worth), (2) lacks standards to judge the importance of observed discrepancies between objectives and performance levels, (3) neglects the value of the objectives themselves, (4) ignores important alternatives that should be considered in planning a program, (5) neglects transactions that occur within the program or activity being evaluated, (6) neglects the context in which the evaluation takes place, (7) ignores important outcomes other than those covered by the objectives (the unintended outcomes of the activity), (8) omits evidence of program value not reflected in its own objectives, and (9) promotes a linear, inflexible approach to evaluation. Collectively, these criticisms suggest that objectives-oriented evaluation can result in tunnel vision that tends to limit evaluation's effectiveness and potential.

To some extent, the rather elaborate technology developed to support this evaluation approach makes its use appear seductively simple to novice evaluators only partially familiar with its philosophical and practical difficulties. The assumption that human service is a technology—a body of techniques leading to prespecified means—has been criticized as the factory model of human services delivery. Many outcomes of human services programs are still highly variable and difficult to predict because of the many influences on human behavior.

A recently passed law in one of our states is a classic example of poor use of the objectives-oriented evaluation approach. The General Assembly mandated that each agency should report once a year both to its local constituency and to the state the extent to which the agency had achieved its stated goals and objectives. All an agency had to do was to announce some general goals and specific objectives, carry out its program for a year, and at the end of the time report how well it had done on those goals and objectives. Although it is often important to know whether an agency is attaining its stated objectives, such is not always the case. It depends largely on whether the goals were worth attaining in the first place. Some goals that are attainable are hardly worth the effort. Some goals are attained because they were set too low or had already been attained, not because the program was effective. The situation is almost analogous to that in which one needs to identify which children are in good health and which are suffering from malnutrition, and height is considered a relevant indicator. There would be at least a measure of foolishness in asking each child to make her own tape measure, use it in measuring her height, and then report how well she has attained the height she desired to reach at that point or whether she is too tall or too short for her age.

A related difficulty lies in the frequent challenge of trying to ascertain the goals or objectives of many human services endeavors. Evaluators have found that the objectives listed on paper do not always match those in the minds of program staff. As a result, their activities may conflict with or deviate from publicly stated objectives, sometimes for good reasons. Professionals will not become slaves to stated objectives if they believe alternative courses of action or goals are desirable. Such individuals tend to argue against strident and unthinking application of an objectives-oriented approach.

A related and perhaps more pervasive problem is the fact that many program directors have not articulated objectives for their programs in any interpretable form. This is not to say they have no idea of where they are going or what they want to accomplish (although that is sometimes unfortunately the case) but rather that they are unaccustomed to thinking or speaking in "behavioral" language familiar to objectives-oriented evaluators. The evaluator may find it necessary to elicit clear statements of intent in an almost Rogerian fashion (e.g., "Tell me more about what you mean when you say you would like your program to . . .") rather than translate those statements into behavioral terms as deemed necessary (not forgetting to ask those whose intentions they reflect whether there have been distortions in the translation). Given the fact that many evaluators, lamentably, are not equipped by disposition or training to assist agencies in this way, the objectives-oriented approach to evaluation frequently results in the verdict that a program cannot be evaluated, when the problem lies more with narrow understanding of the approach and/or the insistence that all must become experts in behavioral specification before this method can be used.

Who really determines the goals and objectives? Do they include all important outcomes? Have all those affected by the program agreed upon these particular goals or objectives? Who has determined that a particular criterion level is more defensible than alternatives? On what evidence? These and other questions must be addressed if an objectives-oriented approach is to be defensible.

Overemphasizing the testing components of this evaluation approach can prove dangerous. "Teaching to the test" may be only human when a teacher's performance is evaluated by how well students do on standardized or statewide assessment tests, but the misinformation that is introduced by such test score pollution (see Haladyna, Nolen, & Haas, 1991) can be very detrimental. Madaus (1983) describes how competency testing invariably turns into *minimum* competency testing when expectations for achievement become bounded by test content. Such narrowing of purposes is a negative, albeit unintentional, consequence this approach may have had.

We should not leave our discussion of limitations of objectives-oriented evaluation without noting that Scriven's (1972) perception of its limitations led him to develop his now widely known proposals for goal-free evaluation. Although intentionally the opposite of objectives-oriented approaches, it seems logical to discuss this proposal here.

Goal-Free Evaluation

The rationale for **goal-free evaluation** can be summarized as follows: First, goals should not be taken as given; like anything else, they should be evaluated. Further, goals are generally little more than rhetoric and seldom reveal the real objectives of the project or changes in intent. In addition, many important program outcomes do not fall in the category of goals or objectives anyway. (For example, establishing a new vocational education center will create additional jobs—a desirable outcome—but never an explicit goal of the center.) Scriven (1972) believes the most important function of goal-free evaluation, however, is to reduce bias and increase objectivity. In objectives-oriented evaluation, an evaluator is told the goals of the project and is therefore immediately limited in her perceptions—the goals act like blinders, causing her to miss important outcomes not directly related to those goals.

For example, suppose an evaluator is told that the goals of a dropout rehabilitation program are (1) to bring school dropouts into a vocational training program, (2) to train them in productive vocations, and (3) to place them in stable jobs. She may spend all her time designing and applying measures to look at such things as how many dropouts have been recruited into the program, how many have been placed and remain placed in paying jobs, and so forth. These are worthwhile goals, and the program may be successful on all these counts. But what about the fact that the crime rate of others (nondropouts) who are receiving employment training has tripled since the dropouts were brought in? Indeed, a hidden curriculum seems to have sprung up: stripping cars. This negative side effect is much more likely to be picked up by the goal-free evaluator than by the objectives-oriented evaluator working behind her built-in blinders.

The following are major characteristics of goal-free evaluation:

- The evaluator purposely avoids becoming aware of the program goals.
- Predetermined goals are not permitted to narrow the focus of the evaluation study.
- Goal-free evaluation focuses on *actual* outcomes rather than intended program outcomes.
- The goal-free evaluator has minimal contact with the program manager and staff.
- Goal-free evaluation increases the likelihood that unanticipated side effects will be noted.

It might be helpful to point out that objectives-oriented and goal-free evaluation are not mutually exclusive. Indeed, they supplement one another. The internal staff evaluator of necessity conducts a goal-directed evaluation. She can hardly hope to avoid knowing the goals of the program, and it would be unwise to ignore them even if she could. Program managers obviously need to know how well the program is meeting its goals, and the internal evaluator uses goal-directed evaluation to provide such administrators with that information. At the same time, it is important to know how others judge the program, not only on the basis of how well it does what it is *supposed* to do but also on the basis of what it *does* in all areas, on *all* its outcomes, intended or not. This is the task for the external goal-free evaluator who knows nothing of the program goals. Thus, goal-directed evaluation and goal-free evaluation can work well together. And while the major share of a program's evaluation resources should not go to goal-free evaluation, it is tragic when all resources go to goal-directed evaluation on a program where the goals do not even begin to include the important outcomes.

APPLICATION EXERCISES

1. Cheryl Brown is a program administrator for the Michigan Department of Social Services. She has been responsible for implementing a parenting program in which the goal is to reduce the incidence of child abuse and child neglect. To evaluate the program she decides that she will depend on one performance measure: the number of cases of reported abuse and neglect.

   Use what you have just learned about Tyler's approach to evaluation, Provus's Discrepancy Evaluation Model, and goal-free evaluation to expand the evaluation design for this program. What would be wrong with basing the evaluation on just the one measure?

2. Jane Jackson is a member of the faculty of Greenlawn Middle School in Antioch, Ohio. Although students are still grouped by grades, within each grade a team of teachers cooperates to develop lessons that are interdisciplinary. Individual members of the team have been assigned responsibility for the areas of English, mathematics, science,

and social studies. Mrs. Jackson has decided to evaluate her area of responsibility: the seventh-grade English section of the instructional program. Her evaluation tentatively includes the following:

a. Administration of a standardized English achievement test in September and June. She plans to compare the means of the pre- and posttest groups with national norms for the tests.

b. Monthly interviews of a 10 percent sample of her class to assess student reaction to the English portion of the instructional program

c. Complete record keeping of students' progress so assessment may be made of their eighth-grade performance

d. Observation by an outside observer twice a month, using a scale she has devised to record pupil interaction during class discussions

e. Comparison of the performance of Mrs. Jackson's seventh-grade class on the standardized tests with the performance of the seventh grade at Martindale Junior High School, a traditional junior high

Using what you have just learned about Tyler's approach to evaluation, how the cube can be used in evaluation, and how Provus's Discrepancy Evaluation Model works, advise Mrs. Jackson on her evaluation design. What questions should she be addressing? How could she organize her evaluation? How might she change her design to make it better?

SUGGESTED READINGS

Affholter, D. P. (1994). Outcome monitoring. In J. S. Wholey, H. P. Hatry, and K. E. Newcomer (Eds.), *Handbook of practical program evaluation.* San Francisco: Jossey-Bass.

Bloom, B. S., Hastings, J. T., & Madaus, G. F. (1971). *Handbook of formative and summative evaluation of student learning.* New York: McGraw-Hill.

Madaus, G. F., & Stufflebeam, D. L. (Eds.). (1989). *Educational evaluation: Classic works of Ralph W. Tyler.* Boston: Kluwer Academic.

Metfessel, N. S., & Michael, W. B. (1967). A paradigm involving multiple criterion measures for the evaluation of the effectiveness of school programs. *Educational and Psychological Measurement, 27,* 931–943. Also in B. R. Worthen & J. R. Sanders (1973), *Educational evaluation: Theory and practice.* Belmont, CA: Wadsworth.

Nowakowski, J., Bunda, M. A., Working, R., Bernacki, G., & Harrington, P. (1985). *A handbook of educational variables.* Boston: Kluwer-Nijhoff.

Provus, M. M. (1971). *Discrepancy evaluation.* Berkeley, CA: McCutchan.

Smith, E. R., & Tyler, R. W. (1942). *Appraising and recording student progress.* New York: Harper & Row.

Tyler, R. W. (1991). General statement on program evaluation. In M. W. McLaughlin & D. C. Phillips (Eds.), *Evaluation and education: At quarter century.* Ninetieth Yearbook of the National Society for the Study of Education, Part II. Chicago: University of Chicago Press.

chapter 6

Management-Oriented Evaluation Approaches

ORIENTING QUESTIONS

1. Why has the management-oriented approach to evaluation been so popular among local administrators and state and federal government leaders?
2. What are the developmental stages of a program and how can management-oriented evaluation help in program development?
3. What techniques are most useful for context evaluation? Input? Process? Product?
4. What are major strengths and limitations of the management-oriented evaluation approach?

The management-oriented evaluation approach is meant to serve decision makers. Its rationale is that evaluative information is an essential part of good decision making and that the evaluator can be most effective by serving administrators, policy makers, boards, practitioners, and others who need good evaluative information. Developers of this method have relied on a systems approach to education in which decisions are made about inputs, processes, and outputs. By highlighting different levels of decisions and decision makers, this approach clarifies who will use the evaluation results, how he will use them, and what aspect(s) of the system he is making decisions about. The decision maker is always the audience to whom a management-oriented evaluation is directed, and the decision maker's concerns, informational needs, and criteria for effectiveness guide the direction of the study.

DEVELOPERS OF THE MANAGEMENT-ORIENTED EVALUATION APPROACH AND THEIR CONTRIBUTIONS

Important contributions to a management-oriented approach to evaluation have been made by many evaluators. In the mid-1960s, Stufflebeam (1968) recognized the shortcomings of available evaluation approaches. Working to expand and systematize thinking about administrative studies and educational decision making, he and others built upon concepts only hinted at in the much earlier work of educational leaders such as Bernard, Mann, Harris, and Washburne. During the 1960s and 1970s, they also drew from management theory (e.g., Braybrooke & Lindblom, 1963). Stufflebeam (1968) made the decision(s) of program managers the pivotal organizer for the evaluation rather than program objectives. In the models proposed by him and other theorists (e.g. Alkin, 1969), the evaluator, working closely with the administrator(s), identifies the decisions the administrator must make and then collects sufficient information about the relative advantages and disadvantages of each decision alternative to allow a fair judgment based on specified criteria. The success of the evaluation rests on the quality of teamwork between evaluators and decision makers.

The CIPP Evaluation Model

Stufflebeam (1971; Stufflebeam & Shinkfield, 1985) has been an influential proponent of a decision-oriented evaluation approach structured to help administrators make good decisions. He views evaluation as "the process of delineating, obtaining, and providing useful information for judging decision alternatives" (Stufflebeam, 1973a, p. 129). He developed an evaluation framework to serve managers and administrators facing four different kinds of educational decisions.

1. *Context evaluation,* to serve *planning decisions.* Determining what needs are to be addressed by a program helps in defining objectives for the program.
2. *Input evaluation,* to serve *structuring decisions.* Determining what resources are available, what alternative strategies for the program should be considered, and what plan seems to have the best potential for meeting needs facilitates design of program procedures.
3. *Process evaluation,* to serve *implementing decisions.* How well is the plan being implemented? What barriers threaten its success? What revisions are needed? Once these questions are answered, procedures can be monitored, controlled, and refined.
4. *Product evaluation,* to serve *recycling decisions.* What results were obtained? How well were needs reduced? What should be done with the program after it has run its course? These questions are important in judging program attainments.

The first letters of each type of evaluation—context, input, process, and product—have been used to form the acronym CIPP, by which Stufflebeam's evaluation model is best known. Table 6.1 summarizes the main features of the four types of evaluation, as proposed by Stufflebeam and Shinkfield (1985, pp. 170-171).

TABLE 6.1   Four types of evaluation

	Context Evaluation	Input Evaluation	Process Evaluation	Product Evaluation
Objective	To define the institutional context, to identify the target population and assess their needs, to identify opportunities for addressing the needs, to diagnose *problems* underlying the *needs,* and to judge whether proposed objectives are sufficiently responsive to the assessed needs	To identify and assess *system capabilities,* alternative program *strategies,* procedural *designs* for implementing the strategies, budgets, and schedules	To identify or predict in process *defects* in the procedural design or its implementation, to provide information for the preprogrammed decisions, and to record and judge procedural events and activities	To collect descriptions and judgments of outcomes and to relate them to objectives and to context, input, and process information, and to interpret their worth and merit
Method	By using such methods as system analysis, survey, document review, hearings, interviews, diagnostic tests, and the Delphi technique	By inventorying and analyzing available human and material resources, solution strategies, and procedural designs for relevance, feasibility, and economy, and by using such methods as literature search, visits to exemplary programs, advocate teams, and pilot trials	By monitoring the activity's potential procedural barriers and remaining alert to unanticipated ones, by obtaining specified information for programmed decisions, by describing the actual process, and by continually interacting with and observing the activities of project staff	By defining operationally and measuring outcome criteria, by collecting judgments of outcomes from stakeholders, and by performing both qualitative and quantitative analyses
Relation to decision making in the change process	For deciding upon the *setting* to be served, the *goals* associated with meeting needs or using opportunities, and the *objectives* associated with solving problems—that is, for *planning* needed changes—and to provide a basis for judging outcomes	For selecting *sources of support,* solution *strategies,* and procedural *designs*—that is, for *structuring* change activities—and to provide a basis for judging implementation	For *implementing and refining the program design and procedure*—that is, for effecting *process control*—and to provide a log of the actual process for later use in interpreting outcomes	For deciding to *continue, terminate, modify,* or *refocus* a change activity, and to present a clear record of effects (intended and unintended, positive and negative)

SOURCE: From *Systematic Evaluation* (pp. 170-171) by D. L. Stufflebeam and A. J. Shinkfield, 1985, Boston: Kluwer-Nijhoff.

As a logical structure for designing each type of evaluation, Stufflebeam (1973b) proposed that evaluators follow these steps:

A. *Focusing the Evaluation*
   1. Identify the major level(s) of decision making to be served; for example, local, state, or national.
   2. For each level of decision making, project the decision situations to be served and describe each one in terms of its locus, focus, criticality, timing, and composition of alternatives.
   3. Define criteria for each decision situation by specifying variables for measurement and standards for use in the judgment of alternatives.
   4. Define policies within which the evaluator must operate.
B. *Collection of Information*
   1. Specify the source of the information to be collected.
   2. Specify the instruments and methods for collecting the needed information.
   3. Specify the **sampling** procedure to be employed.
   4. Specify the conditions and schedule for information collection.
C. *Organization of Information*
   1. Provide a format for the information that is to be collected.
   2. Designate a means for performing the analysis.
D. *Analysis of Information*
   1. Select the analytical procedures to be employed.
   2. Designate a means for performing the analysis.
E. *Reporting of Information*
   1. Define the audiences for the evaluation reports.
   2. Specify means for providing information to the audiences.
   3. Specify the format for evaluation reports and/or reporting sessions.
   4. Schedule the reporting of information.
F. *Administration of the Evaluation*
   1. Summarize the evaluation schedule.
   2. Define staff and resource requirements and plans for meeting these requirements.
   3. Specify means for meeting policy requirements for conduct of the evaluation.
   4. Evaluate the potential of the evaluation design for providing information that is valid, reliable, credible, timely, and pervasive (i.e., will reach all relevant stakeholders).
   5. Specify and schedule means for periodic updating of the evaluation design.
   6. Provide a budget for the total evaluation program. (p. 144)

The UCLA Evaluation Model

While he was director of the Center for the Study of Evaluation at UCLA, Alkin (1969) developed an evaluation framework that paralleled closely some aspects of the CIPP model. Alkin defined evaluation as "the process of ascertaining the decision areas of concern, selecting appropriate information, and collecting and analyzing information in order to report summary data useful to decision-makers in selecting among alternatives" (p. 2). Alkin's model included the following five types of evaluation:

1. *Systems assessment,* to provide information about the state of the system. (Very similar to context evaluation in the CIPP model.)
2. *Program planning,* to assist in the selection of particular programs likely to be effective in meeting specific educational needs. (Very similar to input evaluation.)
3. *Program implementation,* to provide information about whether a program was introduced to the appropriate group in the manner intended
4. *Program improvement,* to provide information about how a program is functioning, whether interim objectives are being achieved, and whether unanticipated outcomes are appearing. (Similar to process evaluation.)
5. *Program certification,* to provide information about the value of the program and its potential for use elsewhere. (Very similar to product evaluation.)

As Alkin (1991) has pointed out, his evaluation model made four assumptions about evaluation:

1. Evaluation is a process of gathering information.
2. The information collected in an evaluation will be used mainly to make decisions about alternative courses of action.
3. Evaluation information should be presented to the decision maker in a form that he can use effectively and which is designed to help rather than confuse or mislead him.
4. Different kinds of decisions require different kinds of evaluation procedures. (p. 94)

Growth and Development of the Early Models

Both the CIPP and UCLA frameworks for evaluation appear to be linear and sequential, but the developers have stressed that such is not the case. For example, the evaluator would not have to complete an input evaluation or a systems assessment in order to undertake one of the other types of evaluation listed in the framework. Often evaluators may undertake "retrospective" evaluations (such as a context evaluation or a systems assessment) in preparation for a process or program improvement evaluation study, believing this evaluation approach is cumulative, linear, and sequential; however, such steps are not always necessary. A process evaluation can be done without having completed context or input evaluation studies. At other times, the evaluator may cycle into another type of evaluation if some decisions suggest that earlier decisions should be reviewed. Such is the nature of management-oriented evaluation.

Work using the CIPP model has produced guides for types of evaluation included in that framework. For example, Stufflebeam (1977) advanced the procedure for conducting a *context* evaluation with his guidelines for designing a needs assessment for an educational program or activity.

A guide for use in *input* evaluation was developed by Reinhard (1972). The input evaluation approach that she developed is called the *advocate team technique.* It is used when acceptable alternatives for designing a new program are not available or obvious. The technique creates alternative new designs that are then evaluated and selected, adapted, or combined to create the most viable alternative design for a new program. This technique has been used successfully by the federal government (Reinhard, 1972) and by school districts (Sanders, 1982) to generate options and guide the final design of educational programs. Procedures proposed by Cronbach (1963) provided useful suggestions for the conduct of *process* evaluation.

Techniques discussed in Chapter 17 of this book provide information useful in conducting *product* evaluations, as do approaches to evaluation discussed in Chapter 7.

Other Management-Oriented Evaluation Approaches

In Chapter 5, Provus's Discrepancy Evaluation Model was described as an objectives-oriented evaluation model. Some aspects of that model are also directed toward serving the information needs of educational program managers. It is systems oriented, focusing on input, process, and output at each of five stages of evaluation: program definition, program installation, program process, program products, and cost-benefit analysis. Even cursory scrutiny of these five types of evaluation reveal close parallels to the CIPP and UCLA evaluation models with respect to their sensitivity to the various decisions managers need to make at each stage of program development.

The utilization-focused evaluation approach of Patton (1986) in one respect could also be viewed as a decision-making approach. He stressed that the process of identifying and organizing relevant decision makers and information users is the first step in evaluation. In his view, the use of evaluation findings requires that decision makers determine what information is needed by various people and arrange for that information to be collected and provided to those persons.

Wholey (1983, 1994) could be considered a proponent of management-oriented evaluation, given his focus on working with management. His writings have concentrated on the practical uses of evaluation in public administration settings.

The systems analysis approach has also been suggested by some to be an evaluation approach (e.g., Rossi & Freeman, 1993). If we agreed completely with those suggestions, we would place systems analysis with other approaches covered in this chapter. However, we do not consider most systems analyses to be evaluative, because of their narrow research focus on (1) establishing causal links between a few preselected variables and (2) cost analyses. Despite their focus on costs (a critical omission in many evaluations), it is the absence of any explicit valuing that causes us to consider most systems studies to be good examples of social research rather than evaluation.

HOW THE MANAGEMENT-ORIENTED EVALUATION APPROACH HAS BEEN USED

The CIPP model has been used in school districts and state and federal government agencies. The Dallas (Texas) Independent School District, for example, established an evaluation office organized around the four types of evaluation in the model. All evaluation activities in that district fall into one or more of these categories.

The management-oriented approach to evaluation has guided program managers through program planning, operation, and review. Program staff have found this approach a useful guide to program improvement.

This evaluation approach has also been used for accountability purposes. It provides a record-keeping framework that facilitates public review of client needs, objectives, plans, activities, and outcomes. Administrators and boards have found this approach useful in meeting public demands for information. Stufflebeam and Shinkfield (1985) described these two uses of the CIPP model as shown in Figure 6.1.

FIGURE 6.1 The relevance of four evaluation types to decision making and accountability

SOURCE: From *Systematic Evaluation* (p. 164) by D. L. Stufflebeam and A. J. Shinkfield, 1985, Boston: Kluwer-Nijhoff.

	Decision Making *(Formative Orientation)*	*Accountability* *(Summative Orientation)*
Context	Guidance for choice of objectives and assignment of priorities	Record of objectives and bases for their choice along with a record of needs, opportunities, and problems
Input	Guidance for choice of program strategy; input for specification of procedural design	Record of chosen strategy and design and reasons for their choice over other alternatives
Process	Guidance for implementation	Record of the actual process
Product	Guidance for termination, continuation, modification, or installation	Record of attainments and recycling decisions

STRENGTHS AND LIMITATIONS
OF THE MANAGEMENT-ORIENTED
EVALUATION APPROACH

This approach has proved appealing to many evaluators and program managers, particularly those at home with the rational and orderly systems approach, to which it is clearly related. Perhaps its greatest strength is that it gives focus to the evaluation. Experienced evaluators know how tempting it is simply to cast a wide net, collecting an enormous amount of information, only later to discard much of it because it is not directly relevant to the key issues or questions the evaluation must address. Deciding precisely what information to collect is essential. Focusing on informational needs and pending decisions of managers limits the range of relevant data and brings the evaluation into sharp focus. This evaluation approach also stresses the importance of the utility of information. Connecting decision making and evaluation underscores the very purpose of evaluation. Also, focusing an evaluation on the decisions managers must make prevents the evaluator from pursuing unfruitful lines of inquiry that are not of interest to the decision makers.

The management-oriented approach to evaluation was instrumental in showing evaluators and program managers that they need not wait until an activity or program has run its course before evaluating it. In fact, educators can begin evaluating even when ideas for programs are first discussed. Because of lost opportunities and heavy resource investment, evaluation is generally least effective at the end of a developing program. Of course, educators have found that it's never too late to begin evaluating, even if a program has been in place for years. The decisions are simply different.

The management-oriented evaluation approach is probably the preferred choice in the eyes of most managers and boards. This is hardly surprising given the emphasis this approach places on information for decision makers. By attending directly to the informational needs of people who are to use the evaluation, this approach addressed one of the biggest criticisms of evaluation in the 1960s: that it did not provide useful information.

The CIPP model, in particular, is a useful and simple heuristic tool that helps the evaluator generate potentially important questions to be addressed in an evaluation. For each of the four types of evaluation (CIPP), the evaluator can identify a number of questions about an undertaking. The model and the questions it generates also make the evaluation easy to explain to lay audiences.

The management-oriented approach to evaluation supports evaluation of every component of a program as it operates, grows, or changes. It stresses the timely use of feedback by decision makers so that the program is not left to flounder or proceed unaffected by updated knowledge about needs, resources, new developments, the realities of day-to-day operations, or the consequences of program interventions.

A potential weakness of this approach is the evaluator's occasional inability to respond to questions or issues that may be significant—even critical—but clash with (or at least do not match) the concerns and questions of the decision-maker who essentially controls the evaluation. In addition, costly programs that lack decisive leadership are not likely to benefit from this approach to evaluation.

Another potential weakness of management-oriented evaluation is the preference it seems to give to top management. If great care is not taken, the evaluator can become the "hired gun" of the manager and program establishment. Thus, one potential weakness of the management-oriented approach is the possibility that the evaluation can become unfair and possibly even undemocratic.

This point is relevant to the policy uses of evaluations by what Cronbach and others (1980) called the *policy-shaping community.* The policy-shaping community includes (1) public servants, such as responsible officials at the policy and program levels and the actual operating personnel, and (2) the public, consisting not only of constituents but also influential persons such as commentators, academic social scientists, philosophers, gadflies, and even novelists or dramatists. Few policy studies have been found to have a direct effect on the policy-shaping community, but evaluations can and do influence these audiences over time. Policy, as a reflection of public values, may be seen as never-ending in that it continues to be molded or revised as issues, reforms, social causes, and social values change or come to the forefront of attention. We need to remember, as Cronbach has noted, that one important role of the evaluator is to illuminate, not to dictate, the decision. Helping clients to understand the complexity of issues, not to give simple answers to narrow questions, is a role of evaluation.

Another limitation is that, if followed in its entirety, the management-oriented approach can result in costly and complex evaluations. If priorities are not carefully set and followed, the many questions to be addressed using a management-oriented approach can clamor for attention, leading to an evaluation system as large as the program itself and diverting resources from program activities. In planning evaluation procedures, management-oriented evaluators need to consider the resources and time available. If the management-oriented approach requires more time or resources than are available, another approach may have to be considered.

As a case in point, consider the classroom teacher who has to make decisions about next week's lesson plans. Because of his time limitations, and the limited information that is readily available to him, this teacher may be able to use only the CIPP or UCLA models informally, as an armchair aid. As with any approach, the management-oriented evaluator needs to be realistic about what work is possible and must not promise more than can be delivered.

Finally, this evaluation approach assumes that the important decisions can be clearly identified in advance, that clear decision alternatives can be specified, and that the decisions to be served remain reasonably stable while the evaluation is being done. All of these assumptions about the orderliness and predictability of the decision-making process are suspect and frequently unwarranted. Frequent adjustments may be needed in the original **evaluation plan** if this approach is to work well.

APPLICATION EXERCISES

1. Using what you have just read about the management-oriented approach to evaluation, identify one or two decisions to be made about a program at your workplace or one with which you are familiar. Who are the decision makers? What information do *you* think they need to make the decisions? What information do *they* think they need to make the decisions? What will influence their decisions? Do you think an evaluation could help them in making these decisions? What kind of evaluation, using the CIPP model, would be most appropriate for each decision?

2. Describe how decisions about programs are typically made in your organization. Would a management-oriented approach work in your organization? Why or why not?

3. A public school system successfully demonstrated its need for federal support for an elementary compensatory education program. They received a $500,000 grant to be spent over a period of three years from July 1, 1995, to June 30, 1998. On March 15, 1995, the superintendent convened a meeting of the assistant superintendent of elementary instruction and 30 principals of elementary schools eligible to participate in the proposed program. It was their decision that a thorough evaluation of the reading and mathematics programs in these schools should be completed by September 30, 1995, to identify needs. Alternative strategies for solving needs would then be evaluated and a program chosen for the elementary compensatory education project. They also decided to establish an evaluation team that would be responsible for

   a. Conducting the evaluation of the reading and mathematics programs of the eligible schools,

   b. Evaluating alternative programs to meet the needs of the 30 schools,

   c. Continually monitoring the program, which would be implemented starting in 1995, and

   d. Collecting information to be reported annually (on June 30 for each year of the grant) to the U.S. Department of Education.

   Using what you have just learned about management-oriented evaluation approaches, advise the evaluation team members about how they should proceed (assuming that it is now March 1995). Be as detailed in your planning as you can be.

SUGGESTED READINGS

Alkin, M. C. (1991). Evaluation theory development: II. In M. W. McLaughlin and D. C. Phillips (Eds.), *Evaluation and education: At quarter century.* Ninetieth Yearbook of the National Society for the Study of Education, Part II. Chicago: University of Chicago Press.

Stufflebeam, D. L. (1983). The CIPP model for program evaluation. In G. F. Madaus, M. Scriven, & D. L. Stufflebeam (Eds.), *Evaluation models: Viewpoints on educational and human services evaluation.* Boston: Kluwer-Nijhoff.

Stufflebeam, D. L., & Shinkfield, A. J. (1985). *Systematic evaluation.* Boston: Kluwer-Nijhoff.

Wholey, J. S. (1983). *Evaluation and effective public management.* Boston: Little, Brown.

Wholey, J. S. Hatry, H. P., & Newcomer, K. E. (Eds.), (1994). *Handbook of practical program evaluation.* San Francisco: Jossey-Bass.

chapter 7

Consumer-Oriented Evaluation Approaches

ORIENTING QUESTIONS

1. Consumers of educational and other human services products (e.g., curriculum materials or training materials) often use product evaluations done by others. If someone were doing a product evaluation for you, what criteria would you want that person to use?

2. What educational or other human services products do you use? How are purchasing decisions made? What criteria seem to be most important in the selection process?

3. What does the consumer-oriented evaluation approach suggest for those involved in curriculum or program development?

4. How has the consumer-oriented evaluation approach been used?

5. What are some major strengths and limitations of the consumer-oriented evaluation approach?

Independent agencies or individuals who have taken responsibility to compile information on educational or other human services products, or assist others in doing so, have promoted the consumer-oriented evaluation approach. Educational and other human services products include a range of materials available in the marketplace: curriculum packages, workshops, instructional media, in-service training opportunities, staff evaluation forms or procedures, new technology, software and equipment, educational materials and supplies, and even services to agencies.

Sales of educational products in the United States alone exceeds $600 million annually. As competition has grown in the educational and human services product industry, marketing strategies have become creative, but seldom are those strategies calculated to serve the best interests of the consumer or client. For this reason, some evaluators have actively urged consumer education, independent reviews of products patterned after the Consumers Union approach, and requirements for objective evidence of product effectiveness. Checklists for rating products and product evaluation reports are two typical outgrowths of this approach.

The consumer-oriented approach to evaluation is predominantly a summative evaluation approach. Developers of products have come to realize, however, that using the checklists and criteria of the consumer advocate while the product is being created is the best way to prepare for subsequent public scrutiny. Thus, the checklists and criteria proposed by "watchdog" agencies have become tools for formative evaluation of products still being developed.

DEVELOPERS OF THE CONSUMER-ORIENTED EVALUATION APPROACH AND THEIR CONTRIBUTIONS

The importance of consumer-oriented evaluation seems to have been first recognized during the mid- and late 1960s as new educational products began to flood the market. Prior to the 1960s, most materials available to educators were textbooks. With the influx of federal education funds earmarked for product development and federal purchases, however, the marketplace swelled.

Scriven's Concerns and Checklists

Scriven (1967) made a major contribution to this approach with his distinction between formative and summative evaluation. The summative role of evaluation, he said, "[enables] administrators to decide whether the entire finished curriculum, refined by use of the evaluation process in its . . . [formative] role, represents a sufficiently significant advance on the available alternatives to justify the expense of adoption by a school system" (pp. 41–42). Criteria that Scriven suggested for evaluating any product included the following:

- Evidence of achievement of important educational objectives
- Evidence of achievement of important noneducational objectives (for example, social objectives)
- Follow-up results

- Secondary and unintended effects, such as effects on the teacher, the teacher's colleagues, other students, administrators, parents, the school, the taxpayer, and other incidental positive or negative effects
- Range of utility (that is, for whom it will be useful)
- Moral considerations (unjust uses of punishment or controversial content)
- Costs

Later, Scriven (1974b) published a product checklist that expanded his earlier criteria. This new product checklist was the result of reviews commissioned by the federal government, focusing on educational products developed by federally sponsored research and development centers and regional laboratories. It was used in the examination of more than 90 educational products, most of which underwent many revisions during that review. Scriven stressed that the items in this checklist were *necessitata,* not *desiderata.* They included the following:

1. *Need:* Number affected, social significance, absence of substitutes, multiplicative effects, evidence of need
2. *Market:* Dissemination plan, size, and importance of potential markets
3. *Performance—True field trials:* Evidence of effectiveness of final version, with typical users, with typical aid, in typical settings, within a typical time frame
4. *Performance—True consumer:* Tests run with all relevant "consumers," such as students, teachers, principals, school district staff, state and federal officials, Congress, and taxpayers
5. *Performance—Critical comparisons:* Comparative data provided on important competitors such as no-treatment groups, existing competitors, projected competitors, created competitors, and hypothesized competitors
6. *Performance—Long term:* Evidence of effects reported at pertinent times, such as a week to a month after use of the product, a month to a year later, a year to a few years later, and over critical career stages
7. *Performance—Side effects:* Evidence of independent study or search for unintended outcomes during, immediately following, and over the long-term product use
8. *Performance—Process:* Evidence of product use provided to verify product descriptions, causal claims, and the morality of product use

9. *Performance—Causation:* Evidence of product effectiveness provided through randomized experimental study or through defensible quasi-experimental, ex post facto, or correlational studies

10. *Performance—Statistical significance:* Statistical evidence of product effectiveness to make use of appropriate analysis techniques, significance levels, and interpretations

11. *Performance—Educational significance:* Educational significance demonstrated through independent judgments, expert judgments, judgments based on item analysis and raw scores of tests, side effects, long-term effects and comparative gains, and educationally sound use

12. *Cost-effectiveness:* A comprehensive cost analysis made, including expert judgment of costs, independent judgment of costs, and comparison to costs for competitors.

13. *Extended Support:* Plans made for postmarketing data collection and improvement, in-service training, updating of aids, and study of new uses and user data

These are stringent standards, to be sure, but defensible and important—although few textbooks or curriculum packages now on the market would satisfy all of them. Perhaps no one product will ever be judged successful on all these criteria, but producers' efforts to meet these standards have a marked effect on improving the efforts of product developers. Scriven adapted this checklist later to use it as a guide for evaluating a program evaluation, titling it the **Key Evaluation Checklist** (Scriven, 1991b).

Scriven continues to be the most avid and articulate advocate of the consumer-oriented evaluation approach, although he is not blind to weaknesses in some of its applications, as noted in the following observation:

> We should add a word about what may seem to be the most obvious of all models for a consumerist ideologue, namely *Consumer Reports* product evaluations. While these serve as a good enough model to demonstrate failures in most of the alternatives more widely accepted in program evaluation, especially educational program evaluation, it must not be thought that the present author regards them as flawless. I have elsewhere said something about factual and logical errors and separatist bias in *Consumer Reports*. . . . Although *Consumer Reports* is not as good as it was and it has now accumulated even more years across which the separatists/managerial crime of refusal to discuss its methodologies and errors in an explicit and nondefensive way has been exacerbated many times, and although there are now other consumer magazines which do considerably better work than *Consumer Reports* in particular fields, *Consumer Reports* is still a very good model for most types of product evaluation. (Scriven, 1984, p. 75)

Other Checklists and Product Analysis Systems

In the mid-1960s, Komoski was a leader in establishing the Educational Products Information Exchange (EPIE) as an independent Product review service modeled after the Consumers Union. Through its newsletter *(EPIE Forum)* and published reports,[1] EPIE has provided much-needed evaluative information to state departments of education and school districts that subscribe to its service. EPIE checklists and curriculum analysis guides have also been valuable tools for the educational consumer.

Likewise, the Curriculum Materials Analysis System (CMAS) checklist developed by Morrisett and Stevens (1967) includes the following useful guidelines for product analysis:[2]

1. *Describe the characteristics of the product:* media, materials, time needed, style, costs, availability, available performance data, subject matter and content, dominant characteristics of curriculum forms.
2. *Analyze its rationale and objectives:* description and evaluation of rationale, general objectives, specific objectives, behavioral objectives.
3. *Consider antecedent conditions in using this product:* pupil characteristics, teacher capabilities and requirements, community and school characteristics, existing curriculum and curriculum organization (vertical and horizontal).
4. *Consider its content:* cognitive structure, skills to be taught, affective content
5. *Consider the instructional theory and teaching strategies used in this product:* appropriateness of teaching strategies, forms, modes, or transactions.
6. *Form overall judgments:* other descriptive data, reported experiences with the product, pilot tryouts, and outside recommendations.

A variety of product evaluation checklists have been developed and used over the past several years by individual evaluators and agencies. Many serve as valuable guides from which one might develop a checklist tailored for one's own situation.

The checklist in Figure 7.1 (p. 112), developed by Patterson (n.d.), provides a good example of a concise review form useful for heuristic purposes.

---

[1] A list of reports is available from EPIE Institute, 475 Riverside Drive, New York, NY 10027.
[2] These categories are drawn from the CMAS outline, which is not reproduced here in its entirety. We take full responsibility for any distortion of intent or content that may have resulted from our selective presentation.

Instructional Materials Review Form: Marvin Patterson
Center for Studies in
Vocational Education
Florida State University

Title(s)_____

_____

Author(s)_____

_____

Publisher_____

_____

Latest Copyright Date_____

☐ Retain for Committee Review
☐ Bibliography Only
☐ Reject (Comments):

Use the following code to rate materials:

+   means yes or good quality   −   means no or poor quality
O   means all right, but not of especially good quality   NA   means not applicable

						Committee Members
						1. Does the content cover a significant portion of the program competencies?
						2. Is the content up-to-date?
						3. Is the reading/math level appropriate for most students?
						4. Are objectives, competencies, or tasks stated in the student materials.
						5. Are tests included in the materials?
						6. Are performance checklists included?
						7. Are hands-on activities included?
						8. How many outside materials are required? + means 0–1 materials O means 2–3 materials − means 4+ materials
						9. Would you use these materials in your training program?
						If the materials to this point appear to be a possible choice for selection, continue with your review. Stop if the materals appear to be too poor for further consideration.
						10. Is a Teacher's Guide included that offers management suggestions for the materials?
						11. Is the material presented in a logical sequence?
						Quality Judgments. Use +,O, − to rate the quality of the products.
						12. Quality of objectives, competencies, and/or tasks
						13. Degree of match between learning activities and objectives
						14. Quality of test items and degree of match with objectives
						15. Quality of performance checklists and degree of match with objectives
						16. Quality of directions for how students are to proceed through the materials
						17. Quality of drawings, photographs, and/or other visuals
						18. Overall design of the learning activities for individualized instruction
						19. Emphasis on safety practices (when needed)
						20. Degree of freedom from bias with respect to sex, race, national origin, age, religion, etc. (see provided guidelines)
						21. Quality of management procedures for teachers (teacher's guides, etc.)
						22. (Optional) List the career-map competencies covered by these materials.

Comments:

FIGURE 7.1   Sample checklist for evaluations

source: The form is from M. Patterson, n.d., Tallahassee, FL: Center for Instructional Development and Services, Florida State University.

HOW THE CONSUMER-ORIENTED EVALUATION APPROACH HAS BEEN USED

As mentioned previously, the consumer-oriented approach to evaluation has been used extensively by government agencies and independent educational consumer advocates such as EPIE to make information available on hundreds of products. As products begin to be developed for use in communities to address youth and other human needs, similar efforts will be needed to sort out the champions from the charlatans.

The Program Effectiveness Panel in the U.S. Department of Education (previously called the Joint Dissemination Review Panel) established a classic example of consumer-oriented evaluation system by setting standards (Tallmadge, 1977) for new educational programs that must be met before the panel will recommend any program for adoption. Those programs that pass the panel's review are approved through the National Dissemination Network for dissemination to school systems throughout the United States.

A role that state departments of education or other governmental agencies could play in consumer protection by using this evaluation approach has been discussed but never implemented. Rather than evaluate products themselves and then disseminate their findings to consumers or merely list available products, governmental agencies have discussed using standard forms to compile and then disseminate evaluation information about any new product. Guidelines developed for this purpose could address four aspects of any product: its processes, content, transportability, and effectiveness. In each case the central concern is, "What does one need to know about a product before deciding whether to adapt or install it?" Questions posed within each category include the following.

Process Information

1. What is the nature and frequency of interactions among (combinations of) students or clients/teachers or service delivery staff/administrators/relevant others? Have these interactions been evaluated?
2. Is the strategy to be employed described so that its appropriateness can be determined? Has the strategy been evaluated?
3. Is the delivery schedule required by the program or product described so that its feasibility can be determined? Has the schedule been evaluated?
4. Are the equipment and facilities required by the program or product described so that their feasibility can be determined? Have they been evaluated?
5. Are the budget and human resource requirements of the program or product listed so that their feasibility can be determined? Have the following requirements been included?
   a. Start-up and continuation budget requirements
   b. Administration/staff/parent or advisory committees/resource requirements
   c. In-service program requirements

6. Is evaluation an integral part of (a) the development and (b) the implementation of the program or product?

Content Information

1. Is the existence or lack of basic program or product elements, such as the following, noted?
   a. Clearly stated outcome objectives
   b. Sufficient directions
   c. Other materials required
   d. Prerequisite knowledge/attitudes required
   e. Fit with knowledge base and existing programs
2. Have the above elements been evaluated?
3. Has the content of the program or product been evaluated by recognized content specialists?
4. Is there sufficient information about the program or product rationale and philosophy to permit a decision about whether it is within the realm of school or agency responsibility or consistent with the organization's philosophy? (For example, school responsibility has traditionally encompassed such areas as intellectual development, personal development, citizenship and social development, educational and personal adjustment, physical growth and development.)
5. Do the objectives of the program or product have cogent rationales? Are they compatible with the school or agency philosophy and the values of the community?

Transportability Information

Three elements relating to transportability appear critical: (1) geography and setting, (2) people, and (3) time.

1. What information is available regarding *settings* in which the program or product has been used effectively, in terms of the following?
   a. Size/numbers
   b. Organization
   c. Political factors
   d. Legal issues
   e. Facilities
   f. Wealth
   g. Occupational factors
   h. Geographical indices (for example, rural/urban)
   i. Cultural factors
   j. Public/nonpublic factors
   k. Philosophical issues

2. What information is available concerning the *individuals or groups* with whom the program or product has been used effectively in relation to the following?
   a. Age/grade
   b. Experience
   c. Entrance knowledge, skills, and behaviors
   d. Expectations/preferences/interests
   e. Ethnic/cultural makeup
3. What information is available regarding the *time of year* in which the program or product has been used effectively?
4. Does the program or product have *special requirements* in areas such as the following?
   a. Training
   b. Organization or facilities
   c. Additional materials or equipment
   d. Research people/specialists

Effectiveness Information

1. Has technically sound information about the effects of the program or product on its target population been obtained using one of more of the following procedures?
   a. Comparison to established base (pre-post)
   b. Prediction (making success estimates using regression techniques or subjective estimation)
   c. Comparison to local or state groups
   d. Comparison against objectives or predetermined criterion levels
   e. Comparison to competing programs or products
2. Is there evidence that the program or product has eliminated a documented need, in addition to management gains such as the following?
   a. Cost savings
   b. Improved morale
   c. Faster improvement rate
3. Is immediate and follow-up effectiveness information available?

These questions could easily be cast into a checklist formed by using the following response categories.

Yes	No	Implied	Not Applicable
Information available:			

Although not necessarily a product evaluation enterprise, the *Mental Measurement Yearbook*s must be mentioned as a form of consumer-oriented evaluation. These yearbooks contain critical reviews of commercially available tests marketed in the United States and several other English-speaking countries. As educational products, these tests deserve the same scrutiny any product receives, and the *Mental Measurement Yearbook*s have provided a valuable service in this regard to educators, psychologists, personnel directors, and any others who use tests or other measurement devices.

STRENGTHS AND LIMITATIONS OF THE CONSUMER-ORIENTED EVALUATION APPROACH

Developers of the consumer-oriented approach to evaluation have provided a valuable service in two ways: (1) they have made available evaluations of products as a service to those who may not have the time or information to do the job thoroughly, and (2) they have advanced the knowledge of consumers about the criteria most appropriate to use in selecting educational or service delivery products. The checklists that have evolved from years of consumer-oriented product evaluations are useful and simple evaluation tools. They have been especially useful in addressing the Values Identification Standard (Standard U4) in *The Program Evaluation Standards* (Joint Committee, 1994).

Consumers have become more aware of commercial sales ploys thanks to the efforts of consumer-oriented evaluators. Consumers are (or should be) less vulnerable to sales tactics than they were 20 years ago. They are (or should be) more discriminating in the way they select products.

The product development industry has a long way to go, however, in being responsive to consumers' needs. Just ask a textbook sales rep for information about the performance or proven effectiveness of his product, and see what kind of information you get. Most of the time it will be either anecdotal testimony and sales information or scanty, poorly conceived product evaluation. Very seldom do corporations spend the time or money needed to acquire acceptable information about their products' performance. Consumers must insist on such information if the product development industry is to take product evaluation seriously.

The consumer-oriented approach to evaluation is not without drawbacks (although they seem small compared to its benefits). It can increase the cost of products. The time and money invested in product testing will usually be passed on to the consumer. Moreover, the use of stringent standards in product development and purchase may suppress creativity because of the risk involved. There is a place for field-trial programs before products are fully adopted. By developing long-term plans for change, educators and other service providers can give untested products a chance without consuming large portions of the budget. Cooperative trial programs with industry may be in the best interests of all.

Finally, the consumer-oriented approach to evaluation threatens local initiative development because local practitioners may become increasingly dependent on outside products and consumer services. Service providers need to place the purchase of outside products in perspective so that they are not overly dependent on the availability of other people's work. We agree with those who contend that we need to be less concerned with developing and purchasing practitioner-proof products and more concerned with supporting product-proof practitioners—those who think for themselves and who take the initiative in addressing human needs.

APPLICATION EXERCISES

1. A company's catalog of resources available to community leaders who work with youth claims that those who apply their approach to youth development will see decreases in alcohol and other drug use, early sexual activity, violence, and school failure. Using what you have learned about consumer-oriented evaluation, what information would you seek before you ordered resource materials from this catalog?

2. Teachers in each academic department of a senior high school are given a choice of curricular programs to use in their classrooms. This policy is designed to take full advantage of the range of capabilities of individual faculty members. All faculty members are required to prepare an evaluation of their program and circulate these reports among the faculty. These evaluations are to be conducted in keeping with the evaluation guidelines established by the curriculum council. The guidelines require

   • a statement from each teacher at year-end about the goals for their course and an assessment of the extent to which these goals were met using the selected program,

   • submission of information from each teacher about the comparison of their pupils' performance and the performance of pupils using a different curricular program,

   • an outside assessment of the appropriateness of the selected program for the teacher's stated goals,

   • a comparison of student performance on standardized tests to national norms, and

   • a complete list of test items are used during the year.

   Results for each item are to be reported.

   Using what you have just learned about consumer-oriented evaluation, what changes in the evaluation process would you suggest to the curriculum council? How could faculty reports be structured so that other schools could benefit from their consumer reports?

SUGGESTED READINGS

Scriven, M. (1974). Standards for the evaluation of educational programs and products. In G. D. Borich (Ed.), *Evaluating educational programs and products*. Englewood Cliffs, NJ: Educational Technology Publications. Also in W. J. Popham (Ed.), (1974), *Evaluation in education*. Berkeley, CA: McCutchan.

Scriven, M. (1991). Key evaluation checklist. In M. Scriven, *Evaluation thesaurus* (4th ed.). Newbury Park, CA: Sage.

Tallmadge, G. K. (1977). *Ideabook: JDRP* (ERIC DL 48329). Washington, DC: U.S. Government Printing Office.

chapter **8**

Expertise-Oriented
Evaluation Approaches

ORIENTING QUESTIONS

1. What are the arguments for and against using professional judgment as the means for evaluating programs?
2. Under what conditions would accreditation, blue-ribbon panels, or connoisseurship be methods of choice for conducting an evaluation?
3. What criteria would you use to screen experts to select the best for an expertise-oriented evaluation?
4. What differences exist between formal and informal professional review systems?
5. What are some major strengths and limitations of the expertise-oriented evaluation approach?

The expertise-oriented approach to evaluation, probably the oldest and most widely used, depends primarily upon professional expertise to judge an institution, program, product, or activity. For example, the worth of a drug prevention curriculum would be assessed by curriculum or subject-matter experts who would observe the curriculum in action, examine its content and underlying learning theory or, in some other way, glean sufficient information to render a considered judgment about its value.

In another case, the quality of a hospital could be assessed by looking at its special programs, its operating facilities, its emergency room operations, its in-patient operations, its pharmacy, and so on, by experts in medicine, health services, and hospital administration. They could examine facilities and equipment/supplies of the hospital, its operational procedures on paper and in action, the qualifications of its personnel, patient records, and other aspects of the hospital to determine whether it is meeting appropriate professional standards.

Although subjective professional judgments are involved to some degree in all the evaluation approaches described thus far, this approach is decidedly different because of its direct, open reliance on subjective professional expertise as the primary evaluation strategy. Such expertise may be provided by the evaluator(s) or by someone else, depending on who offers most in the substance or procedures being evaluated. Usually one person will not own all of the requisite knowledge needed to do the evaluation adequately. A team of experts who complement each other are much more likely to produce a sound evaluation.

Several specific evaluation processes are variants of this approach, including doctoral examinations administered by a committee, proposal review panels, professional reviews conducted by professional accreditation bodies, reviews of institutions or individuals by state or national licensing agencies, reviews of staff performance for decisions concerning promotion or tenure, peer reviews of articles submitted to "refereed" professional journals, site visits of educational programs conducted at the behest of the program's sponsor, reviews and recommendations by prestigious "blue-ribbon" panels, and even the critique offered by the ubiquitous expert who exists to serve in a self-appointed watch-dog role.

To impose some order, we choose to organize and discuss these various manifestations of expertise-oriented evaluation within four categories: (1) formal professional review systems, (2) informal professional review systems, (3) ad hoc panel reviews, and (4) ad hoc individual reviews. Differences in these categories are shown in Table 8.1, along the following dimensions:

1. Is there an existing structure for operating the review?
2. Are published standards used as part of the review?
3. Are reviews scheduled at specified intervals?
4. Does the review include opinions of multiple experts?
5. Do results of the review have an impact on the status of whatever is reviewed?

TABLE 8.1   Some features of four types of expertise-oriented evaluation approaches

Type of Expertise-Oriented Evaluation Approach	Existing Structure	Published Standards	Specified Schedule	Opinions of Multiple Experts	Status Affected by Results
Formal review system	Yes	Yes	Yes	Yes	Usually
Informal review system	Yes	Rarely	Sometimes	Yes	Usually
Ad hoc panel review	No	No	No	Yes	Sometimes
Ad hoc individual review	No	No	No	No	Sometimes

To this we have added a fifth category, namely educational connoisseurship and criticism, to discuss an interesting expertise-oriented approach that does not fit neatly into the other categories or dimensions shown in Table 8.1.

Site visitation, frequently the mode for conducting expertise-oriented evaluations, is not itself an approach to evaluation; rather, it is a method that might be used not only here but also with other evaluation approaches. Site-visit methods and techniques are discussed in Chapter 18, along with other techniques often used by expertise-oriented evaluators. A more comprehensive and detailed discussion of guidelines and procedures for site visits and proposal reviews also appears in Worthen, O'Sullivan, and White (in press).

DEVELOPERS OF THE EXPERTISE-ORIENTED EVALUATION APPROACH AND THEIR CONTRIBUTIONS

It is hard to pinpoint the origins of this approach, for expertise-oriented evaluation has long been with us. It was formally used in education in the 1800s, when schools began to standardize college entrance requirements. Informally, it has been in use since the first time an individual to whom expertise was publicly accorded rendered a judgment about the quality of some endeavor (and history is mute on when that occurred). Several movements and individuals have given impetus to the various types of expertise-oriented evaluations, as described below.

Formal Professional Review Systems

We would define a formal professional review system as one having (1) structure or organization established to conduct periodic reviews; (2) published standards (and possibly instruments) for use in such reviews; (3) a prespecified schedule (for example, every five years) on which reviews will be conducted; (4) opinions of several experts combining to reach the overall judgments of value; and (5) an impact on the status of that which is reviewed, depending on the outcome.

Accreditation.   To many, the most familiar formal professional review system is that of *accreditation,* the process whereby an organization grants approval of institutions such as schools, universities, and hospitals. Beginning in the late 1800s, national and regional accreditation agencies in education gradually supplanted in the United States the borrowed Western European system of school inspections, and these became a potent force in education during the 1930s. Education was not alone in institutionalizing accreditation processes to determine and regulate the quality of its institutions. Parallel efforts were underway in other professions, including medicine and law, as concern over quality led to wide-scale acceptance of professionals' judging the efforts of fellow professionals. Perhaps the most memorable example is Flexner's (1910) examination of medical schools in the United States and Canada in the early 1900s, which led to the closing of numerous schools he cited as inferior. As Floden (1983) has noted, Flexner's study was not accreditation in the strict sense, because medical schools did not participate voluntarily, but it certainly qualified as accreditation in the broader sense: a classic example of private judgment evaluating educational institutions.

Flexner's approach differed from most contemporary accreditation efforts in two other significant ways. First, Flexner was not a member of the profession whose efforts he presumed to judge. An educator with no pretense of medical expertise, Flexner nonetheless ventured to judge the quality of medical training in two nations. He argued that common sense was perhaps the most relevant form of expertise.

> Time and time again it has been shown that an unfettered lay mind, is . . . best suited to undertake a general survey. . . . The expert has his place, to be sure; but if I were asked to suggest the most promising way to study legal education, I should seek a layman, not a professor of law; or for the sound way to investigate teacher training, the last person I should think of employing would be a professor of education. (Flexner, 1960, p. 71)

It should be noted that Flexner's point was only partially supported by his own study. Although he was a layman in terms of medicine, he was an *educator,* and his judgments were directed at medical *education,* not the practice of medicine, so even here appropriate expertise seemed to be applied.

Second, Flexner made no attempt to claim empirical support for the criteria or process he employed because he insisted that the standards he used were the "obvious" indicators of school quality and needed no such support. His methods of collecting information and reaching judgments were simple and straightforward: "A stroll through the laboratories disclosed the presence or absence of apparatus, museum specimens, library, and students; and a whiff told the inside story regarding the manner in which anatomy was cultivated" (p. 79).

Third, Flexner dispensed with the professional niceties and courteous criticisms that seem to typify even the negative findings yielded by today's accreditation processes. Excerpts of his report of one school included scathing indictments such as this: "Its so-called equipment is dirty and disorderly beyond description. Its outfit in anatomy consists of a small box of bones and the dried-up, filthy fragments of a single cadaver. A cold and rusty incubator, a single microscope, . . . and no access to the County Hospital. The school is a disgrace to the state whose laws permit its existence" (Flexner, 1910, p. 190).

Although an excellent example of expertise-oriented evaluation (if expertise as an educator, not a physician, is the touchstone), Flexner's approach is much more like that of contemporary evaluators who see judgment as the sine qua non of evaluation and who see many of the criteria as obvious extensions of logic and common sense (e.g., Scriven, 1973). But today's accreditation systems seem for the most part to have grown up differently. Whereas Flexner's review used the same process and standards for all medical schools reviewed, there is much more variability in contemporary national and regional accreditation systems. Agencies in the United States, such as the North Central Association (NCA) for accrediting secondary schools, the Joint Commission on Accreditation of Healthcare Organizations (JCAHO), or the National Council for the Accreditation of Teacher Education (NCATE), have developed dualistic systems that include some minimum standards deemed important for all institutions, along with an internal self-study component in which institutions can present their unique mission and goals, defend their reasonableness and importance, and report on how well that self-study approach is accomplishing its goals and what capabilities it offers for the foreseeable future. These two facets of accreditation are emphasized to greatly different degrees in various accreditation systems, leading Kirkwood (1982) to criticize accreditation for lacking "similarity of aims, uniformity of process, or comparability among institutions" (p. 9), whereas others complain that the imposition of external standards by accrediting agencies denies institutions the opportunity of developing unique strengths.

Current accreditation systems also depend on the assumption that only members of a profession are qualified to judge the activities of their peers. Not only are accreditation site-visit team members drawn from the profession or occupation whose work they will judge, but also the standards and criteria are developed solely by members of that professional fraternity.[1] For example, "The standards of techniques for accreditation of schools of teacher education have been determined by committees, comprised mainly of practicing teachers and teacher educators" (Floden, 1983, p. 262).

Although accreditation has historically focused on the adequacy of facilities, qualifications of staff, and perceived appropriateness of the processes used, rather than assess the outcomes of programs, several current accreditation systems aspire to justify their criteria and standards on the basis of empirical links of inputs and processes to outcomes. In large part such efforts are reactions to critics of accreditation who have typified accreditation as (in private correspondence from an unnamed colleague) "a bunch of anachronistic old fogies who bumble about with meters, measuring lighting and BTUs and counting the ratio of children per toilet, but failing to measure anything which could be conceived by any stretch of the imagination as related to what children are learning." Though obviously far overdrawn, such a caricature strikes a sensitive nerve among people responsible for accreditation systems, and such criticisms may account, at least in part, for a gradual de-emphasis on such quantitative indicators as square footage per student or number of volumes in the library and a move toward more qualitative indices dealing with purposes of schooling. The same

---

[1] Floden (1983) has noted that jurisdictional disputes *within* professions exist, as with the long-standing tension over who should control accreditation of teacher education programs, elementary and secondary school teachers or faculties of teacher education institutions. Though beyond the scope of this chapter, issues of who should participate in and who should control accreditation processes are obviously important.

issue appeared in a mental health setting where an accreditation team member observed that an organization that received a "solid C" was probably providing better services than one that received an A. His reasoning was that the accreditation focused so much on time-consuming paperwork irrelevant to patient outcomes that an organization that did well on those issues was probably not spending sufficient time for its professionals to provide good therapy.

Some movement has been seen in recent years toward including outcomes in the accreditation process. Regional school accreditation agencies are developing outcomes-based accreditation procedures. Several state commissions on higher education are trying to include outcome standards such as graduation rates, job placement, withdrawal rates, and ratios of the costs of education to eventual salaries of graduates. These efforts have not yet stood the test of long usage, but they do appear promising.

As accreditation systems have matured, they have taken on commonalities that extend to the accreditation of most institutions, permitting Scriven (1984) to describe the distinctive features of contemporary accreditation as including (1) published standards; (2) a self-study by the institution; (3) a team of external assessors; (4) a site visit; (5) a site-team report on the institution, usually including recommendations; (6) a review of the report by some distinguished panel; and (7) a final report and accreditation decision by the accrediting body. Although not every accrediting system follows this prescription completely,[2] this is an excellent description of most accreditation systems today.

Although viewed by some as not truly an evaluative system, others see accreditation as very much evaluative. Regardless of which view one holds, most would agree that accreditation has played an important role in institutional change. It is true that accrediting agencies have little real power over agencies who fail to take their recommendations seriously, as Floden (1983) states:

> If accreditors instruct an institution to make particular changes, three options are open. First, officials may amass the necessary funds and make the changes. Second, they may decide the changes cannot be made and close their doors. Third, they may decide not to worry about what the accreditors say and make no changes. If an institution exercises either of the first two options, the aims of accreditation have been realized. When the third option is taken, the process of accreditation has failed to achieve its main purpose. (p. 268)

Yet, in our experience, the third option is only infrequently exercised. Fully accredited status is, if nothing more, a symbol of achievement highly valued by most institutions. Although there may be much room for improvement in the accreditation process, it appears to be a formal review process that will be with us for a long time and, if the upsurge of thoughtful analyses of accreditation

---

[2] For example, the American Psychological Association omits any self-study by professional psychology programs under its accreditation review.

issues, problems, and potential is any indication, there is reason to be optimistic that its impact can be positive.

Other Formal Review Systems. Despite the wide reach of accreditation, there are those who feel it is an incestuous system that often fails to police itself adequately. As House (1980) has stated:

> At one time it was sufficient for an institution to be accredited by the proper agency for the public to be assured of its quality—but no longer. Parents are not always convinced that the school program is of high quality when it is accredited by the North Central Association. In addition, political control of accrediting activities is shifting to state governments. (p. 238)

Because of such concerns over accreditation's credibility, coupled with the pervasive feeling that decisions "closer to home" are preferable, many state boards or departments are conducting their own reviews of institutions. Although these typically supplement rather than supplant reviews by private accrediting bodies and generally use similar review strategies, they seem of greater consequence to institutions and programs reviewed because negative reviews result not only in loss of status but also possible loss of funding or even termination.

Consider, for example, the Utah State Board of Regents' system for reviewing academic departments within the state's tax-supported universities and colleges.[3] The process and the structure for conducting these reviews have been formalized, general standards exist, a review schedule (every seven years) has been established, teams of experts in the academic discipline (also some "outsiders" to avoid bias and promote breadth of perspective) are used, and the results can influence both the future funding for the department and even its continued existence (though that is a rare outcome, indeed).

Informal Professional Review Systems

Many professional review systems have a structure and a set of procedural guidelines and use multiple reviewers. Yet some lack the formal review system's published standards or specified review schedule. For example, in the United States, state departments of education were required by federal law, over a period of two decades, to establish a system to evaluate all programs and projects funded under a specific funding authorization designed to increase innovation in schools. Compliance varied widely, but those states that conscientiously complied established an evaluation system in which at least a sample of districts receiving such funds were reviewed annually by site-visit teams and the results

---

[3] More information on the Utah review system can be obtained by writing to the Office of the Commissioner of Higher Education, Utah State Board of Regents, Utah System of Higher Education, 3 Triad Center, Suite 550, 355 West North Temple, Salt Lake City, UT 84180-1205.

used to determine future funding levels and program continuation. However, few states had anything resembling published standards, and most site-visit teams were left to develop their own evaluation procedures without the benefit of any guidelines. Clearly, these were informal review systems.

Other examples of informal expertise-oriented review systems include reviews of professors for determining rank advancement or tenure status. Such reviews generally follow loosely institutionalized structures and procedures, include input from several professional peers,[4] and certainly can influence the status of the individual professor. Generally review schedules are set (for instance, some university policies require annual reviews of individuals in any rank lower than professor for five years or more), but sometimes the timing is dependent on the applicant's petitioning for review whenever he feels prepared. Reviewers rarely use prespecified, published standards or criteria. Such standards are developed by each rank and promotion committee (a group of expert peers) within broad guidelines specified by the university and department and possibly by an existing statement of the role the individual is expected to play in contributing to those goals.

A graduate student's supervisory committee, composed of experts in the student's chosen field, is an example of an informal system for conducting expert-oriented evaluation. Structures exist for regulating such professional reviews of competence, but the committee members determine the standards for judging each student's preparation and competence. Few would question whether results of this review system affect the status and welfare of graduate students.

Some may consider the systems for obtaining peer reviews of manuscripts submitted to professional periodicals to be examples of informal professional review systems. Perhaps. Many journals do use multiple reviewers, chosen for their expertise in the content of the manuscript and, sometimes, empaneled to provide continuity to the review board. In our experience, however, the review structure and standards of most professional journals shift with each appointment of a new editor, and reviews occur whenever manuscripts are submitted rather than on any regular schedule. In some ways, journal reviews may be a better example of the ad hoc professional review process discussed below.

Ad Hoc Panel Reviews

Unlike the ongoing formal and informal review systems discussed above, many professional reviews by expert panels occur only at irregular intervals, when circumstances demand. Generally, these reviews are related to no institutionalized structure for evaluation and use no predetermined standards. Such professional reviews are usually "one-shot" evaluations prompted by a particular, time-bound

---

[4] In peer evaluation, a "peer" might be thought of as anyone who is an expert in the substantive and procedural areas in which the individual or group's competence or contribution is being judged—an "expert" being anyone with recognized expertise in such substance or procedures.

need for evaluative information. Of course, a particular agency may, over time, commission many **ad hoc panel reviews** to perform similar functions without their collectively being viewed as an institutionalized review system.

Funding Agency Review Panels. Many funding agencies use peer-review panels to review competitive proposals. Reviewers read and comment on each proposal and meet as a group to discuss and resolve any differences in their various perceptions.[5] Worthen and White (1987) provided a set of proposal review guidelines and instruments for use by external review panels, including (1) preparing for the proposal review (selecting reviewers, structuring review panels, preparing and training reviewers in the use of review instruments); (2) conducting the proposal review (individual evaluation procedures, total panel evaluation procedures, methods for eliminating bias); and (3) presenting results of proposal reviews (summarizing review results). Justiz and Moorman (1985) and Shulman (1985) have also discussed particular proposal review procedures that depend upon the professional judgment of panels of experts. But expert professionals are not the only ones who can be used as evaluators. Many community nonprofit agencies review proposals for United Way and other funding agencies, using committees of volunteers as reviewers. While these reviews are done conscientiously, new, unstated considerations and criteria are often injected into the funding decisions, and the committees are often criticized as not being qualified to judge the funding proposal. If community volunteers are viewed as "experts in the needs of the community," and if they are assisted by subject-matter consultants in some way, then the evaluation process may come closer to the expertise-oriented approach as defined in this chapter.

Blue-Ribbon Panels. A prestigious "blue-ribbon panel," such as the National Commission on Excellence in Education, which was discussed in Chapter 1, is an example of an ad hoc review panel. Members of such panels are appointed because of their experience and expertise in the field being studied. Such panels are typically charged with reviewing a particular situation, documenting their observations, and making recommendations for action. Given the visibility of such panels, the acknowledged expertise of panel members is important if the panel's findings are to be credible. On more local scales, where ad hoc review panels are frequently used as an evaluative strategy on almost all types of educational endeavor, expertise of panel members is no less an issue, even though the reviewers may be of local or regional repute rather than national renown. Although recommendations of ad hoc panels of experts may have major impact, they also may be ignored, for there is often no formalized body charged with the mandate of following up on their advice.

---

[5] "Field readers" who respond individually from afar may collectively make up a panel if they or their opinions are later brought together to arrive at a group judgment concerning that which is evaluated.

Ad Hoc Individual Reviews

Another form of expertise-oriented evaluation resides in the ubiquitous individual professional review of any entity by any individual selected for his expertise to judge its value. Employment of a consultant to perform an individual review of some educational, social or commercial program or activity is commonplace. Such expert review is a particularly important process for evaluating textbooks, corporate training programs, media products, job placement tests, program plans, and the like. Such materials need not be reviewed on site but can be sent to the expert. A good example is the review of commercially available tests used by the Buros Institute of Mental Measurements (see Conoley & Impara, 1995).

Educational Connoisseurship and Criticism

The roles of the theater critic, art critic, and literary critic are well-known and, in the eyes of many, useful roles. Critics are not without their faults (as we shall discuss later), but they are good examples of direct and efficient application of expertise to that which is judged. Indeed, few evaluative approaches are likely to produce such parsimonious and pithy portrayals as that of one Broadway critic who evaluated a new play with a single-line summary: "The only thing wrong with this play is that it was performed with the curtain up!"

Although not championing one-line indictments, Eisner (1991) does propose that experienced experts, like critics of the arts, bring their expertise to bear in evaluating the quality of programs in their areas of expertise. Eisner does not propose a scientific paradigm but rather an artistic one, which he sees as an important qualitative, humanistic, "nonscientific" supplement to more traditional inquiry methods.[6]

Eisner (1975, 1991) has written that this approach requires *connoisseurship* and *criticism*. **Connoisseurship** is the art of appreciation—not necessarily a liking or preference for that which is observed but rather an awareness of its qualities and the relationships between them. The connoisseur, in Eisner's view, is aware of the complexities in real-world settings and possesses refined perceptual capabilities that makes the appreciation of such complexity possible. The connoisseur's perceptual acuity results largely from a knowledge of what to look for (advance organizers, or critical guideposts), gained through a backlog of previous relevant experience.

The analogy of wine tasting is used by Eisner (1975) to show how one must have a great deal of experience[7] to be able to distinguish what is significant about

---

[6] This is an important point lost on some who employ Eisner's notions as the *sole* evaluation of the evaluation object, overlooking the fact that Eisner never proposed his approach as sufficient in and of itself.

[7] We add that Eisner doubtlessly had *quality* of experience in mind as much or more than *quantity*. The lush and the connoisseur of wine are worlds apart.

a wine, using a set of techniques to discern qualities such as body, color, bite, bouquet, flavor, aftertaste, and the like to judge its overall quality. The connoisseur's refined palate and "gustatory memory" of other wines tasted is what enables him to distinguish subtle qualities lost on an ordinary drinker of wine and to render judgments rather than mere preferences. Connoisseurship does not, however, require a public description or judgment of that which is perceived, for the latter moves one into the area of criticism.

"Criticism is the art of disclosing the qualities of events or objects that connoisseurship perceives" (Eisner, 1979a, p. 197), as when the wine connoisseur either returns the wine or leans back with satisfaction to declare it of acceptable, or better, quality. Evaluators are cast as critics whose connoisseurship enables them to give a public rendering of the quality and significance of that which is evaluated. **Criticism** is not a negative appraisal, as Eisner presents it, but rather an educational process intended to enable individuals to recognize qualities and characteristics that might otherwise have been unnoticed and unappreciated. Criticism, to be complete, requires description, interpretation, and evaluation of that which is observed. "Critics are people who talk in special ways about what they encounter. In educational settings criticism is the public side of connoisseurship" (Eisner, 1975, p. 13). Program evaluation, then, becomes program criticism. The evaluator is the "instrument," and the data collecting, analyzing, and judging are largely hidden within the evaluator's mind, analogous to the evaluative processes of art criticism or wine tasting. As a consequence, the expertise—training, experience, and credentials—of the evaluator is crucial, for the validity of the evaluation depends on his perception. Yet different judgments from different critics are tolerable, and even desirable, for the purpose of criticism is to expand perceptions, not to consolidate all judgments into a single definitive statement.

Kelly (1978) has also likened evaluation to criticism by using literary criticism as his analogy. Although different in some features from Eisner's approach, it is similar enough to be considered another example of the expertise-oriented evaluation approach.

HOW THE EXPERTISE-ORIENTED EVALUATION APPROACH HAS BEEN USED

As we noted earlier, this evaluation approach has been broadly used by both national and regional accreditation agencies. Two rather different types of accreditation exist. One is *institutional accreditation,* where the entire institution is accredited, including all of its more specific entities and activities, however complex. In essence, such institutional endorsement means the accrediting body has concluded that the educational institution, in general, meets acceptable standards of quality. The second type is *specialized or program accreditation,* which deals with various subunits in an institution, such as particular academic or professional training programs.[8] As Kirkwood (1982) noted, "institutional accreditation is not equivalent to the specialized accreditation of each of the several programs in an institution" (p. 9). Rather, specialized accrediting processes are usually more specific, rigorous, and prescriptive than are those used in institutional accreditation. Most specialized accreditation bodies are national in scope and frequently are the major multipurpose professional associations (e.g., the American Psychological Association or the American Medical Association), whereas institutional accreditation is more often regional and conducted by agencies that exist solely or primarily for that purpose (e.g., in the United States, the North Central Association or the New England Association).

A good example of how accreditation by private professional agencies and government-sponsored professional reviews are combined comes from Bernhardt's (1984) description of the evaluation processes of state, regional, and national education agencies, which collectively oversee teacher education programs in California.

> Colleges and Universities in California must be accredited or approved by at least three agencies to offer approved programs of teacher education. Private institutions must first have the approval of the State Department of Education's Office of Private Postsecondary Education (OPPE) to offer *degree* programs. Public institutions must be authorized by their respective California State University and University of California systems. Second, institutions must be accredited by the Western Association of Schools and Colleges (WASC). Then, institutions must submit a document that states that the program is in compliance with all CTC guidelines in order to gain the approval of the Commission on Teacher Credentialing (CTC).
>
> In addition to OPPE, WASC, and CTC accreditation, educational institutions often choose to be accredited by the National Council for Accreditation of Teacher Education (NCATE). (p. 1)

Yes, formal professional review systems are alive and well, at least in California.

Other uses of expertise-oriented evaluation are discussed by House (1980), who notes the upsurge of university internal-review systems of colleges, departments, and programs. He notes that such professional reviews are not only useful in making internal decisions and reallocating funds in periods of financial austerity but also may deflect suggestions that such programs should be reviewed by higher-education boards.

Uses (and abuses) of peer review by governmental agencies have been discussed by scholars in many disciplines (see Anderson, 1983). Some funding agencies have also used panels of prestigious educators to evaluate the agencies to which research and development awards had been made. For example, the

---

[8] Obviously, in single-purpose institutions, such as a dental school with no other programs, this distinction is meaningless.

U.S. Department of Education has commissioned review teams to visit and evaluate each member within its federally funded network of regional laboratories and university-based research and development centers, even though the evaluation focused on only some important outcomes.

As for uses of Eisner's educational criticism approach, we are familiar with few applications beyond those studies conducted by his students (Alexander, 1977; McCutcheon, 1978; Vallance, 1978).

STRENGTHS AND LIMITATIONS OF THE EXPERTISE-ORIENTED EVALUATION APPROACH

Collectively, expertise-oriented approaches to evaluation have emphasized the central role of expert judgment and human wisdom in the evaluative process and have focused attention on such important issues as whose standards (and what degree of publicness) should be used in rendering judgments about programs. Conversely, critics of this approach suggest that it often permits evaluators to make judgments that reflect little more than personal biases. Others have noted that the *presumed* expertise of the reviewers is a potential weakness.

Beyond these general observations, the various types of expertise-oriented evaluation approach have their own unique strengths and weaknesses. Formal review systems such as accreditation have several perceived advantages. Kirkwood (1982) lists accreditation's achievements

> (1) in fostering excellence in education through development of criteria and guidelines for assessing institutional effectiveness; (2) in encouraging institutional improvement through continual self-study and evaluation; (3) in assuring the academic community, the general public, the professions, and other agencies that an institution or program has clearly defined and appropriate educational objectives, has established conditions to facilitate their achievement, appears in fact to be achieving them substantially, and is so organized, staffed, and supported that it can be expected to continue doing so; (4) in providing counsel and assistance to established and developing institutions; and (5) in protecting institutions from encroachments that might jeopardize their educational effectiveness or academic freedom. (p. 12)

The thoroughness of accreditation agencies has prevented the sort of oversimplification that can reduce complex educational phenomena to unidimensional studies. Other desirable features claimed for accreditation include the external perspective provided by the use of outside reviewers and relatively modest cost.

Of all these advantages, perhaps the most underrated is the self-study phase of most accreditation processes. Although it is sometimes misused as a public relations ploy, self-study offers potentially great payoffs, frequently yielding far more important discoveries and benefits than does the later accreditation site visit. Together, internal self-study and external review provide some of the advantages of an evaluative system that includes both formative and summative evaluation.

Formalized review systems also have nontrivial drawbacks. We have already commented on public concerns over credibility and increasing public cynicism that professionals may not police their own operations very vigorously. Scriven (1984) has called accreditation "an excellent example of what one might with only slight cynicism call a pseudo-evaluative process, set up to give the appearance of self-regulation without having to suffer the inconvenience" (p. 73). The steady proliferation of specialized accrediting agencies suggests that there may indeed be truth to the suspicion that such processes are protectionist, placing professional self-interest before the interests of the institutions or publics they serve. Further, proliferation of review bodies, whether for reasons of professional self-interest or governmental distrust of private accreditation processes, can place unbearable financial burdens on institutions. Bernhardt (1984) suggests that the California system, which was described earlier, is too expensive to operate under current budgets, that it is not efficient, and that it is effective for determining only institutional compliance, not educational quality. Perhaps one accreditation visit may be relatively cost-efficient, as noted above, but multiple reviews can boost costs to unacceptable levels.[9] Scriven (1984) has cited several problems with accreditation: (1) no suggested weightings of a "mishmash" of standards ranging from trivial to important, (2) fixation on goals that may exclude searching for side effects, (3) managerial bias that influences the composition of review teams, and (4) processes that preclude input from the institution's most severe critics.

Informal peer-review systems and ad hoc professional reviews reflect many of the advantages and disadvantages discussed above for accreditation. In addition, they possess unique strengths and limitations. Some pundits have suggested that such expert reviews are usually little more than a few folks' entering the program site without much information, strolling through the facilities with hands in pockets, and leaving the site with precious little more information but with firm conclusions based on their own preconceived biases. Such views are accurate only for *misuses* of expert-oriented evaluations. Worthen and White (1987) have shown, for example, how on-site ad hoc panel reviews can be designed to yield the advantages of cross-validation by multiple observers and interviewers while still maximizing the time of individual team members to collect and summarize a substantial body of evaluative information in a short time span. Such ad hoc review panels can also be selected to blend expertise

---

[9] One of the present authors resides in an academic department that received four external professional reviews by national professional associations and state regulatory bodies in one two-year period. The costs borne by the department for these reviews so depleted the budget that supplies (e.g., fax paper) were exhausted midway through each academic year.

in evaluation techniques with knowledge of the program and to avoid the naive errors that occur when there is no professional evaluator on the review team (Scriven, 1984).

Disadvantages of expert-oriented peer reviews include the public suspicion that review by one's peers is inherently conservative, potentially incestuous, and subject to possible conflict of interest. If evaluators are drawn from the ranks of the discipline or profession to be evaluated, there are decided risks. Socialization within any group tends to blunt the important characteristic of detachment. Assumptions and practices that would be questioned by an outsider may be taken for granted. These and other disadvantages led us (Worthen & Sanders, 1984) to point to serious problems that can occur if a program is evaluated only by those with expertise in program content.

House (1980) has noted that confidentiality can be another problem because professionals are often reluctant to expose their views boldly in the necessary public report. This normally results, he says, in "two reports, one an inside confidential report revealing warts and blemishes, the 'real' report, and a public report which has been edited somewhat. This dual reporting seems to be necessary for professional cooperation, but of course it makes the public distrustful" (pp. 240–241).

Obviously, the question of interjudge and interpanel reliability is relevant when using expert-oriented evaluation because so much depends on the professionalism and perception of the individual expert, whether working alone or as a team member. The question of whether a different expert or panel would have made the same judgments and recommendations is a troublesome one for advocates of this approach, for by its very definition, replicability is not a feature of expertise-oriented studies. Moreover, the easy penetration of extraneous bias into expert judgments is a pervasive concern.

Finally, the connoisseurship-criticism approach to evaluation shares, generally, the strengths and limitations of the other expertise-oriented evaluation approaches summarized above, in addition to possessing unique strengths and weaknesses. Perhaps its greatest strength lies in translating educated observations into statements about educational quality. Prior training, experience, and "refined perceptual capabilities" play a crucial role in every expertise-oriented approach to evaluation, but they are perhaps best explicated in Eisner's connoisseurship-criticism approach. One cannot study his proposals and still lampoon expertise-oriented evaluation as a mere "hands-in-pocket" stroll through the program site.

The connoisseurship-criticism approach also has its critics. House (1980) has cautioned that the analogy of art criticism is not applicable to at least one aspect of evaluation:

> It is not unusual for an art critic to advance controversial views—the reader can choose to ignore them. In fact, the reader can choose to read only critics with whom she agrees. A public evaluation of a program cannot be so easily dismissed, however. Some justification—whether of the critic, the critic's principles, or the criticism—is necessary. The

demands for fairness and justice are more rigorous in the evaluation of public programs. (p. 237)

R. Smith (1984) is perhaps the harshest critic of the "educational criticism" approach to evaluation, fearing that "educational criticism will be esteemed more for its quality as literature and as a record of personal response than for its correct estimates of educational value" (p. 1). He continues by attacking Eisner's conception of criticism on philosophical and methodological grounds, and two of Smith's points are germane here. First, he quarrels with Eisner's contention that connoisseurs require no special preparation for their role by noting that anyone wishing to be a connoisseur-critic must possess the skills of literary criticism, knowledge of the theories of the social sciences, and knowledge of the history and philosophy of the programs they are evaluating, as well as sensitivity and perceptiveness—no small feat for the person whose primary training may be, for example, as a social worker. How many could really qualify as connoisseurs is an important question. Second, Smith questions whether the same methodology is useful for judging the wide array of objects Eisner includes as potential objects of criticism. "Do the same nondiscursive techniques serve the criticism of classroom life, textbooks, and school furniture?" (p. 14). Probably not.

APPLICATION EXERCISES

1. The Metropolitan Community Action Organization of Los Angeles received federal funds to establish a one-year education program for adults who have been unable to find employment for 18 consecutive months. A program was implemented that had two major components: (1) the teaching of basic skills, such as reading, mathematics, and English as a foreign language, and (2) the teaching of specific vocational skills, such as typing, shorthand, keypunching, and drafting. The program was designed by adult education specialists from a local university and representatives of the employment training task forces of local unions.

   Adults were tested as they entered the program by using standardized test batteries in reading and mathematics. Entrants scoring below a grade equivalent of 8.0 were assigned to appropriate levels of reading and/or mathematics instruction. Individual instruction was also provided for students who were not comfortable using the English language. Vocational offerings varied and depended on the unions' assessment of potential job openings in the Los Angeles area. Many of the vocational classes were held on the premises of places of business or industry. A few were conducted in the facility provided for the adult education program.

   Using what you have learned about expertise-oriented evaluation approaches, indicate how these approaches might be used in the evaluation of this program.

   What purposes could they serve? What could they contribute that other approaches might neglect or not address well? What process and criteria would you use to select your experts and to evaluate their performance?

2. What outside experts review your program or organization?

   a. If you work in an organization that is accredited, review the standards used for accreditation. Do you feel the standards get at the real quality issues of the program or organization? What other standards might you add? Does the accreditation tell the organization's staff something they didn't already know? How are the accreditation findings used?

   b. What other outsiders review your program or organization? How expert are they in your program or organization's context, process, and outcomes? What are the characteristics of the most helpful and least helpful reviewers?

SUGGESTED READINGS

Eisner, E. W. (1991a). Taking a second look: Educational connoisseurship revisited. In M. W. McLaughlin & D. C. Phillips (Eds.), *Evaluation and education: At quarter century.* Ninetieth Yearbook of the National Society for the Study of Education, Part II. Chicago: University of Chicago Press.

Eisner, E. W. (1991b). *The enlightened eye: Qualitative inquiry and the enhancement of educational practice.* New York: Macmillan.

Floden, R. E. (1983). Flexner, accreditation, and evaluation. In G. F. Madaus, M. Scriven, and D. L. Stufflebeam (Eds.), *Evaluation models: Viewpoints on educational and human services.* Boston: Kluwer-Nijhoff.

Kells, H. R., & Robertson, M. P. (1980). Post-secondary accreditation: A current bibliography. *North Central Association Quarterly, 54,* 411–426.

Kirkwood, R. (1982). Accreditation. In H. E. Mitzel (Ed.), *Encyclopedia of educational research* (Vol. 1, 5th ed.), pp. 9–12. New York: Free Press.

National Study of School Evaluation. (1978). *Evaluative criteria.* Arlington, VA: Author.

chapter 9

Adversary-Oriented Evaluation Approaches

ORIENTING QUESTIONS

1. When and why would one want to use an adversary-oriented approach to evaluation?
2. Is the adversary-oriented approach limited to courtroom formats? What variations of this approach might be used for program evaluation? Can you give an example of a use for each variation?
3. Do adversary-oriented evaluations always have two opposing views?
4. What are the major strengths and limitations of adversary-oriented evaluation approaches?

Most approaches to program evaluation rest in part on the assumption that the evaluator should be impartial toward that which she evaluates. Evaluators who hold this view exert considerable effort trying to prevent their personal biases from influencing their findings and judgments.

Yet the truly insightful evaluator is aware that the potential for evaluator bias to influence the outcomes of the study can never be excluded, that even the choice of methods to control bias may be biased. Why did the evaluator choose to collect these particular data as opposed to other data that might have been collected? Why were these particular instruments used instead of others that were available? Why were some individuals interviewed but not others? Each such choice permits personal preferences, prejudices, or preconceptions to slip unnoticed (even by the evaluator) into the evaluation in ways that might significantly alter its outcomes. The evaluator cannot divorce herself from the evaluation.

When one considers other aspects of the evaluator's role, such as interpreting information, framing conclusions, and determining value, the possibility that personal values may influence the results is more obvious. Might the accreditation team's evaluation of the nonsexist counseling course have been more favorable if the team had not been all male? Would the board have been quicker to believe the glowing evaluation of the agency director's favorite drug rehabilitation program if it had not recently reviewed the evaluator's application for the associate director's job? Who will know that the harsh evaluation of a computer-assisted job training program stemmed more from the evaluator's aversion to computers than from any of the program's attributes? In short, the notion that any evaluator can be a paragon of impartiality is naive. The best that any evaluation approach can hope for is to control bias sufficiently so that it does not significantly distort or alter results.

Where most evaluation approaches attempt to reduce bias, the *adversary-oriented approach* aspires to balance it, attempting to assure fairness by incorporating both positive and negative views into the evaluation itself. We would consider an evaluation adversary-oriented if both sides of issues or questions were argued, one side by advocates (those in favor) and the other by adversaries (those opposed). Various types of data (ranging from test scores to human testimony) might be selected and used by either side as evidence to support its arguments. Generally some type of hearing is held so that the opposing views can be presented and debated before whoever serves as "judge" or "jury" to decide on the relative merits of the opposing cases. There is no presumption that the proponents and opponents of a program being evaluated are unbiased in appraising it. On the contrary, we expect their biases to surface as they mount their respective defenses of, or attacks on, the program. And by encouraging biases on both sides to surface, we help ensure a balanced method of gathering information regarding the program.

Adversary-oriented evaluation, then, is a rubric encompassing a collection of divergent evaluation practices that might loosely be referred to as *adversarial* in nature. In its broad sense, the term refers to all evaluations in which there is planned opposition in the points of view of different evaluators or evaluation teams—a *planned* effort to generate *opposing* points of view *within* the overall evaluation.[1] One evaluator (or team) serves as the program's advocate, presenting the most positive view of the program possible from the data, while another evaluator (or team) plays an adversarial role, highlighting any existing deficiencies in the program. Incorporation of these opposing views within a single evaluation

---

[1] As will be shown later, we also consider as adversary-oriented those evaluations where more than two opposing views exist. We use the term to include all cases where opposing advocates or positions, no matter how many, are represented in an evaluation, just so those multiple views are clearly in opposition to one another and the evaluation is structured and conducted to highlight the opposition among the views. For now, however, we prefer to use the simpler, two-view "pro and con" case to make our points more clearly.

reflects a conscious effort to assure fairness and balance and illuminate both strengths and weaknesses of the program. As Levine (1982) has put it,

> In essence, the adversarial model operates with the assumption that truth emerges from a hard, but fair fight, in which opposing sides, after agreeing upon the issues in contention, present evidence in support of each side. The fight is refereed by a neutral figure, and all the relevant evidence is weighed by a neutral person or body to arrive at a fair result. (p. 270)

Several types of adversarial proceedings have been invoked as models for adversary evaluations, including judicial proceedings, congressional and other hearings, and structured debates, each of which we shall consider in this chapter.

DEVELOPERS OF ADVERSARY-ORIENTED EVALUATION APPROACHES AND THEIR CONTRIBUTIONS

Adversary-oriented evaluation approaches can subsume, draw from, and be incorporated within other evaluation approaches. For example, there is considerable dependence on expertise-oriented evaluation (discussed in Chapter 8) in many adversary proceedings (e.g., the use of expert witnesses in trials and congressional hearings). Adversary-oriented evaluation also shares with the evaluation approaches discussed in Chapter 10 dependence on multiple perspectives about what is evaluated. (Indeed, one such approach, transactional evaluation, proposes the use of proponents and opponents of planned changes on evaluation teams charged to study innovations.) We distinguish adversary evaluation, however, by its use of planned, structured opposition as the primary core of the evaluation and by its derivation from metaphors drawn from more venerable adversarial paradigms.

Origins of Adversary-Oriented Evaluation

Rice (1915) proposed an evaluation method intended to eliminate graft and increase governmental efficiency by presenting facts about waste and corruption to a mock "judge and jury." Rice's approach is the first proposed use of "adversary evaluation" with which we are familiar. The idea was not further developed, however, for 50 years. Guba (1965) suggested that educational evaluation might use aspects of the legal paradigm. If trials and hearings were useful in judging truth of claims concerning patents and products, and if human testimony were judged acceptable for determining life or death, as in the judicial system, then might not legal proceedings be a useful metaphor for program evaluation? Might there be merit in evaluation "trials," in taking and cross-examining human testimony, and in using the concept of advocacy to ensure that evaluation fairly examined both sides of issues?

At first, Guba's ideas seemed to fall on deaf ears, for that was the era when evaluators were about the business of refining the application of social science research methods (e.g., experimental design) to program evaluation, as well as developing promising new approaches drawn from other relevant paradigms (management-oriented approaches based on decision theory and systems analysis). But gradually a few colleagues began to test the utility of Guba's suggestions.

The first self-conscious effort to follow a particular adversary paradigm was made in 1970 by Owens. Designed to test the usefulness of a modified judicial model, the evaluation focused on a hypothetical school curriculum and included pretrial conferences, cases presented by the "defense" and "prosecution," a hearings officer, a "jury" panel of educators, charges and rebuttals, direct questioning and redirected questions, and summaries by the prosecution and defense. The reports (Owens, 1971, 1973) were intriguing to the community of evaluators and led to further conceptual and empirical work on the adversary approach (e.g., Kourilsky, 1973; Wolf, 1975; Levine, 1974; Stake & Gjerde, 1974; Kourilsky & Baker, 1976; Worthen & Owens, 1978; Levine & Rosenberg, 1979; House, Thurston, & Hand, 1984). Several of these studies involved what might best be termed *advocate-adversary evaluation,* where an advocate evaluator presents the most favorable review possible and an adversary evaluator presents the most critical and damaging case that might be made, but there are no adversarial interactions or rebuttals surrounding the two stated positions.[2]

As these efforts to develop the adversary approach continued, several evaluations occurred that could be judged truly adversarial in nature (e.g., Hiscox & Owens, 1975; Wolf, 1975, 1979; Stenzel, 1976; Nafziger, Worthen, & Benson, 1977; Levine et al., 1978; Braithwaite & Thompson, 1981; Madaus, 1981; Popham, 1981; Van Mondfrans, 1993). These studies have used widely divergent styles, and reactions to them have been mixed (as will be discussed later).

In the balance of this chapter we shall consider three general approaches to adversary evaluation: (1) adaptations of the legal paradigm and other "two-view" adversary hearings, (2) adaptations of quasi-legal and other adversary hearings where more than two opposing views are considered, and (3) use of debate and other forensic structures in adversary evaluations.

---

[2] Many writers today use the term *advocate-adversary evaluation* to refer to what we call adversary-oriented evaluation in this chapter. Although the advocate-adversary label is not incorrect, because generally one evaluator serves as an advocate and the other an adversary, we prefer to reserve that term to describe cases where opposite views are given but the evaluation is not structured to take full advantage of one of the paradigms underlying truly adversarial evaluation. Also, we prefer the single term *adversary* not only to refer to the roles of the program's advocate and adversary as adversaries to one another's views but also to encompass situations where multiple positions exist, varying in their advocacy or opposition to the program but clearly at odds with one another.

✳The Judicial Evaluation Model and Other "Pro and Con" Adversary Hearings

The "fight theory" underlies most models of litigation for resolving differences among opposing parties. According to Auerbach, Garrison, Hurst, and Mermin (1961), this theory holds that the facts in a case can best be determined if each side tries as hard as possible, in a keenly partisan spirit, to provide the court with evidence favorable to that side. Although not disagreeing with the advantages of this posture, Frank (1949) has cautioned that disadvantages occur when "the partisanship of the opposing lawyers blocks the uncovering of vital evidence or leads to a presentation of vital testimony in a way that distorts it" (p. 81). Efforts to adapt aspects of the legal paradigm for use in program evaluation have attempted to capitalize on the potentials cited by Auerbach and his colleagues while avoiding the pitfall of which Frank warns.

Owens (1973) listed several characteristics of the adversary proceeding that he believed made it more appropriate for program evaluations than more familiar evaluation models:

1. The rules established for handling the adversary proceedings are quite flexible.
2. Complex rules of evidence are replaced by a free evaluation of evidence based solely upon whether the evidence is considered by the hearings officer to be relevant.
3. Both parties can be required before the trial to inform the hearings officer of all relevant facts, means of proof, and names of witnesses.
4. A copy of the charges is furnished to the hearings officer and defendant before the trial and the defendant has the option of admitting in advance to certain charges and challenging others.
5. Witnesses are allowed to testify more freely and to be cross-examined.
6. Experts are often called upon to testify even before the trial.
7. Pretrial conferences of the hearings officer with both parties tend to make the trial less a battle of wits and more of a search for relevant facts.
8. In addition to the two parties involved, other interested groups may be permitted to participate. (pp. 296–297)

Owens also indicated that adversary proceedings should be used not to replace existing designs for data collection and analysis but rather to provide an alternative way of interpreting, synthesizing, and reporting evidence.

The work of Wolf (1975) has been particularly thoughtful in relation to how evaluators might better define evaluation issues, what role personal testimony might play in evaluation, procedures for direct questioning and cross-examination, and rules of admissibility of evidence. Borrowing concepts from both jury trials and administrative hearings, Wolf proposed the *judicial evaluation model,* which included a statement of charges, opposing counselors, witnesses, a judge or hearings officer, and a jury panel. Four stages are proposed:

1. *Issue generation:* identification and development of possible issues to be addressed in the hearing
2. *Issue selection:* elimination of issues not at dispute and selection and further development of those issues to be argued in the hearing
3. *Preparation of arguments:* collection of evidence, synthesis of prior evaluation data to develop arguments for the two opposing cases to be presented
4. *The hearing:* including prehearing discovery sessions to review cases and agree on hearing procedures, and the actual hearing's presentation of cases, evaluation of evidence and arguments, and panel decision.

Wolf (1975, 1979) made clear that his intention was merely to use the law as a metaphor for program evaluation, not to replicate legal procedures. He was also prompted by critiques of problems in applying the legal paradigm to program evaluation (e.g., Popham & Carlson, 1977; Worthen & Rogers, 1980) to argue that his model was not an adversarial debate or adversary evaluation, as such: "the metaphors of law are just that—metaphors. . . . Once the concepts are taken too literally, the object of judicial evaluation then becomes *winning*. This is precisely *not* what the JEM [judicial evaluation model] strives for" (Wolf, 1979, p. 22).[3]

Levine and Rosenberg (1979) have provided an insightful examination of numerous issues in adapting legal analogs for use in evaluation (e.g., the burden of proof and use of presumptive evidence). They point out that although adversary models such as jury trials, administrative hearings, appellate proceedings, and arbitration hearings all have unique ways of using evidence and argument, they also have important similarities, including (1) an existing controversy between two or more parties, (2) formal case presentation by advocates for each position, (3) facts heard and a decision rendered by an impartial arbiter, and (4) a decision based solely upon arguments heard and evidence presented during the proceeding.

Adversary Hearings with More Than Two Opposing Views

Many committee hearings are not adversarial. Some of the review panels discussed in Chapter 8 (such as blue-ribbon panels) may hold public hearings to collect information pertinent to their charge. Appointed commissions charged with the resolution of controversial issues (e.g., the National Commission on Excellence in Education described in Chapter 1) frequently hold hearings to

---

[3] We agree that all adversary models should be concerned with judicious evaluation, but we wonder whether it is realistic to expect that winning will not continue to be such a part of human nature as to suggest this hope may be overly optimistic, as we shall discuss later.

obtain evidence and opinions relevant to their mission. House (1980) has cited as one such example the frequent use in England of commissions and councils headed by prominent citizens to provide guidance to government policy makers. Hearings held by most committees and commissions are decidedly not adversarial in structure, however, for no efforts are made to articulate or contrast opposing points of view.

Several other types of committee hearings are structured to identify and explore all the points of view represented in a particular context. Although not "adversarial" in the strict sense of the word, because, as Smith (1985) has noted, they explore a variety of positions, not just pro and con, we prefer to include them here because (1) they reflect multiple viewpoints, which often are in conflict with one another, thus perhaps qualifying as "multiadversarial" in nature; and (2) they frequently use hearing processes, questioning, cross-examination, interaction concerning alternative viewpoints, and summary statements of the various positions, all procedures typical of the two-sided "pro and con" adversary hearing. St. John (n.d.), in referring to such hearings as the "committee approach" to evaluation, listed as key characteristics the following:

- All of those with a stake in the evaluation—decision-makers, evaluators, program personnel, clients, and other interested persons—are brought together in the same place at the same time for a careful review of the issues at hand.
- A public hearing with testimony, questioning, cross-examination, and summary statements *produces a full exposition of evidence and illuminates differing points of view about that evidence.*
- The committee hearing method consists of public, verbal, face-to-face interactions, and therefore generates a high degree of personal involvement. Consequently, committee hearings are likely to have a strong impact on those involved, as well as on those who observe them.
- Because interaction between different points of view takes place, a process of communication and education occurs, and the evaluation makes its impact as it is happening. (p. 2; italics ours)

St. John also suggested that committee hearings "may be useful . . . when the impact of the evaluation and its follow-through depends on the *consensus of multiple perspectives,* and such consensus is unlikely without significant interaction" (p. 3, italics ours). Had he said "presentation of multiple perspectives," we would agree fully, for there are obviously instances where consensus among disparate views is not attained, yet issues are resolved through hearing and weighing the evidence supporting those alternative viewpoints en route to a decision that may or may not be consensual. We see the focus of such "adversary" committee hearings as the presentation and examination of multiple perspectives that illuminate all legitimate views prior to final resolution of the issues.

The most frequently proposed model for this type of adversary evaluation is the congressional or legislative investigative hearing (Stenzel, 1982; Levine et al., 1978). With origins nearly as old as the origins of parliamentary process, congressional hearings seek to gain information or unveil truth. Although chief counsel and, possibly, minority counsel might be assigned to assist the committee, the viewpoints seldom are dichotomous partisan views but rather reflect a broad spectrum of individual and group positions. (Witness the well-known examples of the Watergate, Iran-Contra, and Whitewater hearings.) Ensuring that all these important views are heard sometimes requires special powers (e.g., subpoenaing witnesses), which would seem more difficult to enact and possibly less appropriate in some settings.

In summary, these "multiadversarial" hearing formats possess many characteristics of adversary-oriented evaluation; although they may not always be as explicitly evaluative as other alternative formats (and some who define evaluation quite strictly may even argue they are not really evaluative at all), we believe they are fully capable of helping to determine the value of a program and thus deserve consideration as an example of this approach to evaluation.

Adversary Debates and Other Forensic Structures

Several approaches that qualify as adversary-oriented do not employ hearing processes. For example, Kourilsky (1973) proposed that pro and con arguments be presented to a decision maker, who would examine the evidence and question the presenters, ultimately arriving at the decision that seemed fair given both positions. Kourilsky and Baker (1976) described an adversary model in which two teams prepared, respectively, affirmative and negative appraisals of that which was evaluated (the preparation stage); met to present the views to one another, cross-examining and critiquing one another's contentions on prespecified criteria (the confrontation stage); and engaged in open-ended discussions until reconciliation of views was attained and translated into written recommendations in a single report. Levine (1974) proposed that a resident adversary or critic might be assigned to a research project to challenge each bit of information collected, searching for other plausible explanations. The Stake and Gjerde (1974) strategy of having two evaluators prepare separate reports summing up opposing positions for and against the program is yet another variant adversarial approach that does not depend on a hearing format. These proposals are all consistent with what has been referred to as "critical evaluation."

Donmoyer (n.d.) proposed a "deliberative" approach to evaluation, which focused on assessing and balancing alternative conceptions of reality and the differing value positions underlying these conceptions. "Because deliberative evaluation is primarily concerned with fostering understanding of alternative conceptions of reality," the evaluator's role is "to foster interaction and facilitate communication *among* representatives of various stakeholder [groups] . . ." (pp. 9–10). Donmoyer saw different worldviews as the cause of underlying disputes, which could be resolved by open presentation of alternative views in some type of forum:

Through the process of communication, those who disagree can, in principle, at least, expand their understanding of an issue by viewing that issue from their opponents' perspectives. (p. 11)

Nafziger and others (1977) described an adversary evaluation design employing a modified debate model for presenting data collected in a comprehensive evaluation to ensure that both sides of controversial issues were illuminated. This model was used in an adversary evaluation of a statewide team-teaching program in Hawaii.

HOW THE ADVERSARY-ORIENTED EVALUATION APPROACH HAS BEEN USED

The Hawaii evaluation conducted by Nafziger and his colleagues (1977) is the only example we know that made an effort to adhere closely to the debate model, as opposed to other forensic models. The program evaluated was a controversial "teamteaching" program. Two evaluation teams were formed, and once they had agreed on the basic design for the evaluation, they were randomly assigned positions as the program's advocate or adversary. Each team drew from the common data provided for in the original design and, in addition, was free to collect supplemental data. The teams wrote and exchanged reports and then prepared written rebuttals. Finally, the team leaders presented their reports and arguments verbally and rebutted their opponents' arguments in a standard debate format, before influential Hawaiian educational, governmental, and private leaders, who were given opportunities to ask questions of both team leaders.

The written final reports and live debates sparked great interest, including wide viewing of two television airings of an hour-long condensed version of the debate. Further, Hawaiian decision makers were very favorable toward the adversarial format of the evaluation (Wright & Sachse, 1977). Despite such receptivity, and selection of this evaluation by the American Educational Research Association as the best all-around evaluation study of 1977, some participants in the study later expressed serious misgivings about aspects of this particular adversary approach (Worthen & Rogers, 1980) or about adversary evaluation in general (Popham & Carlson, 1977).

Van Mondfrans (1993) used a different adaptation of the debate model, in which the evaluator presented the results of a study of the effectiveness of one school district's year-round schools, and then proponents and opponents of year-round education were allowed to argue, respectively, for or against the program, with the stipulation that their arguments must be strictly limited to evidence drawn directly from the evaluation data.

Several adversary-oriented evaluations have incorporated aspects of the legal paradigm. Wolf's judicial evaluation model has been used in (1) the evaluation of Indiana University's undergraduate teacher education programs (Wolf, 1975); (2) examination of the U.S. Bureau of Education for the Handicapped's implementation of a law mandating that all handicapped children have available a free and appropriate education (Wolf & Tymitz, 1977); (3) a study of policy formulation in a local school district (Wolf, 1978); and (4) a formative evaluation of the effectiveness of "networking" among agencies in Virginia's employment and training program (Braithwaite & Thompson, 1981). A modified version of the judicial evaluation model (which omitted the jury or panel whose purpose in previous applications was to make recommendations or decisions) was used in the highly publicized Clarification Hearings on Minimum Competency Testing sponsored by the U.S. National Institute of Education (Herndon, 1980; National Institute of Education, 1981; Madaus, 1981; Popham, 1981).

Other adversary hearings employing legal methods include Owens (1971), described earlier in this chapter, and an evaluation of an experience-based career education program for high school students (Hiscox & Owens, 1975), which produced a videotaped hearing presided over by a law professor serving as "judge," with professors of evaluation as the defense and prosecution "attorneys." In an evaluation of doctoral candidacy procedures in a university psychology program, a public hearing resembling a jury trial was used (Levine et al., 1978).

Aspects of both the legal and debate models were employed in an evaluation of an experimental undergraduate program in liberal arts at the University of Illinois (Stenzel, 1976). A debate consisting of opening arguments, rebuttals, and final summaries of both advocate and adversary positions was presented to a panel of judges, following the appellate court hearing in which such a panel decides issues under contention.

Clyne (1982) summarized the uses of the adversary process in program evaluation: (1) summative evaluation, (2) formative evaluation, (3) social science debate, (4) policy analysis and debate, (5) school governance and local decision making, and (6) issue resolution and policy formation. Worthen and Rogers (1980) reported that a survey of a group of key educators and policy makers showed most (81 percent) thought adversary evaluation was appropriate for summative evaluation, whereas only 15 percent felt it should be used in formative evaluation. Braithwaite and Thompson (1981) disagreed, stating that their study showed adversary evaluation could also serve well in formative evaluation. In their evaluation of the national Clarification Hearings on Minimum Competency Testing, Estes and Demaline's (1982) surveys showed that most participants or potential users of such evaluations view adversarial approaches as more useful for summative than formative decisions.

STRENGTHS AND LIMITATIONS OF THE ADVERSARY-ORIENTED EVALUATION APPROACH

Some strengths and weaknesses transcend particular adversary approaches and speak to the merits of the adversarial concept itself. For example, most observers would agree that building opposing viewpoints into an evaluation tends to illuminate both the positive and negative aspects of a program better than most other evaluation approaches. Adversary approaches also tend to broaden the range of information collected. A strength common to all of the adversary approaches is the interest they create on the part of their intended audiences. Indeed, one of this approach's greatest strengths is that it can satisfy the audience's informational needs in an interesting, informative manner. Nearly everyone loves a contest.

Adversary-oriented evaluation is also sufficiently broad and pluralistic that it can be combined with other approaches. For example, there is nothing to prevent the use of an expertise-oriented evaluation approach by both teams in an adversary-oriented study, nor would it violate this approach for the advocate to use a participant-oriented approach while the adversary employed a management-oriented approach.

Openness to diverse viewpoints and open participation by stakeholders who might be excluded by most other approaches are other advantages. Further, this diversity increases the educative value of the hearings.

Another general advantage to adversary-oriented evaluation is that it anticipates (and largely blunts) the nearly inevitable criticisms offered by anyone whose position is not supported by the findings. It is difficult to argue that an evaluation is unfair if it examines and presents *both* sides of an issue. Use of adversary evaluation to defuse political heat may be an unexpected fringe benefit of this approach.[4] Because opposing views are incorporated *into* the evaluation, most of the pros and cons are argued in an open forum, diverting much subsequent criticism of the evaluation itself. In short, there is more openness to examining issues rather than focus on one particular point of view. This is consistent with findings from social psychology literature in persuasion and communication research (see Paulson, 1964) that suggest opinions are modified more readily when both positive and negative views are reported.

Another advantage is the substantial, rigorous planning required of most adversary evaluations (no one wants to be humiliated by an opponent's gloating over an easy victory). Few evaluation studies are so carefully planned as those with an adversary orientation.

Adversary evaluation also has, in a sense, a built-in **metaevaluation**: an evaluation of the evaluation. The collection, analysis, and interpretation of data used to support any point of view will be painstakingly criticized by those in opposition. All that remains is to do a more general metaevaluation of the overall study.

The use of direct, holistic human testimony is frequently cited as a strength of adversary-oriented evaluation, as is cross-examination of that testimony. Considerable use can be made of expert witnesses, thus enabling experts to draw

---

[4] Madaus (1982) disagrees with us, cautioning that the judicial evaluation approach may be inappropriate for controversial issues such as busing to create ethnic ratios in schools, because of their potential of touching off bitter confrontations by groups on the left and right of the issue, affecting cooperation and data sharing. Perhaps he is correct, at least on the deepest schisms society faces.

inferences that might elude "lay" reviewers. Testing of hidden biases is another strength of this approach, as is examination of alternative interpretations of evidence.

Certain legal metaphors may be particularly useful. For example, the British judicial system's pretrial "exploration for discovery" provides an opportunity for opposing barristers to disclose to one another their cases and supporting evidence in the interest of finding any common ground. When two adversaries agree on any data, interpretation, or conclusion, it lends great credence to that aspect of the evaluation. The requirement that any evidence presented be understandable also precludes the type of obfuscation and "baffle-gab" that permeates many traditional evaluation reports.

To summarize the discussion thus far, we believe an adversary-oriented evaluation approach may be useful when (1) the object of the evaluation affects many people, (2) controversy about the object of the evaluation has created wide interest, (3) decisions are summative, (4) evaluators are external, (5) clear issues are involved, (6) administrators understand the intensity of adversary-oriented evaluations, and (7) resources are available for additional expenses required by adversarial strategies.

Despite their potential for making evaluation findings more interesting and meaningful to decision makers, adversary-oriented approaches to evaluation are not yet sufficiently well developed to serve as a standard or model for future efforts. As yet there is little beyond personal preference to determine whether such evaluations would best be patterned after jury trials, congressional hearings, debates, or other adversarial arrangements. Preoccupation with the respective paraphernalia of these various approaches could cause evaluators to overlook the benefits that might accrue from use of adversary-oriented evaluation, namely, including planned opposition among evaluators. Despite its intriguing possibilities, we are not convinced that the legal paradigm is necessarily the best pattern. Evaluators may forthrightly protest (e.g., Wolf, 1975, 1979) that rigid adherence to a legal model is not intended, yet many continue to cling to the more trivial courtroom rituals that seem unnecessary or downright inappropriate in most evaluations—what Owens (1973) has called "entanglement in legal technicalities." For instance, replicating the theatrical aspects of the courtroom in adversary hearings is distracting and has made a mockery of some adversarial evaluations. Cloaking the person presiding over a hearing in a black robe seems as pretentious and inane as placing powdered wigs on senators presiding over congressional hearings.

Use of the legal paradigm can also result in a seductive slide into what might be termed an "indictment mentality," which can do a disservice both to evaluation efforts and to the programs being evaluated. Adversary-oriented evaluation literature that invokes the legal model tends to use terms such as "statement of charges" (Hiscox & Owens, 1975), "defendant" (Levine & Rosenberg, 1979), "not guilty" (Levine, 1982), "trial by jury" (Wolf, 1975), and the like. That orientation may be appropriate when there is a formal complaint against a program, as in the occasional investigation of some program for malfeasance, misuse of funds, or gross mistreatment of those served by the program. But such situations are rare, and formal complaints, plaintiffs, and litigants are conspicuously absent in the typical program evaluation—and rightly so. Evaluation should aspire to improve programs, not determine their guilt or innocence. Although evaluators must of necessity render judgments of worth, judging merit is not the same thing as determining guilt.

It is not only the vocabulary of the legal model that is problematic but also its characteristic of serving only when there is a problem to be solved. There is already too much tendency to view evaluation as something done when a program is in trouble, when there is a crisis or failing that requires correction. It would be unfortunate if this tendency were exacerbated and evaluations conducted only when a complaint had been lodged, an accusation leveled, an offending program accused. It is precisely this orientation that we fear may be a side effect of basing evaluations on the legal model or on any model meant to be applied only in problem-solving or crisis situations. It would be far more salutary if policy makers and program managers came to view evaluation as something routinely carried out to help them keep programs operating at maximum effectiveness and efficiency.

Of course, one can use aspects of the legal paradigm, such as cross-examination by adversaries, without requiring full or even partial courtroom procedures (as demonstrated by congressional hearings or interviews conducted jointly by partisan interviewers). Wolf (1975) and Hiscox and Owens (1975) have shown that one can adapt portions of the legal model without adopting it in its entirety.

Another general concern with adversary-oriented evaluation is whether it provides decision makers with the full range of needed information. Presentation of strong pro or con positions might increase the probability of an extreme decision. In emphasizing polar positions, stakeholders stand to both gain and lose. They may gain a broader spectrum of data, with more diverse interpretations provided to decision makers; few other evaluation approaches seem likely to push as far in both positive and negative directions. But in broadening that spectrum, they may compromise the very impartiality so essential to rational decision making.

As mentioned earlier, decision makers may place greater confidence in conclusions and recommendations agreed to by both sides. Although this seems patently sensible, experience with adversary evaluation suggests such agreement is unlikely to be a spontaneous by-product of the sparring and jousting that often occurs between adversaries. Most adversary approaches have a competitive element; it is expected that one of the adversaries will win and the other lose. When competition is high, cooperation tends to be lower. Mutual agreements are often abandoned in the adversaries' rush to turn every opposing argument to their own advantage. When winning is at stake, seemingly rational opponents question the obvious. And shared conclusions are not easily come by. Most adversary-oriented evaluation approaches could profit from a better mechanism for seeking and reporting areas of agreement.

Popham and Carlson (1977) point to "disparity in proponent prowess" as a deficit of adversary evaluation, claiming it is all too likely that the case will be decided because of a disparity in skill of the competing teams (or individuals) and that the audience will be influenced more by the persuasiveness of the protagonists than by the strength of the evidence that supports their arguments. The potential that a skilled orator without solid supportive data will sway the "jury" by eloquence alone is, unfortunately, a real possibility.

Assignment of adversaries to pro or con positions is also a difficult matter because of the possible biases that they might bring with them. As noted at the beginning of this chapter, one object of adversary-oriented evaluation is not elimination of bias but rather balancing and publicizing of that bias. Of course, biases are unlikely to be eradicated by assignment to a position. Imagine the plight of Ralph Nader if he were assigned to defend a program or product that he thought was not in the public's best interest.

It may not be an explicit assumption, but many adversary-oriented evaluations proceed as if there were an unspoken *obligation* to present two *equally convincing* cases, pro and con. Naturally, no one would tolerate an advocate who presented a weaker case than the data warranted, but what about one who erred in the other direction, feeling compelled to keep up with the opposition, even if it meant straining or ignoring the data? Such an orientation might be appropriate in a forensic society wherein the result of the debate seldom had much effect on the proposition being argued, but not in an evaluation where the outcome will influence real programs and real people.

Like the legal paradigm, the debate model also has irrelevancies that should be strained out before it is applied to evaluation. The touchstones of debate are polemics and persuasion, not truth, which is central to the validity of evaluation studies. Debaters surely use facts and cannot normally afford to ignore the evidence at hand. But seldom is the debater forced to adhere as tightly to the plain, unadorned facts as is the conscionable evaluator. Logic can provide a permissive climate for manipulating data until the form is favorable. Probably more sophistry results from debaters' perversions of syllogistic logic than any other form of self-deception. A skilled debater can often build a remarkably strong case on a very flimsy foundation.

Many commentators have pointed out that adversary-oriented evaluations are time-consuming and expensive, requiring extensive preparation and considerable investment of human and fiscal resources (e.g., Owens, 1973; Stenzel, 1982; Popham & Carlson, 1977; Van Mondfrans, 1993). Braithwaite and Thompson (1981) said the judicial evaluation model's most serious problem is that it is a "heroic model," requiring

> a large number of participants, many of whom are in important roles. We utilized four case presenters, seven panelists, a hearing officer, a panel facilitator, a nonparticipant observer, and two research assistants in addition to ourselves, 13 witnesses, and two speakers who provided contextual statements at the outset of the hearing. (p. 16)

Levine and others (1978) estimated that over 80 percent of their effort in an evaluation using an adaptation of a jury trial went into preparing the case and managing the process, and less than 20 percent went into the actual hearing. Kourilsky and Baker (1976) noted as a potential snare of adversary evaluation the temptation to report all of the voluminous information collected with this approach. In short, questions have been raised about whether the adversary approach to evaluation is worth its considerable costs.

The real question, however, is not cost but cost-effectiveness or cost-benefit. On these dimensions it seems apparent that benefit must be argued on grounds that adversary evaluation increases representativeness of the data, fairness of the instruments, communication between evaluators and decision makers, and identification of all the pros and cons. Whether adversary evaluation really provides additional benefits must remain an open question until someone sees fit to research the issue.

A final concern of critics of adversary-oriented evaluation is that those who serve as judges are fallible arbiters. Popham and Carlson (1977) have worried about the lack of a process for appealing unwise decisions by arbiters, stating that the lack of a "higher court of appeals" in evaluation precludes rectifying improper judgments.[5] House (1980) echoes this concern and also lists as a criterion the contention that the "adversary model" may resolve conflicts but has limited potential for getting at the truth of a matter. He references a former U.S. attorney general's comment that he couldn't think of a worse procedure for arriving at the truth. We disagree, but then that is what one might expect in a chapter devoted to adversarial behavior.

APPLICATION EXERCISES

1. Select a program or project in your organization or community that is controversial. What ideas does adversary-oriented evaluation give you about how to evaluate this program? How would you structure the evaluation to avoid many of the problems of the adversary-oriented evaluation approach?

2. The curriculum council for a large school district decided that one of the major weaknesses of the elementary curriculum was its writing program. Junior high teachers reported that students were generally unable to write cohesive, descriptive paragraphs. On the recommendation of the council, six elementary schools were selected to participate in a pilot project to develop an elementary writing program. The nucleus of the developmental staff consisted of the faculty of these schools. This staff included also a specialist in creative writing from the local university and a representative from the curriculum council. The staff worked together for eight weeks in the summer to develop a program that would be used in all six grades. When school opened, they

---

[5] Although we would not disagree, we might point out that the same deficit extends to other evaluation approaches, which also lack a mechanism for appealing improper conclusions. Perhaps the visibility associated with the "findings" in an adversary evaluation makes this a more serious concern here, however.

met twice weekly to discuss the way the course was progressing and to act on the recommendations of the evaluation team. The evaluation team had been appointed by the curriculum council and had the following responsibilities: (1) to decide what questions should be asked of the program; (2) to select the appropriate criteria for success of the program; and (3) to gather information about the program and give it to the program staff with recommendations that they either improve, terminate, or maintain the program.

How could adversary-oriented evaluation approaches be used to address the evaluation needs of the council? Provide details about who would be involved, what the procedures would involve, what reports would be generated, and how the results might be used.

SUGGESTED READINGS

Levine, M. (1982). Adversary hearings. In N. L. Smith (Ed.), *Communication strategies in evaluation.* Beverly Hills, CA: Sage.

Owens, T. R. (1973). Educational evaluation by adversary proceeding. In E. R. House (Ed.), *School evaluation: The politics and process* (pp. 295–305). Berkeley, CA: McCutchan.

Stenzel, N. (1982). Committee hearings as an evaluation format. In N. L. Smith (Ed.), *Field assessments of innovative evaluation methods.* New Directions for Program Evaluation, No. 13, 85–100. San Francisco: Jossey-Bass.

Wolf, R. L. (1975). Trial by jury: A new evaluation method. *Phi Delta Kappan, 57,* 185–187.

Worthen, B. R., & Rogers, W. T. (1980). Pitfalls and potential of adversary evaluation. *Educational Leadership, 37,* 536–543.

chapter 10

Participant-Oriented Evaluation Approaches

ORIENTING QUESTIONS

1. What led to the development of participant-oriented evaluation approaches?
2. What are some of the fundamental principles that participant-oriented evaluators follow when they conduct their evaluations?
3. What problems might a naturalistic evaluator have with a client who wants a detailed evaluation plan in hand before allowing the evaluation to begin? How could the evaluator deal with this requirement?
4. Should naturalistic evaluations limit their practice to qualitative methods? Why?
5. How has each of the evaluation approaches described in this chapter been used?
6. What are the major strengths and limitations of participant-oriented evaluation approaches?

Beginning in 1967, several evaluation theorists began to react to what they considered to be the dominance of mechanistic and insensitive approaches to evaluation in the field of education. These theorists expressed concerns that evaluators were largely preoccupied with stating and classifying objectives, designing elaborate evaluation systems, developing technically defensible objective instrumentation, and preparing long technical reports, with the result that evaluators were distracted from what was really happening in the programs they evaluated. Critics of traditional evaluation approaches noted that many large-scale evaluations were conducted without the evaluators' ever once setting foot on the participating program site(s). What began as a trickle of isolated comments grew to a deluge that flooded evaluation literature in education and the social sciences. More and more practitioners began publicly to question whether many evaluators really understood the phenomena that underlie their numbers, figures, charts, and tables. An increasing segment of the education and human services communities argued that the human element, which was reflected in the complexities of everyday reality and the different perspectives of those engaged in providing services, was missing from most evaluations.

Consequently, a new orientation to evaluation was born, one that stressed firsthand experience with program activities and settings. This general approach, which grew quickly after the early 1970s, is aimed at observing and identifying all (or as many as possible) of the concerns, issues, and consequences integral to the human services enterprise.

In large part a reaction to perceived deficits in other evaluation approaches, this orientation encompasses a wide variety of more specific proposals that might be generally tied together by their acceptance of the intuitionist-pluralist philosophy of evaluation (see Chapter 4). Many of those who contributed to the development and use of participant-oriented approaches to program evaluation prefer naturalistic inquiry methods as described later in this chapter, as opposed to conventional nomothetic science. Moreover, most advocates of this approach see as central the significant involvement in the evaluation of those who are participants in the endeavor being evaluated, hence the descriptor *participant-oriented* as a label for this approach.[1]

The evaluator portrays the different values and needs of individuals and groups served by the program, weighing and balancing this plurality of judgments and criteria in a largely intuitive fashion. (By intuitive, we do not mean that the evaluator cannot approach this task in a systematic manner but rather that there is no algorithm he can follow in doing so; his intuition about what weight to put on each criterion will determine how the judgment is shaped). What is judged "best" depends heavily on the values and perspectives of whichever groups or individuals are judging. By involving participants in determining the boundaries of the evaluation, evaluators serve an important educative function by creating better-informed program staff.

DEVELOPERS OF PARTICIPANT-ORIENTED EVALUATION APPROACHES AND THEIR CONTRIBUTIONS

In an important sense, Stake (1967) was the first evaluation theorist to provide significant impetus to this orientation in the field of education. His paper "The Countenance of Educational Evaluation," with its focus on portrayal and processing

---

[1] Obviously "naturalistic" and "participant-oriented" are not synonymous; a naturalistic evaluation could focus on description and portrayal, while ignoring participants' views, just as an evaluation might be built around issues selected by participants without using naturalistic methods. The tendency for the two somewhat different approaches to overlap heavily in practice—most evaluations which are examples of one are also examples of the other—is our justification for intertwining them somewhat here as we discuss this general evaluation approach.

the judgments of participants, was to alter dramatically the thinking of evaluators in the next decade. Along with his later writings (Stake, 1975a, 1975b, 1978, 1980, 1988, 1991, 1994, 1995), he provided conceptions and principles that have guided the evolution of this evaluation approach. Stake's early writings evidenced his growing concern over dominance of program evaluation by parochial, objectivist, mechanistic, and stagnant conceptions and methods. Guba's (1969) discussion of the "failure of educational evaluation" provided further impetus at the time to the search for an alternative to the rationalistic approach to evaluation. Parlett and Hamilton (1976) complained that the predominant "agricultural-botanist" research paradigm was deficient for studying innovative educational programs, and they presented an alternative "illuminative evaluation" approach that followed a social anthropology paradigm. Rippey (1973) decried the insensitivity of existing evaluation approaches to the impact of an evaluation upon the incumbents in roles within the system being evaluated; he proposed "transactional evaluation" as a more appropriate evaluation approach for systems undergoing evaluation and resultant changes. MacDonald (1974, 1976) expressed concern over existing evaluation approaches' misuses of information for questionable political purposes, opting instead for "democratic evaluation," designed to protect the rights and informational needs of the whole "community" involved.

Guba and Lincoln (1981) reviewed the major approaches used in program evaluation and rejected all except Stake's notion of **responsive evaluation**, which they incorporated with naturalistic inquiry to create an evaluation approach they proposed as superior to all alternatives for education. Their subsequent work (Guba & Lincoln, 1989) further delineated an approach that not only rejected the positivist paradigm in favor of that of the constructivist but also focused on evaluation as a means of empowering stakeholders they deemed as disenfranchised with other evaluation approaches. Patton (1975, 1986, 1990b, 1994) added substantially to the literature on participant-oriented evaluation through his reports of his field evaluation experiences. Numerous others have also suggested participant-oriented evaluation approaches, or methodologies that are compatible with them (e.g., Rippey, 1973; MacDonald, 1974, 1976; Parlett & Hamilton, 1976; Fetterman, 1984, 1994, to name only a few).

Diverse as these proposals are for variants of this general evaluation approach, two threads seem to run through all of them. The first, as Wachtman (1978) notes, is

> disenchantment with evaluation techniques which stress a product-outcome point of view, especially at the expense of a fuller, more holistic approach which sees education as a human endeavor and admits to the complexity of the human condition. Each author argues that instead of simplifying the issues of our humanity we should, in fact, attempt to understand ourselves and human services in the context of their complexity. (p. 2)

Second, in most of these writings, value pluralism is recognized, accommodated, and protected, even though the effort to summarize the frequently disparate judgments and preferences of such groups is left to the intuitive sagacity and communication skills of the evaluator.

Those who use participant-oriented approaches to evaluation typically prepare descriptive accounts—"portrayals," as they have come to be called—of a person, classroom, school, district, project, program, activity, or some other entity around which clear boundaries have been placed. Not only is the entity richly portrayed but it is clearly positioned within the broader context in which it functions.

In addition to commonalities noted above, evaluations that use this approach generally include the following characteristics:

1. *They depend on inductive reasoning.* Understanding an issue or event or process comes from grass-roots observation and discovery. Understanding emerges; it is not the end product of some preordinate inquiry plan projected before the evaluation is conducted.

2. *They use a multiplicity of data.* Understanding comes from the assimilation of data from a number of sources. Subjective and objective, qualitative and quantitative representations of the phenomena being evaluated are used.

3. *They do not follow a standard plan.* The evaluation process evolves as participants gain experience in the activity. Often the important outcome of the evaluation is a rich understanding of one specific entity with all of its idiosyncratic contextual influences, process variations, and life histories. It is important in and of itself for what it tells about the phenomena that occurred.

4. *They record multiple rather than single realities.* People see things and interpret them in different ways. No one knows everything that happens in a school or in any but the tiniest program. And no one perspective is accepted as *the* truth. Because only an individual can truly know what he has experienced, all perspectives are accepted as correct, and a central task of the evaluator is to capture these realities and portray them without sacrificing the program's complexity.

Of the many authors who have proposed participant-oriented evaluation approaches, we have selected for further description here a few who have made unique contributions.

Stake's Countenance Framework

Stake's (1967) early analysis of the evaluation process had a major impact on evaluation thinking and laid a simple but powerful conceptual foundation for later developments in evaluation theory. He asserted that the two basic acts of evaluation are *description* and *judgment* (the "two countenances" of evaluation). Thus the two major activities of any formal evaluation study are full description and judgment of that which is being evaluated. To aid the evaluator in organizing data collection and interpretation, Stake created the evaluation framework shown in Figure 10.1.

Using this framework, the evaluator (1) provides background, justification, and description of the program rationale (including its need); (2) lists intended antecedents (inputs, resources, existing conditions), transactions (activities, processes), and outcomes; (3) records observed antecedents, transactions, and outcomes (including observations of unintended features of each); (4) explicitly states the standards (criteria, expectations, performance of comparable programs) for judging program antecedents, transactions, and outcomes; and (5) records judgments made about the antecedent conditions, transactions, and outcomes. The evaluator analyzes information in the description matrix by looking at the congruence between intents and observations, and by looking at dependencies (contingencies) of outcomes on transactions and antecedents, and of transactions on antecedents. Judgments are made by applying standards to the descriptive data.

The countenance structure thus gives evaluators a conceptual framework for thinking through the data needs of a complete evaluation. In reviewing his countenance paper 25 years later, Stake (1991) noted that it underemphasized

FIGURE 10.1 Stake's layout of statements and data to be collected by the evaluator of an educational program

SOURCE: From "The Countenance of Educational Evaluation" by R. E. Stake, 1967, *Teachers College Record, 68,* p. 529. Reprinted by permission.

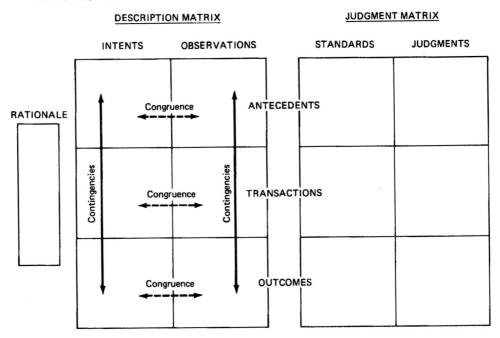

the process of describing the evaluation, a shortcoming that he addressed later in his responsive evaluation paper.

Illuminative Evaluation

Parlett and Hamilton (1976) proposed an evaluation approach, which they called *illuminative evaluation,* that involves intensive study of a program as a whole—its rationale and evolution, operations, achievements, and difficulties in the organizational context. The purpose of their approach, proposed as especially applicable to small-scale programs, was to illuminate problems, issues, and significant program features. Based on the social anthropology paradigm, and somewhat on psychiatry and sociology participant observation research, this approach grew from disenchantment with the classical experimental paradigm, which Parlett and Hamilton termed an *agricultural-botany paradigm,* suggesting that it is a more appropriate paradigm for plants than people. Illuminative evaluation is primarily concerned with description and interpretation, not measurement and prediction. No attempt is made to manipulate or control variables, but rather the complex educational context is taken, as it exists, and the evaluator attempts to understand it.

The importance of studying the context of programs, according to Parlett and Hamilton, is that a variety of factors influence programs in any evaluation, such as constraints (legal, administrative, occupational, architectural, financial); operating assumptions held by staff (arrangement of treatment and service delivery, record keeping); staff members' individual characteristics (working style, experience, professional orientation, private goals); and client perspectives and preoccupations. Also, the introduction of changes within the organizational context sets off repercussions and unusual effects. The evaluator's task is to provide a comprehensive understanding of the complex reality surrounding the program—to "illuminate" by sharpening discussion, disentangling complexities, isolating the significant from the trivial, and raising the level of sophistication characterizing debates. Although illuminative evaluation concentrates on information gathering, not decision making, it is expected that different groups will look to the evaluator's reports to help make difficult decisions. The illuminative evaluator does not pass judgment but rather attempts to discover, document, and discuss what the program comprises and what it is really like to be a participant in it.

The process of evaluation proposed by Parlett and Hamilton has three basic stages.

1. *Observation,* to explore and become familiar with the day-to-day reality of the setting being studied
2. *Further inquiry,* to focus the study by inquiring further on selected issues
3. *Explanation,* to seek to explain observed patterns and cause-and-effect relationships

Progressive focusing is recommended for use throughout the evaluation as a technique for refocusing and narrowing the study, thereby allowing more concentrated attention to emerging issues.

Emphasizing process, subjective information, and naturalistic inquiry, the illuminative evaluation approach depends largely on data from observations, interviews, questionnaires and tests, and documents or background sources. "Triangulative" combinations of such data are proposed to provide a more accurate portrayal of reality. The focus of this approach requires that the illuminative evaluator spend substantial periods of time in the field.

Responsive Evaluation

During the early 1970s, Stake began to expand his earlier (1967) writing more obviously into the realm of participant-oriented evaluation. Although the seeds of this explication lie in his earlier work, Stake's more recent conceptions of responsive evaluation (1972, 1975b, 1978, 1980) are implicitly less formal and explicitly more pluralistic and process focused than his earlier countenance model.

Responsive evaluation's central focus is in addressing the concerns and issues of a stakeholder audience. Stake (1972) noted that he was not proposing a new approach to evaluation, for "responsive evaluation is what people do naturally in evaluating things. They observe and react" (p. 1).[2] Rather, Stake saw this approach as an attempt to develop a technology to improve and focus this natural behavior of the evaluator. Stake stressed the importance of being *responsive* to realities in the program and to the reactions, concerns, and issues of participants rather than being *preordinate*[3] with evaluation plans, relying on preconceptions and formal plans and objectives of the program. Stake (1975a) defined responsive evaluation as follows:

> An educational evaluation is responsive evaluation if it orients more directly to program activities than to program intents; responds to audience requirements for information; and if the different value-perspectives present are referred to in reporting the success and failure of the program. (p. 14)

---

[2] Stake's assertion is confirmed by personal experience. After being skeptical for several years about the usefulness of responsive evaluation, one of the authors of this text was asked to describe in print how he would evaluate a particular curriculum (Worthen, 1981). This expedition into "logic-in-use" (see Kaplan, 1964) was revealing because it forced recognition that Stake's description of responsive evaluation had indeed captured those activities and procedures so long used by many experienced evaluators as to become second nature. Stake has served well by articulating and bringing to a level of public discourse and analysis procedures that have previously existed largely at the subconscious level of practicing evaluators.

[3] "Preordinate" evaluation refers to evaluation studies that rely on prespecification, where inquiry tends to follow a prescribed plan and does not go beyond the predetermined issues and pre-defined problems.

A major reason for proposing responsive evaluation is Stake's perception that the ultimate test of an evaluation's validity is the extent to which it increases the audience's understanding of the entity that was evaluated. Improved communication with stakeholders is a principal goal of responsive evaluation. "The responsive approach tries to respond to the natural ways in which people assimilate information and arrive at understanding" (p. 3).

The purpose, framework, and focus of a responsive evaluation emerge from interactions with constituents, and those interactions and observations result in progressive focusing on issues (similar to the progressive focusing in Parlett and Hamilton's, 1976, illuminative evaluation described earlier). Responsive evaluators must interact continuously with members of various stakeholding groups to ascertain what information they desire and the manner in which they prefer to receive such information. Stake (1975b) described the responsive evaluator's role this way:

> To do a responsive evaluation, the evaluator of course does many things. He makes a plan of observations and negotiations. He arranges for various persons to observe the program. With their help he prepares for brief narratives, portrayals, product displays, graphs, etc. He finds out what is of value to his audience. He gathers expressions of worth from various individuals whose points of view differ. Of course, he checks the quality of his records. He gets program personnel to react to the accuracy of his portrayals. He gets authority figures to react to the importance of various findings. He gets audience members to react to the relevance of his findings. He does much of this informally, iterating, and keeping a record of action and reaction. He chooses media accessible to his audiences to increase the likelihood and fidelity of communication. He might prepare a final written report; he might not—depending on what he and his clients have agreed on. (p. 11)

As one might infer from the above description, responsive evaluators are relatively disinterested in formal objectives or the precision of formalized data collection; they are more likely to be at home working within the naturalistic or ethnographic paradigm, drawing heavily on qualitative techniques. Feedback to the various stakeholders is more likely to include portrayals and testimonials rather than more conventional evaluation data. Such portrayals will frequently feature descriptions of individuals in **case studies** based on a small sample of those affected by the program or process being evaluated. Reports to audiences will underscore the pluralism within the program setting. A single set of recommendations is highly improbable; recommendations are more likely to be of the conditional sort where judgments about the "best" program or the "preferred" course of action will vary, depending on who is doing the judging and what criteria he uses to ascertain value. Maxwell (1984) has published a rating scale that could be used to assess the quality of responsive evaluations.

FIGURE 10.2   Prominent events in a responsive evaluation

SOURCE: From *Program Evaluation, Particularly Responsive Evaluation* (Occasional Paper No. 5, p. 19) by R. E. Stake, 1975b, Kalamazoo, MI: Western Michigan University Evaluation Center. Adapted by permission.

Stake (1975b) used the "clock" shown in Figure 10.2 as a mnemonic device to reflect the prominent, recurring events in a responsive evaluation. Although the evaluator might best begin the evaluation at twelve o'clock and proceed clockwise, Stake has emphasized that any event can follow any other event, and at any point the evaluator may want to move counterclockwise or cross clockwise, if events warrant such flexibility. Further, many events may occur simultaneously; many will occur several times during an evaluation. The "clock" serves to remind evaluators that flexibility is an important part of using this participant-oriented approach.

One revealing comparison of responsive and **preordinate evaluation** approaches was provided by Stake's (1975b) analysis of what percentage of time evaluators of each persuasion would spend on several evaluation tasks.

	Preordinate (%)	Responsive (%)
Identifying issues, goals	10	10
Preparing instruments	30	15
Observing the program	5	30
Administering tests, etc.	10	—
Gathering judgments	—	15
Learning client needs, etc.	—	5
Processing formal data	25	5
Preparing informal reports	—	10
Preparing formal reports	20	10

(p. 20)

Stake (1978) also advanced the participant-oriented approach to evaluation by expanding on its rationale. This approach, he said, has appeal for the following reasons:

1. It helps audiences for the evaluation understand the program if evaluators pay attention to the natural way in which audiences understand and communicate about things.
2. Knowledge gained from experience (tacit knowledge) facilitates human understanding and extends human experience.
3. Naturalistic generalizations, which are arrived at by recognizing similarities of objects and issues in and out of context, are developed through experience. They serve to expand the way in which people come to view and understand programs.
4. By studying single objects, people accumulate experiences that may be used to recognize similarities in other objects. Individuals add to existing experience and human understanding.

We have given more space to responsive evaluation than to other participant-oriented evaluation approaches because, as eclectics, we believe that responsive evaluation can be included in all other approaches. The focus of responsive evaluation is on audience concerns and issues—on the information they want the evaluator to provide. One audience may desire information about program outcomes, another may wish to know about how to improve some process, and a third may be concerned with information that would show stakeholders whether the program is being implemented correctly. Any or all of these needs could be addressed by a responsive evaluator, for his evaluation is tailored to fit ("respond to") whatever informational need the evaluation's clients wish to have addressed.

One might question whether or not responsive evaluation, so broadly defined, may lose its uniqueness and meaning. Such a broad claim for responsive evaluation, misunderstood, could also result in less able evaluators' attempting to pass off inferior evaluations, which would be rejected as examples of any other evaluation approach, by labeling them as "responsive" evaluation. That prospect tempts one to narrow the definition of responsive studies to exclude atrocities that do not deserve inclusion under any rubric. But one may as well rail against use of the term "creativity" because of the largely abortive efforts to define and measure that construct as to argue for limiting the broad perspective of responsive evaluation because those incapable of doing quality evaluation work, by any definition, may try to creep under the shelter of the broader conceptions that Stake and Guba and Lincoln have proposed. In the final analysis, each evaluation must be judged by its usefulness, not its label. Used intelligently and competently, responsive evaluation methods have great potential for enhancing the quality of any evaluation study.

Naturalistic Evaluation

In *The Flame Trees of Thika*, Elspeth Huxley (1982) makes this astute observation:

> The best way to find things out . . . is not to ask questions at all. If you fire off a question, it is like firing off a gun—bang it goes, and everything takes flight and runs for shelter. But if you sit quite still and pretend not to be looking, all the little facts will come and peck round your feet, situations will venture forth from thickets, and intentions will creep out and sun themselves on a stone; and if you are very patient, you will see and understand a great deal more than a man with a gun does. (p. 272)

Huxley's words sum up the spirit of the **naturalistic evaluation** approach better than could any academic description. Yet it is important to move beyond the prosaic to try, as House (1983a) has done, to understand the structure of reality underlying this approach. He labeled as "naturalistic" evaluation any evaluation that

> aims at naturalistic generalization (based on the experience of the audience); is directed more at non-technical audiences like volunteers or the general public; uses ordinary language and everyday categories of events; and is based more on informal than formal logic. (p. 57)

Although House and others had written of naturalistic approaches to evaluation, Guba (1978) provided the first comprehensive discussion of the merits of introducing naturalistic methods into program evaluation. He differentiated between naturalistic inquiry, rooted in ethnography and phenomenology, and "conventional" inquiry, based on the positivist, experimental paradigm. He not only outlined several reasons for preferring naturalistic inquiry but also analyzed major methodological problems confronting naturalistic inquirers. His monograph contributed greatly toward formulation of naturalistic evaluation methodology.

The most significant work in this area, however, is the work of Guba and Lincoln, which carefully linked naturalistic inquiry to Stake's responsive evaluation and then described procedures for implementing this approach. Their more recent work (Guba & Lincoln, 1981, 1989; Lincoln & Guba, 1985) extended their discussion of the naturalistic method of inquiry.

According to Guba and Lincoln, the major role of evaluation is one of responding to an audience's requirements for information in ways that take account of the different value perspectives of its members. By taking a naturalistic approach to evaluation, the evaluator is studying the program activity in situ, or as it occurs naturally, without constraining, manipulating, or controlling it. Naturalistic inquiry casts the evaluator in the role of a learner, and those being studied in the role of informants who "teach" the evaluator. The dominant perspective is that of the informant, because the evaluators learn their perspectives, learn the concepts they use to describe their world, use their definitions of these concepts, learn the "folk theory" explanations, and translate their world so the evaluator and others can understand it.

Guba and Lincoln stress that the criteria used to judge the rigor of scientific inquiry also hold for naturalistic inquiry but require some reinterpretation. For instance, if one were concerned about the "truth" of an evaluation for particular subjects in a particular context, the naturalistic evaluator would be concerned with *credibility* of findings rather than internal validity. Corroboration of data through cross-checking and **triangulation** are two methods used by the naturalistic evaluator to establish credibility.

If one were concerned with the *applicability* of an evaluation in other contexts or for other subjects, the naturalistic evaluator would look at the fit of the evaluation findings rather than external validity. Applicability is enhanced through the use of working hypotheses that should be tested in other contexts and through the use of "thick description," which is a "literal description of the entity being evaluated, the circumstances under which it is used, the characteristics of the people involved in it, the nature of the community in which it is located, and the like" (Guba & Lincoln, 1981, p. 119).

If one were concerned with the *consistency* of evaluation findings (that is, whether the same finding would result if the study were repeated), the naturalistic evaluator would consider the study's *auditability* rather than reliability. By having a second team review the documentation and reasoning underlying the evaluation, the evaluator can determine whether agreement on the findings can be reached. Halpern (1983) has developed an extensive model for auditing naturalistic inquiries.

Finally, if one were concerned about the *neutrality* of the evaluation, the naturalistic evaluator would look at the evaluation's *confirmability* rather than its objectivity. Data should be factual and confirmable. The naturalistic evaluator will require that the information generated by the evaluation can be confirmed.

The naturalistic evaluator proceeds by first identifying stakeholders. Their value positions are important, for it is their perspectives that should be reflected in the evaluation. Concerns and issues are elicited from interviews with the stakeholders and from naturalistic observations by the evaluator.

The naturalistic evaluator's data-collection task is defined by certain kinds of information that are sought.

- Descriptive information about the object of the evaluation and its context
- Information responsive to concerns (documenting concerns, seeking causes and consequences, and identifying possible actions)
- Information responsive to issues (clarifying issues, identifying potential courses of action to resolve them)
- Information about values (clarifying values, finding out about their source and degree of conviction)
- Information about standards to be used in the evaluation (identifying criteria, expectations, and needs).

Through the use of interviews, observations, nonverbal cues, documents, records, and **unobtrusive measures**, the naturalistic evaluator uses field notes and records as the sources of this information. Descriptions are used not only as data but also as a reporting technique.

Looking Back.   The participant-oriented evaluation approaches we have described above collectively reflect a new orientation in the field of program evaluation. They are similar in important ways, yet each is unique. As noted in a review of a collection of actual evaluations that follow this general orientation, they display "a family resemblance, not an enclosed orthodoxy guided by a tacit uniformity of practice" (Hamilton, Jenkins, King, MacDonald, & Parlett, 1977, p. 235). Hamilton (1977) provided a general description of "pluralist evaluation models" that serves to summarize the participant-oriented approaches we have discussed.

> In practical terms, pluralist evaluation models . . . can be characterized in the following manner. Compared with the classic models, they tend to be more extensive (not necessarily centered on numerical data), more naturalistic (based on program activity rather than program intent), and more adaptable (not constrained by experimental or preordinate designs). In turn, they are likely to be sensitive to the different values of program participants, to endorse empirical methods which incorporate ethnographic fieldwork, to develop feedback materials which are couched in the natural language of the recipients, and to shift the locus of formal judgment from the evaluator to the participants. (p. 339)

HOW PARTICIPANT-ORIENTED EVALUATION APPROACHES HAVE BEEN USED

In one sense, given the breadth of this general evaluation approach, one could almost include as examples any program evaluation that has used ethnography, case studies, storytelling, qualitative techniques, and the like. We will resist that temptation, recognizing that many studies may use some of the apparatus of participant-oriented evaluation without being good examples of this approach. Rather, we would point to a few examples that reflect conscious efforts to follow this evaluation approach.

Rippey (1973) has described how the concept of transactional evaluation has been used to aid in the process of change in different types of organizations. Likewise, Parlett and Dearden (1977) provide examples of the use of illuminative evaluation in evaluation of higher-education programs.

The arts was the focus of an extensive evaluation project using the responsive evaluation approach (Stake, 1975a). In this project and an earlier one that evaluated a program for talented youth (Stake & Gjerde, 1974), responsive evaluation procedures were used to address issues of immediate interest to evaluation audiences.

Malcolm and Welch (1981) provide an example of a naturalistic case study of a Catholic junior college in Minneapolis, Minnesota. Of particular interest are the authors' personal reactions to such topics as the evaluators' preparations, note taking in the field, phases in planning for the study, interviewing, data analysis and report writing, and final editing and validation.

Other uses of the participant-oriented approach to evaluation have been reported by Wolcott (1976), Wolf and Tymitz (1977), Patton (1990b), Guba and Lincoln (1981), Spindler (1982), Williams (1986), Fitzpatrick (1992), and Stake (1992, 1994). In addition, Independent Sector (1995) has produced a useful guide to getting people involved in evaluations using this approach.

STRENGTHS AND LIMITATIONS OF PARTICIPANT-ORIENTED EVALUATION APPROACHES

Introduction of evaluations using this approach has prompted more acrimonious debate than almost any development in evaluation within the last two decades. Critics of this approach discount it as hopelessly "soft-headed" and argue that few if any program evaluators are either virtuous or intellectually agile enough to wield masterfully the seductively simple yet slippery and subtle tools that this approach requires. Champions of pluralistic, responsive approaches reply that they can be readily used by any sensitive individual and that they are infinitely richer and more powerful than other approaches and, indeed, can subsume them, because they are flexible and do not preclude the use of other approaches within them, should that be desired by the evaluator's sponsor. Our intent here is not to add to what we see as a largely unproductive, divisive debate but rather to summarize briefly some of the pros and cons thus far advanced for this approach.

It is important to distinguish between participant-oriented approaches to evaluation and qualitative methodologies used in data collection. Participant-oriented approaches can and do use both qualitative and quantitative methods. There is, however, more use of qualitative methods in participant-oriented evaluations than is typical in, for example, objectives- or management-oriented evaluations.

Few would argue against the claim that participant-oriented evaluation has emphasized the human element in evaluation. It directs the attention of the evaluator to the needs of those for whom an evaluation is being done, and it stresses the importance of a broad scope: looking at the program from different viewpoints. Those who use this approach view programs as a complex human undertaking and attempt to reflect that complexity as accurately as possible so that others may learn from it. The potential for gaining new insights and usable new theories about our educational, social, or corporate programs by using this approach stands among its greatest strengths. Other advantages of this method are its flexibility, attention to contextual variables, and encouragement of multiple data-collection techniques designed to provide a view of less tangible but crucial aspects of human and organizational behavior. In addition, this approach can provide rich and persuasive information that is credible to audiences who see it as reflecting genuine understanding of the inner workings and intricacies of the program.

As with other approaches to evaluation, the strengths of this approach may also prove to be its limitations. Attempts to simplify the evaluation process have proven popular and effective in the past, as evidenced by the 50-year dominance of the objectives-oriented evaluation method. Thus, an approach that stresses complexity rather than simplicity may ultimately prove more popular with theorists than with practitioners, however sound it may be on other grounds.

More than any other approach to program evaluation that we have examined, participant-oriented approaches add a political element inasmuch as they foster and facilitate the activism of recipients of program services. In schools, parents and students are only infrequently very active politically. However, recipients of public services or advocates for those services are often considerably more prone to political activism. For example, programs intended to serve AIDS patients, the homeless, the chronically mentally ill, and tenants in public housing programs more often are carved out of a politicized climate. Programs such as these often receive much national and local media attention and have interest groups that are quite well organized.

Critics of the participant-oriented approach have found its subjectivity a serious limitation, even though such arguments could be mounted against every other approach to evaluation (as noted in lengthy discussions of this issue by Guba & Lincoln, 1981). Because of their reliance on human observation and individual perspective, and their tendency to minimize the importance of instrumentation and group data, advocates of this approach have been criticized for "loose and unsubstantiated" evaluations. For example, Sadler (1981) discussed intuitive data processing as a potential source of bias in naturalistic evaluations. Others have noted that ethnographic field work can take so much time to complete that the situation often changes or the administrator has to make a decision before the evaluation findings are available. Moreover, some have claimed that excluding judgment from the evaluator's role makes some participant-oriented approaches nonevaluative. In fact, some worry that these approaches confuse with evaluation the many roles that evaluators can play outside of evaluation (e.g., Stufflebeam, 1994; Mayeske, 1995). Further, failure to suggest ways of weighing or combining individual standards into overall judgments about the program is viewed as making pluralistic, participant-oriented evaluation difficult for all but the most sensitive and skilled evaluators. Even proponents of these approaches concede that dependence on open-ended techniques and progressive focusing in this approach make evaluator partiality a potential problem.[4]

The cost of using participant-oriented approaches to evaluation has been viewed by some as a serious limitation, especially during times of tight budgets. This approach can be labor-intensive, often requiring full-time presence of the evaluator in the field over an extended period. The time it takes to prepare field notes and reports using this approach is at least as long as it takes for the initial observations.

The labor intensity of participant-oriented approaches to evaluation limits the number of cases that can be studied intensively. Consequently, it is critical that cases be selected carefully and, even then, that conclusions not be extended beyond what those cases will allow. On the whole, evaluators using this approach are well advised to be cautious in making interpretations and drawing conclusions. Most results might best be considered contextually anchored facts on which to base—and then test—tentative generalizations.

APPLICATION EXERCISES

1. What current program are you involved with that would benefit from a participant-oriented evaluation? Who are the stakeholders for this program? How would you proceed with the evaluation? How could "thick description" be used?

2. As newly appointed director of student activities for the John F. Kennedy High School, you decide to conduct an evaluation of the student activities program in the school. The most current information about the program is found in the faculty handbook, published at the opening of each school year. This description reads as follows:

   The John F. Kennedy High School offers a wide range of activities for its 2,000 students. Among the various activities are clubs, intramural and varsity sports, band, choir, orchestra, and various service programs such as Red Cross. Clubs are organized by students and assigned a faculty advisor by the dean of students. Meetings are scheduled on Monday to Thursday evenings and held in the cafeteria, auditorium, or gymnasium of the school. Varsity sports activities are directed by members of the physical education faculty. Intramural sports are organized by home rooms and directed by a faculty member appointed by the dean of students. Band, choir, and orchestra are under the direction of members of the music department. Service programs are organized by students who must also find a faculty member who is willing to advise them.

   Feeling that this description does not provide you with sufficient insight into the program, you decide to conduct an evaluation of the current program before undertaking

---

[4] It should be noted that recent advances in the methodology of naturalistic and participant-oriented approaches have largely neutralized these latter concerns, however.

any modifications or restructuring of the program. As a participant-oriented evaluator, how would you proceed to plan and conduct the evaluation?

SUGGESTED READINGS

Cousins, J. B., & Earl, L. M. (Eds.). (1995). *Participatory evaluation in education.* Bristol, PA: Falmer Press.

Fetterman, D. M. (1994). Empowerment evaluation. *Evaluation Practice, 15,* 1–15.

Guba, E. G., & Lincoln, Y. S. (1989). *Fourth generation evaluation.* Thousand Oaks, CA: Sage.

Lincoln, Y. S., & Guba, E. G. (1985). *Naturalistic inquiry.* Beverly Hills, CA: Sage.

Patton, M. Q. (1994). Developmental evaluation. *Evaluation Practice, 15,* 311–320.

Stake, R. E. (1967). The countenance of educational evaluation. *Teachers College Record, 68,* 523–540.

Stake, R. E. (1975). *Program evaluation, particularly responsive evaluation.* (Occasional Paper No. 5). Kalamazoo: Western Michigan University Evaluation Center.

Stake, R. E. (1995). *The art of case study research.* Thousand Oaks, CA: Sage.

chapter 11

Alternative Evaluation Approaches: A Summary and Comparative Analysis

ORIENTING QUESTIONS

1. What are some cautions to keep in mind when considering the alternative evaluation approaches?

2. Did you find one evaluation approach that you feel most comfortable with, or did you find useful ideas coming out of each approach?

3. Would you miss much if you ignored all but one approach, which you then used for all evaluations? What are some dangers of always using the same evaluation approach?

4. What negative metaphors underlie certain evaluation models? Why is that a concern?

5. What has each of the alternative evaluation approaches contributed to the conceptualization of evaluation?

6. What are some of the major contributions that the various evaluation approaches, viewed collectively, make to the practice of program evaluation?

7. How might the various evaluation approaches be used together in an actual evaluation?

In Chapter 4 we presented a variety of ways to classify evaluation approaches—including our schema, which organizes the proposed approaches into six categories: objectives-oriented, management-oriented, consumer-oriented, expertise-oriented, adversary-oriented, and participant-oriented evaluation. Together these six represent major current schools of thought about how to approach program evaluation. And collectively, Chapters 5 through 10 summarize the theoretical and conceptual underpinnings of most of today's program evaluations. It is therefore appropriate to ask how useful these frameworks are.

The answer is "Very useful indeed," as we shall discuss shortly. But first we feel compelled to offer several cautions.

CAUTIONS ABOUT THE ALTERNATIVE EVALUATION APPROACHES

Five cautions about the collective conceptions of evaluation presented in Chapters 5 through 10 are worthy of consideration here.

The Seminal Writings in Evaluation Are neither Models nor Theories

In a young field there is inevitably a good bit of conceptual floundering as notions are developed, circulated, tried out, refined, and challenged by new alternatives. Until a solid knowledge base begins to guide practice, any new field is likely to be guided by the positions, preferences, and polemics of its leaders. Some may argue that this is inappropriate. But the point is that it is also inevitable, for no new field or discipline is born full grown. Yet it is also appropriate to ask how far the conceptions of leaders have led the field, and in what direction.

Given the fact that program evaluation grew in part out of scientific inquiry, it is not surprising that many evaluators have aspired to be scientists. As evaluators turned toward the various evaluation "frameworks" as sources of guidance, many began asking how close program evaluation was to becoming a science or discipline in its own right. Perhaps political, social, or situational naïveté fosters the hope that evaluation will one day grow into a full-grown discipline. That day, if attainable, would seem far off.

Neurath, Cernap, and Morris (1955) noted decades ago that advancement in any field is often directly related to existence of a "univocal language," one in which there is one and only one term for each construct and where each important construct is so named. The semantic undergrowth in the field of evaluation could hardly be termed univocal; some clearing of redundant verbiage is clearly called for.

If one applies standard criteria for scientific models, the various evaluation approaches do not seem to qualify in any but the loosest sense. Even the less rigorous dictionary definitions of "models" seem ill-suited for the current evaluation literature. The most relevant definition is "something eminently worthy of imitation, an exemplar, an ideal," but without clearer operational guidelines and procedures, most evaluation "models" are so vague and general as to elude emulation in any strict sense.

If not models, then what about theories? Here again, our conceptions in evaluation seem not to fit. What we have come to call the theoretical underpinnings of our field lacks important characteristics of most theories. Our evaluation writings are not axiomatic or deductive bodies of knowledge. They do not enable us to develop, manipulate, or interrelate laws and explanations. They do not permit us to predict or explain. They are not tested in the empirical crucible or interrelated with or validated against other relevant bodies of knowledge. In short, they are not theories.

If not models or theories, what are those influential conceptions about evaluation we have used six chapters of this book to present? Quite simply, they are individuals' conceptions about the field of evaluation, their efforts to order the content of a new and partial field into some kind of logical structure. They are sets of categories, lists of things to think about, descriptions of different kinds of evaluation, and exhortations to (perhaps) be heeded. Useful? Very. But theories? Models? No, clearly not.

"Discipleship" to a Particular Evaluation "Model" Is a Danger

> Into the street the Piper stept,
>   Smiling first a little smile,
> As if he knew what magic slept
>   In his quiet pipe the while.
>
> *Robert Browning,* The Pied Piper of Hamelin

Every evaluation approach described in this book has adherents who believe that a better evaluation will result from that orientation than from alternatives. Fair enough. We have no quarrel with those who follow particular persuasions, just so they do so intelligently, knowing when and where their preferred approach is not applicable, as well as when and how to apply it.

What is troublesome, however, is that every evaluation approach also has some unthinking disciples who are convinced that a particular approach to evaluation is right for every situation.[1] There really are evaluators who are CIPP loyalists, or unswerving adherents of the discrepancy evaluation model, or those who hold the tenets of responsive evaluation as articles of faith. Many evaluators unthinkingly follow a chosen evaluation approach into battle without first making certain the proposed strategy and tactics fit the terrain and will attain the desired outcomes of the campaign. Insisting that the judicial evaluation model be used for an internal formative evaluation where the issues, not to mention the program, are vague and amorphous is as foolish as mounting a cavalry attack across a swamp.

Ideally, evaluation practitioners will be sufficiently at home selecting from a variety of evaluation approaches appropriate for the situation rather than distort the interests and needs of the evaluation's audience(s) to make them fit a preferred approach.

---

[1] Readers are reminded of Kaplan's (1964) "law of the instrument" analogy to show the fallacy of such thinking (see Chapter 4).

Calls to Abandon Pluralism and Consolidate Evaluation Approaches into One Generic Model Are Unwise

The proliferation of proposals for how to do program evaluation has frustrated some writers, resulting in calls for consolidating the different approaches to program evaluation into one omnibus, generic model that would encompass all others (e.g., Gephart, 1978). The arguments for consolidation stem from a desire to simplify the task of evaluation. In his call for a synthesis of the alternative evaluation approaches, Gephart lamented that "the multiple model mess has become dysfunctional!" and argued that the only real difference in the models "is the verbiage used to describe the elements of the 'different' models" (pp. 2–3).

On the surface, such calls for synthesis are appealing because they address the desire of many practitioners and clients just to get to the point, namely, "Skip the academic discussions and just tell us how to do program evaluation!" And, were it possible to achieve, a synthesis would unravel evaluation's currently tangled literature, especially if the purpose of the synthesis were limited to identifying similarities in approaches. One might profitably analyze the various evaluation approaches in terms of their concepts and constructs, assumptions and orientations, terminology and (where provided) proposed methodology—and then ask to what extent these approaches really look at different but related evaluation phenomena. Perhaps, with all approaches viewed in aggregate, a more complete portrayal of evaluation would emerge. If a synthesis accomplished nothing more than to bring into the present jungle of terminology some semblance of semantic cultivation, the effort would be useful.

Yet there are inherent dangers in attempting to synthesize alternatives, especially if the intent is to create the "one model" (of which Gephart speaks) generally applicable in program evaluation. Indeed, we would argue against such reductionism for several reasons.

First, the alternative evaluation approaches described in the preceding chapters are based on widely divergent philosophical assumptions. Although some are compatible enough to be fruitfully combined, integrating all would be a philosophical impossibility, for key aspects of some approaches are directly incompatible with central concerns of others.[2] One might "synthesize" diverse ethnic cultures in an unprejudiced societal "melting pot," but there is little hope of creating a similar synthesis of the inhabitants of a zoo. The analogy to program evaluation is distressingly apt. It would be unfortunate if efforts to synthesize diametrically opposed approaches into one "model" resulted in so much philosophical dilution that the whole was truly less than the sum of its parts.

Second, as mentioned earlier, unthinking discipleship is a tendency among at least some evaluators. If a more prestigious synthesized evaluation model were

---

[2] We view this, not lack of interest or effort, as the most likely reason that no synthesis has been forthcoming since the professionwide discussion of that issue in 1977. We should also note that this does not negate the possibility of eclectically combining compatible portions of different approaches, as discussed later in this chapter.

created, it seems likely that disciple-prone evaluators would gather around the new banner in greater numbers than for any previous approach. There would be little advantage in trading provincial bondage to become vassals of a strong centralized monarchy. Intellectual bondage is intellectual bondage no matter where it exists.

A more serious danger lies in the fact that moving toward one omnibus model at this time could bring premature closure to expansion and refinement within the field. Our conceptions are still too untried and our empirical base too weak for us to be very certain of which notions should be preserved and which discarded. How does one go about synthesizing undeveloped, untested hunches and speculative statements? It would seem far preferable to tolerate our contradictory and confusing welter of ideas and make of them what we can than to hammer them into a unified but impoverished conception of evaluation. "The dangers are not in working with models, but in working with too few, and those too much alike, and above all, in belittling any efforts to work with anything else" (Kaplan, 1964, p. 293). Just because we can synthesize does not mean that we should. As Kaplan puts it, consolidation would impose a premature closure on our ideas and thus limit

> our awareness of unexplored possibilities of conceptualization. We tinker with the model when we might be better occupied with the subject-matter itself . . . incorporating it in a model does not automatically give such knowledge scientific status. The maturity of our ideas is usually a matter of slow growth, which cannot be forced. . . . Closure is premature if it lays down the lines for our thinking to follow when we do not know enough to say even whether one direction or another is the more promising. (p. 279)

A final concern has to do with whether we would really be enriched if the multitude of schemes and suggestions for how to do an evaluation could somehow be streamlined into one or two more sophisticated guidelines. Evaluation contexts are so different that it is difficult to conceive of any one or two models that would be relevant to all. For all their crudity and imperfection, diverse frameworks offer a richness of perspectives and serve as heuristics—especially if one uses evaluation approaches eclectically (where philosophical compatibility permits), as we shall propose later.

The Choice of Evaluation Approach Is Not Empirically Based

If one accepts our view that it is useful to have a variety of evaluation approaches, the next logical question is, How will one know which approach is best for a given situation? And that question is devilishly difficult to answer because of one simple fact: There is almost no research to guide one's choice.

Over the years many evaluators have called for a program of research on evaluation (e.g., Stufflebeam et al., 1971; Worthen, 1972, 1977; Shadish, Cook, & Leviton, 1991). For the most part, their calls have fallen on deaf ears. The lack of an adequate empirical base is probably the single most important impediment to development of a more adequate evaluation theory and models. In the absence of relevant evidence about which approach works best under which circumstances, adherence to any one model rather than another is largely a statement of philosophy or a profession of faith. As Scriven (1976) muses,

> There has been a good deal of work on "evaluation models" which are hybrids between ways of conceptualizing evaluation and reminders as to how to do it. These range from the highly relativistic and value free approaches of many Tyler students and Malcolm Provus' Discrepancy Evaluation, through the touchy-feely school of transactional and responsive evaluation (Rippey and Stake respectively) to the extremely far-reaching and absolutistic approach that I have espoused. Each can, I believe, contribute something of value to most clients, but beyond that I can hardly make a dispassionate judgment. (pp. 28–29)

Years after he first pointed out the need for such research, Stufflebeam (1981) was forced to conclude that "there has been very little empirical research on the relative merits of different approaches to evaluation. Clearly, the field of evaluation could profit from systematic examinations of the feasibility, costs, and benefits of competing conceptualizations" (p. 4). In the ensuing 16 years, this situation has not changed much. Until we have solid information about the relative effectiveness of the numerous evaluation approaches, choices among alternatives will remain a matter of the evaluator's preference.

Negative Metaphors Underlying Some Approaches Can Cause Negative Side Effects

In Chapter 4 we discussed how different evaluation metaphors have led to widely diverse evaluation approaches. This leads us to a disquieting fact about these underlying metaphors, namely, that they are predicated upon negative assumptions that fall into one of two categories.

First, several metaphors tacitly assume there is something wrong in the system being evaluated; a patient has died and the cause of death must be discovered (e.g., forensic medicine or pathology); a scandal has emerged and the truth must be uncovered (investigative journalism or investigative social research); or allegations have been made and must be investigated (adversary hearings). Such indictment mentality is shortsighted and should be discouraged.

Second, several metaphors are based on assumptions that people will lie, evade questions, or withhold information as a matter of course. For example, in Douglas's (1976) volume on investigative social research, he notes that most social research techniques are based on a cooperative methodology that assumes candor and honesty once one builds rapport with interviewees, informants, and so forth. Instead, he proposes an alternative confrontive methodology for handling dishonesty and evasion, which he asserts are typical in situations fraught with anxiety and threat. If we accept the premise that evaluation is basically anxiety provoking to those being evaluated, then we could readily conclude that Douglas's methods would be appropriate for collecting data in most program evaluations. But that would be tantamount to saying that individuals whose programs are being evaluated are prone to be deceitful, dishonest, and evasive, which is an absurd generalization on its face. To champion any evaluation methodology that leads to mutual distrust between evaluators and practitioners would not only be wrongheaded but also self-defeating.

Which brings us to a critical question: Can one draw on metaphors such as investigative journalism, investigative social research, congressional hearings, and the like without their serving as Trojan horses to carry insidious assumptions into the precepts and practice of evaluation? We have uneasy visions of educational evaluators marching in the wake of Ralph Nader, evaluating the educational enterprise with no more care than that shown in Nader's assault on the Educational Testing Service and the school testing industry. Or imagine an evaluation analog to Senator Proxmire's "Golden Fleece Awards." Cohen (1978) tells of how irresponsible distortions of his own research by a *National Enquirer* reporter led Proxmire to request the formal report of Cohen's research from the sponsoring National Science Foundation. The specter that evaluation could become a degenerate example of tabloid journalism is frightening—and perhaps not so far-fetched as we'd like to think. It would be unfortunate to try broadening evaluators' perspectives and succeed only in creating a muckraker mind-set.

One way to avoid some of these problems would be to evoke more positive metaphors, such as the health maintenance approach to medicine. Diagnoses and prescriptions (however unpalatable) are likely to be accepted more gracefully if it is apparent from the outset that the primary objective is not only to uncover and eradicate what is wrong but also to identify and strengthen what is working well.

CONTRIBUTIONS OF THE ALTERNATIVE EVALUATION APPROACHES

If, as argued earlier, the evaluation approaches suggested in the literature are not models or theories, and if there is no empirical basis for deciding which to follow when designing and conducting a particular evaluation, then of what worth are they? Of considerable worth, actually. A novice evaluator may not use Scriven's (1974a) modus operandi method of evaluation, but probably no month passes when that evaluator does not somehow make conscious use of the concepts of formative or summative evaluation Scriven introduced to our thinking. Individuals may spend years as evaluators and never once use Stufflebeam's (1971) CIPP model of evaluation, but most likely they have checked one or more of their evaluation designs against Stufflebeam's (1973b) list of steps in designing evaluations. In similar ways, most of the evaluation approaches summarized in prior chapters influence in important ways the practice of evaluation.

Thinking back to evaluations we have done, our colleagues' work was used in this way in almost every study. As noted earlier,

> Although I have developed some preferences of my own in doing evaluations, probably 75 percent of what I do is application of what I have distilled from others' ideas. Doubtlessly, all who have been repeatedly exposed to the evaluation literature have absorbed much "through the pores," as it were, and now reapply it without cognizance of its source. Although few of us may conduct our evaluations in strict adherence to any "model" of evaluation, few of us conduct evaluations which are not enormously influenced by the impact of our colleagues' thinking on our own preferences and actions. (Worthen, 1977, p. 12)

The alternative conceptions about how evaluation should be conducted—the accompanying sets of categories, lists of things to think about, descriptions of different strategies, and exhortations to heed—influence the practice of program evaluation in sometimes subtle, sometimes direct, but always significant ways. Some evaluation designs adopt or adapt proposed approaches. Many evaluators, however, conduct evaluations without strict adherence (or even purposeful attention) to any "model," yet draw unconsciously in their philosophy, plans, and procedures on what they have internalized through exposure to the literature. So the value of the alternative approaches lies in their capacity to help us think, to present and provoke new ideas and techniques, and to serve as mental checklists of things we ought to consider, remember, or worry about. Their heuristic value is very high; their prescriptive value seems much less.

COMPARATIVE ANALYSIS OF CHARACTERISTICS OF ALTERNATIVE EVALUATION APPROACHES

So many new concepts have been presented in Chapters 5 through 10 that the reader might be feeling challenged to assimilate all of it. The matrix in Figure 11.1—a comparative analysis of the characteristics, strengths, and limitations of the six approaches—should help. The aspects of each approach that we have chosen to highlight are as follows:

1. *Proponents*—Individuals who have written about the approach
2. *Purpose of evaluation*—The intended use(s) of evaluation proposed by writers advocating each particular approach or the purposes that may be inferred from their writings
3. *Distinguishing characteristics*—Key descriptors associated with each approach

FIGURE 11.1 Comparative analysis of alternative evaluation approaches

	Objectives-Oriented	Management-Oriented	Consumer-Oriented	Expertise-Oriented	Adversary-Oriented	Participant-Oriented
1. Some proponents	Tyler Provus Metfessel and Michael Hammond Popham Taba Bloom Talmage	Stufflebeam Alkin Provus	Scriven Komoski	Eisner Accreditation Groups	Wolf Owens Levine Kourilsky	Stake Patton Guba and Lincoln Rippey MacDonald Parlett and Hamilton Cousins and Earl
2. Purpose of evaluation	Determining the extent to which objectives are achieved	Providing useful information to aid in making decisions	Providing information about products to aid decisions about purchases or adoptions	Providing professional judgments of quality	Providing a balanced examination of all sides of controversial issues, highlighting both strengths and weaknesses	Understanding and portraying the complexities of a programmatic activity, responding to an audience's requirements for information
3. Distinguishing characteristics	Specifying measurable objectives; using objective instruments to gather data; looking for discrepancies between objectives and performance	Serving rational decision making; evaluating at all stages of program development	Using criterion checklists to analyze products; product testing; informing consumers	Basing judgments on individual knowledge and experience; use of consensus standards, team/site visitations	Use of public hearings, opposing points of view; decision based on arguments heard during proceedings	Reflecting multiple realities; use of inductive reasoning and discovery; firsthand experience on site
4. Past uses	Program development; monitoring participant outcomes; needs assessment	Program development; institutional management systems; program planning; accountability	Consumer reports; product development; selection of products for dissemination	Self-study; blue-ribbon panels; accreditation; examination by committee; criticism	Examination of controversial programs or issues; policy hearings	Examination of innovations or change about which little is known; ethnographies of operating programs

(continued on next page)

FIGURE 11.1 (continued)

	Objectives-Oriented	Management-Oriented	Consumer-Oriented	Expertise-Oriented	Adversary-Oriented	Participant-Oriented
5. Contributions to the conceptualization of an evaluation	Pre-post measurement of performance; clarification of goals; use of objective tests and measurements that are technically sound	Identify and evaluate needs and objectives; consider alternative program designs and evaluate them; watch the implementation of a program; look for bugs and explain outcomes; see if needs have been reduced or eliminated; metaevaluation; guidelines for institutionalizing evaluation	Lists of criteria for evaluating educational products and activities; archival references for completed reviews; formative-summative roles of evaluation; bias control	Legitimation of subjective criticism; self-study with outside verification; standards	Use of forensic and judicial forms of public hearing; cross-examination of evidence; thorough presentation of multiple perspectives; focus on and clarification of issues	Emergent evaluation designs; use of inductive reasoning; recognition of multiple realities; importance of studying context; criteria for judging the rigor of naturalistic inquiry
6. Criteria for judging evaluations	Measurability of objectives; measurement reliability and validity	Utility; feasibility; propriety; technical soundness	Freedom from bias; technical soundness; defensible criteria used to draw conclusions and make recommendations; evidence of need and effectiveness required	Use of recognized standards; qualifications of experts	Balance; fairness; publicness; opportunity for cross-examination	Credibility; fit; auditability; confirmability

7. *Benefits*	Ease of use; simplicity; focus on outcomes; high acceptability; forces objectives to be set	Comprehensiveness; sensitivity to information needs of those in a leadership position; systematic approach to evaluation; use of evaluation throughout the process of program development; well operationalized with detailed guidelines for implementation; use of a wide variety of information	Emphasis on consumer information needs; influence on product developers; concern with cost-effectiveness and utility; availability of checklists	Broad coverage; efficiency (ease of implementation, timing); capitalizes on human judgment	Broad coverage; close examination of claims; aimed toward closure or resolution; illumination of different sides of issues; impact on audience; use of a wide variety of information	Focus on description *and* judgment; concern with context, openness to evolve evaluation plan; pluralistic; use of inductive reasoning; use of a wide variety of information; emphasis on understanding
8. *Limitations*	Oversimplification of evaluation and programs; outcomes-only orientation; reductionistic; linear; overemphasis on outcomes	Emphasis on organizational efficiency and production model; assumption of orderliness and predictability in decision making; can be expensive to administer and maintain; narrow focus on the concerns of leaders	Cost and lack of sponsorship; may suppress creativity or innovation; not open to debate or cross-examination	Replicability; vulnerability to personal bias; scarcity of supporting documentation to support conclusions; open to conflict of interest; superficial look at context; overuse of intuition; reliance on qualifications of the "experts"	Fallible arbiters or judges; high potential costs and consumption of time; reliance on investigatory and communication skills of presenters; potential irrelevancies or artificial polarization; limited to information that is presented	Nondirective; tendency to be attracted by the bizarre or atypical; potentially high labor-intensity and cost; hypothesis generating; potential for failure to reach closure

4. *Past uses*—Ways in which each approach has been used in evaluating prior programs
5. *Contributions to the Conceptualization of an Evaluation*— Distinctions, new terms or concepts, logical relationships, and other aids suggested by proponents of each approach that appear to be major or unique contributions
6. *Criteria for judging evaluations*—Explicitly or implicitly defined expectations that may be used to judge the quality of evaluations that follow each approach
7. *Benefits*—Strengths that may be attributed to each approach and reasons why one might want to use this approach (what it can do *for* you)
8. *Limitations*—Risks associated with use of each approach (what it can do *to* you)

ECLECTIC USES OF THE ALTERNATIVE EVALUATION APPROACHES

The purpose in the foregoing comparative analysis is to provide key information on the strengths, limitations, and primary uses of each approach. The information in Figure 11.1 is not intended to imply that any one approach is "best"; rather, it is our contention that each approach can be useful. The challenge is to determine which approach (or combination of concepts from different approaches) is most relevant to the task at hand.

Perhaps an experience of one of the authors in attempting to answer a question of a student in a graduate evaluation seminar will help make the point.

We were conducting a several-week-long examination of various authors' evaluation approaches and how each might be applied to do an evalua-tion, when one student asked, . . . "What approach do you usually use?" . . . I pointed out that I did not believe there was one best approach, that each has its strengths, and that I simply used whichever approach was most appropriate to the situation at hand.

"How do you know which one is most appropriate?" she queried. I . . . talked about things like looking at the purpose of the evaluation, the kind of decision needed, limitations of the approach, and so on, . . . and concluded . . . that a lot of it was in experience and, although a little tough at first, they would all get the hang of it once they had done a few evaluations.

"Maybe it would help," she stated, "if you could give us a few examples of where you've used one of the approaches and then show us why you picked it."

That seemed like a very useful suggestion, . . . so I began to sort through my mental files to find the very best examples of where I had used one of the evaluation approaches. Then I began to sort to find *any* examples of where I had used one of the approaches. I discarded evaluation after evaluation because I really had not used the approach, whatever it was, fully. There were truncated CIPP evaluations . . . , since I seldom seemed to be called on early enough to do much with context or input evaluations. There were applications of Hammond's cube . . . for selecting variables, but the rest of the evaluation failed to follow Hammond's ideas. Each was incomplete as an example of use of the approaches, and I struggled for more pure examples to offer.

Finally, I remembered using Stake's "countenance" framework in its entirety in evaluating an administrators' training program. That one was memorable because it had been a class project where two students and I took it on . . . so they could get the experience. . . . That one brought others to mind and before long I was able to give examples of using several of the frameworks in the way they were intended to be used. The intriguing realization was that every one of those examples came from class projects conducted jointly with students, where I had intentionally adhered to the models to demonstrate their features. I could not recall a single "lone-wolf" evaluation of my own where I had consciously selected any single approach to guide the study. Instead, for several years I had been designing each evaluation de novo, pulling pieces of different frameworks in as they seemed relevant. Certain features of some models I used frequently, others seldom or never.

That realization seemed worth sharing, although in the process I felt a twinge of disloyalty toward some of my esteemed colleagues and friends for never really using their frameworks in my work. . . . The class was slightly taken aback at first by my heretical revelation, but they seemed comforted when I pointed out that there were distinct advantages in eclecticism, since one was free to choose the best from diverse sources, systems, or styles. Warming to the idea, I argued that one could choose the best features of each approach and weave them into a stronger overall approach—really a classic bit of cake-having and cake-eating. . . .

We talked for the remainder of the class about why each evaluation required a somewhat different mix of ingredients, how synthesis and eclecticism were not identical, and why an eclectic approach may be useful. (Worthen, 1977, pp. 2–5)

The authors of this text are all self-confessed eclectics in our evaluation work, choosing and combining concepts from the evaluation approaches to fit the particular situation, using pieces of various evaluation approaches as they seem appropriate. In very few instances have we adhered to any particular "model" of evaluation. Rather, we find we can ensure a better fit by snipping and sewing together bits and pieces off the more traditional ready-made approaches and even weaving a bit of homespun, if necessary, rather than by pulling any existing approach off the shelf. Tailoring works.

Obviously, eclecticism has its limitations (after all, it has been derided as the discipline of undisciplined minds), and one obviously cannot suggest that we develop an "eclectic model" of evaluation, for that would be an obvious non sequitur. And the uninformed could perform egregious errors in the name of eclecticism, such as proposing that a program's objectives be evaluated as a first step in conducting a goal-free evaluation or laying out a preordinate design for a responsive evaluation. Assuming that one avoids mixing evaluation's philosophically incompatible "oil and water," the eclectic use of the writings presented in the preceding chapters has far more potential advantages than disadvantages, whether that eclecticism means combining alternative approaches or selectively combining the methods and techniques inherent within those approaches.

Evaluators who have urged that more thoughtful attention be given to eclecticism include Talmage (1982), Cronbach and others (1980), Cronbach (1982), Conner, Altman, and Jackson (1984), and Chen (1990). Yet eclectic use of the evaluator's tools is a lamentably infrequent occurrence in program evaluation. This is partly due to the fact that education has been the primary field in which models have been discussed. Other fields such as sociology, criminal justice, and mental health have erred in not considering those approaches for evaluation. By failing to consider these approaches, evaluators in these fields have often failed to consider sufficiently the critical components of their evaluation, such as audiences, purposes, and uses. The evaluations in those fields have remained more applied research than evaluation and have been more summative than formative. Much of evaluation's potential lies in the scope of strategies it can employ and in the possibility of selectively combining those approaches. Narrow, rigid adherence to single approaches must give way to more mature, sophisticated evaluations that welcome diversity. Admittedly, this will be a challenging task, but that does not lessen its importance.

DRAWING PRACTICAL IMPLICATIONS FROM THE ALTERNATIVE EVALUATION APPROACHES

All the evaluation approaches we have presented have something to contribute to the practicing evaluator. They may be used heuristically to generate questions or uncover issues. The literature contains many useful conceptual, methodological, political, communicative, and administrative guidelines. Finally, the approaches offer powerful tools that the evaluator may use or adapt in his work.

Later in this book we will look at practical guidelines for planning and conducting evaluations. Many of these guidelines have been developed as part of a particular approach to evaluation. Fortunately, however, they are generalizable, usable whenever and wherever needed. Just as a skilled carpenter will not use only a hammer to build a fine house, so a skilled evaluator will not depend solely on one approach to plan and conduct a high-quality evaluation.

Let us now turn in the next section of this book to practical uses of the tools that evaluation practitioners, theorists, and methodologists have generated. But first, pause a moment to apply what you have learned in this chapter.

APPLICATION EXERCISES

1. Identify five evaluation studies in a journal of interest to you, or, better yet, collect in-house reports on five evaluation studies. These might be from your own welfare agency, from your school or university, from a city, county, state, or federal office, or from a nonprofit agency. After reading the report, discuss what approach the author used. Is it eclectic or does it follow one model predominantly? What elements of each approach seem to be most useful in guiding the authors in identification of purpose, audiences, data collection methods, and presentation of results?

2. Pupils entering the third grade in a particular small town were routinely tested using a standardized oral reading test. Typically, students from the school scored at or above the established national norms for the test. On the 1995 and 1996 administrations of the test, however, student performance fell significantly below national norms. In attempts to interpret this sudden drop in students' reading scores, school officials compared third-grade classes from 1985 to 1995 on the following characteristics:

   a. Focus of first- and second-grade reading curriculum

   b. Performance on mental ability tests

   c. Previous teachers' education and professional experiences

   d. Socioeconomic background of students.

   e. Mobility of students

   Students entering the second grade in 1995 or 1996 were similar to students from earlier years in socioeconomic backgrounds, performance on mental ability tests, and teachers' prior experiences. However, the mobility of students had greatly increased and, as a result, students coming into the second grade had received a much greater variety of approaches to teaching reading in the first grade. As the small town had begun to grow, many students and their families had relocated from the large city close by to the small town. Approximately one-quarter of the entering second graders had attended first grade in elementary schools outside of the district. These students had experienced a variety of reading approaches, few being the combination of phonics and whole language approaches used by the small town elementary school. Some had received a strictly phonics-based approach. Others had received reading instruction that focused heavily on the whole language approach. As a result, when students entered the second grade, teachers were faced with a much more hetero-geneous group, in terms of reading skills, than they had had in the past when the population of the town was more stable. Further, new research on reading instruction suggested to the teachers that their methods needed to be based more on the individual learning styles of students.

   As a result of these changes, teachers and administrators agreed to adopt a new reading curriculum that focused on matching reading instruction to the learning styles of individual students. Teachers would make use of a variety of strategies based on the needs of individual learners. Since this new curriculum represented a major change in focus, it was agreed that a formative evaluation would be conducted during the first year to provide feedback on the implementation of the program and the achievement of some of its immediate outcomes. The purpose of the evaluation was to provide feedback to teachers and administrators about how to adapt the curriculum to meet the needs of the school and its students. If the curriculum became too unwieldy, summative decisions concerning the continuation of the curriculum might be considered, but the proposed focus was formative.

An evaluation plan was developed to answer the following questions:

a. What were the identified learning styles of new third graders? How many children were classified by each style? How were decisions made about children whose styles were overlapping or difficult to define?

b. Were teachers able to conduct reading instruction to address each style? Which styles were most difficult for teachers to address? How much time was required for new curriculum development and lesson planning?

c. How did students respond to the new curriculum? To what extent did they enjoy the approach they received? What side effects occurred in students as a result of different approaches (greater self-esteem and positive feelings about school overall, classroom management issues, spill-over effects for other content areas)?

d. How did students with each learning style progress in their competencies in oral reading? in their interest in independent reading?

e. What were parents' attitudes and perceptions regarding the reading program? Did parents' satisfaction differ based on the learning style of their child?

Describe how each of the evaluation approaches discussed in Chapters 5–10 would address these evaluation questions. Would each approach agree with the focus of the questions? How might each adapt the questions? For each approach, describe how that approach might lead you to proceed with the evaluation, with data collection, with reporting of results, and so on. Do you think one approach or a particular combination of approaches might be most appropriate for conducting this particular evaluation? If so, describe that approach or combination of approaches and give a rationale for your selection.

SUGGESTED READINGS

Madaus, G. F., Scriven, M., & Stufflebeam, D. L. (Eds.). (1983). *Evaluation models: Viewpoints on educational and human services evaluation.* Boston: Kluwer-Nijhoff.

McLaughlin, M. W., & Phillips, D. C. (Eds.). (1991). *Evaluation and education: At quarter century.* Ninetieth Yearbook of the National Society for the Study of Education. Chicago: University of Chicago Press.

Scriven, M. (1993). *Hard-won lessons in program evaluation.* New Directions for Program Evaluation, No. 58, 1–107. San Francisco: Jossey-Bass.

Shadish, W. R., Cook, T. D., & Leviton, L. C. (1991). *Foundations of program evaluation.* Newbury Park, CA: Sage.

Stufflebeam, D. L., & Shinkfield, A. J. (1985). *Systematic evaluation.* Boston: Kluwer-Nijhoff.

part THREE

Practical Guidelines for Planning Evaluations

$\mathbf{I}$n Part One we discussed the purpose and uses of evaluation, presented some basic evaluation concepts and distinctions, and described the history of program evaluation. In Part Two we examined factors that led to alternative conceptions of evaluation, summarized the key characteristics and the strengths and weaknesses of six general evaluation approaches, and argued for thoughtful use of those approaches, including eclectic combination of features of the alternative approaches, when doing so would be advantageous.

Which brings us to the heart of this book: practical guidelines. In this part we begin to provide guidelines that we believe will be helpful to evaluators, regardless of which evaluation approach or combination of approaches they might elect to use. We also focus on guidelines for planning evaluation efforts (and in Part Four focus on guidelines for conducting and using evaluations). We begin Part Three by examining in Chapter 12 reasons that lead to initiation of program evaluations, considerations in deciding when to evaluate ("always" is a common but incorrect answer), and how to determine who should conduct the evaluation. In Chapter 13 we discuss the importance of the evaluator's understanding the setting and context in which the evaluation will take place, as well as the importance of characterizing accurately that which is to be evaluated. Two crucial steps in evaluation planning—identifying and selecting evaluative questions and criteria, and planning the information collection, analysis, and interpretation—are examined in detail in Chapters 14 and 15. We also include in Chapter 15 a few guidelines for developing management plans for evaluation studies, stressing the importance of establishing evaluation agreements and contracts.

The focus of the chapters that follow is decidedly practical. Although we will continue to quote or reference other sources, these chapters are not intended as scholarly reviews of the content covered. Were such reviews to be included, several of these chapters could each fill a textbook. Our intent is only to introduce enough information to give both the evaluator and user of evaluation (1) an awareness of how to proceed and (2) direction to more detailed coverage of many (especially technical) topics in other textbooks. Experience and further study will have to suffice to teach the rest.

INTRODUCTION OF CASE STUDY

To help readers apply the content of the chapters in this and the following section, we have included a case study, which we will thread through the chapters. At the end of each chapter (in Chapters 12 to 20) is a section titled "Case Study Application," where we attempt briefly to describe how we would apply some of the content of that chapter to one particular evaluation of a public school curriculum. It is important to point out that not *all* of the content in *any* chapter can be applied to the case study; such an attempt would double the length of this book. We have selected only those few concepts to discuss within the case study that we think will be most helpful in making or clarifying our points. We hope that this case study will help to show how at least some of the guidelines we discuss could be applied to a real evaluation.

Setting the Stage: The Radnor Case Study

The case study we will use here appeared in Worthen and Sanders (1987), the predecessor to this book, and has been retained because of positive feedback on it from students and faculty who have used it previously. It describes the "Radnor humanities curriculum," a real curriculum that existed in the Radnor Middle School in Wayne, Pennsylvania (and may still exist, for all we know). A brief description of the Radnor humanities curriculum is provided below, in the form of a short description of an imaginary report of the Radnor humanities curriculum review committee. Beginning in Chapter 12 of this book, and extending through Chapter 20, an account of a *fictional* evaluation of that curriculum is presented, drawing on an earlier, hypothetical description of how such a program could be evaluated.[1]

---

[1] From Worthen (1981), in Brandt (1981), used by permission of the Association for Supervision and Curriculum Development, and adapted and extended as necessary to fit the needs of this text.

Three introductory comments are appropriate. First, we have chosen to apply the rather eclectic "multiple-method" approach we have come to favor to our imaginary evaluation of the Radnor curriculum. If readers wish to see how their other preferred evaluation approaches (such as participant-oriented, expertise-oriented, or decision-oriented evaluation) could be applied to the Radnor curriculum, other chapters in Brandt (1981) illustrate how a variety of evaluation approaches might be applied to a single curriculum. We strongly endorse Brandt's entire book as excellent supplemental reading to this text.

Second, students and faculty who are not educators should not be "put off" by use of this example; a school curriculum is clearly an educational *program,* and those from other fields should be able to transfer important learnings from this case study to programs in their own fields.

Third, we have left the evaluation case study in the informal, singular, first-person form in which it first appeared and have included in Chapter 12 the introduction that provides a framework for the case study as it appears there and throughout the next several chapters of this text.

THE RADNOR HUMANITIES CURRICULUM

How have you evaluated this program?" asked the president of the board of education. She seemed determined to maintain an air of objectivity, but the atmosphere was growing tense in the school library where the board was meeting.

The main business of the evening was a report on the middle school's humanities program. Prepared by a committee of 11 educators and 6 parents, the report was the product of more than 30 committee meetings plus discussions with students, staff, and citizens. It explained philosophy, listed goals and objectives, described the curriculum in detail, made specific recommendations, and included a rationale for each recommendation. It even listed a number of alternatives that had been considered but rejected as undesirable.

All students in the sixth, seventh, and eighth grades were required to take the humanities course, which was taught two days a week by four teachers, including an artist and a musician, all members of a separate humanities department. The arts—everything from literature and drama to architecture and the visual arts—were used to develop the students' "understanding of all that it means to be human." Looking at a van Gogh painting of a Flemish mining family at dinner, for instance, students might be asked, "Would you like to be invited to dinner here?" as well as, "What tones and colors did the painter use?" They might listen to Humperdink's opera *Hansel and Gretel* or "She's Leaving Home" by the Beatles. Examples were drawn from African and Asian cultures as well as from European and American.

The program should be continued, the report said, with some modifications, including a new organizational framework based on the concepts and skills being taught, and increased emphasis on writing and other language skills. Several board members and parents were not satisfied. A woman who was a member of the study committee, but who had not attended most meetings, read a statement expressing concern about the general direction of American education and objected to "values clarification" and "secular humanism" in the program. (The teachers insisted they did not use techniques such as those advocated by proponents of *values clarification.*)

Others said a humanities course would be more appropriate for older students, who would have the background to appreciate it, but that students in the middle school needed more basic knowledge first. One board member asked what impact the program was having on students and how it could be measured.

Pointing out that the program had been in limbo for more than a year, the principal, assistant superintendent for curriculum, and the superintendent gave strong personal endorsement and asked for an immediate decision. Several parents added their support. But when the meeting ended at 11:00 P.M., the board had postponed acceptance of the committee's report until they could talk privately with the principal about how the program could be scheduled and staffed in light of declining enrollments.

Ten days later, a majority of the board members voted to permit continuation of the humanities course. Still, evaluation remained an issue. In reply to the question about measurement, the principal had said it couldn't be done statistically; the course did not teach children *what* to think and feel, it taught them *to* think and feel.

Evaluation of the Radnor Humanities Curriculum

In Chapters 12 to 20, practical guidelines for various aspects of evaluation will be discussed and then applied, in turn, at the end of each chapter, to an imaginary evaluation of the preceding humanities curriculum.

chapter 12

Clarifying the Evaluation Request and Responsibilities

ORIENTING QUESTIONS

1. Suppose you received a telephone call from a potential client asking if you would do an evaluation. What are some of the first questions you would ask?
2. Are there times you would decline a request for evaluation? If so, under what conditions?
3. How can an evaluability assessment help determine whether an evaluation will be productive?
4. What are some advantages and disadvantages in having an evaluation conducted by an external evaluator? By an internal evaluator?
5. What criteria would you use to select an external evaluator?

In the preceding chapters we discussed evaluation's promise for improving programs. The potential and promise of evaluation may create the impression that it is *always* appropriate to evaluate and that every facet of every program should be evaluated.

Such is not the case. The temptation to evaluate everything may be compelling in an idealistic sense, but it ignores many practical realities. In this chapter we discuss how the evaluator can better understand the origin of a proposed evaluation and judge whether or not the study would be appropriate.

To clarify the discussion, we need to differentiate here among several groups or individuals who affect or are affected by an evaluation study: sponsors, clients, stakeholders, and audiences.

An evaluation's **sponsor** is the agency or individual who authorizes the evaluation and provides necessary fiscal resources for its conduct. Sponsors may or may not actually select the evaluator or be involved in shaping the study, but they generally have ultimate authority concerning the evaluation. In some circumstances, the sponsor may delegate that authority to the client.

The **client** is the specific agency or individual who requests the evaluation. In many instances, the sponsor and client are synonymous—but not always. For example, in an evaluation of a domestic violence treatment program operated by a nonprofit agency, the agency (client) requests and arranges for the actual study, but the requirement and funding for the evaluation may both originate with a foundation that is the funding source for the program (sponsor).

Stakeholders are those who have a stake in the program to be evaluated or in the evaluation's results. Sponsors and clients are both stakeholders, but so are program managers and staff, the recipients of program services and their families, other agencies affiliated with the program, interest groups concerned with the program, elected officials, and the public at large. As we will discuss, it is wise to consider all the potential stakeholders in a program when planning the evaluation. Each group may have a different picture of the program and different expectations of the program and the evaluation.

Audiences include individuals, groups, and agencies who have an interest in the evaluation and receive its results. Sponsors and clients are usually the primary audiences and may occasionally be the only audiences. Generally an evaluation's audiences will also include all stakeholders, although that is not always so. For example, elementary school students might be participants in an evaluation of their school's reading program, being observed, tested, or interviewed, but only in some circumstances would they likely display much interest in the results of that evaluation. Sometimes it is appropriate to prepare a community report based on the evaluation findings for a program. In that case, the audience can include the community-at-large. More will be said about evaluation audiences in Chapter 13.

UNDERSTANDING THE REASONS
FOR INITIATING THE EVALUATION

It is important to understand what prompts an evaluation. Indeed, determining the purpose is probably the most important decision the evaluation sponsor will make in the course of an evaluation.[1] And understanding that purpose is probably the most important insight the evaluator can have. If some problem prompted

---

[1] In earlier chapters we noted that evaluation's purpose is always the same—to determine worth or merit. Here and throughout the remainder of this text we also use the term "purpose" as it is commonly used, to refer to the purpose (motives) that lead stakeholders to propose that an evaluation be conducted. It should always be clear from the context which usage of "purpose" is intended.

the decision to evaluate, or if some stakeholder has demanded an evaluation, the evaluator should know about it.

Presumably, the decision to evaluate stemmed from someone's need to know. Whose need? What does he want to know? Why? How will he use the results? The evaluator's first questions should begin to identify these reasons.

Sometimes the evaluation client can answer such questions directly and clearly. Unfortunately, that is not always the case, and the evaluator's task is made more difficult when the client has no clear picture of what the evaluation should accomplish. It is not uncommon to find that the clients or sponsors are unsophisticated about evaluation procedures and have not thought deeply about possible ramifications or results. Sometimes even the persons who commission the evaluation study are not clear about *why* the evaluation is being planned. Frequently the purpose of the evaluation is not clear until the evaluator has carefully read the relevant materials, observed the evaluation object, and probed the aspirations and expectations of stakeholders.

Such probing is necessary to clarify purposes and procedures. Where sponsors or clients are already clear about what they hope to obtain, it is no less crucial for the evaluator to understand their motivations. He can often do so by exploring— with whoever is requesting the evaluation—such questions as these:

1. Why is this evaluation being requested? What is its purpose? What questions will it answer?
2. To what use will the evaluation findings be put? By whom? What others should be informed of the evaluation results?
3. What is to be evaluated? What does it include? Exclude? During what time period? In what settings? Who is the intended client for the program? Who will participate? What are the goals and objectives of the program? What problem is the program intended to address? Who is in charge of it? Has it ever been evaluated before?
4. What are the essential program activities? How do they link with the goals and objectives? What is the program theory?
5. How much time and money are available for the evaluation? Who is available to help with the evaluation? Is certain information needed right away?
6. What is the political climate and context surrounding the evaluation? Will any political factors and forces preclude a meaningful and fair evaluation?

The foregoing questions are only examples, and evaluators might add or subtract others. What is important is that, through careful questioning and listening, the evaluator comes to understand the purpose for the evaluation. Not all purposes are equally valid.

By listening closely to the client's reasons for initiating the evaluation and talking with other stakeholders to determine their information needs and perceptions of the study, the evaluator can learn much about the program that will help ensure that the evaluation is appropriately targeted and useful. The evaluator can also take a proactive role during this phase by suggesting other reasons for evaluating that may prove even more productive (Fitzpatrick, 1989). This strategy is particularly useful when the stakeholders are new to evaluation and unsure of their needs. Such clients may assume that evaluations should only measure whether objectives are achieved (the objectives-oriented approach) when other critical information needs exist that could be served by evaluation. Thus, this phase can begin the important two-way communication process essential to evaluation, in which the evaluator learns as much as he can about the program through careful questioning, observing, and listening and, at the same time, educates the stakeholders about what evaluation can do.

Informational Uses of Evaluation

Evaluation is intended to enhance our understanding of the value of whatever is evaluated. Yet, as we noted at the beginning of this text, evaluation has many different uses. Examples of some of the informational uses of evaluation by policy makers, program managers, and program staff include

1. Determining whether sufficient need exists to initiate a program and describing the target audience;
2. Assisting in program planning by identifying potential program models and activities that might be conducted to achieve certain goals;
3. Describing program implementation and identifying whether changes from the program model have occurred;
4. Examining whether certain program goals or objectives are being achieved at desired levels; and
5. Judging the overall value of a program and its relative value and cost compared to competing programs.

Each of these five uses of evaluation may be directed to an entire program or to one or more of the smaller components of a program. The first two uses are frequently parts of planning and needs assessment (McKillip, 1987; Witkin & Altschuld, 1995). These tasks generally take place during the early stages of a program but may occur at any stage when program changes are being considered. The third use is often described as a monitoring or process study. The fourth use can be characterized as an outcome study, while the final use is achieved through conducting cost-effectiveness or cost-benefit studies. All of these studies serve legitimate uses for evaluation because each one serves an important, informational use: enhancing our understanding of the value of the program.

Noninformational Uses of Evaluation

In addition to the direct "informational" uses described in the previous section, evaluation also has noninformational uses. Cronbach and his colleagues (1980) underscore this use in arguing that the very incorporation of evaluation into a system makes a difference. They conclude that "the visibility of the evaluation mechanism changes behavior" (p. 159), citing as an analog how drivers' observance of speed limits is affected by police officers' patrolling the highways in plainly marked patrol cars. They also suggest that the existence of evaluation may help convince stakeholders that the system is responsive, not impervious, to their feedback.

In her seminal treatise on evaluation, Weiss (1972) noted that evaluation also has several noninformational uses that are seldom acknowledged. Some of the more covert, nefarious, and patently political uses she cites are:

> *Postponement.* The decision maker may be looking for ways to delay a decision. Instead of resorting to the usual ploy of appointing a committee and waiting for its report, he can commission an evaluation study, which takes even longer.
>
> *Ducking responsibility.* . . . There are cases in which administrators know what the decision will be even before they call in the evaluators, but want to cloak it in . . . legitimate trappings. . . .
>
> *Public relations.* . . . The administrator believes that he has a highly successful program and looks for a way to make it visible. . . . The program administrator's motives are not, of course, necessarily crooked or selfish. Often, there is a need to justify the program to the people who pay the bills, and he is seeking support for a concept and a project in which he believes. . . .
>
> *Fulfilling grant requirements.* . . . Many federal grants . . . are tagged with an evaluation requirement. . . . the operators of a project . . . tend to neglect the evaluation [and] . . . see it mainly as a ritual designed to placate the funding bodies, without any real usefulness to them.
>
> Evaluation, then, is a rational enterprise often undertaken for nonrational, or at least noninformational, reasons. (pp. 11–12)

Recent work by Worthen (1995) suggests, however, that such noninformational uses may be more common in federal or national evaluations than in evaluations of programs administered at the state or local level. In an analysis of 108 evaluations, Worthen found that over two-thirds of the evaluations of state and local programs served informational purposes while only 15 percent of those conducted at the federal level served such purposes. While these results are based on a sample of studies conducted by only one institute, the Western Institute for Research and Evaluation (WIRE) and the number of national programs sampled is relatively small, the results do fit rather well our collective experiences in other evaluations. If one can assume that the political tides run stronger in national programs than at lower levels, then these results may be attributable to the impact political forces have on evaluation, as we discuss in Chapter 16.

Evaluation's Educative Function: Another Noninformational Use. Another important use of evaluation is its role in educating others, not simply about the program being evaluated, but also about alternative means for decision making. Smith (1989) writes that one of the most important benefits of evaluability assessment, a method of determining whether the program is ready for evaluation, is improving the skills of program staff in developing and planning programs. Through participating in an extensive series of structured discussions to develop the program model, the staff learn skills that can be used in the next program they develop, even if evaluation is not involved.

Cronbach and his colleagues (1980) emphasize the importance of the educative role of the evaluator in helping the client determine the directions of the evaluation. They note that "the evaluator, holding the mirror up to events is an educator. . . . The evaluator settles for too little if he simply gives the best answers he can to simple and one-sided questions from his clients. He is neglecting ways in which he could lead the clients to an ultimately more productive understanding" (pp. 160–161). Thus, before proceeding with the evaluation, the evaluator must spend a significant period of time learning about the program, its stakeholders, the decision-making process and the culture of the organization in order to accurately determine the purpose of the study.

CONDITIONS UNDER WHICH EVALUATION STUDIES ARE INAPPROPRIATE

Except for some uses cited by Weiss, the foregoing examples all represent *appropriate* uses of evaluation studies. But evaluations are not always used appropriately. Several circumstances in which evaluations are, at best, of dubious value and, at worst, harmful, are outlined here.

Evaluation Would Produce Trivial Information

Heretical as this may sound to some, sometimes a program simply lacks sufficient impact to warrant the expense of formal evaluation. Some programs are one-time efforts with no potential for continuation. Some are provided at such low cost to so few people that the need for more than informal evaluation is unlikely. Common sense must dictate when a program has enough impact to warrant formal evaluation of its effectiveness.

Evaluation Results Will Not Be Used

Too often the professed "need" for an evaluation is merely an unreasoned assumption that every program must be evaluated. Evaluation is of dubious value unless there is commitment by someone to use the results. There may be some value in a "decision-free Nader's Raiders" type of evaluator capability, but given the scarcity of evaluation resources (both financial and human) and the demand for evaluation information to support important decisions, it seems a questionable investment at present.

Sometimes there are important decisions to be made, but it is clear that they will be made for reasons unrelated to evaluative data. A program may, for instance, have sufficient political appeal or public support that administrators are simply unwilling to discontinue or change it drastically, no matter what problems an evaluation study may reveal. In this case, evaluation can play no meaningful role except—assuming the data cooperate—to justify program continuation, a dubious "whitewash" function at best. Evaluators should avoid meaningless, ritualistic evaluations or pro forma exercises where evaluation only appears to justify decisions actually made for personal or political reasons.

Of course, such dubious (and, one hopes, rare) motives are not always apparent. One of the most frustrating situations the evaluator will confront is to learn, *after* the evaluation has been completed, that the client or sponsor was not really open to conclusions that contradicted preconceived notions. If the evaluator learns during the evaluation that certain conclusions are inevitable, it would be best to find ways to truncate the evaluation "sham" at the earliest opportunity.

Evaluation Cannot Yield Useful, Valid Information

Sometimes, despite an important pending decision, it appears highly unlikely that an evaluation study will produce any relevant information. For example, consider a decision about whether to continue a school dropout prevention program. Here information about the program's effects on dropout rates, graduation percentages, and so forth would be relevant. But what if the program only started one month before the school board must make its decision? The probability of obtaining dependable information (even predictive information) about the program's effectiveness in that length of time is so slight that it would seem wiser to spend one's energies convincing the school board to delay the decision. Similarly, a variety of constraints beyond the evaluator's control (e.g., inadequate resources, lack of administrative cooperation or support, limited time in which to collect decent evaluation data, impossible evaluation tasks, and inaccessible data essential to the evaluation) can prevent the evaluator from providing useful information. Well-intentioned but naive clients may request "mission impossible" evaluations that yield only wasted efforts and disappointment. The evaluator needs to recognize when an evaluation is doomed to fail from the beginning. If unreasonable constraints preclude a professionally responsible evaluation, it would be wise not to undertake the evaluation. A bad evaluation is worse than no evaluation at all; poor evaluation data can readily mislead and lull administrators into the false security of thinking the misinformation they have really portrays their efforts.

Evaluation Is Premature for the Stage of the Program

Programs that are in a tryout phase nearly always benefit from well-conducted formative evaluation (barring reasons listed hereafter). But one cannot be so quick to conclude that a summative evaluation would be appropriate. Premature summative evaluations are among the most insidious misuses of evaluation, prompting concerns such as those expressed by Campbell (1984):

> Another type of mistake involved *immediate evaluation,* evaluation long before programs were debugged, long before those who were implementing a program believed there was anything worth imitating.
>
> When any one of them, after a year or so of debugging, feels they have something hot, a program worth others borrowing, we will worry about program evaluation in a serious sense. Our slogan would be, "Evaluate only proud programs!" (Think of the contrast with our present ideology, in which Washington planners in Congress and the executive branch design a new program, command immediate nationwide implementation, with no debugging, plus an immediate nationwide evaluation.) (pp. 35–37)

While today's Washington planners are more likely to be cutting programs than starting new ones, states, local governments, and nonprofit agencies are the sites of many new programs. Unfortunately, they—or their funding source— also often mandate summative evaluations too early in the stage of the program. Tharp and Gallimore (1979) illustrate a more effective approach to evaluation. Their approach requires a long-term commitment to using evaluation for decision making and the development of evaluation questions that are appropriate for the stage of the program and the current information needs of program developers. The process is an iterative one. Results of one study are used to make changes and refinements; the next study examines whether these changes have succeeded.

Propriety of Evaluation Is Doubtful

Evaluations are undertaken for many reasons—some noble and some not. When the evaluator can discern that the reasons for undertaking the study are honorable and appropriate, the chances that the evaluation will be a success are enhanced. But the evaluator must also be able to recognize less noble reasons, including those that strain or violate professional principles. It would be unwise to proceed with any evaluation if its propriety is threatened by conflict of interest, jeopardy to participants in the study, or any other factors.

Ethical evaluators refuse to undertake thinly disguised "hatchet jobs," where an evaluation is structured to "get" a particular person or project. Any immoral or illegal uses of information are to be avoided by the evaluator. Confidential information cannot and should not be released in any form that would harm individuals, groups, or institutions.

DETERMINING WHEN AN EVALUATION
IS APPROPRIATE: EVALUABILITY ASSESSMENT

In the early 1970s, Joseph Wholey and his colleagues at the U.S. Department of Health, Education, and Welfare (now Health and Human Services) saw that the proliferation of program evaluation in the 1960s had not resulted in an increase in the use of program evaluation for decision making (Buchanan & Wholey, 1972). In fact, many of the potential users of evaluation were unhappy with such studies, believing that they often failed to provide useful information.

Wholey and his colleagues developed **evaluability assessment** as a tool to remedy this situation. They saw evaluability assessment as a means for facilitating communication between evaluators and stakeholders, for determining whether a program was "evaluable," and for focusing the evaluation study itself.

The developers of evaluability assessment believed that many evaluations had failed because of discrepancies between "rhetoric and reality" (Nay & Kay, 1982, p. 225). As Nay and Kay point out, different levels of policy makers and program managers have different rhetorical models of the program. The models of high-level policy makers may be quite general, reflecting their role in advocating for resolution of the problem and gaining funding. The rhetorical models of managers closer to program delivery become more specific and closer to reality. Yet even the models of managers relatively close to the program may fail to match reality. Many policy makers and managers may continue to cling to their rhetorical models because they perceive their particular model as necessary for public consumption. In any case, the varying rhetorical models and the gap between rhetorical models and reality make program evaluation difficult. The evaluator is unsure which program "reality" to assess.

Other common barriers to a program's being evaluable include nebulous or unrealistic goals and objectives, failure to link program activities to these goals and objectives, and managers who are unable or unwilling to make program changes on the basis of evaluation information (Horst, Nay, Scanlon, & Wholey, 1974). Other problems Wholey has discussed in more recent work include (1) the failure of evaluators and managers to agree on goals, objectives, and performance criteria for measuring these objectives; (2) the inability to obtain data on program performance; and (3) problems with the particular purposes and uses of the evaluation itself (Wholey, 1983, 1987; Wholey, Hatry, & Newcomer, 1994). Wholey and his colleagues wanted to develop a way to remedy these problems.

Evaluability assessment was devised to help programs meet three criteria they deemed necessary for meaningful evaluation:

1. Program objectives, important side effects, and priority information needs are well defined (that is, program managers have agreed on a set of measurable objectives and program performance indicators in terms of which the program is to be assessed and managed).
2. Program objectives are plausible (that is, there is some likelihood that the objectives will be achieved).

3. Intended uses of information are well defined (that is, program managers have agreed on intended uses of program performance information). (Wholey, 1983, pp. 39–40)

Evaluability assessment was first developed as a precursor to a summative evaluation; if the evaluability assessment revealed that the program did not meet the criteria, the summative evaluation would not proceed. Over the 20 years during which evaluability assessment has been conducted, its uses have expanded. Evaluability assessment is now frequently employed to clarify the purposes of a formative study or as a planning tool in its own right (Smith, 1989). It can serve as an effective method for clarifying the evaluation request for many types of evaluation study.

How Does One Determine Whether a Program Is Evaluable?

The major steps to determining whether a program is evaluable are:

1. Clarify the intended program model or theory.
2. Examine the program in implementation to determine whether it matches the program model and could, conceivably, achieve the program goals and objectives.
3. Explore different evaluation approaches to determine the degree to which they meet stakeholders' information needs and are feasible to implement.
4. Agree on evaluation priorities and intended uses of the study.

These steps are achieved not by the evaluator alone but in conjunction with the intended users of the study. A working group is established to clarify the program model or theory and to define their information needs and expectations for the evaluation. The role of the evaluator is to facilitate these discussions and to listen and learn about the program and the stakeholders. Wholey (1994) writes, "evaluators do not hypothesize the program design. Instead, they *extract* the program design . . . from relevant documentation and key actors in and around the program" (p. 20, italics ours). Too many evaluations fail when the evaluator develops his model of the program and assumes stakeholders agree.

What methods are used to accomplish these tasks? In addition to the facilitation of the working group, the evaluator uses *personal interviews* with stakeholders, *reviews of existing program documentation* (proposals, reports, brochures, etc.), and *site visits* to observe the program's implementation. The interviews and program documents help the evaluator facilitate the early discussions of the working group to achieve consensus on the program model or theory.

The program model or theory should delineate the goals and objectives of the program and the principles that link program actions to these goals and objectives. Frequently, a model will take the form of a flowchart linking program actions and assumptions to the program goals and objectives. Alternative models may be developed as necessary to facilitate communication. Closure occurs when stakeholders achieve consensus on a particular model that is sufficiently detailed for the evaluator to conduct a study.

Site visits and further study of program documents (quarterly reports, resource allocations, other evaluation studies) can then help the evaluator determine whether the program is being implemented according to the model and whether the implementation can feasibly achieve the desired goals. If problems occur in either of these areas, the evaluator should then return to the working group. He can help the working group determine whether the model should be revised to match program reality or program changes should occur so that the program implementation corresponds to the current model. The working group can then also address whether and when the evaluation should proceed. In cases where major adaptations occur, the evaluation might best be postponed until program stability is achieved.

If no problems emerge in program implementation, the working group can then turn to examining various evaluation plans. The evaluator would also facilitate this discussion to provide guidance about what evaluation can accomplish, at what cost, and in what time frame. By this time, the evaluator also should have learned, from his interviews, of different stakeholders' needs. Alternative evaluation plans can be developed specifying the questions the evaluation will answer, data to be collected, time and resources required, and potential outcomes and uses. The working group then needs to select a plan.

At any stage the group and/or the evaluator can conclude that an evaluation is inappropriate at this time or that a quite different evaluation is required. Evaluations might be postponed if

- Consensus cannot be achieved among major stakeholders on the program model;
- Program actions differ greatly from the program model;
- Program actions could not feasibly achieve any stated goals or objectives of the model;
- Major stakeholders cannot achieve consensus on the desired evaluation plan;
- The desired evaluation plan is not feasible given data availability and resources;
- Intended uses of the evaluation are too ambiguous.

The above conditions might lead to the conclusion that the intended evaluation is inappropriate at that time. However, the process may have led to another type of evaluation. Specifically, the working group and/or the evaluator may conclude that although the originally intended outcome study is inappropriate due to lack of agreement on the program model or failure in program implementation, a needs assessment or monitoring study would be useful at this time. The needs assessment study could be used to better define the program model. The monitoring study could determine whether proposed changes in the implementation of the program occur. Thus, this process of determining when an evaluation is appropriate may result in a relatively simple "go" or "no go" or may result in a changed evaluation focus. In either case, the evaluator, through this planning effort, has made a major step toward conducting an evaluation that makes a difference in organizational effectiveness.

How Evaluability Assessment Is Impacted by Alternative Evaluation Approaches

How would the different models reviewed in Chapters 5 to 10 approach the clarification of the evaluation request? Most proponents of the models described in those chapters would not object to the evaluability assessment method described above, and all would include at least some interviews with stakeholders and reviews of existing documents during the planning stage. The differences among models would be of emphasis.

An evaluator ascribing to the objectives-oriented model would focus primarily on the specification of objectives during this stage. He would be more likely to assume that the study would be an outcome study focusing on the achievement of objectives. He would be inclined to conclude an evaluation is inappropriate only if objectives are not clearly defined. In contrast, the management-oriented evaluator would focus more on the decisions to be made and the information needs of the managers who will make those decisions. If these decisions concern objectives, he would focus on those objectives; however, if the decisions concern the program model or implementation, he would readily adapt to a needs assessment or monitoring mode.[2] In contrast to the management-oriented approach, the consumer-oriented evaluator would clarify the request through working with the consumers of the program and identifying their concerns. Similarly, the expertise-oriented evaluator might limit the evaluation by relying on established areas of concern in the discipline of the program (e.g., medical, education, or environmental standards). The clarification might have little focus on the needs of actual stakeholders, as the evaluator would assume that he was hired to define the criteria based on his personal expertise.

The participant-oriented evaluator would involve many more stakeholders than other models in the clarification of the evaluation request. Since the values of these stakeholders are more likely to differ than are those of the more homogeneous managers, meetings of working groups, as proposed by Wholey, may be more acrimonious and achieving consensus more difficult. Further, if the gap between managers and other stakeholders were too great, open discussion might be discouraged. However, such working groups could succeed in identifying issues that might not have been raised in the managerial meetings and, in such a way, further communication between managers and other stakeholders. As an alternative, the participant-oriented evaluator might clarify the evaluation request through interviews with different stakeholder groups, reviews of program documents, and observations of the program, without trying to achieve consensus through a working group of

---

[2] Wholey is considered a management-oriented evaluator (Shadish, Cook, & Leviton, 1991); thus, his evaluability assessment model fits the management-oriented approach. His model has been adapted here to permit addressing other stakeholders.

all stakeholders. The participant-oriented evaluator who is of a constructivist bent is looking for multiple realities, not necessarily consensus.

Checklist of Steps for Determining When to Conduct an Evaluation

The checklist in Figure 12.1 should help the evaluator decide when to initiate an evaluation. However, when the decision is yes, the evaluator may still choose to adopt some of the methods discussed to assist in focusing the evaluation.

FIGURE 12.1   Checklist for determining when to conduct an evaluation

Check one for each item.

	Yes	No
Step 1. *Is there a legal requirement to evaluate?* (If yes, initiate the evaluation; if no, go to step 2.)	_____	_____
Step 2. *Does the object of the evaluation have enough impact or importance to warrant formal evaluation?* (If yes, go to step 3; if no, formal evaluation is unnecessary, and you should discontinue further use of this checklist.)	_____	_____
Step 3. *Is there sufficient consensus among stakeholders on the model for the program? its goals and objectives?* (If yes, go to step 4; if no, consider a needs assessment study.)	_____	_____
Step 4. *If the program has begun, are its actions consistent with the program model? Is achievement of goal(s) feasible?* (If yes, go to step 5; if no, consider a needs assessment or monitoring evaluation to study program modifications.)	_____	_____
Step 5. *Is the proposed evaluation feasible given existing human and fiscal resources and data availability?* (If yes, go to step 6; if no, find more resources before proceeding or revise the scope of your plan.)	_____	_____
Step 6. *Do the major stakeholders agree on the intended use of the evaluation?* (If yes, go to step 7; if no, discontinue or focus on fewer stakeholders who can use the information effectively.)	_____	_____
Step 7. *Are the stakeholders in a position to use the information productively?* (If yes, go to step 8; if no, discontinue or focus on other stakeholders who can use the information to make decisions or take action.)	_____	_____
Step 8. *Will the decisions of your primary stakeholders be made exclusively on other bases and be uninfluenced by the evaluation data?* (If yes, evaluation is superfluous, discontinue; if no, go to step 9.)	_____	_____
Step 9. *Is it likely that the evaluation will provide dependable information?* (If yes, go to step 10; if no, discontinue.)	_____	_____
Step 10. *Is the evaluation likely to meet acceptable standards of propriety?* (See Chapter 16.) (If yes, go to summary. If not, consider other means of data collection or discontinue.)	_____	_____

Summary:
Based on steps 1–10 above, *should an evaluation be conducted?*

SELECTING AN EVALUATOR

In the previous section we discussed *when* to conduct an evaluation. We now consider *who* will conduct the evaluation. The first decision to be made may be choosing whether to use an external or **internal evaluator**. When the decision to be made is summative—whether to continue, expand, or drop a program—an **external evaluator** (also called a third-party evaluator, independent evaluator, evaluation consultant, or evaluation contractor) may be preferable to an internal evaluator. However, as evaluation has grown as a field, some have observed that few evaluations are purely summative (M. F. Smith, 1994). Most evaluations have implications for formative and summative decisions. Nevertheless, internal and external evaluators can present distinct differences.

Advantages of External Evaluations

The advantages of using an external agency or individual[3] to conduct the summative evaluation can be summarized as follows:

1. The external evaluation is likely to be more impartial (i.e., capable of replication with comparable results by different but equally competent evaluators) because the external evaluator has more distance from the program and those involved in its planning and implementation than the internal evaluator.

2. The external evaluation is likely to be more credible to outside audiences, especially if the program is controversial and evaluation findings are to be used in settling a dispute.

3. External evaluation enables an agency to draw on evaluation expertise beyond that possessed by agency staff. Many school systems and other public and nonprofit organizations simply do not find it feasible to hire sufficient numbers of evaluation specialists to conduct the evaluations needed in the system; but they can obtain the necessary expertise through external evaluators. Moreover, external evaluators fit into more flexible staffing arrangements, because there is no need for continuing financial commitment, as is the case with internal evaluators. Thus, the particular skills of several individual external evaluators might be employed at appropriate stages, with each being paid only for the specific services needed.

4. External evaluators bring with them a fresh, outside perspective. Unlike the internal evaluator, they see both the forest and the trees, often detecting unwarranted assumptions that are accepted by insiders.

5. Sometimes persons associated with a program are more willing to reveal sensitive information to outsiders (if trust exists) than they are

---

[3] Individual consultants and external contracting agencies are not treated separately in the remainder of this discussion because procedures for obtaining assistance are similar in both cases.

to on-site evaluators, who they fear may inadvertently breach their confidentiality because they are continually on-site and in contact with others involved in the program.

6. External evaluators can have less concern than internal evaluators with presenting unpopular information or taking action to curtail a study due to concerns over ethical or utilization issues. Specifically, since their future salaries and promotions do not depend on people in the organization, external evaluators can be as blunt and honest as the situation merits. Internal evaluators can be inhibited by future concerns. (This perceived advantage of the external evaluator can, however, be overstated. External evaluators are often interested in further work with the organization and good references, if not permanent employment.)

Advantages of Internal Evaluations

Internal evaluations may be conducted by staff whose full-time responsibilities and training are in the evaluation area or, in small organizations, by persons whose primary responsibilities and training are in other areas. Obviously, the internal person with more evaluation expertise is preferable to his counterpart whose expertise lies less in evaluation and more in other areas. Nevertheless, both types of internal evaluators share some advantages.

1. Internal evaluators have more knowledge of the program model and its history. This advantage can make internal evaluators quite useful in needs assessment and monitoring studies.

2. Internal evaluators are more familiar with the various stakeholders and their interests, concerns, and influence. This knowledge can help increase the use of the study. Further, if the evaluator has formed positive relationships with management and staff, this relationship can help ease anxiety and build trust regarding evaluation (Love, 1991).

3. Internal evaluators know the history of the organization and the typical dynamics involved in decision making. Thus, they can more readily and accurately identify persons who will make productive use of the study and can time and present the study to maximize its use.

4. Internal evaluators will remain with the organization after the evaluation and can continue to serve as advocates for use of its findings.

5. Given that internal evaluators are already employed by the organization and oriented to it and the program, start-up times for the evaluation can be quicker than searching for, selecting, and hiring an external evaluator who, if he has not worked with the organization before, will need to take time to learn its dynamics.

6. Internal evaluators are a known quantity. Their strengths and weaknesses are known to the organization and can be analyzed in reference to the project under consideration.

The definition of an internal evaluator becomes less clear in larger organizations and governmental units. Evaluators from the General Accounting Office (GAO) would probably be considered external evaluators when they evaluate an Executive Branch program in response to a congressional request, even though they are federal employees evaluating a federal program. Is an employee of a state evaluation unit, analogous to the GAO, considered an internal or external evaluator when he evaluates a program in another state organization? What if the evaluator is part of an evaluation unit within the state organization he is evaluating? Now, he would be more likely to be considered an internal evaluator, especially if the organization were a small one.

The prototypical internal evaluator is an employee of a small organization who works daily with program planners and providers; moderate-size nonprofit organizations and many units of local government are examples of organizations that would include such internal evaluators. Conversely, the prototypical external evaluator is an independent consultant or an employee of an organization whose function is to conduct evaluations by contract. Many evaluators lie somewhere between these two extremes. Nevertheless, the contrasts between internal and external evaluators, as with the distinctions between summative and formative evaluations, help us to examine the strengths and weaknesses of the various alternative evaluators we could select to conduct the study. We also can use the continuum from internal to external evaluator to ameliorate some of our concerns. Thus, the concern regarding impartiality or bias of the internal evaluator may be partially remedied by selecting an internal evaluator who is relatively distant, on an organizational chart, from the program. Note, however, that this distance, while improving objectivity, diminishes the typical advantages of the internal evaluator, that is, the evaluator's knowledge of the program and its stakeholders. Duffy (1994), an internal evaluator for the FBI, presents an effective case study for her organization and describes ways that internal evaluation can be organized to prevent abuses. (See Love, 1991, for more on internal evaluation.)

Advantages of Combining Internal and External Evaluation

Internal and external evaluation are far too often viewed as mutually exclusive. They need not be. Combining the two approaches can compensate for several of the disadvantages of each mentioned previously. The external evaluator's lack of familiarity with the program and its stakeholders is less of a problem if he works in tandem with an internal evaluator who can provide the necessary contextual information. Travel costs can be greatly reduced by having the internal evaluator collect the bulk of the necessary data and actively communicate evaluation plans and results to significant internal audiences. Finally, after the external evaluator is gone, the internal evaluator will remain as an advocate for the use of the evaluation.

The external evaluator can then be used to ensure impartiality and credibility as well as to provide specialized knowledge and skills that are not routinely needed in-house. The external evaluator can assist with key tasks where bias

Check one for each item.

	Yes	No

Step 1. *Is there a legal requirement that the evaluation be conducted by an external evaluator?* (If yes, initiate the search for an external evaluator; if no, go to step 2.)

Step 2. *Are financial resources available to support the use of an external evaluator?* (If yes, proceed to step 3; if no, discontinue use of this checklist and conduct the evaluation internally.)

Step 3. *Does the evaluation require specialized knowledge and skills beyond the expertise of internal evaluators who are available to do the evaluation tasks?* (If yes, initiate the search for an external evaluator; if no, go to step 4.)

Step 4. *Is the evaluation concerned with measuring major or highly politicized goals for summative purposes?* (If yes, initiate the search for an external evaluator; if no, go to step 5.)

Step 5. *Is an outside perspective of particular importance to the study?* (If yes, initiate the search for an external evaluator; if no, go to the summary.)

Summary
Based on steps 1 to 5 above, *should this evaluation be conducted by an external evaluator?*

FIGURE 12.2   Checklist for determining whether to use an external evaluator

might inadvertently occur, such as designing the evaluation, selecting or developing instruments, drawing conclusions from data, and the like. The external evaluator can interpret and present sensitive results to stakeholders. External evaluators can also be used to "audit" internal evaluation studies to certify that they are methodologically sound and unbiased (Chen, 1994). Such partnerships incorporate the advantages of external evaluation without requiring that the entire evaluation be conducted externally. Further, through the resulting teamwork, internal evaluators can learn new evaluation methods to be used by the organization in the future.

Checklist of Steps for Determining Whether to Use an External Evaluator

Figure 12.2 is proposed as a checklist for deciding whether or not to use an external agency or individual to conduct the evaluation.

SELECTING AN EXTERNAL EVALUATOR

Selecting an external evaluator is neither simple nor trivial.[4] Once an agency has decided to use an external evaluator, it is important to obtain the services of an individual or consulting firm with the necessary competence and sensitivity

---

[4] This statement and many others made in this section are obviously applicable to the internal evaluator as well; those statements peculiarly applicable to the external evaluator will be apparent.

to do the job well. There is no better way to guarantee a bad evaluation than to turn it over to someone who is inept. Relationships with stakeholders can be irreparably harmed by an insensitive or unresponsive evaluator. Misleading or incorrect information is easy to generate and disseminate but difficult to eradicate. Therefore, great care should be exercised in choosing external evaluators. Before summarizing some criteria that have been suggested for selecting evaluators, it is necessary to consider briefly what competent evaluators must be able to do.

Competencies Needed by Evaluators

There have been several conceptual and/or empirical efforts to identify the tasks required of evaluators and more specific competencies (knowledge, skills, and sensitivities) required to perform those tasks well (e.g., Worthen, 1975; Anderson & Ball, 1978; Covert, 1992; Mertens, 1994). Even summarizing the evaluation competencies listed via these efforts is beyond the scope of this book, but a few comments seem in order.

First, the overlap among various lists is reassuringly high. We would be concerned if there were substantial disagreement among professional evaluators regarding critical competencies—but such is not the case.

Second, the few areas where the lists of competencies do not overlap result, we believe, from (1) different publication dates (new issues and needs in evaluation are being discovered continually); (2) differences in level of detail; and (3) differences in the evaluation philosophy of the authors (some emphasize technical, others subjective or artistic competencies).

We have included in the Appendix a listing of general *areas* of competence we consider important to enable evaluators to conduct high-quality evaluations. An agency can make use of competencies from the literature cited above or those listed in the Appendix to derive the knowledge and skills that are pertinent to their particular evaluation. These competencies would almost certainly include the ability to work with audiences to formulate key evaluation questions; skills in research design, data collection, analysis, and interpretation; the planning and management skills to carry out a study in a timely, cost-effective fashion; the ability to conduct the study in an ethical manner; the communication skills to convey results to varying audiences through oral and written venues; and, finally, the sensitivity to work with a variety of stakeholders in a manner that meets their needs and facilitates the use of results.

Possible Approaches to Selecting an Evaluator

What are the means by which an agency can determine whether an evaluator has these skills? As in any personnel process, selection methods should be matched to the knowledge and skills to be assessed. A résumé and/or past evaluation reports can be useful in judging whether the candidate has the necessary methodological expertise and writing skills. An interview with the

	Evaluator qualifications (Check one for each item.)		
	Yes	No	?
Question 1. *Does the evaluator have the ability to use the methodologies and techniques that may be required in the study?* (Consider education and training, past experience, and philosophical orientation.)			
Question 2. *Does the evaluator have the ability to help articulate the appropriate focus for the study?* (Consider communication skills, ability to work with stakeholder groups, content specialization.)			
Question 3. *Does the evaluator have the mangement skills to carry out the study?* (Consider education and training, past experience.)			
Question 4. *Will the evaluator maintain appropriate ethical standards?* (Consider education, training, talk with references.)			
Question 5. *Will the evaluator be interested in and able to communicate results to desired stakeholders in such a way that they will be used?* (Examine previous evaluation documents; talk with references.)			

Summary
Based on questions 1 to 5 above, *to what extent is the potential evaluator qualified and acceptable to conduct the evaluation?*

FIGURE 12.3   Checklist of questions to consider in selecting an evaluator

candidate—if possible, conducted by representatives of different stakeholders—can be used to assess the candidate's oral communication skills and ability to work with different audiences. An interview can be particularly successful in determining an evaluator's ability to explain complex issues clearly (in describing previous work) and to listen and learn. The candidate's questions and comments during an interview can be judged in terms of his interest in the program and the evaluation, his sensitivity to different stakeholders, and his overall oral communication skills. Finally, talking with others who have used the evaluator can be invaluable in discovering more about the candidate's skills in managing an evaluation responsibly and ethically. References can also provide useful information about the personal style and professional orientation of the evaluator.

Checklist of Questions to Consider in Selecting an Evaluator

Figure 12.3 is proposed as a checklist of criteria to consider in selecting an evaluator.[5] Each can be answered with a simple yes or no, or qualified as necessary.

---

[5] Each item in this checklist is written to apply to an individual. If the potential evaluator is an agency, the question should be recast accordingly.

CASE STUDY APPLICATION

At first, I was fooled by ASCD's (the Association for Supervision and Curriculum Development) request that led to this "case study."[6] The task appeared straightforward enough. "Would you," ASCD editor Ron Brandt had asked over the telephone, "be willing to write a chapter for a book on evaluation? We will give you a description of a real program—sort of a case study—and would like you to explain, in a general way, how you would go about evaluating it." Straightforward. Simplicity itself. So I agreed.

Then the case study arrived; it was a description of a humanities curriculum in a middle school in the Radnor Township (Pennsylvania) School District. It contained the report of the Humanities Curriculum Review Committee and a brief overview that provided an introduction (pp. 188–190). I read the material quickly, worried vaguely that the description was so incomplete that it might not provide much focus for an evaluation, and then dropped the missive into my ASCD file; the deadline was still months away.

Months passed. So did the deadline. A skillfully worded reminder from the editor prodded my conscience, and I retackled the task, beginning by rereading the program description. I had been right. The writing was lucid; it provided a general outline of the humanities program, gave the general context and some issues surrounding it, and even provided some details about rationale, objectives, schedules, and the like. But it struck me as not nearly enough. Somehow I have never learned to design an evaluation that is really "on target" without knowing a good bit about not only the program but also the context in which it is embedded, the personnel who operate it, the population it is intended to serve, availability of resources for the program (not to mention the evaluation), and so on. Without such information, deciding how to aim the evaluation is largely guesswork, and the odds are high that it will miss the mark. How, I wondered, could ASCD expect any evaluator to make a clean hit on such an obscure target?

To put it bluntly, I felt frustrated at the realization that it simply was not feasible to extract, from what I had received, a clear enough picture of the program and the factors influencing it to permit me to design an evaluation I would feel comfortable defending. Were I like some clairvoyant colleagues who seem not to need much information about a program to launch a full-fledged evaluation, or like the enviably certain and single-minded souls who push and pull every evaluation problem until it can be solved by their preferred evaluation approach, I might have worried less. But somehow I have been afflicted with an abiding conviction that the evaluation approach should be tailored to fit the evaluation problem or need, not the reverse. So I continued to fret about the ambiguity of the request.

Then suddenly the realization hit me. The fuzziness of that target was no accident. By providing purposely incomplete information about the Radnor humanities curriculum, ASCD was forcing each author to fill in the gaps, and in so doing, to reveal clearly the personal preferences and predilections that make each evaluator's approach unique and render evaluation still more of an art than a science.

---

[6] This section and parallel sections that follow at the end of chapters are taken from Worthen (1981), with adaptations and expansions as necessary for our purposes here. The Radnor humanities curriculum, which is evaluated in this "imaginary" evaluation, is described in the Part Three introduction.

Finally, I decided to take the liberty of imagining that the evaluation has already been planned and conducted, thus permitting a description of what has already happened. This shift in tense is important, because it allows exploration of the interactive, iterative nature of evaluation design, which is difficult to see when one looks only at the artificially one-dimensional evaluation plan.

I have chosen to use imaginary journal entries and file artifacts to communicate many of my thoughts about how the evaluation might be conducted. In doing so, I have liberally interpreted the Radnor context; I have made many assumptions about what went on as the evaluation unfolded; I have invented fictional characters[7] and events to suit my purposes; and in the process I have probably unintentionally maligned at least some of the principal actors in the Radnor drama. If so, it is hoped that I have at least done so equitably. My sincere apologies are extended to Principal Claire Janson and others for any violence I may have done to their school system or sensibilities.

My journal entries cover a 12-month period during the design, conduct, and reporting of the evaluation of the humanities program. I have also annotated these entries and artifacts under "author comments" to help underscore important points.

Journal Entry: October 11. Today was the first of three days I've agreed to spend here in Battle Creek, Michigan, serving as a member of a panel of evaluators helping the Kellogg Foundation's Evaluation Director operationalize and refine his concept of "cluster evaluation." Tonight at dinner, Harriet Millman, another of the panelists, told me she had recently been asked to recommend an evaluation consultant to do an evaluation for a school district in Pennsylvania which she worked with a couple of years ago to set up a standardized testing program. I'm not quite clear on what it's about, except I believe it's some kind of junior high art program that is drawing fire from some "back to basics" folks; at least that's what she thinks. Not sure I want to get involved, even should they ask me, which is a long shot, since Harriet says they're considering several possible consultants but only have the resources to hire one and may not want to fly someone in.

Guess I'm a bit reluctant since, from what I can gather, the school is being pressured to have the evaluation done, and I'm a bit wary of being brought into situations where the locals have been forced to set up an evaluation but want to let you know that they're not going to be forced to like it. Being unwanted and unwelcome is "unfun," and it makes establishing rapport a real upstream swim. Maybe I'm jumping at shadows, though, because of some prior experiences I'm not eager to repeat, like the time a faculty member in a college several of us were evaluating stood up in a public meeting and defined *waste* as "a busload of evaluators going over a cliff—with two empty seats"! Quaint sense of humor, that.

All I really know about this Pennsylvania art program, however, is that the decision to evaluate it has been made. Anyway, I told Harriet I would be willing to talk about it if they should contact me.

Author Comments. Sometimes the evaluator is identified and selected early enough to help determine whether or not it is appropriate to evaluate a particular educational endeavor. More often, however, the decision has been

---

[7] Any resemblance to persons living or dead is purely coincidental.

made before the evaluator is ever contacted. In such cases, the client has presumably made the right choice in deciding to evaluate or else the decision to evaluate has been made at a higher administrative or governing level—in an equally rational way, one would hope. All the evaluator can do is to be sensitive to the possibility that evaluation may be premature or unwarranted for reasons discussed earlier in this chapter. Should that be the case, the professionally responsible evaluator will so advise, urging that the evaluation not go forward until or unless it is appropriate, as was discussed earlier. The fact that it is idealistic to expect all evaluators, whose earnings may be reduced if the evaluation does not continue, to suggest terminating a premature or otherwise inappropriate evaluation underscores how important it is for those who decide when to initiate an evaluation to consider all the factors in the earlier checklist.

> *October 19.* Received an interesting call today from a Ms. Janson, principal of a middle school in Radnor Township (somewhere near Philadelphia). She asked if I might be willing to consider undertaking an evaluation of the program Harriet Millman told me about. Turns out that it's a somewhat controversial humanities curriculum in her school. Seems board of education members have asked for the evaluation. She made it clear to me that she wasn't asking me to do it but only asking if I'd be interested, since they're still deciding who they want. Harriet gave my card to the superintendent, and Ms. Janson (Claire) says she has inherited the job to call several evaluators to find out who might be interested and available to do the study.
>
> She didn't seem at all hostile toward having part of her school's curriculum evaluated, so maybe it's not as hot an issue as I'd thought. Besides, she said no one would believe the results of the evaluation unless it were conducted by an outsider. Anyway, I told her I would be interested—tentatively, at least—and sent her the résumé she requested. I hoped she might mention who else she was considering, but she didn't. No reason why she should, since I guess this could be viewed as a "competitive" situation, although I'm not really panting over the opportunity. It's been a while since I've been asked to throw my hat into the ring, but no harm, I guess.
>
> *October 24.* Claire Janson's secretary called from Radnor today and asked if I had a graduate transcript I could send. I told her no, saying I doubted if it would be helpful even if I had one, since those courses were taken 20 years ago. She asked if I had much coursework or background in the humanities. I told her no, not much. She seemed a bit flustered asking those questions, until I offered to send her copies of a couple of evaluation reports I had done and a few names of folks for whom I had done evaluation work in the past four to five years. I suggested she ask Ms. Janson if that wouldn't suffice, since it seems a lot more relevant and a whole bunch easier to locate. I've no idea where to look for my transcript.

Author Comments.   Some wisdom should guide the rigor with which information about evaluators might be pursued. The relevance of formal academic preparation fades with the passage of time, and intervening experience becomes more important. Asking for documents or information not only of dubious utility but also not convenient for the evaluator to provide may discourage interest, unless the evaluator is salivating over the opportunity. Of course, if the evaluation is in Tahiti, or the contract is large and lucrative, one can ask for nearly outrageous information and some evaluators will try to provide it. No evaluator should object, however, to being asked for a few work samples or references of clients previously served. If they do object, that should raise a red flag to further discussions.

October 31. Harriet called from Penn State today and said she'd been at Radnor yesterday and heard I was going to be doing the external evaluation. That's news to me—I've not heard a word since I sent the stuff to them last week. Sounds as if they may have made a decision. Harriet said she didn't know who else they were considering, but guessed they may not have had many well-qualified persons interested in the job. I had hung up the phone before I realized what she'd said! Reminds me of my old psychometrics prof who was fond of saying one could always look good if compared to a norm group made up of stuffed owls.

APPLICATION EXERCISES

1. What questions might you want to ask if you were being considered to perform an evaluation?
2. Consider a program you know. Does it meet Wholey's criteria for evaluability? If not, what changes need to occur? Are there any steps you could take as an evaluator to help achieve these changes?
3. Considering the program you identified in exercise 2, would an internal or external evaluator be preferable for this program? Justify your choice.
4. What knowledge and skills would be necessary to evaluate the program you are considering? How would you go about hiring a person to conduct this evaluation (internal or external)?

RELEVANT EVALUATION STANDARDS

The evaluation standards we see as relevant to this chapter's content are the following. These standards are described in Chapter 20 on page 442.

U1—Stakeholder Identification
U2—Evaluator Credibility
F2—Political Viability
P1—Service Orientation
P7—Conflict of Interest
A1—Program Documentation
A2—Context Analysis
A3—Described Purposes and Procedures

SUGGESTED READINGS

Cronbach, L. J., Ambron, S. R., Dornbusch, S. M., Hess, R. D., Hornik, R. C., Phillips, D. C., Walker, D. F., & Weiner, S. S. (1980). *Toward reform of program evaluation.* San Francisco: Jossey-Bass.

Guba, E. G., & Lincoln, Y. S. (1981). *Effective evaluation.* San Francisco: Jossey-Bass.

Joint Committee on Standards for Educational Evaluation. (1994). *The program evaluation standards* (2nd ed.). Thousand Oaks, CA: Sage.

Love, A. J. (1991). *Internal evaluation: Building organizations from within.* Newbury Park, CA: Sage.

Smith, M. F. (1989). *Evaluability assessment: A practical approach.* Boston: Kluwer Academic.

Wholey, J. S. (1983). *Evaluation and effective public management.* Boston: Little, Brown.

chapter 13

Setting Boundaries and Analyzing the Evaluation Context

ORIENTING QUESTIONS

1. Who are the potential audiences for an evaluation? When and how should they be involved in the evaluation?
2. Why is it important to describe the object of the evaluation?
3. What tools does the evaluator use to describe the object of the evaluation?
4. How can presenting more than one budget be useful to the evaluator? What are some ways that costs can be reduced?
5. What should the evaluator consider in analyzing the political context in which an evaluation will occur? What impact would political considerations have on the conduct of the study?

In the preceding chapter we dealt with determining whether to conduct an evaluation, deciding whether to use an internal or external evaluator, and judging the qualifications of competing evaluators. In this chapter we turn our attention to four other important considerations: identifying evaluation audiences, setting boundaries on whatever is evaluated, analyzing available resources, and analyzing the political context.

IDENTIFYING INTENDED AUDIENCES FOR AN EVALUATION

Every evaluation study results in some type of report. It is therefore essential that the evaluator know the various audiences for that report as well as how each might use the evaluation's findings. In this section we discuss the identification and involvement of appropriate evaluation audiences.

Identifying the Multiple Audiences for an Evaluation

An evaluation is adequate only if it collects information from and reports information to all legitimate evaluation audiences. An evaluation of a school program that answers only the questions of the school staff and ignores questions of the school board, parents, students, and relevant community groups is simply a bad evaluation. The evaluator should identify and communicate with each audience to learn its perceptions and concerns about the program and the evaluation. Obviously, because some audiences will usually be more important than others, some weighting of their input will be necessary. Correspondingly, the **evaluation plan** should plan to collect appropriate evaluation information from each audience with a direct interest in the program as well as to provide information to each such audience. But how does one identify all the legitimate audiences?

At the outset, the evaluator must realize that the sponsor and client usually represent a primary audience. Yet there are almost always additional important audiences for the evaluation's results. Indeed, the evaluation's sponsor often supports the study to provide information for other audiences—such as the evaluated program's staff.

Working with the evaluation client and/or sponsor, the evaluator must strike a reasonable balance in deciding whether to define audiences broadly or narrowly. Few evaluations hold sufficient interest to warrant news releases in the *Wall Street Journal* or the *London Times.* But the more frequent mistake is settling on too narrow a range of audiences. Policy makers, managers, and representatives of those working in the "trenches" are usually selected to guide evaluations and consume their products. And community members and representatives of other influence groups are increasingly numbered among the evaluation's audiences. But there is still a regrettable tendency to respond to the squeaking wheel, targeting evaluation studies to those who are vociferous, strident, or powerful. What about the retired folks without school-age children, who are uninvolved in the PTA and who are often regarded only when their numbers and approaching school bond issues or other tax increases for educational purposes make it prudent to ignore them no longer? And what of the high school students and their parents? In introducing empowement evaluation, Fetterman (1994) has argued for the need not only to inform but also to empower the most frequently neglected audience, the clients of the program themselves.

The greater the number and diversity of audiences to be served, the more complex and costly the evaluation. Conversely, for political and practical reasons, the evaluator can ill afford to ignore certain constituents. Thus, the question of who the audiences are and how they are to be served is a crucial one.

It is important that the evaluator begin to identify and consider all potential audiences during the planning stage. Guba and Lincoln (1981) have developed a set of questions to assist the evaluator in identifying potential audiences. Their questions distinguish among audiences involved in supporting or developing the program to be evaluated, audiences potentially benefiting from the program, and audiences for whom the program may present disadvantages or decrements. We have adapted their questions in modifying the checklist shown in Figure 13.1, which is drawn from our 1987 text (Worthen & Sanders, 1987).

It is doubtful that any one evaluation would have all the audiences listed in Figure 13.1, but the viability of each of these audiences should be considered during the planning stage. The evaluator should discuss these audiences with the client and meet individually with representatives of each audience to learn their perceptions of both the program to be evaluated and the evaluation itself. What does each audience perceive as the purpose of the program? How well do they think it works? What concerns do they have about it? What have they heard about the evaluation? Do they agree with its intent? What do they hope to learn from the evaluation? What concerns do they have about it? The evaluator should attempt to meet with audiences with diverse opinions of the program not only to include all audiences but to help her gain a complete picture of the program.

After meeting with representatives of all potential audiences, the evaluator can then make decisions, possibly with the client, about the import and role of each audience in the evaluation. Important audiences might be involved in an advisory group to the study and consulted frequently; some might become involved in data collection and interpretation of results; others might be briefed on a more intermittent basis. Other audiences may have little or no interest in the study, given its present focus. The checklist in Figure 13.1 is intended to help evaluators and clients think broadly of the audiences for the evaluation and the purpose that might be served in involving them in the study or providing them with the evaluation information. Once the appropriate evaluation audiences have been identified, the list should be reviewed periodically as the evaluation progresses because audiences can change.

Of course, as information is provided to each group, it is important to consider what information each audience needs and will use. All audiences are not interested in the same information. Program deliverers and primary managers will be interested in more detail than the general public or policy makers. Differing interests and needs often require that evaluation reports be tailored for specific audiences, in ways discussed further in Chapter 19.

Evaluation Audience Checklist

Entity to be Evaluated				(Check all appropriate boxes.)	
Individuals, Groups, or Agencies Needing the Evaluation's Findings	*To Make Policy*	*To Make Operational Decisions*	*To Provide Input to Evaluation*	*To React*	*For Interest Only*
Developer of the program					
Funder of the program					
Person/agency who identified the local need					
Boards/agencies who approved delivery of the program at local level					
Local funder					
Other providers of resources (facilities, supplies, in-kind contributions)					
Top managers of agencies delivering the program					
Program managers					
Program deliverers					
Sponsor of the evaluation					
Direct clients of the program					
Indirect beneficiaries of the program (parents, children, spouses, employers)					
Potential adopters of the program					
Groups excluded from the program					
Groups perceiving negative side effects of the program or the evaluation					
Groups losing power as a result of use of the program					
Groups suffering from lost opportunities as a result of the program					
Public/community members					
Others					

FIGURE 13.1   Checklist of evaluation audiences

Importance of Identifying and Involving Evaluation Audiences

The aggregated viewpoints of various evaluation audiences provide focus and direction to the study. Unless evaluators direct the evaluation clearly at their audiences from the outset, results are likely to have little impact. Discussing who will use evaluation results, and how, is essential to clarify the purpose of the study.

As noted in Chapter 12, most evaluators have at some time been misled (perhaps inadvertently) into undertaking an evaluation, only to find at some point that its underlying purpose was quite different from what they had supposed. Such misunderstanding is much more likely if an evaluator talks only to one audience. Dialogue with multiple audiences also clarifies the reasons behind an evaluation (except for the rare case where a manipulative individual may intentionally obscure the real purposes—in those cases even contact with multiple audiences would be less useful than truth serum in discerning the real reasons for the evaluation). Vroom, Colombo, and Nahan (1994) report a fascinating case study of such an evaluation.

DESCRIBING WHAT IS TO BE EVALUATED: SETTING THE BOUNDARIES

Setting boundaries is a fundamental step in gaining a clear sense of what an evaluation is all about. No evaluation should be conducted without a detailed description of the program being evaluated. Such a description establishes the boundaries of whatever is to be evaluated. Poor or incomplete descriptions can lead to faulty judgments—sometimes about entities that never really existed. For example, the concept of team teaching has fared poorly in several evaluations, resulting in a general impression that team teaching is ineffective. Closer inspection shows that what is often labeled as "team teaching" provides no real opportunities for staff members to plan or work together in direct instruction. Obviously, better descriptions would have precluded these misinterpretations. One can only evaluate adequately that which one can describe accurately.

The importance of good description increases in proportion to the complexity and scope of what is evaluated. Evaluators are frequently asked to help evaluate entities as vague as "our Parks and Recreation program." Does that include all programs across all seasons, only the summer recreational programs, or only swimming programs? Would such an evaluation focus on training of part-time summer employees, public use of parks, maintenance of parks, or all of the above? Would it determine whether the goals of Parks and Recreation meet the need of the community, whether the program managers are correctly and effectively implementing the policies determined by elected officials, or both? Answering such questions establishes boundaries that help the evaluation make sense.

A **program description** is a description of the critical elements of the program to be evaluated. Such a description typically includes goals and objectives, critical components and activities, and descriptions of the target audience. It may also include characteristics of personnel delivering the program, administrative arrangements, the physical setting, and other contextual factors. Description can include models or flowcharts depicting the theory of the program or why it is expected to achieve the proposed outcomes. Many descriptions are extensive, delineating critical factors in the history of the program and reasons for choices made at various stages. Others are more brief but still convey a picture of the essence of the current program. The critical factor in a program description is that it is sufficiently detailed to provide a foundation for the program evaluation and a common understanding for the parties involved.

Factors to Consider in Characterizing the Object of the Evaluation

The evaluator can demarcate the object of the evaluation and the study itself by answering these questions:

- What problem was the program designed to correct? What need does the program exist to serve? Why was the program initiated? What are its goals? Whom is it intended to serve?
- What does the program consist of? What are its major components and activities, its basic structure and administrative/managerial design? How does it function? What research support exists to link the activities and characteristics of the program and clients with the desired goals?
- What is the program's setting and context (geographical, demographic, political, level of generality)?
- Who participates in the program (direct and indirect participants, program deliverers, managers and administrators, policy makers)? Who are other stakeholders?
- What is the program's history? How long is it supposed to continue? When are critical decisions about continuation to be made?
- When and under what conditions is the program to be used? How much time is it intended to take? How frequently is it to be used?
- Are there unique contextual events or circumstances (e.g., contract negotiations, budgetary decisions, changes in administration, elections) that could affect the program in ways that might distort the evaluation?
- What resources (human, materials, time) are consumed in using the program?
- Has the program been evaluated previously? If so, what outcomes/results were found?

The evaluator should also seek to clarify what is *not* included in the program to be evaluated.

Other models also exist to characterize the object of the evaluation. As discussed in Chapter 12, through his development of the process of evaluability assessment, Wholey (1983, 1987, 1994) has written of the need to develop a program model that conveys the linkages between program goals and objectives and program actions. Thus, he would suggest developing a model that links the program activities described in the second question in the preceding list with the goals identified in the first question. The model would describe how these activities could conceivably achieve the stated goals. If no clear linkage between program activities and goals and objectives emerged, the program might not be ready for evaluation.

Using Program Theory to Describe the Program

Theory-driven evaluation, suggested briefly by Weiss (1972) and Fitz-Gibbon and Morris (1975) but developed fully by Chen and his colleagues (Chen, 1990; Chen & Rossi, 1983), uses program theory as a tool for (1) understanding the program to be evaluated and (2) guiding the evaluation. Chen (1990) defines program theory as "a specification of what must be done to achieve the desired goals, what other important impacts may also be anticipated, and how these goals and impacts would be generated" (p. 43). Program theory consists of two parts: normative and causative theory. Normative theory describes the program as it should be, its goals and outcomes, its interventions and the rationale for these, from the perspectives of various stakeholders. Causative theory makes use of existing research to describe potential outcomes of the program based on characteristics of the clients and the program actions. The information gained from these theories can then be used to develop a plausible program model.

Chen's work was prompted by the often atheoretical approach of evaluators to a program. By failing to understand the program theory, or the complex assumptions that link the problem to be resolved with the characteristics and actions of the program and the characteristics and actions with desired outcomes, evaluations too often have tended to be black-box studies. Such studies measure inputs and outputs but, due to lack of understanding of the program theory itself, fail to explain program failures or successes. What aspects of the program prompted failure? Success? Why did these components fail or succeed? By articulating the theory of the program, the evaluator begins the evaluation with an understanding of the program expectations.

Rossi's (1971) impact model illustrates a simple method for beginning to develop the theory of the program. He proposes three steps: a causal hypothesis, an intervention hypothesis, and an action hypothesis. The causal hypothesis links the problem to be solved or reduced by the program (A) to a purported cause (B). For example: teenagers abuse drugs (A) because they have difficulty dealing with peer pressure to use drugs (B). The intervention hypothesis links program actions (C) to the purported cause (B). Thus: role-playing methods for resisting peer pressure (C) will increase teens' ability to resist peers' invitations to use drugs (B). Finally, the action hypothesis links the program activities with the reduction of the original problem. Thus the action hypothesis would be: role-playing methods for resisting peer pressure (C) will decrease teen drug abuse (A). The evaluator can work with stakeholders to develop an impact model that specifies problems, causes, and program activities and links between these. The initial impact model will be primarily normative, based on the perceptions and experiences of the stakeholders and program developers. A causative model can then be developed linking empirical research to each of the hypotheses or raising questions where empirical evidence is lacking. The normative and causative model can provide the framework for the subsequent evaluation. Thus, a causal hypothesis can lay the foundation for needs assessment questions such as, To what extent does teen drug abuse really exist among our target population? What is the nature of the problem? What drugs are abused? Under what circumstances? Does inability to resist peer pressure really exacerbate the problem? The intervention hypothesis or hypotheses can help identify important components of the program to monitor or describe in formative studies. (Most models will have several intervention hypotheses connecting different parts of the program with various causes of the problem.) The action hypothesis makes the final link between the problem and the program. It exemplifies the question many black-box studies address, namely, Did the program achieve its goal? However, without the important causal and intervention hypotheses, the evaluator may fail to understand and explore the underlying theory of the program.

Methods for Describing the Object of the Evaluation

Answers to questions posed in the preceding section can be obtained in a variety of ways and from a variety of sources. Three basic approaches to collecting descriptive information are (1) reading documents with information about the object, (2) talking with various individuals familiar with the object, and (3) observing the object in action. Each is discussed briefly here.

Descriptive Documents.   Most programs are described in proposals to funding agencies, planning documents, reports, minutes of relevant meetings, correspondence, publications, and so on. Taking time to locate and peruse such documents is an important first step in understanding any entity well enough to describe it correctly.

Interviews.   Helpful as they are, written documents cannot provide a complete or adequate basis for describing the object of the evaluation. The evaluator should talk at length with those involved in planning or operating the program and with those who may have observed it in operation. Stakeholders with alternative perspectives should also be interviewed. In evaluating a treatment program for domestic violence perpetrators, for example, the evaluator would be well advised to learn how the program is (and is supposed to be) operating, not only from the therapists and administrators responsible for delivering the program but also from the state department responsible for providing funding for the program, the participants in the program and their families, judges who make referrals to the program, and so on. It is important to interview representatives of all the relevant audiences to develop a model on which consensus can be reached *and* to understand the different perspectives of the audiences.

Observations.   Much can be learned by observing programs in action. In addition to personally observing the program, the evaluator may wish to ask relevant content or process experts to make observations. Often observations will reveal variations between how the program *is* running and how it is *intended* to run that an evaluator may not discover through interviews or reading.

Having described the object of the evaluation, the evaluator must ensure that the stakeholders agree that the description accurately characterizes the program. Confirmation of this agreement may be achieved through ongoing meetings with a work group that has been involved in developing the program description (as in evaluability assessment), through distribution of a formal description to different audiences, or through meetings with various stakeholders. Recall, however, that the purpose of this stage is also to set boundaries for the evaluation by clarifying exactly what is to be evaluated. To achieve a full understanding of the context of the evaluation, the description may have involved a larger portion of the program than the evaluation will address. If the evaluation is to focus on a smaller piece of the overall program, clarification about the object of the evaluation should occur at this time.

Clarifying what is to be evaluated reduces the chances that the evaluator will later be accused of evaluating the wrong thing, of conducting an evaluation that was too narrow in scope, or of failing to take important factors into account.

Dealing with Different Perceptions

The above discussion assumes that consensus on both the program itself and the boundaries of the evaluation exists. Such is not always the case.

As a case in point, Vroom, Colombo, and Nahan (1994) describe how differences in perceptions of goals and program priorities among managers, staff, and sponsors led to a very problematic evaluation. In an innovative program to use cable technology to help the unemployed find jobs, these stakeholders differed in the priority they attached to the technology and the direct service components of the program. The sponsor was concerned with measuring the direct impact on the unemployed, but the agency staff members were concerned with implementing the new, sophisticated cable technology. While other organizational problems also contributed to the failure of the evaluation, the authors believe that more extensive ongoing discussions and meetings with the stakeholders could have clarified the differences in perspective and helped the evaluation.

House (1988) describes the problems that occurred in the evaluation of Jesse Jackson's PUSH/Excel program when the evaluators' perceptions differed from those of the program administrators and staff. The federal evaluators saw the program as having clearly defined, specific components. When they found that each site did not have these components, they attributed the variations to program failure. Program developers, however, had anticipated adaptation to local concerns; they saw PUSH/Excel as a far less structured entity than did the evaluators. The failure to communicate these differences clearly led to a failure in the evaluation.

In cases where disagreements over the nature of the evaluation object exist, the evaluator is often well advised to look at each interpretation. By letting various audiences attach whatever meaning they wish to the object and then focusing on results that are relevant to that meaning, the evaluator can address the information needs of multiple audiences. Moreover, she can educate audiences by helping them look beyond their particular perspectives.

In cases where the differences of perception are among the primary audiences for the study and those differences are rather major, the evaluator may want to establish a working group of members of the differing audiences to reach an agreement on a program description and the boundaries of the evaluation. If consensus cannot be achieved, the evaluator may conclude that further evaluation should be delayed. (See Chapter 12 for discussion of evaluability assessment.)

Sometimes it is important for evaluators to obtain formal agreement from the client that a description is accurate. Such agreements can help avoid later conflicts between stakeholders and the evaluator about whether or not the evaluator has really understood the evaluation object.

Redescribing the Object As It Changes

It is important to portray the actual character of the object not only as it begins but also as it unfolds. A critical point for evaluators to remember is that the object to be evaluated frequently changes during evaluation. As House (1993) has written, a program is not "a fixed machine." The nature of a program varies and this variation is caused by many factors (McClintock, 1987). The changes may be due in part to the responsiveness of program managers to feedback that suggests useful refinements and modifications. It is also often the case that an object, such as a training program for new supervisors, is not implemented by users in quite the way its designers envisioned. Some adaptations may be justifiable on theoretical grounds, some may result from naïveté or misunderstanding, and some may stem from purposeful resistance on the part of users determined to expunge something objectionable from the original conception. Regardless, the evaluator must describe at the end of the evaluation what was actually evaluated, and that may be quite different from what was originally planned.

Guba and Lincoln (1981) provide an excellent discussion of reasons why changes in the evaluation object (which they call the "evaluand") might occur.

> The evaluator who assumes that an implemented evaluand will be substantially similar to the intended entity is either naive or incompetent. Thus, field observations of the evaluand in use, of the setting as it actually exists, and of the conditions that actually obtain are absolutely essential.

Variations in the entity, setting, and conditions can occur for a variety of reasons. In some cases the reluctance or resistance of the actors in the situation produces unwanted changes. Adaptations to fit the evaluand to the local situation may have to be made. The simple passage of time allows the action of various historical factors to make their contribution to change. Most of all, the continuing activity of the evaluator himself, if it is taken seriously by the actors and if it produces meaningful information, will contribute to a continuously changing set of circumstances. (p. 344)

A Sample Description of an Evaluation Object

To help illustrate the key points in this section, we include a discussion of a program evaluated by one of the authors (Fitzpatrick, 1988). The program to be described is a treatment program for persons convicted of driving under the influence (DUI) of alcohol. The description is organized around the first two bulleted items listed on page 220, under "Factors to Consider in Characterizing the Object of the Evaluation." Program descriptions or models can be organized in many different ways. This presentation is designed to illustrate what might be learned in regard to each factor.

The first set of questions is: What need does the program exist to meet? Why was it initiated? What are its goals? Whom is it intended to serve?

This particular treatment program is designed for offenders who are considered problem drinkers or incipient problem drinkers due to a number of different criteria, including number of DUI arrests, blood-alcohol level at the time of arrest, scores on a measure of alcoholism, and whether an accident was involved in the arrest. The program exists to reduce deaths and accidents due to drunk driving. As with many programs of this type, it was initiated due to public attention to this issue and recognition that some sort of cost-effective treatment might be needed for certain offenders to contain the problem. Its goals are to help offenders to recognize that they have a drinking problem and to seek further treatment. The designers of the program recognize that resources for the program are insufficient to stop problem drinkers from drinking. Thus, the following program theory contains a more immediate, implicit goal. The theory or model of the program is (a) problem drinkers drive under the influence of alcohol because they have problems with alcohol and are not aware of the extent of their problem; (b) if these offenders are exposed to information regarding alcohol use and participate in group discussions regarding their own use, they will recognize their own problem; (c) the treatment program will refer them to places where they can receive extended therapy; (d) by receiving extended therapy, the offenders will reduce their consumption of alcohol and, hence, their frequency of driving under the influence of alcohol. A secondary competing model to achieve the goal is to get participants to use alternative means of transportation and avoid driving when they have been using alcohol. (See below.)

The second set of questions is: What does the program consist of? What are its major components and activities, its basic structure and administrative/managerial design? How does it function? What research support exists to link the activities and characteristics of the program and clients with the desired goals?

> The curriculum and methods used in the treatment program were developed, outlined, and disseminated to treatment sites by the state agency that funds and administers the program. The program is 20 to 30 hours in length delivered over 8 to 12 sessions. The content consists of a combination of lectures, films, group discussions, and exercises. The manual for the treatment is quite specific about the content for each session; however, interviews with the treatment deliverers, who are independent practitioners in the alcohol abuse area, indicate that they often adapt the content based on their perceptions of the group's needs. Observations of a few programs suggested experiential activities may be more limited than expected. The theory on which the treatment is based requires a heavy emphasis on experiential methods rather than didactic approaches to achieve the goal of attitude change with problem drinkers. Offenders who meet the criteria are to be sentenced by the judges to complete the program at the site closest to their home. (Offenders have lost their driver's licenses as part of their punishment.) If they fail to complete the program, they are then sentenced to time in jail.

Another critical component of the program description is characterization of the stakeholders.

> Prominent stakeholders in this program include the judges (who initially sponsored the study), Mothers Against Drunk Driving (MADD, who lobbied the judges to sponsor the study), the program deliverers, and the state division that oversees the program. Other stakeholders include the clients, their families, victims of traffic accidents in which arrests are involved and their families, insurance companies, alcohol treatment centers, and the public at large. The judges are interested in improving their sentencing by learning what kinds of offenders are least likely to complete treatment successfully. MADD is interested in the degree to which the program achieves its goals. The program deliverers are persons with expertise in treating alcohol offenders both through these programs and others. They are most interested in ending alcohol abuse. The state funding source agrees that alcohol abuse is part of the problem and should be remedied but also advocates alternative methods of transportation. Research suggests that treatments that decrease the frequency of driving (removal of license and increase in insurance costs) are more effective at decreasing deaths due to driving under the influence than treatments that address the alcohol abuse itself. However, as most professionals in this field are from the alcohol treatment area rather than the transportation area, the alcohol-ism treatment approach tends to be the dominant focus.
>
> Much research has been conducted in this area nationally, and the state division responsible for overseeing the program collects some routine data from sites. However, little systematic research has been performed on this state program. Current data collection focuses on attendance and change on pre-post knowledge and attitude measures administered at the beginning and end of the programs. No monitoring studies or follow-up outcome studies have been conducted.

The preceding description is designed to illustrate some of the critical factors that an evaluator might note in characterizing the object of the evaluation during the planning phase. To describe the program, the evaluator made use of printed material (state manuals and proposals, local site materials); interviews (judges, MADD, deliverers, state administrators); observations of the program; and a review of literature on treatment programs and solutions for persons convicted of drunk driving. With the information obtained from answering the first two questions, a model can be developed for the program. The model can be depicted with a flowchart or in a narrative manner, as illustrated in this example. Empirical research that both supports and weakens the model should be described. Site visits to the program can then help bring this model to life and assist the evaluator in determining whether program activities correspond to the model. This description, then, can provide the foundation for further communication with audiences in planning the focus of the evaluation.

ANALYZING THE RESOURCES AND CAPABILITIES THAT CAN BE COMMITTED TO THE EVALUATION

Very often, program managers, deliverers, and sometimes clients themselves view resources committed to evaluation as resources taken away from the program itself. If those dollars were only available we could educate more students, treat more patients, serve more clients, create more parks, and so on. However, others in the public and nonprofit sectors have come to recognize that evaluation can be very useful to them. Evaluation can help program managers and deliverers adapt programs to better meet the needs of their clients. The use of Total Quality Management (TQM) in the private sector to assess client satisfaction and delivery of products persuaded many others that evaluation might, in fact, pay for itself. Hodgkinson, Hurst, and Levine (1975) first introduced the doctrine of cost-free evaluation to argue that evaluation is not an "added-on-extra" but a means for identifying "cost-saving and/or effectiveness-increasing consequences for the project" (p. 189). The evaluator should recognize that her purpose is to improve productivity and the quality of the product, either through formative recommendations for program improvement that will lead to better products or result in lower costs or summative recommendations that will result in maintaining or expanding successful, cost-effective programs or eliminating unsuccessful ones.

Analyzing Financial Resources Needed for the Evaluation

Even when the client is converted to the doctrine of cost-free evaluation, determining what resources can be devoted to evaluation is difficult. As Cronbach and others (1980) have noted, "deciding on a suitable level of expenditure is . . . one of the subtlest aspects of evaluation planning" (p. 265).

Ideally, this decision should be made in consultation with the evaluator, whose more intimate knowledge of evaluation costs would be of great help. Unfortunately, there may not be sufficient rapport between evaluator and client to foster such collaborative planning. Indeed, in many situations the client may initially proceed independently to set budgetary limits for the study. Sometimes the evaluator is informed how much money is available for the evaluation. Frequently, however, the amount of money available is not made clear. In such cases, we recommend the evaluator propose two or three different levels of evaluation that differ in cost and comprehensiveness—perhaps a "Chevrolet" and a "Cadillac" evaluation, for example—from which the client can select. Clients are often unaware of the possibilities of evaluation design, of what information evaluations might be able to produce, or of the cost of evaluation services. Faced with decisions about trade-offs and budget limitations, the client also needs to know about alternatives and their consequences in order to make a good decision. Budgeting could be the last step in planning an evaluation. On the other hand, if budget limits are known at the beginning, they will affect (and usually enhance) planning decisions that follow.

Ideally, evaluation plans and budgets should remain flexible, if at all possible. Circumstances will change during the study, and new information needs and opportunities will unfold. If every dollar and every hour of time are committed to an inflexible plan, the results will fail to capitalize on the new insights gained by evaluator and client. Even the most rigid plan and budget should include provisions for how, by mutual agreement, resources might be shifted to accomplish evaluation tasks that take on new priority through changing circumstances.

Analyzing Availability and Capability of Evaluation Personnel

Budget is only one consideration affecting the design of an evaluation study. Personnel is another. Frequently, evaluators can make use of qualified personnel who are on site for reasons other than evaluation. Program staff may be able to collect data. Secretaries can work part-time typing, searching records, or the like, at no cost to the evaluation budget.[1] Graduate students seeking internship experience or working on dissertations or course-related studies can undertake special assignments at minimal cost to the evaluation budget. Volunteers from neighborhood associations and other community groups, parent-teacher associations, church groups, or advocacy groups associated with the project can often perform nontechnical evaluation tasks. Clients themselves can also help. Calls for volunteers from among these various groups often pay off. And involving volunteers not only helps contain costs but also sparks interest in the evaluation among stakeholders.

---

[1] This is not to say there is no cost for such personnel services but only that it may be possible to obtain some assistance with evaluation tasks from on-site personnel within existing operating budgets.

Whenever people who are not evaluation specialists conduct or assist with evaluation tasks, the evaluator faces unique responsibilities that cannot be neglected: orientation, training, and quality control. Evaluation personnel who lack specialized training or relevant experience require orientation to the nature of the study, its purposes, and the role they will be asked to play. They must understand their responsibilities, not only in completing evaluation tasks in a quality and timely manner but also in representing the evaluation team and its sponsoring organization. Naive and unprepared evaluation staff (volunteers or otherwise) can play havoc with an evaluation if they interact abrasively with others, misrepresent the nature or purpose of the study, betray anonymity or confidentiality, or even dress inappropriately for the setting. Evaluation volunteers or adjuncts must also be trained in the skills required to do the tasks assigned. They must follow strict, detailed guidelines, or errors are likely to occur. Even then, careful supervision and spot-checking are usually required.

Whenever "nonevaluator" personnel are used to expand an evaluation effort at low cost, the risk of bias is present. Personal considerations must not influence the way in which these volunteers conduct their evaluation tasks. It is easy to allow presuppositions to color one's perceptions. Although few seem likely to be so unprincipled, it is also easy to alter or distort the data to make it fit one's prior conclusions. Thus, to protect the study's validity and credibility it is essential that an evaluator using "local" personnel in the evaluation use caution and judgment in determining what tasks the volunteers will perform. They should not be assigned tasks that would expose them to confidential information (e.g., neighbors reviewing children's achievement test scores). The evaluator should provide adequate supervision and also audit and authenticate everyone's work by spot-checking and verifying all data collection and analysis. Given conscientious supervision, monitoring, and auditing, local staff or volunteers can make a useful "cost-free" contribution to an evaluation.

Of course, using unskilled personnel may not always be as economical as it first appears. It is in the evaluator's best interest to consider carefully the qualifications of available assistants, including their commitment and responsibility, before including them.

Analyzing Other Resources and Constraints for Evaluations

The availability of existing data, including files, records, previous evaluations, documents, or other data-collection efforts to which the evaluation may be attached, is an important consideration. The more information that must be generated de novo by the evaluator, the more costly the evaluation.

The availability of needed support materials and services is also important. Existing testing programs, computer services, routine questionnaires, or other information services are all possible resources that could be drawn upon at little or no cost to the evaluation if they already exist for other purposes.

The evaluator should also take into account the relevance of existing evaluation approaches and methods for the specific study being considered. The methodological or technological state of the art necessary to respond successfully to a particular evaluation request may be so underdeveloped or new that a major research and development effort will be required before the evaluation can be launched. Pioneering can require considerably more time, effort, and money than either evaluator or sponsor can afford to spend.

Time must be considered a resource. The evaluator does not wish to miss opportunities for making the evaluation useful because of tardy reports or data collection and analysis. Knowing when to be ready with results is part of good planning. It is ideal to have sufficient time to meet all information needs at a pace that is both comfortable and productive. Limited time can diminish an evaluation's effectiveness as much as limited dollars.

ANALYZING THE POLITICAL CONTEXT FOR THE EVALUATION

Evaluation is inherently a political process. Any activity that involves applying the diverse values of multiple constituents in judging the value of some object has political overtones. Whenever resources are redistributed or priorities are redefined, political processes are at work. And consider the political nature of decisions regarding whose values are attended to, how they are weighted, what variables are studied, how information is reported and to whom, how clients and other audiences intend to use evaluative information, what kind of support is given to the evaluation and by whom, what potentially embarrassing information is hidden, what possible actions might be taken to subvert the evaluation, and how the evaluator might be co-opted by individuals or groups.

Political processes begin to work with the first inspiration to conduct an evaluation and are pivotal in determining the purpose(s) to be served and the interests and needs to be addressed. Political considerations permeate every facet of evaluation from planning through the reporting and use of evaluation results.

We have reserved our more extensive discussion of political factors in evaluation for Chapter 16. But we cannot leave this chapter without saying a few words about the importance of analyzing the political context in which the evaluation will be conducted while there is still time to recognize and retreat from a political debacle that could render an evaluation useless.

Upon receiving any new request to undertake an evaluation, the evaluator might consider the following questions:

1. Who would stand to lose/gain most from the evaluation under different scenarios? Have they agreed to cooperate? Do they understand the organizational consequences of an impartial evaluation?
2. Which individuals and groups have power in this setting? Have they agreed to sanction the evaluation? To cooperate?

3. How is the evaluator expected to relate to different individuals or groups? As impartial outsider? Advocate? Future consultant or subcontractor? Confidante? Assistant? What implications does this have for her being co-opted?
4. From which stakeholders will cooperation be essential? Have they agreed to provide full cooperation? To allow access to necessary data?
5. Which stakeholders have a vested interest in the outcomes of the evaluation? What steps will be taken to give their perspective a fair hearing without allowing them to preclude alternative views?
6. Who will need to be informed during the evaluation about plans, procedures, progress, and findings?
7. What safeguards should be incorporated into a formal agreement for the evaluation (e.g., reporting procedures, editing rights, protection of human subjects, access to data, metaevaluation, procedures for resolving conflicts)?

Answers to these questions will help the evaluator determine whether it will be feasible and productive to undertake the evaluation study, a decision we will address shortly. First, it may be helpful to consider briefly how the activities and issues discussed so far in this chapter would be influenced by the evaluation approach being used.

VARIATIONS CAUSED BY THE EVALUATION APPROACH USED

The participant-oriented model has had an important influence on evaluators. Few evaluators today would conduct an evaluation without considering other audiences for the evaluation and the context in which the evaluation is to be conducted. However, as in Chapter 12, the models differ in emphasis.

An evaluator using a pure objectives-oriented approach, a rare case today among trained evaluators, might involve different audiences in defining program objectives but in her single-minded focus on objectives, might fail to obtain an adequate description of the program and an understanding of the political context in which it operates. An objectives-oriented approach tends to be relatively linear and can fail to acknowledge the multiplicity of views about the program, the clients it serves, and the society within which it operates.

Similarly, a management-oriented approach is often criticized for its focus on the manager as the primary decision maker and on providing information only for identified decisions to be made. While sophisticated users of this model would certainly identify and learn about the concerns of other audiences, these audiences would be viewed as secondary. If such audiences were outside the organization (e.g., clients, interest groups), they would almost certainly not be seen as a primary audience because the evaluator following this approach would tend to see them as lacking the power to make decisions that could affect the program dramatically. (Obviously, such evaluators would have failed to consider boycotts!) Similarly, a management-oriented evaluator might focus on defining the decisions to be made and the context for those decisions rather than the context for the program itself.

The consumer-oriented approach will, of necessity, define the program from the eyes of the consumer. In this case, other audiences and other views of the program or products may be neglected. Thus, a consumer-oriented evaluation of the national forests might choose to focus on the satisfaction of campers in these forests. How pleased are they with the camping facilities? The beauty of the site? The access to the campground? Such a focus would neglect other audiences such as ranchers, nonusers who want the land protected, and future generations of users and nonusers.

The expertise-oriented evaluator is likely to be the most narrow in identifying and considering audiences and their descriptions and views of the program. The expertise-oriented evaluator is hired because of her own personal knowledge of such programs. Such knowledge, and the criteria for the evaluation, typically arise from professional education, training, experience in the field, and, often, standards developed by the same profession in which the "expert" is educated. Thus, the audience for the program and the means for describing the program are rather narrowly circumscribed by the profession the program represents (e.g., education for schools, health for hospitals, criminal justice for prisons). The expertise-oriented evaluator may collect data on the program from many different audiences but rarely would consider these audiences' information needs for the evaluation. This evaluator would view her role as reflecting the standards of her field, not those of others.

The participant-oriented model is certainly the most ardent in advocating the inclusion of many different audiences and perspectives in the planning of the evaluation. The evaluator using this model would constantly seek the multiple perspectives of different audiences. She would argue that no one view of the program reflects truth and, thus, she must seek many different perspectives to understand the program in its totality. Such an approach is, of course, likely to consider the most audiences and the largest number of program descriptions. The question becomes one of synthesis. Who makes this synthesis? The evaluator may become an important decision maker with this approach if she is the sole person responsible for such synthesis. Or, alternatively, the evaluator may work with a committee of different users to guide the synthesis. The management-oriented evaluator might accuse the participant-oriented evaluator of being naive about the political sphere. The management-oriented evaluator is betting that the manager she targets as the primary decision maker is the one most interested and most able to make decisions based on the results of the evaluation. The participant-oriented evaluator might retort that few decisions emerge directly from an evaluation. By involving and informing many audiences, her evaluation, she would argue, is most likely to make a difference in the long run.

DETERMINING WHETHER TO PROCEED
WITH THE EVALUATION

In Chapter 12 we talked about identifying reasons for the evaluation; such reasons provide the best indicators of whether an evaluation will be meaningful. In this chapter we have discussed the importance of understanding who will use the evaluation information and how, and we have suggested ways to identify relevant audiences. We have stressed the importance of describing and setting boundaries on what is evaluated and analyzing fiscal, human, and other resources to determine feasibility. And we have cautioned evaluators to consider whether any political influences might undermine the evaluation effort.

Unfortunately, we can offer no simple algorithm for balancing all these factors in making a final decision about whether to proceed with the evaluation. Thoroughness in considering the factors outlined in this and the preceding chapter, insight, thoughtfulness, and common sense are the ingredients essential to a sensible decision about when to agree to do an evaluation. Yet even the most insightful evaluator with considerable experience will sometimes make an unwise decision, which is our cue to return to the case study we left at the end of Chapter 12.

> ### CASE STUDY APPLICATION
>
> ***November 2.*** Claire Janson, the Radnor principal, called today and told me I'd been picked by the committee to do their evaluation, if I would. I agreed tentatively, but told her I couldn't make a final commitment without knowing more about the program, precisely why they want it evaluated, what use they would make of the evaluation findings, the resources available for the evaluation study, and so on. She promised to send some written materials for me to review.

Author Comments.   To agree to undertake an evaluation without first knowing a bit about the program to be evaluated strikes me as a potential disservice to both the program and the evaluator. Only an evaluator who is naive, avaricious, or supremely confident that her evaluation skills or approach will solve any evaluation problem would plunge in with so little information. Having once met all three of those criteria, I have more recently repented, and during the last decade have insisted on learning enough about the program, prior to committing to evaluate it, to be certain I could be of some help.

> ***November 8.*** Spent a few minutes this evening reading through materials I received from Radnor Township School District. They sent a brief report of their Humanities Curriculum Review Committee, which listed committee membership; outlined their activities; gave goals, objectives, and rationale for the curriculum; and included an outline of the content of the program and the schedule for implementation. They also listed other alternatives they had considered and rejected, even explaining why, which is a helpful inclusion. No clue in the materials, however, to some of the more important things I need to know before I decide whether I can be of any real help to them. Spent a while jotting down some questions I want to ask the principal.

Author Comments. Later examination of artifacts in my Radnor School District Evaluation file would reveal the following list of questions (Artifact 1).

ARTIFACT 1

1. How old is the humanities curriculum in the Radnor School District? The Humanities Curriculum Review Committee was launched in 1994, just over a year ago—but what about the curriculum? Is it well established or new? Entrenched or struggling to find root?
2. Have there been any previous efforts to evaluate the humanities program? If so, by whom? When? What were the findings? How did they affect the program?
3. Why does the board want the program evaluated now? What are the political forces at work? If it is controversial, who are the advocates (beyond the obvious)? The opponents? What sparks the controversy?
4. What decision(s) will be made as a result of the evaluation? Will the evaluation really make a difference, or is it merely for show?
5. How broadly did the curriculum committee sample opinions of the public, the students, teachers, administrators, outside specialists? To what extent did those groups really have a chance to give input? Were they well enough informed for their input to be on target? How much do they feel they were really listened to—did their input really shape the outcome?
6. How well is the humanities department at Radnor School integrated with the other departments? Is the relationship congenial? Competitive? Any problems here?
7. What are the costs of the humanities program (dollars, time)? Any problems here?
8. What resources are available to conduct the evaluation? How good a job do they really want? (If evaluation budget is inadequate, are there staff members in the school or district who might be assigned to spend time helping collect some of the data, working under my supervision? May not cost much less overall, considering staff time, but should substantially reduce cash outlay for the district, for consultant time, travel, per diem. Use this only in areas where bias isn't too much of a concern or where I can check and correct pretty well for any bias that creeps in.)
9. What access will I have to collect data I need? Are there any problems with the teachers' association or contracts, policies on testing students, and so forth, that would constrain me if I wanted to observe classrooms, interview teachers, or test students? What about policies concerning control of the evaluation report(s), review or editorial rights they may insist on, my rights to quote, release, and so on?
10. Are there any other materials that might give me a better feel for the program? What are the activities and major components? What methods are used? How do these activities and methods link to the goals and objectives of the program?
11. What do the teachers and curriculum planners see as the theory or model for the program? How do they think the activities and methods of the program lead to achievement of the goals? Have they modeled the program on others they are familiar with?
12. And lest I forget, rhetoric aside, are they really serious about attaining *all* the goals they have laid out? In a mere two hours per week over three school years? Or are those goals just window dressing to sell the program?

Author Comments. Most of these questions simply seek descriptive information essential to know how (or whether) to conduct the evaluation. Questions 3, 4, 5, 7, 8, and 12 may also suggest a hint of cynicism or suspicion, yet the failure to ask and answer such questions has sent more rookie evaluators baying down wrong trails, en route to unproductive thickets of irrelevant findings, than any other single oversight. I don't really expect Ms. Janson to be able to answer all these. Many will require talking with others involved in the project.

But, at least I can get her point of view and see how sensitive they might be to such questions.

> ***November 9.*** Called Claire Janson, principal of Radnor Middle School. She responded to several of my questions, but as we got into the discussion, it became apparent that she couldn't really answer some of them without presuming to second-guess the board or others. After a bit, she asked, in view of all the questions I was posing, how much information I really thought I would need before I could sit down and outline an evaluation design that would tell them what they needed to know. I pointed out that was precisely the problem. I wasn't yet certain just what it was they needed to know; hence, all my questions. I suggested to Ms. Janson that the most feasible way to proceed would be for me to visit the school for two or three days, talk with her and some other members of the committee (including a parent or two), visit with some board members, observe some humanities classes, review the written units, and see if I couldn't get my questions answered, along with a lot of other questions that will probably occur to me in the process. I suggested that I could then leave with her a rough draft of an evaluation plan that I thought would answer their questions; they could review it and decide whether they want me to proceed with any or all of it. That way they would know in advance how I intend to carry out the evaluation and what data I propose to collect rather than discover at the end of the evaluation that they didn't really place much stock in the approach I had used or that I had omitted information they viewed as critical. Ms. Janson immediately saw the wisdom and advantage in my suggestions. She seems delightfully perceptive. I arranged to visit Radnor next week. Before I go, I want to have a graduate student do a quick review of literature on such programs so I can learn a little about methods that have been found to achieve such goals with kids this age.

Author Comments. In reaching agreements about the conduct of an evaluation, the evaluator should not be the only person to exhibit caution. Evaluation clients should also look carefully at what is proposed before they commit precious resources to the evaluation. Although most evaluators of my acquaintance are well intentioned, and a majority of those competent, there are yet too many charlatans and hucksters who lack the scruples and/or the skills necessary to do good evaluation work. Atrocities committed by such have gone far to breed skepticism that many program staff extend undeservedly to well-qualified, reputable evaluators. Even with well-intentioned, competent evaluators, potential clients can have no assurance a priori that their particular approach to evaluating the program will be very helpful.

It is for these reasons that I generally suggest that the evaluator and client interact enough to clarify in some detail what the evaluator is proposing before they "plight their troth." This might require the client to invest a small amount of resources to cover out-of-pocket expenses and a day or two's time for the evaluator (or more than one evaluator) to talk with representatives of the various audiences for the evaluation, probe areas of ambiguity, and provide at least a rough plan to which the client can react. In my judgment, that small investment will yield important returns to the client and avoid the later disenchantment that often occurs as an evaluation unfolds in ways never imagined by a client (but perhaps envisioned all along by the evaluator).

The best possible results of such a "preliminary design" stage are sharper, more relevant focusing of the evaluation and clarity of understanding that will undergird a productive working relationship between evaluator and client throughout the study. The worst that can happen is that a small proportion of the resources will be spent to learn that there is a mismatch between what the evaluator can (or is willing to) deliver and what the client needs. That is small cost compared to discovering the mismatch only after the evaluation is well under way, the resources largely expended, and an untidy divorce the only way out of an unsatisfactory relationship.

The quick review of literature can be supplemented and better focused after the visit, but it is useful to learn a little about what has been found to work, and what *doesn't* work. This information can help the evaluator to ask good questions when talking with the clients about the model for the program. If they're using methods that the literature shows have not been too successful, the evaluator can probe to learn more about why they have chosen that method, whether they know about others' failures with it, and how open they are to hearing about potential failures of some program components.

> ***November 14.*** I just completed an interesting day and evening in the Radnor School District trying to get a fix on their humanities program. Had informative discussions with Claire Janson, Ron Holton (chairman of the committee), two humanities teachers, and one parent who served on the committee. All are staunch "loyalists" for the program, but they don't seem closed-minded about it. Not that they are really clamoring for an evaluation—I gather that interest comes mostly from the board— but they seem open to looking at the program and have been candid in responses to my questions. The humanities teachers were the most guarded; not too surprising, I suppose, for it appears they may have a lot at stake. They and Claire Janson were all quick to record their skepticism about using tests and statistics to measure something as ethereal as the humanities. The humanities teachers seemed dumb-founded to learn that my Ph.D. is not in some branch of the humanities. One asked how anyone except an expert in humanities could presume to evaluate a humanities curriculum. I countered by pointing out that I write doggerel, publish an occasional short story, and once even tried to sell an oil painting. She wasn't easily impressed. I debated whether to trot out my well-practiced arguments about why evaluators need not be specialists in the content of what they evaluate but decided the moment was not right for conversion.
>
> I asked each person I talked with what she or he saw as the major goals of the program and how they thought the program achieved those goals. For those who were hazy on this, I asked them what problems they felt students had before this curriculum began and what caused those problems. I then asked them to talk about how the humanities program could mediate these problems. Many talked about how much rote learning was in the school, and I had to work to get them to focus on the students. However, many noted the program was to help students become more creative and to appreciate the arts and abstract concepts. Some work will be needed to explore what they mean by "understanding of all that it means to be human." But I am

beginning to get a better understanding of the model for the program. I also asked each person what questions they would like an evaluation study to answer and how they would use the findings. I'll do the same tomorrow and try to refine the model and make up a master list of potential questions. For me, this is a crucial step.

Also read lesson plans for several of the units. No obvious clues there, except that some units appear to focus more on stuffing students with facts than engaging them in higher-level mental processes that the literature indicated was needed to achieve their goals. I'll need to look at some other lesson plans to see whether I just pulled a biased sample. Also observed a humanities class in action, much of which focused on varying styles used by artists in the different art periods.

What have I learned so far? Quite a bit, I think, but I'll wait until I complete my observations tomorrow before I try to summarize them.

Author Comments.   Although this journal entry may not really reflect a full day's work for the ambitious evaluator, it reflects some of the types of information the evaluator might try to obtain in informal interviews and perusal of written information and other materials. Whereas the evaluator's thoughtfully prepared questions might be the core of such interviews, often the most useful information comes from probing leads that open during the conversation. Rogerian counseling[2] may yet contribute useful skills to program evaluation.

The discovery that the evaluator is not a specialist in the content or processes at the heart of the program being evaluated is often a rude shock to the client who is honestly confused as to how such a neophyte in the relevant subject matter could possibly be of help. Having concluded that evaluators need not be content specialists except when certain evaluation approaches (e.g., expertise-oriented evaluation) are used, I used to try to convert clients with repeated and lengthy appeals to reason. Experience (and exhaustion) have convinced me of the wisdom of eschewing such appeals in favor of simple promises to obtain judgments of relevant substantive experts as part of the evaluation. Invoking patience is infinitely easier than persuasion and, in this case, seems as productive, because I have never had a client continue to worry this point after the client has seen how relevant content expertise plays a part in the evaluation design.

November 15. Met with three members of the board of education for lunch. Found them all frankly skeptical, in varying degrees, about the value of the middle school's humanities curriculum. One, an engineer, really seemed to have her mind made up. She described the humanities curriculum as a "puff course" and argued there was greater need for more formal reading instruction and work in the sciences at this age level and that the "interdisciplinary frills" could wait until students had mastered the basics. She forecast the outcome of "any honest evaluation" with such certainty that I suspect she may be impervious to any evaluative data that may show the program to have merit.

---

[2] A counseling technique that elicits information by reflective, open-ended questions such as, "Tell me more about that," or "So you feel the program is not working well; can you tell me more about why you think that is the case?"

The other board members seemed less definite, but both called for rigorous, tough evaluation that will "tell it like it is." The board president indicated the program had never been formally evaluated and she felt it was difficult to defend continuation of a program, about which serious questions were being raised, in the absence of objective measurements that show it is working. We talked at length about program costs, what decisions will result from the evaluation, and who will make them. A most useful interview, especially when I got them to list the questions they would like to see addressed by the evaluation. I think board members are leaning but have not yet made up their minds.

Spent the morning reviewing another set of lesson plans. No fact sheets these; on the contrary, they contained much that strikes me as esoteric for the seventh grader. But I'll await the judgment of humanities experts on that one.

Author Comments.   Before beginning any evaluation that relates to continuation or termination of a program, I always try to ferret out whether there is really any need to evaluate; that is, have those who hold the power to make the decision already made up their minds (with little probability they will change them), regardless of the results of the study? That perspective stems from the sad realization that perhaps 75 percent of my first several years as an evaluator was spent generating methodologically impeccable but altogether useless evaluation reports—useless because I wasn't sharp enough to recognize the symptoms of ritualistic evaluation.

Now this doesn't mean that one aborts every evaluation where the decision makers are found to be tilted toward one view or another. To take that stance would be to eliminate evaluations of most programs governed by human beings. But it does mean that one should check and be convinced there really are decision alternatives that the evaluation can influence. If not, I can muster little defense for the expenditure of time and money to carry out the study.

November 15 (continued). This afternoon I met again with Ms. Janson, then with a third humanities teacher, and finally with two teachers, one each from the English and social science departments. Now I feel a need to boil down all the rough notes I've taken to try to see what I have learned and what I yet need to learn about the program (Artifact 2). That should help me be ready for the special session the principal has arranged with the committee tomorrow.

ARTIFACT 2

Memo to the File
November 15
Re: Radnor Humanities Program: Summary of Information Learned On Site, November 14–15

1. Radnor Township School District has had a humanities curriculum for 10 to 11 years, but it has evolved and mutated several times. With the exception of the additional structure and more skill emphasis, the current program has not changed greatly in the past three years.
2. The goal of the program appears to be to introduce students to the range of human creativity and, in so doing, inspire them to be more creative and to have a greater interest

and appreciation for the arts and how they enhance our lives. Activities linked to this goal appear to include both review of different artists, architects, musicians, and writers and their work, and students' creation of their own individual projects in various areas of the arts.

3. The humanities curriculum has never been formally evaluated.

4. During the past year or two, community concerns have risen about the need for more academic content, more basic skills development, and so forth, and the humanities curriculum has come to be viewed increasingly as a frill by important segments of the community, including some board members.

5. "Values clarification" does not appear to be a real issue, except in the minds of a strident few (including one committee member). The real issue seems to be that of devoting more time to the basic subjects versus spending it on an interdisciplinary program aimed at using the arts to help students "understand and appreciate all that it means to be human." The differences appear to be honest ones of philosophy and conviction, not those of convenience or self-interest, at least for the most part. Although there is no public outcry evident, the skepticism reflected by the board seems to reflect the trend in the community (as perceived by those involved).

6. The curriculum committee made no systematic effort to obtain input from a broad or representative sampling of parents or others prior to their October report. They did hold public meetings attended by some parents, and parents on the committee reported conversations they had with other parents, but community input was really quite limited.

7. The humanities department is isolated physically in a separate building from other departments with which it might be expected to be integrated. There does not appear to be much integration across the departments.

8. The fiscal costs of the humanities program really reside in the collective salaries of the four humanities teachers (close to $130,000 in total). There are no texts or other significant dollar costs. There does appear to be an interest on the part of some board members in the possible savings if the program were eliminated, because the board has expressed interest in making any staff reductions that might be made without reducing the quality of schooling offered to its students.

9. "Opportunity costs" are a key issue for those in the community who favor the "back-to-basics" notion discussed above. Within the school, faculty members in science and social science are particularly concerned about this, for time spent on their subjects was cut back to make room for the required humanities courses.

10. Within the school, faculty members in the science and social science departments are reported to be generally unenthusiastic about the program, those in the reading department about evenly split for and against it, and those in the English department generally favorable. The latter may relate to the fact that some of the humanities teachers apparently have good credentials in English plus more seniority in the district than the current staff in the English department. If humanities folds, those staff members might be given jobs in the English department, putting jobs of some of the English faculty on the line. Support under those circumstances may be more pragmatic than idealistic.

11. The board really wants to make a "go–no go" decision and is asking for a summative evaluation to provide them with information to help them decide intelligently. All my instincts tell me that, if there were no evaluation, or if the evaluation were not credible to the board, they would ultimately discontinue the program. But I am equally convinced that an evaluation showing that the program is producing the benefits its sponsors claim for it could yield a positive board decision to allow its continuation.

12. There is apparently about $30,000 available for the evaluation this school year, with any subsequent follow-up funding (if necessary) to be decided by the board. The district is willing to assign some of its staff to assist in collecting data I might specify.

13. District policy will permit me access to whatever data sources I need. The district would not restrict my rights to quote, use, or release the report at my discretion.

14. Other units' lesson plans are available for review, but some may not be currently in use. Other lessons may be being delivered that do not have completed plans.

15. The staff does seem genuine about the program's goals, although some awareness seems to be creeping in that it may be difficult to help students understand "all that it means to be human" in a lifetime, let alone two hours a week for 27 months.

16. The primary audiences for the evaluation seem to be (1) the board, (2) the Humanities Curriculum Review Committee, and (3) district and school staff not included on the committee but influenced by the outcomes. Important secondary audiences would include parents and students.

17. There is a sharp difference in the type of data preferred by the various audiences. The principal represented the point of view of the humanities department staff and a majority of the committee when she said, "Numbers won't tell the story—this type of program defies quantitative evaluation." Board members called for hard data, however, with one saying, "If you can't quantify it somehow, it probably doesn't exist." Others noted they found testimonials unconvincing and would hope for something more substantial. When informed of those sentiments and asked to react to them in light of her own pessimism about quantitative measurement of student outcomes in humanities, Claire Janson said she would love to see some good "numerical" proof that the program was working, for she wasn't sure anything else would convince the board. She acknowledged that testimonials were likely to fall on deaf ears, but she was skeptical that anything else could be produced.

18. Radnor has only one middle school. If one wished to find the most comparable students for a possible control group comparison, the Welsh Valley or Balla Cynwyd Middle Schools in the Lower Merion Township School District, also in the west Philadelphia suburbs, would be the best bets. Or might there be some way to relax temporarily the requirement that all students in the middle school must go through the humanities curriculum, so that some might spend that time in the more traditional subject matter? That may not be feasible, but I need to probe this more. Without some sort of comparison, I worry that we might pick up student gains (losses) and attribute them to the curriculum, whereas they really stem from maturation or the *Classes for Youth* series on Channel 7.

Author Comments.   These simulated conclusions are what I believe, reading between the lines, one might find if one spent a couple of days working in the Radnor School context. Although these conclusions may be inaccurate, they represent the types of information that should be gleaned in an initial visit to a program. In one sense, the evaluation has already begun, and some of these conclusions represent evaluation findings. Yet many are still impressionistic and would need further confirmation before I would lean on them too heavily. For now, their primary utility would be to focus my design and further my data-collection efforts. More important, much of what has been collected constitutes the basic stuff of "program description."

Without using space to comment on each item in my "memo," let me draw attention to two things. First, specification of audiences for the evaluation findings is an essential, often neglected, part of evaluation design. Let us hope memo items 16 and 17 help make that point, if only on one dimension. Second, memo item 18 alludes to the possibility of finding an appropriate comparison group. Space does not permit me to create enough of the context to outline in any sensible way what such a design might look like, for it could take many forms, dependent on the conditions, or might prove inappropriate altogether. The specifics of any comparative design are less important here, however, than the fact that I would probably *try* to include a comparative element in any evaluation of a program such as this one, if feasible. Such an approach can get to the heart of the issues of effectiveness and opportunity cost, where most other approaches are weaker or even speculative in this regard. If one chooses, for whatever reason, to evaluate a program without looking at whether it produces the desired outcomes more efficiently or humanely than alternative programs (or no program at all), one never knows just what has been gained by choosing that particular program or lost by rejecting other, possibly better, alternatives.

Now, lest I be accused of falling prey to the "law of the instrument," let me hasten to note that I probably use a comparative evaluation design in fewer than half of the evaluations I conduct. Sometimes they simply are not feasible; sometimes they are irrelevant to the questions posed; sometimes I find it too much of an uphill struggle to disabuse program staff of the widely held view that comparative experiments are irrelevant or harmful; and sometimes I'm simply not creative enough to come up with one that makes sense. But none of these facts dissuade me from the feeling that one should look carefully at the power of the comparative element in evaluation. Were this a real-life evaluation, I would work hard to see whether a reasonable comparison could be included to get at issues such as relative effectiveness and cost of students' spending time in the humanities curriculum versus other alternatives.

November 16. Held a half-day meeting with Claire Janson, six other members of the curriculum committee, and the president of the board of education. Spent the first hour checking my perceptions about the program to make sure I was on track, and the next hour was devoted to discussing and resolving issues.

First, we talked at length about the polarization that seemed to be developing over the program and discussed the possibility of using an adversary evaluation approach in at least some parts of the study. That unnerved some of the group who felt there were too many adversaries as it was. I explained that I thought the approach had considerable merit when controversy already existed and opposing positions could be highlighted *within* the study rather than a battle waged around the evaluation. I explained that adversary evaluation attempts to ensure fairness through seeking both positive and negative perspectives, that both sides of the issue should be illuminated, and that the range of information collected would tend to be broader. Equally important, critics would be much less likely to discount the evaluation as being biased. After some discussion of costs of collecting parallel information, we decided tentatively that the adversary approach might serve best in three ways: (a) by planning to include the opinions of both strong supporters and detractors of the program—laying out the opposing points of view clearly and collecting data insofar as possible to test these opposing claims; (b) by enlisting the aid of two well-selected evaluators, one assigned to defend and one to attack the program, then having both review my evaluation design to see whether additional data are needed to make their case as strong as possible; and (c) after the data are in, by having my two colleagues review them and, as part of the final report, present and debate their cases, pro and con, on the basis of the evidence yielded by the study. Then the board can be the "jury" and reach a verdict. Not really the full "adversary model" of evaluation, I admit, but the group resonated to some of those concepts from it and felt the concepts would be helpful both in ensuring fair play and in being an excellent report technique. . . .

Author Comments.   Some might suggest a more full-blown application of the judicial "model" of evaluation here, complete with opposing counsel, taking of testimony, cross-examination, and other accoutrements of the courtroom. However, I feel the essence of the adversarial model is not in imitating a courtroom but in planning the study to consciously test and present opposing points of view.

> ***November 16 (continued).*** Second, some of the teachers asked whether I really understood the program well enough to evaluate it. Would the program I evaluated really be *their* program or my misconception of it? I suggested I write a description of the program and send it to Ms. Janson. She and the humanities teachers could correct any errors in it, so we can reach agreement on just what it is that is being evaluated.

Author Comments.   Why would I have the client review my written description of the program? First, because I want them involved in the evaluation. If they're part of it, they will ultimately be more trusting of the results. Their involvement in describing the program and their "sign-off" on the description at this point represents our first collaborative effort in the evaluation. Second, because I want to make sure I *do* understand the basic aspects of the program I am evaluating. While interviews, observations, and reviews of existing documents tell me a lot, I'm not omniscient. They have been involved with the program much longer than I have. It would be arrogant to assume they don't know more about it. My task is to help them summarize the program into a coherent model—something that those intimately involved with a program often have difficulty doing because their knowledge keeps them from "seeing the forest for the trees."

APPLICATION EXERCISES

1. Consider a program with which you are familiar. Who would be the audiences for the evaluation of this program? Use Figure 13.1 to identify potential audiences. Whom might you choose to interview? What might be the perspectives of each? Do you think it would be advisable to select some representatives of the audiences to serve as an advisory committee for the evaluation? If so, whom would you select and why?

2. What critical political factors might the evaluator in the above situation need to be aware of?

3. Through either a literature review or through contact with an agency, find a report describing a program. What is the model for this program? What are the goals and objectives? What are the critical components and activities? Is it feasible that these goals and objectives could be achieved with the specified clients using the described activities? Why or why not? Does the literature review or program description provide any evidence for why the model should work? Does it provide an accurate description of the model? What questions would you like to ask program staff to learn more about the model?

4. Consider the problem of teenage pregnancy. Develop an impact model for this problem with a causal hypothesis, intervention hypothesis, and action hypothesis. First, develop such a model based on your class's knowledge of the problem. Next, interview people in your community who work in this field and develop a normative theory of the problem. Finally, review the research literature and determine the validity of the normative model based on the research you find. What alternative causative models might you develop?

RELEVANT EVALUATION STANDARDS

The evaluation standards we see as relevant to this chapter's content are the following. These standards are described in Chapter 20 on page 442.

U1—Stakeholder Identification

F1—Practical Procedures

F2—Political Viability

A1—Program Documentation

A2—Context Analysis

SUGGESTED READINGS

Brinkerhoff, R. O., Brethower, D. M., Hluchyj, T., & Nowakowski, J. R. (1983). *Program evaluation: A practitioner's guide for trainers and educators.* Boston: Kluwer-Nijhoff.

Chen, H. (1990). *Theory-driven evaluations.* Newbury Park, CA: Sage.

House, E. R. (1988). *Jesse Jackson and the politics of charisma: The rise and fall of the PUSH/Excel program.* Boulder, CO: Westview Press.

McClintock, C. (1987). Conceptual and action heuristics: Tools for the evaluator. In L. Bickman (Ed.), *Using program theory in evaluation.* New Directions for Program Evaluation, No. 33, 43–57. San Francisco: Jossey-Bass.

chapter 14

Identifying and Selecting the Evaluation Questions and Criteria

ORIENTING QUESTIONS

1. What is the function of evaluation questions? Criteria? Standards? When is each necessary?
2. What are good sources for evaluation questions?
3. What role should the evaluator play in determining what questions will be addressed in the evaluation? What role should the client play?
4. In identifying and selecting evaluation questions, what different concerns and activities are involved in the *divergent* and *convergent* phases?
5. Should standards be absolute or relative? What kinds of standards can be specified?

Evaluations are conducted to answer questions and to apply criteria to judge the value of something. The **evaluation questions** provide the direction and foundation for the evaluation. Without them, the evaluation will lack focus, and the evaluator will have considerable difficulty explaining what will be examined, how, and why. **Criteria** are used to delineate the characteristics of a successful program or implementation. **Standards** then designate the level of performance the program must achieve on these criteria to be deemed a success. The evaluation design is not complete without the specification of such standards. The evaluation questions articulate the focus of the study, but without standards the evaluator will be unable to judge the results. Without criteria, he will be unable to judge the program itself.

The evaluator's primary responsibility is to gather and interpret information that can help key individuals and groups improve efforts, make enlightened decisions, and provide credible information to the public.

The process of identifying and defining the questions to be answered and the criteria to be used by the evaluation is critical. It requires careful reflection and investigation, for if important questions are overlooked or trivial questions are allowed to consume evaluation resources, the result could be

- Little or no payoff from the expenditure for the evaluation,
- A myopic evaluation focus that misdirects future efforts,
- Loss of goodwill or credibility because an audience's important questions or concerns are omitted,
- Disenfranchisement of legitimate stakeholders, or
- Unjustified conclusions.

Even though evaluation questions may be poorly articulated, they are usually attended to in some cursory fashion. Not so with evaluation criteria or standards, which are sometimes never articulated at all. It is always disconcerting to read through an evaluation report and be unable to find anywhere a statement of the criteria or standards used to determine whether a program was a success or failure. Yet without such specifications, measurements and observations cannot be translated into value judgments. For example, is an in-service program for supervisors successful if 50 percent of the supervisors attend? That all depends on the rationale for the program and the attendance standard that would signal success or failure. What about a 70 percent attendance rate in a high school mathematics class—is that good or bad? Again, it depends on the standard. If it is a college preparatory class with high attendance expectations—say a standard of 95 percent—70 percent is very poor. If it is a remedial mathematics class for dropouts who are returning to school on a part-time basis, the expectation might be considerably lower—say 50 percent—and an attendance rate of 70 percent might be noteworthy. These oversimplified examples should underscore the point that a statement of criteria and standards is essential to every good evaluation.

Cronbach (1982) uses the terms *divergent* and *convergent* to differentiate two phases of identifying and selecting questions for an evaluation. We will adopt these helpful labels in the discussion that follows.

In the **divergent phase**, as comprehensive a "laundry list" of potentially important questions and concerns as possible is developed. Items come from many sources, and little is excluded, for the evaluator wishes to map out the terrain as thoroughly as possible, considering all possible directions.

In the **convergent phase**, evaluators *select* from the "laundry list" the most critical questions to be addressed. Criteria are then developed for these questions. As we shall see later in this chapter, the process of setting priorities and making decisions about the specific focus for an evaluation is a difficult and complex task.

During the evaluation, new issues, questions, and criteria may emerge. The evaluator must remain flexible, allowing modifications and additions to the evaluation plan when these seem justified. Now let us consider the divergent—and then the convergent—phase in some detail.

IDENTIFYING APPROPRIATE SOURCES OF QUESTIONS AND CRITERIA: THE DIVERGENT PHASE

Cronbach (1982) summarizes the divergent phase of planning an evaluation as follows:

> The first step is opening one's mind to questions to be entertained at least briefly as prospects for investigation. This phase constitutes an evaluative act in itself, requiring collection of data, reasoned analysis, and judgment. Very little of this information and analysis is quantitative. The data come from informal conversations, casual observations, and review of extant records. Naturalistic and qualitative methods are particularly suited to this work because, attending to the perceptions of participants and interested parties, they enable the evaluator to identify hopes and fears that may not yet have surfaced as policy issues. . . .
>
> The evaluator should try to see the program through the eyes of the various sectors of the decision-making community, including the professionals who would operate the program if it is adopted and the citizens who are to be served by it. (pp. 210, 212–213)

If the evaluator is to obtain genuinely diverse viewpoints, he must "throw a broad net" to encompass a wide variety of sources:

1. Questions, concerns, and values of stakeholders
2. The use of evaluation "models," frameworks, and approaches (such as those in Part Two of this book) as heuristics
3. Models, findings, or salient issues raised in the literature in the field of the program
4. Professional standards, checklists, guidelines, instruments, or criteria developed or used elsewhere
5. Views and knowledge of expert consultants
6. The evaluator's own professional judgment

Each of these sources will be discussed in more detail in the following pages.

Identifying Questions and Concerns of Stakeholders

Perhaps the single most important source of evaluation questions, concerns, and criteria is the project or program's stakeholders—its clients, sponsors, participants, and affected audiences. Today, many in the evaluation field acknowledge the importance of consulting concerned stakeholders, but, at the same time, many fail to articulate how these stakeholders should be involved. We cannot overemphasize the importance of garnering the questions, insights, perceptions, hopes, and fears of the evaluation study's stakeholders, for such information should be primary in determining the evaluation's focus.

To obtain such input, the evaluator needs to identify individuals and groups who are influenced or affected by whatever is being evaluated. A tough but not impossible task, as Weiss (1984) observes.

> No procedural mechanisms appear capable of identifying, let alone representing, the entire set of potential users of evaluation results or the questions that they will raise. But in the normal course of events, adequate representation of stakeholders seems feasible. (p. 259)

Identifying stakeholders may be easier if one uses a checklist that includes the following: (1) *policy makers* (such as legislators or governing board members); (2) *administrators* or *managers* (those who direct and administer the program or entity evaluated); (3) *practitioners* (those who operate the program); (4) *primary consumers* (those intended to benefit, such as students, clients, or patients); and (5) *secondary consumers* (citizen and community groups who are affected by what happens to primary consumers). These five groups represent types of stakeholders who are associated with almost any program. Several distinct stakeholders or groups of stakeholders may emerge in each category. For example, administrators and managers for a school program will often include assistant principals, principals, and people affiliated with the program in the central administration, cluster coordinators, and so on. The superintendent may be considered a policy maker or an administrator depending on his relationship to the program. By considering each of the five categories, the evaluator can identify many potential stakeholders.

The checklist of potential evaluation audiences presented in Chapter 13 can also be useful in helping to identify potential stakeholders. That list of audiences is more extensive than the list given here because audiences include groups who have no particular stake in the program but would be interested in the results of the evaluation. Nevertheless, audiences should include all relevant stakeholders.

Once stakeholders are identified, they should be interviewed to determine what they would like to know about the object of the evaluation. What questions or concerns do they have? What is their perception of the program to be evaluated? What do they think it is designed to do, and how well do they think it is doing that? How would they change the program if they had the opportunity?

Many stakeholders who are unfamiliar with evaluation may have difficulty expressing what they would like the evaluation to do because they do not know what evaluations can do. It is, therefore, important that the evaluator ask questions in ways that are meaningful to the stakeholder. Rather than focus on the evaluation, the evaluator should focus on the stakeholders' *perceptions of the program*. The evaluator can then translate these concerns into evaluation questions at a later point. In many cases, as relationships with significant stakeholders evolve, the evaluator may move into an educative role to help the stakeholders learn of the different questions the evaluation could address or to acquaint the stakeholders with relevant research findings or evaluation approaches that would be appropriate. However, at the initial stage, it is important for the evaluator to spend more time *listening* than educating. By listening to the stakeholders' perceptions and concerns, the evaluator will gain an enormous amount of information about the program, its environment, typical methods of decision making, and the values and styles of the stakeholders. Asking why they are concerned about a particular aspect of the evaluation object, why they would value particular outcomes, or what they would do with the answers to particular questions can help the evaluator judge the thoughtfulness and importance of particular questions and criteria proffered by stakeholders.

There is no single technique for eliciting evaluation questions from stakeholders, but we believe a simple and direct approach works best. Before attempting to identify these questions, however, it is useful to first establish a context that will help to make them more meaningful. For example, we might begin this way: "As you know, I've been hired to do an evaluation of the X program. I would like the information that I collect to be useful to people like yourself. At this stage, I'm interested in learning about your perceptions of the program and what the evaluation can do for you. Could we begin by your sharing your current thoughts about the program and this evaluation?" We find it useful to begin in this rather *general* way. What the stakeholder chooses to tell you reflects his priorities. Making the initial questions more focused can result in your missing his major concerns. After you have learned about the stakeholder's general concerns, some probing may enable you to learn his *perception of the model or theory of the program*. For example, if an objectives-oriented approach seems appropriate, you might ask questions such as: "What do you see as the major goals or outcomes of the program? How do you think the program activities lead to those goals? Which activities do you see as most critical for achieving the goals?"

Eliciting Evaluation Questions from Stakeholders. Having learned of the stakeholder's perceptions about the program, you need to determine what questions they want the evaluation to answer. There is no more important—or more frequently neglected—step for assuring that the evaluation will be used by its stakeholders. You might begin by asking: "If I could collect information to answer any question about your program that you would like this evaluation to answer, what question would that be?" Like pickles in a jar, evaluative questions are easier to get out after the first one has been extracted. Some probing may help clients focus their thinking, using questions such as "What information would be most helpful to you to better manage or deliver the program? To decide whether to continue your support? Your participation in it? Which program components or activities do you consider most critical to the program's success? Which program components or activities are most problematic? What questions do you have about program operations?" If stakeholders overlook areas of obvious importance, you might ask, "Are you interested in _____?" The question "What else would you like to know?" often produces abundant responses. This is no time to be judgmental or to point out that some suggested questions may currently be unanswerable. This is the time for generating all the evaluation questions possible. The time for weighing and selecting the subset of questions to be ultimately pursued is later, in the convergent stage. You should, however, briefly describe the process to each stakeholder so that he recognizes that the questions will later be winnowed.

Figure 14.1 illustrates a possible sequence of questions in a stakeholder interview, leading from general questions intended to identify stakeholder views of the program, to more focused questions intended to identify their major evaluation questions. Additional specific procedures for guiding evaluator-participant interactions can be found in the writings of advocates of responsive evaluation (e.g., Stake, 1975a, 1975b, 1980; Guba & Lincoln, 1981; Lincoln & Guba, 1985). Patton's (1986, 1987b) utilization-focused evaluation provides additional guidance for the evaluator in learning of the information needs of stakeholders.

By grounding the evaluation plan in the concerns of key people, the evaluator takes steps to ensure that the evaluation will be useful and responsive

FIGURE 14.1   Information to be obtained in interviews with stakeholders

---

1. What is your general perception of the program? What do you think of it? (Do you think well of it? Badly of it? What do you like about it? What do you not like? Why?)
2. What do you perceive as the purposes (goals, objectives) or guiding philosophy of the program? (Do you agree with these purposes or philosophy? Do you think the problems the program addresses are severe? Important?)
3. What do you think the theory or model for the program is? (Why/how do you think it works? How is it supposed to work? Why would the program actions lead to success on the program's objectives or criteria? Which program components are most critical to success?)
4. What concerns do you have about the program? About its outcomes? Its operations? Other issues?
5. What major questions would you like the evaluation to answer? Why?
6. How could you use the information provided by these questions? (Would you use it to make decisions, to enhance your understanding?)
7. What do you think the answer to the question is? (Do you already know it? Would you be concerned if the answer were otherwise?)
8. Are there other stakeholders who would be interested in this question? Who are they? What is their interest?

---

to constituents who may have differing points of view. For example, consider a leadership training program funded by an external foundation. Interviews with stakeholders of such a program might produce the following questions:

1. (From the program administrator) Are we running on time and within our budget? Are we meeting foundation expectations for this program? Is the program being implemented as planned? What changes have occurred and why? Are participants achieving needed leadership skills?
2. (From program staff) What materials and procedures have been developed in other programs that we might use? How are trainees reacting to the program? Which sessions work best? Worst?
3. (From participants toward whom the program is aimed) Have the leadership skills of participants really improved? What portions of the program are most useful to participants?
4. (From the top managers in the organization) What evidence is there that the program is working? What continuing expenses are going to exist once foundation support terminates? Is this program having the desired impact on the units in which the trainees work? Would this program serve as a model for other change efforts? How is this program changing our organization?
5. (From the foundation) Is the program doing what it promised? What evidence is there that variables targeted for change have actually changed? How cost-effective is this program? Could the program be established in other settings? What evidence is there that the program will continue once foundation funds are terminated?

Using Evaluation Models, Frameworks, and Approaches As Heuristics

In exploring different approaches to evaluation in Part Two of this book, we noted that the specific conceptual frameworks and models developed under each approach play an important role in generating evaluation questions. This is one place in the evaluation process where the conceptual work done by the different evaluation theorists pays considerable dividends.

In reviewing the evaluation literature summarized in Part Two, the evaluator is directed toward certain questions. Sometimes a framework fits poorly and should be set aside, but usually something of value is suggested by each approach, as the following examples illustrate.

The *objectives-oriented approach* guides us to ask whether goals and objectives are defined and to what extent they are achieved. Have the goals and objectives been evaluated? Are they defensible? Achievable? Under what conditions or in what settings? What would prevent their achievement? The Discrepancy Evaluation Model (Provus, 1971) raises other questions about standards, program design, program installation, achievement of process, terminal and ultimate goals, and cost-benefit analysis.

The particular *management-oriented approach* developed by Stufflebeam generates questions about the context (need), input (design), process (implementation), and product (outcomes) for a program. Management-oriented approaches also remind us to learn about the decisions that are to be guided by the evaluation, for example, what do decision makers need to know, and when do they need to know it?

The *participant-oriented approach* reminds us that we should be sure to consider all stakeholders and should listen to what they have to say even during informal conversations. The *process* of the program is critical and we should try to understand the different ways that people view it or the different meanings placed on it. Portraying the program in its full complexity as a means of educating audiences should be of utmost concern. Stake's (1967) Countenance Model offers a framework for us to ask questions about rationale, intents, actual events, and standards. We are reminded that full descriptions of the *actual* object of the evaluation and the context in which it operates should be included in our evaluation.

The *consumer-oriented approach* has generated many checklists and sets of criteria that may be of considerable value to us when considering what components or characteristics to study in an evaluation or what standards to apply. The *expertise-oriented approach* has produced standards and critiques that reflect the criteria and values used by contemporary experts in education, mental health, social services, criminal justice, and other fields. The *adversary-oriented approach* reminds us to look for both strengths and weaknesses of the object we are evaluating and to include evaluation questions, concerns, and criteria from both the strongest proponents and opponents of that which is being evaluated.

To the extent that these conceptual frameworks can stimulate questions that might not emerge from other sources, they are important sources for evaluators to consider in the divergent phase of focusing the evaluation. As noted, many stakeholders are not familiar with the variety of issues an evaluation can address. We have found that stakeholders will sometimes focus only on goals, assuming that an evaluation *must* measure goals. While in many cases such a focus is appropriate, often other concerns are more paramount, given the stage of the program and the needs of stakeholders. Posavac (1994) describes a case in which stakeholders' limited understanding of evaluation led to their advocacy for a summative evaluation when a formative evaluation was a more appropriate strategy. He argues that evaluators must "take an active role in helping their clients to understand what they really need" (p. 75). Evaluation models can help the evaluator consider other areas of focus for the evaluation and educate the stakeholder as to the myriad issues that evaluation can investigate.

Using Research and Evaluation Work in the Program Field

Many evaluators focus their work in a limited number of content areas or fields. Some evaluators work entirely in the field of education; others, in mental health, health education, criminal justice, social services, training, nonprofit management, or some other area. In any case, the evaluator should be conversant with the salient issues in the area and consider their relevance to the present evaluation.

For example, enthusiastic sponsors and participants of a merit pay program for teachers may need to be reminded of the potential impact of the system on teamwork. Or advocates for low-cost housing dispersed throughout the community may fail to address adequately the concerns of existing homeowners regarding the impact of such housing on their property values or quality of life. The evaluator has a responsibility to raise such questions.

Commissions and task forces are sometimes formed by national, regional, or local governments to study particular issues of interest to governmental leaders. The report of the National Performance Review headed by Al Gore (1993), *From Red Tape to Results: Creating a Government That Works Better and Costs Less,* is a good example. Such reports raise provocative questions, and although they occasionally make unsubstantiated claims, they usually reflect current social concerns, issues, and beliefs. They may also serve to draw an informed evaluator's attention to issues that should be raised during a particular evaluation. Questions about important current issues may be omitted if the evaluator fails to raise them, with the result that the evaluation may be considered informative but devoid of information on the "real issues facing the field today." Obviously, we are not proposing a faddish "bandwagon" approach to determine what questions will be addressed by an evaluation study, but it would be naive indeed not to even consider the relevance of educational and social issues permeating current professional literature and other media.

In addition to being familiar with current issues in the field, the evaluator should make use of existing research to help develop causative models and questions to guide the evaluation. Chen (1990) advocates using existing theory and research to develop program models to guide the evaluation. Existing research and theory can be used to identify causes of the problem the program is designed to address, to discover successes and failures in remedying these problems, and to examine conditions that can enhance or inhibit program success with specific populations. The research literature can shed light on the likelihood that the program to be evaluated can succeed. It can be useful for the program evaluator to compare models in the research literature with the existing normative program model. Discrepancies between these models can suggest important areas for evaluation questions. Published evaluations of similar programs can suggest not only questions to be examined but also methods that might be productive for the evaluation study. The evaluator who has worked in this area extensively may be familiar with existing research. Nevertheless, a literature search can be a useful start to any planning process.

Using Professional Standards, Checklists, Guidelines, and Criteria Developed or Used Elsewhere

In many fields, standards for practice have been developed. Such standards can often be useful either in helping generate questions or in specifying criteria. As with existing research and evaluation, standards can signal areas that may have been overlooked in the focus on the existing program. Standards can be helpful for generating questions or criteria that are pertinent to a particular evaluation. They are important resources for evaluators to have in their tool kits.

One caution is important. As Tittle (1984) has pointed out indirectly in her thoughtful analysis of contextual influences on professional standards, standards set by autonomous professional groups are in and of themselves likely to be more convergent than divergent. Tittle states:

> Professional standards codify acceptable practice for a field. In professions which are autonomous, the standards are set by the members of the profession. Such standards are a product of general consensus within the profession, and often represent the results of much negotiation and compromise (p. 3).

Thus, compromise and consensus in developing sets of professional standards may rob them of diversity; using them as only one source in conjunction with others justifies their inclusion in a discussion of the divergent phase of evaluation planning. The same would be true for several of the other sources of evaluative questions and criteria discussed below.

Asking Expert Consultants to Specify Questions or Criteria

Evaluators are often asked to evaluate a program outside of their area of content expertise. The evaluator's expertise in evaluation is needed, but the specific content of the program is relatively new to the evaluator. For example, an evaluator may be called upon to evaluate a school's reading program, even though he knows little about such programs. In these cases, it is essential that the evaluator communicate extensively with the program staff and managers to understand the model for the program and conduct a review of literature to become familiar with issues in the area. In some cases, however, the evaluator may also want to make use of consultants with expertise in the content of the program to provide a more neutral and broader view than he may gain from program staff. Such consultants can be helpful in suggesting evaluation questions and criteria that reflect current knowledge and practice.

That evaluation specialists must elicit input from content experts is widely recognized.[1] Scriven (1973) asks that serious consideration be given to subject-matter experts' opinions of the quality of curriculum materials. Stake (1967) proposes that evaluators seek out, process, and report opinions of "persons of special qualification," presumably including content specialists. Stufflebeam and his colleagues (1971) point out that the evaluator often appropriately plays an "interface role" between content experts and audiences for the evaluation. The

---

[1] Advantages and disadvantages of having the evaluator serve in the dual capacity of expert in both the substantive content and evaluation methods are discussed in Worthen and Sanders (1984).

Joint Committee on Standards for Educational Evaluation (1994) recommends using teams of experts for most evaluations.

In the case of evaluating a school reading program, for example, the consultant could be asked not only to generate a comprehensive list of questions to be addressed but also to identify previous evaluations of reading programs, standards set by professional organizations such as the International Reading Association, and research on the criteria and methods for evaluating reading programs. If there is concern about possible ideological bias, the evaluator might employ more than one independent consultant.

Using the Evaluator's Professional Judgment

The evaluator should not overlook his own knowledge and experience when generating potential questions and criteria. Experienced evaluators are accustomed to describing the object of the evaluation in detail and looking at needs, costs, and consequences. Perhaps the evaluator has done a similar evaluation in another setting and knows from experience what questions proved most useful. Professional colleagues in evaluation and the content field of the program can suggest additional questions or criteria.

Evaluators are trained, at least in part, to be skeptics, to raise insightful (one hopes) questions that otherwise may never have been considered. This training is never more valuable than during the divergent phase of identifying evaluation questions and criteria, for some important questions may be omitted unless the evaluator raises them himself.

An experienced and insightful evaluator looking at a new project might raise questions like these:

- Are the purposes the project is intended to serve really important? Is there sufficient evidence of need for the project as it is designed? Are other more critical needs going unattended?
- Are the goals, objectives, and project design consistent with documented needs? Are scheduled activities, content, and materials consistent with needs, goals, and objectives?
- Have alternative strategies been considered for accomplishing the project's goals and objectives?
- Based on evaluations of other, similar projects, what questions were addressed that should be incorporated into this evaluation?
- Based on experience with other, similar projects, what new ideas, potential trouble spots, and expected outcomes can be projected?
- What indicators of project success will be accepted? Can such indicators be determined with instruments or technical "state of the art"?
- What critical elements and events should be examined and observed as the project develops?

- Have the critical events of the project occurred on time and within budget?
- What impact does the project have on ancillary but crucial side effects?

Summarizing Suggestions from Multiple Sources

Somewhere in the divergent process the evaluator will reach a point of diminishing returns, where no new questions are being generated. Assuming each available resource has been tapped, the evaluator should stop and examine what he has obtained: usually, long lists of several dozen potential evaluation questions, along with potential criteria. So that the information can be more readily assimilated and used later, the evaluator will want to organize the evaluation questions into categories. Here certain evaluation frameworks, such as Stufflebeam's (1971) CIPP model, Stake's (1967) Countenance Model, or Provus's (1971) Discrepancy Evaluation Model may be useful. The evaluator might adopt labels from one of these frameworks or create a new set of categories tailored to the study. Regardless of the source, having a manageable number of categories is essential in organizing potential questions and communicating them to others. Here is a sample of possible questions that might arise in the divergent phase for planning an evaluation of an existing conflict resolution program in the schools:

Context
1. What kinds of conflict occur among students in the schools? Who is most likely to be involved in a conflict (age, gender, characteristics)? What is the nature of the conflict?
2. How were conflicts resolved without conflict resolution? What kinds of problems occurred as a result of this strategy?
3. What communication skills do the students have that conflict resolution could build upon? What problems do the students have that might hinder the learning or use of conflict resolution skills?
4. How many conflicts currently occur? How frequent is each type?
5. What effects do the current conflicts have on the learning environment? The management of the school? The motivation and abilities of the teachers?

Process
1. Are the conflict resolution trainers sufficiently competent to provide the training? Have the appropriate personnel been selected to conduct the training? Should others be used?
2. Do the students selected for training meet the specified criteria?
3. What proportion of students participate in the complete training program? What do these students miss by participating in the training (opportunity costs)?
4. Does the training cover the designated objectives?

5. Do students participate in the training in the intended manner?
6. Where does the training take place? Is the physical environment for the training conducive to learning?
7. Do the teachers encourage use of the conflict resolution strategies? How? Do the teachers use these strategies themselves? How? What other strategies do they use?

Outcomes

1. Do the students who have received the training gain the desired skills? Do they believe the skills will be useful?
2. Do the students retain these skills one month after the completion of training?
3. What proportion of the students have used the conflict resolution strategies one month after program completion? For those who have not used the strategies, why not? (Were they not faced with a conflict, or were they faced with a conflict but used some other strategy?)
4. Under what circumstances were students most likely to use the strategies? Under what circumstances were they least likely to use the strategies?
5. How did other students support or hinder the students' use of the strategies?
6. Did the students discuss/teach the strategies to any others?
7. Was the incidence of conflicts reduced at the school? Was the reduction due to the use of the strategies?
8. Should other students be trained in the strategy? What other types of students are most likely to benefit?

It will be obvious to thoughtful evaluators and stakeholders that it is not feasible to address all identified questions in any one study. Practical considerations must limit the study to what is manageable. Some questions might be saved for another study; others might be discarded as inconsequential. Such winnowing is the function of the convergent phase.

SELECTING THE QUESTIONS, CRITERIA, AND ISSUES TO BE ADDRESSED: THE CONVERGENT PHASE

Cronbach (1982) introduces well the need for a convergent phase of evaluation planning.

The preceding section [the divergent phase] spoke as if the ideal were to make the evaluation complete, but that cannot be done. There are at least three reasons for reducing the range of variables treated systematically in an evaluation. First, there will always be a budget limit.

Second, as a study becomes increasingly complicated, it becomes harder and harder to manage. The mass of information becomes too great for the evaluator to digest, and much is lost from sight. Third and possibly most important, the attention span of the audience is limited. Very few persons want to know all there is to know about a program. Administrators, legislators, and opinion leaders listen on the run.

The divergent phase identifies what could *possibly* be worth investigating. Here the investigator aims for maximum bandwidth. In the convergent phase, on the contrary, he decides what incompleteness is most acceptable. He reduces bandwidth by culling the list of possibilities. (p. 225)

No evaluation can answer responsibly all the questions generated during a thorough, divergent planning phase. So the question is not *whether* to winnow these questions into a manageable subset but rather *who* should do it and *how.*

Who Should Be Involved in the Convergent Phase?

Some evaluators write and behave as if selecting crucial, practical evaluation questions were the sole province of the evaluator. Not so. In fact, under no circumstances should the evaluator assume sole responsibility for selecting the questions to be addressed or the evaluative criteria to be applied. This task requires close interaction with stakeholders. The sponsor of the evaluation, key audiences, and individuals or groups who will be affected by the evaluation should all have a voice.

Indeed, some evaluators are content to leave the final selection of questions to the evaluation sponsor or client. Certainly this lightens the evaluator's task. In our view, however, taking that easy course is a disservice to the client. Lacking the advantage of the evaluator's special training and experience, the client may well wind up posing a number of unanswerable questions for the study.

How Should the Convergent Phase Be Carried Out?

How can the evaluator work with the multiple stakeholders to select the targets for the evaluation? To begin with, the evaluator must determine what criteria should be used to rank the potential evaluation questions. Cronbach and others (1980) propose the following criteria:

So far we have encouraged the evaluator to scan widely; only in passing did we acknowledge that all lines of inquiry are not equally important. How to cut the list of questions down to size is the obvious next topic. . . . simultaneous consideration is given to the criteria . . . [of] prior uncertainty, information yield, costs, and leverage (that is, political importance). These criteria are further explained as follows: The more a study reduces uncertainty, the greater the information yield and, hence, the more useful the research.

Leverage refers to the probability that the information—*if* believed— will change the course of events. (pp. 261, 265.)

We draw on Cronbach's thinking in proposing the following seven criteria for determining which proposed evaluation questions should be investigated:

1. *Who would use the information? Who wants to know? Who will be upset if this evaluation question is dropped?* If limitless resources were available, one could argue that (except for invading rights of privacy) anyone who wishes to know has, in a democratic society, the right to information about what is evaluated. Rarely are resources limitless, however, and even if they were, prudence suggests a point of diminishing returns in collecting evaluative information. Therefore, if no important audience will suffer from the evaluator's failure to address a particular question, one might well give it a lower ranking or delete it.

2. *Would an answer to the question reduce present uncertainty or provide information not now readily available?* If not, there seems little point in pursuing it. If the answer already exists, then the question can be addressed easily with little cost to the evaluator or client.

3. *Would the answer to the question yield important information?* Some answers satisfy curiosity—but little more; these are what we call "nice to know" questions. Important questions are those that provide information that might be acted upon. They may address areas considered problematic by stakeholders with the wherewithal to make or influence changes. Where limited resources force choices, the importance of an answer should be an obvious criterion for inclusion.

4. *Is this question merely of passing interest to someone, or does it focus on critical dimensions of continued interest?* Priority should be given to critical questions of continuing importance. Program theory can help illuminate critical dimensions of the program.

5. *Would the scope or comprehensiveness of the evaluation be seriously limited if this question were dropped?* If so, it should be retained if at all possible.

6. *Would the answer to the question have an impact on the course of events?* If the question could affect policy or operating decisions, there is good reason to address it, if resources permit.

7. *Is it feasible to answer this question given available financial and human resources, time, methods, and technology?* Limited resources render many important questions unanswerable. Better to delete them early than to breed frustration by pursuing impossible dreams. Not all questions are equally costly to answer. Perhaps this seems obvious,

but it is so commonly ignored that Cronbach's (1982) reminder is important.

> The evaluator, working within fixed resources, reduces the initial list of questions to a manageable subset; then he budgets resources unequally over the survivors (holding back some reserves). Not many questions drop entirely out of consciousness. . . . It is sensible to pick up inexpensive information. Recording incidental observations costs almost nothing, while it costs somewhat more to cull data from records produced by normal operations and still more to collect fresh data. (p. 239)

The seven criteria just noted can be cast into a simple matrix (see Figure 14.2) to help the evaluator and client narrow the original list of questions into a manageable subset. Figure 14.2 is proposed only as a general guide and may be adapted or used flexibly. For example, one might expand the matrix to list as many (*n*) questions as exist on the original list, then simply complete the column entries by answering yes or no to each question or, alternatively, assigning some numerical rating. Numerical ratings offer the advantage of helping weight or rank questions. However the matrix is used, the evaluator and client (and representatives of other stakeholder groups, if possible) should work together to complete it. Although the evaluator may have the say on what is feasible, the relative importance of the questions will be determined by the client and other stakeholders. Scanning the completed matrix reveals quickly which questions are not feasible to answer, which are unimportant, and which can and should be pursued.

Of course, this is only one way to narrow down the original list. The evaluator may simply wish to go through the organized laundry list and, for each potential question, jot down a few words or phrases, keeping in mind the criteria summarized in Figure 14.2. The evaluator might place an asterisk (*) beside each question that appears a sure candidate for selection, then review the overall scope of selected questions and the feasibility of answering all of them in a

FIGURE 14.2 Matrix for ranking or selecting evaluation questions

	Evaluation Question						
Would the evaluation question . . .	*1*	*2*	*3*	*4*	*5*	*. . .*	*n*
1. Be of interest to key audiences?							
2. Reduce present uncertainty?							
3. Yield important information?							
4. Be of continuing (not fleeting) interest?							
5. Be critical to the study's scope and comprehensiveness?							
6. Have an impact on the course of events?							
7. Be answerable in terms of							
A. Financial and human resources?							
B. Time?							
C. Available methods and technology?							

quality manner. Has the potential utility of the evaluation been compromised in any way so far? Is feasibility still a concern?

At this point, the evaluator should sit down with the sponsor and/or client to review what could have been addressed in the evaluation (the laundry list), what seems most reasonable (those with asterisks), and what issues still exist in making selections (feasibility, scope, potential utility, any concerns the sponsor or client may have).

Whether the evaluator prefers to work directly from the original laundry list or to use a matrix like that in Figure 14.2, we cannot stress too strongly the importance of conducting this activity—which will focus the entire evaluation study—interactively with the evaluation client. The sponsor or client will likely want to add or subtract selected questions, possibly negotiating an increased or reduced scope for the study or debating rationales for adding or dropping certain questions. The evaluator may find it necessary to defend his own professional judgment or the interests of unrepresented stakeholders. This can be difficult. If the sponsor or client demands too much control over the selection of evaluation questions (e.g., requiring inclusion of unanswerable questions or those likely to yield one-sided answers), the evaluator must judge whether his position has been compromised. If it has, it is probably in the best interest of all concerned to terminate the evaluation at this point. Conversely, the evaluator must refrain from insisting on his own preferred questions and overriding legitimate concerns of the sponsor or client.

Usually the evaluator and client can agree on which questions should be addressed. Reaching a congenial consensus (or compromise) goes far toward establishing the sort of rapport that turns an evaluation effort into a "partnership" in which the client is pleased to cooperate. A feeling of "shared ownership" greatly enhances the probability that evaluation findings will be used.

If the evaluator and the client and/or sponsor have winnowed out all of the evaluation questions, it is important to check the acceptability of the resulting subset with other important stakeholders. To facilitate this, the evaluator provides a list of questions to be addressed with a short explanation indicating why each is important. If the matrix (Figure 14.2) is used, a copy should be provided. The list of questions and/or matrix should be shared with all important stakeholders in the evaluation. They should be informed that this tentative list of questions is being given to them for two reasons: (1) to keep them informed about the evaluation and (2) to elicit their reactions, especially if they feel strongly about adding or deleting questions. Sufficient time should be set aside for their review before the final list is produced.

Concerned comments merit a direct response. The evaluator should meet with any who are dissatisfied with the list of questions and with the sponsor, if need be, to discuss and resolve concerns to everyone's satisfaction before continuing. To push for premature closure on legitimate issues surrounding the scope of the evaluation is one of the worst mistakes the evaluator can make. Unresolved conflicts will not go away, and they can be the undoing of an otherwise well-planned evaluation.

One caution: A timeworn but effective ploy used by those who wish to scuttle an unwanted evaluation is to raise unresolvable objections. The astute evaluator should recognize strident insistence on including biased or unanswerable questions. He can counter them by giving an advisory committee of stakeholders, including the conflicting parties, the task of hearing and making recommendations on the evaluative questions to be addressed. As we have discussed, advisory groups composed of stakeholders are a useful and effective part of many successful evaluation studies.

Specifying the Evaluation Criteria and Standards

Having identified the evaluation questions, the evaluator, in concert with the stakeholders or advisory group, needs to specify standards for each question. If the questions do not make explicit the criteria being used to judge the program, criteria for such judgments should also be developed at this point.

To ensure that the questions have incorporated the desired criteria, the evaluator should discuss with the group the object to be judged. If the purpose of the study is summative, it is critical that the important criteria for judging a program be conveyed in the evaluation questions. The evaluator should ensure that criteria found in the literature to be critical to program success are included. He should then see that the group agrees that the criteria conveyed through the evaluation questions are appropriate. If the purpose of the study is formative, an overall judgment regarding the program may be inappropriate, but a judgment of a particular portion of the program may be required. In a manner similar to that used for the overall program, the evaluator can then help the group to consider whether the questions adequately convey their criteria for judging this portion of the program and its operations.

The specification of standards of performance can be a complex area fraught with uncertainty. Where similar programs exist, such programs can be examined for standards of performance. With new programs, or questions that address process concerns, less information is available to guide the decision. Nevertheless, it is important for the evaluator and the stakeholder group to have some idea of the level of performance that is acceptable and the level that is not acceptable for each area. Without standards at this stage of the evaluation, it is too easy for the unscrupulous program manager to claim that the obtained level of performance was exactly the one desired.

A standard should be developed to reflect the degree of difference that would be considered sufficiently meaningful to adopt the new program. Such a standard might be absolute or relative.

Absolute Standards.   Sometimes policy will require the specification of an absolute standard. As more states move toward establishing graduation requirements and/or pass requirements that require the demonstration of particular knowledge and skills, absolute standards should be specified whenever possible to determine whether new programs can achieve the desired level. Similarly, accreditation requirements or standards for care of patients can lead to the need for absolute standards. When existing performance standards are absent, the evaluator can begin with seeking input from knowledgeable stakeholders about their expectations on each question. As the evaluator learns the range of expectations, he can then lead a discussion of proposed standards with the key stakeholders or an advisory group. Standards should be specific to each criterion. Thus, if attendance were an important criterion for success, the evaluator might ask, "What proportion of students do you expect to complete the program? 100 percent? 90 percent? 75 percent?" or "How much of a reduction in conflict incidents do you expect to occur as a result of the program? 75 percent? 50 percent? 25 percent?" Such questions can prompt a frank discussion of expectations that will be invaluable in judging program results.

On occasion, the answer that stakeholders may come up with is an honest "We don't know," in which case experience with the program may be needed before standards can be established. If the literature has reported on other similar programs, results of these programs may provide some answers, but caution should be used in applying these standards to new target audiences with different characteristics and new staff with different competencies and skills. If standards are established, the evaluator should avoid having program staff purposely set standards too low (to ensure program success) or having program opponents set them too high (to guarantee failure). Working with a group of stakeholders with different perspectives can help avoid such a situation.

Relative Standards. Some argue that absolute standards such as those implied above are unnecessary when the study will involve comparisons with other groups. Thus, Light (1983) argues that outcomes superior to those achieved with a placebo control or comparison group are sufficient to demonstrate program success. Scriven (1980) advocates comparing programs with available alternatives. Such comparisons can be useful in determining program impact and, hence, value. The standard in such cases may be that the new program is significantly better than the alternative method. Care should be taken, however, to define the term "significant." A statistically significant difference may still be too small to have any practical significance. Many evaluators are moving to the use of **effect size**, a measure of the magnitude and practical significance of between-group differences, because they see it as more meaningful than the traditional statistically significant difference. While traditional statistical significance focuses on the probability of the null hypothesis being true (a "true-false" approach), the effect size conveys the size of the difference in a manner similar to that of a Z-score or standard deviation units. The term "effect size" is drawn from the literature on meta-analysis, which is designed to combine results from across a number of studies (Glass, McGraw, & Smith, 1981; Durlak & Lipsey, 1991). It is typically calculated by dividing the difference between the means of the two groups (control and experimental groups) by the pooled, within-group standard deviation. Thus, when evaluations involve the comparisons of two programs, effect size can be used to specify standards. The effect size essentially conveys the degree to which differences between the two groups differ beyond, and in comparison to, the ordinary variability among individuals. As such, the effect size can provide a standard that is relative to typical group performance. Thus, using effect size to specify a standard can be useful when it is difficult, or unnecessary, to specify an absolute standard.

Whether standards are absolute or relative, their importance cannot be overemphasized. The next section cautions, however, against setting standards too rigidly in the beginning of a program.

REMAINING FLEXIBLE DURING THE EVALUATION: ALLOWING NEW QUESTIONS, CRITERIA, AND STANDARDS TO EMERGE

Many evaluations are flawed by evaluators who relentlessly insist upon answering initially agreed-upon questions, regardless of intervening events, changes in the object of the evaluation, or new discoveries. During the course of an evaluation, many occurrences—for example, changes in scheduling, personnel, and funding; unanticipated problems in program implementation; evaluation procedures that are found not to work; lines of inquiry that prove to be dead ends; new critical issues that emerge—require new or revised evaluation questions. Because such changes cannot be foreseen, Cronbach and his associates (1980) propose that

> Choice of questions and procedures, then, should be tentative. Budgetary plans should not commit every hour and every dollar to . . . the initial plan. Quite a bit of time and money should be held in reserve. (p. 229)

When changes in the context or object of the evaluation occur, the evaluator must ask whether that change should affect the list of evaluation questions. Does it make some questions moot? Raise new ones? Require revisions? Would changing questions or focus in the middle of the evaluation be fair? The evaluator should discuss any changes and their impact on the evaluation with the sponsor, client, and other stakeholders. Allowing questions and issues to evolve, not committing to an evaluation carved in stone, fulfills Stake's (1975b) concept of responsive evaluation discussed in Chapter 10.

A word of warning, however: Evaluators must not lose track of questions or criteria that—despite possible changes—remain important. Resources should not be diverted from vital investigations just to explore interesting new directions. Flexibility is one thing, indecisiveness another.

Once the evaluation questions (and/or criteria, standards) have been agreed upon, the evaluator can complete the evaluation plan. The next steps in the planning process are covered in Chapter 15.

Reprise: The reader is reminded that on November 14 and 15, the evaluator, during on-site interviews, had asked all those interviewed (the school principal, three humanities teachers, the Humanities Curriculum Review Committee chairperson, one teacher each from the English and social science departments, one parent, and three members of the school board) what questions they would like the evaluation study to answer. We return to the saga on November 16, midway through a half-day meeting of the evaluator with the principal, six other members of the curriculum committee, and the president of the board of education.

CASE STUDY APPLICATION

November 16 (continued). Having dealt with some other key issues, we spent the bulk of the meeting laying out the skeleton of an evaluation plan, which I suggested we do together. Some of the committee wanted the evaluation to focus on the curriculum goals and objectives, using those as organizers for collecting and reporting the data. But the board president noted that the objectives were only part of the program, and he listed several important questions he felt would be overlooked if we were bound by the objectives. That was tremendous! It usually takes a fair bit of Rogerian counseling to get people to look beyond their written objectives, so I was quick to take the opportunity to tout the advantages of using evaluative questions as key organizers in an evaluation study. To illustrate, I put on the blackboard the questions I had gleaned over the past two days that they and others had said they would like the evaluation to answer. They got involved, started categorizing and collapsing questions, added others, and before we knew it, we had 17 evaluation questions that they all agreed should be dealt with in the study, plus a handful that were left in but viewed as lower in priority.

Before we finalized the list of questions, I proposed they let me review some other professional sources for additional questions we may want to add but might not think of in one short meeting. (I'm sure glad I had Denise do the literature search!) They agreed, and all but two of the committee members said they could get together again tonight. So we agreed to meet again at 7:00 P.M.

Spent the next several hours back in the office they've let me use, trying to think of additional evaluation questions we should consider asking. Several additional questions occurred as I thought a bit about Stake's and Eisner's approaches to evaluating the arts, so now I've inserted some questions on how the various stakeholders view the process of education, as well as what expert humanities "connoisseurs" might say about this program. Also pulled a couple of relevant questions from the Commission on Excellence report. I pulled out Denise Schwartz's review of literature and found one article that described models for using the arts to broaden students' perspectives in middle school. Two others described evaluations of programs in other states that had attempted to achieve similar outcomes. The smartest thing I've done was to put her in touch with Dewey Pitcher, associate dean of the College of Humanities back on campus. He had pointed her in the right direction to find some of these evaluations and models. Seeing how helpful he had been, I decided to give him a call to pump him a little further. I know he used to do a lot of accreditation and site-visit work, and wondered if he could tune me in to any sets of written standards for humanities programs that might be floating around in some relevant professional group. He was really helpful, even though he didn't cite any standards, as such, because he reeled off about two dozen questions he'd want answered about any humanities program and pointed out some of the controversial issues in the area. Even though we had already thought of most of the evaluation questions, there were three or four that were new and struck me as important. Also, there does seem to be disagreement in the field about how receptive middle school students are to such knowledge, given their stage of moral development. He suggested I attend carefully to the ages of the students and past educational experiences. Now I feel ready and armed for tonight's meeting.

Author Comments. It is paramount to include representatives of all important audiences in the design of an evaluation study. Without that step, it is your evaluation design; with their involvement, there is an excellent chance they will see it as their design. What better way to have someone understand evaluation and use its results than to get that person involved as a partner in its conduct?

For me, an easy first step is to ask everyone directly or indirectly involved in the program what questions he would like to see answered by the evaluation study. Evaluators should feel free to inject their questions (and may need them for "pump priming" so others get a feel for what is meant by "evaluation questions"), but a major portion of these questions should be drawn from those with a stake in the outcome of the study.

By examining the relevant research and evaluation literature and perusing the professional writings that describe good and not-so-good humanities programs, I can gain a greater understanding of why the program may or may not work and what its critical components are. This also helps me find seeds to still more evaluative questions. I always ask an expert in the field—someone who "knows the territory"—to help get the literature review started. These computer searches often provide *too much* information. You can't separate the wheat from the chaff! If the expert is knowledgeable, sometimes he can provide a reasonable shortcut to help you identify key issues, questions, models, and seminal articles and evaluations that would not be feasible for you to ferret out on your own.

The examples used in this hypothetical case study may not suffice in a real evaluation, but they should illustrate some of what goes on in the divergent phase of identifying evaluative questions. Now to the convergent phase.

November 16 (continued). Met with the group again tonight and shared with them the additional questions I had generated. I listed several criteria on the blackboard and we used those as yardsticks to determine whether or not to include each question. This is a pleasant group; usually someone has apoplexy over one or more of the questions that threatens some particular sacred cow. Not so this time, except when I asked, "What evidence exists that the goals of the curriculum are really important?" That one raised dust for a minute or two, but they accepted it after the shock wore off that anyone would presume to ask it. After a bit they almost seemed to relish the answer, presuming I'd get the answer they would predict.

With the addition of the new questions, some of the earlier ones dimmed by comparison and were quickly dropped. We reordered the rest by priority and agreed on 14 that are crucial, plus 4 others we'll try to answer if resources permit. The board president had a tough time letting go of one pet question that was just not feasible without a $75,000 study but finally made it.

Once we got set and agreed on the questions, I suggested we spend our remaining time trying to get the group to help me identify where to begin to look for answers to the questions.

Author Comments.   The criteria mentioned in the above journal entry are those shown earlier in Figure 14.2, which I always find useful and prefer to use if possible. Jim Sanders feels more at home with his laundry list and asterisks. Jody Fitzpatrick uses the laundry list and asterisks but with a few criteria designed for that organization. All work. The key is to find that approach that you can use to help stakeholders in the evaluation converge on the subset of evaluation questions that are (1) of most importance and (2) feasible. The importance of narrowing the focus to a reasonable number of important, answerable questions that are satisfactory and interesting to key audiences is so obvious that one might wonder why we trouble to state it. Actually, it really is not so obvious to many evaluation practitioners. We have witnessed numerous studies that were launched with long lists of unranked, unselected evaluation questions, only to end up months later frustrated and confused because they have only produced answers to a few, and those were not the questions the clients cared about most. Indeed, if we had $10 for every case like that we have seen, we would be basking in the Bahamas rather than penning these pages.

APPLICATION EXERCISES

1. Consider an evaluation that would have meaning for you and your organization or employer. If you're at a loss for a program you know, you might select your graduate program. Or try some recent, highly publicized program or policy being considered by city or state officials. Using what you now know about generating and then selecting questions, criteria, and standards for the evaluation, generate a list of evaluation questions you would want to address.

2. What method would you use to cull the above questions in the convergent phase, knowing your organization and the issues involved? Do the criteria in Figure 14.2 serve the purpose? Would you modify them? Are there questions that you *know* must be answered and the laundry list with asterisks would suffice? How would you involve the other stakeholders in the convergent phase?

3. Are criteria and standards necessary for each of these questions? If the evaluation is summative, do the questions convey all the important criteria for the program? Should other questions or criteria be added? Now, set standards for each question as appropriate. Discuss your rationale for each standard.

4. Interview a fellow student about a program with which he is familiar. If possible, interview someone else knowledgeable about the same program. What differences do you discover? Why do you think these differences exist?

5. Obtain a copy of a report from a completed evaluation study. Consider the questions that were addressed. Were there any critical oversights? Was the evaluation limited or comprehensive in scope? Were criteria and/or standards explicitly stated? If not, was their omission acceptable? Why or why not? If they were stated, on what grounds

were they developed? Do you agree with the criteria? Would you have added others? Were standards set at the appropriate level?

RELEVANT EVALUATION STANDARDS

The evaluation standards we see as relevant to this chapter's content are the following. These standards are described in Chapter 20 on page 442.

U1—Stakeholder Identification	F3 —Cost Effectiveness
U3—Information Scope and Selection	P1 —Service Orientation
U4—Values Identification	P5 —Complete and Fair Assessment
F1 —Practical Procedures	A3 —Described Purposes and Procedures
F2 —Political Viability	A12—Metaevaluation

SUGGESTED READINGS

Cronbach, L. J. (1982). *Designing evaluations of educational and social programs.* San Francisco: Jossey-Bass.

Cronbach, L. J., Ambron, S. R., Dornbusch, S. M., Hess, R. D., Hornik, R. C., Phillips, D. C., Walker, D. F., & Weiner, S. S. (1980). *Toward reform of program evaluation.* San Francisco: Jossey-Bass.

Lincoln, Y. S., & Guba, E. G. (1985). *Naturalistic inquiry.* Beverly Hills, CA: Sage.

Patton, M. Q. (1986). *Utilization-focused evaluation* (2nd ed.). Beverly Hills, CA: Sage.

Witkin, B. R., & Altschuld, J. W. (1995). *Planning and conducting needs assessments.* Thousand Oaks, CA: Sage.

chapter 15

Planning How to Conduct the Evaluation

ORIENTING QUESTIONS

1. What are some activities or functions common to all evaluations that must be considered in planning any evaluation study? (*Hint:* One of them is "collection of information.")
2. What should be specified in the evaluation plan?
3. What is the role of the client in developing the plan?
4. How can you organize time, responsibilities, and resources so that all evaluation tasks are accomplished in a first-rate and timely manner?
5. What resources must be considered when developing evaluation budgets?
6. Why would a formal evaluation contract or agreement between evaluator and client be useful?

Much has been said in earlier chapters about the need to "focus" the evaluation study—to understand what is to be evaluated, why the evaluation has been proposed, what the evaluation's sponsor, client, and other stakeholders want to learn, and what criteria they would use to make judgments. But is this evaluation planning? Yes. When the focus of a study has become clear, is the evaluation plan complete? No, for focusing is only one part of developing an evaluation plan.

To explain the relationship between focusing and planning an evaluation, we turn to the earlier work of Stufflebeam (1968, 1973b). He proposes that one first *focus the evaluation* to determine what information is needed. He also proposes four functions common to various kinds of evaluation, namely information *collection, organization, analysis,* and *reporting.* To develop an evaluation design, Stufflebeam maintains one must plan how each of these functions would be carried out. Finally, he proposes that developing a plan for *administering the evaluation* is an integral part of an evaluation design. Stufflebeam's (1973b) resultant structure for developing evaluation designs includes these six activities/functions:

1. *Focusing* the evaluation
2. *Collecting* information
3. *Organizing* information
4. *Analyzing* information
5. *Reporting* information
6. *Administering* the evaluation

In Chapters 12 through 14 we dealt with various aspects of *focusing the evaluation* (phase 1 in the list). Understanding the origin and context of a proposed evaluation and identifying and selecting the evaluation questions, criteria, and standards most appropriate for the study are the major aspects of focusing the evaluation. In this chapter we focus on phases 2 through 6, *collecting, organizing, analyzing,* and *reporting* information and *administering* the evaluation. Before addressing these topics, we wish to remind the reader of two important points:

1. Evaluations should be conducted in a flexible manner. One should not infer that the steps involved in evaluation are sequential and linear. We might have almost as conveniently used here Stake's "clock" (1975b) (shown as Figure 10.2), which emphasizes that one may move back and forth among evaluation functions, from data analysis to more data collection, to reporting, back to reanalysis, and so on. Whatever schematic is used to portray them, all evaluations have in common these facts: (a) they involve data collection, analysis, and interpretation, and (b) the evaluator must plan how these functions will be fulfilled.

2. The evaluator should have a clear understanding of the purpose and role of the evaluation. In earlier chapters we outlined several different approaches to evaluation and described how each might be used to perform different evaluation roles. Then we provided practical guidelines (especially in Chapters 13 and 14) to help the evaluator focus the evaluation study. It would seem difficult for an evaluator to go through activities such as we have proposed without developing a fairly clear notion of the role the evaluation will play and a general idea of the type of evaluation study that will best suit that role. Such conceptual clarity is essential to any good evaluation plan.

Yet far too often evaluators arrive at this point, after considerable interaction with the client and other stakeholders, still unable to articulate clearly the purposes or procedures of the evaluation. By now, the evaluator should exhibit a clear understanding of the particular evaluation she is proposing. Is she planning a formative or summative evaluation? Is it comparative or descriptive?

Is the evaluation to be objectives-oriented, with the design built around the measurement of specific objectives, or goal-free, with the design built around independently generated evaluation questions? Answers to questions such as these should be apparent in any good **evaluation plan**. If they are not, the evaluator should settle them in her mind (and that of the client) before proceeding further. Without clarity on these points, the focus for the evaluation is fuzzy indeed, and it would be an accident if the remainder of the evaluation were anything but a muddle.

IDENTIFYING DESIGN AND DATA-COLLECTION METHODS

In Chapter 14 we dealt with identifying and selecting those evaluation questions that the evaluation study should answer. Once the evaluation questions are known, the next logical step is to determine what information is needed to answer each question. For example, consider the question "Have the critical program activities occurred on time and within budget?" To answer this question, the evaluator would need to know, among other things, which activities were identified as critical; the program time frames and budget, by activity; when each critical activity began and ended; and the total cost of each critical activity.

The information needs in the preceding example seem very straightforward. But in practice they are often much more complex. For example, consider the question, "What impact does the computer-based WANDAH program have on the writing performance of high school students in the Jefferson High WANDAH writing classes?" To answer the question it would be necessary to first identify the appropriate design. Is the program at a pilot stage and the design descriptive? Or is a summative decision to be made and a more experimental design necessary with some type of comparison group? Having determined the design, the evaluator would then need to specify the means for measuring "writing performance." Writing performance could be viewed either holistically or analytically, or both. Holistic measures of students' writing ability might involve judgments made by panels of the overall quality of students' papers, before and after exposure to WANDAH. An analytic approach might include measures of syntactic density, numbers of T-units, percent of *to be* verbs, or average sentence length before and after using WANDAH. Or students' writing performance might be measured according to the extent and effectiveness of revisions from one draft to another. In this armchair example, we can beg the choice, but were we actually conducting the study we would be required to decide which type of design would be best and precisely what variables and measures should be used to answer the question.

The evaluator should obviously involve the client and other stakeholders in deciding what information would best answer each evaluation question. But the evaluator plays an active and pivotal role, as Cronbach and his colleagues (1980) have observed.

The evaluator, then, should be far more than a passive notetaker trying to locate variables to study. From his own knowledge or from his consultation with experts he should come to understand the problem area and the history of similar programs well enough to suggest likely points of breakdown and possible unfortunate side effects. He can reasonably become devil's advocate, imagining the complaints that opponents might voice about the program. The evaluator can also suggest outcome variables that others have failed to mention, so that his clientele can decide whether data are wanted on these. (p. 170)

Using Research Designs in Evaluation

Research designs specify the organization of parts of the study and the manner and methods in which some information will be collected. They also have implications for the sources of data. Thus, the evaluator should consider whether research designs are appropriate and discuss related issues with the stakeholders in the development of the evaluation plan. Many evaluators conceptualize research designs as descriptive or causal. When the evaluation question is a causal one, evaluators will often use experimental or quasi-experimental designs (see Singer & McDowall, 1988; Waldo & Chiricos, 1977). Others may make use of descriptive case studies to examine changes that occur in target groups (see Datta, 1995). In examining the impact of policies that affect whole groups (changes in laws or regulations), evaluators may use multiple regression or other statistical methods to help in answering the evaluation question (see Folz & Hazlett, 1991; Freeman, Klein, Townsend, & Lechtig, 1980).

More often the evaluation question is a descriptive one—to show a trend, to illustrate a process, to convey the status of something, or to describe and analyze a program, process, or procedure. Time series methods may be selected to show a trend, as reflected in the question "Are high school graduation rates declining?" Cross-sectional methods may be used to assess public opinions of a program. Case study methods may be used to describe the critical components of a successful child abuse prevention program. Guba and Lincoln (1981) have used the term "thick description" to refer to certain types of descriptive studies, and such thick description can be most useful in informing stakeholders about what is actually happening in a program. Descriptive designs are commonly used in needs assessments and monitoring or process studies. They also can be useful in impact studies designed to determine whether participants' final performance is at the desired level or to describe performance at critical stages of the program. Many summative evaluations consist of a mix of causal and descriptive designs to avoid a black-box solution that fails to describe connections between the clients and the program.

The evaluator and stakeholders should examine each question carefully to identify any important research design issues relevant to the question. Most evaluations use multiple research designs or combinations of designs to address different questions. Nevertheless, it is important to consider design at this stage.

Agreements may need to be reached on the availability of comparison groups, the appropriateness of random assignment, the time for collecting data from multiple sources, the specification of the cases, the timing of measures, and other issues relevant to the organization of the collection of information.

At this stage the evaluator may be ready to specify the exact design to be used if the intent of the question is quite clear and the limitations and flexibility permitted in data collection have been explored. For example, if the question is specifically to examine a trend—Has the number of pregnant women receiving prenatal care in the first trimester increased over the last five years? Has the number of high school graduates pursuing education at community colleges increased over the last decade?—it may be perfectly appropriate to designate a simple time series design at this point. However, if there is some interest in exploring the *whys* of the trends, the evaluator might need to explore further to determine the extent to which case study or cross-sectional components need to be added. In some cases, the evaluator may be content with simply specifying whether the design will be causal or descriptive and delaying the selection of a specific research design until the details of information needs, feasibility of different designs and methods, costs, and timelines are further developed. Research design concerns should, however, be addressed before the conclusion of the planning process.

The designation of the appropriate design for each question enhances communication between the stakeholders and the evaluator and helps the stakeholders envision how the study will actually be implemented. Through learning the details of the design, the stakeholders can raise any concerns they have about data collection or issues that might constrain the study. Changes can then be made at that point rather than in the middle of data collection.

Identifying Appropriate Sources of Information

Once needed information has been agreed upon, the source(s) of that information must be specified. For example, let us say that to answer the question "Have the critical program activities occurred on time and within budget?" it was agreed that needed information would include program time frames and budget by activity, costs for each activity, and documentation of when each critical activity began and ended. The primary information source for such items would typically be the program administrator and existing program documents. Secondary sources (used as necessary to supplement or cross-check information and perceptions) might be the organization's accountant or budget officer, funding agency officials of the program if externally funded, or program participants (for information on timing and direction of activities).

To answer the question "What impact does the computer-based WANDAH program have on the writing performance of high school students in the Jefferson High WANDAH writing class?" let us assume that it had been decided that information was needed on one holistic measure (teachers' judgments of overall writing quality on one assignment) and one analytic measure (percent of *to be* verbs). The source of information for both would be the students in the WANDAH classes (and students in some non-WANDAH classes, if a comparison group were used). The source is not the teacher or the rater who counts the *to be* verbs; they only judge, score, or transmit information about writing performance, and that information obviously emanates from the students.

Using Existing Data As an Information Source.   Evaluators (and clients) sometimes overlook the fact that not every question must be answered by collecting original data. Evaluators would be wise to see whether information relevant to any of the evaluation questions already exists in readily available form. For example, are there extant evaluation reports, status reports, or data collected for other purposes that might provide complete or partial answers to some evaluation questions? Much of the information necessary to answer the first question posed above—"Have the critical program activities occurred on time and within budget?"—might be available in existing organizational documents. Before moving to collecting new information, the evaluator should always ask the client, program managers, and deliverers of the program whether there are existing sources that might meet the information needs. She then needs to judge the appropriateness of these sources. Internal data, specific to the organization, may or may not be collected and organized in a valid and reliable manner. Such data may, however, provide much information about the environmental context of the program.

Public documents and databases are another major source of existing information. Examples of such data include the reports developed by the U.S. Census Bureau (including the Census of Governments, the Decennial Census of Population and Housing, the monthly Current Population Survey, and Survey of Income and Program Participation); statistics collected by the U.S. Department of Labor and other federal departments; the City-County Data Book; reports and databases of various state, local, and nonprofit organizations; and the like. Such data are typically intended to be used by others. As such, the information is generally collected in a careful, standardized fashion and is likely to be more reliable and valid than much internal existing data. While it is reliable and valid for the purposes for which it is collected, such information may not, however, be reliable and valid, or sufficiently sensitive, for the program evaluation at hand. The evaluator should be certain to learn about the manner in which the information is collected, the definitions of the constructs, the sampling methods used, and the time frame and population sampled to determine whether the data will be appropriate for the current program evaluation. Smith (1982) provides a very useful example of some public data resources that might be consulted in relation to several types of evaluation questions. Chelimsky (1985b) discusses the importance of federal databases to permit comparisons across smaller entities and how budget cuts may threaten these sources. Thoughtful evaluators should identify parallel information resources that might exist at the local level.

One word of caution: Just because data exist does not mean the data must be used. We have no sympathy for the evaluator who permits evaluation questions to be wrested into nearly unrecognizable form only so they can be answered by available information. Such distortion of an evaluation's intent is not excusable by claims of heightened efficiency. In such cases, the evaluator has committed what Patton (1986) calls a "Type III error," answering the wrong question!

Commonly Used Information Sources.   Within each evaluation study, information sources will be selected to answer the particular questions posed. Obviously, information sources may be as idiosyncratic as the related questions. As discussed above, existing data are one important information source. If original information must be collected, the most common sources are these:

- Program recipients (e.g., students, patients, clients or trainees)
- Program deliverers (social workers, therapists, trainers, teachers, physicians, nurse practitioners)
- Persons who have knowledge of the program recipients (parents, spouses, co-workers, supervisors)

Other frequent sources include the following:

- Program administrators
- Persons or groups who might be affected by the program or who could affect its operation (the general public, future participants, organizations or members of interest groups involved in the program)
- Policy makers (boards, CEOs, executive and legislative bodies)
- Persons who planned or funded the program (state department officials, legislators, federal funding agency officials)
- Persons with special expertise in the program's content or methodology (other program specialists, college or university specialists)
- Existing data and documents (existing databases, files, and public documents such as written reports)
- Program events or activities that can be observed directly

Policies That Restrict Information Sources.   It is important to identify, early in planning an evaluation, the organizational policies that may affect the collection of information. For example, contracts or agency policies may restrict how employees can be involved in the evaluation. Employees may be restricted from data collection or other tasks beyond their immediate job responsibilities. Most organizations have policies concerning collecting data from clients or existing files. Such policies are often designed to protect the interests of clients; however, the evaluator needs to be aware of such policies to learn how they may limit or restrict data collection. Many organizations require that surveys or interview questions be approved prior to use. Often, permission of parents or guardians must be obtained before collecting information from children or those unable to give permission themselves. Many constraints exist around the use of personnel information.

In addition to organizational constraints, evaluators have certain ethical principles they must follow to protect those from whom information is collected. Evaluators need to protect confidentiality or anonymity, if that has been promised, and avoid invasion of privacy. If certain potentially harmful information may be subpoenaed later, the evaluator should consider whether it is necessary to collect it in the first place. Protection of Human Subjects committees, established in the United States by the National Research Act of 1974, should have time to review plans and instruments used in the evaluation.

Some evaluators try to ascertain whether any existing policies will affect their study even before they identify the major evaluation questions their study will address. We prefer not to be constrained by policy considerations quite so early, however. Restrictive or enabling policies will become apparent quickly enough if the evaluator identifies the best possible sources of information needed for the study and then asks the client whether there are any policies restricting use of those sources to gather information.

If reconsideration of the policy is deemed inappropriate, the evaluator will have to obtain information from secondary sources or forgo collecting it altogether. Questions that become unanswerable because of policy constraints needn't be tossed out. Retaining them in the evaluation plan can be instructive.

Client Involvement in Identifying Information Sources.   The client's role in identifying information sources is nearly as important as client involvement in determining what information is needed. The evaluator will often, by dint of experience, be able to identify good sources of information that may not have occurred to the client. Almost as often, the client will be able to identify useful sources of information that may otherwise escape the evaluator's attention. It is simple enough to ask the client, "Do you have any suggestions about where we might best obtain such information?" This sort of collaboration not only yields helpful answers but further enhances the shared ownership of the evaluation by the client and evaluator.

Identifying Appropriate Methods and Instruments for Collecting Information

Once the evaluator has specified where or from whom the needed evaluation information will be obtained, the next step is to specify the particular methods and instruments for collecting the needed information. Returning to our earlier examples, information about the timeliness and cost of critical program events might be obtained through personal interviews with the program administrator, budget officer, and program participants or through perusal of program budget and schedule documents. Information about the impact of the WANDAH program on students' writing ability might be collected by the previously mentioned holistic measure (teachers' judgments of overall writing quality on a given assignment) or analytic measure (percent of *to be* verbs in one writing assignment).

There are countless ways to classify data-collection methods and instruments. Although not exhaustive, we have found the following classification scheme[1] useful in prompting neophyte evaluators' thinking about possible methods of data collection.

   I. Data collected directly from individuals identified as sources of information
     A. Self-reports
       1. Paper-and-pencil methods (e.g., structured questionnaires, unstructured surveys, checklists, inventories, rating scales)
       2. Interviews (structured or unstructured, personal or telephone)
       3. Focus groups
       4. Personal records kept at evaluator's request (e.g., diaries, logs).
     B. Personal products
       1. Tests
         a. Supplied answer (essay, completion, short response, problem solving)
         b. Selected answer (multiple-choice, true-false, matching, ranking)
       2. Performances (simulations, role-playing, debates, pilot competency testing)
       3. Samples of work (portfolios, work products of employees)
  II. Data collected by an independent observer
     A. Narrative accounts
     B. Observation forms (observation schedules, rating scales, checklists)
  III. Data collected by a technological device
     A. Audiotape
     B. Videotape
     C. Time-lapse photographs
     D. Other devices
       1. Physical devices (blood pressure, air quality, blood-alcohol content, traffic frequency or speed)
       2. Graphic recordings of performance skills
       3. Computer collation of participant responses
  IV. Data collected with unobtrusive measures
  V. Data collected from existing information resources or repositories
     A. Review of public documents (federal, state, or local department reports; databases; publications)
     B. Review of organizational documents or files (files of client records, notes or products of employees or program deliverers, manuals, reports, audits, publications, minutes of meetings)

---

[1] This set of categories is drawn from Worthen, Borg, and White (1993).

    C. Review of personal files (correspondence or e-mail files of individuals reviewed by permission of correspondent)

Numerous other ways of categorizing information-collection techniques have been developed; of these, the listing of multiple measures provided by Brinkerhoff, Brethower, Hluchyj, and Nowakowski (1983) and Posavac and Carey (1991) are useful examples.

Reviewing the Adequacy of Information-Collection Techniques.   Many evaluators choose data-collection techniques or instruments more for their familiarity than for their appropriateness. Evaluators may frequently find familiar techniques applicable, but equally often, new approaches must be sought. Stufflebeam (1981) makes a similar observation.

> Only recently have evaluators begun to realize that evaluation needs a respectable methodology that is built from the ground up. That is, the techniques of evaluation must be built to serve the information needs of the clients of evaluation. (p. 5)

In addition to making sure the information collected matches the construct of interest, the evaluator should ensure that sufficient information will be collected on each construct. Some phenomena are sufficiently clear-cut (e.g., height, number of children in a classroom, dollars spent) that only one measure is needed. Others, such as writing ability or parenting skills, require multiple measures because no one measure is sufficient to capture the totality of the phenomenon. In such cases, multiple measures, using different sources and different methods, are necessary to ensure the evaluation question is answered completely.

Once information-collection techniques have been specified for each evaluative question, the evaluator should review them, as a set, to assess their technical soundness, availability, relevance, and utility, asking these questions:

- Will the information to be collected provide a comprehensive picture of what is evaluated?
- Are the information-collection procedures legal and ethical?
- Will the cost of any data-collection procedure be worthwhile, given the amount and kind of information it will provide?
- Can the information be collected without undue disruption to the project?
- Can the procedures be carried out within the time constraints of the evaluation?
- Will the information collected be reliable and valid for the purposes of the evaluation?
- Does the data-collection plan make use of already existing data where appropriate data are available?

Role of the Client in Identifying Methods and Instruments.   Typically, the evaluator will have more expertise regarding the array of possible methods than will the client or members of the advisory group. However, having identified possible methods, it is useful to review these methods with the client or advisory group to receive their feedback concerning the appropriateness of the measures. These stakeholders can often provide a fresh perspective on the measures and insights on how those from whom data are to be collected might react. The wording of questions, the focus of the observation, the feasibility of physical measures can all be elements for useful discussion. Finally, these information-collection strategies will form the foundation of the evaluation. If the client does not find them to be credible, the ultimate usefulness of the evaluation may be in question.

In most instances, collecting the evaluation information is the province of the evaluator, not the client, for reasons discussed in earlier chapters (e.g., conflict of interest, technical competence). It is, after all, the evaluator who must guarantee the ultimate quality of the evaluation information—the core of the evaluation. While the evaluator has the responsibility to ensure that data-collection procedures are designed and implemented to ensure quality information, clients may be involved in the data collection. In recent years, many evaluators have moved to involve stakeholders more at this stage. Fetterman (1994) cites many studies that have used evaluations to empower clients to become change makers in their own organizations or communities. In any case, when others are involved it is the evaluator's responsibility to ensure they have the training to carry out the data collection in a responsible manner. (See Chapter 14 for more on involving clients in data collection.)

Determining Appropriate Conditions for Collecting Information

It is not enough to specify only the methods and instruments for collecting information; as noted above, the evaluator must also ensure that the conditions within which those methods and instruments are employed are appropriate. Perhaps the most common concerns are these: (1) Will sampling be used in collecting the information? (2) How will the information actually be collected? and (3) When will the information be collected? A few words about each of these concerns may be helpful.

Specifying Sampling Procedures to Be Employed.   Some innocents have stated that researchers use sampling because they are concerned with generalizing their findings to large populations, whereas evaluators do not use sampling procedures because they are concerned only with describing and judging what exists in the particular case. Such logic misses the key point: Sampling is as useful and efficient for drawing inferences about more circumscribed populations as for large populations.

For example, if an evaluator were asked to evaluate the effect of HMOs on health costs and patient health in California, it is unlikely that she would propose collecting information on every person enrolled in an HMO in California. The cost would likely be prohibitive and probably unjustified as well. Careful use of scientific sampling procedures permits the evaluator to select and test a much smaller sample while still generalizing with a high degree of confidence about the likely impact of HMOs in California. Similarly, no sane educational evaluator, charged with evaluating the effect on student achievement of a statewide, ninth-grade math curriculum in Texas would propose testing every ninth grader in Texas.

However, when the sample is very small, it is advisable, if possible, to collect data from the entire population. In such circumstances, sampling methods are not as likely to result in a sample representative of the population. For example, in an evaluation of an employment training program with 118 trainees, it would be helpful (depending on budget and time) to administer a paper-and-pencil test to each of the 118 trainees enrolled in the program. If the test were group-administered, this could easily be warranted. However, if data collection is costly, sampling might be used for cost purposes. If data needed to be collected through interviews with supervisors or observations of performance on the job, it would seldom be practicable to collect information on all 118 trainees. Purposive sampling could be used to maximize the likelihood that the sample is representative.

Sampling, then, is a tool to be employed by the evaluator whenever resources or time are limited and wherever sampling would not diminish the confidence that could be placed in the results. We have no quarrel (resources permitting) with the evaluator who compulsively insists on using a particular data-collection technique (e.g., a survey) with every individual involved, unless such preoccupation uses up resources and forces the omission of other methods (such as observations, interviews, document analysis, tests) that might yield equally or even more important information. We would usually prefer to see sampling employed with multiple data-collection techniques rather than see all the resources for an evaluation expended to collect data from the entire population using a single instrument.

Specifying How Information Will Be Collected.   For each type of data collection it is necessary to specify *who* will collect the data as well as the *conditions* under which it will be collected.

- Who will collect the information? For methods such as interviews, observations, and focus groups, how will the characteristics of the evaluator influence the data collection?
- What training should be given to the people collecting the data? What sorts of checks need to occur as data collection proceeds?
- In what setting should data collection take place? Is the setting conducive to the respondents' providing the desired information?
- How can anonymity and confidentiality be protected?

- Does the data collection pose any threat to the respondents? What type of debriefing is needed?
- Is any special equipment or material needed for the collection?

If the evaluator is using a method or measure new to her, it is critical that she examine the literature on methods for using such measures accurately and talk with others who have used the method to receive their suggestions. If the method is quite new to the evaluator, she should not implement it without training or assistance from others. Evaluators need a bigger "bag of tools" than researchers because they are examining a wider variety of phenomena than most researchers. As such, it is imperative for the evaluator to reassess continually the methods she knows and seek training concerning new techniques.

Specifying When the Information Will Be Collected.   It seems almost a truism to say that evaluation information collected too late to bear on the relevant course of events is not useful. Timeliness is essential. In determining when information should be collected, the evaluator must consider three criteria.

1. When will the information be needed?
2. When will the information be available?
3. When can the information conveniently be collected?

Knowing when information will be needed establishes the latest allowable date for collecting it because time must be allowed to analyze, interpret, and report results. Availability is also an issue. It is patently absurd to schedule student "posttesting" for early June if the school year ends in late May, yet we have seen evaluators who have discovered this fact too late. Similarly, mailing surveys in mid-December when many people are too busy with holiday activities is not wise planning. It is also inefficient to return repeatedly to the site to collect data that could have been collected only once, given better planning. If the evaluator specifies the time for each data-collection technique, it is easy to see whether data pertaining to other evaluation questions might be conveniently collected at the same time, using the same technique. It seems obvious, doesn't it? Yet this simple bit of planning is often overlooked.

Determining Appropriate Methods and Techniques for Organizing, Analyzing, and Interpreting Information

Evaluators must plan the format in which information will be collected in addition to designating means for coding, organizing, storing, and retrieving it (Stufflebeam, 1973b). An example might underscore this point. A consultant of our acquaintance was once called by a school district to help analyze "some evaluation data we have collected and would like to analyze in the next week or two." Upon asking to see the data, our friend was led to a room nearly half the size of a normal classroom. There were the data—thousands of students' notebook diaries bound in bundles, by classroom and school, filling the room and stacked floor to ceiling, except for passageways. Our friend's first fear was that the data might topple over on her; her second was that district officials might really believe all that data could be analyzed adequately in such a short time. After some discussion with our friend, school officials realized that analyzing a random sample of the data—stratified by school, grade level, classroom, student, and time of day—was all that was possible. It also occurred to them that they could have greatly simplified the lives of the students and spared their time (not to mention the forests of the Northwest) if that had been all the data they had collected in the first place.

Specifying How Information Is to Be Analyzed.   For each evaluation question, the evaluator should describe the way in which collected information will be analyzed. This requires two steps: (1) identifying the statistical or summarizing *techniques* to be employed for analyzing both quantitative and qualitative information, and (2) designating some *means* for conducting the analysis. For instance, in the example above, central tendency and dispersion descriptive statistics could be used with quantitative data, or content analysis for qualitative data. The "means" might refer to the computer and necessary software to be used to analyze the data.

Interpreting the Results.   Statistical reports do *not* speak for themselves. Different people looking at the same results may attach very different interpretations to them, depending on their values, past experiences, and personal expectations. For this reason it is useful to share the results of data analyses as they become available with the evaluation client and other key audiences to elicit their interpretations of what those results mean. For some evaluation questions, the criteria and standards developed will serve as a guide to the interpretations. However, the evaluation plan should allow for the recording of multiple or conflicting interpretations, and all interpretations should take multiple perspectives into consideration.

In later chapters we discuss at greater length helpful procedures for interpreting data analysis results as well as some common misinterpretations of evaluation findings. Here our concern is only with pointing out the importance of carefully planning interpretation procedures.

Determining Appropriate Ways to Report Evaluation Findings

For each evaluation question selected, the evaluator should specify when answers and interpretations should be prepared and for whom. For some questions, frequent periodic reports may be appropriate; for others, a single report may suffice. Some reports should be formal technical documents; others may take the form of memoranda, informal discussions, oral presentations, or meetings.

A good way to plan the reporting of evaluation findings is to use a matrix that specifies for each evaluation question (1) the audience, (2) the content to be included, (3) the reporting format, (4) the date of the report, and (5) the context in which the report will be presented. An example is shown in Figure 15.1.

Once the evaluator has planned reports for each evaluation question, she should review the reports, as a set, to see whether collectively they provide the needed information in a usable form. In Chapter 19 we discuss evaluation reporting at some length. At the planning stage, however, we cannot improve on a very useful set of questions suggested by Brinkerhoff and colleagues (1983):

1. Are report audiences defined? Are they sufficiently comprehensive?
2. Are report formats, content, and schedules appropriate for audience needs?
3. Will the evaluation report balanced information?
4. Will reports be timely and efficient?
5. Is the report plan responsive to rights for knowledge and information with respect to relevant audiences? (p. 48)

FIGURE 15.1 Sample worksheet for planning the evaluation reporting

Evaluation Question	Audience for the Report	Report Content	Report Format	Reporting Schedule	Context for Presenting Report
1. Have the critical program events occurred on time and within budget?	Program staff	Progress to date; problems needing attention	Memorandum and verbal presentation	Beginning of each month	Presentation at staff meeting, with one-page written summary
2. What impact does WANDAH have on students' writing ability?	School principal language arts faculty, school board	Findings of student performance on holistic and analytic measures	Written report, with oral briefing, plus executive summary	Preliminary report on March 15; final report on May 1	Briefing and discussion of preliminary report with faculty and principal; written final report to them and executive summary to board, with oral briefing as requested by board

Use of Simple Worksheets
to Summarize an Evaluation Plan

It may be useful to summarize briefly our discussion of those items that collectively form the outline of an evaluation plan. For each evaluation question (or objective) used to focus the study, it is important to specify the following:

1. *Information required* to answer the question (or determine whether the objective has been attained)
2. *Design(s)* to be used to collect information
3. *Source(s)* of that information
4. *Method(s) for collecting* the information
5. *Information-collection arrangements,* including
   a. Sampling procedure (if any)
   b. Collection procedure (who collects information; under what conditions)
   c. Schedule for collection
6. *Analysis procedures*
7. *Interpretation procedures* (including standards)
8. *Reporting procedures,* including
   a. Audience(s) for report
   b. Report content
   c. Report format
   d. Schedule for reporting
   e. Context for reporting

An efficient way of completing these steps is to use a matrix with the first column listing the evaluation questions (or objectives), and subsequent column headings corresponding to each important element of the plan—as shown in Figure 15.2. Naturally, nowhere is it written that one must use every column of the matrix for it to prove useful. Nor is there anything magical or immutable about the headings we have provided; they can be modified to suit the evaluator. For example, a more simplified matrix such as that shown in Figure 15.3 (p. 286) has proven useful in many evaluation studies. This simpler version is especially useful with clients, who can more readily assist in completing this "short form," and with funding agencies, who have found such matrixes useful in understanding what is proposed by the evaluator. The evaluator can, of course, subsequently add columns and detail as desired, for her own purposes. A simple device of this type is among the most useful tools an evaluator can employ for summarizing or communicating an evaluation plan to clients and other audiences.

SPECIFYING HOW THE EVALUATION WILL
BE CONDUCTED: THE MANAGEMENT PLAN

The final task in planning the evaluation study is describing how it will be carried out. A **management plan** is essential to help in overseeing the project. Who will do what? How much will it cost? Will it be within budget? Conducting

Evaluation Question	Information Required	Design	Information Source	Method for Collecting Information
1. What types of employment did welfare mothers find after completing their employment training? Did it include health benefits? Was the compensation adequate to bring about self-sufficiency?	Job title, responsibilities, sector of employment (public, private, nonprofit), number of hours per week, salary, health benefits, length of time employed, other components as they arise	Descriptive, cross-sectional, possible case study elements	Graduates of employment training who found employment	Survey, interviews, possible focus group

Sampling	Information-Collection Procedures	Schedule	Analysis Procedures
Survey to all (n = 50), interview with sample of 20; focus group with 10	Surveys distributed when client picks up graduation diploma; interviews arranged then and conducted in their home by trained research assistants; focus group conducted by consultant, 15 randomly recruited with compensation of $25 and babysitting provided	Surveys—October; interviews—November; focus group—early December	Descriptive stats and chi square for surveys. Use results for interview. Summarize major themes of interviews. Use results to plan focus groups. Use taped transcript of focus groups for analysis. Integrate all results to describe trends and solutions.

Reporting Procedures

Interpretation Procedures	Audience(s)	Content	Format	Schedule
Are at least two-thirds of those who are employed earning a sufficient amount to sustain their family? Are they able to afford adequate child care? Are health benefits provided? For those whose employment does not establish or appear to lead to self-sufficiency, what solutions are recommended?	Funding sources (city and state departments), project administrators, program deliverers (especially employment counselors), clients, public at large	Help answer question: What is the program doing well? What changes are needed?	Technical report to funding sources and project administrators with one meeting with each funding source to discuss results; several meetings with project administrators and deliverers to discuss their interpretation of results and possible changes; meeting with clients to report results and receive their input; press release to general public	Meetings to discuss results—January; release report—mid-February with press release

FIGURE 15.2 Sample worksheet for summarizing an evaluation plan

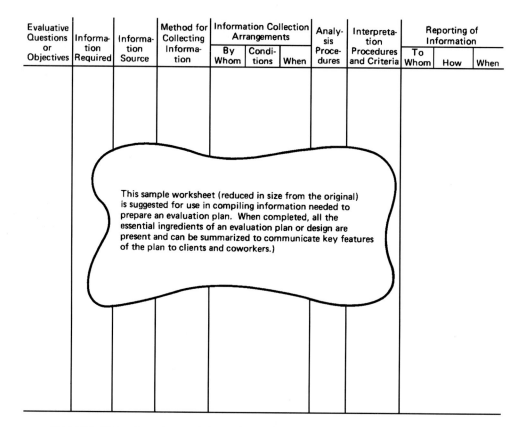

Evaluative Questions or Objectives	Information Required	Information Source	Method for Collecting Information	Information Collection Arrangements			Analysis Procedures	Interpretation Procedures and Criteria	Reporting of Information		
				By Whom	Conditions	When			To Whom	How	When

This sample worksheet (reduced in size from the original) is suggested for use in compiling information needed to prepare an evaluation plan. When completed, all the essential ingredients of an evaluation plan or design are present and can be summarized to communicate key features of the plan to clients and coworkers.)

FIGURE 15.3 Sample worksheet for summarizing an evaluation plan: abbreviated form

a thorough and systematic evaluation study is a complex undertaking. To make the effort successful, the evaluator must effectively manage not only the evaluation activities but also the resources allocated to carry them out.

Evaluation management is multifaceted. An evaluation manager must supervise other staff; serve as liaison to evaluation clients, participants, and other evaluation stakeholders; and identify and cope with political influences. Effective management also demands communication and reporting skills. Needed resources must be identified, allocated, and monitored. Periodically, the manager must review all evaluation activities to ensure that schedules are being respected and that all activities meet the high technical standards expected.

An evaluation, whether a team or single-person effort, cannot afford to be disorganized or haphazard. As the Program Evaluation Standards (Joint Committee, 1994) remind us, professional evaluators are responsible for planning cost-effective evaluations. A management plan is needed to structure and control resources—including time, money, and people. As with the evaluation plan, the management plan must be open to change in response to fluctuating circumstances. But the need for flexibility in no way diminishes the need for a plan.

A good management plan must specify for each evaluation question the following: (1) the tasks to be performed and the timelines for each task, (2) the personnel and other resources required to complete the task, and (3) the cost. Each column builds on the next. Once tasks and timelines are specified, the personnel and resources to perform the tasks can be identified. Complex tasks will require higher-level personnel; time-consuming tasks will require more hours. When tasks are compressed into a short time frame, more personnel will be required. Finally, with the specification of personnel and resources, costs for each question can be determined. Figure 15.4 presents a sample management plan. The sections below will describe how it is developed.

Estimating and Managing Time for Conducting Evaluation Tasks

Among the most common techniques used for estimating time on tasks are **PERT charts** and **Gantt charts**. PERT is an acronym for "Program Evaluation and Review Technique" and was developed by the U.S. Department of Defense as a management tool for complex military projects. It has since been used in many other settings to examine the interrelationships among tasks and the time required to complete both subsets of tasks and entire projects (Cook, 1966; Sylvia, Meier, & Gunn, 1985). PERT charts are most useful in large, complex studies where overlooking details may create unresolvable problems. For many evaluations, PERT may be more cumbersome and time-consuming than it is enlightening. In most evaluation studies, a simplified version of PERT, in which one estimates the time required for each task and links the task with others to be performed either simultaneously or before or after the task at hand, is sufficient. An example of a simplified PERT chart is shown in Figure 15.5 (p. 290).

Gantt charts (Clark, 1952) are simple displays that include proportionate, chronologically scaled time frames for each evaluation task. A Gantt chart lists tasks on the vertical axis and a time scale on the horizontal axis. A horizontal line is drawn for each task to show how long it will take. An evaluator (or anyone) can look at a Gantt chart and tell at a glance when activities will begin and how long each will continue. Gantt charts are easy to prepare, and in addition to their management benefits, they can be effective in communicating evaluation plans. A sample Gantt chart is shown in Figure 15.6 (p. 290).

Charts can help highlight important interim deadlines (or "milestones," as they are often termed by funding agencies) that must be met if the overall evaluation study is to be completed on time. Even if a formal PERT or Gantt chart is not used, the evaluator should develop a list of critical tasks for each piece of data collection and estimate the time required to perform each task. She should then consider which tasks can or should occur simultaneously in order to meet the overall time constraints of the project. Start and end times

FIGURE 15.4 Sample management plan worksheet

Evaluation Question	Tasks	Estimated Task Beginning and Ending Dates	Personnel Involved and Estimated Costs	Other Resources Needed and Costs	Total Task Cost
1. Have the critical events of the program occurred on time and within budget?	1a. List program's critical events, time schedule for each, and budget for each.	1a. First month of program.	1a. Evaluator, 5 days at $300 per day = $1,500	1a. None	1a. $1,500
	b. Monitor progress and expenditures for critical events.	b. Beginning to end of each month of program.	b. Evaluator, 2 days at $300 per day = $600 per month of program	b. None	b. $600 per month
	c. Prepare and present monthly reports.	c. Last week of each month of program	c. Evaluator, 2 days at $300 per day = $600 per month of program	c. .5 day of clerical time = $30 per month of program	c. $630 per month
2. Is there sufficient evidence of need for the program as it is designed? Are there other more critical needs that are not	2a. Search for assessment of needs.	2a. First day of program or before.	2a. Evaluator, 1 day at $300 per day = $300	2a. None	2a. $300

being addressed?

b. If no needs assessment exists, plan and conduct needs assessment.

b. First month of program.

b. Evaluator, 10 days at $300 per day = $3,000

b. Consultants, 1 for 3 days at $350 = $1,050; research assistant, 10 days at $125 = $1,250; reimbursement to focus group participants: 4 groups with 10 members, $25 each = $1,000; rooms and refreshments for focus groups at $50 each = $200; secretarial costs for transcribing tapes, 2 days at $60 per day = $120

b. $6,620

c. Prepare written report for project administrator.

c. Fourth week of program

c. Evaluator, 2 days at $300 per day = $600

c. Clerical time, .5 day at $60 = $30

c. $630

d. Meet with program administrator.

d. End of fourth week of program

d. Evaluator and program administrator, 2 hours at $38 per hour = $76

d. None

d. $76

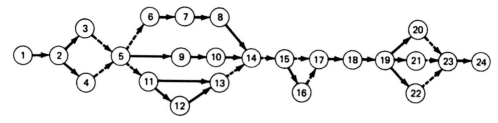

Event Identification

1. Start Project
2. Complete Objectives
3. Complete Data Paradigm
4. Complete Hypotheses
5. Start Item Construction
6. Start Universe Definition
7. Start Sampling
8. Start Sample Selection
9. Start Tryout
10. Start Final Form
11. Start Interviewer Selection
12. Complete Administrative Procedures
13. Complete Schedules
14. Start Field Interview
15. Start Data Coding
16. Complete Follow-up
17. Start Tabulation
18. Start Statistical Tests
19. Complete Tests
20. Complete Interpretation
21. Complete Tables
22. Complete Charts
23. Start Narrative
24. Complete Narrative

FIGURE 15.5   Summary network for survey research project

SOURCE: From *Program Evaluation and Review Technique: Applications in Education* (Monograph No. 17, p. 43) by D. L. Cook, 1966, Washington, DC: U.S. Office of Education Cooperative Research. Reprinted with permission.

for each task should then be specified. This timeline can then be used for effective monitoring of projects.

Bell (1994) observes that well-specified milestones are essential to monitor projects adequately. Monitoring should not be time-specific, such as monthly, but based on identified milestones on the tasks to be completed. Complex or lengthy tasks, or work completed by a new staff person, will require more milestones than other types of task. Milestones for monitoring a large project should not simply be the beginning and end points of information collection

FIGURE 15.6   Example of showing milestones on a Gantt chart

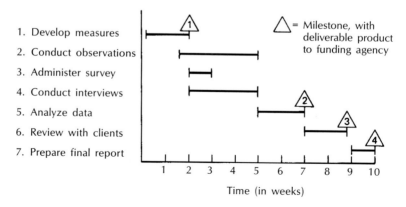

but should include key interim steps during which the evaluation managers can discuss progress and findings with the staff person.

As more time is required for certain tasks, the evaluator should adjust the overall project timeline. This might be accomplished by reducing the time required for future tasks through adding more personnel, reducing the scope of work, or determining whether the time frame for the study can be extended. The timeline is a tool, not a taskmaster. It gives the evaluation manager a means for organizing and monitoring progress. But, as unanticipated events occur, such as unforeseen difficulties in data collection, the need for greater depth or additional collection of information due to ambiguities in results, or a client's requests for additional information, the evaluator can and should adapt the timeline to meet these needs.

It is essential that sufficient time be allowed for all aspects of the evaluation, from focusing the evaluation study through final reporting. Good evaluation management never places key actors under unrealistic constraints that jeopardize the quality of their performance.

Analyzing Personnel Needs and Assignments

The quality of any evaluation depends heavily on the capability and energy of those who carry it out. In some instances, only one individual—the evaluator—may be responsible for everything. Most typically, others—secretarial personnel, evaluation assistants, consultants, or evaluation colleagues—will also be involved.

Perhaps the first concern of any evaluation manager is whether qualified individuals are available to carry out the various evaluation tasks. Answering this question demands specifying clearly the roles and responsibilities of each individual. In proposing how to develop an implementation plan for evaluation, Suarez (1981) outlines "personnel role specifications" as the first step: Specify who would manage the study, complete the evaluation design, select or develop instruments, collect data, analyze data, write summary reports, and so on.

To determine who will do what, consider the skills required for completing each task. Who has these skills? Who has experience and interest in this area? Who has training and experience in content analysis? In recruiting participants for focus groups? In analyzing data with path analysis techniques? In writing clear, interesting reports for the public? For a small project, choices may be among the evaluator and one or two assistants or consultants. For larger projects, the skills of the existing professional staff, and their existing workloads, should be reviewed to determine who is available and most appropriate for each task. Even with a large existing staff, consultants may need to be hired in specialized areas.

Estimating Costs of Evaluation Activities and Developing Evaluation Budgets

There are many nondollar and indirect costs of evaluation, such as opportunity cost or political cost. In the interest of simplicity, we limit our discussion here to direct dollar costs; Alkin and Solman (1983) provide a more complete treatment of other evaluation costs and benefits.

> ***Typical Resources and Their Costs.***   An evaluation budget usually includes the following 10 categories (Sanders, 1983):
>
> 1. *Evaluation staff salary and benefits.* The amount of time that staff members must spend on evaluation tasks and the level of expertise needed to perform particular evaluation tasks both affect costs. Benefits have become an increasingly costly portion of the budget as health insurance costs have risen. Costs in this category are estimated relatively easily by using existing salary and benefit figures. Once the proportion of a person's time devoted to the evaluation is determined, that portion of the staff member's salary and benefits can be charged to the evaluation budget. Most organizations have a set benefit rate that is a percentage of the salary. If a new person must be hired, salaries for the proposed position can be determined by consulting with other organizations with like employees, perusing advertisements and notices in publications advertising for similar positions, and so on.
>
> 2. *Consultants.* As noted, consultants are frequently needed either (a) to provide skills not currently reflected among project staff and not permanently needed in the organization or (b) to provide an independent perspective on the program or the evaluation. Consultants also have the advantage (to the budget, at least!) of not receiving benefits. Costs for consultants can be calculated using their daily or hourly rate.
>
> 3. *Travel and per diem (for staff and consultants).* Costs here depend on the amount of field work and the degree of personal interactions required to design and conduct an evaluation. Some contracts apply restrictions on travel costs (e.g., no billing for travel within the catchment area of the organization). Travel costs can include estimates of automobile mileage for meetings, training, observations, data collection, and other activities outside of the catchment area. Airfare, ground transportation, and per diem costs for lodging and meals should be calculated for long-distance travel.
>
> 4. *Communications (postage, telephone calls, etc.).* This category includes both fixed costs (e.g., continuing monthly billings for telephone hookups, postage meters, networks for e-mail) and variable costs (for special communication efforts, such as long-distance calls, faxes). Fixed costs can be budgeted by multiplying the length of the contract by the proportion of work the organization devotes to that contract. (Be sure not to include anything already counted in indirect or overhead costs.) Variable costs should be estimated based on the nature of the tasks involved. Thus, postage costs will be much higher if mailed surveys are part of the study. These postage costs should be calculated directly based on the number of mailings, postcards, and return envelopes.

5. *Printing and duplication.* Costs here cover preparation of data-collection instruments, reports, and any other documents. Routine costs may be estimated by comparison with other past projects or discussions with others who have overseen similar projects. Often secretarial staff can be helpful in estimating budget costs in this area. Costs of printing and duplicating final reports, binding, or any special graphics should be checked with copying centers.

6. *Data processing.* In the past, most data-processing tasks were performed in conjunction with computer centers that had mainframe computers. Today, most data analysis is performed with personal computers and analyses are conducted by existing staff personnel. Thus, many of the centralized computing costs that used to be separated are not any longer. If specialized software or new hardware are required for the project, the costs of these products could be included in this category. Similarly, charges for computer-based literature searches can also be included in this category.

7. *Printed materials.* This category includes the costs for acquiring data-collection instruments and library materials. If existing instruments are to be purchased or books and materials ordered, these costs can be estimated through consultation with a librarian or the publisher or author of the instruments.

8. *Supplies and equipment.* This category covers the costs of specific supplies as well as equipment that must be purchased or rented. If the primary supplies to be used are routine (pencils, pens, paper, etc.), routine office estimates should be obtained and prorated for the length of the contract. Occasionally, special purchases or rentals are necessary. These could include videotaping equipment, specialized software or hardware required for the project, purchases of existing databases or fees for using existing data, or mechanical devices for collecting data (blood-pressure monitors). Costs of purchasing or renting such special equipment should be obtained from suppliers. In some cases, contracts may require rentals rather than purchases of costly equipment.

9. *Subcontracts.* This category includes expenditures for any contracted services, such as accounting, legal services, test development, and so forth. All subcontracts must be negotiated with the subcontractor before the evaluation budget is completed. Each subcontractor may submit an independent budget. Agencies and institutions often include these costs in their overhead rates. However, small or new agencies may need to bill for these services.

10. *Overhead (facilities, utilities).* The greater the use of external personnel and services, the lower the overhead costs. Typically, however, an institution must bear certain fixed overhead costs (i.e., those of maintaining an adequately equipped physical plant) regardless of what arrangements are made for the evaluation. Most organizations

have fixed percentages of a total budget, or of personnel salaries and benefits, that they charge as operating overhead. Check to see what overhead covers to make sure you are not double-billing. Thus, if overhead includes fixed costs for communication, computers, accounting, or legal services, these should not be billed separately.

Once costs in each budget category have been calculated, a total cost for the evaluation can be determined. This first estimate often exceeds the evaluator's or client's expectations. When this happens, review each line item and ask how the work could be completed at less cost. Some effective cost-saving measures include these:

- Using available volunteers or low-cost workers to reduce staff salaries and benefits (taking care, however, not to compromise quality control)
- Using local specialists for data collection to reduce travel costs
- Asking less-expensive staff to perform nontechnical, routine tasks
- Borrowing (equipment, people, materials, and supplies)
- Seeking "in-kind" contributions from the organization in which the evaluator is employed (often done for good public relations) or the sponsoring agency
- Reducing the scope of the evaluation, perhaps deferring some parts for later
- Using existing instruments, data, or reports
- Using inexpensive data collection when precision can be sacrificed without severe consequences
- Using public media to disseminate results
- Using services when rates are cheapest (e.g., nighttime faxes or mainframe computer runs or evening long-distance telephone calls)
- "Piggybacking" on other studies
- Increasing efficiency through good management

ESTABLISHING EVALUATION
AGREEMENTS AND CONTRACTS

Many potential problems that arise during evaluation can be more readily solved if client and evaluator share a firm understanding. Even among administrators and evaluators with the highest possible professional standards and ethics, conflicts can and do arise—usually in the absence of well-documented agreements concerning important procedures. As Guba and Lincoln (1981) note:

Evaluations are done for clients who commission the evaluation, provide for its legitimization, and pay for it. Since he who pays the piper calls the tune, the evaluator must have a firm understanding with the client about what the evaluation is to accomplish, for whom, and by what methods. The evaluator also needs to be protected against certain arbitrary and possibly harmful or unethical actions by the client, just as the client needs to be protected against an unscrupulous evaluator. The means for achieving these understandings and establishing these safeguards is the evaluation contract. (pp. 270–271)

Anderson and Ball (1978), quoting Samuel Goldwyn's wry comment that "oral agreements aren't worth the paper they're written on," add the following:

> For major evaluation efforts, a formal, legal contract should be negotiated; not to have one would be foolish for both parties. In smaller evaluation efforts, a formal contract might be unnecessary, but even then a letter of agreement . . . makes excellent sense. In either case, the agreement should spell out not only the financial arrangements but also the main elements and requirements of the planned evaluation. (p. 155)

It is obviously too late to draft a formal evaluation agreement after the evaluation is under way; such an agreement should be developed prior to launching the evaluation study. See Worthen, O'Sullivan, and White (in press) for a comprehensive discussion of how to establish evaluation agreements and contracts. The Program Evaluation Standards includes Formal Agreements as a specific standard: "Obligations of the formal parties to an evaluation (what is to be done, how, by whom, when) should be agreed to in writing, so that these parties are obligated to adhere to all conditions of the agreement or formally to renegotiate it" (Joint Committee, 1994, p. 87). They suggest guidelines for the agreement and note common errors in drafting such agreements.

CASE STUDY APPLICATION

November 16 (continued). With the time remaining in our meeting, I proposed we use the evaluation questions we had agreed on to flesh out an evaluation plan. We took a few of the questions and, using a matrix I offered, went through the exercise of identifying information we would need to answer them, listing where and how we would obtain the information, and so on. It was great to see the enthusiasm of several of the group when they began to realize how simple and straightforward it was. Once they had the hang of it, I suggested they fill out as much of the matrix as they could for the remaining questions and then send it to me. I would try to refine it, flesh out the evaluation plan, and send it back to them for their final approval.

Didn't get the plan finished, but I feel good about what we were able to accomplish. More important, this isn't going to be *my* evaluation plan. It is at least *ours,* if not *theirs,* built on questions they posed and answered by information from sources they specified.

> ***December 3.*** Received the draft of the Radnor group's effort to fill out the matrix for the remaining evaluation questions for their study. They got most of it filled out and had some interesting ideas I may not have thought of. Think I'll save a copy and use it in my evaluation seminar to prove my point that much of evaluation planning, sans its mystique, is simple logic and should be shared by the client, with the evaluator providing technical help as and where it's needed.

Author Comments.   Perusal of my handout for spring quarter would reveal the document appearing as Artifact 3, of which only a few samples, and only a few columns of those, are shown here in the interest of space.[2]

Yes, I do think it useful to have the client help identify not only possible sources of information but also possible ways to collect it. Methodological expertise notwithstanding, the evaluator seldom has the client's intimate feel for the program, such as who is really involved, who knows what, and even how certain groups or individuals might respond to proposed data-collection techniques. Obviously the client should not be left to focus the evaluation alone, but there seems little reason for failing to involve the client as a partner at the design stage.

A few comments about the matrix are in order. First, these sample evaluation questions do not pretend to be complete. Several key questions are obviously omitted, for example, questions about students' learning of concepts presented in the curriculum.

Second, this simulated (but realistic) example of how the matrix might look obviously reflects a first draft in need of considerable refinement. Questions should be raised about whether other sources of information should be included or present sources excluded. Strategies for data collection and instruments are still vague in some instances and need to be checked for cost and feasibility.

Third, even when it is refined, there is no claim that this is the only way a good evaluation could be designed. I would argue, however, that it is a systematic way to produce a good evaluation design, where the evaluator can ensure it is technically sound and the client can be sure it is acceptable on other grounds.

Finally, the matrix contains "pieces" of the evaluation that still need to be summarized to yield the real evaluation design. For example, summarizing the columns on methods and arrangements for collecting information will normally identify several questions to be posed to the same source (e.g., teachers), using the same method (such as a mailed questionnaire). Economy of time and effort (and the respondent's patience) will generally result from collecting all the information in a single instrument. Such summarization also quickly reveals inconsistencies and proposals in the draft that are not feasible.

---

[2] Even these samples are only partial, providing the first four columns of a matrix. Subsequent columns that would need to be completed for each evaluation question (but omitted here to conserve space) include *at least* the following: arrangement for collecting information (by whom, when, under what conditions), analysis of information, and reporting of information (to whom, when, how).

ARTIFACT 3   Sample items from the Radnor Township draft evaluation design

Evaluation Questions	Information Required	Source of Information	Strategy/Method of Collecting Information
1. To what extent are the program objectives shared by important groups?	Ratings of importance of objectives	a. Board of education b. Hum. Curr. Review Comm. c. Teachers d. Parents e. Other community members	a–b. Individual interviews c–e. Mailed questionnaire to all teachers, samples of others, using Phi Delta Kappa goal-ranking procedure
2. To what degree does the curriculum address all the stated objectives?	Coverage of stated objectives in lesson plans and other materials	a. Humanities faculty b. External humanities experts	a. Faculty analysis of curriculum, match to objectives b. Review/critique of lesson plans and materials
4. Is the content of the lesson plans faithful to the humanities?	Substantive adequacy of lessons and other materials	External humanities experts	Expert review of lesson plans and materials
5. Are social attitudes in the community such that the curriculum can be successfully implemented here at this time?	Attitudes of community members and influence groups toward the humanities	a. Community members b. Community influence groups (for example, PTA and service club officers)	Mailed questionnaire survey to sample of community's citizens plus all identified "influence leaders"
9. Do the lesson plans and other curriculum materials use sound instructional theory?	Knowledge of instructional theory	Expert in instructional theory	Expert review of lesson plans and materials
13. Do student attitudes demonstrate that the curriculum is producing the desired results?	Attitudes of students toward the values and concepts taught in the curriculum	Students	a. Comparative design, using attitude scales, observation, and unobtrusive measures; and . . . ? b. Simulated situations, role-playing to get at real student attitudes (e.g., attitudes toward cultural differences)

December 6. Completed the evaluation design for the Radnor humanities curriculum today. In the process, I realized we had never explicitly agreed on the criteria or standards the board would use in determining whether or not to continue the program, even though we had discussed them in relationship to the evaluation questions and I had talked individually with some board members about them. So I called Nancy Reese, the board president, and asked her if she might be able to help me with that. We agreed she should go to her colleagues on the board with the list of evaluation questions and ask them, "Do these evaluation questions cover all the important criteria you will use in judging the value of the program? Which criteria are most important?" Then, to help define standards: "What kind of answer

to this question would convince you to continue the program? To discontinue it?" Given answers to those questions, we can make sure we're covering all the important criteria and have some sense for the standards they will apply to each. Their answers will help me decide what emphasis to place on the various kinds of data.

Author Comments.   There are many ways one might go about identifying criteria and setting standards for determining whether an entity like this humanities curriculum should be continued or jettisoned. The example offered here is admittedly somewhat tardy if you believe that the only criteria of importance are those held by the formal decision makers. Yet I find formal decision makers seldom work in a vacuum and are often influenced by what standards other groups use to judge the program. Once I tended to blurt out, within moments of an introductory handshake with a decision maker, "Okay, now what criteria do you intend to use to determine whether or not to continue the program?" I am now more patient. Indeed, I like to share the full range of questions various groups hold to be important with the formal decision makers—in this case, the board—and ask them, in essence, whether the answer to that question would influence them either to continue or to scrap the program. Not only can one generate criteria in this way but there is also the possibility of expanding the horizons of those who must make difficult decisions.

December 13. Nancy Reese called back today after polling the board members on criteria. She reported that she and one other member of the board think all the questions should be used to decide whether to keep the humanities curriculum. But consensus of the board is that the most important criteria relate to three areas: (1) how well students are performing in basic skills (writing and other language skills); (2) whether students are attaining the general and specific goals of the curriculum (critical thinking, appreciation of cultural, ethnic, and social diversity); and (3) whether the patrons of the school wish to see the curriculum continued. On the first criterion, Ms. Reese indicated the board hoped students would be performing at least as well as students from other similar schools while their abilities on the second should be much better. They would like a solid majority of patrons to support the curriculum. With that information, I can complete the evaluation plan and send a copy off to Claire Janson tomorrow.

Author Comments.   Nancy Reese may not have reported formalized standards per se, but she has given the stuff of which standards are made. Further, I now know which questions address the most important criteria. I have nothing against decision makers who tell me they intend to continue a program only if "the mean score of students exceeds the seventy-fourth percentile on the vocabulary section of the ITBS," just as long as they can defend their rationale and chosen instrument. Sometimes such standards are based on criteria relating to program funds controlled by external funding sources or to other such practical considerations. However, I do like to explore the degree to which such criteria are purely arbitrary. If that is the case, it cuts off discussion of important issues. I would much rather have a glimmer of what decision makers really think important (and some future opportunity to help them reflect more specifically on how they intend to apply the criteria) than deal with the artificial precision built into too many of today's so-called criteria.

December 14. Completed the Radnor evaluation plan tonight (Artifact 4). Was disappointed to find I had to cut out some things I feel are important because there simply isn't enough time and/or money to do them. Alas. Still, I think the plan is a good one, given the constraints we're operating under. I did list in a section on "limitations of this evaluation" those things I deemed important but had to sacrifice due to shortage of resources.

ARTIFACT 4   Outline of the humanities program evaluation

I. Introduction
    A. History and description of the humanities curriculum
    B. Purposes of the evaluation
    C. Audiences for the evaluation
    D. Constraints and policies within which the evaluation must operate
II. Evaluation plan
    A. Overview
        1. Possible comparative elements
        2. Planned opposition: use of the adversary evaluation approach
        3. Sequencing and interrelationship of components
        4. Evaluation questions to be addressed by the study
        5. Criteria for judging the program
    B. Work unit 1.0: curriculum analysis
        1. Expert review: humanities specialists
        2. Expert review: instructional design specialist
    C. Work unit 2.0: collection of extant data
        1. Existing records
        2. Unobtrusive measures
    D. Work unit 3.0: mailed questionnaire surveys
        1. Survey populations/samples
        2. Survey instruments
        3. Follow-up techniques
        4. Nonresponse bias checks
    E. Work unit 4.0: student measures
        1. Cognitive measures
            a. Basic skills
            b. Humanities content
        2. Affective measures
            a. Attitude scales
            b. Simulated situation: role-playing
    F. Work unit 5.0: evaluation team on-site visit
        1. Classroom observation
        2. Interviews
            a. Students
            b. Teachers
            c. Parents
            d. Board members

III. Reporting of results
    A. Preliminary report: exit interview of on-site team
    B. Final report and executive summary
    C. Review of draft reports
    D. Debating the pros and cons
IV. Personnel
    A. External evaluation team
    B. Radnor staff (supervised participation)
V. Schedule
    A. Work flow
    B. Deadlines
VI. Budget

Author Comments.   Space prohibits commentary on each of the points in this sketchy outline of the plan, but elaboration may be helpful on a few points that may not be self-evident.

First, for reasons outlined earlier, I would try to get comparative snapshots of the students in the program and other comparable youngsters on variables outlined in work units II-C and II-E. Without more information about the availability of other comparison groups and willingness to allow their use, one could only temporize at this stage, laying out a possible comparative design in II-A and promising, should that not prove feasible, to direct the resources assigned to that effort into more intensive data collection within Radnor on those variables.

Second, within each "work unit" proposed, I would preview *briefly* the type of instrument I would use (listing specific instruments if they are already in existence) and the proposed data analysis.

Third, in work unit 1.0, I would propose sending program goals and lesson plans to the appropriate experts and having them conduct their analyses from afar, unsullied by the rhetoric of the enthusiastic program staff.

Fourth, in work unit 2.0, I would envision collection of information on variables such as instances of in-school problems among different ethnic groups; membership in elective dance, drama, or art classes; participation in extra-curricular arts events; and the like.

Fifth, in work unit 4.0, I would probably depend on a combination of criterion and norm-referenced measures to get at the basic skills. In addition, I would want to sample students' written products, given the emphasis the curriculum places on that area. In the humanities content, local criterion-referenced measures should be constructed, working cooperatively with the humanities faculty to make certain the items reflect important concepts. In addition, I would want to select a good measure of critical thinking to get at those ambitious program goals.

In the affective area, I would look for existing measures of appreciation of the arts and sensitivity to others and talk with stakeholders to see whether they met our needs—there's a lot of research in this area, so there could be something that works. If not, I would again work closely with teachers to design measures that matched the Radnor curriculum. As a supplement, I would structure simulated situations and role-playing opportunities where a smaller sample of students could react directly to stimuli, making choices that reveal relevant attitudes (e.g., stereotypic perceptions of the elderly).

Sixth, I would use an intensive on-site visit of two or three days duration as one of the major sources of data. For all its limitations, there is a great deal to be said for good old-fashioned professional judgment by those who know the territory. So I would be certain to include both humanities experts and evaluation specialists on a team of four or five people. With careful advance scheduling, orientation of the team to the evaluative questions and the interview schedules, splitting the team up to conduct individual interviews, and then coming back to debrief and synthesize findings, a good bit can be accomplished in a reasonably short time (if the team survives the inhumane pace).

Seventh, once the instruments and instructions for their use were completed, I would rely heavily on Radnor district staff to assist with much of the on-site data collection and tabulation, thus greatly amplifying the data that can be collected on a small evaluation budget.

Finally, this evaluation plan proposes what might be called an eclectic, "multiple-source, multiple-method" evaluation, with all the advantages inherent in such an approach.

> *December 15.* Now, for the management plan! As I worked out how I was going to accomplish all this, I could see that some questions could be asked in one operation. For example, questions 2 and 4 [in Artifact 3] involved external experts in the humanities and I could have them responding to both evaluation questions for the same consulting fee. Such efficiency!
>
> I considered combining evaluation questions 1 and 5, too, but then thought better of it because they really address two very different issues, and I thought it might confuse the community members to cover both at once. I also wanted to include community influence groups in getting answers to question 5, while not going to the same sources as for question 1. That reasoning led me to plan to conduct separate surveys for questions 1 and 5.
>
> As I worked out my management plan, it became obvious that I should line up a part-time research assistant right away. Otherwise the good students would be unavailable when I need them. I also needed to reserve some secretarial time at points when I would need it. My department head said it would be OK to use our department secretary, as long as we ran the project through the university and paid the reduced "overhead" costs the university would require. The evaluation budget will reimburse my institution for this shared time.

Author Comments. Again, in the interest of space and simplicity, the document appearing as Artifact 5 is limited to a management plan for the first question listed in Artifact 3.

> *December 15 (continued).* The Gantt chart for the main evaluation questions listed in the plan revealed the following pattern of project activities. [See Artifact 6.] This chart should be a useful tool to communicate the evaluation plan to the folks

ARTIFACT 5 Summary of the management plan

Evaluation Question	Tasks	Estimated Task Beginning and Ending Dates	Personnel Involved and Estimated Costs	Other Resources Needed and Costs	Total Task Cost
1. To what extent are the program objectives shared by important groups?	1a. Develop and pilot-test questionnaire and cover letter to be used for interviews and mail surveys.	1a. January 1–January 15	1a. Evaluator, 2 days at $300 per day = $600; research assistant, 1 day at $125 = $125.	1a. .5 day of clerical time at $60 per day = $30.	1a. $755
	1b. Develop sampling plan.	1b. January 1–January 15	1b. Evaluator, .25 day at $300 per day = $75; research assistant, .75 day at $125 per day = $94	1b. None	1b. $169
	1c. Develop follow-up and nonresponse bias check procedures.	1c. January 1–January 15	1c. Evaluator, 1 day at $300 per day = $300.	1c. None	1c. $300
	1d. Conduct interviews and mail survey with follow-up.	1d. January 20–February 15	1d. Evaluator, 5 days at $300 per day = $1,500; research assistant, 5 days at $125 per day = $625.	1d. Travel expense = $30; postage = $75; duplication = $100; paper = $25; clerical time, 2 days = $120.	1d. $2,475
	1e. Analyze data.	1e. February 20–March 1	1e. Research assistant, 5 days at $125 per day = $625.	1e. None	1e. $625
	1f. Prepare reports.	1f. March 1–March 15	1f. Evaluator, 5 days at $300 per day = $1,500.	1f. 1 day of clerical time = $60; duplication = $100.	1f. $1,660

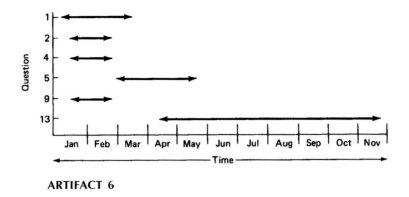

ARTIFACT 6

at Radnor. I didn't break it down by task because the chart got to be too cluttered. I can later develop a Gantt chart for each question to help guide me and the research assistant.

December 15 (continued). It appears that a part-time research assistant and a part-time secretary will serve the needs of this project nicely. Now that my research assistants and I do most of our own word processing on the computer, I find our need for secretarial help is greatly reduced. Nevertheless, the secretary is essential for keeping track of paper work on budgetary issues in the university bureaucracy and for coordinating mailings of surveys and the like. I may want to delegate some of my load to boost up the time of the research assistant on the project while lightening my own. Depends on the reaction to the budget I proposed and the quality of my research assistant [Artifact 7].

ARTIFACT 7

Evaluation staff salaries	$42,208
(evaluator, research assistant, secretary)	
Consultants	8,000
(humanities experts—4,	
instructional theory experts—2,	
case study researchers—2)	
Travel	943
Postage	240
Telephone	70
Duplication	432
Supplies (tapes)	20
Total direct costs	$51,913
Indirect costs (28% of Direct Costs)	$14,536
Budget total	$66,449

December 15 (continued). When I added up this budget, I was utterly amazed—I had no idea it would add up so fast. All the costs are well grounded on detailed planning for this project, but Claire Janson may have a stroke. Yet I realized that I had not even budgeted for some little things like normal office supplies, and my travel budget was low and would only allow me to use fairly local external consultants.

December 21. Claire Janson called today and indicated the board and committee had given the go-ahead on the plan I submitted, with the only suggested changes coming in the deadline and budget. The board has decided they cannot delay a decision about the humanities curriculum as long as they had originally planned. Instead, they want to make a decision by May 15 so they will have time, should they decide to discontinue the program, to plan for its phaseout and provision of alternative curricular offerings for the students. Since the timeline is tighter, they've agreed to let the budget go up to $65,000.

The reduced time frame disappoints me, for it will be a real hurry-up job to develop the instruments, supervise the data collection, coordinate the on-site visit, and orchestrate the expert reviews of the materials by that deadline. Fortunately, most of the design can still be implemented and completed within the deadline, although it will be tight. The greatest problem this new deadline causes is the loss of any chance to look at changes in students over time—something I had intended with the cognitive, affective, and unobtrusive measures of student behavior. So I have taken out the pretest-posttest stuff and will depend much more on the site visit and comparison with other schools on the basic skills. That weakens the evaluation, but one hopes the combination of perspectives left in the study will still be strong enough to yield solid findings. One good thing came from this. They agreed to fold the consultant review into the site visit, using a team that includes both humanities experts and us evaluators, so that should help.

Anyway, I cut out those activities that couldn't be completed by May, revised the Gantt chart and budget accordingly, ready to send it back to Radnor as an appendix to the evaluation agreement I'll draft tomorrow. It does shave the budget a bit, which is good, but not too much, what with increasing the travel budget some.

Author Comments.   The best-laid plans of mice and evaluators often go awry. (That is why evaluators need to be not only intellectually flexible but also emotionally resilient.) It is not uncommon for deadlines to be abruptly shifted for reasons far less reasonable than that which I invented as the rationale of the Radnor board. Let me strike another blow for eclectic, multiple-method evaluation designs; they are considerably more robust to changes than are their more single-minded counterparts. If one depends on a single strategy for collecting information and it so happens that changing circumstances disrupt that strategy, there is much less likelihood that the evaluation will succeed.

December 22. Spent a while this morning trying to draft a written evaluation agreement to send to Claire. Frankly, I couldn't get my heart into it. The sample contract I was trying to copy was so stuffy that I got to where I wanted to choke every time I hit another "whereas," "wherefore," or "party of the second part."

Maybe I'm a bit cowardly, but I can't get my nerve up to send a stiff, legalistic contract to Radnor and ask those people to sign it. I feel like they'd suspect they'd hired a lawyer, not an evaluator. The last thing I want to do is go into this evaluation with them feeling like I don't trust them. I'm already an outsider, and an evaluator, so that's two strikes against me. I'm not about to waste my third strike by creating the impression with them that there is no basis for good, old-fashioned trust. Maybe I'm suffering from an overdose of Christmas spirit, but I think I'll let a brief letter suffice [Artifact 8].

ARTIFACT 8

December 22

Ms. Claire Janson, Principal
Radnor Middle School
13 Ideal Circle
Radnor, PA 19087

Dear Ms. Janson:

I was pleased to learn from you earlier today that you and your colleagues have generally accepted my evaluation plan, subject to the modifications in activities, schedule, and costs on which we have agreed. I have made the necessary alterations and a revised copy is enclosed.

If you would be comfortable with a fairly informal agreement, I see no need for much formality. Will it suffice to say that I will do the evaluation for the $65,000 outlined in the budget attached to my revised plan? Also, let's agree that I'll follow the plan attached, and we can incorporate it by reference into this letter of agreement.

Anything else we need to agree to or modify can be worked out comfortably as necessary, I am sure.

If this is agreeable, please countersign this letter below, retain one copy for your records, and return one to me.

I look forward to working with you.

Sincerely yours,

Author Comments.   The evaluation plan provides a good basis for finalizing the agreement between evaluator and client, but there should be some form of written agreement or letter of understanding that incorporates the plan, agrees on reporting deadlines, budget, and the like. I would urge development of such an agreement in virtually any significant evaluation enterprise. Some may see seeds of distrust in such urging. I agree, but the distrust is not of the motives or character of the principal parties; it is merely distrust of their total recall of an understanding made months earlier.

In larger evaluation studies, a more detailed and formal contractual agreement will be necessary.

The above entry represents two "cop-outs." The first is by our mythical evaluator who would rather be comfy than safe, friendly than correct. I used to feel just like him, *until* I'd been "burned" a few times. Now I get tempted to write down and obtain my teenager's signature on agreements to replace gasoline in the family car. Well, almost tempted. We'll have to wait and see how our evaluator fares and whether his casual approach to evaluation contracting comes back to haunt him at a later date.

Meanwhile, the second-cop out is letting my evaluator cop out, not just to make an instructional point but also to keep the number of pages for this section within bounds. My rationalization is that the reader who really wants to peruse sample evaluation contracts can find several—even one laced liberally with "whereas" and "wherefore"—elsewhere (Worthen, et al., in press).

APPLICATION EXERCISES

1. Using the evaluation questions you developed at the conclusion of Chapter 14, develop an evaluation and management plan to address those questions. What further information do you need to do that? (Subsequent chapters will tell you more about methods.) What stakeholders should you involve in planning the evaluation design? What tasks are involved in each step? Who should do them? When?

2. Select a recent article describing an evaluation from *Evaluation Practice, New Directions for Program Evaluation,* or *Evaluation Review.* Reconstruct an evaluation plan from that article. What were the evaluation questions the study answered? What information was collected? What designs, sources, and methods were used? Were multiple methods used? How were data analyzed and interpreted? How were stakeholders or clients involved in the planning of the evaluation?

3. Interview someone who has conducted an evaluation study. Ask her how she developed her design. What issues were most troublesome at the planning stage? How did she involve stakeholders on the issues? On which issues did stakeholders play a major role? On which did the evaluator hold more decision-making power? Why? How would you have developed the study differently? What aspects of her plan would you now incorporate into your own matrix?

4. During your interview for exercise 3, ask how the evaluator managed the study. What did professional evaluators do? Research assistants? Clerical staff? How did she monitor the timeline? Finally, see if she will give you a copy of the budget and ask her how she determined some of the costs. Did costs change as the project developed? Bring in the budget to class and compare it with budgets obtained by other students.

RELEVANT EVALUATION STANDARDS

The evaluation standards we see as relevant to this chapter's content are the following. These standards are described in Chapter 20 on page 442.

U1—Stakeholder Identification	U4—Values Identification
U2—Evaluator Credibility	U6—Report Timeliness and Dissemination
U3—Information Scope and Selection	F1—Practical Procedures

F2 —Political Viability
F3 —Cost Effectiveness
P1 —Service Orientation
P2 —Formal Agreements
P3 —Rights of Human Subjects
P4 —Human Interactions
P5 —Complete and Fair Assessment
P6 —Disclosure of Findings
P7 —Conflict of Interest
P8 —Fiscal Responsibility
A1 —Program Documentation

A2 —Context Analysis
A3 —Described Purposes and
   Procedures
A4 —Defensible Information Sources
A5 —Valid Information
A6 —Reliable Information
A7 —Systematic Information
A8 —Analysis of Quantitative
   Information
A9 —Analysis of Qualitative Information
A11—Impartial Reporting

SUGGESTED READINGS

Brinkerhoff, R. O., Brethower, D. M., Hluchyj, T., & Nowakowski, J. R. (1983). *Program evaluation: A practitioner's guide for trainers and educators.* Boston: Kluwer-Nijhoff.

Clark, N. (1952). *The Gantt chart.* London: Pitman & Sons.

Cook, D. L. (1966). *Program evaluation and review technique: Applications in education* (Monograph No. 17). Washington, DC: U.S. Office of Education Cooperative Research.

Posavac, E. J., & Carey, R. (1991). *Program evaluation: Methods and case studies.* Englewood Cliffs, NJ: Prentice-Hall.

Sylvia, R. D., Meier, K. J., & Gunn, E. M. (1985). *Program planning and evaluation for the public manager.* Monterey, CA: Brooks/Cole.

Wholey, J. S., Hatry, H. P., & Newcomer, K. E. (Eds.). (1994). *Handbook of practical program evaluation.* San Francisco: Jossey-Bass.

Worthen, B. R., O'Sullivan, R., & White, K. R. (in press). *Tools and techniques for program evaluation.* Boston: Kluwer-Nijhoff.

Practical Guidelines for Conducting and Using Evaluations

In Part Three we provided guidelines for planning evaluations. In Part Four we focus on guidelines for conducting and using evaluations, beginning in Chapter 16 with suggestions for dealing with political, ethical, and interpersonal aspects of evaluation. In Chapter 17 we examine several methods and techniques for collecting, analyzing, and interpreting quantitative information, and in Chapter 18 we provide an overview of selected methods and techniques for analyzing qualitative information. Chapter 19 deals broadly with various aspects of reporting and using evaluation results, and Chapter 20 provides standards and procedures for evaluating evaluation plans, activities, and reports.

None of the chapters in this section purport to treat completely their respective topics. A textbook could be devoted to each chapter (and, indeed, many texts do exist on several of those topics). Each chapter is intended only to introduce the topic and provide practical suggestions for how to use the material in an actual evaluation. References to more extensive discussions of each topic are provided for those who wish more detailed information.

chapter 16

Dealing with Political, Ethical, and Interpersonal Aspects of Evaluation

ORIENTING QUESTIONS

1. What types of bias can result from the evaluator's *interpersonal, financial,* or *organizational* relationships? From his beliefs? How might such biases be minimized or eliminated?
2. What ethical standards and guidelines should be followed in conducting evaluation studies? What is the difference between ethical guidelines and standards of practice? Why is each important?
3. To what extent is evaluation a political activity?
4. What types of political pressures cause the most serious problems in evaluation studies? How can the evaluator cope with such pressures?

By now, we hope we have made the point that evaluation is not only—or even primarily—a methodological and technical activity. Important as methodological and technical expertise are to good evaluation, that importance is often overshadowed by the interpersonal, ethical, and political influences that shape the evaluator's work. Many a good evaluation, unimpeachable in all technical details, has failed because of interpersonal insensitivity, ethical compromises, or political naïveté. It is pointless to promise to collect sensitive data (principals' ratings of teachers, for instance, or AIDS patients' reported incidence of drug use) without first obtaining permission from the office or individual who controls those data. Agreements must be reached early in any evaluation about such issues as access to data and safeguards against misuse. Program staff must be guaranteed opportunities to correct factual errors without compromising the evaluation itself. These issues exist in almost every evaluation, and the more explicitly they are dealt with, the more likely the evaluation is to succeed.

Evaluators can no longer afford to content themselves with polishing and plying their tools for collecting, analyzing, and reporting data. They must consider how evaluation reports will be received by important stakeholders; whether the results of the evaluation will be suppressed, misused, or ignored; how to deal with pressures for immediate data or oversimplified questions; and how to prevent "evaluation anxiety" from disrupting clients or unduly influencing evaluation results. Ignoring such concerns is self-defeating, for human, ethical, and political factors pervade every aspect of an evaluation study. It is folly to ignore them, labeling them as mere nuisances that detract the evaluator from more important tasks. Political, ethical, and human factors are present in virtually every program evaluation, and moving ahead without dealing with them is both incompetent and unethical.

In this chapter we deal with four important, interrelated topics: (1) communication between evaluator and stakeholders; (2) biases inherent in certain client-evaluator interrelationships; (3) ethical issues and considerations in evaluation; and (4) political pressures and problems in evaluation.

ESTABLISHING AND MAINTAINING GOOD COMMUNICATIONS AMONG EVALUATORS AND STAKEHOLDERS

The evaluation literature contains numerous pronouncements that good communications are an essential part of both evaluation and the politics that inevitably surround evaluation studies.[1] Yet we continue to find many criticisms of evaluators' communication practices and many examples of poor communication, for example, the tedious and voluminous technical report offered as the sole end product of an evaluation study. Perhaps the message has not sunk in. Perhaps evaluators get too caught up in technical matters and deadlines to attend to communication. Whatever the reason, poor communication can be lethal to an evaluation.

Sometimes the client needs to be reminded that honest evaluation entails risk. Approval and cooperation need to be obtained from those in power. Reporting procedures must be clear to everyone at the outset, and clients and evaluators should agree on ways to maintain open communications, assure fairness and impartiality in the evaluation, and resolve any conflicts that might arise during the study.

We offer the following practical recommendations for interpersonal communications in evaluation:[2]

---

[1] We shall say more about communication in discussing evaluation reports in Chapter 19.

[2] We are grateful to Vincent Greaney for participating in discussions that led us to formulate these recommendations.

1. *Prepare clients (those who sponsor the evaluation) and other stakeholders for evaluation.* Develop an "evaluation spirit" by informing all participants about the purpose and benefits of the evaluation. Resistance to evaluation comes naturally to most people, and not knowing what to expect can only increase such resistance. Evaluators can minimize defensive attitudes by not forcing stakeholders to participate, especially where their involvement could be optional, while at the same time encouraging participation and making sure no one is excluded. And though the quality of the evaluation cannot be sacrificed for the sake of goodwill, there is always room for negotiation and compromise.

2. *Foster stakeholder participation.* Increase the likelihood of involvement by
   - Providing a clear opportunity for involvement and allowing time for it,
   - Developing awareness of the evaluation (presenting the evaluation's purpose and plan to stakeholders, clarifying what will be looked at or asked about, and sharing written evaluation documents),
   - Clarifying the format and timing for evaluation reports,
   - Capitalizing on various stakeholders' familiarity with the object of the evaluation (recognizing that no one person has the full range of experience with all of the program's functions), and
   - Encouraging constructive criticism (inviting stakeholders to challenge assumptions or weaknesses, encouraging divergent perspectives, encouraging a spirit of fairness and openness).

3. *Plan adequate time for carrying out all of the evaluation.* Consider forming a stakeholder committee to schedule all planned evaluation work and help decide if the evaluation's scope must be reduced to allow time for all planned activities.

4. *Invite and nurture outside participation.* In evaluating a school program, for example, remember that parents, school board members, students, taxpayers, and resident experts are all potential stakeholders. Their participation not only strengthens the evaluation but also signals to school staff that this is an important project. When evaluating programs in health and human services or in corporate settings, the external stakeholders may be different (e.g., citizen groups, families of those receiving treatment, county commissioners, service providers, corporate board members, consumer advocacy groups), but the importance of their involvement is no less.

5. *Foster a spirit of negotiation and compromise rather than unilateral action.* The evaluator should also recognize and respect the power structure within the program setting. Not listening to important stakeholders generally means damaging—or even losing—the trust, respect, and rapport you have worked hard to gain.

6. *Link long-term goals to immediate actions.* People like to see achievements, so set intermediate goals as stepping-stones to long-term goals.

But counsel against discarding long-term goals just because they are not immediately achievable.

7. *Assign responsibilities.* Involving many participants fosters commitment to change and development of new plans.

8. *Put a premium on memos, meetings, and informal "chats."* People need and like to feel informed. The confidence that comes with knowing what's going on helps build an "evaluation spirit" and common understanding about the evaluation.

9. *Recognize and protect the rights of individuals.* The Joint Committee on Standards for Educational Evaluation (1994) proposes the following standard to govern human interactions: "Evaluators should respect human dignity and worth in their interactions with other persons associated with an evaluation, so that participants are not threatened or harmed" (p. 99).

Following these recommendations can provide benefits in the accuracy of the evaluative information that a study yields. For example, Brandon, Lindberg, and Wang (1993) found that involving program beneficiaries in specifying which program attributes an evaluation should address enhances the validity of the evaluation findings. Other benefits of stakeholder involvement will become apparent as we return to that topic in later chapters.

UNDERSTANDING POTENTIAL BIAS RESULTING FROM THE EVALUATOR'S PERSONAL VALUES AND INTERPERSONAL, FINANCIAL, AND ORGANIZATIONAL RELATIONSHIPS WITH OTHERS

The possibility of human beings' rendering completely unbiased judgments seems very slight. There is no reason to believe that evaluators are much less susceptible to bias than are their counterparts in other walks of life. In fact, it is ironic that some evaluators actually could be *more* susceptible to bias, simply because they believe that they are completely unbiased. When biases are left undetected, to function at a subconscious level, they can have a powerful influence on evaluators' judgments, inferences, and decisions.

Perhaps the myth that evaluators are less biased than others is partly attributable to the popular view that evaluation is an "objective" enterprise, involving valid and reliable data and allowing no subjectivity. That optimistic view has been recognized as rather naive, however. Choices are by nature subjective. And evaluators increasingly realize that bias—inadvertent or conscious—can intrude subtly into nearly every choice they make, from selecting an evaluation approach to designing a report. Indeed, the portrait of the completely dispassionate and unbiased evaluator must be hung alongside that of the unicorn and other quaint folklore characters.

A full discussion of sources of bias in program evaluation studies transcends the scope of this book. We have discussed some sources of bias, in passing, while examining topics in earlier chapters. Perloff, Padgett, and Brock (1980) provide a provocative analysis of how various social and cognitive biases can influence evaluation. Here we will treat briefly only a few potential sources of bias. We will consider how the evaluator's values and beliefs can be problematic—in two different ways. We will also examine how the evaluator's relationship to and dependence upon others can seriously bias his judgments. Every evaluation is a reflection of the evaluator's personal beliefs, as well as a complex of interpersonal, financial, and organizational interrelationships between the evaluator and numerous other actors in the evaluation context. We shall discuss briefly how each of these factors can bias the evaluator's judgments.

The Evaluator's Beliefs and Bias

It is probably no revelation to even the newest student that an evaluator's value system and beliefs can readily bias an evaluation he conducts *if* he cannot keep those biases from influencing the evaluation. And he cannot. At least not completely. While several evaluation approaches attempt to control bias,[3] none are completely successful. The values and beliefs of the evaluator enter in at every step, in the decisions about what information should be collected, how to collect it, what analyses are best, and how it should be presented. Subjectivity, a parent of bias, is possible if not inevitable in every such choice. This does not deny that a great majority of experienced evaluators may have found ways to enhance their neutrality and reduce the degree to which their personal values intrude into the evaluation, thus reducing their personal bias. But reducing is not eliminating. Some subjectivity and vestigial bias will always remain.

For example, an evaluator's philosophy or personal feelings about the nature or theory of a program can also bias his evaluation of it. Imagine an educational expert is philosophically opposed to mentor programs because he believes they "let parents off the hook" rather than help parents to take responsibility. He would have real trouble keeping that bias from slanting an evaluation of a "Big Brother" program he might undertake.

All evaluators hold similar philosophical views about programs, and we need to consider how these affect our evaluation approach. For example, we might be very positive about prevention, or we may prefer a treatment orientation. Some evaluators may prefer a client-centered treatment approach, while others favor a larger public orientation. Some may have conservative views. Others may believe in liberal or even libertine philosophy. All of these belief systems have a potential to bias the evaluation if the evaluator is not alert.

A more serious problem occurs when the evaluator has become ethnocentric (believing his own group is superior to others, especially in their values and

---

[3] Or, in the case of adversary-oriented evaluations, to *balance* it.

beliefs). An ethnocentric evaluator has become so blinded by his own values and beliefs that he simply cannot see or comprehend the divergent values of stakeholders and recognize how that has shaped their approach to the program being evaluated. Thus, he may be incapable of developing rapport with stakeholders not from his "group" and, in the extreme, cannot even interact meaningfully with them. Such severe ethnocentrism can seriously bias the outcomes of an evaluation, especially where naturalistic field work is used.

In another concern borrowed from anthropological literature, Lincoln and Guba (1981) identified "going native" as a serious source of evaluator bias. This "evaluators-in-grass-skirts" portrayal is nearly a mirror image of ethnocentrism. "Going native" occurs when the evaluator has consciously or subconsciously adopted the beliefs and values of the group he is studying, thus resulting in his downplaying evaluation findings that would prove detrimental to the group and emphasizing positive findings. These authors point out that the evaluator may intend this to benefit his "adopted" group, but his "going native" and losing perspective may actually do a disservice to the group, as well as to the cause of evaluation.

Lincoln and Guba (1981) suggest that bias caused by either ethnocentrism or "going native" can be controlled, or at least lessened to a considerable degree, by three strategies.

1. Careful keeping of *reflexive logs* of the evaluator's evolving perceptions, day-to-day procedures, methodological decisions, day-to-day personal introspections, developing insights, and hypotheses to help the evaluator "reflect him to himself," to better see how the evaluation design is emerging and how the evaluator is emerging as an inquirer.
2. *Peer debriefing,* to help keep the evaluator and his data collection and interpretation on track, by providing an external check (e.g., "Wasn't that a grass skirt I saw you wearing yesterday, John?").
3. An *audit trail* (modeled loosely on fiscal audits) designed to have an external party review the inquiry processes to determine whether the evaluation procedures used were dependable (fair and adequate, following good procedure) and confirmable (having results properly based on accurate data handling and interpretation).

Whatever methods are used, it is important to be vigilant to see that the evaluator's personal values and beliefs are not allowed to bias the evaluation such that the outcomes will be significantly affected.

Interpersonal Relationships and Bias

It is apparent to even the casual observer that individuals' feelings toward one another can color their judgments, not only about each other but about practically anything with which the other person is perceived to be associated. Hence, we have legal restrictions on testimony about one's spouse, and anti-nepotism policies that prohibit individuals from being placed in positions where they would need to make decisions about the salary, promotion, or job security of a family member.

Obviously an evaluator must decline an invitation to evaluate a displaced homemakers program directed by his sister-in-law. But a less conspicuous source of bias lies in interpersonal relationships that may influence the evaluator in more subtle but equally potent ways. Consider the school district evaluator who is assigned to evaluate a program directed by his weekly tennis doubles partner (a fact unknown to the superintendent who made the assignment). Or the external evaluator who finds himself unable to say anything positive about a health education program directed by an individual whose political and religious views are dramatically opposed to his own. Or the staff member assigned to evaluate nutrition counseling services provided by colleagues who share office space, coffee breaks, and membership on the office's bowling team. But relational entanglements need not be so blatant to be problematical. As Anderson and Ball (1978) noted years ago,

> These relationships . . . influence the morale of the evaluation staff and the program staff. That is, they affect not only such principled and abstract topics as bias and ethics, but also such bread-and-butter issues as the evaluator's mood on Friday afternoon after a week of either repeated friction or relative harmony with program personnel. (p. 127)

They might have gone on to say that the evaluator's mood will in turn affect such principled concerns as bias and ethics, for the impact of affect on behavior is too well-known to require comment here. This does not argue for a cold, aloof evaluator, impervious to human attachments, but for awareness that myriad aspects of interpersonal relationships can color and alter the thinking and judgment of an evaluator, and that these factors must therefore be thoughtfully controlled. Failure to do so will result in the evaluator's being co-opted in ways that are likely to bias seriously the outcomes of the study.

Those who doubt that social relationships can bias an evaluator's judgment should spend a while as an internal staff evaluator charged to evaluate the program in which he is employed. Can he really remain unbiased when his evaluative findings and suggestions are repeatedly accepted? Or repeatedly rejected? When his suggestions are accepted and are woven into the interim reports so tightly that he becomes their silent coauthor (and it becomes *his* program), can his subsequent evaluations of that program have much credibility? Can his evaluative judgments be considered valid and unbiased? Perhaps, for some recent methods and concepts embodied in well-conceived learning organizations and TQM (Total Quality Management) systems illustrate how internal staff—evaluators included—can be encouraged and helped to suspend judgment or step back from an issue and test it, to improve it. Yet these techniques do not alter human nature, and it will continue to be important in all settings to examine the evaluator's interpersonal relationships with others to alter or buffer those relationships as need be to assure that they do not threaten to bias the evaluation's outcomes significantly.

Financial Relationships and Bias

Sir Robert Walpole said that "all men have their price," the implication being that anyone can be bought. And although there are enough examples of incorruptibility and integrity around to prove Walpole's assumptions exaggerated, there are still enough corrupt individuals to give some credence to his cynical view of human nature.

Evaluators hold no claim to moral eminence. There is little reason to believe they are either more or less vulnerable than anyone else to the pressures and influences of financial advantages. We doubt there are many instances of evaluators being bribed to sway an evaluation one way or another, but financial pressures are not always so obvious and direct. For example, consider the unenviable plight of the evaluator who is employed by the very agency whose program he is evaluating. To illustrate how thorny this situation can be, let us describe an actual case.

An evaluator of our acquaintance—we'll call him John—was employed by a U.S. government–supported research center whose mission was to develop and test exemplary programs and practices for schools. Assigned to direct the center's evaluation unit, John in due time completed an evaluation of a center program designed to improve secondary school students' mathematics performance and attitudes toward math: the Accelerated Mathematics Program (AMP). AMP was expensive—Congress had invested over $1 million in its development—and while John found that students liked the program, there wasn't a shred of evidence to suggest that it had *any* impact on students' performance. Troubled by the implications of reporting such information to the funding agency through which Congress had initiated the program, John finally worded his draft report to convey that the *evaluation* was to blame for AMP's failure to produce evidence of success. The summary of his report read as follows (italics ours).[4]

> *Summary.* The results of this study indicate that the Accelerated Mathematics Program (AMP) was somewhat effective in developing positive attitudes toward mathematics, in the sense that students tended to like the AMP materials. The study supplied no evidence, however, from which either long- or short-term student performance changes in mathematics ability can be inferred. *The results do not necessarily indicate that AMP was not effective in promoting change in math performance, but that a variety of shortcomings and limitations of*

---

[4] The names, organizations, and titles in this summary and the following letter have been changed to provide anonymity and "protect the innocent," so to speak. But the essential content has not been altered and is reproduced here verbatim.

the evaluation design did not allow for the identification and measurement of these changes.

And how did the funding agency respond to this obvious effort to soften the bad news? Their reaction to the draft report came in a letter, which is reprinted here.

Dear John:

Thank you for the three draft copies of the AMP Impact study. I look forward to the final report.

I hope that our future efforts will be structured so that statements such as those in the "summary" will not have to be made. Instead, I hope that we will be able to say something *positive* in the final report about changes in important performances. I have heard so many good things about AMP that I am disheartened by the lack of evidence that it has short-term performance effectiveness and that I cannot therefore argue for its potential for long-term effectiveness.

The issue here is straightforward. The best argument for funding centers such as yours that I can make internally here in the Department and externally with the Congress is that our products lead to measurable changes for good in American schools. Regardless of the positive "feelings" I get about AMP, it appears we cannot justify all the effort in terms of performance criteria, as per your draft report. That is a drawback. But one which I think we can overcome in future efforts, hopefully in your final report.

Sincerely,

Lawrence

Lawrence T. Donaldson
Chief Administrator

The message is blatantly clear. John better find something positive to prove AMP and its cohort programs are worth the investment, or funding could be withdrawn, the program would fold, and John himself would be looking for other employment. It would take a robust soul indeed not to feel some ethical strain in such a situation, especially when his salary comes directly from the threatened program! Fortunately, though John equivocated at first, this story eventually had a happy ending. The final report told the true story, and John was able to assume the role of evaluator (with a clear conscience) on the development staff for another program at the same center.

Even when the evaluator is external to the agency whose programs or products are being evaluated, financial dependence can be a potential source of bias. Consider, for example, the delicate balance that must be maintained by an external evaluation consultant or firm dependent on "repeat business." Scriven (1993) points out this potential source of bias rather succinctly: "one key economic insight about evaluation contracting is this: No one ever got rich from one evaluation contract" (p. 84). The possibility of future evaluation contracts or consulting depends on how well the client likes the most recent evaluation completed by the evaluator. No problem here if the client has a penchant for the truth, even if it might reflect negatively on the program. But what if the client goes rigid at the first hint of criticism? The evaluator who wants future work from such a person must, as Brickell (1978) puts it, bite the hand that feeds him while appearing to lick it.

Even if the evaluator is not dependent on repeat business, he may find himself dependent on the client for funds to complete the study in hand. Seldom is an evaluator given all the funds for an evaluation up front. Clients sometimes wish to see interim products before releasing all the dollars necessary to carry the study to completion. The apparent or unspoken desire of the client to see positive results could very well introduce bias to interim evaluation findings, so the remaining payments will not be jeopardized.

In summary, the evaluator's financial relationship with and dependence upon the client must be reviewed carefully to determine whether these factors are likely to bias the study. Scriven (1993, pp. 79–86) has offered cautions that are pertinent to such reviews aimed at detecting bias.

Organizational Relationships and Bias

Organizational relationships may be of greater concern to the evaluator than immediate financial gain. The relationship between the evaluator and the program being evaluated can determine not only his present financial welfare but possibly his future employment. Further, an organization may exert great (or total) control over the evaluator's other perquisites (such things as office space, access to secretarial resources, access to and use of facilities and record-keeping systems—even the convenience of available parking space). The way the organization exercises this control to make the evaluator's life easier or more difficult can certainly cause problems with bias.

To make this point, we present in Figure 16.1 eight possible organizational relationships between the evaluator and the program being the evaluated. Generally, the greatest potential of bias exists in the first row of Figure 16.1, and the least potential of bias exists in the last row.

Generally, the potential for bias is higher when the evaluator is employed by the organization whose program is being evaluated than when the evaluator is employed by an outside agency. In addition, bias is more likely when the "organizationally employed" evaluator reports to the director of the program being evaluated than when he reports to someone outside that program. And as noted earlier, the evaluation consultant who is dependent on repeat business may be more vulnerable to bias because of a perceived need to please the client. In some large organizations, the least bias may result from having the evaluation conducted by an evaluator who is assigned to another unit within the organization, thus being "internal" to the organization but "external" to the program being evaluated. In short, the more control the client (the unit or program being evaluated) has over the evaluator's job security, salary (or future consultant fees),

Evaluator Employed	To Do One Evaluation or Successive Evaluations	Evaluator Reports
1. Within the organization that has responsibility for the program being evaluated	1. Successive evaluations	1. Directly to the director of the program being evaluated
2. Within the organization that has responsibility for the program being evaluated	2. One evaluation	2. Directly to the director of the program being evaluated
3. Within the organization that has responsibility for the program being evaluated	3. Successive evaluations	3. To someone outside the program being evaluated but within the same organization
4. Within the organization that has responsibility for the program being evaluated	4. One evaluation	4. To someone outside the program being evaluated but within the same organization
5. By outside agency	5. Successive evaluations	5. As consultant or contractor to the director of the program being evaluated
6. By outside agency	6. One evaluation	6. As consultant or contractor to the director of the program being evaluated
7. By outside agency	7. Successive evaluations	7. Directly to the outside funding agency that supports the program
8. By outside agency	8. One evaluation	8. Directly to the outside funding agency that supports the program

FIGURE 16.1 Organizational relationships of evaluator to client

and perquisites, the *less* candor and objectivity the evaluator is likely to demonstrate in conducting the evaluation.

Some authors (e.g., Cronbach et al., 1980) are unsympathetic to concerns that the locus of the evaluator's employment may influence the results of the evaluation. Such a stance ignores the very real influence that control of salary and perquisites can have on objectivity and even truth. Any assertion that such mundane matters are unlikely to influence an evaluation's outcome must seem quaint to "in-house" evaluators or evaluation contractors who have survived years of service in political cauldrons in which they have seen (if not felt personally) employment locus and control of perquisites wreak havoc.

Bias in Formative and Summative Evaluation.   The discerning reader has probably already noted that our discussion in the preceding sections omits one important consideration: whether the evaluation is primarily formative or summative. In considering the pros and cons of an evaluator's financial and administrative dependence on or independence from the client, such dependence may be not only tolerable in a formative evaluation but even desirable, for it may prompt the evaluator to be more responsive to particular information needs of the program—information needed to improve the program. Not so for a summative evaluation, where organizational and financial dependence would seem much less tolerable, and positive evaluation results produced by a dependent evaluator would normally be viewed with suspicion. An external, independent evaluator is generally to be preferred in summative evaluations, although as we have noted in the prior section, "independence" is defined by a variety of factors often not considered. For example, it strains credibility to argue that an external evaluator is truly independent when he is selected and paid by the client to carry out a summative study (even though independence is more likely here than if the evaluator were internal, and hence under even more direct client control). Stated differently, co-optation, ego involvement, and bias are undesirable in any evaluation, but they are doubly so in summative evaluation studies, where any conflict of interest is on a direct collision course with the purpose of such studies.

MAINTAINING ETHICAL STANDARDS: CONSIDERATIONS, ISSUES, AND RESPONSIBILITIES FOR EVALUATORS AND CLIENTS

In our earlier text (Worthen & Sanders, 1987) we postulated five forms of "evaluation corruptibility" that result from ethical compromises or distortions.

- Willingness, given conflict of interest or other perceived payoffs or penalties, to twist the truth and produce positive findings
- Intrusion of unsubstantiated opinions because of sloppy, capricious, and unprofessional evaluation practices
- "Shaded" evaluation "findings" resulting from intrusion of the evaluator's personal prejudices or preconceived notions
- Obtaining the cooperation of clients or participants by making promises that cannot be kept
- Failure to honor commitments that could have been honored (p. 289)

House (1995) has listed five ethical fallacies of evaluation that address some of these same problems from a somewhat different perspective.

1. Clientism—the fallacy that doing whatever the client requests or whatever will benefit the client is ethically correct
2. Contractualism—the fallacy that the evaluator is obligated to follow the written contract slavishly, even if doing so is detrimental to the public good
3. Methodologicalism—the belief that following acceptable inquiry methods assures that the evaluator's behavior will be ethical, even when some methodologies may actually compound the evaluator's ethical dilemmas

4. Relativism—the fallacy that opinion data the evaluator collects from various participants must be given equal weight, as if there is no basis for appropriately giving the opinions of peripheral groups less priority than that given to more pivotal groups

5. Pluralism/Elitism—the fallacy of allowing powerful voices to be given higher priority, not because they merit such priority but merely because they hold more prestige and potency than the powerless or voiceless

In discussing the ethical problems evaluators face, House states:

First, they exercise powers over people that can injure self-esteem, damage reputations, and stunt careers. . . . Second, evaluators are engaged in relationships in which they themselves are vulnerable to people awarding future work. . . . Also, evaluators come from the same social classes and educational backgrounds as those who sponsor the evaluations and run the programs. These factors multiply ethical hazards. (p. 29)

Whether such problems as these—or the "forms of corruptibility" we listed earlier—result from the evaluator's incompetence or from more morally reprehensible causes, they still result in seriously compromised or outright discredited evaluations. It may matter greatly, on moral grounds, whether evaluation results are distorted because the evaluator is unconscionably self-serving or because he is simply ignorant of how to discover and portray reality. But in practical terms the result is the same. Therefore, those who conduct and those who are served by evaluation studies share a responsibility for becoming informed about relevant ethical issues. Yet, in a survey of American Evaluation Association members' views on ethical issues, Morris and Cohn (1993) found that many were unaware of major ethical issues, suggesting that many evaluators would benefit from greater understanding of ethical standards for evaluation practice.

Proposed Ethical Standards in Evaluation

Beginning in the mid-1970s, several professional organizations contemplated evaluation's ethical issues. In the early 1980s, two major organizations in the United States published proposed sets of standards for evaluation practice (the Joint Committee on Standards for Educational Evaluation, 1981, and the Evaluation Research Society Standards Committee, 1982). In the latter part of that decade, both the U.S. and Canadian governments revised their standards pertinent to program evaluation. In the United States, the pertinent standards were subsets of the Government Accounting Office's auditing standards (Comptroller General of the United States, 1988) dealing with "general standards" and "performance audits," while in Canada the standards (Office of the Comptroller General, 1989) focused exclusively on program evaluation. In the 1990s, the Joint

Committee on Standards for Educational Evaluation (1994) issued a new edition of *Program Evaluation Standards,* and the American Evaluation Association (1995) published its "Guiding Principles for Evaluators." The Canadian Evaluation Society (1992) developed a draft set of standards for program evaluation in Canada, and the Australasian Evaluation Society developed an "Interim Code of Ethics" and is currently developing a set of guidelines for how to apply the Joint Committee's 1994 *Program Evaluation Standards* in Australia (Amie, 1995). It is abundantly clear that program evaluators are concerned with developing and getting evaluators to adhere to high standards of ethical conduct. Although these various sets of standards or guidelines are dissimilar in level of detail and organization, they all address the issue of ethical conduct in one way or another. (For analyses of similarities and differences in these various sets of standards and guidelines, see Covert, 1995, and Sanders, 1995). For example, in proposing the *Program Evaluation Standards,* the Joint Committee (1994) states that the quality of any evaluation study can be determined by examining its (1) utility, (2) feasibility, (3) propriety, and (4) accuracy. Concern for ethical conduct centers in the third category, that of "propriety," and specific standards in this area include

- Service orientation,
- Formal agreements,
- Rights of human subjects,
- Human interactions,
- Complete and fair assessment,
- Disclosure of findings,
- Conflict of interest, and
- Fiscal responsibility.

The American Evaluation Association's (1995) "Guiding Principles for Evaluators" are elaborations of five basic, broad principles.

1. *Systematic Inquiry:* Evaluators conduct systematic, data-based inquiries about whatever is being evaluated.
2. *Competence:* Evaluators provide competent performance to stakeholders.
3. *Integrity/Honesty:* Evaluators ensure the honesty and integrity of the entire evaluation process.
4. *Respect for People:* Evaluators respect the security, dignity, and self-worth of the respondents, program participants, clients, and other stakeholders with whom they interact.
5. *Responsibilities for General and Public Welfare:* Evaluators articulate and take into account the diversity of interests and values that may be related to the general and public welfare. (p. 20)

None of these principles will be fully satisfied if the evaluator is not scrupulously ethical, but principles 3 to 5 are at the core of ethical conduct. Sanders (1995, p. 50) has shown that there is great overlap of the Joint Committee's propriety standards listed earlier and these three AEA principles.

Other authors and professional organizations have also implicitly or explicitly listed ethical standards for evaluators or researchers (e.g., American Anthropological Association, 1990; American Educational Research Association, 1992; Perloff & Perloff, 1980; Covert, 1988; Honea, 1992; Stufflebeam, 1991). For the most part, their concerns have been well covered by the propriety standards of the Joint Committee (1994); however, drawing on these sources, we expand here on a few of the Joint Committee's standards.

Service orientation is intended to assure that evaluators should serve not only the interests of the agency sponsoring the evaluation but also the learning needs of program participants, community, and society.

Formal agreements goes beyond agreement on technically adequate evaluation procedures and includes such issues as following protocol, having access to data, clearly warning clients about the evaluation's limitations, and not promising too much.

Rights of human subjects are broadly understood to include such things as obtaining informed consent, maintaining rights to privacy, and assuring confidentiality. But human rights extend also into the standard of *human interactions,* which holds that evaluators must respect human dignity and worth in all interactions associated with the evaluation so that no participants are humiliated or harmed.

Complete and fair assessment aims at assuring that both the strengths and weaknesses of a program are portrayed accurately, with no "tilt" in the study to satisfy the sponsor or appease politically potent groups. Reaching a fair balance of the strengths and weaknesses of a program does not mean, however, that an equal number of strengths and weaknesses must be identified, but rather that whatever strengths and weaknesses exist are accurately assessed.

Disclosure of findings reflects an evaluator's obligation to serve not only his client or sponsor but also the broader public(s) who supposedly benefit from both the program and its accurate evaluation. In addition, the evaluator has loyalties to the profession of evaluation and the ethical canons on which it depends. That these canons are not crystal clear and the ethical dilemmas not all resolved is apparent from questions posed by Newman (1995) as still awaiting resolution.

When evaluating a program, evaluators usually observe contexts outside the scope of the specified evaluation domain. If these observations indicate that undue harm is being done, what is our obligation to report the harm? And to whom? Suppose the evaluators become aware of false, limited, or non-dissemination of evaluation findings (for example, stakeholders are denied or have limited access to report findings that could provide them with the necessary data to argue with administrative decisions). What is the evaluators' duty? Do we have an obligation to report findings to stakeholders who are omitted from the decision making process? Are we obligated to inform stakeholders of negative results, or is that the prerogative of the client? (p. 102)

Conflict of interest cannot always be resolved. But if the evaluator makes his values and biases explicit in as open and honest a way as possible, in the spirit of "let the buyer beware," clients can at least be alert to biases that may unwittingly creep into the work of even the most honest evaluator.

Fiscal responsibility does not end with the evaluator's making sure all expenditures are appropriate, prudent, and well documented. Evaluation also carries nontrivial costs to personnel involved in that which is evaluated, including time and effort in providing, collecting, or facilitating the collection of information requested by the evaluator and the time and energy expended in explaining the evaluation to various constituencies.

Ethical Guidelines and Standards Are Not Quite the Same

Despite the overlap between the various sets of evaluation standards and guidelines, standards of practice are not the same as ethical codes or principles. In their study of how well the Joint Committee's (1981) standards matched with Kitchener's (1984) ethical principles proposed as pertinent to professions, Brown and Newman (1992) concluded that (1) experienced professional evaluators were able to match the standards to the ethical principles much more readily than were evaluation novices or consumers, but (2) the principles and standards are not synonymous. Sanders (1995) concurs, noting that the Joint Committee's standards focus on the soundness of one particular evaluation, whereas the AEA's principles address an expected professional lifestyle that permeates and cuts across the evaluator's behavior on all evaluations he may conduct. But Sanders is quick to note that these differences in focus do not suggest disagreement: "there are no conflicts or inconsistencies between the two" (p. 48).

We will say more about these standards and guidelines in Chapter 20. But despite their important contributions to program evaluation, neither of these two efforts has yielded an "accepted code of ethics or ethical principles for evaluators. The literature concerning ethical practice in evaluation is sparse. Given the varied educational backgrounds and professional affiliations of evaluators, they may practice under several different and potentially conflicting ethical codes" (Love, 1994, p. 33).

Ethics Are Not the Sole Responsibility of the Evaluator

Our emphasis on the evaluator's responsibility to carry out his activities in an ethical fashion may seem to suggest that ethics is the sole province of the evaluator. Obviously, such is not the case; ethical responsibilities are shared by evaluation sponsors, participants, and audiences.

Many ethical issues pertain directly to the programs or products being evaluated—the extent to which they are fulfilling their objectives and the impact they have, for better or worse, on the lives of those they serve.

> Much of the work in evaluation ethics (i.e., the moral behavior of an individual as a professional evaluator) which has been done to date has focused on *evaluation* moral issues such as confidentiality of data, protection of human subjects, proper professional behavior, and so on. Little has been done on *program* moral issues, such as: Is this mental hospital placing the community at risk by its early release of patients? Is this nursing home meeting residents' physical needs but at the cost of their human rights of privacy, freedom of movement, and individual expression? Is this educational program for talented students enhancing cognitive skills but reinforcing their emotional dependency on special recognition and privileges? (Smith, 1983, p. 11)

Perhaps it is appropriate to suggest that the ultimate ethical principle, "Do unto others as you would have them do unto you," is no more or less binding on evaluators than it is on the other stakeholders in every program evaluation.

Morris and Cohn's (1993) survey of AEA members netted 459 responses. Of those respondents, nearly two-thirds reported they had encountered ethical problems in their evaluation work. Many of these problems reflect unethical conduct by evaluation participants other than the evaluator. For example:[5]

- Evaluator is pressured by stakeholders to alter presentation of findings.
- Findings are suppressed or ignored by stakeholder.
- Findings are misused by stakeholder (but not to punish anyone).
- Findings are used to punish evaluator.
- Findings are used to punish someone other than evaluator.
- Findings are deliberately modified by stakeholder prior to release.
- Findings are misinterpreted by stakeholder.
- Stakeholder misrepresents authorship or plagiarizes report content.
- Stakeholder prejudges what findings "should be."
- Stakeholder plans to use findings in an ethically questionable fashion.
- Stakeholder declares certain evaluative questions "off limits," despite their obvious relevance.
- Sponsors omit other legitimate stakeholders from planning process.
- Stakeholder pressures evaluator to violate confidentiality.

Clearly it is appropriate to be concerned about ethical lapses not only of the evaluator but also of those he serves.

---

[5] We have altered the wording on some of these to increase clarity (based on our experience and interpretation) and accept responsibility if doing so has altered the authors' original meaning.

Ethics beyond a Code of Ethics

The evaluation standards and guidelines described earlier are, in our judgment, singularly useful in improving the practice of evaluation. We urge anyone aspiring to do high-quality evaluation to become intimately familiar with those standards and guidelines and to apply them diligently. At the same time, we caution that mere adherence to ethical standards—however sound—does not ensure ethical behavior. It is impossible to draft standards that anticipate all potential ethical problems or dilemmas.

Perhaps Sieber (1980) still states it best.

A code of ethics specifically for program evaluators . . . would be a minimum standard; it would only state what the profession expects of every evaluator in the way of honesty, competence, and decency in relation to those ethical problems that are clearly defined at present.

In contrast, *being ethical* is a broad, evolving personal process. . . . Ethical problems in program evaluation are problems having to do with unanticipated conflicts of obligation and interest and with unintended harmful side effects of evaluation. To *be* ethical is to evolve an ability to anticipate and circumvent such problems. It is an acquired ability. . . . As one undertakes new and different kinds of evaluation and as society changes, one's ability to be ethical must grow to meet new challenges. Thus, *being ethical* in program evaluation is a process of growth in understanding, perception, and creative problem-solving ability that respects the interests of individuals and of society. (p. 53, italics ours)

Yet this ideal espoused by Sieber is unlikely to be reached unless evaluators pay greater attention to ethical issues. Honea (1992) found in her case studies of experienced public-sector evaluators that they seldom discussed ethics or values in their work lives. She found four factors that seemed to inhibit such discussions. Specially, her interviewees perceived that

1. They were being ethical if they were following the model of "objective scientist," and lapses in objectivity were viewed as less an ethical than a methodological concern.
2. Participants in evaluation always behave ethically, so discussion of ethics is unnecessary.
3. Being a member of an evaluation team and engaging in team deliberations prevents unethical behavior from occurring.
4. Neither evaluators nor others involved in the evaluation have the time to confront or discuss ethical issues.

If these perceptions of evaluators Honea studied are generalizable, then there is a serious need to capture and focus the attention of evaluators on the centrality of ethical issues in evaluation work.

In her insightful discussion of future efforts necessary to solidify ethical practice in evaluation, Newman (1995) has noted another challenge: What is ethical conduct in one culture or society may be viewed as shocking misconduct in another. Hendricks and Conner (1995) concur, citing important ways in which evaluators from (or experienced in working in) other countries view the AEA's guidelines very differently than do evaluators in their American origins. Much work lies ahead to develop ethical guidelines that can capitalize on the commonalities that cut across cultures and contexts while still accommodating and being sensitive to the cultural diversity of values—and ethics. As Newman (1995) puts it:

> In its current state, the status of ethics in evaluation is at an early stage of development. We know we need ethics to survive; we know we, not others, must develop our ethical system; we know that we must not put off this task. We have begun the discussion; we have developed a preliminary document. We must not let the process stop at this point; we must continue the dialogue and where necessary create and recreate our own path to ethical practice. (p. 110)

COPING WITH POLITICAL PRESSURES AND PROBLEMS IN EVALUATION

In the last section we focused on the importance of ethical conduct of the evaluator. Rightly so. But we do not want to create the erroneous impression that the evaluator is at the root of all ethical problems encountered in program evaluations. Often the evaluator is forced to perform difficult and delicate tasks in high-pressure situations, a task little more enviable than walking a tightrope in a gale.

Chelimsky (1995a) notes that evaluators are often subject to partisan attacks intended to discredit them and their evaluation, for fear of what the evaluation may reveal.

> Efforts to discredit an evaluation based on recognized standards of practice will often follow after pressures on the evaluator—varying from gentle through acute to outright intimidation—have failed. . . . It is true that the shortcomings of evaluators are real and important to address; however, in my experience, the chief barrier to producing useful evaluations lies not in the evaluator but in the evaluation milieu, which may or may not allow the evaluator to be truthful about the merits of the program or policy that has been evaluated. (pp. 53-54)

We agree. Few evaluations ever completely escape the influence of political forces, and those forces are the crux and the cause of many of program evaluation's ethical dilemmas. This view was implicit in the early writings of Suchman (1967) and Cronbach and his colleagues (1980), all of whom hold the view that evaluation is essentially a political activity, underscoring the fact that evaluation of publicly supported enterprises is inextricably intertwined with public policy formulation and all the political forces involved in that process. Evaluators who fail to understand this basic fact squander human and financial resources by conducting evaluations that are largely irrelevant because of their "political naïveté," however impeccably they are designed and conducted. In this section, therefore, we discuss the political nature of evaluation and ways of coping with unwarranted political influences that can otherwise subvert evaluation efforts.

Evaluation as a Political Activity

The term *politics* has been applied so broadly to so many different phenomena that it has all but lost its meaning. It has come to stand for everything from power plays and machinations within a university department to political campaigns or relations between governmental agencies. Even Merriam-Webster's *Collegiate Dictionary* (tenth edition) defines *politics* variously as:

- the art or science concerned with winning and holding control . . .
- activities characterized by artful and often dishonest practices
- the total complex of relations between people living in society (p. 90)

And definitions of *political* are just as divergent.

Against such a permissive backdrop, we feel free to add to the proliferation of definitions two more, one more Aristotelian than the other.

1. First, we see political influence as having to do with obtaining, retaining, and exercising formal or informal control over individuals or collectives of individuals in ways that shape activities, policies, and directions of those entities.
2. Second, and more loosely, we have come to think of political influences as the sum total of everything that operates to influence an evaluation but is outside of the evaluator's personal control (i.e., does not include the methods, techniques, and interpersonal capabilities of the evaluator).

Such descriptions are admittedly more practical than precise, but our discussion of evaluation's political aspects makes no pretense of "political scholarship." Rather, it draws directly on lessons learned in our collective half century of tiptoeing through the political minefields surrounding most of the many program evaluations we have conducted. When so engaged, precise definition of politics seems superfluous. One need not know whether the mine was a Claymore or a "Bouncing Betty" to know it would have been preferable to have tread elsewhere. And most political problems are little more predictable than buried land mines, with the only certainty being that their sudden discovery tends to ruin one's day.

Thus, no matter how one defines politics, many evaluators will likely view it as merely an eight-letter dirty word. That perception is perhaps forgivable, for many evaluators have come to understand political influences in much the same way as a bull's-eye learns about bullets. Yet we suggest there is a more enlightened view. Thoughtful evaluators of publicly funded programs view politics as the way laws and program regulations are made, the way individuals and groups influence the government, and the very essence of what enables governments to respond to the needs of those individuals and groups. Indeed, without politics, government programs would be less responsive, not more.

Even evaluators who believe they are evaluating "nonpolitical" programs and thus can shun the realm of politics altogether fail to perceive the highly political nature of their craft. Effective evaluators must recognize and cope with political influences as they occur. To ignore them or assume "politics can be removed from this study" is both naive and erroneous.

One of the earliest evaluators to describe how political factors influence evaluation was Weiss (1973), who described evaluation as a rational enterprise occurring within a political context. According to Weiss, political factors "intrude" upon evaluations in three ways: (1) the policies and programs with which evaluation deals are themselves the products of political decisions; (2) because evaluation supports decision making, its reports become political documents; and (3) evaluation, by its very nature, makes implicit political statements (such as those challenging the legitimacy of certain program goals or implementation strategies). Twenty years later, Weiss (1993) reaffirmed her belief that "politics impinges on evaluation in the three ways I described" and that these factors "direct attention to what has come to be known as the politics of evaluation" (p. 107).

But even as Weiss was illuminating the political nature of evaluation, others were examining how shifts in the political scene were altering conceptions of evaluation. For example, Sjoberg (1975) described the evolution of "evaluation research" (his phrase, not ours) as due to societal forces. Specifically, he noted that efforts of social scientists to evaluate social programs are fraught with ethical and political dilemmas. In his view, the increasing use of evaluation as a useful tool was brought about by a fundamental shift from industrial to postindustrial economic and political systems.

In looking back on that era, Sechrest and Figueredo (1993) observed that naive program evaluators initially tried to impose their view of social science onto the existing political and policy world. Rebuffed, they began to realize that the realities of the evaluation environment were quite different from their conceptions. Their dilemma was complicated still further by a social revolution from the industrial "mode of management, in both business and government, to a post-industrial era, or cybernetic, mode" (p. 646) that favored multiple decision makers, an information-based society, and a blurred distinction between producer and consumer. Decentralization of policy making led to heterogeneity of program implementation, and the formerly monolithic set of interests, objectives, and policy makers was replaced by an entire social network involved in and influenced by the social program. Faced with this new social ecology, program evaluators were forced to adapt their conceptions and processes of evaluation and, since the 1970s, there have been few evaluators who have not recognized that political processes will be an ever present part of program evaluation.

For example, Palumbo (1987) argued that politics play a major role in the practice of program evaluation, and Patton (1988) noted that politics played a pervasive role in everything from the evaluation's theoretical orientation and design to utilization of the study's results. Perhaps Chelimsky (1987) has contributed most to understanding the political nature of evaluation of programs and policies, especially those at the national level of government. She has spoken of many lessons learned about the politics of program evaluation, including these:

> Evaluators have learned that they . . . must understand the political system in which evaluation operates and the information needs of those policy actors who utilize evaluation.
>
> They have learned to more broadly conceptualize the political system and include all sectors that make the kinds of policy decisions into which evaluation feeds, including executive and legislative branch policymaking. (p. 17)
>
> Taking political processes into account when conducting an evaluation transforms the way in which time is allocated. Evaluators have learned to devote much more time to negotiation, discussion, briefing, accuracy-checking, prioritizing, and presentation than before.
>
> The use of evaluation . . . [is] growing dramatically. But if the profession is making progress, it is due largely to those who . . . focused our attention on the political environment in which evaluators expected to be useful but knew very little about. (p. 19)

Canadian Senator Marsden (1991), speaking to the Canadian Evaluation Society, noted that "there is a great scope and promise in program evaluations for political decision making that remains unexploited" (p. 3). She went on to urge that "evaluations—or at least the clarity of some of the thinking behind program evaluations—[be] brought to bear at three stages of political work: (1) at the introduction of legislation . . . , (2) at . . . times where large cuts, large increases, etc. occur, and (3) at times of crisis" (p. 9).

Desirable as these calls are for program evaluation to be used as a tool to improve federal legislation, some evaluators worry that political forces at the national level are so strong as to threaten to swamp evaluation's ship of state. Suarez (1990) suggested that few national evaluations have as their central goal the provision of impartial information that will inform and shape national policies and decisions. The political stakes are simply so high at the federal level, she claims, that advocacy eventually inundates those who retreat to the high ground in search of valid information for use in rational decision making. Although we agree that her description fits many national evaluations, there are many notable exceptions, such as a majority of studies conducted by the U.S. General Accounting Office.

When one examines the trends in the use of evaluation at state, provincial, and local levels, there is even more room for optimism. Not that politics is absent from local and state/provincial governmental processes. Such a claim would be naive, especially when high-stakes decisions are in the offing. But despite the pervasive presence of politics at every level, there are some data (e.g., Worthen, 1995) that suggest that the political sailing is smoother on state and local tributaries than on major national flood tides where the waters are stirred up by unwanted evaluation mandates. While politically roiled programs can occur at any level, there are at least a large portion of the local and state programs that are free enough of political undercurrents to allow policy makers to use program evaluation to gather information they need to guide future program development.

Partisanship and Political Neutrality

The "politics of evaluation" also influences how evaluators deal with partisan activities meant to influence the conduct of evaluation in ways that favor one group or another. It is essential that the evaluator represents *all* stakeholders, following Cronbach and his colleagues' (1980) advice that the evaluator try to see the program through the eyes of diverse partisans, thus being multipartisan, making the best case he can for each side in turn.

The Joint Committee (1994) also recognizes the importance of the evaluator's sensitivity to the various partisan views of stakeholder groups; the committee proposes the following standard:

> *Political Viability.* The evaluation should be planned and conducted with anticipation of the different positions of various interest groups, so that their cooperation may be obtained, and so that possible attempts by any of these groups to curtail evaluation operations or to bias or misapply the results can be averted or counteracted. (p. 71)

Coping with Political Pressures on Evaluation Studies

> Was it mere naïveté that accounted for the initial failure of evaluation researchers to anticipate the complexities of social and political reality? These researchers [evaluators] were mentally prepared by the dominant Newtonian paradigm of social science for a bold exploration of the icy [unchanging] depths of interplanetary space. Instead, they found themselves completely unprepared for the tropical nightmare of a Darwinian jungle: A steaming green Hell, where everything is alive and keenly aware of you, most things are venomous or poisonous or otherwise dangerous, and nothing waits passively to be acted upon by an external force. This complex world is viciously competitive and strategically unpredictable because [evaluation] information is power, and power confers competitive advantage. The Darwinian jungle manipulates and

deceives the unwary wanderer into serving myriads of contrary and conflicting ends. The sweltering space suits just had to come off. (Sechrest & Figueredo, 1993, p. 648)

This colorful portrayal of evaluators' first forays into the septic and unpredictable environment in which programs wait to be evaluated underscores one point that is perfectly predictable: political pressures are inevitably part of evaluation. And the professional evaluator who prefers to eschew "politics" and deal only with technical considerations has made a strange career choice.

Some political pressures, however, can interfere with evaluation in ways that are patently unethical. We are not concerned here with legitimate political processes or problems that naturally arise whenever an evaluation is conducted but rather with those emanating from the *unethical* use of political influence.

By analogy, one can examine the "tactical research" studies commissioned by sponsors of social causes or commercial products to obtain data that will serve their self-interests. For example, Rossi and Wright (1985) describe how two similar and nearly simultaneous surveys of public opinions on gun control yielded very different results. The survey, funded by the Center for the Study and Prevention of Handgun Violence, concluded that the majority of the public "want handgun licensing and registration," while the survey funded by the National Rifle Association reported that the majority of the public "believe that we do not need more laws governing the possession and use of firearms" (p. 312).

Reichardt (1994) reported how a study by Arthur D. Little Inc. concluded that disposable diapers are not more harmful to the environment than reusable cloth diapers. Suddenly, punitive measures state legislatures had been aiming at throwaway diapers melted away, and critics were quieted. The fact that the study was commissioned, funded, and publicized by the largest producer of disposal diapers, Proctor and Gamble, suggested the possibility that it was fatally flawed by blatant self-interest. But it had its desired effect, a classic contribution to a triumph of a throwaway society over ecological conservatism.

Relatively few program evaluators of our acquaintance have been subjected to naked pressure to bias the outcomes to serve the client's self-interest. But such occurrences are not unknown to program evaluations. Adams (1983) cites several such pressures experienced by internal evaluators and suggests how to cope with them. And Brickell (1978) describes several situations in which evaluators have experienced unethical political influence. We present his examples here, along with our suggestions for coping with the pressures involved in each case.

1. *The client makes it clear from the start what the evaluator should report at the end of the evaluation. Anything different will be unacceptable.* The evaluator could explain how a professional evaluator works and describe the standards (see Chapter 20) of the profession that apply in this situation. If the client persists in prescribing the expected outcomes, the evaluator should abort the evaluation and consider reporting the incident to a higher authority.

2. *The client rewrites the evaluation report, changing the evaluator's findings and interpretations.* Obviously the evaluator should protest and request that such self-interested editing be deleted. If that request is ignored, assuming the evaluator stipulated in the evaluation agreement that he had control of final reports (editing and distribution), he could offer to correct the client's error by distributing the original report, could sue the client for violation of the contract, or could expose the client for unethical practices, perhaps through the public media. Or he might correct the situation simply by offering to have the client's comments appended to the report so that both the evaluator's and the client's undiluted views could be distributed to other stakeholders.

3. *The client alludes to the possibility that obtaining future evaluation contracts is contingent on positive findings in the current evaluation. If the evaluator turns in a negative report, his future work is jeopardized.* If unethical evaluation practice were to result from the evaluator's bowing to this conflict of interest, he would be better off forgoing future work than gaining notoriety through a breach of ethics. The evaluator and client could agree to allow other, independent evaluators to conduct or review the evaluation. The evaluator could appeal to a professionwide group to support him in seeking both employment security and independence. He should also avoid tying his well-being to one client or project.

4. *The client introduces new requests that throw both schedule and budget off, then complains when things are not done on time.* Once the evaluation agreement is signed, all new requests should be accompanied by renegotiation of the agreement (including time frames and budget). The evaluator needs to be careful not to overpromise because of political pressure or a desire to be "nice."

It is the evaluator's responsibility to see that political forces such as these are not allowed to subvert an otherwise good evaluation study. Of course, it is easier to propose coping strategies from an armchair than from one of the hot spots just described. In reality, the difficulty of dealing with unethical political pressures is often acute. For this reason, it is often advisable for evaluators to work in teams rather than alone. There *is* safety—to say nothing of commiseration—in numbers.

After offering several "tongue-in-cheek" rules for escaping the influence of external political factors (Do not work for anyone who has anything to do with the project you are evaluating. . . . Be independently wealthy. . . .), Brickell makes the following serious suggestions for dealing with political influences in evaluation:

1. Try to understand how the client thinks. Find out what he has to gain or lose from the evaluation. . . .

2. Reassure the client at the outset that you can interpret the findings so as to give helpful suggestions for program improvement—no matter what the findings of the study are.

3. Find out what the powerful decision-makers—the client and those who surround him—will actually use as criteria for judging the success of the project. Gather and present evidence addressed to those criteria. You may, if you wish, also gather data on the official objectives of the program or even on objectives that happen to interest you. But never try to substitute those for data addressed to criteria the decision-makers will use.

4. Try to get a supervisory mechanism set up for the evaluation contract that contains a cross section of all the powerful decision-makers. Try to get it designed so that the members have to resolve the conflicts among themselves before giving you marching orders for the study or deciding whether to accept your final report.

5. Write the report carefully, especially when describing shortcomings and placing blame, and do mention any extenuating circumstances. . . . Review the final report draft before submitting it to the client for his review, making sure in advance that you can defend any claim you make.

Following those rules will not help you escape political influences. The most they can do is help you cope with them. (p. 98)

Two decades later, Brickell's suggestions doubtlessly appear overly tilted toward placating management, while ignoring other program participants. In today's more egalitarian view, such studies would be recognized as insufficient if other stakeholder groups were not continually involved in a similar fashion. Through such means, the evaluator may buffer his evaluation from political forces that could otherwise buffet it badly.

Fortunately, the Joint Committee (1994) provides the evaluator with professional standards that emphasize the importance of formal evaluation agreements and the judicious use of an outside consultant to help mediate conflicts. In addition, avoiding conflict of interest and insisting upon open, fair, and complete disclosure of findings are two of the most important principles an evaluator can remember when it comes to coping with unethical political pressures.

Advocacy Evaluation and Political Pressures

So far we have discussed situations where political pressures are exerted on program evaluations to serve unworthy purposes (e.g., greed, usurpation of power, concealment of corruption, unfair competitive advantage). But often program evaluators find that even the most commendable motives can push their evaluation studies off course.

For example, several thoughtful and articulate evaluation theorists and practitioners have argued that the evaluator's clients and/or the public good

chapter 17

Collecting, Analyzing, and Interpreting Quantitative Information

ORIENTING QUESTIONS

1. What precautions should one take in planning and organizing data collection?
2. How does one choose between qualitative and quantitative methods? What is critical multiplism?
3. When can experimental and quasi-experimental designs be useful? When are they feasible?
4. Should you develop your own test or survey or make use of an existing one?
5. When are telephone interviews appropriate?
6. When should you use a cost-effectiveness approach rather than a cost-benefit approach?

> The government is very keen on amassing statistics. They collect them, add them, raise them to the nth power, take the cube root and prepare wonderful diagrams. But you must never forget that every one of these figures comes in the first instance from the village watchman, who just puts down what he pleases. (Sir Josiah Stamp, as quoted by Light & Smith, 1970)

The collection of information is fundamental to evaluation. Although policy makers sometimes joke about "data-free" or "fact-free" evaluations, no reputable evaluator would presume to make evaluative judgments without first assembling a solid base of evidence.

Still, information is situational and changes with every evaluation. Similarly, the methods evaluators use to collect information must also change. Sometimes alternative data-collection methods are available, and the evaluator must make a choice, considering cost, precision (reliability), stability, relevance, validity of measurements, feasibility, political advisability, and acceptability to various audiences. The evaluator must be prepared to use whichever method or methods appear most appropriate. And "being prepared" usually means having prior experience. We advise evaluators to gain experience with any methods that may be new to them—and that means actually using the methods, not just reading about them.

Entire books have been written on a single data-collection technique, instrument, or procedure. We could not hope to cover in comparable detail the many data-collection methods that evaluators have come to use and value. Instead, we devote two chapters to these topics.

QUANTITATIVE AND QUALITATIVE METHODS

During the 1980s and early 1990s many persons working in program evaluation were consumed by controversy over the use of qualitative or quantitative methods. (See Chapter 4 for a discussion of this dispute.) But that debate now seems largely past. Most evaluators now agree that no one method or approach is always appropriate. Rather, the method must be selected based on the question one is trying to answer. Further, as many of the phenomena we examine are amorphous or difficult to measure directly, these phenomena will require multiple measures to adequately assess the issue. Such multiple measures should not all be of the same type; the purpose of multiple measures is to observe the phenomenon from different perspectives. Thus, often when multiple measures are used, those measures will include a combination of qualitative and quantitative approaches. As Cronbach (1982) has noted, "Evaluations should not be cast into a single mold [scientific]. For any evaluation, many good designs can be proposed, but no perfect ones" (pp. 1–2).

We believe the qualitative-quantitative debate has been useful for the field in informing evaluators from different backgrounds and disciplines of the alternative approaches and measures available and encouraging evaluators to consider multiple sources and methods. Evaluators address many different types of questions, from needs assessments to outcome and cost studies, and measure a wide array of concepts, from blood pressure to self-esteem, from computational skills to quality of life. Given the breadth of their tasks, evaluators must have a broad array of "tools" that encompass both qualitative and quantitative methods.

In this chapter we briefly discuss the most commonly used quantitative methods and suggest references for those wanting additional information. In Chapter 18, we provide comparable coverage of qualitative methods. However, the reason for separating these chapters into quantitative and qualitative approaches is not to divide the methods that the evaluator should use, but rather to permit us to present a large number of methods that, in combination, should permit the evaluator to address many important questions.

Using Critical Multiplism to Blend Both Approaches

Shadish (1993) has proposed using critical multiplism to unify the qualitative and quantitative approaches and assist the evaluator in conducting an evaluation. He proposes seven technical guidelines for the evaluator in planning and conducting her evaluation.

1. Identify the tasks to be done.
2. Identify different options for doing each task.
3. Identify the strengths, biases, and assumptions associated with each option.
4. When it is not clear which of several defensible options for doing a task is least biased, select more than one to reflect different biases, avoid constant biases, and overlook only the least plausible biases.
5. Note convergences of results over options with different biases.
6. Explain differences of results yielded by options with different biases.
7. Publicly defend any decisions to leave a task homogeneous (pp. 19-20).

Critical multiplism is an extension of triangulation, or the use of mixed methods to assess the same construct. (See Chapter 18 for more on triangulation.) Cook (1985), in introducing critical multiplism, argued that the concept of triangulation should be applied not only to the measurement phase of the evaluation but to other stages of the evaluation as well. Thus, at the question-generation stage, the evaluator would use differing theoretical perspectives, opposing or differing political views and value systems, and the like, to identify potential evaluation questions.

In this chapter and the next we will encourage you to use multiple, mixed methods on the frequent occasions when one method does not prove sufficiently unbiased to proceed. In selecting different methods, the evaluator should choose ones that have different biases. Interpretation is strengthened when results from these different methods converge. Where differences occur, the evaluator must search for explanations. In this way, qualitative and quantitative approaches add to our ability to judge the value of the evaluation object.

Before discussing specific methods and techniques, we need to comment briefly on dealing with protocol and other potential problems in collecting evaluation data, as well as the importance of establishing procedures for information control, organization, storage, and retrieval.

PLANNING AND ORGANIZING THE COLLECTION OF INFORMATION

As discussed in Chapter 15, data-collection methods must be sanctioned by the proper authorities. These authorities can include Protection of Human Subjects committees or other review committees within the organization, the client, administrators of the program to be evaluated, program staff and program participants, or clients, depending on the nature of the data collection. In addition to seeking approval through proper channels and following organizational policies, it is important that the evaluator seek the input of those who will be involved actively or passively in the collection of information (e.g., responding to surveys, helping to administer tests, observing activities or being observed, and the like). These audiences' cooperation can be vital to successful data collection. If they object to the data-collection methods or procedures or fail to understand the purpose, they can sabotage the collection of valid information by providing false or misleading information or encouraging others to do so. Others simply may not take the data collection seriously. Explaining the importance of their cooperation can prevent many potential problems. Guaranteeing confidentiality or anonymity can be helpful. Rewards—such as released time or feedback from the study—may also encourage full cooperation. Adherence to ethical practices that protect participants' rights is also essential to ensure access to data sources.

Technical Problems in Data Collection

The evaluator's version of Murphy's law goes something like this: "If anything can go wrong in collecting information, it will." A comprehensive list of potential problems would fill this chapter. But here are a few of the major ones:

- *Unclear directions lead to inappropriate responses, or the instrument is insensitive or off-target.* (Always pilot-test your methods.)
- *Inexperienced data collectors reduce the quality of the information being collected.* (Always include extensive training and trial runs. Eliminate potential problem staff before they hit the field. Monitor and document data-collection procedures.)
- *Partial or complete loss of information occurs.* (Duplicate records; keep records and raw data under lock and key at all times.)
- *Information is recorded incorrectly.* (Always check data collection in progress. Cross-checks of recorded information are frequently necessary.)
- *Outright fraud occurs.* (Always have more than one person supplying data. Compare information, looking for the "hard to believe.")
- *Procedures break down.* (Keep logistics simple. Use supervisors. Minimize control for responsible evaluation staff. Avoid mailing critical information. Keep copies of irreplaceable instruments, raw data, records, and the like.)

Information Control, Organization, and Retrieval

An aspect of information collection that proves troublesome in many evaluations is the handling of data. Let us consider four steps involved in managing information: organization, control, checks, and storage and retrieval.

Information organization requires a filing system so important information is not misplaced. Consider how information for each method of data collection should be stored and the format for that storage.

Information control requires assurance that nothing is lost, overlooked, released prematurely, or used inappropriately in violation of evaluation policy or human rights. As information manager, the evaluator has a responsibility to see that collected information is safeguarded. Staff who have access to data should be thoroughly trained in procedures for storage, release, and confidentiality.

Information checks provide assurance that both quantitative and qualitative information is recorded accurately. Samples of information should be double-checked for coding accuracy. Confirmation and cross-checks should be used to reduce misinterpretation.

Information storage and retrieval may occur either in computer files or in raw data files. Raw data should be kept in locked storage rooms and stored for at least three years. Follow-up studies, reanalyses, and questions about the evaluation can all require the use of the raw data. If using raw data files, appropriate mechanisms for retrieval must be planned.

DESIGNS FOR COLLECTING CAUSAL AND DESCRIPTIVE INFORMATION

Experimental Designs

Misuses of experimental designs have been legitimately criticized (Lincoln & Guba, 1985; Patton, 1986; House, 1990; Johnston & Swift, 1994), yet we disagree with those who contend that the experimental paradigm is inapplicable in program evaluations. Comparative experimental and quasi-experimental designs have legitimate and valuable uses in evaluation when effects of well-defined treatments need to be estimated. An experimental or quasi-experimental design can be appropriate when the primary purpose of the evaluation is to answer questions of effectiveness by comparing the program outcomes achieved by one program with those of another program being actively considered as an alternative. Such decisions occur with relative frequency in the public sector. Principals ask, "Should we resume our old phonics-based approach to reading or should we continue with our new whole language approach?" Health administrators ask, "Is our new outreach program for pregnant teens, designed to encourage early prenatal care, more successful than the old method?" To make this choice, these stakeholders want information that compares the outcomes of the two programs in a responsible way. Ideally, the new programs have had time to "work out the kinks" and formative evaluation has been used to describe program actions and outcomes and work for improvement. But, after this period of pilot-testing and revising to maximize the model, an impact study may be appropriate to help administrators and other stakeholders make the choice. Such designs are not a magical way to attribute causality. No design can completely prove causality. But these designs, along with theory building and the collection of other information, can be quite helpful in demonstrating the effects of various programs.

Experimental designs, *if feasible,* are preferable to quasi-experimental designs in that they can counter more threats to the internal validity of the study. Experimental designs include pre-post and posttest-only designs. Other experimental designs, such as the Solomon-4, are used rarely. Each of these designs involves randomly assigning program participants to a group. Through random assignment of a sufficient number of people to each group, experimental designs maximize the chances that the groups are equal on many factors that could influence their response to the program, namely, individual characteristics and attitudes, past history, things going on in their lives currently, and so on. While individuals in the groups are not equal, the groups as a whole are viewed as equivalent. Thus, differences that emerge between the groups on measures taken after the program can be more validly attributed to the program than if the composition to the groups were determined in some other way.

Posttest-only designs are the least complicated of the experimental designs and require simply using a random numbers table (or computer-generated random numbers) to assign participants to two groups (or more, if more comparisons are desired) and collecting information after the program ends (the posttest) to determine whether differences occurred. The name of the design, posttest-only, does not dictate the measure to be used. Post-treatment measures can be surveys, interviews, observations, tests, or any other measure deemed appropriate. The term "posttest-only" refers only to the time at which information will be collected. No pretest information is collected with the posttest-only design because it is assumed the two groups are equivalent due to the random assignment of individuals or units (offices, schools, classrooms) to the programs or treatments.

The **pre-post design** is employed when a pretreatment measure can supply useful information. For example, if the groups are small, there may be concern about their equivalence. A pretest can help confirm their equivalence, though only on the measures collected. If there is concern that many participants may drop out of the program, and thus scores on the posttest may not represent equivalent groups, pretest scores can be used to examine differences in the two groups as a result of dropouts. (Dropouts would be a legitimate concern in evaluating a training program for the hard-core unemployed but would probably not be a concern in a month-long program for fourth graders.) Pretests can provide useful information with both small groups or groups where dropout rates may be high.

Many use pretests as benchmarks to report the change that has occurred in those participating in the program from before the program to its conclusion. These reports are often appealing to stakeholders; however, pre-post comparisons can be misleading because the change from pre to post also includes other factors in the participants' lives (e.g., maturation, other learning, and intervening events). Instead, the postmeasure of the comparison group is generally the more appropriate comparison. If the decision to be made is whether to deliver a new program or an old one, the comparison group should receive the old intervention, and the stakeholders should focus on the differences between the posttest scores of the two groups. The posttest score of the comparison group represents what the treatment group would have achieved if they had been assigned to that treatment. The real choice for stakeholders is between one program and another, as represented by the post scores of the two groups, not between their previous state and their current state. If, in fact, the choice to be made is between no program and an existing or new one, a comparison group can be constructed to receive no treatment. The posttest scores of this comparison group will then reflect how participants in the treatment group would have changed if they received no treatment at all.

In response to those who argue that comparative experiments are not feasible in field studies, Cook and Campbell (1979) list several situations when randomized experiments or quasi-experiments are entirely appropriate and possible:

- When lotteries or other chance drawings are expected
- When demand outstrips supply
- When an innovation cannot be delivered in all units at once
- When experimental units can be temporarily isolated
- When experimental units are spatially separated or interunit communication is low
- When change is mandated and solutions are unknown
- When a tie can be broken
- When some persons express no preference among alternatives

Many argue against random assignment to treatments on an ethical basis. Such concerns can be very legitimate. Often new programs have been carefully planned, have a firm theoretical foundation, and offer great promise to participants. However, we often fail to consider the ethical issues involved in failing to study the treatment thoroughly. Is it ethical to expose people to treatments or programs that may, in implementation, be *less successful* at achieving the goal than the currently accepted method? Is it right to raise the expectations of those in need and then dash them with an untried method? In a time of declining resources for those in need, is it ethical to continue expenditures on an untested method when these resources could be used to effectively meet needs in other proven ways? There are no easy answers to these questions. The consequences of randomization need to be considered carefully for each circumstance. What are the *risks* to each group? How much do we know about the new treatment? About the old? How long will the experiment last? Under what circumstances could it be halted and the better treatment delivered to all? Dennis and Boruch (1989) present a set of threshold conditions that should be attained before considering randomized experiments. While their conditions are applied to developing countries, they can be easily extrapolated to other settings. Passamani (1991) provides a thoughtful discussion of the ethics of random assignment, or clinical trials, in medical settings. For more information on implementing experimental designs in the field, their effects on construct validity, and the ethical and personal issues faced by evaluation and program staff in such designs, see Conrad (1994).

Quasi-Experimental Designs

For many programs, random assignment is neither feasible nor desirable. In such cases, a **quasi-experimental design** can be more appropriate. These designs do not involve random assignment but are an improvement over the nonexperimental design in countering some threats to internal validity. The most commonly used quasi-experimental designs are the interrupted time-series design and the nonequivalent comparison group design.

The **interrupted time-series design** involves collecting data many times prior to the program and then many times after its introduction. This design is used frequently when the intervention, or program, is a law or policy that must apply to everyone in the city, state, or nation. New clean air standards could not be randomly assigned to some households and not others. Changes in the laws for prosecuting juveniles cannot be applied to some juveniles and not others. However, for both of these "programs" information will have been routinely collected on phenomena of interest prior to and after the new laws or standards are imposed. Environmental agencies routinely collect data on air quality; juvenile justice agencies collect such data on juvenile crime. These existing data can be analyzed to assess program effects.

While, theoretically, an interrupted time-series design can be used in many settings, in fact its most frequent application is with existing data that have been collected routinely prior to the intervention. The value of the interrupted time-series study is the measures made prior to the intervention. These measures help demonstrate trends in the absence of the program. Changes in the trend lines after the introduction of the program may then be attributable to the new standard or law. (Caution should be used, however, as these changes may be caused by other reforms that were instituted at the same time. Very often in the public sector, we institute a package of *many* reforms to deal with a serious problem. This package may help us to address the problem comprehensively, but it hinders us in discovering which aspects of the package worked.) One other caution: An interrupted time-series design is most appropriate with programs that expect a relatively quick change. If the change is gradual, the change in the trend line will be gradual and it will be more difficult to attribute the change to the program. Of course, one can lengthen the time between points of data collection to attempt to have the trend line show a more immediate effect, but the longer the time between points, the more likely it is that other factors may have caused the change.

A **nonequivalent comparison group design** is similar to the experimental pre-post design, but participants or students are not randomly assigned to groups. Instead, we try to find an existing group very similar to the one that will receive the new program. The pretest is a more important component of this design than it is in the experimental designs because it helps demonstrate equivalence of groups, if only on the premeasure. If intact groups in large organizations are being studied (e.g., offices, classrooms, schools, wards) and the program is short-lived, it may be relatively easy to find a comparable comparison group. However, if the organization is small (a single elementary school with three classrooms per grade or a school district with two high schools) it is likely that the different units will have some significant differences. If the program is long, the groups may begin as relatively equal, but other differences may occur through the course of the program (e.g., different teachers or staff with different motivations, skills, and emphases).

Another quasi-experimental design is the **regression-discontinuity design**. This design is particularly useful when eligibility for the program to be studied is determined by a person's "scoring" above or below a certain point on the eligibility criterion (e.g., high blood pressure or cholesterol levels). Thus, patients may be eligible for a special weight-reduction program based on being at least 30 percent above standard weight guidelines for their height and gender. The design then compares outcomes for these patients with outcomes for people who were not eligible for the program, using regression methods. A "discontinuity" in the line, or a difference in the regression line, for the two groups suggests a program effect. This design can be useful when programs are limited to those most in need or most qualified, such as a program for highly gifted students, and eligibility is determined by a clearly defined cut point. See Trochim (1984) and Reichardt, Trochim, and Cappelleri (1995) for more information on this design.

Cook and Campbell (1979) provide more information on design in general and quasi-experimental designs in particular. One of the newer issues in design concerns the failure to adequately consider statistical power in planning designs. As a result, Type II errors, or failure to find significant differences between groups when such differences really exist, occur far more frequently than we are aware. Such errors can cause us to reject beneficial programs because we believe they make no difference when, in fact, small sample sizes and/or large group variability may have limited our ability to detect differences. Lipsey (1990) discusses methods for planning designs to avoid such problems.

Descriptive Designs

In addition to experimental and quasi-experimental designs, which are typically considered quantitative in their foundation and are undergirded by the positivist paradigm, there are other designs that are generally associated with the quantitative tradition. The purpose of these designs, however, is not to attribute causality but to describe something. These designs include the cross-sectional design and the time-series design. Unlike the qualitative case study design, these designs do *not* provide in-depth descriptions. They are fairly simple designs but are used frequently to answer rather straightforward questions.

The **cross-sectional design** is intended to show a "snapshot in time." This design typically makes use of a survey approach to collect information on the attitudes, behaviors, opinions, or lives of various groups, either total populations or subgroups sampled from those populations. The purpose of this design is both to describe trends across all groups and to identify any differences among the subgroups. A cross-sectional design might be used to answer any one of the following questions: A principal asks, "What do parents think of our school? What do they see as the strengths and weaknesses of the school environment, facilities, curriculum, personnel? Do parents differ in their opinions based on the grade their child is in? Their child's performance? Their ethnicity? The parents' education and expectations?" The director of an outpatient unit of a mental health center asks, "How do our clients hear of us? What are their expectations about mental health treatment? What problems typically prompt their first visit? Do these opinions differ by the age, income, education, or ethnicity of clients? By the nature of their presenting problem?" These questions might be posed in the context of a needs assessment or formative evaluation. At this initial stage, the primary interest is in identifying problems or priorities. Further evaluation may move into a case study mode to explore the viability of solutions to problems discovered through the cross-sectional design.

A **time-series design** is intended to demonstrate trends or changes over time. As with the cross-sectional design, the question to be answered is relatively simple and straightforward. A health administrator might ask, "Is the number of premature births in our hospital declining?" A high school principal may ask, "Is the proportion of our student body needing ESL classes increasing or decreasing?" A police chief might ask, "What is the trend of juvenile crime in our city? Which juvenile crimes are increasing? Which are decreasing? Which are remaining stable? How do these trends compare with the number of juveniles in our population? Will the number of juveniles remain the same in the next decade?" The latter includes a number of different questions that will help the chief and her staff in planning, but all would be addressed through simple time-series designs. As with interrupted time-series designs, the time-series design often makes use of existing information in order to obtain enough observations over time. Key decisions involve the time ranges to use (quarterly, semiannually, yearly) and the number of data-collection points to obtain. As the evaluator collects information from points increasingly farther back in time, she must make sure the data-collection methods themselves have not changed. Changes in the manner of data collection or definition of terms (What is a juvenile? What is a felony? Which crimes are recorded? What is an ESL class? What is a premature birth?) can make it appear that there is a change in the phenomenon being measured when in fact the change is due to an instrumental change in data collection. Variations of the time-series design are the panel and cohort designs, which are often labeled as longitudinal studies, in which the same or similar persons are followed across time. See O'Sullivan and Rassel (1995) for more information on time-series and cross-sectional designs.

COMMON METHODS FOR COLLECTING QUANTITATIVE INFORMATION

In this section we will discuss other commonly used quantitative methods for collecting information that may be needed to carry out an evaluation, along with references to more detailed treatments of each. The methods covered in this section might be considered an inventory of methods that the professional evaluator should be able to employ. None is to be used indiscriminately in every evaluation. Each should be used only after careful thought has been given to (1) the information that is required to answer the evaluation questions and (2) the extent to which the proposed methods will provide satisfactory answers to those evaluation questions.

Testing

Tests are one method for collecting evaluative information. For educational evaluators, tests constitute a major source of information. Knowledge acquisition is often the primary objective of educational programs, and the acquisition of knowledge is generally, but not always, measured by tests. Evaluators in other fields also make use of tests, though less extensively than educational evaluators. Evaluators in training settings may use tests, though their ultimate objective is often application on the job or effect on the organization (see Chapter 22). Evaluators in the health field may make use of tests for the many educational programs conducted for clients or for health education programs for practitioners. Evaluators in social services may make use of tests to measure outcomes in employment or parenting programs. Thus, all evaluators need to have some knowledge of tests as a data-collection instrument.

Four approaches to achievement testing have emerged:[1] norm-referenced testing (NRT), criterion-referenced testing (CRT), objectives-referenced testing (ORT), and domain-referenced testing (DRT). These four strategies have many elements in common, but depending on which strategy is chosen, the procedures for test development and interpretation can be quite different. **Norm-referenced tests** are intended principally to compare students' performance against others taking the same test. They are the tests routinely administered in most school districts to assess progress. The California Achievement Test, the Comprehensive Test of Basic Skills, and the Iowa Test of Basic Skills are common examples. The strength of such tests is that they permit comparison with established norm groups; as such, they can be helpful in answering questions such as "How is our school doing in conveying commonly accepted knowledge and skills compared to other schools in the nation?" Their chief weakness is that the content

---

[1] Here we are focusing only on using *tests* to measure student achievement. We discuss closely related but clearly different methods of assessing student performance—most often referred to as direct assessment, performance assessment, or alternative assessment—later in this section.

may not be valid for the curriculum being evaluated. To be very useful, care should be taken to ensure that the content of the NRT items and the knowledge and skills called upon to respond correctly match reasonably well the instructional objectives of the program to be evaluated.

In contrast to norm-referenced tests, **criterion-referenced tests** are developed specifically to measure performance against some absolute criterion. The items on the tests are typically written to address a specific curriculum and may be used to evaluate individual students' progress on the curriculum. Such tests have more content validity for purposes of evaluating a curriculum than would norm-referenced tests. Programs may be judged by the proportion of students attaining the criterion by a certain point in time. Norm-referenced testing and criterion-referenced testing, however, both provide a standard for judging students' performance: the norm group or the criterion, respectively.

Objectives-referenced testing and domain-referenced testing do not provide such standards. Instead, they yield descriptive data about student performance with no judgments attached. **Objectives-referenced tests** make use of items keyed to specific instructional objectives. Such tests are most useful for formative evaluation for the teacher or trainer. **Domain-referenced tests** are used to estimate a student's knowledge of a domain of content. The items are not linked to a curriculum but rather to the content domain being measured (e.g., American history, comparative anatomy). These items, too, can be useful for evaluative purposes, though such tests are costly to develop compared to objectives-referenced and criterion-referenced tests. They can, however, be used to answer questions such as "How much do our graduates know about X content?" Standards can be developed to reflect the school's or organization's expectations regarding the amount of knowledge a graduate or a student finishing a course should have.

The series of *Mental Measurements Yearbook* volumes and *Tests in Print* (developed originally by O. K. Buros and currently managed by the Buros Institute at the University of Nebraska) are invaluable reference works when selecting a test for data collection. The most recent of these is Conoley and Impara's (1995) *Twelfth Mental Measurements Yearbook,* which reviews almost 400 tests and attitude scales. Sweetland and Keyser (1986) also provide a useful review of tests.

Alternative Assessment Methods

In schools, standardized achievement tests are routinely used to measure achievement. However, in recent years there has been a move away from using only standardized tests to measure progress. Significant stakeholders, including many parents, teachers, and administrators, question whether such tests measure students' abilities accurately and comprehensively. Further, many teachers and administrators have not found the information useful to them in revising or managing the educational process. A national study of the use of tests in science education found that "existing standardized and text-embedded tests (publisher-supplied tests) are inadequate to support reform in science and mathematics education" (Harmon, 1995, p. 32). Alternatives Harmon sees emerging are changing the content of multiple-choice tests (she cites the National Assessment of Educational Progress as an example of a test that measures higher-order thinking in science), open-ended written items, structured interviews, and performance assessment.

Several labels have been used to describe alternatives to standardized tests, with the most common being *direct assessment, authentic assessment, performance assessment,* and the more generic *alternative assessment.* Although these various descriptors reflect subtle distinctions in emphasis, the several types of assessment all reflect two central commonalities. First, they are all viewed as *alternatives* to traditional multiple-choice, selected-answer achievement tests. Second, they all refer to *direct* examination of student *performance* on significant tasks relevant to life outside of school.

Some of these alternatives reflect the positive influence advocates of qualitative methods have had on the measurement field. These alternatives also remind us that testing can be accomplished both by paper-and-pencil measures and by performance measures. (See the list of data-collection methods on page 277 in Chapter 15.) Paper-and-pencil tests that are criterion referenced, objectives referenced, or domain referenced can be included in an evaluation to inform stakeholders about progress and strengths and weaknesses. But performance measures, such as simulation devices, student portfolios, or oral debates, can also be appropriate, given the content to be measured, in assessing knowledge or skills. As with any evaluation, the key is to select the method or methods that provide the best match to the content to be measured and the purpose of the evaluation. In measuring conversational ability in a foreign language, a structured language proficiency interview would clearly be more appropriate than a paper-and-pencil test. In measuring the skill to use scientific equipment to perform an experiment, a performance assessment in the lab would probably be most appropriate. And in measuring the ability to recognize and correct grammatical and spelling errors, a paper-and-pencil test may be most efficient.

For more detailed discussions of alternative testing methods and test development, see Perrone (1991) and Worthen, Borg, and White (1993). For information on using performance assessment for educational evaluations, see Mitchell (1992).

Questionnaires

Questionnaires (sometimes referred to as "surveys")[2] may be developed to measure attitudes, opinions, behavior, life circumstances (income, family size, housing conditions, etc.) or other issues. Questionnaires have in common the fact that they are paper-and-pencil measures designed for respondents to report information. The measures may be administered individually, in groups, or by mail. Item types include open-ended items for which content analysis is used;

---

[2] "Survey" more appropriately refers to the general method, while "questionnaire," "interview protocol," and the like refer to instruments used to collect the actual data.

short-answer open-ended items (e.g., number of children); multiple-choice items; items with adjectival responses (e.g., rating items using excellent, very good, good, fair, poor); items with adverb responses (always, frequently, etc.); and Likert-scale items, to be discussed later in this section.

As with any type of information to be collected, the evaluator should first consider whether there are existing questionnaires that would be appropriate to use in the current study. The *Mental Measurements Yearbook* volumes (see Conoley & Impara, 1995) describe and reference numerous attitude scales. More specialized references of attitude scales include the *Handbook of Scales for Research in Crime and Delinquency* (Brodsky & Smitherman, 1983) for questionnaires on attitudes toward crime and police or self-reports of criminal behavior. *Measures for Clinical Practice: A Sourcebook* (Corcoran & Fisher, 1987) contains tested measures of phenomena such as self-concept, satisfaction with life, loneliness, anxiety, and depression, which can be used by nonclinicians. *The Clinical Measurement Package: A Field Manual* (Hudson, 1982) presents measures on such issues as parental attitudes, peer relations, family relations and other issues. McDowell and Newell (1987) describe questionnaires for use in the health arena. Another way to learn of recent, commonly accepted measures is through the review of literature conducted by the evaluator during the planning stage. Note the measures used by other evaluators in these studies and consider their appropriateness for your own purposes.

When the purpose of the survey is to measure opinions, behaviors, attitudes or life circumstances quite specific to the program to be evaluated, the evaluator is likely to be faced with developing her own instrument. In this case, we recommend developing a design plan for the questionnaire analogous to the evaluation design used for the entire evaluation. In the first column, list the questions (not the item) to be answered by the survey. That is, what questions should the results of this survey answer? In the second column, indicate the item type(s) that should be used to obtain this information. A third column may be used after items are developed to reference the numbers of the items that are to answer this question. A fourth column can then specify the means of analysis. Figure 17.1 provides an illustration. This design then becomes a guide for planning the survey and analyzing the information obtained. It helps the evaluator to make sure she includes a sufficient number of items to answer each question. (Some questions need more items than others.) The design also helps avoid items that sound interesting but in fact don't really address any of the evaluation questions. The evaluator may decide to include such items, but their purpose should be further explored. Items that do not answer a question of interest lengthen the questionnaire and show disrespect for the time and privacy of the respondent.

In selecting a type of item, consider that many variables can be measured with several different item formats. Yet attitudes are probably most appropriately measured with **Likert-scale items**. These items consist of sentences that reflect an attitude on the construct of interest. Responses are made on a "strongly agree-strongly disagree" continuum. Behaviors are perhaps best measured with

Question	Item Type	Item Number	Analysis
1. What is clients' overall opinion of the agency?	Likert 5-point scale	2–20	Descriptive for each item and total score
2. How did clients first learn of the agency?	Multiple-choice	21	Percentages
3. What type(s) of services do they receive from the agency?	Checklist	22–23	Percentages
4. Do opinions differ by type of service required?		Score on 2–20 with 22–23	t-tests and ANOVA, explore

FIGURE 17.1 Sample design plan for questionnaire

multiple-choice items (to select a behavior) or adverbial items (to report frequency of behaviors), while opinions might best be obtained by using adjectival items (for ratings of favorability) or multiple-choice items (for preference of options). Information concerning life circumstances might best be measured with multiple-choice items (presenting numeric ranges, alternatives, or yes-no responses) or short-answer, open-ended items. If the questionnaire is to be mailed, open-ended items should be used sparingly unless the audience is quite motivated; requiring much writing can greatly decrease the response rate. Nevertheless, open-ended items at the conclusion of the questionnaire can provide useful additional information and give the respondents an opportunity to voice alternative views.

Careful development of the questionnaire draft, instructions, and cover letter (if distributed by mail) then follow. A first draft of the questionnaire should meet these criteria:

1. *Sequencing questions*
   a. Are later responses biased by early questions?
   b. Does the questionnaire begin with easy, unthreatening, but pertinent questions?
   c. Are leading questions (ones that "lead" to a certain response) avoided?
   d. Is there a logical, efficient sequencing of questions (e.g., from general to specific questions; use of filter questions when appropriate)?
   e. Are closed- or open-ended questions appropriate? If closed, are the categories exhaustive *and* mutually exclusive? Do responses result in the desired scale of data for analysis (i.e., nominal, ordinal, interval)?
   f. Are the major issues covered thoroughly while minor issues are passed over quickly?
   g. Are questions with similar content grouped logically?
2. *Wording questions*
   a. Are questions stated precisely? (Who, what, when, where, why, how?)
   b. Does the questionnaire avoid assuming too much knowledge on the part of the respondent?

    c. Does each item ask only one question?

    d. Is the respondent in a position to answer the question, or must she make guesses? If so, are you interested in her guesses?

    e. Are definitions clear?

    f. Are emotionally tinged words avoided?

    g. Is the vocabulary at the reading level of the audience? If any technical terms, jargon, or slang are used, are they the most appropriate way to communicate with this audience?

    h. Are the methods for responding appropriate? Clear? Consistent?

    i. Are the questions appropriately brief and uncomplicated?

3. *Establishing and keeping rapport and eliciting cooperation*

    a. Is the questionnaire easy to answer? (Questions are not overly long or cumbersome.)

    b. Is the time required to respond reasonable?

    c. Does the instrument look attractive (i.e., layout, quality of paper, etc.)?

    d. Is there a "respondent orientation"?

    e. Does the cover letter provide an explanation of purpose, sponsorship, method of respondent selection, anonymity?

    f. Is appropriate incentive provided for the respondent's cooperation?

4. *Giving instructions*

    a. Is the respondent clearly told how to record her responses?

    b. Are instructions for return clear? Is a stamped return envelope provided?

More information on constructing questionnaires and other survey instruments can be found in Sudman and Bradburn (1982) and Fowler (1984). Many evaluators make use of Dillman's Total Design Method for constructing and mailing questionnaires (Dillman, 1978). Aday (1989) provides advice for developing questionnaires in the health area.

Telephone Interviews

As many of you know—especially those who have been greeted by a phone call from a professional survey firm during the middle of cooking dinner and juggling children and homework—telephone interviews have become a much more commonly used method of collecting information. While the information obtained from telephone interviews could be considered qualitative by some, we have included it in this chapter because we see it as more akin to a questionnaire administered orally than to a personal interview. A telephone interview is like the former in that it must be brief to encourage participation and the questions rarely require long responses. Unlike the personal interviewer, the telephone interviewer has difficulty in establishing rapport due to the lack of eye contact and other nonverbal cues. While branching is often used in telephone interviews to skip questions inappropriate for the current respondent, the interviewer is seldom encouraged to adapt questions as in an unstructured personal interview. Instead, standardization is encouraged.

The questions asked in telephone interviews are often quite similar to those one would use in a questionnaire except that items with long stems or response alternatives that may be difficult to comprehend when received orally are discouraged. But open-ended items can be more frequent in telephone interviews than in mailed questionnaires because respondents are more willing to speak a sentence or even a paragraph than write one. Telephone interviews can result in obtaining information more quickly than questionnaires distributed through the mail. In spite of disputes over costs, the costs of each method can be relatively similar, depending on the number of respondents, the length of the questionnaire or interview, and the availability of staff to administer telephone surveys. The categories of costs are simply different. Costs in mailing question-naire include secretarial time, paper, copying, postage, postcards, and envelopes. Costs in telephone surveys are primarily the costs of staff involved in conducting and monitoring the surveys. Long-distance charges, the rental of facilities for telephoning and training, and the purchase of phones may also be factors.

Telephone surveys should be considered as preferable to mailed surveys when there is a need for speed, respondents may be reluctant or unable to complete written surveys but could be reached by telephone, and the questions to be asked lend themselves to being delivered by phone. Good references for telephone surveys include Dillman (1978) and Lavrakas (1987).

Delphi Techniques and Q-Sorts

Both Delphi techniques and Q-sorts are quantitative techniques or procedures that have been used successfully to obtain the opinions of groups, often for needs assessment studies. The **Delphi technique** is designed to move a group to consensus and makes use of a series of mailings of specially styled ques-tionnaires to respondents. The first mailing solicits opinions on the issue. Subsequent mailings show statistical summaries of results to previous mailings (reporting medians and interquartile ranges) and remind the respondent of her earlier responses. The respondent is permitted to change her response or justify it, if it is outside the interquartile range. This method is often used with panels of experts who are geographically dispersed and who therefore would be costly, if not impossible, to bring together. It can also be useful when respondents desire anonymity. A recent study by Woudenberg (1991) cautions that while the Delphi method achieves consensus among the group, this consensus is due more to group pressure than to finding any "true" expert opinion. See McKillip (1987) for more information on this technique. Clark and Friedman (1982) demonstrate an interesting application in the mental health area.

The **Q-sort** is similar to the Delphi technique in that it obtains opinions on needs or objectives; however, it does not strive for consensus or make use of a series of mailings. Briefly, a Q-sort uses lists of need statements or goal (objective) statements that have been assigned numerals and placed on cards. Participants are asked to rank the issues listed on the cards. A structured Q-sort includes a set of rules whereby a certain number of cards (needs or objectives) must be placed in each of a certain number of piles. In an unstructured Q-sort, a person is asked merely to place the cards into a predetermined number of piles according to her own perceptions. This approach, in essence, "lets the cards fall where they may." The ordinal data that result from the sorts may be analyzed to yield a number of useful statistics.

SAMPLING

Sampling is a means of drawing a portion of a target population for study. If we were to test only a portion of the children in the state for an evaluation of immunization rates, we would be sampling. If our sample had been carefully selected, we could then use the information collected from the sample to make inferences about immunization rates and patterns of the entire target population (in this case, all the children in the state).

Sampling is not necessary in all evaluations. If the population of interest, or the group to which the results of the study will be extended, is small, it may be wise to collect information from the entire group. If the population is large, however, sampling can reduce the costs of collecting information while still allowing the conclusions to be generalized to the larger group. In *basic research* and in *polling,* sampling is almost always appropriate because the population of interest is very large (i.e., all children in the United States, all voters).[3] Evaluators, however, should not immediately assume sampling is called for in all studies, especially if the population is small. If sampling is required the evaluator must determine the desired sample size. The variability of the phenomenon to be examined and the desired degree of accuracy both affect the sample size. (See Krejcie & Morgan, 1970, for a guide to estimating sample sizes.)

Not all methods of sampling are equally successful. One common method of sampling is haphazard or **convenience sampling**. With convenience sampling, individuals or other units from whom data will be collected are selected on the basis of accessibility, with little concern for the composition of the sample as a whole. If we were to select the first four people coming into an agency for our sample, regardless of who they were, we would be drawing a convenience sample. Conclusions about a whole population based on a convenience

---

[3] Though random sampling is appropriate in much basic research because the purpose is to extend the results to a much larger population, it is, in fact, rarely used. Scan research journals in various fields and one rarely finds a study in which random sampling was used, much less one in which the sample was drawn from the population of interest. When random sampling is used in basic research, the researcher tends to sample from an available subset of the population. In such cases, the random sampling only permits the empirical generalization to the subset from which the sample was drawn. The researcher then must use reasoning (logic, argument, statistics comparing the available group to the entire population) to generalize the results to the population of interest. Sampling from the true population of interest (e.g., all four-year-olds in the United States, or all children at risk for drug abuse) is generally not feasible.

sample are very likely to be erroneous. Nevertheless, mall surveyors and television "man-on-the-street" interviews seem quite happy with this method!

Judgment or **purposive sampling**, while seemingly more carefully considered than convenience sampling, presents similar risks in generalizing to the population as a whole. However, this method is often used successfully in qualitative evaluations for different purposes. Purposive sampling can be helpful to describe a subgroup and, hence, to obtain a better understanding of the program as a whole. In this approach, a sample is drawn based on particular purposes or judgments. Students who are deemed the greatest discipline problems by teachers might be selected to describe the types of discipline problems teachers encounter. Or a group of "typical" clients in a budget counseling program might be selected for study to determine the types of problems these "typical" clients encounter in applying information from the program. Such samples can be helpful for descriptive purposes, but care should be used not to extend the results beyond the group from whom data are collected. If our purposes are to generalize beyond our sample to a larger population, this sampling strategy may not be the wisest to use.

In contrast, *probability sampling* does permit the evaluator to generalize the results to the population from whom the sample is drawn. With probability sampling, each unit in the population has a known probability of being selected. With simple **random sampling**, a type of probability sampling, each unit has an equal and independent chance of being selected. Samples drawn in this method, if large enough, are more likely to represent the population than samples drawn through convenience or purposive sampling. Most large assessment projects (e.g., the U.S. National Assessment of Educational Progress [NAEP]) and public opinion polls use probability sampling.

What does probability sampling involve? First, let us define a few terms: A *sampling unit* is an element or collection of elements in the target population. Sampling units could be individuals; classrooms, offices, departments or like units; or entire institutions such as schools, hospitals, or prisons. Care must be taken to select a sampling unit that is consistent with the element about which one would like to make inferences. That is, if we want to draw conclusions about individual schools, we should use schools as the sampling unit, not classrooms or individual pupils.

A *sample design* is the plan by which a sample is to be drawn. This is to be distinguished from *sample selection,* which is the actual drawing and listing of specific sampling units to be observed.

A *sampling frame* is the list, map, directory, or other source in which sampling units are defined and from which a set of units is selected. If the target population were all small elementary schools (fewer than 200 children) in Iowa, our sampling frame would be a list or directory of those schools. In selecting a sampling frame, the evaluator should consider the degree to which the sampling frame includes all the population of interest. (Are all elementary schools with fewer than 200 children in Iowa included in the list? Have some new schools started since the list was developed?). Conversely, it is important to determine whether the sampling frame includes units that are not currently part of the population of interest. (Does the list contain schools that have grown to be larger than 200 pupils since the publication of the document?) The degree to which the sampling frame includes the entire target population, and no others, greatly influences the accuracy of your sampling process.

To draw a random sample, the evaluator must first define the population of interest for the evaluation and specify the sampling unit. Then, she must find the sampling frame that contains all the population, and no others, in the unit of interest. Some adjustments to the sampling frame may be required to exclude units no longer in the population and add units new to the population. If simple random sampling is to be used, the evaluator could then use a table of random numbers to select those from whom information will be collected from the sampling frame. Computer programs are also available to assist in this process.

Two common variants on simple random sampling are stratified random sampling and cluster sampling. **Stratified random sampling** is used when the evaluator is interested in examining differences among subgroups in the population, some of which are so small that they may not be represented in sufficient numbers in a simple random sample. (If all subgroups of interest are large, stratifying is unnecessary.) Thus, if an evaluation were examining parents' attitudes about schools, one might stratify for parents with children in special needs classes to make sure such parents are sufficiently represented for the evaluator to be able to confidently report their attitudes as an important subgroup. Often, samples are stratified for race or ethnicity if it is believed that racial or ethnic minorities may have different opinions and they represent only a small proportion of the population. Company surveys might stratify for level of position to make sure that administrators are sampled in sufficient numbers. Stratified random sampling divides the population into "strata" representing the subgroups of interest. Simple random sampling is then used to select units within each strata.

Cluster sampling serves a different purpose and is most commonly used in national studies for cost-saving purposes. Cluster sampling involves drawing a series of random samples of geographic clusters (i.e., blocks or voter precincts rather than individual units). If your population of interest were the entire midwestern United States, simple random sampling would result in extensive travel for each individual unit sampled. Cluster sampling can condense that travel and cost by permitting more intense data collection in each geographic area selected. Of course, cluster sampling is *only* useful if the method of data collection requires face-to-face interviews or observations. The costs for mailed surveys or phone surveys would not be reduced through cluster sampling. Random digit dialing has largely replaced traditional sampling methods in conducting phone surveys.

A comprehensive discussion of sampling appears in Henry (1990). We also recommend that the evaluator study the well-designed sampling procedures used by large-scale assessment projects such as the NAEP or survey studies such as those conducted by the Institute for Social Research at the University of Michigan. Many existing sampling designs can be adopted or adapted by the evaluator.

COST ANALYSIS

Most program managers are not econometricians and should not be expected to be skilled in identifying all the financial, human, or time costs associated with programs they operate. That leniency cannot extend to the evaluator, however, for it is her job to bring precise information on costs to the attention of developers, deliverers, and administrators who are responsible for their products or programs. Educators and other public administrators are often faulted for choosing the more expensive of two equally effective programs—just because the expensive one is packaged more attractively or advertised more widely. The real fault lies with the program evaluation's having failed to consider cost along with the other variables. As any insightful administrator knows, sound decision making depends on knowing how much program X will accomplish *at what cost.*

Analyzing costs and benefits for public-sector programs can be a quite complex undertaking. Public administrators, elected officials, and the public at large are very concerned with the cost of public programs today. Thus, cost studies are important. However, it is essential to distinguish among the different types of cost studies that can be conducted. Each type is useful but serves different questions, choices, and program stages. We have found Levin's (1983) discussions of cost-benefit, cost-effectiveness, cost-utility, and cost-feasibility analyses to be a useful guide to what is possible.

Cost-benefit analysis is defined as the analysis of well-defined alternatives by comparing their costs and benefits when both costs and benefits are expressed in monetary terms. Each alternative is examined to see whether benefits exceed costs, and the ratios of the alternatives are compared. The alternative with the highest benefit-to-cost ratio is then selected.

Conducting a cost-benefit study essentially involves identifying all costs and all benefits associated with a program and translating any nonmonetary costs or benefits into dollars. While determining all costs and monetizing them (converting them to dollars) can be difficult, monetizing benefits is often more problematic. The outcomes of most public-sector programs are difficult to convert to dollar terms. What is the monetary value of better mental health? Clean air? An additional year of education? One less murder? Educational benefits are often translated into projected gains in earnings or into the amount of money one would have to pay for educational services if they were not provided. Other outcomes that contribute to greater longevity (health programs, clean air) or greater productivity (training, better mental health) also make use of earnings to monetize benefits. Benefits for national parks have been monetized by determining the amount people pay to travel to and visit them (Mills, Massey, & Gregersen, 1980). The evaluator is advised to review the literature on cost-benefit studies in the discipline of the program to be evaluated to identify the commonly accepted benefits used and means for converting these benefits to dollars.

The disadvantage in cost-benefit analysis, of course, is that it can be very difficult to translate all benefits into dollar terms. While gains in earnings are one benefit of education, other benefits are accrued through the impact of education on the quality of life and the educational aspirations of the next generation, to name only two. Further, cost-benefit studies can involve quite technical issues, using discounting to put all costs in the same time frame ($1,000 in 1950 is not worth the same amount in 1997) and opportunity costs to convey the costs of *not* pursuing other options (Yes, you may earn more after going to college, but be sure to consider also the income lost due to not working full-time during that period of attending school *and* lesser seniority and experience once one enters the job market). These methods can improve the accuracy of the final ratio but add further to the complexity and estimation or judgment involved in conducting such a study.

One of the most important things for evaluators to remember, and to convey to stakeholders, about cost-benefit studies is that, in spite of the fact that the study ends with nice, neat numerical ratios, these numbers are quite *fallible*. Many judgments and estimates are involved in determining the costs and benefits to be included and how to change these to dollars. Good studies often present several ratios (called "sensitivity analysis") to show how changes in assumptions will change the ratios.

The term "cost-benefit" has become popular and, on more than one occasion, the authors have been asked to conduct a cost-benefit study when in fact such a study would not address the information needs of the client. Given *their* costs, cost-benefit studies are *only* cost-effective when stakeholders are trying to make summative decisions about programs with quite different outcomes. Should we rebuild the playground or purchase new books? Which program deserves more funding: public television or children's immunizations? When a choice is to be made among programs with like outcomes, other types of cost studies that do not require monetizing benefits can be more appropriate.

Cost-effectiveness analysis involves comparing the costs of programs designed to achieve the same or similar outcomes. When selecting among alternatives for attaining a particular objective, this method would be the correct choice. It is among the most useful decision-making approaches in many fields. Like cost-benefit analysis, cost-effectiveness analysis results in a ratio. However, the benefits side of the ratio is not expressed in monetary terms. Instead, it is expressed as one unit of outcome that would be desired for the programs being compared. The outcome might be one additional year of life, one year's increase in reading ability, an employment or college placement, or one less violent crime. The ratio then shows the cost of each program per outcome achieved. Programs can then easily be compared for their cost-effectiveness in achieving the desired outcome. Only programs with common goals and common measures of effectiveness can be compared using this method.

Since many programs have multiple goals, judgment is involved in determining the goal to focus on in the ratio. Several ratios may be calculated to reflect the different goals of the programs. A cost-effectiveness study of two reading programs might, quite appropriately, calculate one ratio with the outcome of gains in reading ability and another ratio with the outcome of books read voluntarily in the next year to measure the success of the programs in instilling a desire to read. While several ratios may complicate the decision to be made, such ratios can be useful in conveying the comparative values of programs. An advantage of cost-benefit ratios is that they have the potential to include all program benefits or outcomes on the benefit side of the ratio through monetizing. The cost-effectiveness study must develop different ratios for each benefit. However, if the benefits are difficult to translate to monetary terms and the program has only two or three major outcomes, several cost-effectiveness ratios may be preferable.

Many excellent examples of the use of cost-effectiveness analysis are available. Levin, Glass, and Meister (1987) use cost-effectiveness analysis to compare several different methods of improving math and reading performance in elementary education. They find peer tutoring to be more cost-effective than the options of computer-assisted instruction, smaller classes, and longer days. McBride, Bertrand, Santiso, and Fernandez (1987) demonstrate the use of cost-effectiveness analysis to compare five methods of service delivery for contraceptive services in rural Guatemala.

The last two cost-analysis methods are used prior to the implementation of a program. Thus, estimates of costs and benefits are made rather than relying on actual program expenditures and outcomes. These analyses involve even more assumptions than the studies reviewed above but can serve useful needs assessment decisions.

Cost-utility analysis is used to analyze alternatives by comparing their costs and estimated utility. Estimated utility is a subjective estimate of the probability of a unit gain (e.g., one grade-equivalent level) and of the value of the outcome (scored, e.g., on a 0-to-10 scale). Estimated utility can be calculated by multiplying the subjective probability by the estimated utility for each program outcome, then summing these across all outcomes to obtain an estimated utility for the program. This can be done for each program or alternative being considered and the final sums can then be compared. The subjectivity of this method makes it hard to replicate and defend the results. It is a method that a planner might use, however, when time and data are minimal.

Cost-feasibility analysis is used to determine whether the costs of an alternative prohibit its consideration. The evaluator simply looks at the costs of each alternative and compares those costs to the available budget. Cost-feasibility studies should be conducted before too much has been invested in program development.

Levin (1983) provides the following set of questions that should help the evaluator judge the utility of cost-analysis reports:

1. What is the decision framework? What criteria will be used to guide the decision?
2. Which alternatives are considered?
3. How are costs estimated?
4. Are the costs analyzed according to who pays them? Are costs categorized by constituents?

5. Are costs presented in an appropriate mode?
6. Is the criterion of effectiveness appropriate?
7. Are there different effects across subpopulations?
8. Does the estimate of effects meet technical standards (e.g., design, measurement, data-analysis standards)?
9. Are the cost comparisons appropriate?
10. How generalizable are the results to other settings?

We hope this brief discussion of cost analysis provides a sufficient overview to help the reader understand basic approaches and necessary steps. Extensive discussions of cost analysis of education may be found in Levin (1981, 1983), Scriven (1974a, 1984), and Thompson (1980). Yates (1996) discusses ways to conduct cost-effectiveness and cost-benefit analysis in human service settings and provides useful examples of its application to substance abuse, suicide prevention programs, residential programs, and other settings. Williams and Giardina (1993) provide an interesting discussion of cost-benefit analysis as approached internationally; they include examples from the areas of health and transportation. Layard and Glaister (1994) review methods and problems in cost studies using cases in the environmental, health, and transportation fields. Scott and Sechrest (1992) discuss cost studies from Chen's theory-driven approach. Skaburskis (1987) discusses the ethics and problems of using cost-benefit analysis in studying rapid transit decisions.

ANALYSIS OF QUANTITATIVE INFORMATION

Evaluations involve processing mountains of information that, if not organized in a form that permits meaningful interpretation, is often worthless or, worse, misleading. The aim of *data analysis* is to reduce and synthesize information—to "make sense" out of it—and to allow inferences about populations. When considering alternative methods for data analysis or interpretation, the evaluator should ask herself these questions:

1. What methods of data analysis and interpretation are appropriate for the *questions* I am trying to answer, the *information* that I plan to collect, and the *method* I will use to collect information?
2. What methods of data analysis and interpretation are most likely to be *understood* and to be *credible* to the audiences who will receive reports?
3. What is the *measurement scale* of my data, and which statistical methods are appropriate to use to analyze such data?

One major choice in data analysis will be whether to use descriptive or inferential statistics to answer the question of interest. Before moving immediately into high-powered inferential techniques, the evaluator should spend much time exploring the data that have been collected using descriptive statistics and graphics. Always know your data thoroughly before moving to summarize with scores or comparisons. What are the central tendencies with each item? What are the frequencies or, for continuous data, the shape of the distribution? Who are the "outliers"? What is the spread of the distribution? Are the respondents very homogeneous or quite different in their responses? Which options were selected more than anticipated? Which were selected less? In addition to looking at overall trends, spend some time analyzing the responses of subgroups. Do younger respondents differ from older ones? Do those with families differ from single respondents? Are there differences by geographic region? By where or when services are received? By the nature of service delivered?

Many things can be discovered (including errors in data collection, coding, or entry) by carefully exploring the data. More than once, an evaluator has been asked to help an agency with a complex statistical problem, only to discover that the in-house data analyst, concerned about being "sophisticated," has failed to use adequate descriptive methods to learn about the information she has. Our goal is not to impress with complexity but to convey information that will help the stakeholder know more about the program. Patton (1987b) encourages involving the stakeholder in data analysis at this beginning stage. Meeting with the client or important stakeholders to review results item-by-item can demystify the data-analysis stage and actively involve the user. The evaluator can learn the types of information that are of most interest to the client or different stakeholders and the most effective ways of presenting that information. Working with the client or group, the evaluator will learn new questions and issues that the data analysis can address. Many important questions of concern to stakeholders can be answered with descriptive, rather than inferential, statistics.

For questions concerned with causality or relationships, inferential statistics are appropriate. Here, the evaluator should select the method that matches the scale of data collected and make sure the data meet the assumptions of the statistic. Chi-square and other nonparametric methods can be useful for examining relationships between ordinal and nominal variables. ANOVA and t-tests can be used to examine relationships between nominal and interval or ratio variables. Finally, multiple-regression methods and their extensions can be useful in exploring relationships among variables or in exploring the independent effects of many variables on one dependent variable.

Easily read texts on quantitative data-analysis methods have been prepared by Jaeger (1983) and Giventer (1996). Brinkerhoff, Brethower, Hluchyj, and Nowakowski (1983) have provided a succinct summary of data-analysis techniques that are frequently employed in evaluation.

In using inferential statistics, the evaluator should remember to caution clients that statistics do not establish causality but simply demonstrate relationships. Statistics, logic, and design must all be used synergistically to establish cause-and-effect relationships. Another common error is to confuse statistical significance with practical significance. Finding that a particular program produces statistically significant reductions in drug use by students only means that the finding is not likely to be a fluke. That is, the difference between the compared scores of the two groups is real. The reductions may or may not be *managerially* significant; perhaps the reductions are great enough to warrant continuation of the program, perhaps not.

Statistical significance is influenced by many factors, not the least of which is the sample size. The more observations or measurements included in the analysis, the more likely it is that differences not due to chance will be found. The more critical question is whether these differences are sufficiently large to be meaningful for program decisions. Effect sizes are frequently used to enhance significance testing and convey more about the practical significance of the difference. (See Chapter 14 for a more extended discussion of effect size.) Standards developed during the planning stage can be helpful in determining the programmatic significance of the findings. Such determination is a judgment and should rarely be made by the evaluator alone. The client and other stakeholders who know what they want from the program are often in a better position to determine practical significance of the findings. See Lipsey (1990) for more information on determining practical significance.

CASE STUDY APPLICATION

January 15. I'm beat tonight, having spent all day working on methods for collecting the data we agreed to collect for the Radnor evaluation. Thinking is tiring work.

But the day was productive. I was able to think through the design a little more carefully. While our purpose is generally causal—to demonstrate the effect of the humanities curriculum—an experimental design is not feasible. The program is already going for the year. Too bad, because some of those board members probably would have responded well to randomly assigning some students to the humanities program and others to a traditional program. The teachers would have objected initially, I suspect, but if I could have had a chance to persuade them that this is the best way to show the advantages of their program *and* that the students taking the traditional approach could take the humanities curriculum next semester, I think it could have worked. But time is a problem! So, a quasi-experimental design is my best solution. An interrupted time-series design is out—there are no existing data on the issues we're concerned with. I'll have to compare the program with performance in some similar schools. The nonequivalent comparison group design will have to do.

Many of the evaluation questions concerning the content of the curriculum, the instructional methods used, and community attitudes are descriptive. A cross-sectional design will be appropriate for these. I'm mainly interested in an overall picture of the adequacy of the content and methods and the flavor of the community opinion. I will want to examine how community opinions of the program differ among some of the important constituencies to determine who's most supportive of the program and who objects the most.

Author Comments.   Many people underestimate the feasibility of experimental designs. In this case, time is a problem. But, given the importance of the issue and the controversy surrounding it, many audiences might have been willing to accept a short-term, one-semester random assignment of students to the options to permit a more fair comparison than the nonequivalent comparison group design will allow. In a small town like this, any schools used as a comparison are bound to have significant differences. In all likelihood the school adopting the humanities program has administrators, faculty, students, and parents who are more interested in the humanities than a school that has not adopted such a program. This interest could influence other parts of their curricula and make their students' skills in this area better than those of students in the comparison school even without the program!

But, as with most evaluation studies, most of the questions of interest did not call for a complicated causal design. I've found that the vast majority of questions stakeholders want answered are descriptive: What was the program like? Was it implemented as planned? What changes were made? What did participants think of it? What does the public or other stakeholders think of the program? Policy makers might argue that while the majority of questions evaluations respond to are descriptive, the *most important* ones are causal. And, depending on the decision, that might be the case. For summative decisions about ending, continuing, or expanding programs, one of the most important criteria is certainly whether the program has the intended effect. However, politicians and administrators are not immune to public opinion. If all governmental decisions were based on whether programs achieved their intended effects, we would undoubtedly have quite different programs. Unfortunately, those making the decisions are faced with a public who wants decisions based on effectiveness *and* decisions based on what they want. Since influential supporters can be found for every existing government program, results based on causality are often secondary concerns.

For *formative* decisions, however, which many evaluations serve, descriptive questions are often the most useful. Answers to such questions help the program managers and staff decide what to change and how to change it.

> *January 15 (continued).* I've also given some thought to sampling strategies. For questions concerning student outcomes, the population is too small to draw a sample of students in the Radnor humanities program. We'll have to collect data from each student for questions concerning learning. However, purposive sampling can be used for student interviews and observations in the classroom. We don't have the budget to conduct interviews with every student. I'd rather select some students to interview, based on teacher recommendations and scores on some of the achievement measures. I'd like to interview some students who are doing well in the program and others who are doing poorly, to get their reactions. In sampling classroom sessions to observe, since I have a concern with whether the instructional methods being used are sufficiently interactive and not simply didactic lectures, I would like to select sessions that should have much interaction and instruction geared to high-level objectives. I'll look over the curriculum and also ask the external reviewers to recommend some sessions they think should be most interactive.
>
> Probability sampling for the community surveys to parents and other stakeholders will work; however, I think stratified sampling will be necessary. Since the number

of community leaders is small, relative to the other groups, I will probably survey all of them and analyze their data separately. However, I want to stratify for the other groups to make sure I get a sufficient number of questionnaires back from parents with students in the program and the minority population. Radnor has relatively small Asian and Hispanic populations. Since the curriculum deals with diversity, I want to make sure I get enough returns from these groups to accurately determine their responses. I considered using the student directory as the sampling frame so I can use surnames to identify Hispanic and Asian students and their parents. However, reflecting on how diverse our culture has become, I realized this wouldn't work—not all people have last names that match their ethnicity. Perhaps I'll just ask the school to give me names of all children and their ethnic identification. Schools are required to keep that. I'll use the enrollment lists for the humanities classes to identify the parents with students enrolled.

Author Comments.   When groups are small, such as with the students enrolled in the program, it is best to collect information from all of them. However, when data collection becomes costly, as with interviews or observations, sampling is necessary. Some might think that random sampling should always be used. However, random sampling for interviews and observations could result in data that are representative but not very useful for the intended purpose. The purpose in the interviews and observations is to explore strengths and weaknesses of the curricula. Thus, selecting students who have done well and poorly will help in exploring these issues. One must be careful not to assume that these results can be generalized to all students.

Some might think that selecting those sessions *most likely* to have interactive activities is biasing the study. It certainly won't give us a representative sample. However, that's not our purpose. Some sessions don't lend themselves to interaction. Our concern is whether those sessions *most likely to have interaction* really do have it. We could waste a lot of time observing a random sample of sessions and finding nothing interactive going on in most. Instead, we can observe those which are most likely to include such activities. If they don't, it's unlikely that others will.

January 15 (continued). I have some ideas for how I want to collect data. Certainly, we will need to construct parent questionnaires. Since I don't have the staff in Radnor to conduct phone interviews and I *do* have the time it takes to wait for mailed surveys with postcards and two distributions to be returned, I will probably go with that method of distribution. Materials sent home by the school will provide a low-cost way of letting parents know a questionnaire is coming. However, I think I will distribute them by regular mail rather than through school folders. Middle school students are notorious for forgetting to share information with their parents! Such distribution could create a quite biased sample!

However, I'm going to hold on the other measures for the time being. Given the nature of the curriculum, qualitative measures will be very important for assessing student learning. A mix of "tests" and "authentic assessment" will be necessary to capture all types of learning and persuade the stakeholders of the curriculum's effect. The interviews and observations of classrooms will require qualitative approaches. Finally, selection of measures should consider all options. Therefore, I'll delay this discussion until the end of the next chapter, where I can demonstrate combining methods.

APPLICATION EXERCISES

1. Recheck your evaluation plan worksheets from Chapter 15. Are there plans that you would like to change, using what you just learned in this chapter? Would you want to add procedures? Approach things a little differently?

2. Develop a chart, listing each of the methods covered in this chapter, and then for each method describe some types of information that might be collected to answer a question of interest in your organization.

3. Find a cost-benefit study in your field. Read it and consider the assumptions made. How were benefits quantified? What costs were considered? Whose perspective was used in the ratio (the client, the public)? Were sensitivity analyses conducted? What types of decision was the study to serve? Would cost-effectiveness analysis have been a more appropriate approach?

4. In small groups, plan and develop a survey to measure attitudes toward your university. First, develop the questions the survey is to answer. (This may be done as a large group before going into small groups or as part of the small-group exercise.) Then, consider the appropriate item types to answer each question. Develop draft items complete with an introduction and instructions. "Pilot-test" your questionnaire on another group and discuss their responses and interpretations. How would you revise your instrument? Was a questionnaire the best way to gain this information? Why or why not?

5. Identify two evaluation questions relevant to your community that could be answered with experimental designs. Why would an experimental design be appropriate? How would it be conducted? Which experimental design would you use? Assuming that you are unable to get permission to use an experimental design, what type of quasi-experimental design would you use and why?

RELEVANT EVALUATION STANDARDS

The evaluation standards we see as relevant to this chapter's content are the following. These standards are described in Chapter 20 on page 442.

U3 —Information Scope and Selection	A4 —Defensible Information Sources
F1 —Practical Procedures	A5 —Valid Information
F2 —Political Viability	A6 —Reliable Information
P3 —Rights of Human Subjects	A7 —Systematic Information
P4 —Human Interactions	A8 —Analysis of Quantitative
P5 —Complete and Fair Assessment	Information
A3 —Described Purposes and Procedures	A10—Justified Conclusions

SUGGESTED READINGS

Aday, L. A. (1989). *Designing and conducting health surveys: A comprehensive guide.* San Francisco: Jossey-Bass.

Cook, T. D., & Campbell, D. T. (1979). *Quasi-experimentation: Design and analysis issues for field settings.* Chicago: Rand McNally.

Demaline, R., & Quinn, W. (1979). *Hints for planning and conducting a survey and a bibliography of survey methods.* Kalamazoo: Western Michigan University Evaluation Center.

Dillman, D. A. (1978). *Mail and telephone surveys: The Total Design Method.* New York: Wiley.

Fowler, F. J., Jr. (1984). *Survey research methods.* Beverly Hills, CA: Sage.

Frey, J. H. (1983). *Survey research by telephone.* Beverly Hills, CA: Sage.

Gall, M. D., Borg, W. R., & Gall, J. P. (1996). *Educational research: An introduction* (6th ed.). White Plains, NY: Longman.

Henry, G. (1990). *Practical sampling.* Newbury Park, CA: Sage.

Jaeger, R. M. (1983). *Statistics: A spectator sport.* Beverly Hills, CA: Sage.

Levin, H. M. (1983). *Cost-effectiveness: A primer.* Beverly Hills, CA: Sage.

Lipsey, M. W. (1990). *Design sensitivity: Statistical power for experimental research.* Newbury Park, CA: Sage.

McKillip, J. (1987). *Needs analysis: Tools for the human services and education.* Newbury Park, CA: Sage.

Mitchell, R. (1992). *Testing for learning.* New York: Free Press.

O'Sullivan, E., & Rassel, G. R. (1995). *Research methods for public administrators* (2nd ed.). White Plains, NY: Longman.

Worthen, B., Borg, W. R., & White, K. R. (1993). *Measurement and evaluation in the schools.* White Plains, NY: Longman.

chapter **18**

Collecting, Analyzing, and Interpreting Qualitative Information

ORIENTING QUESTIONS

1. What do qualitative methods add to evaluation?
2. When is a case study appropriate? What does it tell us?
3. What is the difference between structured and unstructured observations? How important are one's initial observations of a program?
4. What is the role of a moderator in a focus group?
5. Can we synthesize the results obtained from qualitative and quantitative methods?
6. How does analysis differ from interpretation? Who should be involved in interpreting results?

Few, if any, evaluation studies would be complete without including some qualitative information. Descriptive studies, monitoring studies, and needs assessments rely heavily on qualitative information. Outcome studies are not complete without a description of the program being evaluated. Too many "black-box" evaluations that failed to describe the program, assuming it was delivered as planned, have lacked credibility and proven useless. Further, few outcomes can be studied comprehensively with only quantitative methods.

As noted in Chapter 17, we believe the evaluator should select the method that is most appropriate for answering the evaluation question at hand. He should consider the best source for the information: Who knows the most about the issue to be measured? Having chosen the source, he should select the most appropriate method for collecting information from that source: Which method will result in the highest quality information, involve the least bias and intrusion, and be both feasible and cost-effective to collect?

In many cases, more than one method will be needed. If so, the methods should be selected to reflect different biases or provide information in a different manner. Shotland and Mark (1987) note that many evaluators fail to achieve their purpose in using multiple methods because they use methods with the same biases. Two different paper-and-pencil tests are likely to be insufficient in breadth to substantially add to the validity of the data collection. Similarly, individual interviews and focus groups with the same individuals over a short time frame would provide some useful additional information, but the methods fail to differ sufficiently to constitute a complete assessment of the phenomenon of interest. The evaluator also fails to achieve his purpose with multiple methods if he uses those methods to measure different phenomena. Shotland and Mark caution that another common mistake in using multiple methods is using different methods to examine different questions. If the methods are not intended to address the same phenomenon, the evaluator is then simply using single measures of each phenomenon in the study and has not made use of multiple measures for establishing validity.

In addition to pairing qualitative and quantitative methods to obtain a more complete picture of the phenomenon of interest, evaluators will often use qualitative and quantitative methods in sequence so that the results of each data-collection effort provides information for the next. For example, program observations may be used to identify some concerns about the process of program implementation. If many programs are offered across a wide geographic area, surveys of participants and/or program deliverers at different sites might then be conducted to see if the respondents report similar occurrences at their sites. Finally, focus groups might be held at a few selected sites to get feedback from participants on these program implementation issues. What changes would they recommend? Why? What did they think of the changes that did occur? How do they think they would react to a program like one delivered at another site? The acceptability of final solutions generated by the focus group to the population as a whole could be assessed with a final brief survey to all participants. Such a pairing of qualitative and quantitative methods makes good use of each type. Representativeness is facilitated with the survey that is mailed to all participants, but it fails to provide information of sufficient depth. The focus groups permit probing and reaction to new ideas generated by the group but risk bias through the participation of those more interested or disturbed by the program or those with more free time to spend in a focus group.

As with the previous chapter on collecting evaluative information, this chapter will only introduce readers to concepts and provide references for further exploration. Again, entire books are written on each method introduced here. Our purpose is to make you aware of the methods available, their purposes, advantages and disadvantages, and how they might be used. The additional references will provide much more extensive information on the actual development and use of each method.

One last comment: Some methods are not so easily classified into qualitative and quantitative categories. Paper-and-pencil multiple-choice tests, Likert-scale attitudinal measures, or close-ended questionnaires are clearly quantitative measures. Results are typically presented numerically, using scores, percentiles, and descriptive statistics. Focus groups and unstructured interviews are clearly qualitative measures. Their results do not lend themselves to simple numerical reductions but rather to narrative interpretations. But what about telephone interviews? Open-ended responses to surveys? Content analyses? Program observations?

For example, observations in which a research assistant makes use of a stopwatch to measure students' "time on task" (whether students are attending to the educational task occurring) and observes designated individual students at particular time intervals in a highly structured manner hardly qualifies as a qualitative measure. Such data collection is not designed to record more than what is specifically instructed and reported in a numerical fashion. Yet many observations are purely qualitative, using narrative description of critical incidents, themes, or whatever focus the study might provide.

Similarly, while some telephone interviews are designed as unstructured efforts to build on the remarks of the respondent, *most* telephone interviews conducted by firms that specialize in this method are quite structured. Interviewers would no more be permitted to deviate from prespecified questions (other than through a carefully prepared probe) than would the research assistant observing the students' time on task. Thus, observations and telephone interviews must be explored further to determine just how they are used and whether they might be considered qualitative or quantitative in approach.

We have included telephone interviews in the previous chapter because we believe most telephone interviews are relatively structured. Though they permit more probing and clarification than a questionnaire, to persuade a typical respondent to participate the interview must be rather short and, hence, structured. Little opportunity is presented for establishing rapport either through body language or verbally. In contrast, *most* observations are qualitative and thus are treated here. Forms may be used to structure the observations to a degree, but the evaluator is always alert for additional information. The purpose of most observations in evaluation, as with the site visit, is to obtain a feel for the program; a sense for the lives, needs, and desires of participants; a view of the services delivered; and a perception of the overall environment and context. Regardless of the placement of the method in these two chapters, each method represents a valid way of learning more about a program, policy, or product and should be part of the evaluator's overall inventory of methods.

METHODS FOR COLLECTING QUALITATIVE INFORMATION

The **case study** is a frequently used approach to gathering qualitative information about a program. The focus of a case study is on the case itself. Such an approach may be particularly appropriate in evaluation when there is a need to provide in-depth information about the *unit,* or case, at hand, not so much to generalize to a larger population. With case studies, generalizability is obtained not through scientific external validity but through logical, "naturalistic generalization." The goal is to develop "thick descriptions," or a *thorough, complete* understanding of the case, to help others understand and judge its worth and the context within which it has operated (Lincoln & Guba, 1985). As noted in Chapter 10, Stake (1978) has been a strong advocate of case studies. He emphasizes the unit itself, or the case, and notes that the case can be as broad or narrow as one desires to define it: "The case need not be a person or enterprise. It can be whatever 'bounded system' (to use Louis Smith's term) is of interest. An institution, a program, a responsibility, a collection, or a population can be the case" (p. 7).

Unlike quantitative designs, a case study does not have a clearly delineated method. In fact, some writers focus on the case study more as a form for reporting results (Guba & Lincoln, 1981; Lincoln & Guba, 1985). Others describe it more in terms of what it is to accomplish and how it might be characterized. Thus, Stake (1978) writes that

> most case studies feature: descriptions that are complex, holistic and involving a myriad of not highly isolated variables; data that are likely to be gathered at least partly by personalistic observation; and a writing style that is informal, perhaps narrative, possibly with verbatim quotation, illustration, and even allusion and metaphor. Comparisons are implicit rather than explicit. Themes and hypotheses may be important, but they remain subordinate to the understanding of the case. (p. 7).

More recently, Stake (1994) has written: "Perhaps the simplest rule for method in qualitative case work is this: Place the best brains available into the thick of what is going on" (p. 242). He writes that the person doing the case study should make use of his observational and reflective skills to obtain a greater understanding of the case at hand.

Case studies typically make use of many methods of data collection but lean most heavily toward qualitative methods such as observations, interviews, and the study of documents. The design is descriptive but, unlike the cross-sectional study or the time-series study, there is an emphasis on depth of description. To achieve that depth, many methods must be used. The methods may be selected or adapted as the evaluator achieves a better understanding of the case. That is, the design is *responsive* to the case and the circumstances at hand. It is adaptive and continues to adapt until the evaluator believes he has a good understanding of the case.

The writing of the results becomes an integral part of the case study, as results should be conveyed in a way that "focuses the reader's attention and illuminates meanings" (Guba & Lincoln, 1981, p. 376). Guba and Lincoln describe the case study as "holistic and lifelike. It presents a picture credible to the actual participants in a setting, and it can easily be cast into the 'natural language' of the involved audiences" (p. 376). Such case studies can lead to greater utilization because the report is both more easily understood and more compelling than the typical report. For more information on case studies, see Stake (1981, 1994) and Yin (1984). Lincoln and Guba (1985) discuss the case reporting format, and Hebert (1986) provides an example of a case study in the qualitative style.

Existing Documents and Records

The evaluator's first consideration for sources and methods of data collection should be existing information, or documents and records. **Documents** include personal or agency records that have not been prepared specifically for research or investigation. **Records**, in contrast, are official documents or data summaries prepared for use by others (Lincoln & Guba, 1985). Records are typically collected more carefully because they are intended for use by others. On the other hand, documents may show the perspectives of various individuals or agencies. Guba and Lincoln (1981) also distinguish between their uses. Records are typically used statistically for tracking, such as employment records or data from the U.S. Census Bureau. Documents, because of their nature, require more qualitative methods for analysis, such as content analysis of a therapist's notes or of the minutes of a town meeting.

We recommend considering existing information for three reasons: (1) Using existing information can be considerably more cost-effective than original data collection; (2) such information is *nonreactive* or not changed by the act of collecting or analyzing it, while other methods of collecting information typically affect the respondent and may bias the response; (3) far too much information is already collected and not used sufficiently. In our excitement to evaluate a program, we often neglect to explore what information may already exist to answer some of the evaluation questions.

Remember that while such information can be cheaper, the cost will not be worth the savings if the information is not valid for the purposes of the *current* evaluation study. Unlike data collected originally for the study, this information has been collected for other purposes. These purposes may or may not match those of your evaluation. (See Chapter 15 for a discussion of existing data and records that can be useful to evaluators.)

Observations

Observations are essential for almost all evaluations. At minimum, such methods include site visits to observe the program in operation and use of one's observational skills to note contextual issues in any interactions with stakeholders. Observation can be used more extensively to learn more about the program operations and outcomes, participants' reactions and behaviors, interactions and relationships among stakeholders, and other factors vital to the study.

Observation methods for collecting evaluation information may be quantitative or qualitative, structured or unstructured, depending on the approach that best suits the evaluation. We have chosen to discuss both types of observations together here for convenience.

Unstructured Observations.   Unstructured methods are especially useful during the initial phase of the evaluation. The evaluator should make use of his observational skills to note critical features during his first interactions with stakeholders. Jorgensen (1989) writes

> the basic goal of these largely unfocused initial observations is to become increasingly familiar with the insiders' world so as to refine and focus subsequent observation and data collection. It is extremely important that you record these observations as soon as possible and with the greatest possible detail because never again will you experience the setting as so utterly unfamiliar. (p. 82)

Unstructured observations remain useful throughout the evaluation if the evaluator is alert to the opportunities. Every meeting is an opportunity to observe stakeholders in action, to note their concerns and needs and their methods of interacting with others. If permitted, informal observations of the program being evaluated should occur frequently. Such observations give the evaluator a vital picture of what others, (e.g., clients, staff, administrators) are experiencing, as well as the physical environment itself. Each member of the evaluation staff should be required to observe the program at least once. Those most involved should observe frequently to note changes and gain a greater understanding of the program itself. Too many evaluations occur in which the evaluator only has a brief glimpse of the program in action or, worse, a paper description of the delivery model.

Structured Observations.   Structured and quantitative observation methods become useful when the evaluator desires to observe specific behaviors or characteristics. What specific behaviors or characteristics might be observed? For many public-sector programs, critical characteristics may be *physical* in nature: park maintenance, road quality, playground facilities, arrangement of classrooms, library collections, physical conditions and/or density of program facilities, and so forth. Other observations can involve *interactions* between program staff and participants: teacher-student interactions, teacher-administrator interactions, student-administrator interactions, physician-nurse-patient interactions, social worker-client interactions, therapist-client interactions, receptionist-client interactions, and so on. Of course, many such observations may be confidential or require informed consent, and the evaluator should be aware of any ethical violations that observations may produce.

A final category of interactions involves participants' *behaviors.* What behaviors might one observe? Imagine a school-based conflict resolution program designed to reduce playground conflicts. Observations of playground behaviors provide an excellent method for observing outcomes. Imagine a new city recycling program in which there is question about the level of interest and nature of participation. The frequency of participation and the amount and type of refuse recycled can be easily observed. While many programs focus on outcomes that are difficult to observe (e.g., self-esteem, drug abuse prevention), many others lead to outcomes that can be observed. This is particularly the case when the target audience or program participants are congregated in the same public area (e.g., hospitals, schools, prisons, parks, or roads).

Structured methods of observation typically involve using checklists or forms for recording observations. These are often called **observation schedules**. Simon and Boyer (1974) have collected observation instruments that may be used to study educational processes. As with attitude measurement, the procedures required for developing good observation checklists and schedules can be complex and costly. Whenever quantitative observation data are needed, we advise reviewing the literature for existing measures and adapting an instrument that already exists. Other concerns in structured observation involve training observers, ensuring interrater reliability among observers, selecting sites and participants for observation, and avoiding reactivity, or changes in the participants, due to their being observed. Structured observations can also be a costly endeavor if a large number of observations are desired or if participants are geographically dispersed. Sechrest (1985) also discusses instances in which structured observations can be useful and describes the means for using these methods in the field. He notes examples of evaluations of the performance of emergency medical technicians and the implementation of programs for developmentally disabled persons. For more information on structured evaluations, see Greiner (1994).

Qualitative Observation Methods.   Qualitative observation depends less on available instruments and more on the evaluator or observer. Checklists may be used, but typically they are less structured. Denzin (1978) has distinguished between the following arrangements for qualitative observation: the complete participant, the participant as observer, the observer as participant, and the complete observer. These terms convey in words the extent to which the observer may become, or desire to become, involved in the program itself. The observer-as-participant role is frequently taken in anthropological research but may also be used in evaluating, for example, adult learning programs in which the evaluator needs to experience the curriculum as a participant. An observer in a training program may often choose the observer-as-participant role to minimize the other trainees' reactivity to the observation. The assistant in a focus group, however, is typically the complete observer, making no effort to blend in with the group but instead focusing on carefully observing the verbal and nonverbal cues of the participants. One should carefully consider which role will be most appropriate for collecting the desired information. In circumstances where those being observed will be inhibited or otherwise influenced by the observation, more participative roles can be desirable. Such participation can also help the observer appreciate the position of those being observed.

Guba and Lincoln (1981) make the following recommendations regarding the means for organizing and recording one's observations:

1. *Running notes:* a pad used to jot down observations as they occur
2. *Field experience log or diary:* detailed notes on a particular concern, such as how an administrator organizes a staff meeting or how a staff member delivers a service to a client
3. *Notes on themes:* detailed notes on a particular theme, such as how teachers work together to revise a curriculum or how participants respond to a particular part of the program
4. *Chronologs:* a step-by-step running account over a unit of time (e.g., a day)
5. *Context maps:* a diagram of the contextual layout in which observations take place
6. *Taxonomies or category systems:* predetermined categories for which instances are sought in open-ended fashion
7. *Schedules:* specified place and time, duration of observation, and method of notation for the observation
8. *Sociometrics:* relational diagrams indicating social intercourse
9. *Panels:* periodic observations of the same persons over time
10. *Debriefing questionnaires:* questionnaires completed by the observers, not the subjects of the observation
11. *Unobtrusive methods:* use of concealed devices or indirect measures

The stages of qualitative observation often include (1) thorough preparation through reading or "chatting" with informants; (2) articulating the purpose of your observations; (3) looking *at* (not *for*) what occurs; (4) listening; (5) asking questions (*after* listening and observing); (6) assimilating and synthesizing information; (7) checking working hypotheses; and (8) triangulating, confirming, and cross-checking.

Let us focus for a moment on what we mean by these steps. First, as with all evaluation, you should talk with stakeholders and read documents and records to learn more about what you might observe and why. What do they hope to learn from the evaluation? Next, articulate the purposes of your observation. These purposes might be relatively unstructured: to see what the classroom looks like, to watch what patients or clients do during the program. Or they may be more pointed: to see how reception staff greet visitors and clients and to determine whether their methods seem welcoming. In any case, with the purpose articulated, one can then observe. Point 3 is important: Look *at* (not *for*) what occurs. Observe the clients or receptionists. What happens? Who speaks first? What does he say? What is his tone? Does he make eye contact? What other body language occurs? What is the response? Take detailed notes of what you are seeing. Don't look *for* "friendliness" or "warmth." Look *at* the people interacting and note your observations. Listen to what occurs. If you are surprised by what you observe, ask questions of either those observed or those knowledgeable about their actions. Assimilate and synthesize what you've learned. Look at your notes across many observations. What trends do you observe? How do these match your expectations? Those of others? Finally, seek other data to confirm or cross-check your hypotheses. To **triangulate**, seek data from sources with different biases; for example, interview those interacting to determine their interpretations. For more information on unstructured observation methods, see Jorgensen (1989) and Adler and Adler (1994).

Site Visits.   A special category of observation methods is the **site visit**, frequently used to evaluate a program in its natural setting. This method is a primary example of the application of the expertise-oriented evaluation approach discussed in Chapter 8. Regulatory agencies, such as accrediting bodies, frequently use site visits as a method for evaluation or a requirement for funding. Though most frequently used for summative evaluation or for educational or financial audits, site visits can also be very useful for formative evaluation (Worthen, O'Sullivan, & White, in press). Stake (1970) has noted that site visits can be criticized because site-visit observers are frequently shown only the best sides of programs, yet he sees site visits as an eminent method of evaluation because they make use of "the most sensitive instruments available—experienced and insightful [people]" (p. 193). He recommends using training of site visitors and careful planning of observations to strengthen the process.

Inadequate preparation limits the usefulness of many site visits. Completing the following activities will greatly enhance the success of the visit itself:

1. *Identifying specific information needed*
2. *Developing evaluation questions* to be posed during on-site interviews
3. *Developing on-site instruments* (e.g., interview forms, checklists, or rating scales)
4. *Selection of on-site visitor(s)*
5. *Previsit communications and arrangements*
6. *Conducting the on-site evaluation visit,* considering
   a. Amount of time to be spent on site
   b. An initial on-site team meeting, prior to meeting with on-site administrators or staff, to reemphasize the purpose, procedures, and expected products of the visit
   c. An initial briefing by site administrator(s) and/or staff to orient the team to specific nuances or idiosyncratic information not readily available in previsit materials
   d. Efficient interviewing and observation by splitting the team up to cover more activities or interviewees, having the entire team together only for key events or interviews with key personnel
   e. Interspersed team meetings to debrief and share impressions, and a final team formulation of their overall evaluation
   f. Exit interview with the site administrator(s) and, if appropriate, site staff

7. *Writing, disseminating, and using the final report of the on-site evaluation*

For a comprehensive, detailed discussion of on-site evaluation guidelines and procedures, see Worthen and others (in press). That text includes examples of on-site evaluation interview forms, rating scales, previsit information forms, team-training materials, and sample exit and final reports.

Interviews

A major difference between paper-and-pencil surveys and collecting data via personal interviews is that interviews allow clarification and probing. Interviews are useful when the purpose of data collection is less clear, greater depth in information is needed, or audiences might be unreceptive to a written survey. Personal interviews require more time than questionnaires and can therefore cost more if many people are to be interviewed. However, they can provide a wealth of information. Exploratory interviews with a variety of stakeholders during the beginning of the evaluation process can be invaluable in shedding light on stakeholders' perspectives and concerns. Later in the evaluation, more structured interviews designed to answer particular evaluation questions can be used with individuals from the same group.

However, good interviewing *is* a skill. Do not assume that inexperienced assistants, simply supplied with questions, will be capable of conducting good interviews. Extensive training with practice sessions and "scripts" for answering common questions is essential preparation.

When using an interview as a method for information collection, consider the evaluation question you are trying to answer. What information do you need to answer the question? Can it be obtained most successfully in a structured or an unstructured interview? The more specific the information desired, the more structured the interview should be. If the information needed is more general, less structured questions are appropriate. An unstructured interview would be appropriate for answering the following types of evaluation question: "What do respondents think of the program? Do they think they have changed as a result of participating? If so, how?" In contrast, a more structured interview might be used to answer the evaluation question "What type of assistance do parents give their children on homework?" Structured questions for this evaluation might include "How often during the last month did you help your child with his homework? When was the last occasion? Could you describe the help you gave then? What prompted you to give this assistance?"

Having considered the degree of structure required for the interview, the evaluator should then develop the questions to be asked, making sure that they cover the spectrum required to address the evaluation question of interest.

The evaluator should also plan the introduction of the interview. The introduction is designed to develop rapport with the respondent and explain the general procedures. Be sure to introduce yourself, explain the purpose and length of the interview, discuss confidentiality and anonymity, and try to put the respondent at ease. If a tape recorder is being used, explain the purpose. (Evaluators differ in their views regarding the use of tape recorders. Some feel it frees the interviewer to make more eye contact and establish rapport while still documenting the dialogue; others prefer handwriting notes, feeling that the presence of the tape recorder can inhibit discussion by intimidating the interviewee.) Give the interviewee time to ask you any questions. Use eye contact and body language to establish rapport. Typically, interviewees are most responsive to people they perceive to be like them. Attempt to match interviewers to critical characteristics of interviewees (e.g., gender, race and ethnicity, age). Interviewers' dress and demeanor, while remaining professional, should match that of the respondent.

One of the most common errors of an interviewer is to talk too much. After rapport is successfully established, the interviewer is present primarily to listen and encourage responses. A good interviewer should become comfortable with pauses and not feel compelled to fill gaps hurriedly. Respondents often pause to convey difficult or sensitive information. If the interviewer rushes in to break the silence, such information is lost. Similarly, the interviewer should be prepared with prompts and phrases to continue discussion. "Tell me more about that," "That's interesting," "Oh, yes," or even "Uh-huh" show you are listening and encourage the interviewee to continue without the interviewer's determining the direction. Reflecting on the last statement of the interviewee can be helpful in encouraging the respondent to continue, though the interviewer should be careful not to add his own interpretation but only to reflect the comments of the respondent: "You say you were concerned when you couldn't understand the instructions?"

Following are some helpful hints for developing interview questions:

1. Keep the language pitched to the level of the respondent. Questions posed to specialists can rely on the terminology with which they are familiar. But questions posed to the general public *must* use language more commonly understood.
2. Try to choose words that have the same meaning for everyone. If two groups lack a common language (or dialect), questions for each group should differ.
3. Avoid long questions. They often become ambiguous and confusing.
4. Do not assume that your respondent possesses factual or firsthand information. A mother may be able to report what books her child reads, but only the child can tell you accurately how much he enjoys reading.
5. Establish the frame of reference you have in mind. For example, if interested in reader preferences in magazines, don't ask, "*How many* magazines do you read?" Ask, "*Which* magazines do you read?"
6. Either suggest all possible answers to a question or don't suggest any. Don't ask, "Do you think the husband should be the primary wage

earner in the family?" Ask, "Who do you think should be the primary wage earner, the husband or the wife? Or do you think it matters?"

7. Protect your respondent's ego. Don't ask, "Do you know the name of the Chief Justice of the Supreme Court?" Ask, "Do you happen to know the name of the Chief Justice of the Supreme Court?"

8. If you are after unpleasant orientations, give your respondent a chance to express his positive feelings first, so that he is not put in an unfavorable light. First ask, "What do you like about X?" Then ask, "What don't you like about X?" or "What bothers you about X?"

9. Decide whether you need a direct question, an indirect question, or a combination. An example of a direct question is "Do you ever steal on the job?" An indirect question might be "Do you know of anyone's ever stealing on the job?" A combination might be "Do you know of anyone's ever stealing on the job?" followed by "Have you ever taken anything while on the job?"

Guba and Lincoln (1981) provide an excellent discussion of interviews and guidelines for interviewers in naturalistic evaluations that has broad applicability. Other sources include Fontana and Frey (1994) and Rubin and Rubin (1995), both of whom review interviewing from a qualitative perspective. Babbie (1992) discusses interviewing methods from a more traditional research perspective. These sources are highly recommended for evaluators who plan on using interviews to collect information.

Focus Groups

Focus groups have become an increasingly popular method of obtaining qualitative information from a group of individuals. Focus groups are like an interview in that they involve face-to-face interaction; however, they build on the group process. A skilled focus group facilitator will make use of ideas or issues raised by participants in the focus group to obtain reactions from others in the group. Discussion in focus groups is not always interviewer to interviewee, but often dialogue continues among focus group participants themselves. Thus, the interview is very much a *group* process.

Focus group techniques emerged from the field of marketing, where such techniques were used to gauge potential customers' reactions to new products and to learn more about customers' needs and wants in regard to the product. Focus group methods have now been adapted to be used in many different settings where there is a need to obtain information on how individuals react to either planned or existing services, policies, or procedures and to learn more about the needs and circumstances of these individuals. Thus, in addition to reacting to issues, focus group participants may suggest new methods or describe circumstances that pose problems with old ones. Focus groups are particularly useful in needs assessments and monitoring studies and for formative evaluations. Participants can tell you their reactions to what they have experienced or what

you are considering, what changes would make it better for them, and circumstances in their lives or beliefs or attitudes that they have that might facilitate
or hinder the success of your program. Focus groups can help confirm or
disconfirm program theories during the planning stages or programs. They can
raise new, novel ideas based on participants' *own* experiences. Focus groups can
also be useful in discovering more about program outcomes, such as how
participants have used what they gained, what barriers they faced, or what
changes they would make in the program.

Focus groups typically consist of 8 to 12 individuals who are relatively homogeneous but unknown to each other. Some focus group specialists
(e.g., Krueger, 1994) recommend smaller groups of 5 to 7 for complex topics.
Homogeneity is desired to facilitate group interaction; noticeable differences in
education, income, prestige, authority, or other characteristics can result in
hostility or withdrawal by those who are lower on those dimensions. Where
input from different groups is desired, it is best to compose focus groups for
each distinct group.

The role of the leader is to facilitate discussion through posing initial and
periodic questions and by moderating the responses of more vocal members and
encouraging responses of quieter members. The leader may also ask questions
to clarify ambiguities or get reactions from other group members. Leading an
effective focus group requires a good knowledge of group dynamics and good
interviewing skills. As focus groups have become popular, many group leaders
have emerged who lack sufficient training. Moderating a focus group successfully
is more difficult than it may seem, and we encourage new users to seek training
and observe others before using the method.

One frequent error in focus groups is to rely too extensively on short,
forced-choice questions (e.g., yes or no) or to have group members respond by
raising hands. The focus group then really becomes a structured group interview,
not a focus group, because it has lost the key focus group characteristics of
member interaction, openness, and exploration.

Employees, or someone known to the focus group participants, should *never*
be used as a focus group leader. The position or attitudes of the leader can
influence such discussions in undesirable ways. In selecting a moderator, consider
how that moderator's characteristics and background can enhance or impede
group discussion. It can be desirable, though not always necessary, to match
moderator and group characteristics on critical demographic variables such as
age, gender, race, or ethnicity. At a minimum, the moderator should have a good
knowledge of the culture or lifestyles of the participants in order to understand
and interpret comments and effectively facilitate interactions.

Groups are typically led by one moderator, who has an assistant to observe
body language and interactions and to assist in interpreting the results. Sessions are
usually tape-recorded, and participants are typically reimbursed for their time.
Sessions generally last one and a half to two hours. The environment for the
focus group is important. Generally, refreshments are available and the room is
arranged to be conducive to conversation. Results are interpreted through

analysis of tape transcripts or replaying tape segments. These results may be analyzed by themes or responses to questions posed by the moderator.

Though focus groups have been used widely in many fields, Flores and Alonso (1995) note that qualitative evaluators in education have neglected focus groups for interviews and observations. They show how focus groups can be used successfully to obtain teachers' perspectives on change. Vaughn, Schumm, and Sinagub (1996) have developed a useful guide to conducting focus groups in educational and psychological settings. They give particular attention to conducting focus groups with children and adolescents. Basch (1987) discusses how focus groups can be used more effectively in the health field. Hoppe, Wells, Morrison, Gillmore, and Wildson (1995) describe ways to use focus groups to discuss sensitive topics with children. For more information on focus groups, see Krueger (1994).

Content Analysis

In reviewing documents, **content analysis** procedures have much to offer. These procedures are used to describe, analyze, and summarize trends observed in written documents, including data collected from focus groups, interviews, and field notes. While the very term "content analysis" correctly denotes that this is a data-analysis technique, it also plays a role in data collection (or at least, "data organization"), especially in its use for organizing and reducing unwieldy qualitative data preparatory to final analysis.

Content analyses of minutes of meetings, publications, newspaper articles, annual reports, and other written documents can provide important clues as to the context of an evaluation. Qualitative content analysis provides summaries of documents. Quantitative content analysis seeks to quantify content objectively, according to explicitly formulated rules and mutually exclusive and exhaustive categories. Historically, content analysis has been quantitative in focus, but Guba and Lincoln (1981) emphasize that "both quantitative and qualitative approaches are now deemed suitable, depending on the questions that need to be answered by the research" (p. 242).

With quantitative content analysis, the content analyst actually counts *coding units* (e.g., words, themes, paragraphs) and places them within categories. The task of the evaluator is to develop a set of categories, select a unit of analysis (sentence, paragraph, chunk of words), and then interpret each unit of analysis assigning appropriate codes. Patton (1987b) notes that categories may be terms expressed by stakeholders themselves or themes identified by the evaluator but reminds us that the categories should serve the purposes of the evaluation. That is, the categories should be designed to answer an evaluation question. Holsti (1969) notes that the most important issue in content analysis is not whether the analysis is qualitative or quantitative (though he favors quantitative) but whether the analysis addresses the right question.

Categories may focus on "what is said" or "how it is said" (Guba & Lincoln, 1981). A sample set of categories (Sanders & Cunningham, 1974) reflecting themes in newspaper articles on sex education is shown in Figure 18.1.

Newspaper:	Date:	Story Source:

– (Negative)	+ (Positive)
Expressions of opposition to sex education	Expressions favoring sex education
Actions in opposition to sex education	Actions in support of sex education
Statements attacking proponents of sex education	Statements supporting proponents of sex education
Statements listing opponents of sex education	Statements listing proponents of sex education
Provisions of alternate plans	Statements opposing alternate plans
Some other plan satisfactory	Authorities insist on current objectives
Miscellaneous–	Miscellaneous+

0 (Neutral)	Other themes
School board to discuss issue	
School board vote to be close	
Possible areas of compromise	
Miscellaneous	

Content totals	Headline	Headline Content
+ _____	Head size _____	(+1,–1, or 0)
– _____	Location on page _____	
0 _____	Length _____	
	Total score and direction _____	

FIGURE 18.1   Sample set of content analysis categories

SOURCE: From "Techniques and Procedures for Formative Evaluation" by J. R. Sanders and D. J. Cunningham, 1974, in G. D. Borich (Ed.), *Evaluating Educational Programs and Products*, Englewood Cliffs, NJ: Educational Technology. Reprinted by permission.

Content analysis has many uses in evaluation. Thematic analyses of board meetings or editorials in professional journals, or word counts on federal policy statements, can help identify and clarify values in an objective way no other source can match. Detailed discussions of content analysis may be found in Holsti (1969), Guba and Lincoln (1981), Miles and Huberman (1984), and Manning and Cullum-Swan (1994).

Unobtrusive Measurements

An unfortunate side effect of many information-collection methods is that subjects alter their behavior when they know information is being collected about or from them. Webb, Campbell, Schwartz, and Sechrest (1966) suggest many ways to get around this reaction, including reliance on the following data sources:

1. *Physical traces:* physical evidence left from some past behavior. Such evidence would include natural erosion (worn carpeting in front of a particular painting in an art museum), natural accretion (deposits of information such as creative work done by past civilizations), controlled erosion measures (such as pre- and postmeasures of shoe wear on children), and controlled accretion measures (such as lightly sealing with glue the pages of a book to detect how many and which pages are read).

2. *Archival records:* the ongoing, continuing records of society, including actuarial records, political and judicial records, government records, and mass media files

3. *Private records:* those not ordinarily left open to the public, including sales records, institutional records, and written documents such as diaries

4. *Contrived observation:* the use of hardware devices for observation (videotapes, audiotapes). When hardware devices are used, they should be a familiar part of the environment, or hidden, if reactivity is to be minimized.

Metfessel and Michael (1967) inventoried alternative ways of unobtrusively collecting information about educational outcomes. Their list of unobtrusive indicators includes attendance records, anecdotal records, appointments, news items, assignments, awards, program changes, citations, disciplinary actions, dropouts, grades, groupings, leisure activities, library cards, PTA participation, and even telephone calls from parents or other interested parties. Observations in other settings may include records of appointments, minutes of meetings, client records, physicians' or direct service workers' notes, newsletters to clients and employees, awards, firings, employee disciplinary actions, records of telephone calls, or computer e-mail records. Many of these, of course, are subject to client privilege or privacy concerns. Such records and documents should only be used with the explicit consent of those involved.

Guba and Lincoln (1981) provide some guidance for identifying unobtrusive measures by distinguishing between *accidental measures* and *systematic measures.* Accidental unobtrusive measures are "measures that one happens upon." (p. 266). The evaluator who is a good observer may note behaviors or phenomena that tell more about the setting. Displays of students' work or other materials in a classroom, physical arrangements of office space, and the like can provide clues as to the environment of the program to be evaluated. Employees' nonverbal behavior at meetings can be analyzed for evidence of program support or relationships with managers. Systematic unobtrusive measures are "those that grow out of the logic of the inquiry itself." To identify such measures, the evaluator considers carefully the nature of the program to be evaluated or the phenomenon to be measured and considers what evidence might be left to illuminate these phenomena. Thus, interest or support for a new piece of playground equipment might be demonstrated by students' use of that equipment, student requests for training or games related to the equipment, wear or repairs to the piece of equipment, and so on. Guba and Lincoln (1981) and Sechrest (1980) argue that to increase our use of unobtrusive measures we need more taxonomies or structures to help in identifying unobtrusive measures.

One word of caution: Unobtrusive measures tend to be unreliable. (For example, is worn-out floor covering in front of a particular art exhibit an indication that it is popular with the masses or that the custodian has a fixation with that artist and sweeps that particular piece of floor at much greater length?) Never base a conclusion on just one measurement. Always triangulate, confirm, and cross-check.

Investigative Journalism

Investigative journalism is a method that has received relatively little attention but is useful in providing a model or metaphor for an approach to evaluation. (Although this might be thought of as an *approach* to evaluation, like those we covered in Chapter 5 to 10, we see it as less developed at this time and therefore more fitting to cover here as a data-collection method). Guba (1981) notes that investigative reporting, which can focus on both *events* and *processes,* requires disclosure of information that may be secret, inaccessible, not easily observed, or hard to discover. Investigative journalism is ostensibly done in the public interest and requires great personal effort on the part of the reporter. It is evident there are a few parallels between program evaluation and investigative reporting.

What can the evaluator learn from investigative journalism? Guba (1981) suggests that evaluators pay heed to these journalistic methods and principles:

1. *Pursuing a variety of sources of information.* Many evaluation studies depend on information from one or a handful of traditional sources. Yet it is clear to the investigative reporter that the most critical information often comes from nontraditional sources. Investigative journalists depend not only on routine information sources but also on tips, repetitive questioning of sources, legwork (getting out and seeing people), insights gained from other investigations, their own observations and experiences, conversations with contradictory sources, and the like. "Truth," for the journalist, evolves through multiple, not limited, sources.

2. *Decision points.* Several times during most inquiry activities, the investigator asks, "Should I continue?" One must be willing to abort a study if it becomes evident that the payoff will not justify the cost of continuing.

3. *The "fast study."* Investigative journalists immerse themselves quickly in the context of their inquiry. Evaluators, too, must learn to

assimilate background information rapidly—to "get smart" and learn the territory early.

4. *Key interviews.* Interviews with key actors in the study should be characterized by (1) preparation—full background briefing; logical, organized questions; and preparation with at least one other interviewer (being sure to define roles and responsibilities); (2) control—ensuring that the interviewer remains in control throughout; and (3) information collection—not only checking existing information but also ferreting out new and elusive details.

5. *Reporting.* Selecting themes, checking accuracy, and arranging follow-up are important tasks for the reporter and evaluator. Like the reporter, the evaluator should ask
   • What is this story about?
   • Who cares?
   • Why will my primary audience care?

6. *Skepticism.* It is often realistic to suspect that people may be selectively providing or even withholding information. The reporter uses this skepticism to his advantage as a motivator for checking additional sources, probing, questioning, and verifying all facts. The evaluator, too, can make his skepticism work to his advantage.

7. *Use of records.* Contrary to popular belief, not all public records are legally open to the public. Not all evaluators know how to locate or access records, though like reporters they need this skill.

8. *Confrontation.* Sometimes it is necessary to take the offensive if information is being withheld. Some techniques used by reporters include
   • Increasing the specificity of questions
   • Showing documentation that supports allegations
   • Demonstrating contradictions as they occur
   • Registering indignation if an interviewee is lying or continues to do so
   • Shifting gears if the confrontation becomes too heated (changing topics or switching to another interviewer)

9. *Dealing with constraints.* Investigators need to recognize and work within certain constraints. Some common constraints in investigative reporting include
   • Resources (time, staff, budget, lost opportunities)
   • Law (libel, slander, censorship, access to data)
   • Attitudes among management (the boss may want to avoid controversy or negative public response)
   • Attitudes among reporters (unwillingness to offend, personal pressures, peer pressure, lack of stamina)
   • Skills (lack of training, experience, ability)
   • Hazards (physical, psychological, legal harassment)
   • Provincialism (lack of trust in work done by others)

10. *Circling, shuffling, and filling.* In order to extend and check information, the investigator may (1) run information obtained from one source past cooperative informants for refutation or confirmation (circling); (2) run information obtained from one source past others who are assumed to be uncooperative, pressing for details, asking what *really* did happen, and then passing new information by other informants (shuffling); or (3) build boundaries around a subject area and then fill in the gaps (filling).

For a comprehensive treatment of the use of investigative journalism in evaluation, the reader is referred to Guba (1981) and Nelson (1982). Smith (1992) broadens Guba's metaphor of the investigative journalism to explore investigative evaluation. His edited volume on the issues of investigative evaluation explores the evaluator as an investigator from several different perspectives.

ANALYSIS OF QUALITATIVE INFORMATION

Wilcox (1982) has noted that the analysis of qualitative data depends on the nature of the data and the conceptual framework employed in the analysis. Methods for qualitative data analysis range from narrative description to quantitative analyses of narrative components, as in content analysis.

Analysis methods for qualitative data usually involve some form of analytic induction. Discussions of specific techniques such as the "key incident" approach (Wilcox, 1982), analysis in the field (Bogdan & Biklen, 1982), and searching for patterns and categories (Guba, 1978; Guba & Lincoln, 1981; Patton, 1990a; Bogdan & Biklen, 1982) have given evaluators direction in processing qualitative information.

The **key incident approach** described by Wilcox (1982) involves analyzing qualitative descriptions of incidents or events that the evaluator identifies as key incidents or concrete examples of an abstract principle. Erickson (1977) describes this approach as follows:

> This involves pulling out from field notes a key incident, linking it to other incidents, phenomena, and theoretical constructs, and writing it up so others can see the generic in the particular, the universal in the concrete, the relation between part and whole. (p. 16)

Wilcox (1982) notes that

> the key incident approach may involve massive leaps of inference over many different kinds of data from different sources, including field notes, documents, elicited texts, demographic information, unstructured interviews, and so on. (p. 462)

The process of "analysis in the field," as described by Bogdan and Biklen (1982), directs the evaluator to spend time each day (some have estimated that one hour of data analysis for each hour of observation is realistic) reviewing field notes, reflecting on what has been learned and what merits further study, writing "observer's comments" into the field notes while experiences are still fresh, and writing short summaries about what is being learned. This continuous data analysis encourages the evaluator to draw tentative conclusions that can then be checked. Evidence supporting conclusions or validating facts can be gathered for use when reports are written.

Searching for patterns and categories is part of the analytic induction that undergirds all qualitative analysis. This search "builds levels of confidence" in the evaluation's ultimate conclusions through these steps:

1. *Exploring and forming impressions,* recorded in field notes
2. *Identifying themes,* recorded in memos or short concept statements
3. *Focusing and concentrating,* using "working hypotheses" as focal points for further observation and documentation. As these working hypotheses are "tested," those that are supported receive further attention, whereas those that are not supported are noted, along with the evidence used to reject them. Meanwhile, the exploring and forming of impressions (step 1 above) continues.
4. *Verification.* Working hypotheses are given the status of tentative conclusions; scenarios and thick, detailed descriptions are developed to make them come alive. These tentative conclusions are then tested for authenticity by the subjects in the study. Confirmation checks and triangulation are used to increase the certainty that these conclusions are accurate. (See page 391 for a description of triangulation.)
5. *Assimilation.* Conclusions are placed in the broader context of what else is known about the object of the evaluation.

Whereas much qualitative data analysis is conducted while the study is in progress, some analyses are delayed until after the evaluator leaves the field. Patton (1990a) outlines several steps for processing the voluminous amount of qualitative data most evaluations will generate, including the following:

1. Make sure it is all there.
2. Make copies for safe storage, for writing on, and for cutting and pasting.
3. Organize the data into topics and files. Bogdan and Biklen (1982), suggest an excellent set of coding categories for this purpose. Lincoln and Guba (1985) and Huberman and Miles (1994) also discuss category systems for organizing qualitative data.
4. Look for causes, consequences, and relationships.
5. Validate the findings of the analysis, using
   a. Examinations of rival explanations;
   b. Reviews of negative cases (exceptions);

    c. Triangulation; reconciling qualitative and quantitative data; comparing multiple qualitative data sources and multiple perspectives from multiple observers;

    d. Design checks (examining distortions due to design decisions);

    e. Evaluator effects (reviewing distortions due to the evaluator's perspectives or behavior);

    f. Quality of the data;

    g. Reactions to reported data and analyses by stakeholders and subjects; and

    h. Intellectual rigor (justification of conclusions).

Triangulation involves examining the consistency of results from different sources and methods for measuring the same construct. (Picture a triangle: In the center is the amorphous phenomenon we hope to measure or describe. It is bounded by lines on three sides—i.e., measures—and each side illustrates a different facet of the phenomenon. By using all three—or more—measures, each of which has a different strength and source of bias than the others, we are better able to capture the phenomenon itself.) When different methods or information from different sources result in similar findings, this convergence adds to the strength of the results. Where results from different methods and/or sources show differences, further data collection or exploration may be necessary to determine the nature of the difference and, hence, more accurately describe the phenomenon. Greene, Caracelli, and Graham (1989) have found that many studies using triangulation fail to examine differences in results when they occur. Such actions not only defeat the purposes of triangulation but neglect the opportunities such differences present. Exploration of the reasons for different results can provide vital insights and demonstrate subtleties about program operations and effects. Shotland and Mark (1987) discuss some of the means for using triangulation to enhance the interpretation of results and some hazards to avoid.

    For detailed discussions of qualitative data-analysis methods, the reader is referred to Miles and Huberman's (1994) text detailing methods for qualitative data analysis and Williams's (1986) monograph on qualitative methods. Richards and Richards (1994) and Weitzman and Miles (1995) describe some of the new computer methods and software for organizing and analyzing qualitative data. Denzin and Lincoln's (1994) *Handbook of Qualitative Research* provides much useful information in this area.

Components of Interpreting Data Analyses

Data analysis focuses on organizing and reducing information and making logical or statistical inferences; interpretation, on the other hand, attaches meaning to organized information and draws conclusions. Analysis may be thought of as organizing and verifying facts; interpretation as applying values, perspective, and conceptual ability to formulate supportable conclusions.

Interpretation should be characterized by careful, fair, open methods of inquiry. Anyone who claims that the "data speak for themselves" is either naive or a shyster.

Interpretation means judging the object of the evaluation and considering the implications of those judgments. Recall that Stake's (1967) Countenance Model (discussed in Chapter 10) includes in the "judgment matrix" both *standards* and *judgments*. These are part of interpretation, but there is more.

The evaluator's perspective also influences his interpretation of the data. Perspective is a result of experience, of unique views and orientations developed over idiosyncratic life histories, and of a tendency to attend to certain details. Thus, all interpretations, to some extent, are personal and idiosyncratic. Consequently, not only interpretations but the *reasons* behind them should be made explicit.

Conceptual ability can also affect interpretation. Each evaluator looks at the evaluation information, twists it around, discovers nuances, and generates insights—things that others may never have seen without the evaluator's help—in an individual way that affects the outcomes of the evaluation. If evaluation is to serve an educational function, as Cronbach and his associates (1980) claim, results must be interpreted so that audiences know how best to use or consider them.

Guidelines for Interpreting Data Analyses

Useful interpretation methods that have served well include:

1. Determining whether objectives have been achieved
2. Determining whether laws, democratic ideals, regulations, or ethical principles have been violated
3. Determining whether assessed needs have been reduced
4. Determining the value of accomplishments
5. Asking critical reference groups to review the data and to provide their judgments of successes and failures, strengths and weaknesses
6. Comparing results with those reported by similar entities or endeavors
7. Comparing assessed performance levels on critical variables to expectations of performance or standards
8. Interpreting results in light of evaluation procedures that generated them

Interpretation of data analyses is not the sole province of the evaluator. No one is omniscient. Most evaluators have learned that interpreting and summarizing results in isolation is generally an unsound practice. The evaluator brings only one of many pertinent perspectives to bear and, in fact, is sometimes less well prepared to offer insightful interpretations than others who can look at the data through fresh eyes.

One method for bringing multiple perspectives to the interpretation task is to use *stakeholder meetings*. Small groups of five to eight people meet for several hours to discuss their interpretations of printouts, tables, charts, and other information collected and analyzed during the evaluation. Stakeholders can be supplied in advance with the results, along with other pertinent information such as the evaluation plan and the list of questions, criteria, and standards that guided the evaluation; that way, meeting time can be devoted to discussion rather than presentation. At the meeting, findings are systematically reviewed in their entirety, with each participant interpreting each finding. Examples of questions that might be asked include: What does this mean? Is it good, bad, neutral? Consequential or inconsequential? What are the implications? What, if anything, should be done?

Besides contributing his own interpretations, the evaluator serves as transcriber so that all interpretations and the reasons for them can be recorded and included in the evaluation reports. These interpretative sessions not only capture diverse perspectives and original thinking but also frequently disclose values previously undetected. All this contributes to the utility of the evaluation while ensuring that those who should be involved are.

Other methods of interpretation suggested by the Joint Committee on Standards for Educational Evaluation (1981) include the following:

- Having different teams write advocacy reports representing the various perspectives
- Conducting a jury trial or administrative hearing to review evidence concerning the object of the evaluation
- Seeking convergence of opinion about interpretation of results through use of a Delphi study

Some additional useful guidelines suggested by Brinkerhoff, Brethower, Hluchyj, and Nowakowski (1983) for interpreting the results of analysis include the following:

- Seeking confirmation and consistency with other sources of information
- Dealing with contradictory and conflicting evidence, not forcing consensus when none exists
- Not confusing statistical significance with practical significance
- Considering and citing limitations of the analysis

COMBINING QUALITATIVE AND QUANTITATIVE METHODS

Mixed-Method Evaluation Designs

While the research and evaluation designs reviewed in this chapter and in Chapter 17 reflect common qualitative and quantitative approaches, respectively, many evaluations are moving toward mixed-method designs. Greene and others (1989) have proposed a very useful conceptual framework for considering such designs. Their framework is based on their study of 57 evaluations using mixed-method designs in a variety of fields. They identified five distinct *purposes* of mixed-method studies: triangulation, complementarity, development, initiation, and expansion. Triangulation is, of course, the use of mixed methods to measure the same construct and thus increase the validity of results for that construct. However, the delineation of the remaining purposes is most enlightening. Below are their definitions:

> Complementarity seeks elaboration, enhancement, illustration, clarification of the results from one method with the results from the other method.
>
> Development seeks to use the results from one method to help develop or inform the other method, where development is broadly construed to include sampling and implementation, as well as measurement decisions.
>
> Initiation seeks the discovery of paradox and contradiction, new perspectives of frameworks, the recasting of questions or results from one method with questions or results from the other method.
>
> Expansion seeks to extend the breadth and range of inquiry by using different methods for different inquiry components. (Greene et al., 1989, p. 259)

Greene and her colleagues found most studies did not use mixed methods for the purpose of triangulation: "Triangulation in its classic sense is actually quite rare in mixed method practice" (p. 266). Instead, the most common purposes of mixed-method designs were complementarity and expansion. Complementarity differs from triangulation in that the purpose is not so much to increase measurement validity as to shed more light on the meaning and nature of the construct. Triangulation, to be successful, *must* measure the same construct. Complementarity may, purposely, attempt to measure a different facet of the construct, expecting to get somewhat different results but believing that these differences will help us learn more about the object of interest. Greene, Caracelli, and Graham characterize triangulation as "cross-checking"; complementarity, as "overlapping." This construct much better matches the purpose of many evaluation studies using mixed methods. The goal is to learn more about the construct being measured by studying it with different measures, not to add to construct validity.

Mixed-method designs are considered to be used for the purposes of expansion when the goal is to learn more, not just about the single construct but about the program or phenomenon being evaluated as a whole. The expansion studies reviewed by Greene, Caracelli, and Graham tended to use quantitative measures to assess outcomes and qualitative measures to describe program implementation. Greene and her colleagues feel such studies have merit but have not maximized their potential. At least in their sample, most expansion studies failed to synthesize results across the methods or to use the results interactively to inform the evaluation.

Development studies, then, make use of mixed methods *in sequence* to inform the evaluator for the next measurement. Thus, interviews and observations may precede a mailed survey to facilitate questionnaire development. A focus group may follow the questionnaire to provide more depth and insight on issues identified through the questionnaire.

Greene and her colleagues note of initiation studies that "purposeful initiation may well be rare in practice" (p. 268). However, studies that were open to this approach—truly integrating results, searching for questions and paradoxes, using different models and paradigms—often yielded very useful and insightful information. This purpose was the only one that they found lent itself to using different paradigms (positivist and naturalist) as well as mixed methods. The use of different paradigms helped reveal paradoxes and new interpretations.

Green and her colleagues also specify seven characteristics of mixed-method designs: using similar or different methods, measuring the same or different phenomena, employing the same or different paradigms, giving equal or unequal status to the measures used, implementing measures interactively or independently, and scheduling measures sequentially or simultaneously. They use these characteristics to make recommendations for achieving the different purposes of such designs. Thus, they argue certain purposes are best achieved by using specific characteristics. For example, mixed-method designs with *developmental purposes* would, of course, use *sequential timing* of measures and *interactive implementation* of the measures—using each to inform the other. *Expansionist designs* are distinguished by measuring different *phenomena,* for example, program implementation and outcomes. As noted, *initiation designs* are the only type to usefully employ different *paradigms.* To discover new perspectives or contradictions, the evaluator needs to explore more creatively; this exploration is facilitated with the use of different paradigms. The characteristic of *independence* in implementing the different methods is only important in *triangulation designs* where, for purposes of construct validity, one would not want one method influenced by another. The purpose of triangulation designs is to show that different *independent* measures of the *same* phenomenon yield the same results. In contrast, in studies in which *complementarity* is the purpose, *interactive implementation* can be useful as each method helps explain or describe the phenomenon being measured in a different way. Subsequent methods and analyses can build on these results *if* they are used interactively.

The identification of these five purposes for mixed-method designs and the discussion of ways in which designs might vary to serve each purpose is most useful. Such discussions further our understanding of the importance of matching design characteristics with the purpose of the evaluation and confirm that there is no one "perfect" design.

Synthesizing Qualitative and Quantitative Results

One concern when using qualitative and quantitative methods is how to synthesize results from these two different methods. To a degree, the analytical methods suggested above for qualitative methods should be used to synthesize the findings from the different methods. Thus, confirmation checks, triangulation, and weighting of evidence may be used to synthesize. Maxwell, Bashook, and Sandlow (1986) provide an interesting and unusual example of synthesizing quite different types of information (ethnographic and experimental) in their evaluation of medical care evaluation committees in physician education.

There is, however, some disagreement over whether such results from qualitative and quantitative methods can be synthesized. Kidder and Fine (1987) argue that triangulation and synthesis can occur between quantitative and what they call "small q" qualitative measures (e.g., open-ended responses on a question-naire), because the deductive approach to these two methods is likely to be the same. However, they argue that triangulation between quantitative and "big Q" work is much more difficult. Big Q qualitative work is "field work, participant observation, or ethnography; it consists of a continually changing set of questions without a structured design" (p. 59). It is inductive and, as such, different in nature from qualitative research. They write:

> The difference between deductive and inductive research lies not in the percentage of structured and unstructured questions but in how open-ended the research process itself is. Researchers who work deductively gather data to test specific hypotheses, not to generate new hypotheses, and serendipitous findings are considered interesting but unreliable. By contrast, researchers who work inductively continue to generate hypotheses and look for new questions even as they gather data. (p. 60).

Interestingly enough, their description, from the qualitative perspective, of the distinctions between big Q qualitative research and quantitative research parallels the writings of Sechrest and Figueredo (1993) from the quantitative perspective. Sechrest and Figueredo argue that the dichotomy between qualitative and quantitative methods fails to identify the real differences in the paradigms. The distinction between the two, they write, is in purpose: The primary purpose of qualitative research is for exploration; the primary purpose of quantitative research is for confirmation.

Synthesis, or triangulation, across these two types is very difficult because they are serving different purposes. Greene and McClintock (1985) provide an excellent example. They describe their efforts at using the positivist and constructivist paradigms to evaluate an adult community education program. While they found the use of the two different paradigms somewhat helpful for understanding the program, they felt the results of the two efforts were too different to use to enhance validity as in triangulation. They suggest that triangulation is only possible within paradigms.

While many evaluations may combine qualitative and quantitative measures, few would combine the positivist and constructivist approach as Greene and McClintock. Instead, results from the constructivist and positivist paradigms would be more likely to be combined *across* studies. Kidder and Fine (1987) see this as not only the greatest challenge for evaluators but also the greatest opportunity for learning about the program. Trend (1978) provides an excellent example of such synthesis or triangulation. He shows how two evaluations of a low-income housing program, one Qualitative and one quantitative, initially appeared to show very different results. However, further exploration of the differences provided a much more full description of the program. Mark and Shotland (1987) discuss bracketing and complementary purposes, as demonstrated by Greene and McClintock, as other means for synthesizing results from qualitative and quantitative methods.

CASE STUDY APPLICATION

January 20. I've been working several days planning data collection—considering sources and methods. I was able to get several instruments developed, in first-draft form at least. Did review the *Mental Measurements Yearbook* and the social psychology handbook of tests and found some possibly useful tests for humanities knowledge, and ordered specimen sets of those. Picked up a possible instrument for testing critical thinking also. But for the most part, it looks like a do-it-yourself instrument development effort. So far I have completed a first draft of the following:

> Interview schedules for students, teachers, parents, and board members, using the questions I know so far to be important. I'll probably add others suggested by the site-visit team of experts, once they're selected.

> A classroom observation instrument. This is somewhat open-ended. I'm wanting to get a sense for the method of instruction used and how students respond. Dewey Pitcher, my humanities expert, cautioned me that classroom involvement is critical for achieving the kind of goals they have outlined.

> A survey to students with a lot of Likert-scale items to get at some of the attitudinal stuff. I borrowed some of the items from existing attitude measures for adults, but I want to review these with the Radnor staff to make sure these items address their concerns and are appropriate for middle school kids. I've adapted the vocabulary a little, but I'll of course need to pilot-test them with kids this age first. I wonder if I could use one of my son's classrooms for pilot-testing?

> A very rough draft of some criterion-referenced tests, mostly useful, I suspect, as a starting place to work with the Radnor humanities faculty. Even though I pulled the concepts from their materials, I'm not certain my items reflect the concepts they view as important.

> Variations of the community survey questionnaire that I hope will get at a lot of opinions and factual information that might otherwise fall through the cracks. People who dash off casual questions surely fall under the "ignorance is bliss" rubric. By the time I'd torn up my third draft today, I was almost wishing I had never minored in sociology.

We're also going to be able to make use of quite a few existing documents and records. We've decided to compare absenteeism in these classes with those of others as an unobtrusive measure of student interest. We're going to look at student participation in humanities-related extracurricular activities and elective classes— things like enrollments in drama, music, and art electives, participation in clubs, Odyssey of the Mind, Inter-Scholastic League writing competitions, etc. We'll compare Radnor's participation in such events with those of other schools. We can't attribute all differences to the program, but these indicators do reflect the real goal of getting students to have a lifelong interest in the humanities and they will help us get a better picture of the broader effects of the program. We're going to review some teacher products (curriculum revisions, faculty meeting minutes) to get a sense of the evolution of the program. And, finally, it looks like we'll be able to examine some student products that occur throughout the program, a major paper and a humanities "creation" of the students' choice—art, music, an essay or fictional piece—to actually describe the outcomes occurring among students. We'll have our site visitors look at these things as well as do some detailed content analysis ourselves.

Author Comments.   Were I actually to conduct this evaluation, I would turn quickly to the *Mental Measurements Yearbook* volumes or other collections that may contain well-developed instruments for some of the paper-and-pencil measures—which are quite a few in this study. I would also contact the authors of some of the published evaluation studies in this area to inquire about instruments they had used. Even though I am never too optimistic about finding just the right instrument, I suspect useful instruments on variables such as critical thinking, writing and language arts, and attitudes toward different cultural groups and ethnicity could be located in these sources.

Even if one did not find usable instruments, there is a high probability of finding useful strategies and formats for asking questions that will make instrument design an easier task.

Where no instruments exist—and I suspect that would be the case for most of the specific content of the humanities curriculum—homemade (do not misread that as *carelessly* made) cognitive measures would need to be fashioned. How to construct those with an eye to validity and other technical considerations is another day's tale. Suffice it to say here that I would work closely with the humanities faculty and members of the Humanities Curriculum Review Committee in designing those instruments. That not only ensures relevance but also is an excellent way to build rapport and trust with those whose program is being evaluated. I would also pilot drafts of the resulting criterion-referenced instruments with small samples of students. The strategy for designing affective measures would be similar.

Although knowledge measures are often viewed as the most difficult to construct, the most poorly designed instruments in many evaluations are usually questionnaires or interview schedules. If one traces the professional genealogy of most evaluators, their parentage is frequently found to consist of educational and psychological methodologists. Small wonder that our evaluators seem to have inherited an ancestral sneer toward mailed questionnaire surveys or interview studies. Most educational and psychological methodologists have long misunderstood (or worse, never studied) the data-collection methods and strategies of the sociometrician or the public opinion polls of political scientists. Rather than expand on a pet peeve here, let me simply indicate that the design of good questionnaires and interview schedules is a task that demands every bit as much time and creativity as the design of more traditional cognitive and affective measures.

While the questions of the evaluation lead us to several paper-and-pencil measures, qualitative data collection will be an important part of this study. We need qualitative data—observations of the program itself, interviews with students, the site visit—to help us judge the overall curriculum and make recommendations concerning its strengths and weaknesses. Finally, we need this information to be able to *describe* the program and convey to the board members and members of the public what the program really is. They may not really have a sense for what the program is and may be reacting to political issues and superficial labels. The observations, interviews, and, most important, the student products will help us provide a picture of that. While decision makers want numbers (remember the engineer!), they also want stories. Many scholars in the management field today are talking about how managers learn by stories. They're right! People remember a telling anecdote more than a figure. The qualitative data will be more than an anecdote; it will convey the whole picture of the program.

> *April 20.* Sorry, journal, for the neglect, but these past few months have been "the pits," as my son would say. My heaviest teaching load always comes during winter and spring, so, with the addition of the Radnor contract I took on, this year "my cup runneth over," so to speak.
>
> Anyway, things are nearly back to normal, and I'm catching up. The Radnor evaluation is almost on schedule, and the data-collection effort is nearly completed. The site visit is the only major evaluation activity still ahead, and it appears my idea of having the humanities experts on that team also do the expert review of the humanities curriculum materials will work out well. No hitches in the testing or attitude measurement, and the second follow-up on the mailed questionnaire to of parents and community leaders has boosted the response rate to over 70 percent and still climbing. Guess there is some genuine interest in this program to get that good a response rate (or perhaps those Dillman strategies for increasing response rates really do work!). I'd rather work to get a good response rate than have to fall back on checking nonresponse bias any day.
>
> Anyway, as soon as we get the last data in, we'll be able to start thinking about analysis and reporting. Of course, we're getting a pretty good picture already about opinion data, etc., from the interviews, and we'll soon know what the experts think. But I'll try to keep an open (don't read that as empty) mind until all the data are in and analyzed.

Author Comments.   Most of the information-collection activities I might actually have conducted in an evaluation of this type can be readily inferred from the evaluation plan outlined in Artifact 4 in Chapter 15, but three comments may be helpful.

First, it is important to capitalize on what is known about survey methods if one intends to obtain an adequate response rate to a mailed questionnaire. There exists a body of literature on how to increase response rates (see Worthen & Valcarce, 1985; Dillman, 1978; Dillman & Sangster, 1991, for information and references in this area). In addition, it would be important to know and use appropriate techniques for assessing whether respondents and nonrespondents differ significantly on relevant variables that might bias the results.

Second, little has been said about observation within classrooms, yet I would see that as a pivotal part of the study. Here I would want the humanities specialist(s) to accompany me or perhaps take the lead. The evaluator should be able to get a fairly good feel for the classroom climate, the effectiveness of the instruction, whether the curriculum objectives are being translated into learning activities for students, and how students react to those activities. The humanities expert is needed, however, to get at the more subtle nuances to judge whether what students are learning in the classroom is really the essence of what is important for them to know about the humanities.

Finally, although I may nowhere label it as such, a data-collection effort such as that outlined here is obviously an instance of multiple-method, multiple-source evaluation.

May 4. For once I believe I did something right. Remember all the time I spent last year planning for the analysis of all of the data that I would collect on the Radnor evaluation? Well, it's paying off now. There is nothing more frustrating than to get to the end of a long and expensive data-collection effort only to find that you can't analyze the data in important ways because of the methods used to collect them (e.g., the scale of data is inappropriate for certain analyses, or the categories and methods used for content analyses don't match the evaluation questions). It's usually too late to go back and do it again by the time data analysis is begun. But this time things worked out well.

I've collected both quantitative and qualitative data in this evaluation and thus used a variety of procedures for data analysis. Claire Janson asked how I would be analyzing the data, so I summarized that briefly and sent it off to her today (see Artifact 9).

ARTIFACT 9

Data	Quantitative or Qualitative?	Techniques Used for Analysis
1. Interviews with students, teachers, parents, and board members	1. Qualitative and quantitative	1. Descriptive statistics (means, standard deviations, frequency distributions) were used for the structured, standard questions. A content analysis and summary of response types with their frequencies were done for the qualitative, probing, and follow-up questions.
2. Classroom observations	2. Quantitative and qualitative	2. Percentages, means, and standard deviations were used to convey the proportion of time spent on interactive exercises in each session observed. In addition, I had asked observers to write short, descriptive narratives about what went on in each classroom so that we could get a sense of what it was like to be there. I had two independent readers read these accounts and then list what they

thought were important events or transactions. They then compared their analyses and resolved any differences between them. Both the full descriptions and the readers' analyses will be used in our reports.

3. Survey data on Likert-scale items; data on attitudes toward values and concepts taught in the curriculum	3. Quantitative	3. There is some debate over whether data collected with such scales should be considered interval or ordinal. I consider each item ordinal. Thus, I reported medians and percentages responding to each option on the item-by-item analysis. But, to give some sense of the overall trend, I also calculated overall scores and subscores on a few dimensions identified through factor analysis. I consider these scores "approaching interval," as they include many data points. Thus, I reported means for these. In comparing the scores of students in the program with the comparison group, I used t-tests. I must be a little cautious in reporting these results, as these were homemade measures and more research is needed to validate them. My factor analysis of the instruments revealed that several possible dimensions were present. It was tempting to report summary, summated ratings for each resulting dimension, but without further research on the instruments I was uncertain enough about stability of these dimensions so that I avoided using them in the analysis.
4. Criterion-referenced test results	4. Quantitative	4. I had spent a lot of time pilot-testing the CRT items and was relatively confident that every item correlated highly with total test scores. My internal consistency (KR_{20}) for the test was high. I used the test to collect pre- and posttest data on participating classrooms and the comparison school. I used an analysis of covariance to determine whether the scores of the two groups differed using the pretest scores as the covariate. This helps control for differences between

(continued)

ARTIFACT 9   *(Continued)*

Data	Quantitative or Qualitative?	Techniques Used for Analysis
		the groups—at least on the pretest. I also calculated an effect size to provide some information on the practical significance of the change. Finally, I compared the change and the posttest scores with the standards we had set during the planning stage.
5. Survey questionnaires	5. Qualitative and quantitative	5. For the structured items, I used frequencies and percentages to report responses on each individual question. I also looked at cross tabulations, using chi-square tests for certain demographic variables crossed with the responses for certain questions. A content analysis was conducted of responses to the open-ended items. Percentages of respondents making each type of response were calculated. We also saved some sample responses to illustrate the nature of the comments.
6. Faculty analyses of curriculum; expert reviews of lesson plans and materials (from site visit)	6. Quantitative and qualitative	6. I used a standard analysis form for these analyses and then allowed reviewers to provide open-ended comments as well. Responses to the structured questions were summarized with frequency distributions and with the appropriate measure of central tendency and dispersion for each question (e.g., mode/median/mean, semi-interquartile range/standard deviation). There were so few on-site reviewers that I reported their open-ended comments verbatim in the report of my analyses.

Author Comments.   Several precautions are in order as the raw data from the instruments are prepared for data analysis. With the advent of desktop microcomputers, it is possible to do most of the analyses right in the office. No need exists to remove the raw data from the office, and a strict policy of keeping the data secure is in place. Before any data can be entered into the computer, a coding handbook should be developed and checked by a colleague. After each form has been coded and entered, a printout of the entered data should be prepared and checked for accuracy. (I'm grateful that some computer software will now check the accuracy for you.) As a last safeguard, the numbers on the printouts should be checked to make sure they are reasonable and within the range of possibilities.

There is nothing (well, almost nothing) more embarrassing than to discover that some particular point I am stressing heavily in the report is wrong, attributable to human error in the analysis. My credibility is also at stake, and no evaluator can afford to lose that.

Confidentiality is also a concern at this point, and I need to make sure that the raw data are stored in a secure area. I promised my respondents that their names would never be associated with their responses. Their trust and my professional integrity are at stake here, so I must be careful. The data entered into the computer only had ID numbers associated with the responses—I am safe there. But the raw data are going to be locked in a data-storage cabinet, never to be opened (unless a reanalysis is in order) for several years to come. My rule of thumb is not to discard any raw data from projects for at least three years.

> ***May 10.*** The numbers have been cranked out of the computer and the last qualitative data summary has just been received from my faithful typist. Enough copies have been made of each for me to distribute them to my steering committee (made up of trusted representatives of each stakeholder group) for their review and interpretation. These aren't reports—just data summaries, tables, graphs, and the best of my narratives. And, of course, the site-visit information is missing, because that occurs later this week.
>
> A half-day meeting has been scheduled at the high school for us to go through the results, instrument by instrument, question by question, and to share our reading and interpretation of the preliminary findings. What do they mean to us? What conclusions can we draw? I am doing my homework now, and I am sure each of the stakeholders will also. This step is important to all of us, because it ensures a place for our values to be reflected in the report. So much the better if we all agree on an interpretation. But if we don't, there is a place for multiple interpretations of the same results. This is part of the educational process—where people learn about differing perspectives and expectations. I am really looking forward to this meeting.

APPLICATION EXERCISES

1. Examine your evaluation plan worksheets from Chapter 15. Have you included qualitative methods as appropriate? What additional qualitative methods would you add? Why?

2. Plan an interview to be conducted with fellow students on their reactions to this course. How does it meet their needs? How will they use the information in the future? Design the interview to answer these questions and two others of your own formulation. Develop the questions to ask in the interview. Then, interview individually three other students. What differences do you find in responses? Does your interviewing style change? Improve? How? Is an interview the best way to answer this question? How does it compare to the use of the questionnaire in the previous chapter? Under what circumstances would you use each approach? Both approaches?

3. Consider your place of work. What documents and records exist there that might be useful for evaluation? How are the documents different from the records? What problems might you encounter in accessing either type of information?

4. Find an evaluation study that uses one or more of the evaluation methods reviewed in this chapter. How does the method or methods shed light on the program? What types of questions do the methods answer? Is the approach of the study inductive or deductive (big Q or little q)? Does it integrate quantitative information? If so, how does it synthesize the results?

5. Develop two evaluation questions that would be amenable to using observational methods to answer. What is observed? How would you observe it?

6. Assume you want to learn more about how small, task-oriented work groups operate for your evaluation of the implementation of Total Quality Management (TQM) in your organization. You believe observation is an essential strategy. Discuss how you would plan and make choices regarding the details of your observation. Would you use a log? How would you record your observations? Develop a log to use to observe a *few* behaviors and pilot-test it through observing two meetings at your workplace.

7. Read the Greene, Caracelli, and Graham (1989) article on mixed-method designs to learn more about their conceptual framework. Use their framework to critique your own evaluation plan as developed in exercise 1 and the study you reviewed in exercise 4. What is the primary purpose of your study? Of the one you critiqued? Do the characteristics of your design match Greene, Caracelli, and Graham's recommendations for designs serving that purpose? What changes would they recommend?

RELEVANT EVALUATION STANDARDS

The evaluation standards we see as relevant to this chapter's content are the following. These standards are described in Chapter 20 on page 442.

U3 —Information Scope and Selection	A3 —Described Purposes and Procedures
F1 —Practical Procedures	A4 —Defensible Information Sources
F2 —Political Viability	A5 —Valid Information
F3 —Cost Effectiveness	A6 —Reliable Information
P3 —Rights of Human Subjects	A7 —Systematic Information
P4 —Human Interaction	A9 —Analysis of Qualitative Information
P5 —Complete and Fair Assessment	A10—Justified Conclusions

SUGGESTED READINGS

Denzin, N. K., & Lincoln, Y. S. (Eds.). (1994). *Handbook of qualitative research.* Thousand Oaks, CA: Sage.

Douglas, J. D. (1985). *Creative interviewing.* Beverly Hills, CA: Sage.

Greene, J. C., Caracelli, V. J., & Graham, W. F. (1989). Toward a conceptual framework for mixed-method evaluation designs. *Educational Evaluation and Policy Analysis, 11,* 255-274.

Guba, E. G., & Lincoln, Y. S. (1981). *Effective evaluation.* San Francisco: Jossey-Bass.

Krueger, R. A. (1994). *Focus groups* (2nd ed.). Thousand Oaks, CA: Sage.

Lincoln, Y. S., & Guba, E. G. (1985). *Naturalistic inquiry*. Beverly Hills, CA: Sage.

Miles, M. B., & Huberman, A. M. (1984). *Qualitative data analysis: A sourcebook of new methods*. Newbury Park, CA: Sage.

Patton, M. Q. (1987). *How to use qualitative methods in evaluation.* Newbury Park, CA: Sage.

Tesch, R. (1990). *Qualitative research: Analysis types and software tools.* New York: Falmer Press.

Yin, R. K. (1984). *Case study research.* Beverly Hills, CA: Sage.

chapter 19

Reporting and Using Evaluation Information

ORIENTING QUESTIONS

1. What considerations are important in tailoring an evaluation report to audience needs?
2. What components should be included in an evaluation report? Why is each of them important?
3. If someone asked you how to make an evaluation report effective, what suggestions would you give?
4. How can you present an oral evaluation report so that it will have substantial impact on your audience?
5. What factors have been found to influence the use of evaluation information?

In the prior two chapters we have discussed the collection, analysis, and interpretation of evaluation information. Obviously, these activities are not ends in themselves but terribly important means to making evaluation information useful. It seems obvious that such information is not likely to be used effectively unless it has been communicated effectively. Yet reporting is too often the step to which many evaluators give the least thought. That is distressing to many evaluation audiences; for example, Newman and Brown (1996) cite their earlier research that found that educational administrators and teachers perceive inadequate reporting as a pervasive problem in program evaluation.

In this chapter we address the following topics: clarifying reporting purposes; timing reports for maximum effectiveness; tailoring reports to meet the needs of various audiences; shaping content; presenting information effectively;

protecting clients' and participants' rights and sensitivities; avoiding common reporting failures; and understanding factors that influence the use of evaluation reports.

PURPOSES OF EVALUATION REPORTS

We noted in Chapter 1 that evaluation (and evaluators) can play many different roles, and the information produced can be put to very different uses. We noted, for example, that formative evaluation information is typically used by those wanting to improve a program they are developing or operating, whereas summative evaluation information is typically used by funders and potential consumers, as well as program staff, to certify a program's utility.

The purpose of an evaluation report is directly linked to the use intended for the evaluation. If the evaluation is formative, its overall purpose is to improve the program, and the report should inform program staff early about how the program is functioning and what changes must be made to improve it. If the role of the evaluation is summative, the report should provide information and judgments about the mature program's value to those who (1) may wish to adopt it, (2) will determine resource allocation for its continuation, or (3) have a right to know about the program for other reasons.

Given that the purpose of an evaluation report follows naturally from the role the evaluation plays, it is apparent that evaluation reports can serve many purposes. Patton (1986), Cousins and Leithwood (1986), and King (1988) have discussed the range of ways evaluation findings can be used. As should be apparent from our discussion in Chapter 16, evaluation reports may often serve political or public relations purposes. Brinkerhoff, Brethower, Hluchyj, and Nowakowski (1983) also underscored this point, listing—in addition to decision making—nine other possible purposes served by evaluation reports:

- To demonstrate accountability
- To convince
- To educate
- To explore and investigate
- To document
- To involve
- To gain support
- To promote understanding
- To promote public relations

Indeed, evaluation reports serve many purposes. Central to all of them, however, is that of "delivering the message"—informing the appropriate audience(s) about the findings and conclusions resulting from the collection, analysis, and interpretation of evaluation information.

IDENTIFYING AUDIENCES FOR EVALUATION REPORTS

In Chapter 12 we discussed the importance of identifying the multiple audiences for an evaluation and suggested procedures for how to do so. An evaluation report obviously cannot be well targeted without clear definition of its audience(s) and the types of questions that audience is likely to raise about findings. Writing an evaluation report before defining the audience is like firing a gun blindfolded, then hurrying to draw the bull's-eye in the path of the speeding bullet. As Lee and Holley (1978) note, "Identify your audience" may be an obvious, overworked platitude, but unfortunately it is often an overlooked step. They cite some common mistakes that have particular relevance for evaluation reports.

> Most evaluations have many audiences. Not identifying all of them is a common mistake. An ignored audience can on occasion get pretty testy and introduce a lot of undesired commotion into the situation. More typically, an audience who needs certain information but never gets it, will make its decisions in ignorance of some perhaps vital information.
> . . .
> Another mistake you can make in identifying your audience is to identify too broad or too narrow an audience. An example of this would be for an evaluator to think a parent committee is the evaluation audience, when the actual audience is the committee chairperson. (She is the respected opinion leader of the group and always determines the action the committee will take on any issue.) Therefore, the majority of the evaluator's dissemination efforts toward the committee should be directed at informing and persuading the chairperson of the validity and implications of the evaluation information. (p. 2)

TAILORING EVALUATION REPORTS TO THEIR AUDIENCE(S)

Different audiences have different informational needs. Knowledge of the values held by those who receive information from the evaluator can help her to shape communications effectively. We suggest that an *audience analysis* should be completed for all pertinent stakeholders for the evaluation. Such an audience analysis would involve determining what information that particular audience should be receiving or is interested in receiving and the best channels and procedures to transmit such information.

For example, when an evaluator completes an evaluation, her methodologically oriented colleagues will be interested in a complete, detailed report of the data-collection procedures, analysis techniques, and the like. Not so for the typical policy maker, manager, client, or public interest group. Neither school superintendents, parole officers, corporate trainers, nor immunization staff will be interested in wading through descriptions of an evaluation's methodology.

These audiences do not share the evaluator's grasp of technical details, her interest in confirmability of naturalistic methods, or her concern over the appropriate choice of an error term in a randomized blocks design. The evaluator will have to tailor reports for these groups so that they depend on nontechnical language and avoid overuse of tabular data presentation. Yet she still needs to satisfy those who would not view her study as credible without knowing all of its technical aspects. Thus, ideally an evaluation might end up with one omnibus technical evaluation report that self-consciously includes all the details and one or more nontechnical evaluation reports aimed at important audience(s). In preparing an evaluation report, the evaluator should consider what type of evidence her audiences will find most compelling, as well as the particular medium, format, and style they are likely to appreciate.

Tailoring Report Content to the Evaluation's Audience(s)

Because of their diverse backgrounds, interests, preferences, and motivations, those who receive and use evaluation reports look for different things. The evaluator who neglects to identify her audiences' needs and preferences will generally find that audiences respond by neglecting her evaluation reports.

In addition to including the specific content important to each audience, the evaluator must also account for differences in the ways audiences interpret and accept evaluation reports. One group may find inferences drawn from certain information credible and useful, whereas another group may scoff at the same conclusions (no matter how "scientifically" defensible). In evaluating a school program, testimonials of students and teachers may be the most persuasive information possible for some audiences, whereas others would insist on statistical summaries of student test performance. The evaluator must also take into account the criteria various audiences will use to make judgments and what standards they will employ to determine the success or failure of that which is evaluated. Evaluation reports must present results in a believable way.

Evaluators can learn from the research of Weiss and Bucuvalas (1980), who state that evaluation reports are most likely to be heard and used by policy makers if they meet two criteria: those of truth value and utility value for the recipient. *Truth value* refers to the technical quality of the study and to whether the findings correspond to policy makers' previous understanding and experience with how the world works (expectations). *Utility value* refers to the extent to which the study provides explicit and practical direction on matters the policy makers can do something about and challenges the status quo (with new formulations and approaches).

Tailoring Report Format, Style, and Language to the Evaluation Audience(s)

Evaluation reports are often thought of as written documents. But slide-tape presentations, oral reports, e-mail broadsides sent via a list server, or a variety of other forms can also be effective. Good evaluations seldom depend solely on the printed word. Ripley (1985) found that audiences who received evaluation information only in a written report were less likely to agree with the evaluator's conclusions and recommendations than were those who only received the information in a nonwritten form. An important challenge for the evaluator is to present the report in the medium and format that will both appeal to and convince the evaluation's audience(s).

Whatever the form of the report, it is also important to tailor the language and level of sophistication so that evaluation findings can be clearly understood. The evaluator must decide whether the report should be general or specific, technical or nontechnical. Cousins and Leithwood (1986) found that a combination of oral and written reports, delivered in nontechnical language, had a higher impact on the evaluation's audience(s) and led to their being more aware of the evaluation and having greater appreciation of its results.

In tailoring the presentation of findings to audience needs, the evaluator might choose from many different media and modes of display.

- Written reports
- Photo essays
- Audiotape reports
- Slide-tape presentations
- Film or videotape reports
- Multimedia presentations
- Dialogues/testimonies
- Hearings or mock trials
- Product displays
- Simulations
- Scenarios
- Portrayals
- Case studies
- Graphs and charts
- Test score summaries
- Questions/answers

E-mail Reports

The advent of e-mail and the mushrooming use of the Internet has added an entirely new dimension to evaluation reporting. The obvious advantages of e-mail include its potential for instant and frequent communication between individuals or among members of a group networked by a common list server. Its capacity for ongoing dialogues and its flexibility make it a prime medium not only for routine evaluation reporting, especially interim reports and preliminary drafts of final reports, but also for atypical reporting. For example, evaluators can send preliminary findings and conclusions to the client(s) in bite-size segments, asking for their prompt reactions. Clients can thus be involved in shaping the report, incrementally, while also enhancing the probability that evaluation results will be used. Much more could be said about the great potential for electronic messaging for evaluation reporting, but e-mail is doubt-lessly so well-known to today's students that it would be superfluous. You will likely conceive of innovative uses of e-mail in evaluation reporting in ways we had never dreamed of.

Audiences Can Help Tailor Reports to Fit Their Needs

Patton (1986) points out that evaluation data are used more if the evaluator discusses and negotiates the format, style, and organization of evaluation reports with primary users. Brinkerhoff and his colleagues (1983) suggest some ways audiences might be involved in influencing the evaluation reports: (1) suggesting dates on which they need information, (2) stating in advance what information would be of interest, (3) requesting specific kinds of recommendations, and (4) suggesting displays and graphs they would find useful. It is beyond the scope of this book to discuss specifics of all the alternative reporting schedules, types, and formats the evaluator might use, but we will deal in the following sections with the issue of timing of reports and the two most common types of reports: written and oral.

TIMING OF EVALUATION REPORTS

As purposes and audiences for evaluation reports vary, so obviously will the timing of those reports. Formative evaluation reports designed to inform program administrators of needed improvements in a developing pilot program obviously cannot be delivered after the program has been completed (although that might be appropriate for a summative evaluation report to the program's sponsors or regulatory agency). An evaluation report that is limited in scope and perhaps even in rough draft form, but presented prior to relevant decisions, is preferable to a polished, comprehensive report that is delivered after those decisions have been made. Even informal verbal briefings that serve an early warning function are preferable to formal but tardy reports. Timeliness is critical in evaluation.

The scheduling of evaluation findings must be guided in a general way by the role of the study. It is obvious, for example, that early reporting will be more customary in a formative evaluation than in a summative study. But it would be an error to conclude that summative reporting is restricted to formal, written reports. Indeed, too much formality may well lessen the likelihood that evalua-tion findings will be used, for an evaluation's primary audience often will not take the time to study a report. Higher-level administrators and policy makers often hear evaluation findings only from underlings or others who have read the report and distilled from it the particular message they prefer. The evaluator who wishes her message to be heard by managers has to rely largely on informal interim reports, using "nonprint" strategies such as these:

- Being around and available to provide information that managers request
- Talking to those trusted people on whom the manager relies
- Using examples, stories, and anecdotes to make succinct, memorable points
- Talking often, but briefly, and in the audience's language

These suggestions are compatible with Cousins and Leithwood's (1986) report that use of evaluation results is enhanced by ongoing communication and/or close geographical proximity between evaluator and decision maker.

Scheduled Interim Reports.   Throughout the planning and implementation of the program that is evaluated, it is often appropriate to schedule a report of whatever evaluation information is available at that time. For example, we spoke in Chapter 15 of evaluation "milestones"; an interim evaluation report may well coincide with (or represent) each of these milestones (e.g., completion or acceptance of the evaluation plan and/or data-collection instruments, a report of results obtained at the conclusion of each exploratory test, a report of a pilot test or field test of a treatment's implementation, or the end-of-year report). Interim reports may also coincide with natural milestones in whatever is being evaluated (e.g., completion of each successive draft of a traffic safety manual, or student performance at the end of each semester in a particular university program). In addition, interim reports may be scheduled at regular time intervals (monthly, semiannually, annually) or to precede or coincide with major events for which the evaluation information is particularly relevant (e.g., scheduled funding decisions about the evaluation object; scheduled meetings of review committees, governing boards, or regulatory bodies; or scheduled legislative sessions).

Unscheduled Interim Reports.   The need for interim evaluation reports cannot always be seen in advance. No matter how carefully interim reports have been scheduled, there will be additional times when available evaluation information should be shared. In a formative evaluation, for example, the evaluator may discover a major problem or impediment, such as the fact that video monitors used in an experimental program designed to train federal meat inspectors are too small for trainees beyond the third row to see the critical indicators of possible contamination. It would be a gross disservice to withhold that information until the next *scheduled* interim report, which might be weeks away, and then deliver the not-too-surprising message that a majority of the new generation of meat inspectors did not seem to be learning much from the experimental program that would serve the cause of public safety. Helpful evaluators will deliver many unscheduled interim reports, as the information is needed, whenever unexpected events or results pop up. For this reason, we propose that the formative evaluator maintain some form of "hot line" to key managers and policy makers so that even informal evaluation results can be transmitted as soon as the evaluator is sufficiently certain of her data. Of course, unscheduled sharing of evaluation information is not limited to formative evaluation; as was noted earlier, the summative evaluator who wishes to see her results used by managers learns to "be around" to share the emerging results of the evaluation informally and frequently.

Final Reports.   Final reports are so familiar as to require no further comment here except to note that (1) they may be incremental (i.e., a preliminary final report released for review and reaction by stakeholders, followed by a later *final* report) and (2) they need not necessarily be written, depending on the desires of the client. Since most clients *do* still request a written final report, however, we turn our attention to that topic.

IMPORTANT INGREDIENTS IN A GOOD WRITTEN EVALUATION REPORT

No one best outline or suggested table of contents fits all written evaluation reports. Evaluation roles, objects, and contexts are simply too diverse to permit that. Each evaluation contains idiosyncracies peculiar to itself, and reports must be tailored to reflect such uniqueness.

Yet there are some important items that should be included in almost every written evaluation (at least every formal, final evaluation report, and interim reports as appropriate). These items are the core of most good written evaluation reports.

We believe that one must worry much more about the form of formal reports intended for external audiences. We see the following outline as applicable in other situations as well, however, and offer it as a heuristic checklist evaluators might consider as they prepare any written evaluation report.

In our judgment, a written, comprehensive, technical evaluation report will typically contain the sections listed in the following "generic" table of contents:

I. Executive summary
II. Introduction to the report
   A. Purpose of the evaluation
   B. Audiences for the evaluation report
   C. Limitations of the evaluation and explanation of disclaimers (if any)
   D. Overview of report contents
III. Focus of the evaluation
   A. Description of the evaluation object
   B. Evaluative questions or objectives used to focus the study
   C. Information needed to complete the evaluation
IV. Brief overview of evaluation plan and procedures
V. Presentation of evaluation results
   A. Summary of evaluation findings
   B. Interpretation of evaluation findings

VI. Conclusions and recommendations
    A. Criteria and standards used to judge evaluation object
    B. Judgments about evaluation object (strengths and weaknesses)
    C. Recommendations
VII. Minority reports or rejoinders (if any)
VIII. Appendices
    A. Description of evaluation plan/design, instruments, and data analysis and interpretation
    B. Detailed tabulations or analyses of quantitative data, and transcripts or summaries of qualitative data
    C. Other information, as necessary

A brief discussion of each of these major sections and their contents follows.

Executive Summary

One feature of many evaluation reports that makes them so formidable is their organization, which often requires that the busy reader ferret out from a compulsively detailed report why and how the study was conducted and what important information it yielded. Sometimes a brief summary of essential information is wedged somewhere between the presentation of the findings and the appendices, but often readers are left to sift out the most valuable nuggets of information for themselves.

Most evaluation audiences do not have (or will not take) the time or energy necessary to read a thick report laden with tabular information or narrative details. It makes good sense, therefore, to provide a brief executive summary in one of the following forms.

Executive Summary within a Report.   For most evaluation studies, an executive summary might best be included within the report itself, preferably right up front where it is the first thing the busy administrator sees when the report is opened. We also propose that the executive summary be printed on a different color paper to draw attention to it. This summary should usually be somewhere between two and six pages in length, depending on the scope and complexity of the evaluation. In addition to a very brief description of the study's purpose, and a very brief word about how data were obtained (e.g., "Data were collected with questionnaires mailed to plant workers and a focus-group interview with plant managers"), the summary should contain the most important findings, judgments, and recommendations, perhaps organized in a simple question-and-answer format. The summary should also contain references directing the reader to further information on salient points. If the evaluation report is large and interest in it broad, then it is sometimes more economical to distribute a *separately bound executive summary* similar in all other respects to that described previously.

Executive Abstract.   With a large evaluation audience, it may be necessary to condense the executive summary to a one- or two-page abstract that contains only the major findings and recommendations without any supporting documentation. Such abstracts are often useful in communicating evaluation results to large legislative bodies, parents, citizens at large, community leaders, members of professional associations, and the like.

In one statewide evaluation of a controversial program conducted by one of the authors, three interrelated written evaluation reports were prepared: (1) a large, detailed technical report containing most of the information called for in the earlier outline; (2) a medium-size summary of major interpretations and judgments drawn from the data; and (3) a brief executive summary of the study procedures, findings, and conclusions. Availability of these three reports was broadly announced in the newspapers and on television. Readership was estimated by the number of people who requested a copy or checked one out in the several repositories in which they were made available. Nearly 400 individuals read the executive summary, 40 read the midsize interpretive report, and only one person ever even requested the complete report (and he was an expert methodologist hired by opponents of the evaluation to see if he could find fault with it). As these results show, shorter reports will often be most widely disseminated.

Introduction to the Report

Despite its prominent placement in the report, the executive summary is only a brief abstract, not an introduction. An adequate introduction will set the stage for the remainder of the report by outlining the basic purpose(s) of the evaluation and the audiences the report is intended to serve. For example, is the evaluation intended to provide information to legislative budget analysts who will determine future funding of a statewide domestic violence program, or is it to document the performance of Mid-City's new, state-supported family violence prevention program in a true field test? Is the evaluation audience the state legislature, the administrators and staff operating the state-supported Mid-City program, or both?

One good way to ensure that a report will be relevant is to describe thoroughly the rationale for the evaluation. The rationale should address such questions as: Why was the evaluation conducted? What is the evaluation intended to accomplish? What questions was it intended to answer? Why was the evaluation conducted the way it was? Once this information is provided, audiences can determine whether the report is relevant by asking how well each question is answered.

The introduction is also one logical place to caution the reader about limitations that affect the collection, analysis, or interpretation of information. Such limitations should be openly disclosed here (or in a later section dealing with evaluation procedures). Similarly, disclaimers are sometimes placed at the beginning of a report (e.g., in the preface or on the title page) to clarify what

- Presenting strengths first generally helps those responsible for the evaluation object to accept the weaknesses listed thereafter.

The discussion of strengths and limitations must be sufficiently complete to allow the audience(s) to see the rationale and judgments on which later recommendations are based.

Another useful format familiar to planners in corporate and higher education settings is the SWOT format (strengths, weaknesses, opportunities, and threats). Although we strongly prefer the inclusion of recommendations, there are times when they might be appropriately omitted. In an adversary-oriented evaluation hearing, for instance, it may be best to use all the evaluation's resources to present the best cases possible, but leave the "jury" to draw the final conclusions and make recommendations. Even here, however, each team could add recommendations they viewed as logical, allowing the jury to sift out the pros and cons. But for most evaluations, recommendations are a key responsibility of the evaluator.

This does not necessarily mean, however, that the evaluator's recommendations should automatically be adopted. Evaluators may be better at identifying how well things are working than they are at recommending how necessary corrections should be made, suggesting that evaluator and client should work together to design corrective action. The client and other audiences may have more confidence in coauthored recommendations.

Minority Reports or Rejoinders

Sometimes, under circumstances discussed in a later section, it may be important to include a section in which those who disagree with the evaluator's judgments, conclusions, or recommendations are provided space to share their distaff views. Or, if one member of an evaluation team disagrees with the majority view, it seems sensible to insert any rebuttals or "minority reports" as a last section.

Appendices

Supporting appendices (bound within the report or as a separate volume) are the place where one should present any information needed to help the reader understand such things as what (if any) sampling procedures were used, how the information was collected to ensure its accuracy, what specific statistical or narrative analysis procedure was used, and why. In short, this is where the evaluator provides the methodological and technical information needed not only by primary audiences but also by fellow evaluators who will decide whether the conduct of the study was adequate to make its results believable. The evaluator cannot forget that fellow evaluators keenly interested in methodological and technical adequacy will be perusing those reports. It is wise to remember Campbell's (1984) insistence on "having available (along with the data available for reanalysis) a full academic analysis for cross-examination by our applied social science colleagues" (p. 41). The appendix is the best place for such detailed descriptions of evaluation procedures, detailed data tabulations or analyses, observation logs, complete transcripts of important interviews, and other information that is relevant but too detailed to present in the body of the report. Appendices might also include the actual data-collection instruments and any other information (e.g., boundary maps of sampling units in a community survey) deemed of interest and importance to the audiences but inappropriately detailed and/or too extensive for inclusion in the body of the report. Appropriate use of appendices will make the report itself much more streamlined and eminently more readable.

SUGGESTIONS FOR PRESENTING INFORMATION IN WRITTEN EVALUATION REPORTS

Written evaluation reports are nearly as varied as those who write them. But the great majority share a common characteristic: They make tedious and tiresome reading. Indeed, their variety seems limited only by the number of ways that can be found to make written information boring. Many deserve Mark Twain's waggish description of a particular book: "chloroform in print." One sometimes wonders whether such dreadful dullness reflects a purposeful design to discourage readers.

Not that all evaluation reports are awful. Now and then one appears that is both interesting and informative, both enlightening and entertaining, both comprehensive and captivating. But these, like other gems, are rare. In this and the following section we suggest several considerations to help make the evaluator's written presentation effective, interesting, and fair.

Accuracy, Balance, and Fairness

It goes without saying that evaluation reports should not be unfair, imbalanced, or inaccurate. Yet truth is elusive, and even the most scrupulous evaluator must struggle to see that carefully collected and analyzed information is not later distorted, intentionally or unintentionally, in its presentation. As the Joint Committee (1994) states: "all acts, public pronouncements, and written reports of the evaluation [should] adhere strictly to a code of directness, openness, and completeness" (p. 109).

Similarly, the evaluator must make certain that nothing is allowed to color the presentation of information. Suppose the personality traits of a program director offend the evaluator. It is important to prevent that fact from negatively tainting the judgments and language in the evaluation report (unless, of course, the program director also offends others in ways that have a negative effect on the program). Fairness in reporting is the hallmark of a professional evaluator.

Finally, there are two or more sides to every story. It is essential that legitimate positions be reported in a balanced way. No evaluator will ever be completely free of bias, but every effort must be made to control bias in reporting.[2] The Joint Committee, evidencing its concern in this area, articulated the following as one standard of propriety:

> *Balanced Reporting.* The evaluation should be complete and fair in its presentation and recording of strengths and weaknesses of the program being evaluated, so that strengths can be built upon and problem areas addressed. (p.105)

Communication and Persuasion

Communication plays an important role in all stages of evaluation. Good communication is essential if the evaluator is to understand the origins and context for an evaluation, elicit the evaluative questions and criteria from stakeholders, reach agreements with clients concerning the evaluation plan, deal with political and interpersonal aspects of evaluation studies, maintain rapport and protocol during data collection, and so on. But nowhere is clarity of communication more central than during reporting. The quality of that communication will determine whether the evaluator's message comes through clear or garbled.

Construed broadly, communication may be thought of as all the procedures one person uses to inform another. Presenting information in a way that it is not understood is simply poor communication (no matter how *correct* the information). Presenting statistical summaries to lay audiences who do not understand statistics is poor communication (or noncommunication), regardless of how well a more statistically oriented audience might receive the same information. It is equally foolish to summarize rich qualitative data in prose that is truly literary and erudite when the audience consists of relatively uneducated stakeholders whose vocabulary and reading ability are badly overmatched by the evaluator's show of erudition.

It is absolutely essential that the evaluator tailor every presentation to make it understandable to its audience(s). This requires care and creativity. To present statistical evaluation results to audiences who are not schooled in statistics, Brager and Mazza (1979) suggest using (1) analogies; (2) graphs or pictorial displays; (3) well-explained summaries to highlight selected findings; (4) a television newscast format to underscore concise, important findings; and (5) a minimal number of judiciously inserted statistics.

No matter how dispassionate the presentation, if the communication seeks to bring the reader to the same conclusions the evaluator has reached, then its intent is not only to inform but also to persuade. House (1980) analyzed in one study the contrast between impersonal, neutral presentation of evaluation

---

[2] Of course, in an adversary-oriented evaluation, balance exists not *within* one set of evaluation findings, as is the goal of most evaluation approaches, but in the balance *between* the two alternative viewpoints built into the evaluation.

procedures and the dramatic use of imagery in presenting the implications for action. But, as House notes, both are used to persuade. Describing the discussion of methodology in the study as being "conducted with painstaking neutrality," he observes that

> The resulting "scientific" style is clinical, detached, impersonal, and lacks imagery. The author presents the external world and allows it to persuade the reader. The style suggests that the observer is governed by method and by the rules of scientific integrity. (p. 99)

In speaking of the study's implications for action, House notes that facts are converted to imagery; he comments:

> Imagery, dramatic structure, and mode of presentation are central considerations for the import of an evaluation. These elements, often thought of as merely cosmetic, can affect what people believe and do. (p. 100)

House also relates both styles of presentation to the coherence he believes is essential, a coherence he says can be attained through "storytelling."

> Every evaluation must have a minimum degree of coherence. The minimum coherence is that the evaluation tell a story. . . .
>
> There are at least two conventional ways of telling the story. One way is to present the evaluator as a neutral, scientific observer. In this case, the story line is implied. It runs something like, "I am a detached, neutral observer who has made measurements according to the canons of science and have found certain things to be so. The program was conducted as I have described it, and I have found the following outcomes. . . ." Usually the story line concludes that "the program was implemented, and such and such were the results." Actual description is often sparse. . . . The usual presentation is to describe the project or the goals of the project, the treatment, the results or effects, and the conclusions.
>
> The second major way of telling the story is for the evaluator to stand closer to the program, as reflected in the narrator's "voice," and to tell the story by describing the events in detail. To this end the evaluator may use emotionally charged language and a narrative presentation. The story may look like a newspaper report. (pp. 102–103)

The importance of telling a story through the evaluation, whether that be through careful narrative description or usual displays, cannot be overemphasized. Whatever tactic is used, it is imperative that the evaluator take pains to communicate her message clearly and persuasively.

Level of Detail

The notion that all evaluators suffer from obsessive-compulsive personality disorders may be an unfounded rumor, but it is probably rooted in some real-world evaluation reports. We have all seen (if not produced) such reports, two inches or more in thickness, crammed full of all conceivable (and some inconceivable) details about the evaluation study and everything associated with it. Some evaluators confuse the call for comprehensiveness with the compulsion to collect. Cronbach and his colleagues (1980) made this wry observation:

> comprehensive examination of a program does not necessarily justify an exhaustive report. . . .
>   Many evaluations are reported with self-defeating thoroughness. . . . A normal human being will try to assimilate only so many numbers, and not much more prose. When an avalanche of words and tables descends, everyone in its path dodges. (p. 186)

How much detail should be included in an evaluation report? Only as much as the audience needs. A program's manager(s) and staff members may be interested in specifics, but that is seldom true of policy makers. A particular program director may be primarily interested in a discussion of how recommendations could be used to improve the program, while community persons may simply be interested in a single sentence summarizing how the program performed on a particular objective. Thus, a written evaluation report should be organized so that various audiences can quickly assess the information of particular interest to them.

Technical Writing Style

Earlier we spoke about communication and persuasion in a broader sense. There we were concerned mostly with communicating clearly, avoiding unnecessary ambiguity, and making certain the evaluation story was clearly understood. In a written report, the use of language, as well as pictures, graphs, and tabular displays, will determine whether or not the communication is effective.

Nothing is as tiresome as reading tedious, unnecessarily convoluted, imprecise, and sometimes inconvenient and awkward expression. (See what we mean?) Wouldn't it have been better if we had said simply, "Nothing is as tiresome as reading complicated writing"?

We offer these few rules for improving writing style in evaluation reports:

- *Avoid jargon.* (If you don't know what it is, you're probably using it.)
- *Use simple, direct language.* (Make certain the level of language is appropriate for the audience; don't ramble.)
- *Use examples, anecdotes, illustrations.* (Don't forget, a picture is worth a thousand words—and don't be flippant by asking why we did not illustrate this text.)

- *Use correct grammar and punctuation.* (And spelling should also be appropriate for the country in which the report is to be used.)
- *Avoid cluttering narrative with reference notes.* (Yes, we know we have done just that, but then this is a text *and reference* book, not an evaluation report, and you are not the typical evaluation audience.)
- *Use language that is interesting, not dull.*

Appearance of the Report

It would be interesting to do a bit of "free-response research" to determine what is the first descriptive word that pops into people's minds when they hear "evaluation report." We cannot predict the most common responses, but we would be amazed if they included "attractive," "handsome," or "visually appealing." Concern with aesthetics has historically been as common among evaluators as compassion has been among tax collectors. Most evaluators have been preoccupied with what the report said, not with how attractively the message was packaged.

Appearance counts, however, because it will often influence how (or whether) a document will be read. Market analysts and advertising specialists know much that would be useful to evaluators who want their products used (such as how long it takes the average administrator to transmit most items from the "incoming" mailbox to the "outgoing" wastebasket).

Until a decade or so ago, many evaluators seemed reluctant to adopt the "slick and glossy" visual tricks of advertising. Now most evaluators are concerned with the "cover appeal" of their report, as well as the attractiveness of its contents. Many evaluators frequently produce high-quality brochures and pictures when reporting evaluations of important programs to their various publics. Much knowledge from the marketing, commercial art, and publishing fields can be tastefully applied to make evaluation reports more visually appealing and readable. Five suggestions follow:

1. *Print quality.* If you have ever tried to read a faded, smudged copy of a report reproduced on some ink-dry printer or nearly worn-out copier, you know that only a rare report will be judged worth the effort. Sharp, dark printing in standard size or larger is essential.
2. *Graphics.* Evaluators (and their secretaries) are not necessarily competent in drafting or in art. Yet that is no longer an acceptable excuse for failure to include high-quality graphics and art, when appropriate, in evaluation reports. A nearly endless array of computer software packages now allows even artistically impaired evaluators to develop attractive and sophisticated graphs and art. The changes introduced by home publishing software, the various "paintbrush" programs, and affordable color printers have left evaluators with no excuse for dull and drab reports. Visual displays should be used in evaluation reports wherever they would be helpful in telling (or

better yet, *showing*) the story. Photographs and other illustrations (while not technically "graphics") can also help greatly.

3. *Page appearance.* Far too many evaluation reports are overwhelmed with a sense of "grayness"—page after page of long, uninterrupted paragraphs with nothing to relieve the monotony. (Small wonder the eye sometimes responds by closing.) Good production editors have long since learned the advantage of "breaking up the page," using strategies such as these:
   - White space (to separate and relieve printed sections)
   - Varied headings (regular and boldface)
   - Underlining or italics (not only to give emphasis but also to add interest)
   - Use of numbered or "bulleted" lists (such as this one)
   - Insertion of visuals (graphs, pictures, or even cartoons)
   - Boxes (or other visual displays of selected materials)

   Several computer programs now have "auto-format" features that show a recommended format that incorporates several of these features.

4. *Color.* Careful use of color can make an evaluation report more attractive, as well as more functional. When the executive summary appears as the first section in an evaluation report, we prefer to print it on colored paper. This not only gives some visual appeal but also draws attention to the summary and makes it easy for the reader to locate it later. Consider printing appendices on yet another color. It will be easy to turn to, and the combination of colors with the predominantly white body of the report enhances the visual appeal of the whole.

5. *Cover.* Obviously not all written evaluation reports warrant preparing and printing a cover. A typed and stapled cover page will serve well in many formative evaluation studies, and possibly some summative evaluation studies as well. But a more attractive report cover may entice readers and suggest that the evaluator thought the information contained in the report was worthy of a professional presentation. Of course, no cover will compensate for an inadequate evaluation report.

HUMAN AND HUMANE CONSIDERATIONS IN REPORTING EVALUATION FINDINGS

Many evaluators become so preoccupied with preparing and presenting their messages that they forget the impact that those messages will have. If an evaluation report labels the U.S. Coast Guards's new officer training curriculum as ill-conceived and its implementation as inadequate, the personal egos (and perhaps the professional reputations) of the curriculum designer and the trainer(s) implementing the program will not go unscathed. This doesn't mean that truth should be diluted to protect feelings but only that it be communicated as carefully, sensitively, and professionally as possible. Beyond apparent idealistic reasons for protecting the rights and sensitivities of those on whom the evaluation might reflect, there are also some obvious (if you think about it for a moment) pragmatic reasons. For example, in many evaluations, results are reported directly to those responsible for planning or running the program. Evaluators far too wise to tell any mother that her baby is ugly may tactlessly tell an administrator and staff that the program to which they have devoted three years of their lives is a disaster. Not surprisingly, the program practitioners may exercise the limits of their ingenuity in seeking ways to discount both the evaluation and the evaluator. The opportunity for the message to be of use may have been irretrievably lost.

The evaluator must take appropriate steps to protect the rights and sensitivities of all those involved in the evaluation. For the practicing evaluator, this means that raw technical facts must be buffered by sensitivity to the maxim that truth must be told with tenderness and in a context of trust. In this section we offer our suggestions for (1) delivering negative messages and (2) providing those affected with the opportunity to review a draft report (and suggest modifications) prior to its final release.

Delivering Negative Messages

In olden days, the messenger who delivered news to the king lived a life fraught with risk. If the news was bad, the messenger might lose his tongue—or even his head. Nowadays, the bearers of bad evaluation tidings may still find themselves savaged (though in a somewhat more polite manner).

Sometimes evaluation clients (or others involved with the evaluation) are so sensitive to any criticism or any hint of imperfection that it would not matter much how negative findings were reported—the reaction would still be defensive. But more often we have observed that defensive reactions are exacerbated by the manner in which the negative results are conveyed.

Earlier we proposed one simple solution: to present the strengths of the program first. (To those who say they cannot find any strengths to report, we suggest they are not very thorough or insightful; in even the most awful program, one can usually comment sincerely on the efforts, dedication, and hard work of the staff.) We also reiterate the following steps recommended by Van Mondfrans (1985) for helping those involved in evaluation to "swallow bitter pills":

1. In an oral debriefing where the major events of the evaluation are reviewed and where the major findings are previewed, the negative information is stated in as positive a context as possible. It seems easier for clients to accept negative information in an oral form in a relatively friendly encounter.
2. A preliminary written report is presented in which the negative information is described in a straightforward factual manner but in as positive a perspective as possible. Often a personal visit needs to

follow in which the preliminary report is discussed and the client allowed to propose changes if the information is viewed as unfair. If changes are needed in the preliminary report, they should not obscure negative information or allow it to be misinterpreted; however, it may be that in discussing the negative information, the client will bring up other factors not known to the evaluator at the time the preliminary report was written. These other factors may be included in the final report in juxtaposition with the negative information, thus allowing better interpretation.

3. A final written report is prepared in which the negative information is accurately and fully presented. Having undergone previous steps, the client is better prepared to deal with the negative information, having had a chance to review it several times, to think of other factors which are relevant, and present those to the evaluator. The evaluator has the opportunity to review other factors and include them in the report if they aid the interpretation of the negative information. (pp. 3–4)

Benkofske (1994a, 1994b) has also suggested ways to prepare stakeholders to receive negative findings about their program's performance. In her view, this is especially important when the negative findings are distilled from qualitative data. She reports that most of her clients have heard so much about the benefits of qualitative data that they inappropriately come to expect it to yield glowing descriptions of their programs. Thus, she finds it important to engage clients early on in a discussion of what they would do if the qualitative data turn out negative. In her words:

> clients all come believing their program **needs** a qualitative study. I have found, however, that stakeholders need to be prepared for the evaluation results if the qualitative data are not positive. It is my personal experience that qualitative data hurts; it stings like hell to see in print pages of quoted material that describes in vivid detail problems with a program. While qualitative data can "brighten the portrait" when positive, it can wound deeply when negative. (p. 2)

Earlier in this chapter we mentioned that disclaimers could be inserted early in an evaluation report to protect both client and evaluator. Such disclaimers are intended to prevent misinterpretation and to put any negative messages in proper perspective. An example of such a disclaimer follows:

> This report describes the procedures and results of a (*state whether formative or summative*) evaluation of (*name of program/project*). The client, (*name of client*), reserves all rights to this information. The purpose of this evaluation was to (*state purpose*). Any other use of this report may be subject to serious errors since the information was

collected with the above purpose as the sole focus. Information relevant to other purposes was either not collected or not reported.

It is often useful to expand on such cryptic disclaimers. Errors and misunderstandings can arise if evaluation results are used for purposes other than those intended.

Providing an Opportunity for Review of the Report

Only the most arrogant evaluator would assume that her work and the report that presents it are completely accurate and fair in all regards. Small factual errors can lead to nontrivial errors in judgments and conclusions. Interpretations can overlook contextual factors that the evaluator failed to understand and thus be spurious. And the evaluator's bias can creep into evaluation narratives unnoticed, especially by the evaluator.

For all of these reasons, we strongly urge that the evaluator circulate a draft of her evaluation report to the client and other key stakeholders for comments, asking that they point out (and correct where appropriate) all

- Minor errors (for example, misspellings),
- Factual errors (wrong names or titles, errors in numbers of persons participating, etc.), and
- Interpretive errors.

Reviewers should be asked not only to challenge anything that they perceive to be an error but also to provide substantiation for the alternative facts or interpretations that they propose as correct. Reviewers should be informed that the evaluator is under no obligation to accept their suggestions (the intent is not to allow clients to rewrite the report any way they wish) but only to give those suggestions serious consideration. The evaluator reserves the right to ignore suggestions and to make only those changes that are warranted.

Circulating a preliminary draft report can increase the number of individuals who read the report carefully; shared responsibility for the report's accuracy is a good motivator. Some may worry that use of drafts may lessen interest in the final report. That concerns us less than the very real possibility that many key persons who are not asked to review a draft may never read the report at all.

What if the evaluator refuses to accept a proposed change in the report, but the reviewer who suggested it continues to contend that the report is inaccurate, misleading, or unfair? Simple. Invite the reviewer to share that view, in writing, and include it in a concluding section of the report, as we proposed earlier. We see no problem with permitting reviewers to include their rebuttals, rejoinders, or contrary comments. If the evaluator's data collection, analysis, interpretation, judgments, and conclusions are on solid ground, they should not be harmed by such detraction. If they are shaky and cannot withstand such challenge, then they deserve to be challenged.

SUGGESTIONS FOR EFFECTIVE ORAL REPORTING

Written evaluation reports, although very common, are not necessarily the most effective medium for evaluation reporting. Oral reports, supported by appropriate visual aids, can be even more effective.

Many of the earlier suggestions for improving written reports are pertinent for oral reports as well. Audiences who listen to oral reports need an introduction that explains the purpose of the evaluation, what was evaluated, the questions addressed, and the evaluation procedures used. Presenting positive conclusions followed by negative conclusions and recommendations is still appropriate. And the evaluator should still be as concerned about such items as the following:

- Accuracy, balance, and fairness
- Communication and persuasion
- Level of detail
- Use of simple, direct, correct, and interesting language
- Avoidance of jargon and unnecessary technical language
- Use of examples, anecdotes, and illustrations
- Sensitivity to the rights and feelings of those involved

Oral reports also require particular attention to audiovisual presentation of information. Obviously the suggestions commonly offered in speech and communications courses and texts are relevant here. But the following tips are particularly relevant for making effective oral evaluation reports:

1. Begin with an outline of the message(s) you want to communicate; sequence and weave them together into the story you want to tell to your audience.
2. Decide who should tell the story. It is not essential that the lead evaluator also be the lead storyteller; what *is* essential is that the story be told well. If the lead evaluator has that capability, then she would obviously be the best choice. But using another member of the evaluation team (or even an outside "reporter") is far preferable to having a good evaluation destroyed in its telling by an evaluator who is not a strong presenter but is too egocentric to abandon center stage. Usually the lead evaluator(s) can be involved in at least a *part* of the presentation so that any awkwardness can be minimized.
3. Choose the oral report medium (verbal narrative, videotape, staged debate, etc.). Make the presentation format interesting and varied using multiple media, multiple presenters, or other variations. Don't use the format the audience expects; do something different to maintain interest.
4. Make visuals to accompany the presentation. Make them large and simple, using only a few words on each. Use high-quality presentation techniques, such as computer-generated 35-mm transparencies.

5. Develop a presentation that feels natural and comfortable to you, then practice until you are at ease delivering it. Use effective highlighting techniques, such as a laser pointer or computer stylus. Practice using it. You don't want your laser beam to hit a client in the eye!

6. Involve the audience in the presentation through questions and answers, show of hands, or other interaction; give them three minutes to talk in trios or couples to identify other issues they would like you to address and the like.

7. Develop and adhere to an agenda, with appropriate breaks. Protracted oral reports will have people slumping in their seats (or worse, out of their seats).

A CHECKLIST FOR GOOD EVALUATION REPORTS

Ingredients of a good evaluation report can readily be inferred from our earlier suggestions, but here, for convenience, is a checklist of things that would typify most good evaluation reports.
Check each that applies.

_____ Interim and final reports provided in time to be most useful

_____ Report content tailored to the audience(s)

_____ Report format and style tailored to the audience(s)

_____ Involvement of audiences in determining the format and style of the report

_____ An executive summary

_____ An adequate introduction to "set the stage"

_____ Mention of limitations of the study

_____ Adequate presentation of evaluation plan and procedures (primarily in appendices)

_____ Effectively organized presentation of results

_____ All necessary technical information provided (preferably in appendices)

_____ Specification of standards and criteria for evaluative judgments

_____ Evaluative judgments

_____ Lists of *both* identified strengths and weaknesses

_____ Recommendations for action

_____ Protection of clients' and stakeholders' interests

_____ Sensitivity to those affected by the evaluation findings

_____ Provision for minority reports or rejoinders

_____ Accurate and unbiased presentation

_____ Effective communication and persuasion through "telling the story"

_____ Appropriate level of detail

_____ Lack of technical jargon

_____ Use of correct, uncomplicated, and interesting language

_____ Use of examples and illustrations

_____ Attention to visual appearance and eye appeal

THE USE OF EVALUATION REPORTS

The utility of any evaluation is a prime criterion for judging its worth (Joint Committee, 1994). If an evaluation is not used, it must be judged harshly regardless of its technical, practical, and ethical merits.

Cost-effectiveness is an important argument for using evaluation. Evaluation is justified only to the extent that it saves the client resources or adds substantially to the community's well-being. For these reasons, we believe it is important to examine (1) research on the ways in which evaluation has been used and (2) research on factors found to influence its use.

Research on Use of Evaluation

Much research of the late 1970s and early 1980s focused on the use of evaluation results. Compilations of that research have been published by several evaluators, including Weiss (1977), Patton (1986), and Cousins and Leithwood (1986). In his review of that literature, Thompson (1994) noted that the results of this early research found that, on the whole, the evaluation results were often disregarded.

However, more recent research on this topic has been published by King (1988), Greene (1988), Newman (1988), and Patton (1991). In general, these studies found increased utilization of evaluation results over that reported by the earlier research. Thompson (1994) attributed these increases to changes in the way evaluators defined "use." This view seems to parallel Patton's (1986) statement:

> Our findings, then, suggest that the predominant issue of non-utilization that characterizes much of the commentary on evaluation research can be attributed in substantial degree to a definition of utilization that is too narrow in its emphasis on seeing immediate, direct, and concrete impact on program decisions. (p. 37)

From all of this earlier research and conceptual activity, we have learned that evaluation is used in many different ways, some of which are difficult to document (Patton, 1986). Yet evaluation's uses are becoming increasingly clear. King (1988) defined four categories of evaluation use:

1. *Instrumental or allocative uses*—direct use of evaluation to make decisions or changes. Only infrequently does a single evaluation study

or a particular piece of information resulting from an evaluation get used immediately for decision making.

2. *Persuasive uses*—use of the evaluation for some kind of personal gain, usually to persuade funders of the program's success.

3. *Conceptual uses*—indirect and cumulative uses of evaluation to shape the thinking of the policy-shaping community. Cronbach and his colleagues (1980) saw this use as the typical and most effective use of evaluation. By drawing attention to critical variables or issues, evaluation affects discussions that eventually lead to changes or new initiatives.

4. *Symbolic uses*—evaluation used for other than that for which it may have been intended. Examples of such use include pro forma submission of a mandated evaluation report just to fulfill funding requirements; uses of evaluation information to support or attack a point of view that may or may not have been associated with the evaluation; drawing from evaluation findings as needed to prepare a new proposal or program design; using evaluation findings to legitimate decisions; and showing the public that evaluation indeed is being done.

These four are not discrete, nonoverlapping categories. In fact, evaluation may be used for any or all of these uses by the same or different users.

Research on Factors Found to Influence Evaluation Use

As was mentioned earlier in this chapter, evaluators can learn from the research of Weiss and Bucuvalas (1980) the importance of producing reports that are viewed by audiences as truthful and useful. Other researchers have investigated additional variables. For example, Alkin, Stecher, and Geiger (1982) concluded that six factors were most responsible for the use of evaluation information: (1) the reputation of the evaluator; (2) the evaluator's commitment to evaluation use; (3) the interest of decision makers and the community in the evaluation; (4) the extent to which the evaluation focused on local needs; (5) the degree to which evaluation was presented in graphic, nontechnical form; and (6) the development of procedures that assisted decision makers to use the information.

Leviton and Hughes (1981) found five clusters of factors that affect evaluation use: (1) relevance of evaluation to decision maker's needs, (2) credibility of the evaluation and the evaluator, (3) communication of evaluation results, (4) translation of evaluation results into specific implications, and (5) evaluation-user involvement and advocacy.

Cousins and Leithwood (1986) found several factors that affected the utilization of the evaluation results: (1) evaluation quality, (2) the evaluator's credibility, (3) relevance of the evaluation, (4) the quality of communication between evaluator and stakeholders, (5) findings of the study (Are they congruent or incongruent with the decision maker's expectations?), (6) timeliness, (7) the needs of the organization, (8) political climate, (9) competing information (in addition to the evaluation results), (10) personal characteristics of the decision maker, and (11) user commitment or receptiveness to evaluation.

Barrios and Foster (1987) found relevance to decision-making, political context, and evaluation-user characteristics to be the main factors in evaluation use. Less consistent factors were user involvement, credibility of information, credibility of evaluator, and quality.

Turner, Hartman, Nielsen, and Lombana (1988) looked at four highly utilized program evaluations and found the four evaluations had the following factors in common: a variety of data-collection methods, a high degree of interest on the part of the evaluator in the program, an assortment of information sources, the evaluation model used, frequent feedback to stakeholders, the substance of the report, the timeliness of the report, user involvement in evaluation planning, and reporting format. Thompson (1994) found a higher probability of evaluation use when the program was novel and the evaluation required only moderate changes in the program.

Patton (1991) has indicated that evaluation use is related to the perceived credibility, accuracy, fairness, and believability of the evaluation. Earlier, Patton (1988) reported that a *personal factor* (an individual takes personal responsibility for getting the information to the right people) is a critical determiner of evaluation use. This proactive stance is evident in the form of "utilization activism" reported by Kennedy, Apling, and Neumann (1980), who found several methods that internal evaluation units were using to promote evaluation use. These included "staff development through workshops and inservice programs, participation on committees, discussions with participant groups, and encouraging policymakers to develop policies regarding information use" (p. 113). They also found evaluators promoting evaluation use by negotiating with potential users during the design stage of the evaluation (e.g, by requiring program managers to respond in writing) and by demonstrating to governing boards how evaluation studies can save money.

Most reviews of research on factors affecting the use of evaluation also show that involving potential users throughout the evaluation is a critical ingredient to evaluation use. They need to be involved at the beginning so that their expectations for the evaluation are understood. They need to feel ownership in the evaluation design and its methods of operation. They need to be kept informed while the evaluation is in progress. They need to understand the evaluation's findings and its implications for action. They need to be involved in evaluation decisions. Failure in any of these forms of involvement and communication are likely to reduce the potential for the use of the information yielded by the evaluation.

As can be seen from the foregoing discussion of research on evaluation use, an empirical basis for making decisions about evaluation is beginning to emerge. As this research literature matures, we expect to see increasing sophistication in the practice of evaluation. In the meantime, the literature does not provide clear-cut and unanimous conclusions to guide evaluation practitioners. For example, Cousins and Leithwood (1986) reported that the quality of the evaluation itself is the factor that seems to be most strongly associated with evaluation use. Yet Weiss and Bucuvalas (1980) found that agreement with the evaluation's conclusions was the factor that most affected use, and users only attended to the "quality" (the correctness of the methods) if they disagreed with the results. The different samples used in these and other studies of evaluation use, their different operational definitions of "use" and "quality," and other variables doubtless account for these differences and other inconclusiveness in the present body of research on evaluation use.

Until there is greater clarity in the empirical research on this topic, we would hazard the following general suggestions for evaluators who want the results of their labors to be used:

1. Identify the key evaluation issues. Structure the evaluation efforts around the information priorities of the program decision makers. Involve them and other stakeholders in the conceptualization of the evaluation, whenever possible.
2. Be sensitive to the context in which the evaluation is taking place. Pay attention to the political climate. Be sensitive to the stakeholders' opinions and feelings. Build rapport with them.
3. Use multiple methods of data collection and analysis. Don't rely on only one form of proof. Use both quantitative and qualitative methods. Be eclectic in your evaluation approach; the breadth of data will help you speak to a broader evaluation audience.
4. Present information in a timely fashion. Be on time with required reports. Provide interim reports.
5. When possible and appropriate, make recommendations.

CASE STUDY APPLICATION

May 11. Today I had the first of the usual flurry of requests for preliminary information that come on nearly every evaluation. But we've not even held our steering committee meeting to review the preliminary data analyses yet, and anything we said at this point would be too subjective for my taste. I usually don't mind giving a few impressions, if people will remember that's all they are, but my sense is that this humanities program is controversial enough that it's likely some people might extract only the message they want to hear from whatever we say. I know we can't guard against that completely, even with the most polished final report, but if I do the best I can to present data I'm confident of, in as careful and balanced a fashion as possible, then I can sleep easier at night if someone misuses it than I can if I contribute to the misuse through casual or careless communication.

Of course, key folk on the committee are now aware of *some* of the preliminary analyses, but that's not in very "disseminable" form, even if we had finished interpreting it, which we haven't. So, there is a need for some interim information; I don't think it necessary to keep everyone waiting with bated breath right up to the final written report. Methinks I'll let the site-visit exit interview later this week be the first interim report—probably the only one, really, with the final report coming on fairly soon.

Author Comments.   Few evaluation reports hold such general interest that they are media events. In contexts like the Radnor humanities curriculum, however, several individuals and groups will generally press to get a preview of the findings at the earliest possible moment. The more visible the evaluation, the more curious the local folks get about the outcomes. When outside experts begin roaming through, requests for evaluation findings often spring up in their wake.

In the Radnor case, I would probably restrict early release of information to the previously mentioned exit interview at the conclusion of the on-site evaluation visit. This is a natural and expected time to share at least general impressions of the evaluation team. The audiences for the report (probably the humanities staff, the principal, and representatives of the humanities committee and the board) should be reminded that this is only one facet of the evaluation and that the results of the on-site evaluation will have to be integrated with those from the other evaluation activities (being reviewed by the steering committee) into a more comprehensive report before they will have the full picture that the evaluation will provide.

> ***May 25.*** I thought I had learned not to procrastinate, but the last few days have been hectic and the final report on the Radnor program is due next week. Time to start writing. Lots of the basic stuff is already there in our data summaries, on-site visit reports, etc., but it needs to be pulled together into a cohesive, coherent report, complete with executive summary and all the trimmings. I promised Claire Janson a draft copy for review by her and the other audiences by the end of next week, so I'd best get busy. Maybe I can get the draft off to her by UPS on Monday.

Author Comments.   In preparing the final report, I would produce a complete first draft, including at least the following:

1. An introduction describing the humanities curriculum, purposes and audiences for the evaluation, and an overview of the rest of the report
2. A list of evaluative questions used to guide the study
3. A very brief overview of the evaluation plan and procedures, with a supporting appendix to provide detail
4. Discussion of findings, probably organized around the evaluative questions (Again, detailed presentations of findings generated by each instrument could be provided in an appendix.)
5. Judgments, in the form of strengths and weaknesses, along with recommendations, with sufficient rationale and linkage to findings to demonstrate that the recommendations are warranted

Once it is completed, I would submit the draft copy of the final report to the principal and ask that she review it and also have it reviewed by the head of the humanities faculty, other selected members of the humanities study committee, and the board president. The intent of this review would be twofold:

first, to identify any factual inaccuracies; second, to challenge any inferences, conclusions, or recommendations these partisan reviewers think are inappropriate, unwarranted, or unfair. It is important, in asking for these reviews, to communicate that you will take them very seriously and will consider carefully each suggested revision, whether it be minor editing or deletion of a major recommendation. It is equally important to make very clear that the ultimate decision for what goes into the final draft report belongs to the evaluator and that there is no guarantee that all of their suggestions will be incorporated. Failure to get these ground rules clear at the outset can lead to all manner of problems.

Having the client review a draft of the report and vouchsafe its factual accuracy is good insurance against the evaluator's committing serious blunders. Helpful clients have saved me embarrassment by correcting nontrivial errors I failed to spot in draft reports (like the "typo" that turned an intended compliment of a program director as single-minded into the much less complimentary "simple-minded").

Even small factual errors, uncorrected, give comfort to the critic bent on discrediting the report. Consider, for instance, the PTA president who had opposed a new curriculum designed to teach reading through a study of local cultures, only to find that our evaluation showed clearly that the curriculum was having a very positive effect on student learning. "How," he thundered at a collective PTA and school board meeting, "can you believe anything else is accurate if the evaluator can't even spell the name of the school or its principal right!" (Now before you judge too harshly, you should try to evaluate the curriculum at Tchesinkut School, where Mr. Nakinilerak presides.) It was there, in the Alaskan bush, that I first learned the value of asking clients to review and share responsibility for accuracy of the final report.

Several references have been made previously to an executive summary. This might take the form of a parsimonious introductory chapter to the evaluation report, including a synopsis of the findings and references to other sections of the report of interest to particular audiences. Or the executive summary might be a separate, self-contained document of 5 to 10 pages for use with interested parties who need results but are not concerned with details. In larger evaluations, where more people need to be informed, a brief evaluation abstract of one or two pages might be useful.

One ethical consideration that should not be neglected in report writing is preserving desired confidentiality and anonymity. Evaluators generally promise that individual responses or test scores will not be divulged (except with the individuals' express approval). Unfortunately, that promise is sometimes forgotten at the report-writing stage.

APPLICATION EXERCISES

1. Apply the "good evaluation report" checklist from this chapter to an evaluation study of your choosing. Do the strengths and weaknesses of the reporting process you reviewed suggest procedures that you will want to adopt in the future?

2. List questions that you think future research on evaluation reporting and use should answer. What questions do you have for which there are no good answers?

RELEVANT EVALUATION STANDARDS

The evaluation standards we see as relevant to this chapter's content are the following. These standards are described in Chapter 20, page 442.

U1—Stakeholder Identification	P6 —Disclosure of Findings
U2—Evaluator Credibility	A1 —Program Documentation
U3—Information Scope and Selection	A3 —Described Purposes and
U4—Values Identification	Procedures
U5—Report Clarity	A4 —Defensible Information Sources
U6—Report Timeliness and Dissemination	A7 —Systematic Information
U7—Evaluation Impact	A10—Justified Conclusions
P5 —Complete and Fair Assessment	A11—Impartial Reporting

SUGGESTED READINGS

Cousins, J. B., & Leithwood, K. A. (1986). Current empirical research on evaluation utilization. *Review of Education Research, 56,* 331–364.

Greene, J. G. (1988). Stakeholder participation and utilization in program evaluation. *Evaluation Review, 12,* 91–116.

King, J. A. (1988). Research on evaluation use and its implications for evaluation research and practice. *Studies in Educational Evaluation, 14,* 285–299.

Newman, D. L., & Brown, R. D. (1996). *Applied ethics for program evaluation.* Beverly Hills, CA: Sage.

Patton, M. Q. (1986). *Utilization-focused evaluation* (2nd ed.). Beverly Hills, CA: Sage.

Smith, N. L. (Ed.). (1982). *Communication strategies in evaluation.* Beverly Hills, CA: Sage.

Thompson, B. (1994, April). *The revised Program Evaluation Standards and their correlation with the evaluation use literature.* Paper presented at the annual meeting of the American Educational Research Association, New Orleans.

Weiss, C. H., & Bucuvalas, M. J. (1980). Truth tests and utility tests: Decision-makers' frames of reference for social science research. *American Sociological Review, 45,* 302–313.

chapter 20

Evaluating Evaluations

ORIENTING QUESTIONS

1. Why should evaluations be evaluated? When would you want to commission a metaevaluation?
2. What are the attributes of good evaluation?
3. What guidelines and steps would you use in carrying out a metaevaluation?
4. What are the major contributions of the Joint Committee on Standards for Educational Evaluation?

Any evaluation study is going to be biased to some extent. Decisions that an evaluator makes about what to examine—what methods and instruments to use, whom to talk to and whom to listen to—all influence the outcome of the evaluation. Even the evaluator's personal background, biases, professional training, and experience all affect the way the study is conducted.

Both evaluator and client must be concerned about evaluation bias: the evaluator because his personal standards and professional reputation are at stake; the client because he doesn't want to invest (either politically or financially) in findings that are off target. Both have a lot to lose if an evaluation is shown to be deficient in some critical aspect.

This is why *metaevaluation*—the evaluation of an evaluation—is important. Formative metaevaluation can improve an evaluation study before it is irretrievably too late. Summative metaevaluation can add credibility to final results.

In this chapter we discuss the concept of metaevaluation, standards and criteria for evaluating evaluations, and metaevaluation procedures that can be used to enhance the quality of evaluations.

THE CONCEPT AND EVOLUTION OF METAEVALUATION

Not even the most enthusiastic advocate would assert that all evaluation activities are intrinsically valuable or even well intentioned. Thoughtful observers have even asked, from time to time, whether evaluation results warrant their cost in human and other resources. As Nilsson and Hogben (1983) correctly point out, metaevaluation refers not only to the evaluation of particular studies but also to evaluation of the very function and practice of evaluation itself.

This broader definition of metaevaluation, however, goes beyond the scope of both this chapter and book. By now our bias must be clear to the reader: We are thoroughly convinced of evaluation's importance. *Properly practiced,* evaluation has led to direct and incontestable improvements in systems, programs, and practices—improvements that would have occurred in no other way. Given the number and frequency of evaluation failures, however, we understand why some question the basic concept. When evaluation goes wrong, the fault lies, we believe, not with the concept but with the way in which the evaluation is conducted. The purpose of metaevaluation is to help evaluation live up to its potential. For this chapter, then, we restrict our discussion to evaluation of individual evaluation designs, studies, and reports.

The Evolution of Metaevaluation

In an informal sense, metaevaluation has been around as long as evaluation, for someone has had an opinion about the quality of every evaluation study ever conducted. During the 1960s, however, evaluators began to discuss formal meta-evaluation procedures and criteria, writers began to suggest what constituted good and bad evaluations (e.g., Scriven, 1967; Stake, 1970; Stufflebeam, 1968), and unpublished checklists of **evaluation standards** began to be exchanged informally among evaluators. In addition, several evaluators published their proposed guidelines, or "metaevaluation" criteria, for use in judging evaluation plans or reports (Stake, 1969; Stufflebeam et al., 1971; Stufflebeam, 1974; Scriven, 1974b; Rossi, 1982).

In general, evaluators welcomed these lists of proposed metaevaluation criteria. In addition, several authors of the criteria attempted to make them useful to evaluation consumers, thinking that perhaps if evaluation clients were more skillful in judging an evaluation's adequacy, the number of unhelpful and wasteful evaluations might diminish. Clients can demand high quality only if they can recognize what it is that makes one evaluation better or worse than another. For this to occur, evaluators and those they serve must reach shared agreements about what constitutes a good evaluation, in terms both can understand.

However, the many different sets of proposed criteria proved disconcerting to evaluators and consumers alike. Was one set better than another? Which was best? Which was most acceptable?

No one could answer such questions well, for none of the proposed sets of criteria offered by evaluators carried any widespread consensus. Consequently, an ambitious effort was launched in the late 1970s to develop a comprehensive set of standards explicitly tailored for use in educational evaluations and containing generally agreed-upon standards for quality evaluation. Development of these standards began in 1975, under the direction of Daniel Stufflebeam, at Western Michigan University's Evaluation Center. Guidance and authorization were provided by a Joint Committee on Standards for Educational Evaluation (hereafter referred to as the Joint Committee) (Ridings & Stufflebeam, 1981).[1] The result of the Joint Committee's work was the *Standards for Evaluations of Educational Programs, Projects, and Materials* (Joint Committee, 1981), which has received widespread attention in education.

These standards were revised and applied to settings beyond K–12 schools in 1994 (Joint Committee, 1994). In the introduction to the *Standards,* as we shall call the book, the Joint Committee stated that development of sound standards could provide the following benefits:

> a common language to facilitate communication and collaboration in evaluation; a set of general rules for dealing with a variety of specific evaluation problems; a conceptual framework by which to study the often-confusing world of evaluation; a set of working definitions to guide research and development on the evaluation process; a public statement of the state of the art in educational evaluation; a basis for self-regulation and accountability by professional evaluators; and an aid to developing public credibility for the educational evaluation field. (Joint Committee, 1981, p. 5; stated similarly in the Introduction of the Joint Committee, 1994)

---

[1] The following professional organizations appointed members to the Joint Committee: American Association of School Administrators, American Educational Research Association, American Evaluation Association, American Federation of Teachers, American Psychological Association, Association for Supervision and Curriculum Development, Canadian Evaluation Society, Canadian Society for the Study of Education, Council of Chief State School Officers, Council on Postsecondary Accreditation, National Association of Elementary School Principals, National Council on Measurement in Education, National Education Association, National Legislative Program Evaluation Society, and National School Boards Association. In addition, numerous professional evaluators assisted in the development of standards, testing them, and drafting instructional materials to help others apply them.

THE JOINT COMMITTEE'S STANDARDS FOR PROGRAM EVALUATION

The Joint Committee's *Standards* is a set of 30 standards, each with an overview that provides definitions and a rationale for the standard, a list of guidelines, common errors, illustrative cases describing evaluation practices that could have been guided by that particular standard, and an analysis of each case. The result is a work so comprehensive that it fills a book (Joint Committee, 1994). A similar set of standards—for personnel evaluation—was published by the Joint Committee in 1988.

One of the most important insights that the Joint Committee provides with the *Standards* is the concept that the quality of an evaluation study can be determined by looking at its (1) utility, (2) feasibility, (3) propriety, and (4) accuracy. The 30 Program Evaluation Standards are grouped according to their potential contribution to each of these four attributes. Utility is purposely listed first for program evaluation, for the Joint Committee recognized that without utility, a program evaluation will be judged harshly, no matter how well it focuses on feasibility, propriety, and accuracy. Following are the Joint Committee's 30 Program Evaluation Standards, with a brief explanation of each.

SUMMARY OF THE PROGRAM EVALUATION STANDARDS

Utility Standards

The utility standards are intended to ensure that an evaluation will serve the information needs of intended users.

U1 *Stakeholder Identification.* Persons involved in or affected by the evaluation should be identified, so that their needs can be addressed.

U2 *Evaluator Credibility.* The persons conducting the evaluation should be both trustworthy and competent to perform the evaluation, so that the evaluation findings achieve maximum credibility and acceptance.

U3 *Information Scope and Selection.* Information collected should be broadly selected to address pertinent questions about the program and be responsive to the needs and interests of clients and other specified stakeholders.

U4 *Values Identification.* The perspectives, procedures, and rationale used to interpret the findings should be carefully described, so that the bases for value judgments are clear.

U5 *Report Clarity.* Evaluation reports should clearly describe the program being evaluated, including its context, and the purposes, procedures, and findings of the evaluation, so that essential information is provided and easily understood.

U6 *Report Timeliness and Dissemination.* Significant interim findings and evaluation reports should be disseminated to intended users, so that they can be used in a timely fashion.

U7 *Evaluation Impact.* Evaluations should be planned, conducted, and reported in ways that encourage follow-through by stakeholders, so that the likelihood that the evaluation will be used is increased.

Feasibility Standards

The feasibility standards are intended to ensure that an evaluation will be realistic, prudent, diplomatic, and frugal.

F1 *Practical Procedures.* The evaluation procedures should be practical, to keep disruption to a minimum while needed information is obtained.

F2 *Political Viability.* The evaluation should be planned and conducted with anticipation of the different positions of various interest groups, so that their cooperation may be obtained and so that possible attempts by any of these groups to curtail evaluation operations or to bias or misapply the results can be averted or counteracted.

F3 *Cost Effectiveness.* The evaluation should be efficient and produce information of sufficient value, so that the resources expended can be justified.

Propriety Standards

The propriety standards are intended to ensure that an evaluation will be conducted legally, ethically, and with due regard for the welfare of those involved in the evaluation as well as those affected by its results.

P1 *Service Orientation.* Evaluations should be designed to assist organizations to address and effectively serve the needs of the full range of targeted participants.

P2 *Formal Agreements.* Obligations of the formal parties to an evaluation (what is to be done, how, by whom, when) should be agreed to in writing, so that these parties are obligated to adhere to all conditions of the agreement or formally to renegotiate it.

P3 *Rights of Human Subjects.* Evaluations should be designed and conducted to respect and protect the rights and welfare of human subjects.

P4 *Human Interactions.* Evaluators should respect human dignity and worth in their interactions with other persons associated with an evaluation, so that participants are not threatened or harmed.

P5 *Complete and Fair Assessment.* The evaluation should be complete and fair in its examination and recording of strengths and weaknesses of the program being evaluated, so that strengths can be built upon and problem areas addressed.

P6 *Disclosure of Findings.* The formal parties to an evaluation should ensure that the full set of evaluation findings along with pertinent limitations are made accessible to the persons affected by the evaluation and to any others with expressed legal rights to receive the results.

P7 *Conflict of Interest.* Conflict of interest should be dealt with openly and honestly, so that it does not compromise the evaluation processes and results.

P8 *Fiscal Responsibility.* The evaluator's allocation and expenditure of resources should reflect sound accountability procedures and otherwise be prudent and ethically responsible, so that expenditures are accounted for and appropriate.

Accuracy Standards

The accuracy standards are intended to ensure that an evaluation will reveal and convey technically adequate information about the features that determine worth or merit of the program being evaluated.

A1 *Program Documentation.* The program being evaluated should be described and documented clearly and accurately, so that the program is clearly identified.

A2 *Context Analysis.* The context in which the program exists should be examined in enough detail so that its likely influences on the program can be identified.

A3 *Described Purposes and Procedures.* The purposes and procedures of the evaluation should be monitored and described in enough detail so that they can be identified and assessed.

A4 *Defensible Information Sources.* The sources of information used in a program evaluation should be described in enough detail so that the adequacy of the information can be assessed.

A5 *Valid Information.* The information-gathering procedures should be chosen or developed and then implemented so that they will ensure that the interpretation arrived at is valid for the intended use.

A6 *Reliable Information.* The information-gathering procedures should be chosen or developed and then implemented so that they will ensure that the information obtained is sufficiently reliable for the intended use.

A7 *Systematic Information.* The information collected, processed, and reported in an evaluation should be systematically reviewed and any errors found should be corrected.

A8 *Analysis of Quantitative Information.* Quantitative information in an evaluation should be appropriately and systematically analyzed, so that evaluation questions are effectively answered.

A9 *Analysis of Qualitative Information.* Qualitative information in an evaluation should be appropriately and systematically analyzed, so that evaluation questions are effectively answered.

A10 *Justified Conclusions.* The conclusions reached in an evaluation should be explicitly justified, so that stakeholders can assess them.

A11 *Impartial Reporting.* Reporting procedures should guard against distortion caused by personal feelings and biases of any party to the evaluation, so that evaluation reports fairly reflect the evaluation findings.

A12 *Metaevaluation.* The evaluation itself should be formatively and summatively evaluated against these and other pertinent standards, so that its conduct is appropriately guided and, on completion, stakeholders can closely examine its strengths and weaknesses.

Utility of the Standards

Evaluators and their clients may use the *Standards* in planning or reviewing evaluations, organizing preservice and in-service education in evaluation, and monitoring or auditing formally commissioned evaluations. In our judgment, the Joint Committee's *Standards* continues to be the ultimate benchmark against which both evaluations and other sets of metaevaluation criteria and standards should be judged. We are not alone in that judgment. The states of Louisiana, Hawaii, and Florida are using the Program Evaluation Standards as a guide for evaluations of education and public-sector programs.

Application of the Standards

The Program Evaluation Standards are not a cookbook list of steps to follow. Rather, they are a compilation of commonly agreed upon characteristics of good evaluation practice. In the final analysis, choices and trade-offs relating to each standard are the province of the evaluator. A checklist (based on the *Standards*) for judging the adequacy of evaluation designs and reports could be developed easily using a format somewhat like that shown in Figure 20.1 (p. 446).

AEA GUIDING PRINCIPLES FOR EVALUATORS

We cannot leave this discussion without noting the Guiding Principles of the American Evaluation Association (Shadish, Newman, Scheirer, & Wye, 1995). The AEA principles are lifestyle expectations for professional evaluators rather than a set of standards to be applied to any one specific study. The AEA principles promote a lifestyle of systematic inquiry, professional development, honesty, respect, and concern for society. As such they permeate the day-to-day activities of the evaluator over an entire career.

The AEA Guiding Principles for Evaluators

The Guiding Principles of the AEA are as follows:

A. *Systematic Inquiry:* Evaluators conduct systematic, data-based inquiries about whatever is being evaluated.

Title of evaluation document: _____

Name of reviewer: _____

		Criterion Met?			*Elaboration*

Standard: Stakeholder Identification

Specific Criteria

a. Are the audiences for the evaluation identified?	Yes	No	?	NA
b. Have the needs of the audiences been identified?	Yes	No	?	NA
c. Are the objectives of the evaluation consistent with the needs of the audiences?	Yes	No	?	NA
d. Does the information to be provided allow necessary decisions about the program to be made?	Yes	No	?	NA

Standard: Reliable Information

Specific Criteria

a. Are information-collection procedures described well?	Yes	No	?	NA
b. Will care be taken to ensure minimal error?	Yes	No	?	NA
c. Are scoring or coding procedures influenced by the evaluator's own perspective?	Yes	No	?	NA
d. Is information generated using evaluation instruments verifiable?	Yes	No	?	NA

Standard: Practical Procedures

Specific Criteria

a. Are the evaluation resources (time, money, and personnel) adequate to carry out the projected activities?	Yes	No	?	NA
b. Are management plans specified for conducting the evaluation?	Yes	No	?	NA
c. Has adequate planning been done to support the feasibility of conducting complex activities?	Yes	No	?	NA

FIGURE 20.1 Sample checklist for judging evaluation reports and designs

1. Evaluators should adhere to the highest appropriate technical standards in conducting their work, whether that work is quantitative or qualitative in nature, so as to increase the accuracy and credibility of the evaluative information they produce.

2. Evaluators should explore with the client the shortcomings and strengths both of the various evaluation questions it might be productive to ask and the various approaches that might be used for answering those questions.

3. When presenting their work evaluators should communicate their methods and approaches accurately and in sufficient detail to allow others to understand, interpret, and critique their work. They should make clear the limitations of an evaluation and its results. Evaluators should discuss in a contextually appropriate way those values, assumptions, theories, methods, results, and analyses that significantly affect the interpretation of the evaluative findings. These statements apply to all aspects of the evaluation, from its initial conceptualizations to the eventual use of findings.

B. *Competence:* Evaluators provide competent performance to stakeholders.

   1. Evaluators should possess (or, here and elsewhere as appropriate, ensure that the evaluation team possesses) the education, abilities, skills, and experience appropriate to undertake the tasks proposed in the evaluation.

   2. Evaluators should practice within the limits of their professional training and competence and should decline to conduct evaluations that fall substantially outside those limits. When declining the commission or request is not feasible or appropriate, evaluators should make clear any significant limitations on the evaluation that might result. Evaluators should make every effort to gain the competence directly or through the assistance of others who possess the required expertise.

   3. Evaluators should continually seek to maintain and improve their competencies, in order to provide the highest level of perform-ance in their evaluations. This continuing professional development might include formal coursework and workshops, self-study, eval-uations of one's own practice, and working with other evaluators to learn from their skills and expertise.

C. *Integrity/Honesty:* Evaluators ensure the honesty and integrity of the entire evaluation process.

   1. Evaluators should negotiate honestly with clients and relevant stakeholders concerning the costs, tasks to be undertaken, limita-tions of methodology, scope of results likely to be obtained, and uses of data resulting from a specific evaluation. It is primarily the evaluator's responsibility, not the client's, to initiate discussion and clarification of these matters.

   2. Evaluators should record all changes made in the originally negotiated project plans and the reasons why the changes were made. If those changes would significantly affect the scope and likely results of the evaluation, the evaluator should inform the client and other important stakeholders in a timely fashion (barring good reason to the contrary, before proceeding with further work) of the changes and their likely impact.

   3. Evaluators should seek to determine, and where appropriate be explicit about, their own, their clients', and other stakeholders' interests concerning the conduct and outcomes of an evaluation (including financial, political, and career interests).

   4. Evaluators should disclose any roles or relationships they have concerning whatever is being evaluated that might pose a signifi-cant conflict of interest with their role as an evaluator. Any such conflict should be mentioned in reports of the evaluation results.

   5. Evaluators should not misrepresent their procedures, data, or findings. Within reasonable limits, they should attempt to prevent or correct any substantial misuses of their work by others.

6. If evaluators determine that certain procedures or activities seem likely to produce misleading evaluative information or conclusions, they have the responsibility to communicate their concerns, and the reasons for them, to the client (the one who funds or requests the evaluation). If discussions with the client do not resolve these concerns, so that a misleading evaluation is then implemented, the evaluator may legitimately decline to conduct the evaluation if that is feasible and appropriate. If not, the evaluator should consult colleagues or relevant stakeholders about other proper ways to proceed. (Options might include, but are not limited to, discussions at a higher level, a dissenting cover letter or appendix, or refusal to sign the final document.)

7. Barring compelling reason to the contrary, evaluators should disclose all sources of financial support for an evaluation and the source of the request for the evaluation.

D. *Respect for People:* Evaluators respect the security, dignity, and self-worth of the respondents, program participants, clients, and other stakeholders with whom they interact.

1. Where applicable, evaluators must abide by current professional ethics and standards regarding risks, harms, and burdens that might be engendered to those participating in the evaluation; regarding informed consent for participation in evaluation; and regarding informing participants about the scope and limits of confidentiality. Examples of such standards include federal regulations about protection of human subjects, or the ethical principles of such associations as the American Anthropological Association, the American Educational Research Association, or the American Psychological Association. Although this principle is not intended to extend the applicability of such ethics and standards beyond their current scope, evaluators should abide by them where it is feasible and desirable to do so.

2. Because justified negative or critical conclusions from an evaluation must be explicitly stated, evaluations sometimes produce results that harm client or stakeholder interests. Under this circumstance, evaluators should seek to maximize the benefits and reduce any unnecessary harms that might occur, provided this will not compromise the integrity of the evaluation findings. Evaluators should carefully judge when the benefits from doing the evaluation or in performing certain evaluation procedures should be forgone because of the risks or harms. Where possible, these issues should be anticipated during the negotiation of the evaluation.

3. Knowing that evaluations often will negatively affect the interests of some stakeholders, evaluators should conduct the evaluation and communicate its results in a way that clearly respects the stakeholders' dignity and self-worth.

4. Where feasible, evaluators should attempt to foster the social equity of the evaluation, so that those who give to the evaluation can receive some benefits in return. For example, evaluators should seek to ensure that those who bear the burdens of contributing data and incurring any risks are doing so willingly and that they have full knowledge of, and maximum feasible opportunity to obtain, any benefits that may be produced from the evaluation. When it would not endanger the integrity of the evaluation, respondents or program participants should be informed whether and how they can receive services to which they are otherwise entitled without participating in the evaluation.

5. Evaluators have the responsibility to identify and respect differences between participants such as differences in their culture, religion, gender, disability, age, sexual orientation, and ethnicity, and to be mindful of potential implications of these differences when planning, conducting, analyzing, and reporting their evaluations.

E. *Responsibilities for General and Public Welfare:* Evaluators articulate and take into account the diversity of interests and values that may be related to the general and public welfare.

1. When planning and reporting evaluations, evaluators should consider including important perspectives and interests of the full range of stakeholders in the object being evaluated. Evaluators should carefully consider the justification when omitting important value perspectives or the views of important groups.

2. Evaluators should consider not only the immediate operations and outcome of whatever is being evaluated but also the broad assumptions, implications, and potential side effects of it.

3. Freedom of information is essential in a democracy. Hence, barring compelling reason to the contrary, evaluators should allow all relevant stakeholders to have access to evaluative information and should actively disseminate that information to stakeholders if resources allow. If different evaluation results are communicated in forms that are tailored to the interests of different stakeholders, those communications should ensure that each stakeholder group is aware of the existence of the other communications. Communications that are tailored to a given stakeholder should always include all important results that may bear on interests of that stakeholder. In all cases, evaluators should strive to present results as clearly and simply as accuracy allows, so that clients and other stakeholders can easily understand the evaluation process and results.

4. Evaluators should maintain a balance between client needs and other needs. Evaluators necessarily have a special relationship with the client who funds or requests the evaluation. By virtue of that relationship, evaluators must strive to meet legitimate client needs

whenever it is feasible and appropriate to do so. However, that relationship can also place evaluators in difficult dilemmas when client interests conflict with other interests, or when client interests conflict with the obligation of evaluators for systematic inquiry, competence, integrity, and respect for people. In these cases, evaluators should explicitly identify and discuss the conflicts with the client and relevant stakeholders, resolve them when possible, determine whether continued work on the evaluation is advisable if the conflicts cannot be resolved, and make clear any significant limitations on the evaluation that might result if the conflict is not resolved.

5. Evaluators have obligations that encompass the public interest and good. These obligations are especially important when evaluators are supported by publicly generated funds; but clear threat to the public good should never be ignored in any evaluation. Because the public interest and good are rarely the same as the interests of any particular group (including those of the client or funding agency), evaluators will usually have to go beyond an analysis of particular stakeholder interests when considering the welfare of society as a whole.*

THE ROLE OF METAEVALUATOR

We note that metaevaluation was added as a standard by the Joint Committee in 1994. No longer is metaevaluation seen as merely a nicety. It is now an expectation. As we implied earlier, nearly everyone does informal metaevaluation. But *formal* evaluation is something else entirely. Ostensibly, a metaevaluator must possess at least as much evaluation acumen as whoever conducted the original study. As Brinkerhoff, Brethower, Hluchyj, and Nowakowski (1983) state, "Not only should they [metaevaluators] be competent enough to *do* the original evaluation, but they also have to be able to tell if it was a good or bad one and be able to convince others that they know the difference" (p. 208).

Accurate as this observation is, it does create a dilemma: It calls for development of a "superevaluator" with sufficient competence to evaluate almost any evaluation that is done. But who then will be competent to evaluate the superevaluator's work? Other superevaluators? Or will it be necessary to develop *super*-superevaluators who are even more competent than the superevaluators whose work they judge?

Of course, the answer to such circular concerns is that in metaevaluation, as in many other efforts, we simply do the best we can. Much as we would prefer to have every metaevaluation conducted by a second superbly skilled

---

* From "Guiding principles for evaluators," American Evaluation Association, 1995, in W. R. Shadish, D. L. Newman, M. A. Scheirer, & C. Wye (Eds.) *Guiding principles for evaluators.* New Directions for Program Evaluation, No. 34, 22–26. Reprinted by permission.

evaluator, that is often not feasible. Often the best metaevaluators are evaluation advisory panels put together to capture different kinds of relevant expertise.

We see all of the following persons as being appropriate individuals to conduct metaevaluations. At the same time we recognize that the sophistication, certainty, and impartiality of their judgments are likely to vary according to their competence and conflict of interest.

1. *Metaevaluation conducted by the original evaluator.* We discussed earlier the possible biases that can accrue from evaluating one's own work. The evaluator is not immune to personal biases, and it is always advisable to have another evaluator review one's work—even if it is only a critique by a friendly but frank colleague down the hall. Should that not be possible, however, we think it better for an evaluator to measure his own evaluation work against the Joint Committee Standards and AEA Guiding Principles than to allow it to go unassessed simply because there is a risk of bias.

2. *Metaevaluation conducted by evaluation consumers.* Often the evaluation sponsor, client, or other stakeholders are left to judge the adequacy of an evaluation plan or report without assistance from a professional evaluator. The success of this approach depends heavily on the technical competence of the consumer to judge how well the evaluation meets such standards as "valid information" or "analysis of quantitative information." The Joint Committee Standards and the AEA Guiding Principles, however, do not require specialized technical training. It may be quite feasible for a client to apply most of these criteria effectively, calling on a technical expert to clarify anything that seems complex or unclear. Of course, if the evaluation is judged to be irrelevant, unintelligible, biased, or untimely, its technical adequacy may be of little concern.

3. *Metaevaluation conducted by competent evaluators.* This would seem to be the best arrangement, all else being equal. Still, there are important choices to be made. As Brinkerhoff and others (1983) remind us, (1) external metaevaluators are generally more credible than internal metaevaluators, and (2) a team may bring a greater range of skills to a metaevaluation than can an individual evaluator.

SOME GENERAL GUIDELINES
FOR CONDUCTING METAEVALUATIONS

Evaluators are well advised to plan both internal and external reviews of evaluation at critical points: once after an evaluation plan or design has been finalized, at periodic intervals during the evaluation to check progress and identify problems, and at the end of the evaluation to review findings and reports and to audit the evaluation procedures and conclusions. Many evaluators use internal and external reviews to guide their work.

The *internal review* can be conducted by an evaluation committee or advisory group. While the evaluation is in progress, the evaluator could enlist a group of stakeholders and evaluation staff, asking for their reactions to the evaluation plan, its implementation, the relative timeliness and costs of various evaluation tasks, and the need for any revisions. The minutes of such meetings provide useful progress reports for the client.

The *external review* is best conducted by a disinterested outside party with successful experience in similar evaluations. If called in early enough, the outside evaluator can review the evaluation design and offer recommendations for strengthening it. An external reviewer can also provide technical assistance during the evaluation and, at the end of the project, can review evaluation procedures, findings, and reports. The external reviewer may need to schedule a site visit at each review stage to gain full access to evaluation files, instruments, data, reports, and audiences. Such an arrangement takes both planning and knowledge of how and where to access pertinent evaluation information. The evaluator should be able to show how the evaluation has been adjusted in response to recommendations by the external reviewer.

Brinkerhoff and his colleagues (1983) provide a helpful list of procedural options (Figure 20.2) from which one might choose in focusing a metaevaluation. As noted above, one can evaluate evaluation plans, designs, activities, reports, or even the financing and management of an evaluation. We choose to emphasize in the remainder of our discussion the evaluation of the evaluation design.

In evaluation, design is critical. Poor designs do not lead to satisfactory evaluations. Yet metaevaluation has to cover more than evaluation design. It is equally important to monitor the evaluation in progress and to review reports

FIGURE 20.2 Procedural options for doing the metaevaluation

SOURCE: From *Program Evaluation: A Practitioner's Guide for Trainers and Educators* (p. 221) by R. O. Brinkerhoff, D. M. Brethower, T. Hluchyj, and J. R. Nowakowski, 1983, Boston: Kluwer-Nijhoff. Adapted by permission.

Focus of the Metaevaluation

	Formative Uses		**Summative Uses**
	Evaluating Evaluation Plans	*Evaluating Evaluation in Progress*	*Evaluating Evaluation after Its Completion*
Procedures for Doing the Metaevaluation	hire consultant (e.g., evaluator, measurement specialist, or content specialist)	independent observers (e.g., metaevaluator, evaluation team, review panel)	review of final reports (e.g., send reports to evaluator, consultant, advisory group)
	review panel (e.g., advisory group)	review of progress reports (e.g., logs, interim reports, budget update, management plan, collection schedule)	metaevaluator (e.g., sponsors or funding agent, advisory panel, professional evaluator[s])
	review of evaluation plans (e.g., design, contract management plan)		

to ensure that the promises outlined in evaluation plans have been kept. It would be foolish to wait until the report is filed to assess the adequacy of the evaluation and thus find it too late to correct many deficiencies that might otherwise be identified. In short, a complete metaevaluation includes

- Reviewing the proposed design to ensure it is feasible and sound;
- Monitoring the design to see that tasks are completed as planned and within budget;
- Checking the quality of instruments, procedures, and products (such as data and reports);
- Reviewing the design for possible midstream revisions (especially in light of the utility the evaluation has shown so far for important audiences or of problems the evaluation was running into); and
- Checking the effects of metaevaluation on the evaluation.

Because of limited space, we limit this discussion and our remaining examples to evaluating the design. Readers should easily be able to extrapolate criteria from this discussion for metaevaluations of other aspects of an evaluation.

Steps to Take in Evaluating an Evaluation Design

The following steps are proposed for conducting a metaevaluation of an evaluation design:

1. *Obtain a copy of the design in a form ready for review.* Formative evaluation of a metaevaluation is obviously desirable once the design is sufficiently formulated to make such a review productive. There is little utility in telling an evaluator that his unfinished design is incomplete.
2. *Identify who will do the metaevaluation.* Check our comments in the previous section "The Role of Metaevaluator" for help in this decision.
3. *Ensure that authorization exists to evaluate the design.* If you are a sponsor or client and you receive a design submitted by an evaluator who proposes to contract with you to do an evaluation, you are obviously free to evaluate it, and normally there would be no professional or legal restraint on your arranging for another competent "metaevaluator" to assist you in doing so. Conversely, suppose the chair of a Concerned Citizens Against Homeless Shelters committee asks you to find flaws in an internal evaluation design the local homeless shelter proposes to use in evaluating its program. You should question the appropriateness of that role, especially if you find the design is in rough-draft form, circulated only for internal reactions, and surreptitiously spirited from the shelter to the

committee by a disgruntled shelter custodian. Metaevaluators (like evaluators) can find themselves used as "hired guns," and it is important before buckling on the holster to be certain that the metaevaluation desired by your paymaster will not violate ethical or legal principles.

4. *Apply standards to the evaluation design.* The Joint Committee encourages use of the Program Evaluation Standards by appending a checklist to its publication.

5. *Judge the adequacy of the evaluation design.* No evaluation design is perfect. The question is whether, on balance, after summarizing judgments across scales, the evaluation seems to achieve its purposes at an acceptable level of quality.

A NEED FOR MORE METAEVALUATION

With any luck we have convinced the reader that the concept of metaevaluation is useful and that there are appropriate tools that can be used for that purpose. Despite the wide publicity, acceptance, and availability of the Joint Committee's standards, however, few evaluations are being subjected to any closer scrutiny now than before their publication. Even casual inspection reveals that only a small proportion of evaluation studies are ever evaluated, even in the most perfunctory fashion. Of the few metaevaluations that do occur, most are internal evaluations done by the evaluator who produced the evaluation in the first place. It is rare indeed to see an evaluator call in an outside expert to evaluate his evaluation efforts. Perhaps the reasons are many and complex why this is so, but one seems particularly compelling: Evaluators are human and are no more ecstatic about having their work evaluated than are professionals in other areas of endeavor. It can be a profoundly unnerving experience to swallow one's own prescriptions. Although the infrequency of good metaevaluation might be understandable, it is not easily forgivable, for it enables shoddy evaluation practices to go undetected and, worse, to be repeated again and again, to the detriment of the profession.

> ### CASE STUDY APPLICATION
>
> *June 4.* My final report went to Claire Janson today, so this evaluation is completed at last! Or is it? I did suggest to the folks at Radnor that it would be in their best interest to have the completed evaluation reviewed by an outside evaluator. Masochistic as this may seem, I strongly believe that there is more to be learned by involving other eyes and ears, perspectives, experience, and, of course, expertise, in any evaluation. To the extent that we become aware of limitations and strong points in the evaluation, I and my Radnor friends can weigh how much confidence to place in the results. We can also learn something that can help us when we undertake evaluation in the future. The learning process in evaluation never stops. That's one reason why I keep at it, I guess. Of course Brad's orthodontics bill is another.

June 16. Just received a package from Radnor. Claire got a professor who teaches evaluation courses in Philadelphia to agree to review the evaluation as a volunteer service to the school district. She used the Joint Committee *Standards* as the basis for his review. Claire kindly sent me a copy of the review. Brief, but helpful.

ARTIFACT 10

Ms. Janson, my reaction to the external evaluation you had conducted for your district is summarized below, using only the category headings for the Joint Committee's *Standards* we discussed. Sorry time did not permit me to provide more detail.

1. Utility of the evaluation. It appears that the groundwork has been laid for producing an evaluation report that has impact. It remains to be seen, however, whether the utility of the evaluation will be worth its cost. You should follow up with the recommendations that resulted from the evaluation and should monitor changes in the program. Because the evaluator has become so knowledgeable about the program, he is a resource that might be tapped in the future for advice on follow-up reviews. My advice to you is not to look at this evaluation as a one-shot study; build on it, continue your reviews, and use further internal evaluation for planning and development. Strong points of this study related to utility were stakeholder involvement throughout the evaluation, the credibility that the evaluator established for himself and the evaluation, the scope of the evaluation, the integration of multiple value orientations into the study, and clarity and timing of the report.

A possible limitation may be the question of commitment of top administrators to the program itself as well as to using the evaluation. Although they have said they are committed, actions speak louder than words.

2. Feasibility of the evaluation. The evaluation was tailored to meet budget and time constraints of the client. The logistics of all phases of the evaluation were kept manageable and enabled the study to be completed on time and within budget. The evaluator did a nice job of not overpromising. He delivered what he said he would. Political viability was built by involving everyone who wanted to be involved or who had something to say about the program.

An unknown yet is the cost-effectiveness of the evaluation, and this is something you can affect. The way in which the evaluation is used should justify its cost. A lot of money and energy that might have been better spent on other work will have been wasted if this evaluation has no demonstrable impact. On the other hand, considerable cost savings could occur if the evaluation prevents investments in future unproductive program activities. This remains to be seen.

3. Propriety of the evaluation. This aspect of the evaluation looks fairly good. A brief agreement clarified most expectations for the evaluation, and everything that was promised was delivered in a quality manner. (But the agreement was a bit too brief and I suspect you and the evaluator must have developed a fair bit of mutual trust to get through the study without major misunderstandings.) There were no conflicts of interest evident in the evaluation. It was wise to hire an impartial and independent evaluation methodologist for the study. Reports were full, frank, and fair, and the rights of participants and informants were respected and protected. Strengths and weaknesses of the program were both addressed. Interactions during the evaluation appeared to be very professional and respectful.

4. Accuracy of the evaluation. The evaluator compensated well for his lack of expertise in humanities education. The use of outside experts and humanities instructors from Radnor rounded out the team of evaluators that, in my judgment, was needed to do a good job of evaluating this program. The evaluator was at somewhat of a disadvantage in that instruments for data collection were not readily available, so that several had to be developed ad hoc. This is a fairly common circumstance in evaluation, but instrument development is expensive and time consuming. The evaluator did a good job of balancing resource allocations to instrument development with his constraints, maybe even an outstanding job, given the limitations placed on him. By using multiple methods and sources, he was able to triangulate in gathering information that is not misleading. It was evident that if he had used just one source and one method (interviews), he might have been led to far different findings that would have been off target. His methods of data control, data analysis, and interpretation addressed the standards of systematic data control, analysis of quantitative and qualitative information, justified conclusions, and objective reporting.

The one limitation that I saw in the reports was the lack of thoroughness of object identification and context analysis. Although the informed reader is well informed about the program and its context, the uninformed reader of the evaluation reports is left wondering about pertinent characteristics of the school district and participating faculty and students. History and philosophy of the program received too little attention, as did implications of the evaluation for other educators who might be considering a similar undertaking. Perhaps a separate report for other educators is in order, so that they can be better informed about its transportability, processes, content, and impact.

Author Comments.   Just as I thought. Well done, but not perfect. There was something to be learned from having the evaluation evaluated by an impartial expert in evaluation. There always is.

October 10. Had a telephone call from Pennsylvania today, requesting some extra copies of the evaluation report I wrote last spring. I was interested to learn that the Radnor folk *did* use that evaluation to make some very sensible decisions about their humanities program. That's the good news. But the bad news is that they've just launched a new districtwide, computer-assisted math curriculum, with absolutely no plans to evaluate it to see how well it works. Claire said she argued vigorously that an evaluation should be built in from the outset, but she lost out.

It beats me why evaluation isn't a regular part of every school's planning, budgeting, program development, textbook and test selection, performance reviews and staff development, educational reform, school board deliberations, mileage requests, and the like. I suspect the problem is that few leadership figures in education, in politics, and in the community have much real understanding about evaluation. There are few who are aware of the potential or who have seen the impact that evaluation can have. There are few who have seen *good* evaluation, in fact. And there are probably many who have seen or experienced poorly done evaluations. We have come a long way during the past 30 years in our understanding of the role and proper conduct of evaluation. We are still learning, but I shouldn't forget that we now know a lot more than we did then.

Seems to me evaluators should be working with school districts, school boards, politicians, and community groups to share what they know and to work out plans for using evaluation effectively. Wouldn't it be something if more administrators figured out how to recognize and reward exemplary evaluation efforts, or maybe even some sensible way to penalize those who spend large chunks of public funds without any effort to evaluate the quality or usefulness of those expenditures? With that kind of leadership, and real effort from the evaluation community, we should be able to make evaluation more useful so it will be used more often and more intelligently.

My word—I just reread this entry, and I wonder where I left my drums and bugle. If I'm not careful, I'll be marching forth, flags flying, to increase the *esprit de évaluation!* Best put a leash on my enthusiasm, I guess. I'd rather hate having my colleagues discount me as some wild-eyed fanatic who gets high by ranting about how evaluation can vanquish the evils of the world. That would surely be a totally exaggerated caricature. Well, at least a somewhat exaggerated caricature.

Author Comments.   And so we come to the end of our fictional evaluation. Yet I have only scratched the surface of what actually happens in carrying out any real evaluation. Most evaluation studies are complex and comprehensive enterprises. Beneath the complexity, however, lie many simple, straightforward steps on which the evaluator and client can work as partners. I hope my imaginary case study has been instructive on some of those practical guidelines. I also hope it has shown that evaluation studies are strongest when tailored specifically to meet the client's needs, drawing as necessary on multiple perspectives rather than follow the prescriptions of any one evaluation model or method. It would be disappointing if my contrived evaluation failed to make that point.

I must confess that writing this fictional Radnor evaluation has been therapeutic. It is the only evaluation I have ever conducted from the comfort of my armchair, and it is the only evaluation where no one has raised questions about my design or my motives, or even my ancestry. Yes indeed, doing these make-believe evaluations could prove addictive.

APPLICATION EXERCISES

1. Use the Joint Committee's Program Evaluation Standards to evaluate a completed evaluation study of your choice. For what aspects of the study do you lack information? What can you learn from the strengths and weaknesses of the work of other evaluators?

2. Select a class of evaluation studies (e.g., program evaluations in a state or federal human services agency completed from 1985 until the present). Use the Program Evaluation Standards to evaluate each study. From these data, can you draw any inferences about program evaluation in the agency? Are there any patterns that emerge? You could repeat this exercise with other classes of evaluations, looking for patterns and drawing conclusions.

RELEVANT EVALUATION STANDARDS

The entire set of 30 standards is pertinent here (which should not be surprising, since this chapter focuses on metaevaluation, the very process for which the 30 metaevaluation standards were created).

SUGGESTED READINGS

Joint Committee on Standards for Educational Evaluation. (1994). *The Program Evaluation Standards* (2nd ed.). Thousand Oaks, CA: Sage.

Shadish, W. R., Newman, D. L., Scheirer, M. A., & Wye, C. (Eds.). (1995). *Guiding principles for evaluators*. New Directions for Program Evaluation, No. 66, San Francisco: Jossey-Bass.

Stufflebeam, D. L. (1974). *Metaevaluation* (Occasional Paper No. 3). Kalamazoo: Western Michigan University Evaluation Center.

part FIVE

Emerging and Future Settings for Program Evaluation

Throughout the prior sections of our text we have described how program evaluation has served important uses in a variety of educational, public, and private-sector settings. We have given examples of program evaluations in local school districts and national education programs, in federal and state health and human services programs, in local community programs aimed at social or environmental problems, in military and scientific endeavors, in nonprofit agencies, and in business and industrial settings. In this final section, we expand our discussion of two settings that are becoming increasingly familiar in today's evaluation scene.

First, in Chapter 21 we discuss several different ways in which multiple-site program evaluations have been used in the past, examine some pitfalls and potentials of multiple-site evaluations, and consider some new conceptions of multiple-site evaluations that are becoming more widely used.

Second, in Chapter 22 we discuss in greater detail how program evaluation is emerging as a dominant force in private and nonprofit settings and describe its role in organizational renewal and improvement of training efforts. We discuss how evaluation fits with and enhances efforts to improve quality and relevance through Total Quality Management, front-end analysis, performance appraisals, customer satisfaction surveys, and other similar corporate endeavors.

Finally, in Chapter 23 we briefly discuss what we and other commentators see as the future of program evaluation.

Because these chapters deal with a wide variety of settings, we have not attempted to extend our Radnor case study into this final section of our text.

chapter **21**

Conducting Multiple-Site Evaluation Studies*

ORIENTING QUESTIONS

1. What is a multiple-site program evaluation and how does it differ from a single-site program evaluation?
2. What are the major reasons for conducting multiple-site program evaluations?
3. What are the three most common types of multiple-site evaluations?
4. What are the primary advantages and disadvantages of multisite evaluation (MSE)? What purposes does it serve?
5. What are the primary advantages and disadvantages of on-site evaluation at multiple sites? What purposes does it serve?
6. What are the primary advantages and disadvantages of cluster evaluation?
7. What major differences exist between MSE, cluster evaluation, and on-site evaluation at multiple sites?

In the preceding chapters, we have discussed procedures for planning and conducting program evaluations without devoting much attention to one very important consideration: Do the evaluation approaches and methods we have presented work equally well for evaluating (a) a program that exists at only one site, in a single agency, and (b) a program that exists at multiple sites, either within the same agency or in different agencies? For example, does the content of prior chapters apply as readily to an evaluation of Arizona's statewide, elementary school, English as a Second Language (ESL) program as to an evaluation of the ESL program in the Frost Elementary School in Mesa? Are the

---

* Portions of this chapter draw on an article by the senior author, in press, in the international journal *Evaluation*.

evaluation approaches and methods we have presented as applicable to evaluating the Rockefeller Foundation's national, six-site Minority Female Single Parent (MFSP) program as they are to evaluating the Atlanta MFSP program? Will the processes and principles we have outlined serve as well in evaluating IBM's overall, nationwide technician training program as in evaluating the effectiveness of the technician training program operated by IBM-Memphis?

For the most part, we would answer these questions affirmatively. Most of what we have said is as applicable to a multiple-site program evaluation as to the evaluation of a single-site program. Evaluations of either a single- or multiple-site program could opt to use a management-oriented evaluation approach or an objectives-oriented approach. Either would need to be focused by determining the purposes for the evaluation, identifying precisely what aspects of the program are to be evaluated, and deciding what specific questions the evaluation is intended to answer. Either would need to be planned by deciding what specific methodology the evaluation would employ, what ethical issues exist and how they can be resolved, and who should receive reports and in what format. In short, most of the contents of this text are applicable to both multiple-site and single-site evaluations.

There are, however, some special evaluation procedures and issues that pertain to evaluation of multiple-site programs. In this chapter, we briefly discuss reasons why multiple-site evaluations can be advantageous; distinguish between three different, general types of multiple-site evaluations; and discuss some special considerations and concerns relating to each of these three types. While some forms of multiple-site evaluation have been with us for decades, others we describe in this chapter are newly emerging or evolving in ways that will likely impact on how many program evaluations are conducted in the future.

PURPOSES AND CHARACTERISTICS
OF MULTIPLE-SITE EVALUATIONS

There are several reasons for conducting program evaluations that span multiple sites. Some of the major reasons are these:

- To determine the overall effect of the program, when effects are aggregated across all program sites
- To evaluate the program in a sample of representative sites so as to estimate the effect of the program across all sites
- To determine whether the program works under the variety of conditions and circumstances that exist where it has been implemented
- To study how the program interacts with specific site characteristics (e.g., demographic differences in program participants, varying placements of the program within agencies' governing structures)

- To monitor individual site compliance in implementing the program according to its specifications or standards
- To compare program performance across sites to identify the most effective and ineffective ways of operating the program
- To determine which sites should be continued or discontinued in the program
- To facilitate cross-site sharing of "effective practices," "lessons learned," and other insights gained in one site that could be beneficial to other sites
- To have program administrators and staff at each site understand that their site may be included in an evaluation (thus serving one of evaluation's primary noninformational purposes)
- To develop collaborative evaluation efforts among evaluators at specific sites to improve evaluation at each site and across sites

And doubtlessly there are other good reasons for multiple-site evaluations that we have overlooked. Those we have listed have contributed to a variety of specific forms of multiple-site evaluations, of which we will discuss the three most common in the remainder of this chapter.

Three Common Types of Multiple-Site Evaluations

Multisite Evaluations. One of the most conspicuous uses of multiple-site evaluation is the conduct of large-scale experimental or quasi-experimental studies of major social or human services programs in areas such as health care, education, mental health, criminal justice, or public welfare. We will refer to this particular type of multiple-site evaluation as "multisite," in keeping with prominent literature on this type of evaluation (e.g., Turpin & Sinacore, 1991).

On-Site Evaluation at Multiple Sites. A second common approach to evaluating multiple-site programs is the use of on-site evaluation teams to visit all or a sample of sites implementing the program. Typically, the purpose of such visits is to determine the value and effectiveness of the individual programs and/ or the overall program, when individual site findings are aggregated, as described by Worthen, O'Sullivan, and White (in press).

Cluster Evaluation. A third, emerging form of multiple-site evaluation is cluster evaluation, a multiple-site, multilevel evaluation approach developed and used within the W. K. Kellogg Foundation to evaluate "clusters" of projects either funded by a specific, targeted funding initiative or clustered together because they deal with the same theme or topic.

These three types of multiple-site evaluations are intended to serve rather different purposes, which may be more readily understood by examining some specific dimensions on which these three types differ.

Two Dimensions on Which
Multiple-Site Evaluations Differ

Sinacore and Turpin (1991) categorized multiple-site evaluations (which they termed "MSEs") into *prospective* and *retrospective*. In the former, the evaluator "intends to use multiple sites at the beginning of an evaluation," while in the latter the use of multiple sites is an afterthought "in which data from different evaluations on a similar topic are brought together for an analysis" (p. 6). These authors also distinguish between two subtypes of MSE as follows:

> One subtype of MSE is an evaluation of a program that is implemented in the *same way* at different geographical locations. . . .
> Another subtype of MSE is an evaluation of a program that is implemented in *different ways* at different geographical locations. (p. 6)

FIGURE 21.1   Dimensions for a typology of multiple-site evalutions

Decision to Use Multiple Sites Is Made

<table>
<tr><th rowspan="2">Program Implementation in Multiple Sites Is</th><th></th><th>Before Evaluation Begins
(Prospective)</th><th>After Evaluation Data
Are Collected
(Retrospective)</th></tr>
<tr><td>Controlled (The
Same in All Sites)</td><td>1.   **Controlled
Prospective**

Multiple sites
selected early;
uniform program
implementation
attempted</td><td>2.   **Controlled
Retrospective**

Retrospective analysis of
data from multiple sites
found (after the fact) to
have used the same
implementation</td></tr>
<tr><td>Uncontrolled
(Different across Sites)</td><td>3.   **Uncontrolled
Prospective**

Multiple sites
selected early; no
effort made to
make program
implementation
uniform</td><td>4.   **Uncontrolled
Retrospective**

Retrospective
analysis of data
from multiple
sites found to
have been
implemented
dissimilarly</td></tr>
</table>

From Sinacore and Turpin's discussion of MSEs, one can conceive of four different types, as shown in Figure 21.1.[1] For now, let us merely say that the *Controlled Prospective* variant (cell 1) is perhaps the most common form of multiple-site evaluation, while the *Controlled Retrospective* variant (cell 2) is more rare, since the probability of finding program implementation the same without prior planning is not too high. It may occur, however, when evaluators become aware that they have counterparts laboring in similar vineyards where the grapes and methods of harvesting them are sufficiently similar to allow the results to be combined into an evaluation "wine" that contains a blend of the individual program evaluations. More often, however, such retrospective analyses discover that the program implementation in the various sites was so dissimilar (e.g., very dissimilar program participants) that the evaluation slides into cell 4, *Uncontrolled Retrospective* multiple-site evaluations, which is appropriately shunned by most evaluators as having little to offer in generating useful information about the program. *Uncontrolled Prospective* multiple-site evaluations (cell 3) are useful in that the clustering of sites has a thoughtful, preordinate rationale, but they are problematic in that it is difficult to sort out the effects of the specific site from the effects of the program. Yet this approach to multiple-site evaluation is preferred by advocates of cluster evaluation, as we will discuss shortly.

MULTISITE EVALUATION (MSE)

Turpin and Sinacore (1991) have coined the term **multisite evaluations (MSEs)** to refer to common evaluations of large-scale social programs such as an evaluation of health services provided by 172 U.S. Department of Veterans Affairs medical centers dispersed throughout the nation. Based on social science research methods, MSEs typically use experimental or quasi-experimental designs, complete with randomization, coupled with sophisticated statistical analysis. MSEs are marked by careful efforts to standardize and control both implementation of the program and the procedures for collecting, verifying, and analyzing the evaluation data. Careful sampling of sites for inclusion in the evaluation is another attribute of most well-conducted MSEs. Thus, the MSE is the archetypical example of a *Controlled Prospective* multiple-site evaluation (cell 1 in Figure 21.1).

Greenberg, Meyer, and Wiseman (1994) define MSE as "a multisite design in which similar program features have been tested simultaneously at several different local administrative offices" (p. 679). Sinacore and Turpin (1991) state:

---

[1] While the two major structuring dimensions shown in Figure 21.1 are suggested by Sinacore and Turpin (1991), the present authors have combined and juxtaposed them in new ways and are thus solely responsible if doing so has altered the meaning or significance of those dimensions.

The distinguishing feature of an MSE is its implementation at different sites with an analysis of *original* data. MSEs should not be confused with metanalyses in which investigators study the effects of programs by examining the summary statistics of numerous published and unpublished evaluations. (p. 7)

Purposes of MSE

The most widely agreed-upon purposes of MSEs are those listed simply by Turpin and Sinacore (1991):

It appears that many evaluators conduct MSEs for similar reasons: to increase generalizability of findings, to maximize sample size, and to respond to a variety of political and social demands. (p. 1)

These authors note that increasing the generalizability of findings greatly increases their external validity, since collecting data from multiple sites helps to pinpoint how well the program works with different types of clients in different contexts. They also point out that using multiple sites increases the sample size, thus raising the statistical power of data analyses and the reliability and validity of the results.

Cottingham (1991) points out that not only are MSEs proposed as a fast means of learning about a program's universality and replicability but, if the program works, its use in multiple sites is viewed as useful in speeding acceptance and adoption of the new program. Greenberg and his colleagues (1994) have provided, in the following quotation, a good sense of the purposes MSEs can serve. They addressed the question of why one might opt to undertake an experiment at multiple sites.

Since it is obvious that, with a given sample size, it is more costly to conduct and evaluate a multisite experiment than a single-site experiment, a useful starting point is to ask what purposes are served by the former that cannot be served by the latter. There are at least three potential advantages of multisite experiments. First, a multisite design can be used to determine whether the program being tested "works" under a variety of conditions. For example, sites may vary in the characteristics of the population being served, economic and other environmental conditions, and program components and inputs. Second, impact estimates can be based on an evaluation sample that is pooled across sites, thereby producing measures that are "representative" of potential program effects over broad geographical areas such as a state or the nation as a whole. Third, multisite evaluations can be used to draw inferences about underlying production relationships by examining how program effects vary with cross-site differences in participant characteristics, environmental conditions, and program features. (p. 680)

Issues in MSE

There are a variety of issues that must be addressed in planning an MSE. First, there is the natural tension between maintaining standardization and control of the program implementation versus the need to adapt the program to local needs and circumstances. While we have said that efforts to control implementation typify the MSE, that is not to say that all those who propose MSE advocate that programs mindlessly force each site to implement the program in the prescribed pattern if (a) it is obvious that local circumstances would cause that prescription to fail but (b) slight adaptations would allow the program to work well. But how much adaptation can be tolerated before one no longer has an evaluation of a single program at multiple sites but rather a series of evaluations of quite different programs? If an MSE of a drug-free schools program shows poor results, is the program to blame, or was the failure due to lack of fidelity in implementing the program? This is an important issue to resolve early in any MSE. Readers who wish more depth in this area are referred to Mowbray and Herman (1991), Cottingham (1991), and Tushnet (1995).

A second issue in MSE is how sites should be selected for inclusion in the evaluation. What seems to be a straightforward issue ("Just draw a random sample") turns out to be somewhat more complex. As Sinacore and Turpin (1991) put it:

> Statistically speaking, deliberate sampling for heterogeneity does not allow one to generalize in meaningful ways to a larger population. This is because selection is not random. However, the variation in participants that is created by using multiple sites allows the evaluator to examine the extent to which a program influences different types of people. For example, if it were shown that the reading program in question was successful at all the sites, it would be known that children across three socioeconomic levels were affected by the program. Given this outcome, something would be learned about the efficacy of the program relative to specific groups of different socioeconomic levels. It would not be known if the same results would be found with a stratified random sample, but at least it can be said that an effect was obtained across the particular range of children involved in the evaluation. (p. 8)

Groups and organizations, like individuals, have "personalities" that can seriously affect program outcomes and cannot be ignored as mere nuisance effects. Therefore, one needs to consider such institutional dimensions before selecting specific sites, using everything that is known about the specific social, political, and organizational characteristics of sites in selecting the best cross section of sites for the MSE. Sinacore and Turpin (1991) concur, noting that

> In sum, a high-quality MSE depends on the evaluator's knowledge about the sites—their organizations and personnel—before including them in

the study. A common wisdom in the Department of Veterans Affairs states, "When you have seen one VA, you have seen one VA." This message should be well heeded. The wise evaluator verifies any claims regarding similarity of prospective sites while planning an MSE. (p. 11)

A third issue in MSE is how to obtain adequate cooperation from each participating site. This has to do both with obtaining the necessary sanction to conduct the evaluation activities at that site and with how relationships, tasks, and arrangements for data collection can be structured to ensure that the needed access to data sources will not be closed off.

There are also many practical issues in conducting MSEs. We enumerate several such issues below, drawing on Sinacore and Turpin (1991), Hedrick and her colleagues (1991), and the authors' experience with MSEs.

1. Understanding the System.   The evaluator's success in conducting an MSE will be determined to a large degree by how well she understands the system within which the program "lives."

2. Staffing the MSE.   A functional staffing plan is essential to the success of any MSE. Whether each site has a separate site coordinator, whether that person has supervisory responsibility for internal program staff and/or external data collectors, whether a central staff will travel to collect all the site data, and so on will vary with each MSE. We can offer no guidelines except that careful guidelines for staffing MSEs must be developed and followed.

3. Staff Training.   For MSEs to be feasible, all evaluation staff must be well trained in how to perform their various tasks. Training may depend on training manuals with separate sections for data collectors, site coordinators, and the like. Training videos may be useful. Workshops to train site evaluation staff may be held at some central location, or a traveling trainer may make a circuit ride, training site evaluators in their own local sites.

4. Budgeting.   Whether an MSE costs more or less than a single-site evaluation with a similar overall magnitude of effort depends on individual circumstances. In general, however, the MSE will be more expensive because of travel costs, personnel time needed to arrange the travel, and long-distance communication (telephone, fax, mail). Budgets for MSEs can sometimes become rather complicated and must be carefully developed and applied.

5. Identifying and Overcoming Cross-Site Obstacles.   The success of an MSE depends on a variety of sensitive and intricately balanced issues. One is stakeholder "buy-in" to the evaluation; involvement of stakeholders in the MSE is important to enhance their ownership of the evaluation activities and results. Communication barriers and social gaps can scuttle the MSE, since it requires such a high degree of communication and cooperation. And nowhere is the ability to analyze and cope with political issues more important than in an MSE. As Sinacore and Turpin (1991) aptly put it:

> While most of us are aware of the political aspects of evaluation research, the multiple political environments of an MSE can be easily overlooked. Even if there is a strong central figure for the study who has influence over participation, there are frequently gatekeepers at each site who can influence data quality. Therefore, it is imperative for evaluators to become aware of the political climate at each site and to respond accordingly. (p. 11)

6. Maintaining Quality Control.   The greater the number of sites in an MSE, the greater the challenge is to maintaining quality of the evaluation data. Standardization across sites of some, if not all, of the evaluation data is the sine qua non of MSE. For data to be "aggregatable," the procedures for collecting, organizing, and verifying all site data must be followed carefully.

7. Conducting Appropriate Statistical Analyses.   Combining data across multiple sites poses challenges not confronted by the single-site evaluator. Even a cursory discussion of those special challenges concerning units of analysis, pooling, and interaction effects would exceed our space here, but interested readers are referred to Sinacore and Turpin (1991).

8. Conducting Multi-Level MSEs.   Many MSEs are already complicated enough when the evaluation of the program is all at the same level. Sometimes, however, an MSE may contain two or more levels of evaluation, such as (a) site-specific program evaluations that attempt to determine the value of specific program variations and (b) a cross-site evaluation of the program intended to provide judgments about the program's overall quality and value.

Future of MSEs

Those who prefer to use social science research methods in their evaluations will likely continue to use MSEs to evaluate human services and other public-sector programs. According to Sinacore and Turpin (1991), MSEs are becoming more popular, and more evaluators will need to prepare themselves to conduct such studies. In their words:

> Use of MSEs is slowly on the rise. Indeed, some evaluators are presently conducting MSEs without realizing that the techniques involved are emerging as a new area of methodological expertise in professional evaluation. Therefore, evaluators who are aware of the advantages and the demands of MSEs will be prepared to conduct the best evaluations of this type. As interest in MSEs continues to grow over the next few years, we expect that many evaluators will come to recognize the potentially rich data sets that MSEs can offer. (p. 17)

ON-SITE EVALUATION AT MULTIPLE SITES

On-site evaluation, where an external evaluator or team visits the program site, collects data, and judges the program on specified evaluative criteria, is one of the most frequently used strategies to evaluate programs in education, health and human services, and nonprofit programs. The popularity of on-site evaluation is doubtless due, at least in part, to the fact that it can be a simple and straightforward approach that is not dependent on extensive technical expertise in psychometrics, statistics, or data manipulation. For those who view professional judgment as constituting the core of evaluation, on-site evaluation is often the preferred approach. Further, on-site evaluation is a flexible method that can be used as a part of a wide variety of evaluation approaches, in either single- or multiple-site programs (although we will focus particularly on the latter in this section). We discussed on-site evaluation briefly as a method in Chapter 18, for it can be used to collect data *within* either MSEs or cluster evaluations, its two companions in this chapter. However, it also qualifies as a form of multisite evaluation in its own right and is therefore treated more fully in this chapter.

There are two related reasons why on-site evaluation visits are made: (1) they are often required by legislation or by some funding or regulatory agency and (2) on-site evaluation is viewed as a valuable technique in assisting programs to reach their full potential. Consequently, on-site evaluation can be used for either formative or summative purposes, although the latter is more common.

On-site evaluation is often used to judge the effectiveness or value of large-scale programs where (1) it is not feasible or desirable to use experimental or quasi-experimental designs for the evaluation; (2) there are no readily available objectives, quantitative indices that can be used as a basis for determining program effects (e.g., test scores, hours of volunteer service, pregnancy rates among specified populations); and (3) program sponsors/funders want relevant evidence beyond the usual rhetoric or unsupported opinions offered by program directors and staff as the basis for judgments about the worth of the programs they operate. For educational programs that are not intended to raise student scores on standardized tests, on-site evaluation is perhaps the most common form of evaluation. In secondary and higher education institutions, accreditation site visits are familiar examples of on-site evaluation, but accrediting agencies' requirements and procedures are tailored to the particular needs and programs they serve and are seldom adaptable for efforts to develop an on-site evaluation procedure appropriate for use with other multiple-site programs. Thus, we will not discuss the philosophy or conduct of accreditation site visits in this chapter. (See Chapter 8, where accreditation is discussed).

Except for accreditation site visits, on-site evaluation is frequently conducted in such a haphazard fashion that it is often discounted as a useful evaluation method. Critics — including staff in programs evaluated by site-visit teams—have complained that site visitors have wandered randomly through their programs, asked apparently aimless questions, and ended up making subjective judgments based on unarticulated criteria. While this may be a caricature of some on-site evaluations, it is such an uncomfortably accurate description of so many that one could almost conclude that the bad reputation of on-site evaluation is deserved. Our view is that it is not. Like any other form of evaluation, on-site evaluation can be done well or poorly. Our focus here is on the development and use of high-quality on-site evaluation procedures, processes, and systems to evaluate the effectiveness of multiple-site programs. Based on our experience with designing, implementing, and monitoring evaluation site visits to various funded programs in multiple sites, we are convinced that well-developed on-site evaluation can be a very effective and very flexible evaluation technique. For example, we believe on-site evaluation can be used to serve the following purposes in multisite evaluations:

- To monitor program compliance with funding agency regulations or guidelines
- To interview program staff and other program participants (through individual or focus-group interviews) to understand how the program operates and how they feel about it
- To collect data with on-site instruments, such as classroom tests or attitude scales, "on-the-spot" handout questionnaires for clinic patients, or observation checklists for use in recording prospective pilots' behavior and performance in commercial pilot training programs
- To probe to understand anomalies or contradictions in data provided previously by sites
- To provide funding agencies with qualitative descriptions of how well each site is accomplishing the agency's program goals and how successful the overall program is when viewed across sites
- To rate each site on specific criteria and provide the funding agency with a summative "score" that might be used in decisions about continuing or discontinuing funding

Obviously, several of these purposes might be accomplished simultaneously, depending on how the on-site evaluation system was set up. And there are doubtless many more purposes we have not thought to list.

The Issue of Control in Multiple-Site On-Site Evaluation

An ideal on-site evaluation of a multiple-site program should, in our judgment, be a Controlled Prospective evaluation (cell 1 in Figure 21.1), where (1) the decision to use multiple evaluation sites is made before the evaluation begins and (2) program implementation is uniform across sites, allowing site-visit teams to develop and use common measures across all program sites. Where implementation of the program is intended to be the same, this would qualify as a "controlled implementation" approach.

In many multisite programs, however, considerable latitude is given to sites in how they implement the program. In such cases, the Uncontrolled Prospective evaluation (cell 2 in Figure 21.1) could allow evaluation to proceed so that evaluation procedures at each site are different and each site-visit team develops its own approach to match the form of the program they encounter in the particular site. Far too often this is the form that multiple-site on-site evaluation takes. While there will be cases where programs are so dissimilar across sites that a series of case studies is the only sensible evaluation approach, in most structured, multisite programs there are essential ingredients that should be present and specific criteria that should be met, *without which the program is not fulfilling, in that site, the intent of those who funded it.* In such cases we believe it is important for the on-site evaluation procedures to be standardized across sites, so that they will provide program sponsors with critical data on how each site is performing, at least on those key dimensions. (This would shift the evaluation back to cell 1 in Figure 21.1.).

We recognize that it is not as easy to standardize on-site evaluation procedures across program sites as is the case with the more structured MSE approach we discussed earlier. But we believe that much more can and should be done to move as far as possible in that direction. Space does not permit us to detail here how that might be done, but we refer readers to a description by Worthen, O'Sullivan, and White (in press) of a detailed set of guidelines and procedures for on-site evaluation of multiple-site programs that outline how to do the following:

- Develop the evaluative questions that will be used in all sites.
- Develop on-site instruments, including rating scales to be used by site-visit teams.
- Make all necessary arrangements for site visits in ways that will reduce or eliminate site-visitor biases.
- Train team members in use of the instruments to standardize data collection and ratings through use of rating-scale anchor points.
- Summarize and report site-visit results so that both cross-site commonalities and specific site idiosyncracies can be understood.

Other Issues in Using Multiple-Site On-Site Evaluation

Several issues need to be considered as one determines how to make the best use of on-site evaluations. The way in which each of the following issues is resolved will determine how the specific on-site evaluation system is designed. In a multiple-site program, general on-site evaluation procedures and instruments should be designed for use in each of the separate on-site evaluations. These will include a general set of questions, criteria, and instruments developed at the outset so evaluators can be trained to use them thereafter with the multiple sites. Essential activities include the following:

1. Selecting the On-Site Evaluation Sample.   If resources are limited, it will be necessary to conduct on-site evaluations of only a sample of the sites in which the program has been implemented. This sample might be selected systematically to include particular sites important for reasons peculiar to that program or to assure as much variability as possible along dimensions such as (a) funding level, (b) geographical location, (c) number of clients served, and so on. Usually a preferable strategy would be to stratify on such variables thought to be important and draw a stratified random sample. This also has the advantage of all sites' knowing they may be included, thus allowing the evaluation to provide some sense of accountability for all sites.

2. Collecting Data before the On-Site Visit.   It is not necessary for site-visit teams to go into a site uninformed about how the program is being used in that site. Mailed questionnaire surveys can be used very effectively to elicit key information about program parameters and details at that site before the site team arrives. The information produced by the questionnaire (or previsit telephone calls, examination of site documents, reports, etc.) also often provide clues of possible problems or issues that should be probed in greater depth during on-site visits.

3. Determining the Duration of the Site Visit.   On-site evaluation visits can vary in duration and intensity from a brief, informal stroll through a program site to an intensive and extensive week-long observation and examination of virtually every facet of the program's operation and activities at that site. Theoretically, site visits could last indefinitely, or at least until the evaluation budget runs out. Practically, however, the cost of maintaining evaluators on site (e.g., lodging and food) usually prohibits use of ethnography and other methods that are time-extensive. In fact, in most program evaluations, a site visit of one to three days in duration may be adequate.

4. Deciding on the Number of Team Members.   On-site teams can obviously vary in size from a single evaluator to a large team presided over by a team leader or coordinator. It seems obvious that, all things being equal, larger, more complex programs require larger numbers of team members to provide adequate coverage. It is also apparent that greater diversity of expertise can be represented in on-site teams with more team members. Typically, most on-site guidelines and procedures assume a two- or three-person team and, with some minor adjustments, can be used with larger on-site teams.

5. Assigning Responsibility for Managing a Multiple-Site System of On-Site Evaluation.   On-site evaluation systems can be managed directly by the funding agency or they can be managed by an agency contracted to coordinate the overall on-site evaluation system. Management of on-site evaluations by either the funding agency or a contracted agency is greatly preferable (unless the evaluation is formative) to having the site arrange for their own site-visit team to conduct the on-site evaluation. This latter arrangement seems too similar to the dubious practice of allowing a bank to audit its own books.

A list of specific site-visit activities that must be planned and conducted appears in Chapter 18; those who wish much greater detail are referred to Worthen, O'Sullivan, and White (in press).

Before leaving this section, however, we should note that some multiple-site evaluations are hybrids of the type of on-site evaluation outlined here and the MSE approach discussed earlier in this chapter. For example, in a national, 12-site evaluation of a major technology vendor's computerized curriculum for elementary school students (Worthen & Van Dusen, 1992), carefully standardized program implementation and student testing followed the MSE strategy, with site coordinators, a quasi-experimental design, and data aggregation across all sites. But additional data were collected by a series of intensive on-site visits to each of the 12 sites, not only collecting still more data on common dimensions and using standardized procedures but also having the on-site team collect some data on unique attributes of each site.

Another type of hybrid between these two multiple-site evaluation strategies is the "multisite/multimethod" variation (Louis, 1982), in which less structured, qualitative data are viewed as coequal in the evaluation with more structured data collected by familiar MSE procedures.

CLUSTER EVALUATION

A third form of multiple-site program evaluation that originated in the W. K. Kellogg Foundation (WKKF) is a two-level approach that its developers termed **cluster evaluation**.[2] Compared to the two more venerable approaches discussed previously, cluster evaluation is an emerging approach that is still in its adolescent stage, if not its childhood. Prior to 1992, cluster evaluation was almost unknown among professional evaluators, and the still-sparse literature on cluster evaluation has all been produced since then. Yet it appears as if cluster evaluation may well be here to stay. In their book *Evaluation for Foundations,* the Council on Foundations (1993) described the Kellogg approach to evaluating clusters of grants as "A Model for Foundation Programs" (p. 232). The American Evaluation Association (AEA) officially established a Topical Interest Group on Cluster Evaluation in 1994. In a recent book on educating health professionals for the communities they serve (Richards, 1995), cluster evaluation is portrayed as a key element in building essential partnerships to foster such advances in community health. And WKKF's Director of Evaluation Ricardo Millett is chair of the AEA Cluster Evaluation Group and is using both that role and his Foundation position to create a continuing dialogue among evaluation experts aimed at refining and

---

[2] The term "cluster evaluation" was first coined in 1988 by WKKF's director of evaluation, Ron Richards, in an evaluation of a Foundation-funded health initiative; the concept was further developed by him and his successors in that position, Jim Sanders and Ricardo Millett.

improving the concept, design, and conduct of cluster evaluation. It appears that the energy and openness exist that are needed to shape a new approach to the point where it can become broadly useful in conducting evaluations.

A Description of Cluster Evaluation and Its Rationale

Cluster evaluation's purposes and philosophical assumptions are quite different from those of the two approaches we have discussed so far in this chapter. These differences will be obvious as we define and describe cluster evaluation more specifically.

First, cluster evaluation should not be confused with cluster sampling. Rather, WKKF officers use the term in situations where several of their individual, local projects (usually funded under one broad program initiative) are collectively considered to constitute a "cluster" of projects that are similar in either sharing a common mission, a common strategy, or a common population. Although the projects are bound together by that common thread, each project has its unique context and is relatively autonomous in how it proposes to accomplish the broad program mission or goals for which the Foundation holds it responsible. These projects are each expected to have a local project evaluation to provide information specific to that project. In addition, WKKF commissions a cluster evaluation intended to examine broader knowledge by looking across all the projects in the cluster.

Just how this is done varies widely across clusters. As O'Sullivan and O'Sullivan (1994) have noted, "Kellogg has defined the cluster evaluation components but has not prescribed the cluster evaluation process." Nonetheless, a cluster evaluation plan is expected by Kellogg (1) to be driven by evaluation questions that deal with priority issues of Foundation officials, (2) to identify common information needed on all projects in order to provide a composite overview of the overall success or failure of the cluster, and (3) to outline methods to collect such data. Further, the WKKF (1991) has identified four key characteristics of the cluster approach:

1. It looks across a group of projects to identify *common threads and themes* that, having cross-confirmation, take on greater significance;
2. It seeks not only to learn *what happened* with respect to a group of projects but *why* those things happened;
3. It happens in a *collaborative* way that allows all players—projects, foundation, and external evaluators—to contribute to and participate in the process so that what is learned is of value to everyone; and
4. The relationship between the projects and the external evaluators conducting the cluster evaluation is *confidential.* Evaluation findings of the cluster evaluation are reported back to the Foundation only in aggregate for the entire cluster and never for the individual projects. This ensures an environment in which projects can be comfortable in sharing with the cluster evaluators the realities of the work they have

undertaken—problems and frustrations as well as triumphs. It greatly increases the usefulness of evaluation findings.

Thus, WKKF's overall strategy for cluster evaluation involves multiple responsibilities for both the Foundation staff and for the cluster evaluators. For the former, it is their responsibility to form the cluster of projects and to manage that cluster across the multiple years of funding. Meanwhile, it is the cluster evaluator's responsibility to evaluate the cluster by developing the methodology for the cluster evaluation, managing it for its duration, and negotiating and maintaining the respective roles, responsibilities, and relationships of cluster and project evaluators.

Various purposes for cluster evaluation have been articulated in WKKF documents and meetings of cluster evaluators the Foundation has sponsored. Each of the following statements is drawn from one or more of the handouts, overheads, brochures, handbooks, or conference proceedings produced and used by WKKF staff, stating that the purpose of cluster evaluation is to do the following:

- Answer the questions *What happened?* and *Why?* for the cluster of projects as a whole.
- Strengthen projects in the cluster through the cluster evaluator's providing technical assistance in evaluation to project evaluators.
- Strengthen projects through the cluster evaluators' facilitating or creating evaluation networking among the projects.
- Strengthen Foundation programs and policy making through collection of information about the context, implementation, and outcomes of the cluster.
- Identify common themes and threads that, having cross-project confirmation, take on greater significance.
- Identify pertinent "lessons learned" by one project that may allow other projects to avoid problems or enhance success.
- Summarize or synthesize the project evaluations.
- Determine how well the collective cluster of projects has succeeded in achieving the funding objectives.
- Translate individual project findings into broad recommendations about the program/area under which the cluster is funded.

The WKKF evaluation staff have also stated unequivocally that it is *not* the purpose of cluster evaluation to do the following:

- Evaluate the success or failure of individual projects.
- Serve as a means for the Foundation to identify weak projects that should be terminated.

- Direct or oversee the project evaluations.
- Engage in metaevaluations of the project evaluations.
- Be intrusive to projects.
- Report information about any specific project(s) in the cluster to WKKF staff; only data aggregated across the cluster or lessons learned from *unidentified* projects would be shared with the Foundation.

Understanding Cluster Evaluation's Context

These statements about cluster evaluation may be better understood when viewed against the philosophy and value orientation WKKF holds for program evaluation. Stated most simply, the Foundation (WKKF, 1994) believes that "evaluation functions 'to improve, not to prove'" (p. 4). In operationalizing these values, WKKF asks cluster evaluators to assemble evidence that its program strategies contribute to their desired ends but cautions that it is unlikely that the Foundation will fund costly experimental studies that will "answer questions of attribution" or that "can provide rigorous (reliable/valid in methodological terms) causal effect estimates" (p. 4). Thus, cluster evaluators are asked to provide *compelling conclusions* to enable two of cluster evaluation's key audiences (WKKF's Board of Trustees and program staff) to answer the central question of whether the strategy that led to funding the cluster of projects was a wise investment of Foundation resources—without traditional methods for determining causation. No small challenge.

An additional part of the context that complicates efforts to gain wisdom by looking across cluster evaluations is the fact that WKKF officers have not standardized cluster evaluation procedures, and thus those procedures have evolved in quite different directions, depending on the evaluation philosophy and methodological preferences of the various cluster evaluators and the conception of cluster evaluation held by the Foundation's various program directors. Tolerance for such diversity is an inevitable by-product of the value WKKF officers place on autonomy, flexibility, empowerment, and change, values held so deeply that some Foundation staff would likely resist any significant degree of standardization of cluster evaluation designs or procedures. Yet if cluster evaluation is allowed to be whatever circumstances and personalities dictate it should be, then it may never become more than an evaluation "shape-shifter," appearing and reappearing in various forms, depending on who within the Foundation is responsible at the moment for interpreting what cluster evaluation should be and do.

Thus, the challenges confronting cluster evaluation are in part a product of the culture and personality of its parent organization (WKKF) and the dynamic, open, and empowering nature of the Foundation's modus operandi. The lack of uniformity in the conception and definition of what cluster evaluation is, what its purposes are, or how it should be conducted reflects WKKF's valuation of high autonomy for grantees and the Foundation's willingness to sacrifice central control—and any form of coerced cohesiveness—in the interests of empowerment and trust of grantees. One can applaud such guiding principles and premises, even while fretting that they make it difficult to describe with any precision just what cluster evaluation is or how it should be conducted. The WKKF (1994) recognizes this difficulty in noting that its

> cluster evaluation model is a relatively new concept in Foundation program evaluation. The concept and practice is evolving. Its operational definition, purposes, and assumptions have varied in practice across W. K. Kellogg Foundation program areas. (p. 4)

All of which suggests that (1) relationships of some cluster evaluations to existing types of evaluation may not hold for all other cluster evaluations and (2) relationships that exist today may not hold tomorrow if cluster evaluation is significantly changed during its further evolution.

These difficulties notwithstanding, there are some characteristics of cluster evaluation that seem to be at its core. We can depend on these in attempting to examine how cluster evaluation fits with our earlier "typology" of multiple-site evaluation strategies.

Comparing Cluster Evaluation and MSE

Returning to Figure 21.1, careful examination reveals that most cluster evaluations, as currently conducted, would fit best—if not exclusively—in cell 3, Uncontrolled Prospective multiple-site evaluations. Conversely, cell 1 is the preferred cell for MSE, where control of program implementation is emphasized. When program implementation is allowed to vary across sites (a hallmark of most cluster evaluations), MSE is viewed by many authors as seriously weakened, because increased site autonomy has resulted in program-by-site interactions that confound outcomes. As Sinacore and Turpin (1991) put it:

> it is not clear whether those differences [observed differences in outcomes among the sites] are caused by the various program formats or by the unique features of the sites in which the program are provided." (p. 7).

Yet this is exactly the type of variation that typically exists in cluster evaluations, where efforts to control variance are replaced with attempts to capitalize on it by studying the relative impact of naturally varying implementation across projects to identify successes and failures calculated to help projects learn from one another. Moreover, a key difference between cluster evaluation and most other forms of MSE lies in the absence of control, except by persuasion, that cluster evaluators have over the site-specific evaluations. (See Hedrick et al., 1991, for a discussion of the issue of centralized control over site evaluations in MSE.)

In short, while cluster evaluation can be categorized as a subtype of MSE, its similarities are mostly superficial, and the contrasting perspectives and purposes of cluster evaluation and MSE suggest that they are actually rather distant conceptual relatives, not the close conceptual cousins they may appear to be upon casual inspection. This fact has been recognized by Schmitz (1994), who contrasted the cluster evaluation she is directing for the WKKF with traditional conceptions of MSE, on several dimensions, as follows:[3]

Multisite Evaluation *"Evaluation for Confirmation"*	*Cluster Evaluation* *"Evaluation for Learning"*
• Single model, centrally designed, implemented at different sites	• Multiple models, designed by different sites, according to local needs, resources, and constraints
• Specifics of model known, pretested, fixed	• Specifics unknown; "cutting edge" and evolving models
• Limited number of narrowly defined goals that lead to dependent variables, common across sites	• Multiple possible goals, broadly defined, somewhat site specific; not all goals or benefits known in advance
• Good framework for testing hypotheses, causal linkages, and generalizability	• Good framework for strengthening programs trying to operationalize guiding philosophy or set of principles at local level
• Top-down project management and evaluation	• Autonomous, locally driven project management; dual levels of evaluation
• Assumes controls can be established to maintain reliability and validity; believes in value of "generic model"	• Assumes some common goals, questions, experiences; believes that sharing information increases knowledge about "what" and "how"; values practical knowledge

Cluster Evaluation's Contribution to the Field of Evaluation

As one could infer from our earlier comments, we see cluster evaluation as still in its early developmental stages. Perhaps it is being in the throes of adolescence's awkwardness that raises so many issues that still need to be resolved.[4] Yet adolescence has its positive aspects as well (after all, adolescents are energetic, idealistic, and creative), and the same is true of cluster evaluation. If

---

[3] We have altered slightly C. Smith's (1994) presentation and format and take responsibility if so doing has misunderstood or misrepresented her intent.

[4] A discussion of the challenges confronting cluster evaluation has been provided by Worthen and Matsumoto (1994).

the issues confronting it are resolved, there is great potential for cluster evaluation to make a broader contribution, for many philanthropic, state, and federal
agencies fund programs with multiple projects that could use such a strategy, if
cluster evaluation can be captured conceptually in ways that allow its use to be
clearly understood by potential users in various contexts where a noncausal form
of multiple-site evaluation is deemed appropriate. And there is reason to believe
that this might occur. For example, Sanders (in press) has laid out steps that
cluster evaluations might follow and proposed common elements for inclusion
in all cluster evaluations. Only future experience can assess the impact of these
suggestions. In the meantime, Sanders contends that cluster evaluation is built
on some of the same philosophical and methodological underpinnings as are
other, more venerable ways of determining merit or fact.

> The stages of inquiry reflected in cluster evaluation design are not
> unique to cluster evaluation. Starting with the classic work of Glaser
> and Strauss . . . , there is a strong and well-documented tradition of
> the methodology used in cluster evaluation found in the literature under
> such labels as qualitative methods, case study methods, and naturalistic
> methods. What is unique about cluster evaluation is the combination
> of four characteristics . . . : (1) it is holistic, (2) it is outcome oriented,
> (3) it seeks generalizable learning, and (4) it involves frequent communi-
> cations and collaborations among the partners. It is an approach to
> evaluation that is intrusive and affects the thinking and practices of
> project staff, the parent or funding organization, and the cluster eval-
> uator along the way. It does not seek to establish causation through
> controlled comparative designs, but instead depends on naturalistic
> observations of many people to infer and test logical connections. The
> underlying paradigm is one of argumentation and rules of evidence such
> as those found in our legal system. It strives for documentation and
> logical conclusions that have been tested as fully as possible given
> resources, time, and methodological constraints of the evaluation. In
> terms of *The Program Evaluation Standards* (Joint Committee, 1994)
> it places a premium on all four attributes of sound program evaluation:
> utility, feasibility, propriety and accuracy.

OTHER APPROACHES
TO MULTIPLE-SITE EVALUATION

Earlier in this chapter we gave an example of how an evaluation of a multiple-
site program could combine aspects of MSE with on-site visits to the multiple
program sites. One could easily envision how combinations of cluster evaluation
and multiple-site on-site evaluation could be used very effectively. (It is less clear
how MSE and cluster evaluation could be combined, based as they are on
strikingly different priorities and premises.)

We make no pretense that the three types of multiple-site evaluations we have presented are all-encompassing. For example, descriptions of nine illustrative case studies of multiple-site evaluations conducted within foundations (Council on Foundations, 1993) reveal that five do not fit precisely into any one of the three types of multiple-site evaluations we have discussed. Yet we believe the three types we have covered are not only the most common and most useful but are also illustrative of the range of approaches that can be used to enhance evaluation of multiple-site programs.

APPLICATION EXERCISES

1. Identify and explain the similarities and differences between multisite evaluation (MSE) and cluster evaluation, and between MSE and multiple-site on-site evaluation.
2. Select a multiple-site program with which you are familiar. Analyze how each of the three major types of multiple-site evaluations described in this chapter might be applied to it, and decide which approach you think would be best. Explain why.
3. Discuss which of the cells in Figure 21.1 you think would yield the best evaluation. The worst. Justify your judgments.

SUGGESTED READINGS

Council on Foundations. (1993). *Evaluation for foundations: Concepts, cases, guidelines, and resources.* Chapter 11: The Kellogg approach to evaluating clusters of grants (pp. 232–251). San Francisco: Jossey-Bass.

Sinacore, J. M., & Turpin, R. S. (1991). Multiple sites in evaluation research: A survey of organizational and methodological issues. In R. S. Turpin & J. M. Sinacore (Eds.), *Multisite evaluations,* New Directions for Program Evaluation, No. 50, 5–18. San Francisco: Jossey-Bass.

Worthen, B. R., O'Sullivan, R., & White, K. R. (in press). *Tools and techniques for program and project evaluations.* Section II: On-site evaluation guidelines and procedures. Boston: Kluwer-Nijhoff.

chapter **22**

Conducting Evaluation of Organizations' Renewal and Training in Corporate and Nonprofit Settings

ORIENTING QUESTIONS

1. How does evaluation in nonprofit organization differ from evaluation in public agencies?

2. What typical questions are asked in the evaluation of training? What should be the focus of new questions?

3. How have trends in personnel evaluation mirrored those in program evaluation?

4. Is Total Quality Management (TQM) a mode of empowerment evaluation?

5. What can evaluators learn from strategic planning? How do quality control (QC) and quality assurance (QA) differ from program evaluation?

While much of program evaluation takes place in the public sector, the tools of evaluation are now used in many different settings. The *independent sector,* or nonprofit organizations, now delivers many services which were previously delivered by state or local governments, school districts, and other public institutions. Yet these services and the stakeholders of these services still need evaluation information to make decisions and learn about these new approaches to service delivery. *Training* has become a major focus of organizations as the global economy and technological change require that workers are constantly retrained to meet the demands of the competitive corporate world. With this training, keyed more than ever to organizational performance, come new demands for training in evaluation. *Personnel evaluation,* performance appraisal and its incumbent tools, have become an integral part of the career of some evaluators. Finally, the corporate world, followed by the public and nonprofit sectors, have adopted new methods for organizational assessment that, though called by other names, are related to evaluation and have implications for the evaluator's work. These methods include *strategic planning, Total Quality Management, quality control,* and *quality assurance.* They are similar to evaluation in that they are designed to determine or to ensure a thing's value (a process, a goal, a strategy) and they call for the systematic collection of information to make these determinations and ensurances. This chapter will discuss some of these new settings and methods and their implications for evaluation.

Though these methods are new to some in program evaluation, others have noted that evaluation encompasses more than simply program evaluation. Scriven (1993) writes that "the term *program evaluation* has become a label for a limited approach, covering only part of what is required in order to do adequate program evaluation. . . . A widening of one's perspective on program evaluation helps one to avoid reinvention of the wheel and omission of relevant aspects of what one is supposed to be evaluating" (p. 3). The Joint Committee on Standards for Educational Evaluation (1988) expanded their focus to personnel evaluation in 1988 with the publication of standards in that field. Chelimsky (1985a), though narrower in her focus, describes how the definition of evaluation has broadened over the years to entail more than program results or effectiveness.

The methods to be reviewed in this chapter, then, can be viewed broadly as part of the total purview of evaluation. As evaluation expands its scope, evaluators find themselves being employed in increasingly diverse settings. May, Fleischer, Scheirer, and Cox (1986) found that 17 percent of recent doctoral graduates in evaluation were working in business and industry and 15 percent were working as private consultants serving customers in many sectors. Evaluators need to be ready and able to adapt their knowledge and skills to new approaches and contexts. This chapter is designed to introduce readers to some of these applications.

EVALUATION IN THE NONPROFIT SECTOR

One of the legacies of the Bush and Reagan administrations has been **privatization—** the move by various government agencies to contract out services that they previously delivered. Typically, these services are contracted to organizations in the nonprofit, or independent, sector though contracting to for-profit corporations has also occurred. (Providing school lunches and maintaining school buildings are among the functions that have been contracted out to private corporations. Some school districts are contracting with the Edison Project and similar organizations to manage and deliver instruction for entire schools.) The **nonprofit sector** has been defined as "a set of organizations that is privately incorporated but serving some public purpose, such as the advancement of health, education, scientific progress, social welfare, or pluralism" (Salamon,

1992, p. 5). In the United States, these nonprofit organizations have a special tax status. Though nonprofit organizations have existed in the United States since the 1700s, their role is changing dramatically with the massive move to privatization of public services (O'Neill, 1989).

The independent sector is growing. Today, its workforce is three times the size of the federal civilian workforce (Zimmermann, 1994). The largest proportion of nonprofit organizations are focused on the health arena; education is the second largest sector (Clotfelder, 1992). Other major areas of nonprofit service delivery include social services, mental health, youth programs, employment and training, and child care. As a result, many of the programs typically studied by program evaluators are being contracted out to this sector. Most of those who work in the nonprofit arena expect the current trends to continue well into the future (Milward, 1994).

Those who work in these settings have concerns about the impact of privatization. Health care professionals worry about less access for the poor as nonprofit and for-profit hospitals compete for resources (Salkever & Frank, 1992). Education professionals worry that the needs of low-income students will be ignored or that the public schools will be left with students whose needs are increasingly difficult and costly to meet (Schwartz & Baum, 1992). Those working in the independent sector worry about their increasing dependence on government resources (Smith & Lipsky, 1993). The term "independent sector" could well become an oxymoron for nonprofits.

The Impact of Privatization on Evaluation

While these questions illustrate some of the concerns of managers and policy makers, there are also concerns for evaluation. How will privatization affect evaluation? What will be the role of the evaluator in the contracting organization? In the nonprofit organization? In many ways, evaluation will take on a much more primary role for government agencies as they contract out services. Once a public agency rids itself of the direct responsibility of delivering the service, its role then becomes *primarily* one of monitoring the contract. The public expects the government to make sure that services are delivered efficiently and effectively, that fraud does not occur, and that legislative intents are met. The demand for privatization has centered around the belief that other sectors can deliver services in better ways than have government agencies. Someone will need to determine whether this is so. In its role as contractor, the public agency will have many information needs. With privatization, the agency is further removed from the delivery of services and thus will have even less knowledge of which clients are being served and the nature of the services being delivered. Questions addressed might include these:

- To what extent is the target audience reached?
- Are services delivered as planned, with the desired expertise and the proper intensity? Are the services congruent with the program model?

- Are desired outcomes achieved?
- What is the impact of service delivery on the community as a whole? What side effects exist?

With privatization, evaluation will address many of the usual questions of program evaluation as well as new ones associated with privatization itself, such as:

- Is the delivery of services by other sectors more efficient than delivery of the services through government agencies?
- Is it more effective?
- If it is more efficient or more effective, what are the costs?

As public agencies struggle to define their role as contractor and evaluator, others question whether government agencies will be capable of fulfilling the role. Milward, Provan, and Smith (1994) note that government's lack of ability to manage contracts with nonprofits is a major problem. Milward (1994) writes:

> Policy design, control of the implementation process, and evaluation of the quality of the contracted services can, and often do remain, the job of the public agency. However, the capacity limitations that led to contracting out in the first place may extend to the guidance and evaluation functions of government. (p. 76)

While some express concerns about the ability of the public agency to monitor and evaluate nonprofit contracts, others, especially those in the non-profit sector, express concerns with the overbearing role of the funding agency in controlling and mandating the specifics of evaluation. One of the present authors worked with a training organization whose state funder wanted a comprehensive evaluation of each of the over 250 training programs delivered by the organization to county social services agencies each year, without regard to the status of the program or the information needs of any stakeholders. The policy was simply that all training programs, regardless of length, longevity, or past evaluations, should be evaluated comprehensively each year. If carried out, the evaluations would have cost more than the training! Ignorance of the use and methods of evaluation and fear of *not* monitoring adequately can lead to excesses. Thus, a major challenge to evaluators and managers in contracting agencies will be defining their role. This role will include determining the nature of questions that *must* be answered to adequately monitor government resources and those questions that should be adapted or developed by the agency delivering the services to help them to improve delivery.

We think the solution in regard to evaluation roles will eventually be a delineation of (1) evaluation questions typically answered by all contractors, to serve summative decisions regarding future contracts, and (2) evaluation questions that may be selected (perhaps from a list provided by contractors) or developed by the nonprofit agency itself (with sign-off by the contractor). This second category of questions would be studied primarily for formative purposes to improve service delivery. Both sets of questions would be developed with each new contracting initiative or, perhaps, with each new contractor. While the mandated questions to be answered would be somewhat similar across contracts, there is no magic set of questions that *all* contractors should answer in *all* circumstances. The optional, or formative, questions would, of course, need to be rather specific to the contract(s) at hand. We recommend that a sample of such questions be developed by the public agency, because often nonprofit organizations, particularly small ones, are new to evaluation and may not know the types of helpful questions that evaluation could address. Nonprofit organizations that have experience with evaluation should, of course, be permitted to develop their own questions.

We have found through our work with nonprofit organizations that they often see evaluation as solely for the funding agency to meet accountability concerns. In the course of defining roles, it will be critical for the public funding agency to demonstrate to nonprofit deliverers that evaluation can be used to meet *their own* information needs. This will be a difficult balancing act, because the public funding agency will need data for themselves to make summative decisions and meet the public demand for accountability. However, if evaluation is to be used to improve the delivery of services, we have learned it must be close to those delivering the product. Funding agencies can demonstrate their commitment to the use of evaluation for formative purposes by deliverers by recognizing that some evaluation information is *not* for the funding source but solely for the provider's information needs. Two excellent guides for internal evaluation by nonprofit organizations are available to help nonprofit organizations develop their effectiveness on a continuing basis (Gray, 1993; Gray & Stockdill, 1995).

The Role of Evaluation within the Nonprofit Agency

We have discussed how privatization or contracting out will change the role of evaluation in the funding agencies. What about the role of evaluation in the independent sector itself? Nonprofit organizations increasingly require the expertise of evaluators to help them meet the demands of government contracts even as they work to improve their capacity to do their own evaluation. Larger nonprofit organizations have and will develop internal capacities for evaluations; other, smaller organizations will continue to rely on external evaluators for special projects. The challenge to the evaluator in these settings will be negotiating the evaluation responsibilities of the nonprofit organization with the funding agency and helping the nonprofit organization view evaluation as something that can help it in managing and delivering services. In many organizations, bringing about this attitude change among potential internal users and stakeholders will be the greatest challenge facing the evaluator. If the funding agency is uncooperative, the job will be made doubly hard.

Another facet of the independent sector that is pertinent for the evaluator is the structure and financing of the organization itself. Directors of nonprofit organizations are responsible to a board of directors. The board is typically composed of individuals with varying backgrounds who have volunteered to serve in this capacity. Board members are often selected for their personal fund-raising capabilities in the community. Relations with the board can be a major concern of managers. Individual board members' interests and attitudes can have a major influence on the operation of the organization. These relationships are new to evaluators who have worked only in public settings. But the evaluator new to nonprofits would do well to spend some time getting to know the board and considering its influence on the organization. Similarly, fund-raising and community relations are a major focus of nonprofit organizations. Recruiting and training of volunteers can be an important activity. These and other characteristics of the independent sector distinguish it from the public agency. These differences can change the nature of evaluation as they create new evaluation questions and arenas of investigation and new configurations of stakeholders.

EVALUATING TRAINING PROGRAMS

Corporations today are struggling to compete in the global economy. New technologies in the work world demand an adaptable workforce with the knowledge and skills required for work that is constantly changing. Business today requires continuous training and retraining of the work force to remain competitive. As a result, there has been enormous growth in the training field. Carnevale, Gainer, and Villet (1990) estimate that employers in the United States spend approximately $30 billion annually on formal training programs. Brinkerhoff (1989) writes: "The investment of private industry in education and training rivals, in scope and resources, the total public education enterprise" (p. 1). However, the nature of the training industry is changing dramatically. In 1989, Brinkerhoff predicted that "the days of the richly endowed training department with its fat program catalogs are numbered" (p. 1). In 1994, Galagan showed his prediction to be correct. Costcutting, downsizing, and reorganizing have led to the "restructuring" of training. A survey by *Training and Development* journal found that 55 percent of trainers reported working in companies that reorganized or restructured training in the past year, while 18 percent reported changing jobs (Galagan, 1994).

What is happening? Those in the training field note that, in today's competitive environment, organizations are more concerned with performance and the impact of training on the organization. Swanson (1987) has described two models of training: the psychology model and the economics model. The *psychology model* focuses on the individual. The goal of training is to add to trainees' expertise and/or reduce trainees' anxiety. Much of training in the 1980s focused on this model. Trainers' knowledge and skills were in the areas of instructional development and design, the adult learning model, and training techniques and methods. The *economic model* focuses on training to reduce or contain costs to the organization. Swanson sees this model as more compatible with the goals of profit-minded organizations. And, in fact, organizations in the 1990s are restructuring training for high performance. Galagan (1994) observes "a seismic shift in the role of training in organizations that are in search of better performance" (p. 22). In a survey of human resource development managers, Carnevale and Carnevale (1994) found the biggest current trend was the creation of the high-performance work organization. Work is reorganized, redesigned, and reengineered to improve performance. They urge trainers to "think performance."

In predicting this trend in training in 1989, Brinkerhoff argued that evaluation could be "the key to the success of training in the future" (p. 1). This success can occur by trainers' expanding their roles or through evaluators' becoming more involved in training or, more likely, some of both. Currently, the most common evaluator of training is the trainer himself (Brandenburg, 1989). Trainers must expand their role to be less involved in instructional design and more involved in planning and evaluation for the organization. In this role, the trainer helps identify problems in the organization that hinder productivity and recommends solutions. Training is thus one of a number of possible solutions the "trainer" might recommend. In this manner, the trainer becomes more of a specialized program evaluator or an industrial psychologist. Given many trainers' limited skills in evaluation, evaluators may need to be partners in this process. (Or trainers will need to get more training!)

Alternative Models for Evaluating Training

What has been the role of evaluation in training? Probably the best-known model for evaluating training was proposed by Kirkpatrick (1977, 1983). Kirkpatrick indicates that training can be evaluated at four levels, as shown in Figure 22.1.

This model has been predominant in the field of training evaluation for some time. However, a competing model for evaluating training is one that has already been presented in this book: the CIPP model, with its four levels of evaluation, namely, context, input, process, and product. A study of members of the American Society of Training and Development (ASTD) revealed that users of the CIPP

Level	*Questions*
1. Reaction	Were the participants pleased with the program?
2. Learning	What did the participants learn in the program?
3. Behavior	Did the participants change their behavior based on what was learned?
4. Results	Did the change in behavior positively affect the organization?

FIGURE 22.1 Kirkpatrick's model of evaluation training

model outnumbered users of the Kirkpatrick model (Galvin, 1983). We find the Kirkpatrick model useful here, however, to illustrate the different questions the evaluator might address in a training setting.

With the current emphasis on the high-performance organization, training evaluation will need to focus more on the fourth level of the Kirkpatrick model. That is, the evaluation of training must show the impact of that training, not only on the individual but on the organization as well. However, traditionally the most common means of evaluating training have been in-class questionnaires (satisfaction) and pre-post testing of learners' performance (LDG Associates, 1986). These methods address only levels 1 and 2 in Kirkpatrick's model.

Other Considerations in Evaluating Training

In addition to needing to focus more on results and organizational impact, trainers and evaluators need to be involved more in needs assessment. One type of needs assessment for training is **front-end analysis** (Robinson & Robinson, 1989), which involves collecting data to assist in the evaluation of a training program. To maximize the likelihood that training will have an impact, trainers need to examine the nature of the performance problem. What is going wrong? What is decreasing productivity? How can productivity be increased? Will improved knowledge and skills solve the problem? Will increased motivation? Retraining of supervisors? Training for better teamwork or creative problem solving? New tools or technology? Who will it be most productive to train? Or is reengineering or job design the solution? The trainer/evaluator should spend much time exploring the nature of the problem in front-end analysis. The results of such analysis can then provide useful information for targeting the training to the right audience, with the right methods and follow-up on the job. Further, if the solution is to be found in alternatives other than training, the evaluator/ trainer can recommend these alternatives.

Brinkerhoff (1989) describes three zones for the evaluation of training: before, during, and after training. He argues that the greatest returns are in studying zones 1 and 3. Questions that would be addressed by each zone include the following:

> Zone 1: What is the problem? Who would benefit most from training? What is the payoff of training likely to be? Whose support is needed to make the training work? What organization and individual per-formance barriers will impede training results? What kind of training works best?
>
> Zone 2: How well do trainees learn? How much do trainees like the training? What learning activities are working best? How is the training going? What about the training should be changed? How well is the instructor doing?
>
> Zone 3: How much of the training is being used? Who is using the training best? Why is the training not being used? What is happening

that is undermining the training? How is the training being supported? What kind of benefits results from the training? (p. 13)

These questions require that the traditional program evaluator use his evaluation skills to address new questions, to apply them to a different entity (training) and in a new setting (corporations). Are these different questions the *only* differences in evaluating training in the corporate setting and program evaluation? No. Just as the evaluator working in the nonprofit sector must be cognizant of the different environment and context for his evaluation, the evaluator in the corporate sector must learn the customs of this environment. What is different? Everything. While this may be a bit of an exaggeration, the differences between the private and public sectors are great. In the private sector, profitability is the bottom line. Compared to the ambiguity of the primary outcomes in the public sector, profitability is easily measured. Decision makers in the corporate setting must use this as their primary standard to remain successful.

In contrast, decision makers in the public sector report to many audiences: federal, state, and local legislative and executive officials; interest groups; clients; the public in general; and so on. By its very nature, evaluation in the public sector is more public. Evaluation in corporations is not public information.

Other differences abound. Swanson (1989) appears skeptical about the ability of evaluators, whom he sees as having a primarily public-sector orientation, to adapt to corporate environments. He characterizes decisions made in the corporate world as those made by the venture capitalist who must make big decisions quickly based on limited information. In contrast, he sees the public sector–oriented evaluator as more like an accountant who "tediously adds up pennies . . . waiting for all the data before filing an accurate report" (p. 72). While we think that Swanson may have confused evaluators too much with accountants and may not be sufficiently aware of the changing environments in which public-sector evaluators work, his description helps illustrate what many see as major contextual differences. Ultimately, in corporate settings, the stakeholder is the organization and the bottom line is profit. The evaluator of training in the corporate setting must be prepared to work proactively to develop programs that will improve productivity and to measure the impact of such programs on the organization's productivity.

PERSONNEL EVALUATION

As in the training field, the roles of program evaluators and industrial psychologists may overlap when it comes to personnel evaluation. However, the skills of program evaluators are particularly useful in this area for both methodological and political reasons. Methodologically, program evaluators can bring new approaches to personnel evaluation even though it has been a highly specialized and technical field. Traditionally, most personnel evaluation has been supervisory-based.

Industrial psychologists have used other sources, such as peers, teams, subordinates, and customers or clients, to provide input (Cascio, 1991; Halachimi, 1995). But such sources often fail to be credible within the organization in spite of studies in industrial psychology that show the validity of some of these sources. Program evaluators who frequently combine quantitative and qualitative methods from several different sources to assess the same construct bring new skills to the evaluation of personnel or, as the term is more traditionally known, **performance appraisal**. Politically, program evaluators have been working in environments fraught with many political concerns. Their training and experience dealing with the concerns of various stakeholders can help them enter this sensitive arena.

What is performance appraisal or personnel evaluation? It is the assessment of an individual employee's abilities and performance. Performance appraisal can occur for many reasons. Two quite different reasons are employee development (training, future promotion) and compensation. Those in the field of performance appraisal urge that these two purposes be addressed separately (Sylvia, 1994). The first, performance appraisal for employee development, is future-oriented and works best when the employee works collaboratively with the supervisor to identify areas for further training and development. Such areas might be to remedy deficiencies or to permit the employee to progress toward personal career goals or acquire new knowledge and skills needed by the organization. Performance appraisal for employee development is primarily an individualized activity. Comparisons with others are *not* integral to the process. In contrast, performance appraisals for purposes of compensation in merit pay situations *must* involve comparisons across employees and, as such, the collection of information must be more uniform. While some argue that individual performance appraisals and merit pay are not an effective means of increasing productivity in today's team-centered environments, performance appraisal continues in most organizations (Bowman, 1994). Nevertheless, it is important that the person developing the performance appraisal distinguish between these two purposes, as the nature of the information collected for the performance appraisal will differ.

To develop a performance appraisal system, the personnel specialist must first identify the *critical components* of the job to be evaluated. These tasks, or the knowledge, skills, behaviors, or traits necessary to perform the tasks, might be identified from job analysis studies or other methods specific to performance appraisal. Forms are developed and completed, typically by the supervisor, to collect information on the respondent's (supervisor's) perceptions of the employee's job performance. Forms vary from those that measure rather general traits (e.g., punctuality, loyalty, or ability to work with others) to behaviorally anchored rating scales (BARS), which list critical behaviors and examples of various levels of behavior. BARS probably represent the most sophisticated of the relatively well-known procedures for performance appraisal and involve (1) collecting data from job incumbents and supervisors regarding critical components of the job and (2) brief narrative examples of work at various levels (poor to outstanding) for each component (Smith & Kendall, 1963). These examples are called "critical incidents" (Flanagan, 1954). Other tasks for the personnel specialist in performance appraisal include training supervisors in the use of the forms and means for providing feedback to employees.

An important new set of guides for the evaluation of teachers, school administrators, and educational specialists has been developed by CREATE, the Center for Research on Educational Accountability and Teacher Evaluation (Farland & Gullickson, 1995). These guides provide models and procedures for conducting personnel evaluations of teachers. The CREATE materials were designed to meet the Personnel Evaluation Standards (Joint Committee, 1988).

Performance appraisal comes out of the scientific school of management and has been highly quantitative in focus, though narrative feedback forms and Management by Objective (MBO) methods have been used when the purpose of the appraisal is employee development. The original goal of performance appraisal was to find a valid, reliable, and completely unbiased way of measuring employee's work behavior. While such goals seem naive, they reflect the strong beliefs in the United States that pay should be "fair"—that is, based on performance, not politics—and that good employees should be rewarded with greater compensation. In the 1980s, dissatisfaction with the measurement focus arose primarily because managers and supervisors felt left out of the picture and organizations often saw little link between performance appraisals and organizational goals and productivity (Nigro & Nigro, 1994). Lovich (1990) characterizes these differences as the distinction between technique and process. Those interested in the techniques of appraisal have a primary concern with "the perfection of the test; that is, the focus of attention is the identification of problems associated with the measurement of performance (e.g., halo effect in ratings, or response bias in rating categories)" (pp. 91-92). For those concerned with process, "The problem of appropriate measurement of past performance is less important than attention to future performance" (p. 92). From this school a concern emerges with the *process* of communications between supervisors and employees and the development of means to improve performance through improving the dialogue between supervisors and employees about individual performance.

These current trends in performance appraisal are highlighted to illustrate some of the debates in personnel evaluation that mirror those occurring in program evaluation. Thus, at about the same time personnel specialists were hearing the need to abandon their focus on measurement validity and focus on the manager's and the organization's needs, program evaluators were hearing Cronbach (1982) declare that internal and external validity should not be as important in evaluation as the user's own judgment of the validity of the study. Campbell (1969) depicted knowledge in disciplines as overlapping like the scales of a fish. He argued that we need to examine more assiduously the scales overlapping our own, and those overlapping them, to learn. Through examining performance appraisal and its history, we learn more about evaluation.

OTHER METHODS
OF ORGANIZATIONAL ASSESSMENT

Total Quality Management

Total Quality Management (TQM) is today being used by many public-, private-, and nonprofit-sector organizations to improve organizational productivity. By 1991, TQM had been adopted by over 3,000 corporations and 40 governments in the United States (Milakovich, 1991). By 1992, 80 percent of the Fortune 1000 companies had quality improvement programs (Lawler, Mohrman, & Ledford, 1992). The U.S. General Accounting Office reported in 1992 that over two-thirds of federal agencies were using some form of TQM. TQM has also influenced the public sector through Osborne and Gaebler's (1992) popular book *Reinventing Government: How the Entrepreneurial Spirit Is Transforming the Public Sector*, which adopted many TQM principles. Vice President Al Gore's (1993) report of the National Performance Review has now applied these methods to many ventures in the public sector.

What is TQM? Ironically, the developer of Total Quality Management published an article on evaluation in the first volume of the *Handbook of Evaluation Research* (Deming, 1975). W. Edwards Deming, the unlikely guru of TQM, is a statistician who worked on organizational efficiency issues in the corporate world. Becoming dissatisfied with the failure of American companies to adopt his techniques, he went to Japan after World War II to help in efforts to reestablish their economy. His methods for improving organizational processes became quite successful in that country, while he remained relatively unknown here. In 1980, Americans watched *NBC White Paper: If Japan Can Do It, Why Can't We?* which introduced many to Deming's methods (Fellers, 1992). TQM has spread through the corporate world and, as noted, is now being adopted widely in the public and nonprofit sectors.

Total Quality Management involves several components. First, it is designed to improve organizational efficiency and productivity through examining suppliers, the work process itself, and customer satisfaction. Taking a systems perspective, these might be viewed as elements of the input, process, and output functions. *Suppliers* are defined broadly as anyone or anything that provides information or materials necessary to perform the task at hand. Suppliers could be companies delivering hard products, other units or people in the organization providing information, or other agencies supplying resources, technical assistance, or even clients. Similarly, customers might be internal or external to the corporation or organization. To improve efficiency, the organization uses TQM to examine how interactions with the suppliers can improve organizational efficiency. In other words, how can the right supplies be received more quickly at the right place and in the right amount? The *work process* itself is then examined and broken into steps to determine how it might be made more efficient or effective. Are any of the present steps unnecessary or duplicative? Why is each step performed? What is its purpose, goal, or objective? Are these purposes and objectives necessary to achieve the desired end product? Can any step be eliminated? (Deming, 1986).

Finally, though not necessarily last, TQM examines *customer satisfaction* as the ultimate outcome. If customers are not satisfied, the process is reexamined. The *ultimate* goal in all TQM work is meeting customer needs and satisfying customers. In the corporate world, the ultimate customer is obviously the person who buys the product, though even in the corporate world there are other customers. Customers for training programs can include trainees, supervisors, managers, and the organization. Customers for the purchasing department are those employees within the organization ordering the product. Defining customers in the public setting becomes a little more difficult, and some question the utility of TQM in the government setting for precisely this reason (Swiss, 1992). Who is the customer for a welfare department? The welfare client? Employers? The general public? Who is the customer for the U.S. Department of Commerce? Large or small businesses? Employees? All citizens? Obviously, those in government must work harder to define their customer(s), but it can be done, as demonstrated in case studies by Rago (1994) in a state mental health agency and Cohen and Eimicke (1994) in a metropolitan parks and recreation department. While TQM began in manufacturing settings, it is now used widely in both public and private organizations whose focus is on service rather than production. As these case studies demonstrate, like manufacturing tasks, service tasks can be broken into steps and studied for quality and improvement.

These are the components TQM examines or studies, but TQM has two critical characteristics that link it to evaluation today. First, being a statistician, Deming (1986) urged that these components be studied through systematic collection of data. Data, through interviews, monitoring, or existing information, are collected to examine current operations or problem areas. Results of this data-collection process are reviewed and new systems are proposed. These systems are then pilot-tested and new information is collected. Processes are revised or replaced, based on these pilot tests. TQM envisions the organization in a *constant* process of testing and examination. Employees are asked to question standard operating procedures (SOPs) and to change continually to achieve quality. (Perhaps Deming read Campbell's "Reforms As Experiments," published in the same edition of the *Handbook of Evaluation*?)

Second, TQM is not conducted by methodological experts, though they can serve as facilitators, but by worker teams. This attribute is critical to the success of TQM. Deming (1986) believed the workers closest to the job knew the most about the work process and hence were in the best place to identify problems and recommend improvements. TQM gives those workers the opportunity to *question* processes and *make* changes while encouraging them to define their goals in relation to *quality products* and *customer needs*. This element of TQM is not so akin to the traditional, social science experimental views of evaluation as to those of the new "empowerment evaluation" (Fetterman, 1994). Just as Fetterman argues that stakeholders can do the evaluation and become empowered, Deming and other TQM advocates argue that worker teams can be trained to collect data on work and make recommendations for improvement. And, as in Fetterman's empowerment approach, worker participation leads to better questions, better solutions, and, most important, better adoption of those solutions by the workers themselves. TQM empowers the worker to question, study, and change the workplace to better meet customer needs.

How does TQM differ from evaluation? One major difference is that its scope is often narrower. TQM rarely evaluates "programs." Instead, TQM focuses on "production line operations." Its primary focus of study is SOPs, or standard operating procedures. As such, TQM is often concerned with monitoring processes, although causes to problems in standard operating procedures are sought. Hackman and Wageman (1995) note that "the single most commonly used [TQM] technique is formation of short-term problem-solving teams with the overall objective of simplifying and streamlining work practices" (p. 315). The principal outcomes examined are length of time to complete certain tasks and customer satisfaction. Like evaluation, TQM collects data from many sources, and data collection can make use of both qualitative and quantitative methods. Extensive use is made of interviews, customer satisfaction surveys, and checklists for monitoring purposes, as well as specialized TQM measures, but any method appropriate to the purpose can be used.

What are the implications of TQM for evaluation? TQM, like Fetterman's (1994) empowerment approach, brings evaluation to the layperson. If successful, TQM can encourage organizations and employees to question and assess new ventures. TQM changes the organizational culture from blind advocacy to healthy skepticism. One of the major problems evaluators face in many organizations is the fear of evaluation and a high degree of loyalty to the present mode of delivery. Scriven (1993) writes: "The roots of resistance to evaluation go very deep indeed, and it is wise not to underestimate their strength. For many people, to concede that their work needs evaluation is to concede that they lack competence. It is part of the ego's survival repertoire to be self-sufficient" (p. 88). Years ago, Campbell (1975) advised managers that they should act as advocates for the problem they are trying to solve, not the solution. In such a manner, they can feel more comfortable in testing new modes of delivery without fear that failure of this mode will jeopardize their future. Instead, by advocating for the problem and testing the solution, they have shown the wise ability to recognize that solutions are tough and must be constantly evaluated. Managers have *not* responded to Campbell's suggestion enthusiastically! And, evaluators have continued to struggle with managers' allegiance to programs and resistance to evaluation. TQM could bring about this long-desired change. That is, it could make questioning and open discussion of failure acceptable in the organizational culture. And that would ease the work of program evaluators enormously.

Some wonder if TQM may be another passing fad, like MBO, Quality Circles, or Planning, Programming, and Budgeting System (PPBS). Perhaps. As with any method, its advocates often promise too much. (See Matthews, 1993, for a discussion of some disillusionments with TQM.) Hackman and Wageman (1995) note: "TQM, in our view, is far more likely gradually to lose the prominence and popularity it now enjoys than it is to revolutionize organizational practice"

(p. 338). They note further, with regret, that recent implementations of TQM tend to ignore the empirical elements of TQM (monitoring, data collection and analysis, pilot-testing) and focus instead on the interpersonal skills and group process techniques of TQM: "Science is fading, the slogans are staying, and the implications are worrisome" (p. 338).

Nevertheless, each of these "fads" leaves something behind. That is, each method has some lasting influence on the organizational culture. MBO led organizations to think more about goals and objectives. Quality Circles left an impact on participatory management. TQM's legacy might be to change the organizational culture to a questioning environment, to use the systematic collection of information to improve organizational processes, or to involve employees at the line level to identify problems and solutions. Each of these legacies will be beneficial to program evaluation.

Strategic Planning

Strategic planning has been around longer than TQM. It became popular in the 1970s in corporate settings and began to be adopted by many public-sector organizations in the early 1980s. **Strategic planning** has been defined as

> a management process that combines four basic features: (1) a clear statement of the organization's mission; (2) the identification of the agency's external constituencies or stakeholders, and the determination of their assessment of the agency's purposes and operations; (3) the delineation of the agency's strategic goals and objectives, typically in a 3- to 5-year plan; and (4) the development of strategies to achieve them. (Berry, 1994, p. 323)

Some research has shown that strategic planning has not been successful in the corporate sector (Mintzberg, 1994). However, strategic planning continues to be used widely in public agencies. Between 1980 and 1991, more than 264 state agencies, from almost every state, initiated strategic planning (Berry, 1994). Recent surveys have shown that strategic planning is used in 60 percent of state agencies. Further, directors of these agencies view strategic planning positively and see it as helpful for decision making (Berry & Wechsler, 1995).

Strategic planning provides important input for program evaluation. It highlights the major goals and directions of the organization. If the planning is longitudinal, it can show changes or shifts in the focus of the organization. The goals and objectives defined through strategic planning can provide early information for planning an evaluation. Through interviews, the evaluator can determine whether these goals and objectives are still being pursued and, if so, what progress is being made toward achieving them. In cases where a goal or objective has been neglected or purposely put on the back burner, learning more about the history of this goal and reasons for its neglect can tell the evaluator much about the environmental context of the evaluation and the influence of various stakeholders. If a goal or objective is linked to the question to be answered in the evaluation, the strategies developed during strategic planning to achieve these related goals and objectives can provide milestones for process evaluation or, at minimum, provide foundation for discussion of progress with stakeholders. Were the strategies followed? If so, what progress was made? Did the stakeholder view the strategy as the appropriate one to take? What problems were encountered in implementing the strategy? What changes were made? Why? In other words, the strategic plan can provide the evaluator with crucial information about both the context of the evaluation and, possibly, the evaluation object itself.

Evaluators have not often been heavily involved in strategic planning. Few references to strategic planning are noted in the evaluation literature. However, evaluators should not shy away from this area. Like needs assessment, strategic planning provides information for decision-making about future directions. Strategic planning differs from needs assessment in that it does not focus on a particular program or population but on the future of the organization as a whole. Thus, it is higher-level planning. But, if evaluators are to have real impact on organizations, both public and private, they must be involved in decisions at many different levels. In the context of corporate training, Brinkerhoff (1989) has suggested that evaluators have been most successful not when they have tried to win support for evaluation as a separate activity but rather when they "have sought ways to weave evaluation thinking and activities into already existing and valued operations" (p. 2). Strategic planning provides an opportunity for evaluators to do just that. In an issue of *Evaluation Practice* on the theme "Past, Present, and Future Assessments of the Field of Evaluation" (highly recommended reading!), many of the authors argue that evaluators must become more involved in planning in the future (Patton, 1994; Reichardt, 1994; Chen, 1994). While these authors refer primarily to program planning, strategic planning provides the opportunity for the inclusion of evaluation thinking at the highest levels.

Quality Control/Quality Assurance

Quality control and **quality assurance** are terms used in corporations and some public-sector settings (e.g., hospitals), to refer to processes akin to monitoring evaluation. As such, evaluators should be familiar with these terms and their application. To illustrate the relationship of quality control and quality assurance to evaluation, Brandenburg (1989) describes them under the heading "New Terms for Familiar Functions" (p. 85). Brandenburg views quality control as the monitoring of inputs and processes primarily for formative purposes; he defines quality assurance as the monitoring of products for summative purposes. We disagree with the linking of formative evaluation with quality control and summative evaluation with quality assurance, fearing that it reflects the old problem of considering all outcome studies summative and process studies formative. Formative and summative evaluations refer to the decisions that will be made from the evaluation, not the thing to be evaluated. Nevertheless, Brandenburg helps in distinguishing quality control and quality assurance based on the *factors* they monitor. *Quality control* mechanisms are designed to provide managers with feedback about whether things are going smoothly at the beginning and middle of the process. The term *quality assurance* begins to be used more when the object to be monitored is closer to the end of the process. However, it would be misleading to imply that quality assurance always measures final outcomes. Instead, it simply measures things that are closer to the end product than quality control does. Because of this ambiguity (When is the thing measured *close enough* to the end product to be considered quality assurance rather than quality control?), the terms are often used interchangeably and what might be labeled "quality control" at one organization is "quality assurance" at another.

Both quality control and quality assurance mechanisms are monitoring devices for collecting routine information on program processes. We would argue that both serve primarily formative decisions because the audience is typically workers and line managers who are responsible for decisions about improving programs, not policy makers who typically make the more summative decisions. Quality assurance and quality control systems are often designed by managers or worker teams who work with the process. They are the primary audience. Sometimes, management information systems (MIS) specialists are involved if the information is to be collected or analyzed by computer. Most MIS products serve a quality control or quality assurance function. Evaluators are rarely involved because the information to be collected is relatively straightforward, (e.g., inventories, supplies, treatment plans, lesson plans, or attendance).

In the public sector, quality assurance is used heavily in hospital and mental health settings and refers to the review of medical or clinical care records. The Joint Commission on Accreditation of Hospital Organizations (JCAHO) uses quality assurance methods for its reviews of institutions. The emphasis is on compliance. The question they are trying to answer is, Do the hospital records comply with JCAHO standards for accountability? Data collection is primarily devoted to sampling records and using checklists to determine the degree of compliance on each standard. Client outcomes are not examined. The assumption is that if the records show appropriate and adequate care, desired outcomes will be achieved. A mental health administrator observed to one of the present authors that a good mental health center should strive for a C from JCAHO; receiving an A probably means you are spending too much time on *records* and too little time on *patient care!* Of course, the examination of existing documents *is* cheaper than validly assessing client outcomes, but the comment does help to illustrate the distinction between program evaluation and quality assurance. Other differences include the nature of use. Quality assurance information can be used with routine frequency (daily, weekly) and is often used to improve the performance of individual workers (e.g., clinicians whose treatment plans are not in compliance are asked to improve). Evaluation results, even with our moving toward sharing results with stakeholders as they emerge, are generally available less frequently and typically do not identify individual workers at fault but rather processes that could be improved.

As with program evaluation, some quality assurance efforts have emerged due to legislative mandates. The 1972 amendments to the Social Security Act (PL 92-603) established Professional Standards Review Organizations to use quality assurance to make sure that funds for Medicare, Medicaid, and the Maternal and Child Health Programs were spent on "medically necessary and high quality care" (Tash & Stahler, 1984). And, like program evaluation, quality assurance and quality control mechanisms aim to provide feedback to improve programs. Coulton (1987) writes :"A successful organization continually looks for, finds, and solves problems. In this context, quality assurance—with its cycle of monitoring, in-depth problem analysis, and corrective action—serves as a self-correcting function within an organization" (p. 443).

Some (Royse, 1992) see the boundaries between quality assurance and program evaluation beginning to blur. As with the other strategies reviewed in this chapter, quality control and quality assurance mechanisms provide opportunities for evaluators to use their skills in the defining of information needs and the collection of information to meet those needs. These actions address Brinkerhoff's (1989) suggestion of using other methods for instilling evaluation thinking into the organization and, in so doing, helping it deliver a better product. As with TQM, quality control and quality assurance focus mostly on process. Unlike TQM, the data collection in quality control and quality assurance systems tends to focus on more stable, or less transitory, information needs.

Through work in each of these arenas—evaluation in the nonprofit sector, corporate training evaluation, personnel evaluation, and the organizational assessment strategies reviewed here (TQM, strategic planning, quality control, and quality assurance)—the evaluator broadens his own skills and experience. Just as visiting other countries helps the traveler learn more about his own culture, working in different settings can help evaluators recognize new characteristics of their own traditional evaluation context. Similarly, evaluating new things or working with other methods of organizational appraisal can expand the evaluator's view of potential evaluation questions and data-collection methods and strategies.

APPLICATION EXERCISES

1. Interview a manager in the nonprofit sector. How does his organization conduct evaluation? How does it differ from the approaches you have read about in this text? How is it like the approaches you have learned? Compare what you learn with others in your class.

2. You have been hired to conduct an evaluation of a program for training new supervisors in how to conduct performance appraisals. What would you do first to plan the evaluation? What types of questions might you suggest the evaluation address? What kinds of measures would you use to address process? Outcomes?

3. Find an article in the library that makes use of quality control or quality assurance measures. How do these measures differ from those typically used in evaluation? How are they like typical evaluation measures? How does the context differ from evaluation? How is it like evaluation?

4. Read one of the case studies on TQM referenced in this chapter. How does its application differ from evaluation? How does it differ from Fetterman's (1994) empowerment approach? (Read the Fetterman reference.)

5. Which do you think should be more important in performance appraisal, the accuracy of the assessment of the individual's performance or the ability of the feedback process to lead to improvement in performance? Why? Does your priority on these two issues mirror your priorities in evaluation? Why or why not?

SUGGESTED READINGS

Berry, T. H. (1991). *Managing the Total Quality Transformation*. New York: McGraw-Hill.

Brinkerhoff, R. O. (Ed.). (1989). *Evaluating training programs in business and industry.* New Directions for Program Evaluation, No 44. San Francisco: Jossey-Bass.

Deming, W. E. (1986). *Out of the crisis.* Cambridge: Massachusetts Institute of Technology, Center for Advanced Engineering Study.

Gies, D. L., Ott, J. S., & Shafritz, J. M. (Eds.). (1990). *The nonprofit organization: Essential readings.* Pacific Grove, CA: Brooks/Cole.

Hackman, R., & Wageman, R. (1995). Total Quality Management: Empirical, conceptual, and practical issues. *Administrative Science Quarterly, 40,* 309–342.

Nutt, P. C., & Backoff, R. W. (1992). *The strategic management of public and third sector organizations.* San Francisco: Jossey-Bass.

Osborne, D., & Gaebler, T. (1992). *Reinventing government: How the entrepreneurial spirit is transforming the public sector*. Reading, MA: Addison-Wesley.

Salamon, L. M. (1992). *America's nonprofit sector: A primer.* New York: Foundation Center.

chapter 23

The Future of Evaluation

ORIENTING QUESTIONS

1. How are future program evaluations likely to be different from current evaluations in
   - the way in which political considerations are handled?
   - the methods that will be used?
   - the involvement of stakeholders?
   - how they are reported?
2. What is the likely future of programs for training evaluators (both for graduate degrees and for in-service training)?
3. What do the authors believe will be important developments for evaluation in the future?
4. What do other evaluation scholars think about the future of evaluation?

We have reached the last chapter of this book. But we have only begun to share what is known about program evaluation. Even the abundance of references we have made to other writings we consider especially important reflect only a fraction of the existing literature in this growing field. In choosing to focus attention on (1) alternative approaches to program evaluation and (2) practical guidelines for planning, conducting, reporting, and using evaluation studies, we have tried to emphasize what we believe is most important to include in any single volume that aspires to give a broad overview of such a complex and multifaceted field. We hope we have selected well. But we encourage students and evaluation practitioners to go beyond this text to explore the richness and depth of other evaluation literature. In this final chapter, we share our perceptions and those of a few of our prominent evaluation colleagues about evaluation's future.

THE FUTURE OF EVALUATION

Hindsight is inevitably better than foresight, and ours is no exception. Yet present circumstances permit us to hazard a few predictions that we believe will hold true for program evaluation in the next few decades. History will prove whether or not our predictions are sufficiently accurate to allow prophecy to be added to the repertoire of techniques useful to evaluators.

We believe that evaluation will continue to spread rapidly around the globe, until there are few countries, territories, provinces, states, and locales in which program evaluations are not at least an occasional occurrence. The spreading interest in program evaluation has been evident for some years in the international participation in evaluation conferences. For example, participants at a 1988 conference on evaluation of educational programs, held in North Berwick, Scotland, represented Austria, Belgium, Canada, Denmark, France, West Germany, Greece, Iceland, Luxembourg, The Netherlands, Norway, Portugal, Sweden, and the United Kingdom (Scottish Council for Research in Education, 1990). At the International Evaluation Conference held in Vancouver, British Columbia, in 1995, over 1,600 persons from 61 countries attended. Such diversity, coupled with the rise of the several professional associations for evaluators we cited in Chapter 3, makes it very safe to say that evaluation will permeate our globe in the coming decades. It may have been more bold and no less accurate to predict that it will be carried into humankind's first long-term space stations as an important partner in improving the many programs needed to sustain not only life but also civilization, as we expand into space and other spheres.

We also believe that evaluation will become an increasingly useful force in the following ways:

- Improving programs, and thus improving the lot of those intended to benefit from those programs
- Improving policy making by governing boards, legislators, and congressional and parliamentary bodies
- Aiding in corporate or public "quality improvement" efforts
- Improving societies through improving their various institutions
- Improving even itself

If these predictions seem overly optimistic, it may underscore our earlier point that evaluators may not always be completely unbiased. Yet these forecasts do not strike us as unrealistic or overdrawn; we are willing to submit them to the test of time.

We also predict that evaluation will expand into other fields, beyond its now venerable role in education, psychology, and health, and its more recent role in the other social sciences, including criminal justice, economics, and family welfare, to play important roles in natural sciences and the variety of other fields as yet less touched by program evaluation. In some fields evaluation will prove nearly as important for its noninformational uses (remember the metaphor of the state trooper patrolling the freeway?) as for its role in providing information to decision makers. We also believe that evaluators' roles will be increasingly expanded into related areas, such as needs assessment and strategic planning, where their skills are very relevant.

We believe evaluation will become increasingly institutionalized in the United States and in other developed countries as the pressure for accountability weighs heavily on governments and as other institutions and evaluators become more skilled in providing useful information to decision makers. Virtually every trend points to more, not less, evaluation in the public, private, and nonprofit sectors in the future. In U.S. education, for example, in addition to calls for evaluation from educational practitioners, the federal courts have begun to use and even order evaluations, and state lawmakers have passed laws requiring that all public education programs and/or all university and college undergraduate programs be evaluated.

We believe that evaluations (and evaluators) of the future will be more politically sophisticated than has been the case previously. The age of innocence when evaluators proclaimed that their studies were merely technical, not political, endeavors is long past. Recognition that evaluation plays political roles beyond that of democratic representation of stakeholders' interests will lead to new conceptualizations of how evaluation can deal with its political nature without being discounted as merely another political (and hence non-credible) activity. This will require evaluators to become more knowledgeable and skillful in working within political systems without sacrificing their essential technical skills.

As a profession, program evaluation will grow slowly but steadily. The American Evaluation Association (AEA) and other societies of practicing evaluators and/or evaluation theoreticians will continue to contribute to evaluation's maturation. Although evaluation will continue to possess many attributes of a distinct profession, we suspect it will still lack means for credentialing evaluators or accrediting evaluation training programs for some time. It seems unlikely that any professional association will soon be equipped to grapple with those thorny and often litigious endeavors (although recent appointment of an AEA Task Force on Certification and discussions in the Canadian Evaluation Society may prove us wrong). Yet we predict that increasingly sophisticated evaluation clients will request information about the competence and credentials of potential evaluators. While the evaluator's less formal "credentials," such as training, experience, prior track record, and references, may suffice for a time, we anticipate this pressure will one day be sufficient to give professional evaluation associations the necessary nudge for them to take the plunge into formal certification of evaluators. We think this day is still far off, however.

It seems safe to predict that the present evaluation standards and ethical guidelines—and their future descendants—will be used increasingly in the years ahead. This will be especially true if, as Berk (1994) predicts, evaluation is increasingly used in litigation. The good old days when evaluators could be at all blasé about legal and ethical issues will soon seem as far removed as the era when distrust or disrespect for politicians was the exception rather than the norm.

The future evaluation literature will increase in both quantity and quality, but relatively little of it will be research based. Current funding agencies do not seem interested in supporting research on the evaluation process. Thus, the *empirical* knowledge base in evaluation will increase very slowly and much of that will be primarily a by-product of training, as experienced evaluation faculty supervise graduate students in conducting original studies that will add to what is known about evaluation. In a field where much of what is written is opinion and conjecture, this development will be important, even though small in scope.

We predict that the opportunity for careers in evaluation will gradually increase as demands for evaluation permeate further into society. Graduate programs in evaluation are unlikely to expand significantly, however, despite increasing demand for evaluators. There may be some growth in existing programs, where institutions have already invested in training of evaluators, but the demand will not be well enough understood by university administrators to result in significant numbers of universities and colleges' initiating programs for training evaluators. Rather, many evaluators will receive their basic training in more traditional disciplines' training programs. The need for in-service education in evaluation will expand dramatically as educators, public and nonprofit administrators, corporate officers, and those in a variety of other roles are asked to assume some responsibility for carrying out evaluation studies alongside their other professional duties. We also expect that evaluation training will become more applied, in coming years, with much of it coming through internships on ongoing evaluation studies or in evaluation agencies where such internships might span several program evaluations.

We believe internal evaluation will, despite its risks, become more important, because of its benefits. We predict there will be increased cooperation between internal and external evaluators, as well as a trend toward limited involvement of external evaluators in formative evaluations, in part to provide a preview of what external evaluators may use as criteria during later summative evaluations.

As for the several alternative approaches to evaluation we described earlier in this book, we predict they and other approaches will be used in more eclectic and less doctrinaire fashions than in the past. Their usefulness will lie less in having any one of them serve as a model to be followed slavishly but rather, as House (1994a) has suggested, as collectively comprising the "grammar of evaluation" that evaluators must understand and be skilled in using:

> [One] might see the evaluation models as something like model sentences in a grammar of evaluation. . . . As one progresses, . . . one does not need to think about the models consciously, except to correct particular errors or study the grammar itself.

Similarly, . . . experienced evaluators can construct evaluation designs which do not depend explicitly on particular models. Actual evaluation designs can be combinations of elements from different models, . . . just as speakers can produce novel grammatical sentences once they have learned the basic grammar of a language. (pp. 241–242)

We also foresee increasing efforts to democratize evaluation not only by broadening participation in evaluation to all legitimate stakeholders, and having representatives of stakeholder groups serve on advisory committees for evaluation studies, but also by using evaluation as an instrument to identify inequality and injustice in society and its various institutions. But we believe that efforts to redefine evaluation as primarily an instrument of social justice rather than a means of determining merit or worth will be gradually replaced with a vision that the two are not incompatible; evaluation of any social policy or institution can quickly show it to be without merit on egalitarian or other worthy grounds, thus aiding the cause of social justice immeasurably without confusing evaluation *with* social justice.

As for its philosophical and methodological future, program evaluation will continue to be pluralistic, and fundamental differences will continue to separate some who will adhere to divisive, polarized views of epistemology and methodology. However, these differences will be of interest to very few evaluation practitioners. The stridency over alternative paradigms and methods has largely subsided, as pragmatic evaluators have found it both possible and productive to draw on both the objectivist and subjectivist traditions in developing multiple approaches to describing the programs they evaluate. Single-method evaluations will be increasingly seen as simplistic and inadequate for evaluation of complex programs or those serving diverse populations. Triangulation, cross-validation, and critical multiplism will be used more routinely to allow the complementarity of qualitative and quantitative approaches to enrich evaluation studies.

We expect to see more longitudinal evaluation as limitations of "snapshot" evaluation studies become more apparent. Not only will matrix sampling be used in quantitative data collection to maximize the validity of results while minimizing intrusions in collecting data, but the logic of such sampling will be extended to qualitative data collection by evaluators equally comfortable with both qualitative and quantitative approaches but desirous of ensuring representativeness of their data. This trend is already occurring, but we expect it to mushroom. And statistical significance of quantitative findings will continue to fade in importance (but not into obscurity) when compared to practical significance. Evaluators will use increasingly sophisticated and precise techniques as they study the causes of success or failure of educational, social, and commercial programs. For example, many techniques discussed in Walberg and Haertel (1990) illustrate promising new tools that will be adopted or adapted by program evaluators.

No predictions of the future would be complete without considering the impact of electronic and other technological advances. Such advances will inevitably alter techniques of data collection and analysis in evaluation. Readers who can still remember the "card sorter" may have had difficulty at that time envisioning today's multiple uses of microcomputers in program evaluation. We expect that new software developments, relational databases, and trend analysis of existing databases will open new vistas for evaluation, but we are reluctant to hazard any specific predicition except that the collective impact of advances in computer technology will be momentous. Similarly, our efforts to predict how other technology will affect evaluation seem likely to be mere guesswork. But it seems certain that other technological advances will permit data collection to be much more rapid, reliable, and valid than is now the case. Perhaps some readers will live to see the day when evaluators (and perhaps teachers) will possess pocket-size instruments that can scan a classroom, record individual and group attitudes and moods, and monitor their level of intellectual readiness or their grasp of specific content. If that occurs during our professional lifetime, it will be time for us to say, "Beam us up, Scotty"—we will have seen enough.

Finally, we predict technology will also alter the way evaluators report. While most current evaluation reports appear in print version, we believe electronic, audio, and video reports are certain to increase in popularity. Perhaps we will live to see evaluation "holograms," where virtual reality could elevate evaluation reporting to levels now nearly unimaginable (although we are not counting on living *that* long). But whatever the medium, we believe there will be a trend toward viewing evaluation reporting as "storytelling," with case studies, scenarios, and typical profiles increasingly used as part of the written narrative or visual portrayal that constitutes the story.

Of course, any—or many—of our specific predictions may prove to be wrong. But we are confident of one final, more general prediction: Program evaluation will greatly improve the practice and products of the programs that are evaluated in the years ahead. It is our hope that analysts looking back in the year 2010 will be able to buttress this assertion with demonstrable evidence that proves, after all, that our confidence in evaluation is more than an article of faith.

So much, then, for our prophecies about evaluation's future. But what of the predictions of other evaluators? Do they see a similar or a different future? At least some seem to concur with our views. For example, Chelimsky (1992) states:

> I believe the truth here is that program evaluation, these days, has begun to hit its stride. We at GAO [the U.S. General Accounting Office] have been developing new methods and using evaluation successfully in our work for the Congress over the past 10 years. Moreover, some remarkable evaluation offices have been developed to serve state legislative and executive information needs. For example, fine evaluations are being done under Minnesota's Office of the Legislative Auditor and Florida has conducted excellent studies of programs for the aged. Inspector General offices increasingly are developing evaluation branches. In fact, auditor generals all over the world—for example, Sweden, Canada, Australia, Israel, Pakistan, South Korea, and so forth—are beginning to include program evaluation as one of their most important areas. . . .
>
> So program evaluation *is* important, governmental effectiveness stands to gain from it, and this is now being recognized worldwide. My sense,

therefore, is that evaluation is moving up and that its future is strong. (pp. 187–188)

House (1994a) adds:

> In summary, I hold an optimistic view of the future of evaluation around the world and its potential power to improve societies and itself. Evaluation's capacity to evaluate itself, to be self-reflective, is more critical than in other fields. The authority to make value judgments about public actions is a formidable social force, and the responsibilities incumbent on such a role are not likely to diminish as evaluation spreads into areas unimaginable only a few years ago. (p. 246)

POTHOLES IN EVALUATION'S PATHWAY

We are not so naive as to think that the road to realization of our positive predictions about evaluation's future will be smooth and straight. On the contrary, we expect that evaluators will experience many frustrations and disappointments along the way as society learns about evaluation and how to maximize its usefulness. Indeed, we predict that the field of evaluation will suffer detours that will discourage many. For example, the recent decision of the U.S. General Accounting Office (GAO) to disband its Program Evaluation and Methodology Division (PEMD) and scatter the few evaluators they retained among other GAO divisions must be considered a serious setback (see Grasso, in press). For 15 years, PEMD was a vital force in evaluation, until recent congressional budget squeezes and downsizing, combined with leadership changes in PEMD and higher government levels, resulted in a regrettable decision to terminate the evaluation unit and disperse the few survivors, ostensibly to "leaven the evaluation loaf" in other GAO divisions. Yet we see this as merely a detour, not the end of evaluation's road, even in GAO.

The basis of our optimism is simple. Short of a collapse in our world economy, we see no force or influence that will prevent enlightened program managers and stakeholders from doing whatever is necessary to obtain information they need to develop, implement, and improve their programs. As long as that need exists, program evaluation can be expected to grow and expand in proportion to the growth and expansion of our society and its economy, despite jolts it may receive from periodic events like closure of GAO's PEMD.

CONCLUSION

We leave the reader with two final thoughts.

First, all that experience and research can teach convinces us that evaluation, properly conducted, has great potential for improving programs and practices in education, human services, business—virtually every area of society. Evaluators have become self-consciously aware that evaluation studies are often misused or ignored, with the result that some individuals have argued for decreased emphasis on the evaluative process. But that seems no more sensible than abandoning medical diagnosis because science has not yet successfully eliminated all disease. Knowledge about evaluation has grown impressively in the near quarter century since our first book was published, but its conclusion still rings true:

> Most systems have most of the earmarks of classical bureaucracies and, historically, have been reasonably successful in resisting change in practices and policies. Recently, strong social forces have coalesced to push many systems out from behind their barriers; change has become a much more frequent reality. However, without a tradition of planned change or systematic inquiry into the effectiveness of potential new programs, the changes which are occurring can be often little more than random adoption of faddish innovations. Perhaps the most important deficiency which fosters such a situation is the lack of dependable information in the performance of available products, practices, and programs. Without such information, practitioners cannot readily correct deficiencies or malfunctions in present practices or intelligently select new products or practices for adoption.
>
> Evaluation . . . holds great promise in providing field workers with badly needed information which can be used to improve the processes of human service. While obviously not a panacea, evaluation can have a profound impact on the human services professions. (Worthen & Sanders, 1973, pp. 348–349)

The second thought we wish to leave with readers is this: Despite great strides, it is increasingly apparent how little we really do know about evaluation, compared to what we need to know. It is our earnest hope that this book has added to that knowledge and thus helped to illuminate the thousand points of darkness that still constitute current processes for creating and implementing the policies and programs intended to improve the lot of humankind.

APPLICATION EXERCISE

Relax. We think you've done enough. Besides, we have no idea how to have you meaningfully apply our predictions about evaluation's future. If *you* do, we will welcome your suggestions for future editions.

SUGGESTED READINGS

Smith, M. F. (1994). Evaluation: Review of the past, preview of the future. *Evaluation Practice, 15*, 215–227.

Wye, C., & Sonnichsen, R. (1992). Another look at the future of program evaluation in the federal government: Five views. *Evaluation Practice, 13*, 185–195.

appendix

Some General Areas of Competence Important in Educational Evaluation

The following (drawn from Sanders, 1979) describes 11 general areas of competence important for evaluators to conduct high-quality educational evaluations. We do not propose the list as all-inclusive of all the areas of competence necessary in the broad range of evaluation approaches that might be applied in education. No doubt some abilities important to conduct certain educational evaluations have been omitted, but we believe these 11 areas are representative areas of competence that cut across almost all educational evaluations.

We believe, then, that the competent evaluator must be able to:

1. *Describe the object of an evaluation*—that is, be able to communicate to others what is being evaluated, what its limits are, and what its important characteristics are. This is necessary, regardless of the object being evaluated (a program, a project, an idea, human performance, materials, etc.). Objects change over time, with different staff, in new settings, from plans to actual operations. Labels are not enough to communicate what has been evaluated.

2. *Describe the context of an evaluation*—that is, be able to communicate to others what factors in the environment have affected the object of an evaluation as well as the evaluation itself. The results of most educational evaluations are specific to a particular setting, time, and set of human actors. The findings are often idiosyncratic because factors in the environment affect the object and its performance in a way that cannot be replicated. Taking knowledge about these factors into account can greatly help us to understand evaluation findings.

3. *Conceptualize appropriate purpose and frameworks for evaluation*—that is, be able to use existing information to make decisions about the most appropriate framework for planning the evaluation. Does the situation call for a formative or summative design? Should the study be objectives-oriented or

511

expertise-oriented? Should the unit being studied be an individual, a classroom, a curriculum, a school system, a region, or a state.[1]

4. *Identify and select appropriate evaluation questions, information needs, and sources of information*—that is, be able to determine what we need to know about an object before judgments can be made and where we might learn about those characteristics. Determining what we need to know is dependent on the criteria that will be used to determine value. Standard criteria can be found in books and articles dealing with entities similar to the object of the evaluation, and these criteria are linked to substantive theory and earlier research. There are also expectations of important evaluation stakeholders that help establish criteria. Finally, proposed evaluation approaches and evaluation textbooks suggest additional criteria. Evaluators must be able to set priorities and justify them for collecting information when lists of information needs become unwieldy. Evaluators must also be able to sort out which of the alternative source of information (e.g., students, parents, administrators, teachers, files, etc.) will provide the best information (objective, reliable, valid, representative, relevant) within our constraints (time, cost, personnel, logistics).

5. *Identify, select, and apply appropriate techniques and procedures for information collection, processing, and analysis*—that is, be able to develop and select various types of information-gathering instruments (tests, scales, questionnaires, interview schedules, observation checklists, or other forms) and procedures (experimental design, survey methods, or the like), being able to record and process various types of information (qualitative and quantitative measurement, coding and computer storage and retrieval), and being able to analyze the information (data reduction and summarization, statistical analysis, assimilation of qualitative data). These technical skills involve identifying and selecting the best approach and then being able to do it. Evaluators need to be skilled technical generalists. Fortunately, graduate course work and textbooks in many relevant skill areas are available to build this competence, but it does take time and opportunity to apply newly gained knowledge.

6. *Determine value of the object of an evaluation*—that is, be able to apply criteria to descriptive information about an object in order to arrive at defensible value statements. There are several routes to determining value, and no one basis for value can be claimed as the correct one. Nevertheless, the competent evaluator must be able to proceed in a systematic and justifiable way to the point of preparing judgments or value statements.

7. *Communicate evaluation plans and results effectively*—that is, be able to understand the information needs of important audiences, prepare appropriate messages, and deliver each message in a way that it will be heard. Written

---

[1] The analysis of different evaluation frameworks provided in Chapters 4 through 11 should prove useful in sorting out and choosing among various frameworks for evaluation, but there are many more details to be determined than any textbook can teach. This competency is somewhat subjective, an art that requires wisdom that only experience can provide.

documents and long technical reports are usually expected from evaluators, but they are not necessarily the best way to communicate plans or results. They might best serve as necessary supporting documents that are available for anyone wanting to pursue a particular point. The evaluator must know the audience for evaluative information, select the most appropriate way to bring that information to the attention of the audience, and then do so in an understandable and timely way. Follow-up communication with an audience is often an important part of the overall communication process.

8. *Manage evaluations*—that is, be able to plan evaluation activities, allocate human and fiscal resources to carry out evaluation tasks, and provide leadership throughout the study, supporting, monitoring, and supervising as necessary other personnel to complete a high-quality evaluation. The competent evaluator must be able to use available resources to produce on schedule a quality evaluation that delivers on all the promises made when the study was commissioned. This requires task orientation, expertise in working with people, planning skills, and good decision-making skills.

9. *Maintain ethical standards*—that is, be able to demonstrate professional behavior during all aspects of an evaluation. Knowing laws regarding protection of human subjects and freedom of information is certainly one part of this competency. In addition, evaluators frequently deal with confidential information, produce value judgments, affect the work and well-being of others, give people "bitter pills" to swallow, and address moral issues. Knowing and maintaining ethical principles as an evaluator is part of professional behavior.

10. *Adjust for external factors that affect an evaluation*—that is, be able to remain flexible during an evaluation. The competent evaluator must be able to assimilate new information into the procedures of the evaluation as such information becomes known. Constraints that may affect even the most well-conceived plan include those that are legal, logistical, political, administrative, human, and methodological. The competent evaluator cannot be dogmatic in implementation of the evaluation plan.

11. *Evaluate the evaluation (metaevaluate)*—that is, be able to critique, revise, and learn from evaluation experiences. Evaluation is a young profession and there is much to be learned. Furthermore, no evaluation can be bias-free. The competent evaluator will include procedures to review plans, techniques, and procedures, and apply appropriate criteria (see criteria for use in evaluating evaluations discussed in Chapter 20) to improve the quality of an evaluation.

Although perhaps hinted at in items 9 and 10 above, professional, ethical, and interpersonal sensitivities are essential for any educational evaluator. As Sechrest (1980) concluded:

> In many ways, attitudes or outlook may be as important as specific skills. Certainly the evaluation researcher must have an ability to work closely with others in a sensitive way. The field is no place for loners nor for those inclined to be oblivious to the attitudes, feelings, and problems of others. Attitudes and outlook are difficult to impart by

direct instruction, but must be carefully nurtured in students who were selected because they seemed hospitable to the learning. (p. 90)

Certainly one would hope to select an evaluator who possesses not only these sensitivities but also those reflected in the 11 general areas of competence outlined above.

Glossary

Accreditation. A system and process of reviewing programs against certain quality standards for purposes of credentialing the program.

Ad hoc panel reviews. Professional reviews by expert panels occurring whenever prompted by a need for information, usually as one-shot or irregularly occurring events. Ad hoc reviews are generally unrelated to any institutionalized structure for evaluation.

Adversary-oriented evaluation. Any evaluation in which planned opposition in the points of view of different evaluators or evaluation teams is the result of efforts to *balance* bias by generating opposing views *within* the overall evaluation.

Audiences. Individuals, groups, and agencies who have an interest in the evaluation and receive its results.

Case study. A data-collection design used in the naturalistic paradigm. It makes use of multiple, often qualitative, methods to provide a thorough understanding of the program, case, or unit of interest.

Client. The specific agency or individual who requests the evaluation.

Cluster evaluation. A multiple-site, multilevel evaluation approach developed and used to evaluate "clusters" of projects that either have things in common with each other or that are funded under a specific funding initiative.

Cluster sampling. A method of random sampling used to permit cost-effective sampling when face-to-face data collection is required across a large geographic area. It involves drawing a series of random samples of geographic blocks or "clusters" of successively smaller geographic units.

Confirmative evaluation. An evaluation conducted after the program has been implemented and is in operation for a significant period to see how well it retains its effectiveness across time, as opposed to the more usual summative evaluation conducted immediately upon completion of the implementation phase.

Connoisseurship. The art of appreciation of an object based on an awareness of its qualities and the relationships among them.

Constructivism. A paradigm that holds that reality does not exist objectively but is constructed by each of us. (Also referred to as **interpretivism**.)

Content analysis. A method for analyzing, describing, and summarizing trends in written documents such as minutes of meetings, publications, newspaper articles, annual reports, field notes, transcripts from focus groups or interviews, and other similar documents. The analysis can take a qualitative or quantitative approach.

Convenience sampling. Haphazard sampling in which individuals from whom data are collated are sampled on the basis of their accessibility. This method does not permit generalizing to the population as a whole.

Convergent phase. A phase in the planning of an evaluation in which the evaluator, working with the client or a group of stakeholders, selects (from the questions generated during the divergent phase) the questions to be addressed in the current study.

Cost-benefit analysis. A method of cost analysis of well-defined program alternatives that involves comparing their costs and benefits when both costs and benefits are expressed in monetary terms. This method is most useful when comparing programs with different outcomes because it changes the benefits into like terms (dollars).

Cost-effectiveness analysis. A method of cost analysis that involves comparing the costs of alternative programs designed to achieve the same or similar outcomes. This method is most useful when comparing programs with like outcomes because it avoids the need to convert benefits to dollars.

Cost-feasibility analysis. A method of cost analysis used to determine whether a particular option is feasible to implement, given its costs and the available budget. This method is used for planning prior to the implementation of a program.

Cost-utility analysis. A method of cost analysis used to analyze alternatives by comparing their costs and estimated utility; used prior to the implementation of a program.

Criteria. Indicators of merit that delineate the characteristics of a successful program or implementation. Although sometimes implicit in the evaluation questions themselves, the criteria to be used for judging program worth should generally be made explicit.

Criterion-referenced tests. Tests developed specifically to measure performance against some absolute criterion.

Criticism. The art of disclosing the qualities of objects that connoisseurship perceives.

Cross-sectional design. A design used when the purpose of the evaluation is descriptive and the interest is in describing attitudes, opinions, or behaviors of groups or subgroups at one point in time. The design typically makes use of surveys to collect information.

Delphi technique. A method of data collection designed to move a group toward consensus through a series of surveys in which respondents report their opinions and in subsequent surveys are provided with information on the opinions of the other group members.

Descriptive design. A design that describes rather than attributes causality.

Divergent phase. A phase in the planning of the evaluation in which a comprehensive list of potentially important questions and concerns, which may come from a wide variety of sources, is developed.

Documents. Personal or agency records that have not been prepared specifically for research or investigation.

Domain-referenced tests. Tests used to estimate a student's knowledge of a particular domain of content (e.g., comparative anatomy). Test items are not linked to a specific curriculum but rather are considered a sample of the universe of similar items possible in that content domain.

Effect size. A means of setting practically significant standards to serve as an alternative to using only statistical significance when the evaluation issue concerns comparing two programs on the same outcome.

Epistemology. The theory of knowledge or the study of the nature of knowledge.

Evaluability assessment. A method for determining whether a program is evaluable, communicating with stakeholders, and planning the evaluation. It involves determining whether the program to be evaluated has well-defined objectives that could plausibly be achieved based upon current program actions, clearly defined information needs, and specified uses for the evaluation.

Evaluation. The identification, clarification, and application of defensible criteria to determine an evaluation object's value (worth or merit), quality, utility, effectiveness, or significance in relation to those criteria.

Evaluation plan. The blueprint for the evaluation study. It is prepared at the conclusion of the planning stage and documents the evaluation questions to be answered, information sources and methods, means for collecting the information including sampling procedures, methods to be used for analyzing the information, interpretation guidelines, and reporting procedures.

Evaluation questions. Questions that provide the direction, foundation, and focus for the evaluation. They specify exactly what the evaluation will answer and guide the design and planning of the evaluation.

Evaluation research. A term used by many social scientists to denote any evaluation that employs a rigorous social science research methodology, as opposed to evaluations conducted with other methods.

Evaluation standards. Commonly agreed-upon principles of professional practice in program evaluation (Joint Committee, 1994).

Experimental designs. Designs used when the purpose of the study is to determine causation of observed effects. These designs counter many threats to internal validity. They require random assignment of participants to groups that are equal on as many factors as possible except one: the treatment being evaluated.

External evaluators. Evaluators who are not permanent employees of the organization conducting the program being evaluated. (Also called third-party evaluators and independent evaluators.)

Focus groups. A method of group interviewing designed to yield information that results from guided interaction among group members; produces different types of information from that provided in traditional one-on-one or structured group interviews.

Formative evaluation. Any evaluation conducted to provide program staff with evaluative information useful in improving the program. It is most typically conducted while the program is being developed.

Front-end analysis. Collecting data to assist in the planning of a training program; a type of needs assessment for training. Such studies typically attempt to define the nature of the organizational performance or problem, the causes of the problem, and the most appropriate means for resolving the problem.

Gantt chart. A simple graphical display that includes proportionate, chronologically scaled time frames for each evaluation task. A Gantt chart lists tasks on the vertical axis and a time scale on the horizontal axis, indicating how long a task will take. Gantt charts are effective in communicating evaluation plans at a glance.

Goal-free evaluation. A method used to reduce bias in program evaluation by shielding the evaluator from knowing the goals of the program being evaluated. This causes the evaluator to concentrate on what the program is actually doing rather than on what it is trying to do.

Goals. General aims or desired outcomes (more general than objectives).

Internal evaluators. Evaluators who are employees of the organization conducting the program being evaluated.

Interpretivism. See **constructivism**.

Interrupted time-series design. A quasi-experimental design in which data are collected many times before the introduction of the program or policy and many times after its introduction. A change in the trend of the data at the point of introduction of the policy may be attributed to the program if no other plausible causal factors were present at that time.

Intuitionist-pluralist evaluation. An evaluation that assumes that the value of a program can only be judged by determining the impact of the program on *each* individual.

Key evaluation checklist. A general checklist of points proposed as necessary for reviewing any program evaluation (Scriven, 1991a).

Key incident approach. A means for analyzing qualitative information. This method involves identifying key incidents and linking them to other events, phenomena, or constructs to illustrate the larger picture.

Likert-scale items. Items used on instruments designed to measure attitudes. These items consist of sentences that reflect an attitude on the construct of interest. Responses are made on a "strongly agree–strongly disagree" continuum.

Logical positivism. An early form of positivism marked by dogmatic certainty and unthinking determination and reductionism. (See also **positivism**.)

Management plan. The blueprint for implementing an evaluation study. For each evaluation question, it specifies each task to be performed, the beginning and end dates for conducting the task, who will conduct the task, the resources needed to complete it, and the total cost of the task.

Metaevaluation. An evaluation of an evaluation; determining the merit or worth of an evaluation itself.

Multisite evaluation. A form of multiple-site evaluation that depends on large-scale experimental or quasi-experimental studies of major social or human services programs.

Naturalistic evaluation. Evaluation of an object as it occurs naturally in its everyday form without constraining, manipulating, or controlling it.

Nonequivalent comparison group design. A quasi-experimental design in which the pre- and posttest performances of two similar (but *not* randomly constituted) groups are compared to examine program effect. Such designs try to identify a comparison group that is quite similar to the treatment group in characteristics and past and present experiences so that differences between the groups on the posttest may be more safely attributed to the treatment.

Nonprofit sector. Organizations, neither public nor private, governed by legal regulations preventing profit taking, which generally serve a public purpose. Nonprofit organizations are legally defined as those qualifying for 401C designation by the federal government. Also known as the independent sector.

Norm-referenced tests. Tests intended primarily to compare students' performance against large (usually regional or national) samples of similar students taking the same test (referred to as "norm groups"). Items on such tests may not provide sufficient information for evaluating specific programs because the content of the items may not match the curricula.

Objectives. Specific intents. Objectives may be intended conditions, activities, processes, or results (either intermediate or ultimate results).

Objectives-referenced tests. Tests that use items keyed to specific instructional objectives. Such tests are most useful for formative evaluation for the teacher or trainer.

Objectivism. An evaluation approach that requires that evaluation information be scientifically objective, that is, that it use data-collection and -analysis techniques that yield reproducible and verifiable results.

Observation schedules. Checklists or forms used for recording structured observations.

On-site evaluation. Evaluation conducted during a visit to the program site. In multiple-site evaluations, it involves on-site evaluation teams' visiting all or some of the sites implementing the program.

Ontology. The theory of reality or existence.

Paradigm. A philosophy or school of thought; a general conception of or model for a discipline or subdiscipline (Scriven, 1991a).

Performance appraisal. Formal mechanisms for evaluating the performance of individual employees and providing them with feedback to improve performance. Performance appraisals may be used for employee development, promotions, and compensation.

Performance. Actual observable behaviors or change in measurable variables. Performance is often compared to objectives to see whether there is a discrepancy between the two.

PERT (Program Evaluation and Review Technique) **charts.** A graphic, flowchart technique used to plan and monitor the implementation of complex projects. It demonstrates the interrelationships among tasks and the time required to complete various tasks and subsets of tasks.

Phenomenology. A paradigm that holds that all knowledge is of phenomena and all existence draws more on the senses than on thought. (See also **constructivism**.)

Positivism. A paradigm that holds that knowledge is based on natural phenomena and their properties and relations as verified by the empirical sciences.

Post-positivism. A later form of positivism marked by a view of knowledge as fallible and facts as value-laden and explainable by many different theories. (See also **positivism**.)

Posttest-only designs. An experimental design in which study participants are randomly assigned to levels of treatment, and post-treatment measures are collected. Pre-treatment measures are not collected as it is assumed that random assignment guarantees equivalence.

Preordinate evaluation. Evaluation that relies on preconceptions and formal plans rather than by evaluation design after the realities in the program are understood.

Pre-post design. An experimental design in which study participants are randomly assigned to levels of treatment and measures are collected before and after the treatment. The collection of pretreatment measures can be helpful if drop-out from treatments are expected to bias posttreatment measures.

Privatization. The move by various government agencies to contract out to private or nonprofit organizations services previously delivered by those government agencies.

Program description. A description of the critical elements of the program. Such a description typically includes goals and objectives, critical components and activities, and descriptions of the target audience and may go on to include characteristics of personnel delivering the program, administrative arrangements, the physical setting, and other contextual factors.

Program theory. A description of the critical elements of the program focusing on what the program is intended to achieve and how it is intended to do so. A model for why the program elements should bring about the desired change with the intended target audience. May make use of research findings and/or program planners' perceptions.

Purposive sampling. A form of sampling in which units are selected based on a judgment that these units have certain desired characteristics. The method does not permit generalizing the results to the larger population but can be useful for descriptive purposes.

Q-sorts. A method of data collection used to obtain ratings of groups on various options. The method requires individuals to prioritize or rank-order their preferences by sorting cards stating each option. It is similar to the Delphi technique in that it obtains opinions on needs or objectives, but it does not strive for consensus or make use of a series of surveys.

Qualitative inquiry. Research that is typically conducted in natural settings, uses the researcher as the primary "instrument," emphasizes "rich description" of the phenomenon being investigated, employs multiple data-gathering methods, and uses an inductive approach to data analysis.

Quality assurance. Mechanisms for monitoring the quality of a product as it approaches the end or outcome stage. It serves as a final check on the quality of the product.

Quality control. Mechanisms for monitoring the quality of a product during the beginning and middle stages of product development.

Quantitative inquiry. Research that focuses on the testing of specific hypotheses, uses structured designs and statistical methods of analysis, and encourages standardization, precision, objectivity, and reliability of measurement as well as replicability of findings.

Quasi-experimental designs. Designs used when the purpose is causal and random assignment is not feasible. These designs counter some threats to internal validity and are therefore an improvement over nonexperimental designs.

Random sampling. A common type of probability sampling in which each individual or unit in the population has an equal and independent probability of being selected for data collection. This method maximizes the chances that the sample will be representative of the population from which the sample is drawn and thus permits generalization to that population.

Records. Official documents or statistics prepared for use by others. Such existing information can be more valid, reliable, and cost-effective than other information if the purposes match those of the current evaluation study.

Regression-discontinuity design. A quasi-experimental design in which subjects who meet a certain criterion are compared to those who fail to meet that criterion. A difference in the regression line for the two groups suggests a program effect.

Responsive evaluation. Evaluation that addresses the emerging concerns, issues, and requirements for information of a stakeholder audience during and throughout the evaluation, insofar as feasible.

Sampling. A means of selecting a portion of a target population for study.

Site visit. A special case of observation used most frequently in the expertise-oriented evaluation approach. Used frequently in accreditation and audits, it typically involves a team of external reviewers' collecting information to make a judgment about many aspects of a site, including a possible summative decision regarding accreditation. (See also **on-site evaluation.**)

Sponsor. The agency or individual who authorizes the evaluation and provides necessary fiscal resources for its conduct.

Stakeholder. An individual who has a stake in or may be affected by the program to be evaluated or the evaluation's results.

Standards. Designated levels of performance the program must achieve on the criteria to be deemed a success. Standards may be absolute (e.g., specific numbers or proportions) or relative (e.g., better than a control or comparison group as demonstrated through statistical significance or effect size). Different stakeholders may have different expectations for the program and, consequently, define "success" differently. Thus, there may not be one set of standards that is *the* standard of performance.

Strategic planning. An organizational method designed to improve performance by defining the organization's mission and constituencies and specifying organizational goals and objectives and strategies for achieving those objectives. The method is used by many public-sector organizations for long-range planning.

Stratified random sampling. A method of random sampling used when the evaluator is interested in examining differences among subgroups in the population, some of which are so small that they may not be represented in sufficient numbers in simple random sampling. Stratified random sampling divides the population into strata representing the subgroups of interest.

Structured observations. Observations conducted when the evaluator desires to focus on specific behaviors or characteristics.

Subjectivism. An evaluation approach that emphasizes the experience of the evaluator rather than scientific knowledge. The validity of such an evaluation depends upon the evaluator's background, qualification, and perspicacity.

Summative evaluation. Any evaluation conducted to provide program decision makers and potential consumers with judgments about that program's worth or merit, in relation to important criteria, to determine adoption, continuation or expansion, or termination.

Time-series design. A design used when the purpose of the evaluation is descriptive and the interest is in describing a trend over time. This design typically makes use of existing data.

Total Quality Management (TQM). A management approach for improving organizational efficiency and effectiveness. Its goal is to improve customer satisfaction and organizational efficiency by examining relationships with suppliers, work processes, and customer concerns.

Transdiscipline. A term sometimes used to refer to an emerging discipline, but more accurately denoting a "cross-discipline" whose subject matter is the study and improvement of specific tools for other disciplines (e.g., statistics).

Triangulation. The practice of comparing results from data designed to measure the same construct but that are collected from different sources and/or by different methods to increase certainty about the validity of the construct.

Unobtrusive measurements. Collecting data about subjects without their knowledge, such as archival and private records, physical traces, and contrived observations.

Unstructured observations. Initial, unfocused, wide-ranging observations, usually employed to become more familiar with the program context so as to refine and focus subsequent observation and data collection.

Utilitarian evaluation. An evaluation that determines value by assessing the *overall* impact of a program on all those affected (i.e., assessing group outcomes as opposed to individual outcomes).

References

Adams, K. A. (1983, April). *When to "hold em" and when to "fold em": Ethical problems of internal evaluators.* Paper presented at the annual meeting of the American Educational Research Association, Montreal.

Aday, L. A. (1989). *Designing and conducting health surveys: A comprehensive guide.* San Francisco: Jossey-Bass.

Adler, P. A., & Adler, P. (1994). Observational techniques. In N. K. Denzin & Y. S. Lincoln (Eds.), *Handbook of qualitative research.* Thousand Oaks, CA: Sage.

Affholter, D. P. (1994). Outcome monitoring. In J. S. Wholey, H. P. Hatry, & K. E. Newcomer (Eds.), *Handbook of practical program evaluation.* San Francisco: Jossey-Bass.

Alexander, R. R. (1977). *Educational criticism of three art history classes.* Unpublished doctoral dissertation, Stanford University. (University Microfilms No. 78-2125)

Alkin, M. C. (1969). Evaluation theory development. *Evaluation Comment, 2,* 2-7.

Alkin, M. C. (1991). Evaluation theory development: II. In M. W. McLaughlin & D. C. Phillips (Eds.), *Evaluation and education: At quarter century.* Ninetieth Yearbook of the National Society for the Study of Education, Part II. Chicago: University of Chicago Press.

Alkin, M. C., & Solmon, L. C. (Eds.). (1983). *The costs of evaluation.* Beverly Hills, CA: Sage.

Alkin, M. C., Stecher, B. M., & Geiger, F. L. (1982). *Title I evaluation: Utility and factors influencing use.* Northridge, CA: Educational Evaluation Associates.

Altschuld, J. W., Engle, M., Cullen, C., Kim, I., & Macce, B. R. (1994). The 1994 directory of evaluation training programs. In J. W. Altschuld & M. Engle (Eds.), *The preparation of professional evaluators: Issues, perspectives, and programs.* New Directions for Program Evaluation, No. 62, 71-94. San Francisco: Jossey-Bass.

American Anthropological Association. (1990). *Statements on ethics: Principles of professional responsibility.* Arlington, VA: Author.

American Educational Research Association. (1992). Ethical standards. *Educational Researcher, 21,* 23-26.

American Evaluation Association. (1995). Guiding principles for evaluators. In W. R. Shadish, D. L. Newman, M. A. Scheirer, & C. Wye (Eds.), *Guiding principles for evaluators.* New Directions for Program Evaluation, No. 34, 19-26.

Amie, M. (1995). The Australasian Evaluation Society. *Evaluation, 1,* 124-125.

Anderson, R. C. (1983). Reflections on the role of peer review in competitions for federal research. *Educational Researcher, 12,* 3-5.

Anderson, S. B., & Ball, S. (1978). *The profession and practice of program evaluation.* San Francisco: Jossey-Bass.

Auerbach, C., Garrison, L. K., Hurst, W., & Mermin, S. (1961). The adversary system. In C. Auerbach & S. Mermin (Eds.), *The legal process.* San Francisco: Chandler.

Babbie, E. (1992). *The practice of social research* (6th ed.). Belmont, CA: Wadsworth.

Bailey, M. T. (1992). Do physicists use case studies? Thoughts on public administration research. *Public Administration Review, 52,* 47-54.

Baker, E. L., & Niemi, D. (in press). School and program evaluation. In D. C. Berliner & R. C. Calfee (Eds.), *Handbook of education psychology.* New York: Macmillan.

Barrios, N. B., & Foster, G. R. (1987, April). *Utilization of evaluation information: A case study approach investigating factors related to evaluation utilization in a large state agency.* Paper presented at the annual meeting of the American Evaluation Association, Boston. (ED 292 814)

Basch, C. E. (1987). Focus group interviews: An underutilized technique for improving theory and practice in health education. *Health Education Quarterly, 14,* 411-448.

Bell, J. B. (1994). Managing evaluation projects step by step. In J. S. Wholey, H. P. Hatry, & K. E. Newcomer (Eds.), *Handbook of practical program evaluation.* San Francisco: Jossey-Bass.

Benkofske, M. (1994a). Personal communication. Reprinted with permission.

Benkofske, M. (1994b, November). When the qualitative findings are negative. Paper presented at the annual meeting of the American Evaluation Association, Boston.

Berk, R. A. (1986). Minimum competency testing: Status and potential. In B. S. Plake & J. C. Witt (Eds.), *The future of testing* (pp. 84-144). Hillsdale, NJ: Lawrence Erlbaum.

Berk, R. A. (1994). Three trends in evaluation research. *Evaluation Practice, 15,* 261-264.

Berliner, D. C., & Biddle, B. J. (1995). *The manufactured crisis.* Reading, MA: Addison-Wesley.

Bernhardt, V. L. (1984, October). *Evaluation processes of regional and national education accrediting agencies: Implications for redesigning an evaluation process in California.* Paper presented at the annual meeting of the American Educational Research Association, New Orleans.

Berry, F. S. (1994). Innovation in public management: The adoption of strategic planning. *Public Administration Review, 54,* 322-329.

Berry, F. S., & Wechsler, B. (1995). State agencies' experience with strategic planning: Findings from a national survey. *Public Administration Review, 55,* 159-168.

Bickman, L. (1994). An optimistic view of evaluation. *Evaluation Practice, 15,* 255-259.

Bloom, B. S., Engelhart, M. D., Furst, E. J., Hill, W. H., & Krathwohl, D. R. (1956). *Taxonomy of educational objectives: Handbook I. Cognitive domain.* New York: David McKay.

Bloom, B. S., Hastings, J. T., & Madaus, G. F. (1971). *Handbook of formative and summative evaluation of student learning.* New York: McGraw-Hill.

Bogdan, R. C., & Biklen, S. K. (1982). *Qualitative research for education.* Boston: Allyn & Bacon.

Boruch, R. F., & Cordray, D. S. (Eds.). (1980). *An appraisal of educational program evaluation: Federal, state, and local agencies.* Washington, DC: U.S. Department of Education.

Bowman, J. S. (1994). At last an alternative to performance appraisal: Total Quality Management. *Public Administration Review, 54,* 129-136.

Bracey, G. W. (1995, October). The fifth Bracey report on the condition of public education. *Phi Delta Kappan,* 149-160. (Prior reports in this series appeared each year in the October issue of the *Phi Delta Kappan,* 1991-1994.

Brager, G. L., & Mazza, P. (1979). The level of analysis and the level of presentation are not the same. *Educational Evaluation and Policy Analysis, 3,* 105-106.

Braithwaite, R. L., & Thompson, R. L. (1981). Application of the judicial evaluation model within an employment and training program. *Center on Evaluation, Development, and Research (CEDR) Quarterly, 14,* 13-16.

Brandenburg, D. C. (1989). Evaluation and business issues: Tools for management decision making. In R. O. Brinkerhoff (Ed.), *Evaluating training programs in business and industry.* New Directions for Program Evaluation, No. 44, 83-100. San Francisco: Jossey-Bass.

Brandon, P. R., Lindberg, M. A., & Wang, Z. (1993). Involving program beneficiaries in the early stages of evaluation: Issues of consequential validity and influence. *Educational Evaluation and Policy Analysis, 15,* 420-428.

Brandt, R. S. (Ed.) (1981). *Applied strategies for curriculum evaluation.* Alexandria, VA: Association for Supervision and Curriculum Development.

Braybrooke, D., & Lindblom, C. E. (1963). *A strategy of decision.* New York: Free Press.

Brickell, H. M. (1978). The influence of external political factors on the role and methodology of evaluation. In T. D. Cook, M. L. Del Rosario, K. M. Hennigan, M. M. Mark, & W. M. K. Trochim (Eds.), *Evaluation studies review annual* (Vol. 3). Beverly Hills, CA: Sage.

Brinkerhoff, R. O. (1989). Using evaluation to transform training. In R. O. Brinkerhoff (Ed.), *Evaluating training programs in business and industry.* New Directions for Program Evaluation, No. 44, 5-20. San Francisco: Jossey-Bass.

Brinkerhoff, R. O., Brethower, D. M., Hluchyj, T., & Nowakowski, J. R. (1983). *Program evaluation: A practitioner's guide for trainers and educators.* Boston: Kluwer-Nijhoff.

Brodsky, S. L., & Smitherman, H. O. (1983). *Handbook of scales for research in crime and delinquency.* New York: Plenum Press.

Brown, R. D., & Newman, D. L. (1992). Ethical principles and evaluation standards: Do they match? *Evaluation Review, 16,* 650-663.

Buchanan, G. N., & Wholey, J. S. (1972). Federal level evaluation. *Evaluation, 1,* 17-22.

Campbell, D. (1969). Ethnocentrism of disciplines and the fish-scale model of omniscience. In M. Sheriff & C. Sherif (Eds.), *Inter-disciplinary relationships in the social sciences.* Chicago: Aldine.

Campbell, D. (1975). Reforms as experiments. In E. Struening & M. Guttentag (Eds.), *Handbook of evaluation research* (Vol. 1). Beverly Hills, CA: Sage.

Campbell, D. T. (1984). Can we be scientific in applied social science? In R. F. Conner, D. G. Altman, & C. Jackson (Eds.), *Evaluation studies review annual* (Vol. 9). Beverly Hills, CA: Sage.

Campbell, D. T., & Stanley, J. C. (1966). *Experimental and quasi-experimental designs for research.* Chicago: Rand McNally.

Canadian Evaluation Society (1992). Standards for program evaluation in Canada: A discussion paper. *Canadian Journal of Program Evaluation, 7,* 157-170.

Carnevale, A. P., & Carnevale, E. S. (1994). Growth patterns in workplace training. *Training and Development, 48,* 22-28.

Carnevale, A. P., Gainer, L. J., & Villet, J. (1990). *Training in America.* San Franscisco: Jossey-Bass.

Cascio, W. F. (1991). *Applied psychology in personnel management.* Reston, VA: Reston.

Chelimsky, E. (1985a). Old patterns and new directions in program evaluation. In E. Chelimsky (Ed.), *Program evaluation: Patterns and directions.* Washington, DC: American Society for Public Administration.

Chelimsky, E. (1985b). Program evaluation and the use of extant data. In L. Burstein, H. E. Freeman, & P. H. Rossi (Eds.), *Collecting evaluation data.* Beverly Hills, CA: Sage.

Chelimsky, E. (1987). The politics of program evaluation. In D. S. Cordray, H. S. Bloom, & R. J. Light (Eds.), *Evaluation practice in review.* New Directions for Program Evaluation, No. 34, 5-21. San Francisco: Jossey-Bass.

Chelimsky, E. (1992). "Views of Eleanor Chelimsky." Quoted in C. Wye & R. Sonnichsen, Another look at the future of program evaluation in the federal government: Five views. *Evaluation Practice, 13,* 185-195.

Chelimsky, E. (1994). Evaluation: Where are we? *Evaluation Practice, 15,* 339-345.

Chelimsky, E. (1995a). Comments on the guiding principles. In W. R. Shadish, D.L. Newman, M. A. Scheirer, & C. Wye (Eds.), *Guiding principles for evaluators.* New Directions for Program Evaluation, No. 66, 53-54. San Francisco: Jossey-Bass.

Chelimsky, E. (1995b). Preamble: New dimensions in evaluation. In R. Picciotto & R. C. Rist (Eds.), *Evaluating country development policies and programs: New approaches for a new agenda.* New Directions for Program Evaluation, No. 67, 3-11. San Francisco: Jossey-Bass.

Chelimsky, E., & Shadish, W. R. (Eds.). (in press). *Evaluation for the 21st century: A resource book.* Thousand Oaks, CA: Sage.

Chen, H. (1990). *Theory-driven evaluations.* Newbury Park, CA: Sage.

Chen, H. (1993). Emerging perspectives in program evaluation. *Journal of Social Service Research, 17,* 1-17.

Chen, H. (1994). Current trends and future directions in program evaluation. *Evaluation Practice, 15,* 229-238.

Chen, H. (1996). A comprehensive typology for program evaluation. *Evaluation practice, 17,* 121-130.

Chen, H., & Rossi, P. H. (1983). Evaluating with sense: The theory-driven approach. *Evaluation Review, 7,* 283-302.

Clark, A., & Friedman, M. J. (1982). The relative importance of treatment outcomes: A Delphi weighting in mental health. *Evaluation Review, 6,* 79-93.

Clark, N. (1952). *The Gantt chart.* London: Pitman & Sons.

Clotfelder, C. T. (Ed.). (1992). *Who benefits from the nonprofit sector?* Chicago: University of Chicago Press.

Clyne, S. F. (1982). *The judicial evaluation model: A case study.* Unpublished doctoral dissertation, Boston College, Boston.

Cohen, S. (1978). Science and the tabloid press. *APA Monitor, 9*(3), 1.

Cohen, S., & Eimicke, W. (1994). Project-focused Total Quality Management in the New York City Department of Parks and Recreation. *Public Administration Review, 54,* 450-456.

Comptroller General of the United States (1988). *Government auditing standards.* Washington, DC: U.S. General Accounting Office.

Conner, R. F., Altman, D. G., & Jackson C. (Eds.). (1984). *Evaluation studies review annual* (Vol. 9). Beverly Hills, CA: Sage.

Conoley, J. C., & Impara, J. C. (1995). *The twelfth mental measurements yearbook.* Lincoln, NE: University of Nebraska Press.

Conrad, K. J. (Ed.). (1994). *Critically evaluating the role of experiments.* New Directions for Program Evaluation, No. 63. San Francisco: Jossey-Bass.

Cook, D. L. (1966). *Program evaluation and review technique: Applications in education* (Monograph No. 17). Washington, DC: U.S. Office of Education Cooperative Research.

Cook, T. D. (1985). Postpositivist critical multiplism. In R. L. Shotland & M. M. Mark (Eds.), *Social science and social policy.* Beverly Hills, CA: Sage.

Cook, T. D., & Campbell, D. T. (1979). *Quasi-experimentation: Design and analysis issues for field settings.* Chicago: Rand McNally.

Cook, T. D., & Reichardt, C. S. (Eds.). (1979). *Qualitative and quantitative methods in evaluation research.* Beverly Hills, CA: Sage.

Corcoran, K., & Fisher, J. (1987). *Measures for clinical practice: A sourcebook.* New York: Free Press.

Cordray, D. S., & Lipsey, M. W. (1987). Evaluation studies for 1986: Program evaluation and program research. In D. S. Cordray & M. W. Lipsey (Eds.), *Evaluation studies review annual* (Vol. 5, pp. 17–44). Beverly Hills, CA: Sage.

Cottingham, P. H. (1991). Unexpected lessons: Evaluation of job-training programs for single mothers. In R. S. Turpin & J. M. Sinacore (Eds.), *Multisite evaluations.* New Directions for Program Evaluation, No. 50, 59–70. San Francisco: Jossey-Bass.

Coulton, C. J. (1987). Quality assurance. In S. M. Rosen, D. Fanshel, & M. E. Lutz (Eds.), *Encyclopedia of social work.* Silver Spring, MD: National Association of Social Workers.

Council on Foundations. (1993). *Evaluation for foundations: Concepts, cases, guidelines, and resources.* San Francisco: Jossey-Bass.

Cousins, J. B., & Leithwood, K. A. (1985). *The state of the art of empirical research on evaluation utilization.* Toronto: Ontario Institute for Studies in Education.

Cousins, J. B., & Leithwood, K. A. (1986). Current empirical research on evaluation utilization. *Review of Educational Research, 56,* 331–364.

Covert, R. W. (1988). Ethics in evaluation: Beyond the standards. *Evaluation Practice, 9,* 32–37.

Covert, R. W. (1992, November). *Successful competencies in preparing professional evaluators.* Paper presented at the annual meeting of the American Evaluation Association, Seattle.

Covert, R. W. (1995). A twenty-year veteran's reflections on the guiding principles for evaluators. In W. R. Shadish, D. L. Newman, M. A. Scheirer, & C. Wye (Eds.), *Guiding principles for evaluators.* New Directions for Program Evaluation, No. 66, 35–45. San Francisco: Jossey-Bass.

Cronbach, L. J. (1963). Course improvement through evaluation. *Teachers College Record, 64,* 672–683.

Cronbach, L. J. (1982). *Designing evaluations of educational and social programs.* San Francisco: Jossey-Bass.

Cronbach, L. J., Ambron, S. R., Dornbusch, S. M., Hess, R. D., Hornik, R. C., Phillips, D. C., Walker, D. F., & Weiner, S. S. (1980). *Toward reform of program evaluation.* San Francisco: Jossey-Bass.

Datta, L. (1994). Paradigm wars: A basis for peaceful coexistence and beyond. In C. S. Reichardt & S. F. Rallis (Eds.), *The qualitative-quantitative debate: New perspectives.* New Directions for Program Evaluation, No. 61, 53-70. San Francisco: Jossey-Bass.

Datta, L. (1995). Multimedia evaluations: A landscape with case studies. Paper presented at the International Evaluation Conference, Vancouver, Canada.

Deming, W. E. (1975). The logic of evaluation. In E. Struening & M. Guttentag (Eds.), *Handbook of evaluation research* (Vol. 1). Beverly Hills, CA: Sage.

Deming, W. E. (1986). *Out of crisis.* Cambridge, MA: Massachusetts Institute of Technology, Center for Advanced Engineering Study.

Dennis, M. L., & Boruch, R. F. (1989). Randomized experiments for planning and testing projects in developing countries: Threshold conditions. *Evaluation Review, 13,* 292-309.

Dennis, M. L., Fetterman, D. M. & Sechrest, L. (1994). Integrating qualitative and quantitative evaluation methods in substance abuse research. *Evaluation and Program Planning, 17,* 419-427.

Denzin, N. K. (1978). *The research act.* Chicago: Aldine.

Denzin, N. K., & Lincoln, Y. S. (Eds.). (1994). *Handbook of qualitative research.* Thousand Oaks, CA: Sage.

Dickey, F. G., & Miller, J. W. (1972). *A current perspective on accreditation.* Washington, DC: American Association for Higher Education.

Dillman, D. A. (1978). *Mail and telephone surveys: The Total Design Method.* New York: Wiley.

Dillman, D. A., & Sangster, R. (1991). *Mail surveys: A comprehensive bibliography, 1974-1989.* Chicago: Council of Planning Librarians.

Dodson, S. C. (1994). *Interim summative evaluation: Assessing the value of a long term or ongoing program, during its operation.* Unpublished doctoral dissertation, Western Michigan University, Kalamazoo.

Donmoyer, R. (n.d.). *Evaluation as deliberation: Theoretical and empirical explorations* (Grant No. G 810083). Ohio State University, Columbus, National Institute of Education.

Douglas, J. D. (1976). *Investigative social research.* Beverly Hills, CA: Sage.

Duffy, B. P. (1994). Use and abuse of internal evaluation. In C. J. Stevens & M. Dial (Eds.), *Preventing the misuse of evaluation.* New Directions for Program Evaluation, No. 64, 25-32. San Francisco: Jossey-Bass.

Durlak, J. A., & Lipsey, M. W. (1991). A practitioner's guide to meta-analysis. *American Journal of Community Psychology, 19,* 291-332.

Eash, M. J. (1970, April). *Developing an instrument for the assessment of instructional materials.* Paper presented at the annual meeting of the American Educational Research Association, Minneapolis.

Eisner, E. W. (1975, April). *The perceptive eye: Toward the reformation of educational evaluation.* Invited address at the American Educational Research Association, Washington, DC.

Eisner, E. W. (1979a). *The educational imagination: On the design and evaluation of school programs.* New York: Macmillan.

Eisner, E. W. (1979b). The use of qualitative forms of evaluation for improving educational practice. *Educational Evaluation and Policy Analysis, 1,* 11-19.

Eisner, E. W. (1991). Taking a second look: Educational connoisseurship revisited. In M. W. McLaughlin & D. C. Phillips (Eds.), *Evaluation and education: At quarter century.* Ninetieth Yearbook of the National Society for the Study of Education, Part II. Chicago: University of Chicago Press.

Erickson, F. (1977). Some approaches to inquiry in school community ethnography. *Anthropology and Education Quarterly, 8,* 58-69.

Estes, G. D., & Demaline, R. E. (1982). Outcomes of the MCT clarification process. In E. R. House, S. Mathison, J. A. Pearsol, & H. Preskill (Eds.), *Evaluation studies review annual* (Vol. 7). Beverly Hills, CA: Sage.

Evaluation Research Society Standards Committee. (1982). Evaluation Research Society standards for program evaluation. In P. H. Rossi (Ed.), *Standards for evaluation practice*. New Directions for Program Evaluation, No. 15, 7-19. San Francisco: Jossey-Bass.

Farland, D. S., & Gullickson, A. R. (1995). *Handbook for developing a teacher performance evaluation manual: A metamanual*. Kalamazoo, MI: Center for Research on Educational Accountability and Teacher Evaluation.

Fellers, G. (1992). *The Deming vision*. Milwaukee, WI: ASQC Quality Press.

Fetterman, D. M. (1984). *Ethnography in educational evaluation*. Beverly Hills, CA: Sage.

Fetterman, D. M. (1992). In response to Lee Sechrest's 1991 AEA presidential address: Roots: Back to our first generation. *Evaluation Practice, 13,* 171-172.

Fetterman, D. M. (1994). Empowerment evaluation. *Evaluation Practice, 15,* 1-15.

Finnan, C., & Davis, S. C. (1995, April). *Linking project evaluation and goals-based teaching evaluation: Evaluating the accelerated schools*. Paper presented at the annual meeting of the American Educational Research Association, San Francisco.

Fitz-Gibbon, C. T., & Morris L. L. (1975). Theory-based evaluation. *Evaluation Comment, 5*(1), 1-4.

Fitzpatrick, J. L. (1988). *Alcohol education programs for drunk drivers*. Colorado Springs: Center for Community Development and Design.

Fitzpatrick, J. L. (1989). The politics of evaluation with privatized programs: Who is the audience? *Evaluation Review, 13,* 563-578.

Fitzpatrick, J. L. (1992). Problems in the evaluation of treatment programs for drunk drivers: Goals and outcomes. *Journal of Drug Issues, 22,* 155-167.

Fitzpatrick, J. L. (1994). Alternative models for the structuring of professional preparation programs. In J. W. Altschuld & M. Engle (Eds.), *The preparation of professional evaluators: Issues, pespectives, and programs*. New Directions for Program Evaluation, No. 62, 41-50.

Flanagan, J. C. (1954). The critical incident technique. *Psychological Bulletin, 51,* 327-358.

Flexner, A. (1910). *Medical education in the United States and Canada* (Bulletin No. 4). New York: Carnegie Foundation for the Advancement of Teaching.

Flexner, A. (1960). *Abraham Flexner: An autobiography*. New York: Simon & Schuster.

Floden, R. E. (1983). Flexner, accreditation, and evaluation. In G. F. Madaus, M. Scriven, & D. L. Stufflebeam (Eds.), *Evaluation models: Viewpoints on educational and human services evaluation*. Boston: Kluwer-Nijhoff.

Flores, J. G., & Alonso, C. G. (1995). Using focus groups in educational research. *Evaluation Review, 19,* 84-101.

Folz, D. H., & Hazlett, J. M. (1991). Public participation and recycling performance: Explaining program success. *Public Administration Review, 51,* 526-535.

Fontana, A., & Frey, J. H. (1994). Interviewing: The art of science. In N. K. Denzin & Y. S. Lincoln (Eds.), *Handbook of qualitative research*. Thousand Oaks, CA: Sage.

Fowler, F. J., Jr. (1984). *Survey research methods*. Beverly Hills, CA: Sage.

Frank, J. N. (1949). *Courts on trial*. Princeton, NJ: Princeton University Press.

Freeman, H. E., Klein, R. E., Townsend, J. W., & Lechtig, A. (1980). Nutrition and cognitive development among rural Guatemalan children. *American Journal of Public Health, 70,* 1277-1285.

Galagan, P. (1994). Reinventing the profession. *Training and Development, 48,* 20–27.

Galvin, J. G. (1983). What can trainers learn from educators about evaluating management training? *Training and Development Journal, 37,* 52, 54–57.

Gephart, W. J. (1978). *The facets of the evaluation process: A starter set.* Unpublished manuscript. Bloomington, IN: Phi Delta Kappan.

General Accounting Office (1992). *Quality management: A survey of federal organizations.* Washington, DC: U.S. General Accounting Office.

Giventer, L. L. (1996). *Statistical analysis for public administration.* Belmont, CA: Wadsworth.

Glass, G. V., McGraw, B., & Smith, M. L. (1981). *Meta-analysis in social research.* Newbury Park, CA: Sage.

Goodlad, J. (1979). *What schools are for.* Bloomington, IN: Phi Delta Kappa Educational Foundation.

Gore, A. (1993). *From red tape to results: Creating a government that works better and costs less: The report of the National Performance Review.* New York: Plume.

Gough, P. B. (1996). A sea change? *Phi Delta Kappan, 77,* 588.

Grasso, P. G. (in press). The Program Evaluation and Methodology Division of the U.S. General Accounting Office: An appreciation. *Evaluation Practice.*

Gray, S. T. (Ed.). (1993). *A vision of evaluation.* Washington, DC: Independent Sector.

Gray, S. T., & Stockdill, S. H. (1995). *Evaluation with power.* Washington, DC: Independent Sector.

Greenberg, D., Meyer, R. H., & Wiseman, M. (1994). Multisite employment and training program evaluations: A tale of three studies. *Industrial and Labor Relations Review, 47,* 679–691.

Greene, J. C., Caracelli, V. J., & Graham, W. F. (1989). Toward a conceptual framework for mixed-method evaluation designs. *Educational Evaluation and Policy Analysis, 11,* 255–274.

Greene, J. G. (1988). Stakeholder participation and utilization in program evaluation. *Evaluation Review, 12,* 91–116.

Greene, J. G., & McClintock, C. (1985). Triangulation in evaluation: Design and analysis issues. *Evaluation Review, 9,* 523–545.

Greiner, J. M. (1994). Use of ratings by trained observers. In J. S. Wholey, H. P. Hatry, & K. E. Newcomer (Eds.), *Handbook of pratical program evaluation.* San Francisco: Jossey-Bass.

Guastello, S. J., & Guastello, D. D. (1991). How organizations differ: Implications for multisite program evaluation. In R. S. Turpin & J. M. Sinacore (Eds.), *Multisite evaluations.* New Directions for Program Evaluation, No. 50, 71–81. San Francisco: Jossey-Bass.

Guba, E. G. (1965). *Evaluation in field studies.* Address at evaluation conference sponsored by the Ohio State Department of Education, Columbus.

Guba, E. G. (1969). The failure of educational evaluation. *Educational Technology, 9,* 29–38.

Guba, E. G. (1978). *Toward a methodology of naturalistic inquiry in educational evaluation* (Monograph Series No. 8). Los Angeles: University of California, Center for the Study of Evaluation.

Guba, E. G. (1981). Investigative reporting. In N. L. Smith (Ed.), *Metaphors for evaluation: Sources of new methods.* New Perspectives in Evaluation (Vol. 1). Beverly Hills, CA: Sage.

Guba, E. G., & Lincoln, Y. S. (1981). *Effective evaluation.* San Francisco: Jossey-Bass.

Guba, E. G., & Lincoln, Y. S. (1989). *Fourth generation evaluation.* Thousand Oaks, CA: Sage.

Guba, E., & Lincoln, Y. S. (1994). Competing paradigms in qualitative research. In N. K. Denzin & Y. S. Lincoln (Eds.), *Handbook of qualitative research.* Thousand Oaks, CA: Sage.

Hackman, R., & Wageman, R. (1995). Total Quality Management: Empirical, conceptual, and practical issues. *Administrative Science Quarterly, 40,* 309-342.

Halachimi, A. (1995). The practice of performance appraisal. In J. Rabin, T. Vocino, W. B. Hildreth, & G. J. Miller (Eds.), *Handbook of public personnel administration.* New York: Marcel Dekker.

Haladyna, T. M., Nolen, S. B., & Haas, N. S. (1991). Raising standardized achievement test scores and the origins of test score pollution. *Educational Researcher, 20*(5), 2-7.

Halpern, E. S. (1983, April). *Auditing naturalistic inquiries: Some preliminary applications. Part I. Development of the process. Part 2. Case study application.* Paper presented at the annual meeting of the American Educational Research Association, Montreal.

Hamilton, D. (1977). Making sense of curriculum evaluation: Continuities and discontinuities in an educational idea. In L. Shulman (Ed.), *Review of research in education* (Vol. 5). Itasca, IL: Peacock.

Hamilton, D., Jenkins, D., King, C., MacDonald, B., & Parlett, M. (Eds.). (1977). *Beyond the numbers game: A reader in educational evaluation.* Berkeley, CA: McCutchan.

Hammond, R. L. (1973). Evaluation at the local level. In B. R. Worthen & J. R. Sanders, *Educational evaluation: Theory and practice.* Belmont, CA: Wadsworth.

Harmon, M. (1995). The changing role of assessment in evaluating science education reform. In R. G. O'Sullivan (Ed.), *Emerging roles of evaluation in science education reform.* New Directions for Program Evaluation, No. 65, 31-51. San Francisco: Jossey-Bass.

Hebert, Y. M. (1986). Naturalistic evaluation in practice: A case study. In D. D. Williams (Ed.), *Naturalistic evaluation.* New Directions for Program Evaluation, No. 30, 3-21. San Francisco: Jossey-Bass.

Hedrick, S. C., Sullivan, J. H., Ehreth, J. L., Rothman, M. L., Connis, R. T., & Erdly, W. W. (1991). Centralized versus decentralized coordination in the adult day health care evaluation study. In R. S. Turpin & J. M. Sinacore (Eds.), *Multisite evaluations.* New Directions for Program Evaluation, No. 50, 19-31. San Francisco: Jossey-Bass.

Hedrick, T. E. (1994). The quantitative-qualitative debate: Possibilities for integration. In C. S. Reichardt & S. F. Rallis (Eds.), *The qualitative-quantitative debate: New perspectives.* New Directions for Program Evaluation, No. 61, 45-52. San Francisco: Jossey-Bass.

Hendricks, M., & Conner, R. F. (1995). International perspectives on the Guiding Principles. In W. R. Shadish, D. L. Newman, M. A. Scheirer, & C. Wye (Eds.), Guiding principles for evaluators. *New Directions for Program Evaluation,* No. 66, 77-90. San Francisco: Jossey-Bass.

Henry, G. (1990). *Practical sampling.* Newbury Park, CA: Sage.

Herman, J. L., Aschbacher, P. R., & Winters, L. (1992). *A practical guide to alternative assessments.* Alexandria, VA: Association for Supervision and Curriculum Development.

Herndon, E. B. (1980). *NIE's study of minimum competency testing: A process for the definition of issues.* Washington, DC: National Institute of Education.

Hiscox, M. D., & Owens, T. R. (1975, May). *Attempts at implementing an educational adversary model.* Paper presented at the third annual Pacific Northwest Educational Research and Evaluation Conference, Seattle.

Hodgkinson, H., Hurst, J., & Levine, H. (1975). *Improving and assessing performance: Evaluation in higher education.* Berkeley, CA: University of California Center for Research and Development in Higher Education.

Holsti, O. (1969). *Content analysis for the social sciences and humanities.* Reading, MA: Addison-Wesley.

Honea, G. E. (1992). *Ethics and public sector evaluators: Nine case studies.* Unpublished doctoral dissertation, University of Virginia, Department of Educational Studies.

Hoppe, M. J., Wells, E. A., Morrison, D. M., Gillmore, M. R., & Wildson, A. (1995). Using focus groups to discuss sensitive topics with children. *Evaluation Review, 19,* 102–114.

Horst, P., Nay, J. N., Scanlon, J. W., & Wholey, J. S. (1974). Program management and the federal evaluator. *Public Administration Review, 34,* 300–308.

House, E. R. (1976). Justice in evaluation. In G. V. Glass (Ed.), *Evaluation studies review annual* (Vol. 1). Beverly Hills, CA: Sage.

House, E. R. (1980). *Evaluating with validity.* Beverly Hills, CA: Sage.

House, E. R. (1983a). Assumptions underlying evaluation models. In G. F. Madaus, M. Scriven, & D. L. Stufflebeam (Eds.), *Evaluation models: Viewpoints on educational and human services evaluation.* Boston: Kluwer-Nijhoff.

House, E. R. (Ed.). (1983b). *Philosophy of evaluation.* New Directions for Program Evaluation, No. 19. San Francisco: Jossey-Bass.

House, E. R. (1988). *Jesse Jackson and the politics of charisma: The rise and fall of the PUSH/Excel program.* Boulder, CO: Westview Press.

House, E. R. (1990). Methodology and justice. In K. A. Sirotnik (Ed.), *Evaluation and social justice: Issues in public education.* New Directions for Program Evaluation, No. 45, 23–36. San Francisco: Jossey-Bass.

House, E. R. (1993). *Professional evaluation.* Newbury Park, CA: Sage.

House, E. R. (1994a). The future perfect of evaluation. *Evaluation Practice, 15,* 239–247.

House, E. R. (1994b). Integrating the quantitative and qualitative. In C. S. Reichardt & S. F. Rallis (Eds.), *The qualitative-quantitative debate: New perspectives.* New Directions for Program Evaluation, No. 61, 13–22. San Francisco: Jossey-Bass.

House, E. R. (1995). Principled evaluation: A critique of the AEA Guiding Principles. In W. R. Shadish, D. L. Newman, M. A. Scheirer, & C. Wye (Eds.), *Guiding principles for evaluators.* New Directions for Program Evaluation, No. 66, 27–34. San Francisco: Jossey-Bass.

House, E. R., Thurston, P., & Hand, J. (1984). The adversary hearing as a public forum. *Studies in Educational Evaluation, 10,* 111–123.

Howe, K. R. (1988). Against the quantitative-qualitative incompatibility thesis, or dogmas die hard. *Educational Researcher, 17,* 10–16.

Huberman, A. M., & Miles, M. B. (1994). Data management and analysis methods. In N. K. Denzin & Y. S. Lincoln (Eds.), *Handbook of qualitative research.* Thousand Oaks, CA: Sage.

Hudson, W. W. (1982). *The clinical measurement package: A field manual.* Homewood, IL: Dorsey Press.

Huxley, E. (1982). *The flame trees of Thika: Memories of an African childhood.* London: Chatto & Windus.

Independent Sector. (1995). *Evaluation with power.* Washington, DC: Author.

Jaeger, R. M. (1983). *Statistics: A spectator sport.* Beverly Hills, CA: Sage.

Jaeger, R. M. (1989). Certification of student competence. In R. L. Linn (Ed.), *Educational Measurement* (3rd ed., pp. 485–514). London: Collier Macmillan.

Johnston, P., & Swift, P. (1994). Effects of randomization on a homeless services initiative: A comment. In K. J. Conrad (Ed.), *Critically evaluating the role of experiments.* New Directions for Program Evaluation, No. 3. San Francisco: Jossey-Bass.

Joint Committee on Standards for Educational Evaluation. (1981). *Standards for evaluations of educational programs, projects, and materials.* New York: McGraw-Hill.

Joint Committee on Standards for Educational Evaluation. (1988). *Personnel evaluation standards.* Newbury Park, CA: Corwin Press.

Joint Committee on Standards for Educational Evaluation. (1994). *The Program Evaluation Standards* (2nd ed.). Thousand Oaks, CA: Sage.

Jorgensen, D. L. (1989). *Participant observation: A methodology for human studies.* Newbury Park, CA: Sage.

Justiz, M. J., & Moorman, H. N. (1985). New NIE peer review procedures. *Educational Researcher, 14*(1), 5-11.

Kaplan, A. (1964). *The conduct of inquiry.* San Francisco: Chandler.

W. K. Kellogg Foundation (WKKF). (1991). *Information on cluster evaluation.* Battle Creek, MI: Author.

W. K. Kellogg Foundation (WKKF). (1994). *Improving cluster evaluation: Some areas for consideration.* Battle Creek, MI: Author.

Kelly, E. F. (1978). Curriculum criticism and literary criticism: Comments on the anthology. In G. Willis (Ed.), *Qualitative evaluation.* Berkeley, CA: McCutchan.

Kennedy, M., Apling, R., & Neumann, W. (1980). *The role of evaluation and test information in public schools.* Cambridge, MA: Huron Institute.

Kidder, L. H., & Fine, M. (1987). Qualitative and quantitative methods: When stories converge. In M. M. Mark & R. L. Shotland (Eds.), *Multiple methods in program evaluation.* New Directions for Program Evaluation, No. 35, 57-75. San Francisco: Jossey-Bass.

King, J. A. (1988). Research on evaluation use and its implications for evaluation research and practice. *Studies in Educational Evaluation, 14,* 285-299.

King, J. A., Thompson, B., & Pechman, E. M. (1981). *Evaluating utilization: A bibliography.* New Orleans: New Orleans Public Schools.

King, J. A., Thompson, B., & Pechman, E. M. (1982). *Improving evaluation use in local schools* (Final Report for NIE-G-80-0082). New Orleans: New Orleans Public Schools.

Kiresuk, T. J., Smith, A., & Cardillo, J. E. (Eds.). (1994). *Goal attainment scaling: Applications, theory, and measurement.* Hillsdale, NJ: Lawrence Erlbaum.

Kirkpatrick, D. L. (1977). Evaluating training programs: Evidence vs. proof. *Training and Development Journal, 31,* 9-12.

Kirkpatrick, D. L. (1983). Four steps to measuring training effectiveness. *Personnel Administrator, 28,* 19-25.

Kirkwood, R. (1982). Accreditation. In H. E. Mitzel (Ed.), *Encyclopedia of educational research* (Vol. 1, 5th ed.), pp. 9-12. New York: Free Press.

Kitchener, K. S. (1984). Intuition, critical thinking, and ethical principles: The foundation of ethical decisions in counseling psychology. *The Counseling Psychologist, 12,* 43-55.

Kourilsky, M. (1973). An adversary model for educational evaluation. *Evaluation Comment, 4,* 3-6.

Kourilsky, M., & Baker, E. (1976). An experimental comparison of interaction, advocacy, and adversary evaluation. *Center on Evaluation, Development, and Research (CEDR) Quarterly, 9,* 4-8.

Krathwohl, D. R., Bloom, B. S., & Masia, B. B. (1964). *Taxonomy of educational objectives: Handbook II. Affective domain.* New York: David McKay.

Krejcie, R. V., & Morgan, D. W. (1970). Determining sample size for research activities. *Educational and Psychological Measurement, 30,* 607-610.

Krueger, R. A. (1994). *Focus groups* (2nd ed.). Thousand Oaks, CA: Sage.

Lavrakas, P. J. (1987). *Telephone survey methods: Sampling, selection, and supervision.* Newbury Park, CA: Sage.

Lawler, E. E., III, Mohrman, S. A., & Ledford, G. E., Jr. (1992). *Employee involvement and Total Quality Management: Practices and results in Fortune 1000 companies.* San Francisco: Jossey-Bass.

Layard, R., & Glaister, S. (Eds.). (1994). *Cost-benefit analysis.* New York: Cambridge University Press.

LDP Associates, Inc. (1986). *What companies do to evaluate the effectiveness of training programs.* Gardner, MA: Author.

Lee, A. M., & Holly, F. R. (1978, April). *Communicating evaluation information: Some practical tips that work.* Paper presented at the annual meeting of the American Educational Research Association, Toronto.

Lessinger, L. M., & Tyler, R. W. (Eds.). (1971). *Accountability in education.* Worthington, OH: Charles A. Jones.

Levin, H. M. (1981). Cost analysis. In N. L. Smith (Ed.), *New techniques for evaluation.* New Perspectives in Evaluation (Vol. 2). Beverly Hills, CA: Sage.

Levin, H. M. (1983). *Cost-effectiveness: A primer.* Beverly Hills, CA: Sage.

Levin, H. M., Glass, G. V., & Meister, G. R. (1987). Cost-effectiveness of computer-assisted instruction. *Evaluation Review, 11,* 50-72.

Levine, M. (1974). Scientific method and the adversary model. Some preliminary thoughts. *American Psychologist, 29,* 661-677.

Levine, M. (1982). Adversary hearings. In N. L. Smith (Ed.), *Communication strategies in evaluation.* Beverly Hills, CA: Sage.

Levine, M., Brown, E., Fitzgerald, C., Goplerud, E., Gordon, M. E., Jayne-Lararus, C., Rosenberg, N., & Slater, J. (1978). Adapting the jury trial for program evaluation: A report of an experience. *Evaluation and Program Planning, 1,* 177-186.

Levine, M., & Rosenberg, N. (1979). An adversary model of fact finding and decision making for program evaluation: Theoretical considerations. In H. C. Schulberg & F. Baker (Eds.), *Program evaluation in the health field* (Vol. 2). New York: Behavioral Publications.

Levitan, S. A. (1992). *Evaluation of federal social programs: An uncertain impact.* Washington, DC: George Washington University Center for Social Policy Studies.

Leviton, L. C., & Hughes, E. F. X. (1981). Research on the utilization of evaluations: A review and synthesis. *Evaluation Review, 5,* 524-548.

Light, R. J. (Ed.). (1983). *Evaluation studies review annual* (Vol. 8). Beverly Hills, CA: Sage.

Light, R. J., & Smith, P. V. (1970). Choosing a future: Strategies for designing and evaluating new programs. *Harvard Educational Review, 40,* 1-28.

Lincoln, Y. S. (1991). The arts and sciences of program evaluation. *Evaluation Practice, 12,* 1-8.

Lincoln, Y. S., & Guba, E. (1981, October). *Do evaluators wear grass skirts? "Going native" and ethnocentrism as problems in utilization.* Paper presented at the annual meeting of the Evaluation Research Society, Austin, TX.

Lincoln, Y. S., & Guba, E. G. (1985). *Naturalistic inquiry.* Beverly Hills, CA: Sage.

Lincoln, Y. S., & Guba, E. G. (1992). In response to Lee Sechrest's 1991 AEA presidential address: Roots: Back to our first generation. *Evaluation Practice, 13,* 165-170.

Lincoln, Y. S. & Guba, E. G. (1994). RSVP: We are pleased to accept your invitation. *Evaluation Practice, 13,* 179-192.

Lipsey, M. W. (1990). *Design sensitivity: Statistical power for experimental research.* Newbury Park, CA: Sage.

Louis, K. S. (1982). Multisite/multimethod studies: An introduction. *American Behavorial Scientist, 26,* 6–22.

Love, A. J. (1991). *Internal evaluation: Building organizations from within.* Newbury Park, CA: Sage.

Love, A. J. (1994). Should evaluators be certified? In J. W. Altschuld & M. Engle (Eds.), *The preparation of professional evaluators: Issues, perspectives, and programs.* New Directions for Program Evaluation, No. 62, 29–40. San Francisco: Jossey-Bass.

Lovich, N. P. (1990). Performance appraisal. In S. W. Hays & R. C. Kearney (Eds.), *Public personnel administration: Problems and prospects.* Englewood Cliffs, NJ: Prentice-Hall.

MacDonald, J. B. (1974). An evaluation of evaluation. *Urban Review, 7,* 3–14.

MacDonald, J. B. (1976). Evaluation and the control of education. In D. Tawney (Ed.), *Curriculum evaluation today: Trends and implications.* Schools Council Research Studies series, London: Macmillan.

Madaus, G. F. (1981). NIE clarification hearing: The negative team's case. *Phi Delta Kappan, 63,* 92–94.

Madaus, G. F. (1982). The clarification hearing: A personal view of the process. *Educational Researcher, 11*(1), 4, 6–11.

Madaus, G. F. (1983). *The courts, validity, and minimum competency testing.* Boston: Kluwer-Nijhoff.

Madaus, G. F., Scriven, M., & Stufflebeam, D. L. (Eds.). (1983). *Evaluation models: Viewpoints on educational and human services evaluation.* Boston: Kluwer-Nijhoff.

Madaus, G. F., & Stufflebeam, D. L. (Eds.). (1989). *Educational evaluation: Classic works of Ralph W. Tyler.* Boston: Kluwer Academic.

Madey, D. L. (1982). Some benefits of integrating qualitative and quantitative methods in program evaluation, with illustrations. *Educational Evaluation and Policy Analysis, 4,* 223–236.

Mager, R. F. (1962). *Preparing instructional objectives.* Palo Alto, CA: Fearon Press.

Malcolm, C., & Welch, W. (1981). *Case study evaluations: A case in point. An illustrative report and methodological analysis of case study evaluations.* Minneapolis: University of Minnesota, Minnesota Research and Evaluation Center.

Manning, P. K., & Cullum-Swan, B. (1994). Narrative, content, and semiotic analysis. In N. K. Denzin & Y. S. Lincoln (Eds.), *Handbook of qualitative research.* Thousand Oaks, CA: Sage.

Mark, M. M., & Shotland, R. L. (1987). Alternative models for the use of multiple methods. In M. M. Mark & R. L. Shotland (Eds.), *Multiple methods in program evaluation.* New Directions for Program Evaluation, No. 35, 95–99. San Francisco: Jossey-Bass.

Marsden, L. R. (1991, May). *Program evaluations and politicians.* Paper presented at the annual meeting of the Canadian Evaluation Society, Vancouver.

Matthews, J. (1993, June 6). "Totaled Quality Management." *Washington Post,* pp. H1, H16.

Maxwell, G. S. (1984). A rating scale for assessing the quality of responsive/illuminative evaluations. *Educational Evaluation and Policy Analysis, 6,* 131–138.

Maxwell, J. A., Bashook, G., & Sandlow, C. J. (1986). Combining ethnographic and experimental methods in educational evaluation. In D. M. Fetterman & M. A. Pitman (Eds.), *Educational evaluation: Ethnography in theory, practice, and politics.* Beverly Hills, CA: Sage.

May, R. M., Fleischer, M., Scheirer, C. J., & Cox, G. B. (1986). Director of evaluation training programs. In B. G. Davis (Ed.), *Teaching of evaluation across the disciplines.* New Directions for Program Evaluation, No. 29, 71–98. San Francisco: Jossey-Bass.

Mayeske, G. W. (1995). Letter to the editor. *Evaluation Practice, 16,* 211–212.

McBride, M. E., Bertrand, J. T., Santiso, R., & Fernandez, V. H. (1987). Cost-effectiveness of the APTOGSM program for voluntary surgical contraception in Guatemala. *Evaluation Review, 11,* 300–326.

McClintock, C. (1987). Conceptual and action heuristics: Tools for the evaluator. In L. Bickman (Ed.), *Using program theory in evaluation,* New Directions for Program Evaluation, No. 33, 43–57. San Francisco: Jossey-Bass.

McCutcheon, G. (1978). Of solar systems, responsibility, and basics: An educational criticism of Mr. Clement's fourth grade. In G. Willis (Ed.), *Qualitative evaluation.* Berkeley, CA: McCutchan.

McDowell, I., & Newell, C. (1987). *Measuring health: A guide to rating scales and questionnaires.* New York: Oxford University Press.

McKillip, J. (1987). *Need analysis: Tools for the human services and education.* Newbury Park, CA: Sage.

Merriam-Webster's Collegiate Dictionary (7th ed.). (1967). Springfield, MA: Merriam-Webster.

Mertens, D. M. (1994). Training evaluators: Unique skills and knowledge. In J. W. Altschuld & M. Engle (Eds.), *The preparation of professional evaluators: Issues, perspectives, and programs.* New Directions for Program Evaluation, No. 62, 17–27. San Francisco: Jossey-Bass.

Mertens, D. M. (1995). Identifying and respecting differences among participants in evaluation studies. In W. R. Shadish, D. L. Newman, M. A. Scheirer, & C. Wye (Eds.), *Guiding Principles for evaluators,* New Directions for Program Evaluation, No. 66, 91–97. San Francisco: Jossey-Bass.

Metfessel, N. S., & Michael, W. B. (1967). A paradigm involving multiple criterion measures for the evaluation of the effectiveness of school programs. *Educational and Psychological Measurement, 27,* 931–943.

Middleton, R. P. (1995). Personal correspondence, October 14.

Milakovich, M. E. (1991). Total Quality Management in the public sector. *National Productivity Review, 10,* 195–213.

Miles, M. B., & Huberman, A. M. (1984). *Qualitative data analysis: A sourcebook of new methods.* Newbury Park, CA: Sage.

Miles, M. B., & Huberman, A. M. (1994). *Qualitative data analysis.* Thousand Oaks, CA: Sage.

Mills, A. S., Massey, J. G., & Gregersen, H. M. (1980). Benefit-cost analysis of Voyageurs National Park. *Evaluation Review, 4,* 715–738.

Milward, H. B. (1994). Nonprofit contracting and the hollow state. *Public Administration Review, 54,* 73–77.

Milward, H. B., Provan, K. G., & Smith, L. J. (1994). Human service contracting and coordination: The market for mental health services. In J. L. Perry (Ed.), *Research in public administration* (Vol. 3). Greenwich, CT: JAI Press.

Mintzberg, H. (1994). *The rise and fall of strategic planning.* New York: Free Press.

Misanchuk, E. (1978). Descriptors of evaluation in instructional development: Beyond the formative-summative distinction. *Journal of Instructional Development, 2,* 267–290.

Mitchell, R. (1992). *Testing for learning.* New York: Free Press.

Morell, J. A. (1990). Evaluation: Status of a loose coalition. *Evaluation Practice, 11,* 213–219.

Morris, L. L., & Fitzgibbon, C. T. (1978). *How to deal with goals and objectives.* Beverly Hills, CA: Sage.

Morris, M., & Cohn, R. (1993). Program evaluators and ethical challenges: A national survey. *Evaluation Review, 17,* 621–642.

Morrisett, I., & Stevens, W. W. (1967). *Steps in curriculum analysis outline.* Boulder: University of Colorado, Social Science Education Consortium.

Mowbray, C. T., & Herman, S. E. (1991). Using multiple sites in mental health evaluations: Focus on program theory and implementation issues. In R. S. Turpin & J. M. Sinacore (Eds.), *Multisite evaluations.* New Directions for Program Evaluation, No. 50, 45–57. San Francisco: Jossey-Bass.

Nafziger, D. H., Worthen, B. R., & Benson, J. (1977). *3 on 2 evaluation report: Vol. I. Technical report.* Portland, OR: Northwest Regional Educational Laboratory.

National Commission on Excellence in Education. (1983). *A nation at risk: The imperative for educational reform.* Washington, DC: U.S. Government Printing Office.

National Institute of Education. (1981). *Minimum competency testing clarification hearing, transcript* (Vols. 1–3). Washington, DC: Author.

Nay, J., & Kay, P. (1982). *Government oversight and evaluability assessment.* Lexington, MA: Heath.

Nelson, D. E. (1982). Investigative journalism methods in educational evaluation. In N. L. Smith (Ed.), *Field assessments of innovative evaluation methods.* New Directions for Program Evaluation, No. 13, 53–73. San Francisco: Jossey-Bass.

Neurath, O., Cernap, R., & Morris, C. (Eds.). (1955). *Fundamentals of the unity of science: Toward an encyclopedia of unified science.* Foundations of the Unity of Science series (Vols. 1–2). Chicago: University of Chicago Press.

Newman, D. L. (1988, April). *Teacher's willingness to participate in evaluation: The effect of past participation and perceptions of usefulness.* Paper presented at the annual meeting of the American Educational Research Association, New Orleans.

Newman, D. L. (1995). The future of ethics in evaluation: Developing the dialogue. In W. R. Shadish, D. L. Newman, M. A. Scheirer, & C. Wye (Eds.), *Guiding principles for evaluators.* New Directions for Program Evaluation. No. 66, 99–111. San Francisco: Jossey-Bass.

Newman, D. L., & Brown, R. D. (1996). *Applied ethics for program evauation.* Beverly Hills, CA: Sage.

Nigro, L. G., & Nigro, F. A. (1994). *The new public personnel administration.* Itasca, IL: Peacock.

Nilsson, N., & Hogben, D. (1983). Metaevaluation. In E. R. House (Ed.), *Philosophy of evaluation.* New Directions for Program Evaluation, No. 19, 83–97. San Francisco: Jossey-Bass.

Nowakowski, J., Bunda, M. A., Working, R., Bernacki, G., & Harrington, P. (1985). *A handbook of educational variables.* Boston: Kluwer-Nijhoff.

Office of the Comptroller General (1989). *Working standards for the evaluation of programs in federal department and agencies.* Ottawa, Canada: Supply & Services Canada.

O'Neill, M. (1989). *The third America: The emergence of the nonprofit sector in the United States.* San Francisco: Jossey-Bass.

Osborne, D., & Gaebler, T. (1992). *Reinventing government: How the entrepreneurial spirit is transforming the public sector.* Reading, MA: Addison-Wesley.

O'Sullivan, E., & Rassel, G. R. (1995). *Research methods for public administrators* (2nd ed.). White Plains, NY: Longman.

O'Sullivan, R. G., & O'Sullivan, J. M. (1994, May). *Evaluation voices: Promoting cluster evaluation from within programs.* Paper presented at the annual meeting of the Canadian Evaluation Society, Montreal.

Owens, T. R. (1971, February). *Application of adversary proceeding for educational evaluation and decision making.* Paper presented at the annual meeting of the American Educational Research Association, New York.

Owens, T. R. (1973). Educational evaluation by adversary proceeding. In E. R. House (Ed.), *School evaluation: The politics and process.* Berkeley, CA: McCutchan.

Palumbo, D. J. (1987). *The politics of program evaluation.* Newbury Park, CA: Sage.

Parlett, M., & Dearden, G. (Eds.). (1977). *Introduction to illumination evaluation: Studies in higher education.* Cardiff-by-the-Sea, CA: Pacific Soundings Press.

Parlett, M., & Hamilton, D. (1976). Evaluation as illumination: A new approach to the study of innovatory programs. In G. V. Glass (Ed.), *Evaluation studies review annual* (Vol. 1). Beverly Hills, CA: Sage.

Passamani, E. (1991). Clinical trials: Are they ethical? *New England Journal of Medicine, 324,* 1589-1592.

Patterson, M. (n.d.). *Instructional materials review form.* Tallahassee: Florida State University, Center for Instructional Development and Services.

Patton, M. Q. (1975). *Alternative evaluation research paradigm.* Grand Forks: North Dakota Study Group on Evaluation.

Patton, M. Q. (1986). *Utilization-focused evaluation* (2nd ed.). Beverly Hills, CA: Sage.

Patton, M. Q. (1987a). The evaluator's responsibility for utilization. *Evaluation Practice, 9,* 5-24.

Patton, M. Q. (1987b). *How to use qualitative methods in evaluation.* Newbury Park, CA: Sage.

Patton, M. Q. (1988). Politics and evaluation. *Evaluation Practice, 9,* 89-94.

Patton, M. Q. (1990a). The challenge of being a profession. *Evaluation Practice, 11,* 45-51.

Patton, M. Q. (1990b). *Qualitative evaluation and research methods* (2nd ed.). Newbury Park, CA: Sage.

Patton, M. Q. (1991). Towards utility in reviews of multivocal literatures. *Review of Educational Research, 61*(3), 287-292.

Patton, M. Q. (1994). Development evaluation. *Evaluation Practice, 15,* 311-320.

Paulson, S. F. (1964, November). The effects of the prestige of the speaker and acknowledgment of opposing arguments on audience retention and shift of opinion. *Speech Monographs,* pp. 267-271.

Perloff, R. E., & Perloff, E. (Eds.). (1980). *Values, ethics, and standards in evaluation.* New Directions for Program Evaluation, No. 7. San Francisco: Jossey-Bass.

Perloff, R. M., Padgett, V. R., & Brock, T. C. (1980). Socio congnitive biases in the evaluation process. In R. E. Porloff & E. Porloff (Eds.), *Values, ethics, and standards in evaluation.* New Directions for Program Evaluation, No. 7, 11-26. San Francisco: Jossey-Bass.

Perrone, V. (1991). *Expanding student assessment.* Alexandria, VA: Association for Supervision and Curriculm Development.

Peshkin, A. (1993). The goodness of qualitative research. *Educational Researcher, 22,* 23-29.

Popham, W. J. (1975). *Educational evaluation.* Englewood Cliffs, NJ: Prentice-Hall.

Popham, W. J. (1981). The case for minimum competency testing. *Phi Delta Kappan, 63,* 89-91.

Popham, W. J., & Carlson, D. (1977). Deep dark deficits of the adversary evaluation model. *Educational Researcher, 6*(6), 3-6.

Popham, W. J., Eisner, E. W., Sullivan, H. J., & Tyler, L. L. (1969). *Instructional objectives* (American Educational Research Association Monograph Series on Curriculum Evaluation No. 3). Chicago: Rand McNally.

Posavac, E. J. (1994). Misusing program evaluation by asking the wrong question. In C. J. Stevens & M. Dial (Eds.), *Preventing the misuse of evaluation.* New Directions for Program Evaluation, No. 64, 69–78. San Francisco: Jossey-Bass.

Posavac, E. J., & Carey, R. (1991). *Program evaluation: Methods and case studies.* Englewood Cliffs, NJ: Prentice-Hall.

Provus, M. M. (1971). *Discrepancy evaluation.* Berkeley, CA: McCutchan.

Provus, M. M. (1973). Evaluation of ongoing programs in the public school system. In B. R. Worthen & J. R. Sanders, *Educational evaluation: Theory and practice.* Belmont, CA: Wadsworth.

Rago, W. V. (1994). Adapting Total Quality Management (TQM) to government: Another point of view. *Public Administration Review, 54,* 61–64.

Raizen, S. A., & Rossi, P. H. (1981). *Program evaluation in education: When? How? To what ends?* Washington, DC: National Academy Press.

Reichardt, C. S. (1994). Summative evaluation, formative evaluation, and tactical research. *Evaluation Practice, 15,* 275–281.

Reichardt, C. S., & Cook, T. D. (1979). Beyond qualitative versus quantitative methods. In T. D. Cook & C. S. Reichardt (Eds.), *Qualitative and quantitative methods in evaluation research.* Beverly Hills, CA: Sage.

Reichardt, C. S., & Rallis, S. F. (1994). Qualitative and quantitative inquiries are not incompatible: A call for a new partnership. In C. S. Reichardt & S. F. Rallis (Eds.), *The qualitative-quantitative debate: New perspectives.* New Directions for Program Evaluation, No. 61, 85–91. San Francisco: Jossey-Bass.

Reichardt, C. S., Trochim, W. K., & Cappelleri, J. C. (1995). Reports of the death of regression-discontinuity analysis are greatly exaggerated. *Evaluation Review, 19,* 39–63.

Reineke, R. A. (1991). Stakeholder involvement in evaluation: Suggestions for practice. *Evaluation Practice, 12,* 39–44.

Reinhard, D. (1972). *Methodology for input evaluation utilizing advocate and design teams.* Unpublished doctoral dissertation, Ohio State University, Columbus.

Rice, J. M. (1915). *The people's government: Efficient, bossless, graftless.* Philadelphia: John C. Winston.

Richards, R. V. (Ed.). (1995). *Building partnerships: Educating health professionals for the communities they serve.* San Francisco: Jossey-Bass.

Richards, T. J., & Richards, L. (1994). Using computers in qualitative research. In N. K. Denzin & Y. S. Lincoln (Eds.), *Handbook of qualitative research.* Thousand Oaks, CA: Sage.

Ridings, J. M., & Stufflebeam, D. L. (1981). Evaluation reflections: The project to develop standards for educational evaluation: Its past and future. *Studies in Educational Evaluation, 7,* 3–16.

Ripley, W. K. (1985). Medium of presentation: Does it make a difference in the reception of evaluation information? *Educational Evaluation and Policy Analysis, 7,* 417–425.

Rippey, R. M. (Ed). (1973). *Studies in transactional evaluation.* Berkeley, CA: McCutchan.

Robinson, D. G., & Robinson, J. C. (1989). *Training for impact: How to link training to business needs and measure the results.* San Francisco: Jossey-Bass.

Rossi, P. H. (1971). Boobytraps and pitfalls in the evaluation of social action programs. In F. G. Caro (Ed.), *Readings in evaluation research.* New York: Sage.

Rossi, P. H. (Ed.). (1982). *Standards for evaluation practice.* New Directions for Program Evaluation, No. 15. San Francisco: Jossey-Bass.

Rossi, P. H., & Freeman, H. E. (1985). *Evaluation: A systematic approach* (3rd ed.). Beverly Hills, CA: Sage.

Rossi, P. H., & Freeman, H. E. (1993). *Evaluation: A systematic approach* (5th ed.). Newbury Park, CA: Sage.

Rossi, P. H., & Wright, J. D. (1985). Social science research and the politics of gun control. In R. L. Shotland & M. M. Mark (Eds.), *Social science and social policy.* Beverly Hills, CA: Sage.

Royse, D. (1992). *Program evaluation.* Chicago: Nelson-Hall.

Rubin, H. J., & Rubin, I. S. (1995). *Qualitative interviewing.* Thousand Oaks, CA: Sage,

Sadler, D. R. (1981). Intuitive data processing as a potential source of bias in naturalistic evaluations. *Educational Evaluation and Policy Analysis, 3,* 25-31.

Salamon, L. M. (1992). *America's nonprofit sector: A primer.* New York: Foundation Center.

Salkever, D. S., & Frank, R. G. (1992). Health services. In C. T. Clotfelder (Ed.), *Who benefits from the nonprofit sector?* Chicago: University of Chicago Press.

Sanders, J. R. (1979). The technology and art of evaluation. A review of seven evaluation primers. *Evaluation News, 12,* 2-7.

Sanders, J. R. (1982). *A design for improving level 2 and low achieving student performance in the Shaker Heights City School District.* Kalamazoo: Western Michigan University, Evaluation Center.

Sanders, J. R. (1983). Cost implications of the standards. In M. C. Alkin & L. C. Solman (Eds.), *The cost of evaluation.* Beverly Hills, CA: Sage.

Sanders, J. R. (1995). Standards and principles. In W. R. Shadish, D. L. Newman, M. A. Scheirer, & C. Wye (Eds.) *Guiding Principles for evaluators.* New Directions for Program Evaluation, No. 66, 47-52. San Francisco: Jossey-Bass.

Sanders, J. R. (in press). Cluster evaluation. In E. Chelimsky & W. R. Shadish (Eds.), *Evaluation for the 21st century: A resource book.* Thousand Oaks, CA: Sage.

Sanders, J. R., & Cunningham, D. J. (1973). A structure for formative evaluation in product development. *Review of Educational Research, 43,* 217-236.

Sanders, J. R., & Cunningham, D. J. (1974). Techniques and procedures for formative evaluation. In G. D. Borich (Ed.), *Evaluating educational programs and products.* Englewood Cliffs, NJ: Educational Technology.

Sanders, J. R., & Sachse, T. P. (1977). Applied performance testing in the classroom. *Journal of Research and Development in Education, 10,* 92-104.

Schmitz, C. C. (1994). What kind of evaluation is the CBPH cluster evaluation? (Mimeo, 3 pp.)

Schofield, J. W., & Anderson, K. M. (1984). *Combining quantitative and qualitative methods in research on ethnic identity and intergroup relations.* Paper presented at the Society for Research on Child Development and Study Group on Ethnic Socialization, Los Angeles.

Schwartz, S., & Baum, S. (1992). Education. In C. T. Clotfelder (Ed.), *Who benefits from the nonprofit sector?* Chicago: University of Chicago Press.

Scott, A., & Sechrest, L. (1992). Theory driven approaches to benefit cost analysis: Implications of program theory. In H. Chen & P. H. Rossi (Eds.), *Using theory to improve program and policy evaluations.* New York: Greenwood Press.

Scottish Council for Research in Education. (1990). The evaluation of educational programmes: Methods, uses, and benefits: Part A, Volume 24. *Report of the Educational Research Workshop. North Berwick, Scotland, November 22-25, 1988.* Bristol, PA: Taylor & Francis.

Scriven, M. (1967). The methodology of evaluation. In R. E. Stake (Ed.), *Curriculum evaluation.* (American Educational Research Association Monograph Series on Evaluation, No. 1, pp. 39-83). Chicago: Rand McNally.

Scriven, M. (1972). Pros and cons about goal-free evaluation. *Evaluation Comment, 3,* 1–7.

Scriven, M. (1973). The methodology of evaluation. In B. R. Worthen & J. R. Sanders, *Educational evaluation: Theory and practice.* Belmont, CA: Wadsworth.

Scriven, M. (1974a). Evaluation perspectives and procedures. In W. J. Popham (Ed.), *Evaluation in education.* Berkeley, CA: McCutchan.

Scriven, M. (1974b). Standards for the evaluation of educational programs and products. In G. D. Borich (Ed.), *Evaluating educational programs and products.* Englewood Cliffs, NJ: Educational Technology.

Scriven, M. (1976). *The intellectual dimensions of evaluation research.* Paper presented at the fourth annual Pacific Northwest and Evaluation Conference, Seattle, WA.

Scriven, M. (1980). *The logic of evaluation.* Interness, CA: Edgepress.

Scriven, M. (1984). Evaluation ideologies. In R. F. Connor, D. G. Altman, & C. Jackson (Eds.), *Evaluation studies review annual* (Vol. 9). Beverly Hills, CA: Sage.

Scriven, M. (1986). New frontiers of evaluation. *Evaluation Practice, 7,* 7–44.

Scriven, M. (1991a). Beyond formative and summative evaluation. In M. W. McLaughlin & D. C. Phillips (Eds.), *Evaluation and education: At quarter century* (pp. 19–64). Ninetieth Yearbook of the National Society for the Study of Education. Chicago: National Society for the Study of Education.

Scriven, M. (1991b). *Evaluation thesaurus* (4th ed.). Newbury Park, CA: Sage.

Scriven, M. (1993). *Hard-won lessons in program evaluation.* New Directions for Program Evaluation, No. 58, 1–107. San Francisco: Jossey-Bass.

Scriven, M. (1994). The final synthesis. *Evaluation Practice, 15,* 367–382.

Scriven, M. (1996). Types of evaluator and types of evaluation. *Evaluation Practice.*

Sechrest, L. (Ed.). (1980). *Training program evaluators.* New Directions for Program Evaluation, No. 8, San Francisco: Jossey-Bass.

Sechrest, L. (1985). Observer studies: Data collection by remote control. In L. Burstein, H. E. Freeman, & P. H. Rossi (Eds.), *Collecting evaluation data.* Beverly Hills, CA: Sage.

Sechrest, L. (1992). Roots: Back to our first generation. *Evaluation Practice, 13,* 1–7.

Sechrest, L. (1994). Program evaluation: Oh what it seemed to be! *Evaluation Practice, 15,* 359–365.

Sechrest, L., Babcock, J., & Smith, S. (1993). An invitation to methodological pluralism. *Evaluation Practice, 14,* 227–235.

Sechrest, L., & Figueredo, A. J. (1993). Program evaluation. *Annual Review of Psychology, 44,* 645–674.

Shadish, W. R. (1993). Critical multiplism: A research strategy and its attendant tactics. In L. Sechrest (Ed.), *Program evaluation: A pluralistic enterprise.* New Directions for Program Evaluation, No. 60, 13–57. San Francisco: Jossey-Bass.

Shadish, W. R. (1994). Need-based evaluation theory: What do you need to know to do good evaluation? *Evaluation Practice, 15,* 347–358.

Shadish, W. R., Cook, T. D., & Leviton, L. C. (1991). *Foundations of program evaluation.* Newbury Park, CA: Sage.

Shadish, W. R., Newman, D. L., Scheirer, M. A., & Wye, C. (Eds.). (1995). *Guiding principles for evaluators.* New Directions for Program Evaluation, No. 66. San Francisco: Jossey-Bass.

Shotland, R. L., & Mark, M. M. (1987). Improving inferences from multiple methods. In M. M. Mark & R. L. Shotland (Eds.), *Multiple methods in program evaluation.* New Directions for Program Evaluation, No. 35. San Francisco: Jossey-Bass.

Shulman, L. S. (1985). Peer reviews: The many sides of virtue. *Educational Researcher, 14,* 12–13.

Sieber, J. E. (1980). Being ethical: Professional and personal decisions in program evaluation. In R. E. Perloff & E. Perloff (Eds.), *Values, ethics, and standards in evaluation.* New Directions for Program Evaluation, No. 7, 51–61. San Francisco: Jossey-Bass.

Simon, A., & Boyer, E. G. (1974). *Mirrors for behavior III: An anthology of observation instruments.* Philadelphia: Research for Better Schools.

Sinacore, J. M., & Turpin, R. S. (1991). Multiple sites in evaluation research: A survey of organizational and methodological issues. In R. S. Turpin & J. M. Sinacore (Eds.), *Multisite evaluations.* New Directions for Program Evaluation, No. 50, 5–18. San Francisco: Jossey-Bass.

Singer, S. I., & McDowall, D. (1988). Criminializing delinquency: The deterrent effects of the New York Juvenile Offender Law. *Law & Society Review, 22,* 521–535.

Sjoberg, G. (1975). Politics, ethics, and evaluation research. In M. Guttentag & E. L. Struening (Eds.), *Handbook of evaluation research* (Vol. 2). Beverly Hills, CA: Sage.

Skaburskis, A. (1987). Cost-benefit analysis: Ethics and problem boundaries. *Evaluation Review, 11,* 591–611.

Smith, C. C. (1994). *What kind of evaluation is the CBPH cluster evaluation?* (Mimeo, 3 pp.)

Smith, E. R., & Tyler, R. W. (1942). *Appraising and recording student progress.* New York: Harper & Row.

Smith, J. K., & Heshusius, L. (1986). Closing down the conversation: The end of the quantitative-qualitative debate among educational inquirers. *Educational Researcher, 15,* 4–12.

Smith, M. F. (1989). *Evaluability assessment: A practical approach.* Boston: Kluwer Academic.

Smith, M. F. (1994). Evaluation: Review of the past, preview of the future. *Evaluation Practice, 15,* 215–227.

Smith, M. L. (1986). The whole is greater: Combining qualitative and quantitative approaches in evaluation studies. In D. D. Williams (Ed.), *Naturalistic evaluation.* New Directions for Program Evaluation, No. 30, 37–54. San Francisco: Jossey-Bass.

Smith, N. L. (Ed.). (1981). *Metaphors for evaluation: Sources of new methods: New perspectives in evaluation* (Vol. 1). Beverly Hills, CA: Sage.

Smith, N. L. (1982). *Public data resources for educational policy analysis and evaluation* (Paper and Report Series No. 75). Portland, OR: Northwest Regional Educational Laboratory, Research on Evaluation Program.

Smith, N. L. (1983). *Dimensions of moral and ethical problems in evaluation* (Paper and Report Series No. 92). Portland, OR: Northwest Regional Educational Laboratory, Research on Evaluation Program.

Smith, N. L. (1985). *Adversary and committee hearings as evaluation methods* (Paper and Report Series No. 110). Portland, OR: Northwest Regional Educational Laboratory, Research on Evaluation Program.

Smith, N. L. (Ed.). (1992). *Varieties of investigative evaluation.* New Directions for Program Evaluation, No. 56. San Francisco: Jossey-Bass.

Smith, P. C., & Kendall, L. M. (1963). Retranslation of expectations: An approach to the construction of unambiguous anchors for rating scales. *Jounal of Applied Psychology, 47,* 149–155.

Smith, R. (1984). *The new aesthetic curriculum theorists and their astonishing ideas: Some actual observations.* (The Monograph Series). Vancouver, Canada: University of British Columbia, Center for the Study of Curriculum and Instruction.

Smith, S. R., & Lipsky, M. (1993). *Non-profits for hire: The welfare state in the age of contracting.* Cambridge: Harvard University Press.

Spindler, G. (Ed.). (1982). *Doing the ethnography of schooling.* New York: Holt, Rinehart, & Winston.

Stake, R. E. (1967). The countenance of educational evaluation. *Teachers College Record, 68,* 523–540.

Stake, R. E. (1969). Evaluation design, instrumentation, data collection, and analysis of data. In J. L. Davis (Ed.), *Educational evaluation.* Columbus, OH: State Superintendent of Public Instruction.

Stake, R. E. (1970). Objectives, priorities, and other judgment data. *Review of Educational Research, 40,* 181–212.

Stake, R. E. (1972). *Responsive evaluation.* Unpublished manuscript.

Stake, R. E. (1975a). *Evaluating the arts in education: A responsive approach.* Columbus, OH: Merrill.

Stake, R. E. (1975b). *Program evaluation, particularly responsive evaluation* (Occasional Paper No. 5). Kalamazoo: Western Michigan University Evaluation Center.

Stake, R. E. (1978). The case study method in social inquiry. *Educational Researcher, 7,* 5–8.

Stake, R. E. (1980). Program evaluation, particularly responsive evaluation. In W. B. Dockrell & D. Hamilton (Eds.), *Rethinking educational research.* London: Hodeder & Stoughton.

Stake, R. E. (1981). Case study methodology: An epistemological advocacy. In W. Welch (Ed.), *Case study methodology in educational evaluation.* Minneapolis: Minnesota Research and Evaluation Center.

Stake, R. E. (1988). Case study methods in educational research: Seeking sweet water. In R. M. Jaeger (Ed.), *Complementary methods for research in education.* Washington, DC: American Educational Research Association.

Stake, R. E. (1991). Retrospective on "The countenance of educational evaluation." In M. W. McLaughlin & D. C. Phillips (Eds.), *Evaluation and education: At quarter century.* Ninetieth Yearbook of the National Society for the Study of Education, Part II. Chicago: University of Chicago Press.

Stake, R. E. (1992). A housing project school. In J. Nowakowski, M. Stewart, & W. Quinn (Eds.), *Monitoring implementation of the Chicago Public Schools' systemwide school reform goals and objectives plan.* Oakbrook, IL: North Central Regional Educational Laboratory.

Stake, R. E. (1994). Case studies. In N. K. Denzin & Y. S. Lincoln (Eds.), *Handbook of qualitative research.* Thousand Oaks, CA: Sage.

Stake, R. E. (1995). *The art of case study research.* Thousand Oaks, CA: Sage.

Stake, R. E., & Gjerde, C. (1974). An evaluation of T-CITY, The Twin City Institute for Talented Youth. In R. H. P. Kraft, L. M. Smith, R. A. Pohland, C. J. Brauner, & C. Gjerde (Eds.), *Four evaluation examples: Anthropological, economic, narrative, and portrayal* (AERA Monograph Series on Curriculum Evaluation No. 7). Chicago: Rand McNally.

Stenzel, N. (1976). *Adversary processes and their potential use in evaluation for the Illinois Office of Education.* Springfield, IL: Illinois Department of Education.

Stenzel, N. (1982). Committee hearings as an evaluation format. In N. L. Smith (Ed.), *Field assessments of innovative evaluation methods.* New Directions for Program Evaluation, No. 13, 83–100. San Francisco: Jossey-Bass.

Stephan, A. S. (1935). *Prospects and possibilities: The New Deal and the new social research.* Chapel Hill: University of North Carolina Press.

Stone, L. (1984, April). *Results from a global curriculum project evaluation: Practical problem-theoretical solutions.* Paper presented at the annual meeting of the American Evaluation Research Association, New Orleans.

St. John, M. (n.d.). Committee hearings: Their use in evaluation (Contract No. 400-80-0105). *Evaluation Guides, 8,* 2-12. Portland, OR: Northwest Regional Educational Laboratory.

Stufflebeam, D. L. (1968). *Evaluation as enlightenment for decision making.* Columbus: Ohio State University Evaluation Center.

Stufflebeam, D. L. (1971). The relevance of the CIPP evaluation model for educational accountability. *Journal of Research and Development in Education, 5,* 19-25.

Stufflebeam, D. L. (1973a). An introduction to the PDK book: Educational evaluation and decision-making. In B. R. Worthen & J. R. Sanders, *Educational evaluation: Theory and practice.* Belmont, CA: Wadsworth.

Stufflebeam, D. L. (1973b). Excerpts from "Evaluation as enlightenment for decision making." In B. R. Worthen & J. R. Sanders, *Educational evaluation: Theory and practice.* Belmont, CA: Wadsworth.

Stufflebeam, D. L. (1974). *Metaevaluation* (Occasional Paper No. 3). Kalamazoo: Western Michigan University Evaluation Center.

Stufflebeam, D. L. (1977, April). *Working paper on needs assessment in evaluation.* Paper presented at the American Educational Research Association Evaluation Conference, San Francisco.

Stufflebeam, D. L. (1981). *A review of progress in educational evaluation.* Paper presented at the annual meeting of the Evaluation Network, Austin, TX.

Stufflebeam, D. L. (1991). Professional standards and ethics for evaluators. In M. W. McLaughlin & D. C. Phillips (Eds.), *Evaluation and education: At quarter century.* Ninetieth Yearbook of the National Society for the Study of Education, Part II. Chicago: University of Chicago Press.

Stufflebeam, D. L. (1994). Empowerment evaluation, objectivist evaluation, and evaluation standards: Where the future of evaluation should not go and where it needs to go. *Evaluation Practice, 15,* 321-338.

Stufflebeam, D. L., Foley, W. J., Gephart, W. J., Guba, E. G., Hammond, R. L., Merriman, H. O., & Provus, M. M. (1971). *Educational evaluation and decision making.* Itasca, IL: Peacock.

Stufflebeam, D. L., & Shinkfield, A. J. (1985). *Systematic evaluation.* Boston: Kluwer-Nijhoff.

Suarez, T. (1981). *A planning guide for the evaluation of educational programs.* Unpublished manuscript, Chapel Hill, University of North Carolina.

Suarez, T. (1990, November). *Living with the mixed message: The effect of government-sponsored evaluation requirements on the practice of evaluaton.* Paper presented at the annual meeting of the American Evaluation Association, Washington, DC.

Suchman, E. (1967). *Evaluative research.* New York: Sage.

Sudman, S., & Bradburn, N. M. (1982). *Asking questions: A practical guide to questionnaire design.* San Francisco: Jossey-Bass.

Swanson, R. A. (1987). Training technology system: A method for identifying and solving training problems in industry and business. *Journal of Industrial Teacher Education, 24,* 7-17.

Swanson, R. A. (1989). Everything important in business and industry is evaluated. In R. O. Brinkerhoff (Ed.), *Evaluating training programs in business and industry.* New Directions for Program Evaluation, No. 44, 71-82. San Francisco: Jossey-Bass.

Sweetland, R. C., & Keyser, D. J. (1986). *Tests: A comprehensive reference for assessments in psychology, education, and business.* Kansas City, MO: Test Corporation of America.

Swiss, J. (1992). Adapting Total Quality Management to government. *Public Administration Review, 52,* 356-362.

Sylvia, R. D. (1994). *Public personnel administration.* Belmont, CA: Wadsworth.

Sylvia, R. D., Meier, K. J., & Gunn, E. M. (1985). *Program planning and evaluation for the public manager.* Monterey, CA: Brooks/Cole.

Tallmadge, G. K. (1977). *Ideabook: JDRP* (ERIC DL 48329). Washington, DC: U.S. Government Printing Office.

Tallmadge, G. K., & Wood, C. T. (1976). *Users guide: ESEA Title I evaluation and reporting system.* Mountain View, CA: RMC Research Corporation.

Talmage, H. (1982). Evaluation of programs. In H. E. Mitzel (Ed.), *Encyclopedia of educational research* (5th ed., pp. 592-611). New York: Free Press.

Tash, W. R., & Stahler, G. J. (1984). Current status of quality assurance in mental health. *American Behavioral Scientist, 27,* 608-630.

Tessmer, M., & Wedman, J. (1992, April). *The practice of instructional design: A survey of what designers do, don't do, and why they don't do it.* Paper presented at the annual meeting of the American Educational Research Association, San Francisco.

Tharp, R. G., & Gallimore, R. (1979). The ecology of program research and evaluation: A model of evaluation succession. In L. Sechrest, S. G. West, M. A. Phillips, R. Rechner, & W. Yeaton (Eds.), *Evaluation Studies Review Annual, 4,* 39-60.

Thompson, B. (1994, April). *The revised Program Evaluation Standards and their correlation with the evaluation use literature.* Paper presented at the annual meeting of the American Educational Research Association, New Orleans.

Thompson, M. S. (1980). *Benefit-cost analysis for program evaluation.* Beverly Hills, CA: Sage.

Tittle, C. K. (1984, April). *Professional standards and equity: The role of evaluators and researchers.* Paper presented at the annual meeting of the American Educational Research Association, New Orleans.

Travers, R. M. W. (1983). How research has changed American schools. Kalamazoo, MI: Mythos Press.

Trend, M. G. (1978). On the reconciliation of qualitative and quantitative analysis: A case study. *Human Organism, 37,* 345-354.

Trochim, W. M. K. (1984). *Research design for program evaluation: The regression-discontinuity approach.* Newbury Park, CA: Sage.

Turner, S. D., Hartman, J., Nielsen, L. A., & Lombana, J. (1988). Fostering utilization through multiple data-gathering methods. *Studies in Educational Evaluation, 14,* 113-133.

Turpin, R. S., & Sinacore, J. M. (Eds.). (1991). *Multisite evaluations.* New Directions for Program Evaluation, No. 50. San Francisco: Jossey-Bass.

Tushnet, N. C. (1995, April). *Toward a general approach to multisite program evaluation.* Paper presented at the annual meeting of the American Educational Research Association, San Francisco. (ERIC No. 383 733)

Tyler, R. W. (1942). General statement on evaluation. *Journal of Educational Research, 35,* 492-501.

Tyler, R. W. (1950). *Basic principles of curriculum and instruction.* Chicago: University of Chicago Press.

Tyler, R. W. (1991). General statement on program evaluation. In M. W. McLaughlin & D. C. Phillips (Eds.), *Evaluation and education: At quarter century.* Ninetieth Yearbook of the National Society for the Study of Education, Part II. Chicago: University of Chicago Press.

U.S. Department of Health and Human Services, Office for Substance Abuse Prevention. (1991). *Prevention plus III.* Rockville, MD: Author.

U.S. General Accounting Office. (1992). *Quality management: A survey of federal organizations.* Washington, DC: Author.

Vallance, E. (1978). Scanning horizons and looking at weeks: A critical description of "The Great Plains Experience." In G. Willis (Ed.), *Qualitative evaluation.* Berkeley, CA: McCutchan.

Van Mondfrans, A. (1985). *Guidelines for reporting evaluation findings.* Unpublished manuscript, Brigham Young University, College of Education, Provo, UT.

Van Mondfrans, A. (1993). Personal communication.

Vaughn, S., Schumm, J. S., & Sinagub, J. M. (1996). *Focus group interviews in education and psychology.* Thousand Oaks, CA: Sage.

Vroom, P. E., Colombo, M., & Nahan, N. (1994). Confronting ideology and self-interest: Avoiding misuse of evaluation. In C. J. Stevens & M. Dial (Eds.), *Preventing the misuse of evaluation.* New Directions for Program Evaluation, No. 64, 49–59. San Francisco: Jossey-Bass.

Wachtman, E. L. (1978, March). *Evaluation as a story: The narrative quality of educational evaluation.* Paper presented at the annual meeting of the American Educational Research Association, Toronto.

Walberg, H. J., & Haertel, G. D. (Eds.). (1990). *The international encyclopedia of educational evaluation.* New York: Pergamon Press.

Waldo, G. P., & Chiricos, T. G. (1977). Work release and recidivism. *Evaluation Quarterly, 1,* 87–105.

Waples, D., & Tyler, R. W. (1930). *Research methods and teacher problems.* New York: Macmillan.

Webb, E. J., Campbell, D. T., Schwartz, R. D., & Sechrest, L. (1966). *Unobtrusive measures: Nonreactive research in the social sciences.* Chicago: Rand McNally.

Weiss, C. H. (1972). *Evaluation research: Methods for assessing program effectiveness.* Englewood Cliffs, NJ: Prentice-Hall.

Weiss, C. H. (1973). Where politics and evaluation research meet. *Evaluation, 1,* 37–45.

Weiss, C. H. (1977). *Using social research in public policy making.* Lexington, MA: Lexington Books.

Weiss, C. H. (1984). Toward the future of stakeholder approaches in evaluation. In R. F. Conner, D. G. Altman, & C. Jackson (Eds.), *Evaluation studies review annual* (Vol. 9). Beverly Hills, CA: Sage.

Weiss, C. H. (1987). Evaluating social programs: What have we learned? *Society, 25,* 40–45.

Weiss, C.H. (1991). Evaluation research in the political context: Sixteen years and four administrations later. In M. W. McLaughlin & D. C. Philips (Eds.), *Evaluation and education: At quater century.* Chicago: University of Chicago Press.

Weiss, C. H. (1993). Politics and evaluation: A reprise in mellower overtones. *Evaluation Practice, 14,* 107–109.

Weiss, C. H., & Bucuvalas, M. J. (1980). Truth tests and utility tests: Decision-makers' frames of reference for social science research. *American Sociological Review, 45,* 302–313.

Weitzman, E. A., & Miles, M. B. (1995). *Computer programs for qualitative data analysis.* Thousand Oaks, CA: Sage.

Wholey, J. S. (1983). *Evaluation and effective public management.* Boston: Little, Brown.

Wholey, J. S. (1986). Using evaluation to improve government performance. *Evaluation Practice, 7,* 5–13.

Wholey, J. S. (1987). Evaluability assessment: Developing program theory. In L. Bickman (Ed.), *Using program theory in evaluation.* New Directions for Program Evaluation, No. 33, 77–92. San Francisco: Jossey-Bass.

Wholey, J. S. (1994). Assessing the feasibility and likely usefulness of evaluation. In J. S. Wholey, H. P. Hatry, & K. E. Newcomer (Eds.), *Handbook of practical program evaluation*. San Francisco: Jossey-Bass.

Wholey, J. S., Hatry, H. P., & Newcomer, K. E. (Eds.). (1994). *Handbook of practical program evaluation*. San Francisco: Jossey-Bass.

Wholey, J. S., Scanlon, J. W., Duffy, H. G., Fukumoto, J. S., & Vogt, L. J. (1970). *Federal evaluation policy: Analyzing the effects of public programs*. Washington, DC: Urban Institute.

Wilcox, K. (1982). Ethnography as a methodology and its application to the study of schooling. In G. Spindler (Ed.), *Doing the ethnography of schooling*. New York: Holt, Rinehart, & Winston.

Williams, A., & Giardina, E. (Eds.). (1993). *The theory and practice of cost-benefit analysis*. Brookfield, VT: Edward Elgar.

Williams, D. D. (Ed.). (1986). *Naturalistic evaluation*. New Directions for Program Evaluation, No. 30. San Francisco: Jossey-Bass.

Winston, J. A. (1995). *Defining program*. An e-mail message sent by Jerome Winston (Director of Program for Public Sector Evaluation, Royal Melbourne Institute of Technology, Victoria, Australia) to multiple recipients of the American Evaluation Association Discussion List, EvalTalk, July 25, 1993.

Witkin, B. R., & Altschuld, J. W. (1995). *Planning and conducting needs assessments*. Thousand Oaks, CA: Sage.

Wolcott, H. (1976). Criteria for an ethnographic approach to research in schools. In J. T. Roberts & S. K. Akinsanga (Eds.), *Schooling in the cultural context*. New York: David McKay.

Wolf, R. L. (1975). Trial by jury: A new evaluation method. *Phi Delta Kappan, 57,* 185–187.

Wolf, R. L. (1978). *Studying school governance through judicial evaluation procedures*. Bloomington: Indiana Center for Evaluation.

Wolf, R. L. (1979). The use of judicial evaluation methods in the formulation of educational policy. *Educational Evaluation and Policy Analysis, 1,* 19–28.

Wolf, R. L., & Tymitz, B. (1977). Toward more natural inquiry in education. *Center on Evaluation, Development, and Research (CEDR) Quarterly, 10,* 7–9.

Worthen, B. R. (1972, April). *Impediments to the practice of educational evaluation*. Paper presented at the annual meeting of the American Educational Research Association, Chicago.

Worthen, B. R. (1975). Competencies for educational research and evaluation. *Educational Researcher, 4,* 13–16.

Worthen, B. R. (1977, April). *Eclecticism and evaluation models: Snapshots of an elephant's anatomy?* Paper presented at the annual meeting of the American Educational Research Association, New York.

Worthen, B. R. (1978, April). *Metaphors and methodologies for evaluation*. Paper presented at the annual meeting of the American Educational Research Association, Toronto.

Worthen, B. R. (1981). Journal entries of an eclectic evaluator. In R. S. Brandt (Ed.), *Applied strategies for curriculum evaluation*. Alexandria, VA: Association for Supervision and Curriculum Development.

Worthen, B. R. (1994). Is evaluation a mature profession that warrants the preparation of evaluation professionals? In J. W. Altschuld & M. Engle (Eds.), *The preparation of professional evaluators: Issues, perspectives, and programs*. New Directions for Program Evaluation, No. 62, 3–15. San Francisco: Jossey-Bass.

Worthen, B. R. (1995). Some observations about the institutionalization of evaluation. *Evaluation Practice, 16*, 29–36.

Worthen, B. R. (in press). A survey of *Evaluation Practice* readers. *Evaluation Practice.*

Worthen, B., Borg, W. R., & White, K. R. (1993). *Measurement and evaluation in the schools.* White Plains, NY: Longman.

Worthen, B. R., & Byers, M. L. (1971). *An exploratory study of selected variables related to the training and careers of educational research and research-related personnel.* Washington, DC: American Educational Research Association.

Worthen, B. R., & Matsumoto, A. (1994, November). *Conceptual challenges confronting cluster evaluation.* Paper presented at the annual meeting of the American Evaluation Association, Boston.

Worthen, B. R., O'Sullivan, R., & White, K. R. (in press). *Tools and techniques for program evaluation.* Boston: Kluwer-Nijhoff..

Worthen, B. R., & Owens, T. R. (1978). Adversary evaluation and the school psychologist. *Journal of School Psychology, 16,* 334–345.

Worthen, B. R., & Rogers, W. T. (1980). Pitfalls and potential of adversary evaluation. *Educational Leadership, 37,* 536–543.

Worthen, B. R., & Sanders, J. R. (1973). *Educational evaluation: Theory and practice.* Belmont, CA: Wadsworth.

Worthen, B. R., & Sanders, J. R. (1984). *Content specialization and educational evaluation: A necessary marriage?* (Occasional Paper No. 14). Kalamazoo: Western Michigan University, Evaluation Center.

Worthen, B. R., & Sanders, J. R. (1987). *Educational evaluation: Alternative approaches and practical guidelines.* New York: Longman.

Worthen, B. R., & Valcarce, R. W. (1985). Relative effectiveness of personalized and form covering letters in initial and follow-up mail surveys. *Psychological Reports, 57,* 735–744.

Worthen, B. R., & Van Dusen, L. M. (1992). *Executive summary to a two-year comprehensive assessment of Basic Learning System implementation models.* Logan, UT: Western Institute for Research and Evaluation/Utah State University Department of Psychology.

Worthen, B. R., & White, K. R. (1987). *Evaluating educational and social programs: Guidelines for proposal reviews, onsite evaluation, evaluation contracts, and technical assistance.* Boston: Kluwer-Nijhoff.

Woudenberg, F. (1991). An evaluation of Delphi. *Technological Forecasting and Social Change, 40,* 131–150.

Wright, W. J., & Sachse, T. (1977, April). *Payoffs of adversary evaluation.* Paper presented at the annual meeting of the American Educational Research Association, New York.

Yates, B. T. (1996). *Analyzing costs, procedures, processes, and outcomes in human services.* Thousand Oaks, CA: Sage.

Yin, R. K. (1984). *Case study research.* Beverly Hills, CA: Sage.

Zemke, R. (1985). The systems approach, a nice theory but . . . *Training, 10,* 103–108.

Zimmermann, U. (1994). Exploring the nonprofit motive (or: What's in it for you?). *Public Administration Review, 54,* 398–402.

Author Index

549

Subject Index